NO WAY OUT

NO WAY OUT

BREXIT: FROM THE BACKSTOP TO BORIS

TIM SHIPMAN

WILLIAM
COLLINS

William Collins
An imprint of HarperCollins*Publishers*
1 London Bridge Street
London SE1 9GF

WilliamCollinsBooks.com

HarperCollins*Publishers*
Macken House, 39/40 Mayor Street Upper
Dublin 1, D01 C9W8, Ireland

First published in Great Britain in 2024 by William Collins

1

A catalogue record for this book is
available from the British Library

HB ISBN 978-0-00-830894-0
TPB ISBN 978-0-00-871203-7

Set in Minion Pro
Printed and bound in the UK using 100%
renewable electricity at CPI Group (UK) Ltd

This book contains FSC™ certified paper and other controlled
sources to ensure responsible forest management.

For more information visit: www.harpercollins.co.uk/green

for Lily,
who arrived between meaningful votes one and two,
and changed my world

and for Charlotte,
who is my world

'Politics is the art of the possible, the attainable
– the art of the next best'

– Otto von Bismarck

CONTENTS

PART THREE: FOUND OUT
Negotiating with Brussels
July to November 2018

PART FOUR: NO WAY OUT
Negotiating with Parliament
November 2018 to July 2019

PART FIVE: TIME OUT
Cometh the Hour ...
June to July 2019

INTRODUCTION

'Primer és saber què fer. Després, saber com fer-ho!'
('First you have to know what to do. Then you
have to know how to do it!')

– Pep Guardiola

This is the third in what is now a four-part sequence of books designed to tell the full story of the most explosive period of domestic British politics since the Second World War. *All Out War: The Full Story of Brexit* (2016) was the first – and remains the only – all points narrative covering the inside story of the EU referendum campaign. The book was runner-up for the Orwell Prize for political writing. It became the basis for *Brexit: The Uncivil War*, the Emmy-nominated 2019 film, scripted by James Graham, in which Benedict Cumberbatch played Dominic Cummings. The author acted as a political consultant on the film.

Fall Out: A Year of Political Mayhem (2017) followed a year later. It recounts how a new government, under Theresa May, set out to tackle Brexit. The bulk of the book is taken up with the story of the 2017 election, revealing how political hubris mixed with inept execution can quickly turn to nemesis. It ends with a disastrously weakened May beginning to negotiate terms with Brussels and the arrival, centre-stage, of the Northern Ireland border issue.

Together the first two books provide evidence for a theory of power which, I will argue, this and the concluding volume prove beyond doubt. Those who succeed in politics know where they want to go strategically, how to get there tactically and have the necessary skills to execute their plans, so that they can turn goals into reality. Politicians lacking any one of these three attributes struggle; those lacking two, fail; those lacking all three are an irrelevance or an embarrassment to themselves.

No Way Out and the final volume, *Out*, have been six years in the making. This book begins by revisiting May's December 2017 Joint Report agreement with Brussels on Northern Ireland, the moment when *Fall Out* concludes. At the time this was a crucial hurdle for May, when her premiership lay on the line. A deal, almost any deal, had to be done to keep her show on the road. Only later, in the genesis of this third volume, did it become clear that the events of that December were utterly pivotal to the Brexit settlement and to the future of her government. The first section also covers how MPs, led by Dominic Grieve, secured the right to a 'meaningful vote' on the Brexit deal, which, alongside the Joint Report, did most to shape the rest of May's premiership. Part One concludes with a flashback chapter, recounting May's early errors, drawing on interviews with those unable to talk openly when the first two books were written.

The rest of Part One recounts the story of May's three great negotiations: first, with her cabinet, then with the EU and finally with Parliament. Part Two covers the tortuous negotiations within government over what Britain wanted the Brexit settlement to look like, first defined in a meeting at Chequers in early 2018, expanded further in May's Mansion House speech and then, when that was rejected by the EU, the prime minister's secret pivot to a deal more aligned with Brussels. That was unveiled at a second meeting at Chequers in July, which prompted the resignations of both David Davis and Boris Johnson, the two most prominent Brexiteers in her government. Part Three recounts May's negotiations with Brussels, via the disastrous Salzburg summit, to the signing of a Withdrawal Agreement deal in November 2018, which led to the resignation of a second Brexit secretary, Dominic Raab.

What then followed was perhaps the most turbulent twelve months in Parliament for a century. Part Four is the story of May's attempts to negotiate with Parliament to pass her deal, a period which saw three meaningful votes, two votes of no confidence – one in the prime minister and one in her government – cross-party talks and constitutional innovation by despairing MPs (aided by an activist speaker) to seize control from the executive to prevent a no-deal departure. This section ends with the fall of May.

Part Five sees Boris Johnson winning the keys to Downing Street after a leadership election in which all the candidates learned from May's experiences and errors and pledged to pursue Brexit negotiations in a different way towards a different end. The chaos and contradictions laid bare here during Johnson's quest for power sowed the seeds of his success, but also fuelled the hubris and nemesis which would follow during his premiership. That and the governments of Liz Truss and Rishi Sunak are the story of volume four, published later this year.

A project once finite in length took on a life of its own as events overtook me. My punishment was to see other authors till the same soil. My goal has been to dive deeper and wider than others, to provide the level of granularity that readers of the *Sunday Times* and the two previous books have come to expect, without losing sight of the big picture.

Like many in Westminster I am a devotee of the works of Robert Caro, whose magisterial multi-volume biography of Lyndon B. Johnson is the gold standard for all political writers. *No Way Out* is firmly in the 'Caro school' (in its length and themes if not in its elegance or insight), in that it aims to be a study of power: how people find it, hold it and use it and the ends for which they do so. My contention is that Brexit, which surprised both victors and vanquished in the 2016 referendum and was a mystery to both, was the greatest political conundrum visited on the British ruling class in eighty years. It destroyed David Cameron then consumed the careers and attention, directly and indirectly, of his three immediate successors. Brexit was, for some, a huge problem to solve or to mitigate, to others it was a once-in-a-generation opportunity to grasp. The story of this sequence, and this book in particular, is that of how Britain's leading politicians sought to navigate both hurdles and opportunities, while not agreeing on which were which. In doing so, both sides would push themselves and Britain's unwritten constitution to breaking point.

This was a political, parliamentary, legal and diplomatic drama, but most of all it was a human drama, red in tooth and claw. As I wrote at the start of *All Out War*, this is not an explanation about why Brexit happened, nor a political argument about its merits. This is elitist history, which focuses on the actions of the politicos around Theresa May who made the decisions; the senior civil servants tasked with enacting them;

the senior Commission and Council personalities they negotiated with; and the major factions in Parliament who sought to thwart them.

If pre-2016 Westminster was largely obsessed with the clever idealism of *The West Wing*, marinated in the farce of *The Thick of It*, the parable of these years became *Game of Thrones*, the pseudo-medieval swords and shagging epic pitching warring factions against each other in the quest for the iron throne. For the Mayites, the Corbynistas, the Johnsonians, the Lib Dems, SNP, ERG and the DUP, for the Labour moderates, the Tiggers and the numerous branches of the Remainer Bresistance – the pro-dealers, Norway-Plus people, customs union fans, People's Voters and full-blown revokers – read the Lannisters, Starks, Baratheons, Martells, Greyjoys and Tyrells. There is a parallel too in the mysterious actors across the Narrow Sea (aka the Channel) who were better organised and frequently misunderstood – able to deploy dragons against the unicorns of others.

Much of the story of book three is the tale of an entrenchment of views, of yawning splits in the Conservative Party and Parliament, but also of the deepest divisions in society in my adult lifetime. My goal is to explain what people were trying to achieve and why – and then how those competing desires interacted to determine events. My intention is not to make moral judgements about the outcomes people sought. In the introduction to their magisterial work on Stanley Baldwin, Keith Middlemas and John Barnes quote the difficulties of scraping 'away the layers' of politicians' judgements to find what Baldwin referred to as the 'many-sidedness of truth'. My goal is to present as many of those truths as possible and leave the reader to decide which to embrace.

Tim Shipman, Blackheath, February 2024

ACKNOWLEDGEMENTS

No Way Out and its companion volume *Out* are based on countless contemporaneous conversations and more than 260 formal interviews. Many of these were conducted in 2019 after the May government fell, with updates in 2020 on the events of the second half of 2019 and further interviews in 2021 on the 2020 Brexit deal. I began a final wave of interviews in late 2022 and early 2023 on the collapse of the Johnson administration, the rise and fall of Liz Truss and Rishi Sunak's accession, Windsor deal and duel for power with Johnson.

After *All Out War*, where I named a large number of sources, I have not identified those who agreed to talk since it makes life easier for them. I am hugely grateful to each and every one of my sources, some of whom gave me four or five interviews. I could name on the fingers of one hand the people who refused to talk. Those I interviewed include three prime ministers, thirty-nine cabinet ministers, another thirteen ministers, sixteen senior civil servants, seven Brexit negotiators, forty-seven Downing Street political advisers (across four governments), thirty-one special advisers, twenty-seven Labour aides, frontbenchers and MPs, seven senior figures in the Brussels institutions, plus more than a dozen other MPs, a handful of diplomats and multiple sources in the Lib Dems, the Brexit Party and the DUP.

I have also drawn on a range of contemporary papers and other media. These include leaked cabinet minutes and government documents, letters from cabinet ministers to their prime minister, political strategy memos, emails, texts and WhatsApp messages – as well as several recordings of meetings made by the participants for their own use.

Special thanks must go to those who helped turn more than 300 hours of interviews into more than 3.3 million words of transcripts. Richard Assheton, Megan Baynes, Christy Cooney, Daniel Gayne, Eleanor Langford, Anna Menin, Holly Pyne and Joseph Wardropper were particularly industrious. I'm also grateful to Louis Ashworth, Frankie Crossley, Lizzie Deane, Tony Diver, Felix Forbes, Todd Gillespie, George Greenwood, Sam Hall, Fergus Horsfall, Megan Kenyon, Lucy Knight, Michael Mander, Harriet Marsden, Matt Mathers, Oliver Milne, Alex Oscroft, Josh Stein and Jan-Peter Westad. In the seven years which this book took to write it was a great pleasure to see many of these young journalists go on to build very promising careers.

None flourished more than Gabriel Pogrund, my helper on both *All Out War* and *Fall Out*, who is now one of the best reporters on Fleet Street. With Patrick Maguire he wrote *Left Out*, the definitive account of Jeremy Corbyn's leadership. In seeking to fill the hole he left behind, I was lucky to secure the services of Katherine Forster, who conducted insightful interviews with more than a dozen key figures.

As in the first two books, I conducted most interviews 'on background', allowing me to use information without direct quotation, or 'off the record', allowing quotation but no attribution. My goal has been to reconstruct what happened without stating the origin of each scene or quote. Where I have described people's words, thoughts or feelings, they were imparted by that individual, someone in whom they confided or another witness to the episode. The obvious source is often not the correct one. I have also drawn heavily on the Brexit Witness Archive, a hugely valuable series of on-the-record interviews with key players, conducted by UK in a Changing Europe, a project established by Anand Menon. Where I have drawn from these interviews, I have footnoted them, but where sources said broadly the same to me, I have tended to use the words they used in my interviews.

Throughout the writing of this book, I have been lucky enough to work with extremely talented colleagues in the *Sunday Times* political team: Caroline Wheeler, my partner in mischief, and Harry Yorke. Both have been useful sounding boards and have contributed delicious nuggets. I have been lucky enough to work for three editors – Martin Ivens, Emma Tucker and Ben Taylor – and news editors – Ben Preston, Lindsay McIntosh and Becky Barrow – who all promoted politics in the paper and (eclipsing that in importance in about 2020) on the *Sunday Times* website.

I would like to express my gratitude to Nick Robinson, who interviewed a lot of the same people for his documentary *Britain's Brexit Crisis*. Nick suggested lines of inquiry that he had not had time to pursue and introduced me to Max Stern, who acted as a fixer with key figures in Brussels and Whitehall. He accompanied me on several excursions, including one memorable visit to Vienna. Ameet Gill made several key introductions to people who might not otherwise have agreed to talk. Laura Kuenssberg shared transcripts of several of her documentary series. Few reporters did a better job, or suffered more abuse for it, during those years. She has both my thanks and my admiration.

For *No Way Out* it became more important to balance the Westminster narratives with perspectives from Brussels and the major European capitals. I am grateful to Bojan Pancevski, the former *Sunday Times* Brussels correspondent now in Berlin for the *Wall Street Journal*, for opening doors in both his old parish and new. I am also indebted to David Rennie for an introduction to some of Donald Tusk's team and to Mark English and Federico Bianchi of the European Commission office in London, and Daniel Ferrie in Brussels, for an introduction to Michel Barnier's, Maros Sefcovic's and Ursula von der Leyen's aides.

The Brexit story is a complicated one and is not something any one reporter can own. I am conscious of standing on the shoulders of giants. I am particularly grateful to Katy Balls, Alex Barker, Sam Coates, Harry Cole, Tony Connelly, Pippa Crerar, James Crisp, James Forsyth, Peter Foster, Tom McTague, Glen Owen, George Parker, Sebastian Payne, Jim Pickard, Dennis Staunton, Steven Swinford, Bruno Waterfield, Nick Watt, Alex Wickham, Oliver Wright and Henry Zeffman, each of whom has broken great stories on the Brexit saga and the Tory civil war. Antonello Guerrero of *La Repubblica*, the most enterprising foreign correspondent in London, shared several interviews with key characters.

Unlike my first two books, which were written in parallel with rivals, other authors have trodden some of this turf first. I am grateful to Anthony Seldon and Raymond Newell, Tom Baldwin and Peter Foster – all of whom shared copies of their books before publication. Seldon, the doyen of Downing Street historians, also gave me helpful suggestions about how to approach the introduction and conclusion over an enjoyable viva/dinner. A full bibliography appears at the end of the book.

At A. M. Heath, Victoria Hobbs was a rock as both agent and therapist when the going got tough. I am blessed, too, with one of the best (and most patient) editors in the business, the incomparable Arabella Pike who had the improvisational nerve to reshape this project into four volumes as deadline approached. At William Collins I would also like to thank Iain Hunt, the best copy editor in the business, who trimmed the manuscript with sensitivity and intelligence; Sam Harding, who sourced the pictures; Matt Clacher for his social media expertise; and Katherine Patrick for her energy and enthusiasm in promoting the book.

In the race to finally finish, Jessie Wraight at the Workers' League in Blackheath presided cheerfully over a calming space in which to write. Andy Taylor read the manuscript and contributed immensely valuable observations. Rosa Prince also gave encouragement and advice. Both helped me make cuts to keep this narrative manageable.

I'd like to thank all the 'Warriors' for their support, their friendship and for keeping me vaguely sane throughout this process.

My greatest thanks are reserved for my family who endured countless absences and ruined holidays as this project spiralled out of control and seemed, at several points, like it would never be completed. My wife Charlotte (aka Lady Shippers) deserves that peerage, at least, for enduring everything I put her through while producing two beautiful daughters, Lily and Ettie. I would also like to thank her wonderful circle of friends who provided support to our family. I will be forever in the debt of my in-laws – Kate and Michael Todman – for their help with childcare as my first born became aware of this strange inanimate rival for my time and attention. 'When you finish your book, Daddy, I think people will be reading it for a million years,' she said, a comment on the time it took to write, rather than its durability. If you buy several copies I will be able to afford to take her on a nice holiday to say 'thank you'.

T.J.S.

TIMELINE

2016

23 Jun – Britain votes to leave the European Union by a margin of 52 per cent to 48 per cent

29 Jun – Other 27 member states agree a 'no negotiations without notification' stance on Brexit talks and Article 50

13 Jul – Theresa May becomes prime minister

2 Oct – In Brexit speech to party conference, May says she will trigger Article 50 before the end of March

2017

4 Jan – Ivan Rogers resigns as Britain's permanent representative to the EU

17 Jan – In a speech at Lancaster House May announces Britain will seek a hard Brexit leaving the single market, the customs union and the jurisdiction of the European Court of Justice. She says 'no deal is better than a bad deal'

29 Mar – May signs letter triggering Article 50

8 Jun – General election: the Conservatives win 317 seats, down 13 and lose their majority. Labour gains 30 seats

19 Jun – Brexit negotiations begin after UK accepts EU's demands on sequencing

18 Sep – Oliver Robbins leaves DExEU to run the Cabinet Office Europe Unit

22 Sep – During a speech in Florence, May says Britain will seek a transition lasting two years

19 Oct – At Brussels summit, May asks EU leaders to declare that 'sufficient progress' has been achieved on citizens' rights, money and Northern Ireland to begin talks on future trade talks. They refuse

4 Dec – DUP pulls the plug on May's planned exit deal

8 Dec – May strikes phase one deal but has to accept a Joint Report spelling out details of a 'backstop' plan for Northern Ireland

13 Dec – Dominic Grieve wins the right for MPs to pass judgement on the final Brexit deal in a 'meaningful vote'

2018

8–9 Jan – Theresa May's botched cabinet reshuffle undermines her authority

Mid Jan – Every minister in DExEU agrees May should seek a Canada-style trade deal with the EU, not a Norwegian-style relationship

17 Jan – Group of Labour MPs meets at Fair Oak Farm to discuss a possible breakaway from the party

12 Feb – Jeremy Corbyn's aides try to bounce Keir Starmer into backing a Labour plan which stops short of customs union membership

23 Feb – Theresa May's Brexit 'war cabinet' meets at Chequers to finally decide Britain's negotiating strategy. They agree Britain should seek the ability to diverge from some EU rules

26 Feb – In a speech in Coventry, Corbyn vows that a Labour government would seek to negotiate a new customs union with the EU

28 Feb – EU publishes a draft legal text of the Joint Report which removes the nuance and Barnier said was designed to 'provoke' the UK

2 Mar – May's Mansion House speech outlines the proposal finalised at Chequers

4 Mar – Sergei and Julia Skripal are poisoned in Salisbury with the Soviet-era nerve agent Novichok

16 Mar – Donald Tusk says the best Britain can hope for is a Canada-style deal with some side deals

19 Mar – Legal text of the Withdrawal Agreement published which says the backstop will apply 'unless and until' another solution is found

21 Mar – Second Fair Oak Farm meeting for Labour MPs considering a split

22–23 Mar – EU Council rejects May's Mansion House proposals causing the prime minister to rethink her approach

23 Mar – It emerges that Jeremy Corbyn backed the artist behind an antisemitic mural on Facebook

26 Mar – Labour MPs attend a Jewish vigil in Parliament Square against antisemitism in Labour; Western countries launch a wave of expulsions of Russian intelligence officers

7 Apr – Syrian forces launch a chemical attack on rebel-held Douma

14 Apr – Britain joins the US and France in launching cruise missile attacks on Syrian military targets

18 Apr – Government defeated in the House of Lords on membership of the customs union

24 Apr – David Davis writes to May calling her customs plan 'politically unpalatable and technically deficient'

29 Apr – Amber Rudd resigns as home secretary over the Windrush scandal

2 May – Brexit war cabinet rejects May's hybrid customs plan with Boris Johnson yelling 'It's six-five!'

11 May – Downing Street sets up two working groups of ministers to examine the Max-Fac and the New Customs Partnership (NCP) proposals

17 May – Cabinet agrees that the backstop will come into force if there is no deal, an arrangement Brexiteers fear will leave the UK a de facto member of the customs union

23 May – At third Fair Oak Farm meeting, Gavin Shuker asks Labour MPs to say whether they will join a breakaway

6 Jun – David Davis threatens to resign over whether the backstop will be time limited. Boris Johnson makes a speech condemning the Treasury as 'the heart of Remain' and says Britain would get a better deal if Donald Trump was doing the negotiating

8–9 Jun – At the G7 summit in Canada, May stands up to Trump as he angers his Western allies by rejecting the rules-based international order

12 Jun – Phillip Lee resigns as a justice minister over Brexit

14 Jun – Tory Remainers furious when a government amendment, which Robert Buckland had thrashed out with Dominic Grieve, is rewritten at the last moment on the orders of David Davis

17 Jun – May announces huge boost to NHS spending but fails to point out that she had fulfilled the promise made on the Vote Leave bus in 2016

20 Jun – Government wins crunch vote to pass the Withdrawal Bill after the Grieve amendment (now disowned by Grieve) is defeated by 319 votes to 303

23 Jun – It emerges that Boris Johnson said 'fuck business'

30 Jun – 49 Labour MPs rebel to back an amendment calling on Britain to remain in the single market and customs union

2 Jul – Downing Street briefs the BBC that there is now a 'third way' on customs. May denies this to Davis

3 Jul – May visits Dutch premier Mark Rutte to explain her Chequers plan

4 Jul – Johnson hosts a meeting of Brexiteer cabinet ministers at the Foreign Office to plot a joint strategy to oppose May's plan

5 Jul – At second Brexiteer gathering in the Foreign Office, Davis says it is better not to present an alternative plan. May explains her plan to Angela Merkel

6 Jul – At the second Chequers summit, the cabinet approves May's plan to remain in the single market for goods following a 'common rulebook'

8 Jul – David Davis resigns at midnight

9 Jul – Boris Johnson resigns. Dominic Raab appointed Brexit secretary. Geoffrey Cox becomes attorney general

12–13 Jul – Donald Trump visits Britain and tells the *Sun* May has botched Brexit

14 Jul – European Research Group (ERG) sets up its own 'Buddies' whipping operation to defeat the government

16 Jul – May accepts four ERG amendments to the customs bill, enraging Remainer MPs. Guto Bebb resigns to oppose the government

17 Jul – Labour's NEC rejects adopting the international definition of antisemitism

23 Jul – Steve Baker tells ERG steering group about his plan for 'controlled chaos'

24 Jul – Over dinner at the home of Jacob Rees-Mogg, leading Brexiteers devise 'Chuck Chequers' plan

26 Jul – In his second meeting with Barnier, Raab gets what he thinks is an admission that the backstop is finite

30 Jul – Rees-Mogg and Baker agree to back Johnson for the leadership

2 Aug – May meets Emmanuel Macron at Fort Bregançon and rejects Chequers proposals

21 Aug – In his third meeting with Raab, Barnier erupts with rage when told that a hard border in Ireland would be the EU's fault

4 Sep – Labour's NEC finally adopts the international definition of antisemitism in full against Corbyn's wishes

10–11 Sep – Downing Street hosts dinner for MPs to try to win them over

11 Sep – Calls for May to be removed at ERG meeting

12 Sep – ERG unveils its plan for the Northern Ireland border

13 Sep – The first cabinet meeting devoted to preparations for no-deal

18 Sep – In *Panorama* interview, May fails to make an effective case for her plan

19 Sep – May publishes article in *Die Welt* arguing that only her plan can command cross-community support in Northern Ireland

20 Sep – Salzburg EU summit is a disaster when Tusk rejects Chequers

21 Sep – May flies home to give defiant speech demanding 'respect' from Brussels

25 Sep – Keir Starmer makes coded pro-Remain speech to Labour's conference which is widely interpreted as a leadership positioning

3 Oct – Cox introduces May, who uses her conference speech to warn the party should unite or risk no Brexit

11 Oct – Robbins and Barnier's team enter 'The Tunnel', the final push for a deal. The EU finally agrees there can be a UK-wide backstop

14 Oct – Raab dashes to Brussels to stop Robbins signing a deal, which May had already torpedoed

15 Oct – Cox outlines the legal issues with the deal to the cabinet 'Pizza Club'

22 Oct – Iain Duncan Smith leads Eurosceptic delegation to Brussels and wrongly concludes that Barnier backs alternative arrangements

29 Oct – In his second budget of the year, Philip Hammond, the chancellor, declares an end to austerity

30 Oct – Raab and Simon Coveney have dinner. The Irish brief that the Brexit secretary wanted to escape the backstop after three months

2 Nov – The EU accepts the backstop is 'temporary' but the UK agrees not to seek an 'arbitrary time limit'

4 Nov – Jeremy Heywood dies in his sleep

9 Nov – Robbins concedes that the customs plan in the Withdrawal Agreement will be the starting point for future trade negotiations, turning the backstop into a 'frontstop'

12 Nov – Final text of the Withdrawal Agreement agreed

13 Nov – Jeremy Hunt warns May the deal will not get through Parliament and that it will be the end of her premiership. The DUP and the ERG both reject the deal. Geoffrey Cox's legal advice says there is no legal way out of the backstop. Nikki da Costa resigns

14 Nov – Cabinet meets for five hours to discuss the deal. Esther McVey demands a vote. May addresses the nation from Downing Street

15 Nov – Raab and McVey resign. Rees-Mogg and Baker tell ERG meeting they have submitted letters of no confidence. In a press conference outside the Commons they call for May to go

22 Nov – Political declaration on the future trade deal published

2 Dec – *Sunday Times* reveals leaked extracts from Cox's legal advice

3 Dec – Cox provides MPs with a summary of his legal advice. Commons votes 311 to 293 to hold the government in contempt of Parliament for refusing to publish the whole thing

10 Dec – May pulls the first meaningful vote, scheduled for 12 December, after being warned the government will lose by more than 200 votes

11 Dec – Graham Brady, chairman of the 1922 Committee, receives a 48th letter of no confidence, triggering a secret ballot on May's future as Tory leader

12 Dec – May wins the confidence vote by 200 votes to 117 but is badly damaged

14 Dec – PM confronts Jean-Claude Juncker in Brussels for calling her Brexit policy 'nebulous'

18 Dec – Cabinet agrees that no-deal is now the 'principal operational focus' of the government. May invites Rees-Mogg and nine other MPs to Chequers to try to find common ground

2019

9 Jan – John Bercow, the Commons speaker, overrules his clerks and announces that he will allow Dominic Grieve's amendment to a government business motion, establishing the principle that MPs can take over the parliamentary timetable

14 Jan – Juncker and Tusk sign a letter to May confirming that the EU did not want to enter the backstop either and pledging to work quickly towards an alternative

15 Jan – May loses the first meaningful vote by 432 votes to 202, the largest government defeat in parliamentary history

17 Jan – The government wins a vote of no confidence called by Labour with 325 votes to 306 for the opposition. The Cooper-Boles bill

20 Jan – May calls together MPs for another Chequers unity lunch

21 Jan – Kit Malthouse convenes a group of key Brexiteers and Remainers to seek a compromise deal

28 Jan – May forced to adopt both the Brady amendment and the Malthouse Compromise at a factious 1922 Committee meeting

29 Jan – The Cooper-Boles attempt to seize control of the Commons fails. The Brady amendment passes

5 Feb – May's visit to Northern Ireland cements her view that a soft Brexit is needed to preserve the Union

7 Feb – Pro-deal cabinet ministers in the 'Croissant Club' sign a letter to May expressing huge concerns about no-deal

11 Feb – Oliver Robbins overheard in the Sofitel hotel in Brussels disparaging MPs

15 Feb – Under pressure from Number 10, Amber Rudd withdraws an article condemning the ERG

18 Feb – Seven Labour MPs announce they are leaving the party to form the Independent Group. They are nicknamed 'Tiggers'. Geoffrey Cox arrives in Brussels for the first of four trips to try to renegotiate the Withdrawal Agreement

19 Feb – Joan Ryan becomes the eighth Labour MP to leave. The ERG hardcore begin referring to themselves as 'the Spartans'

20 Feb – Anna Soubry, Heidi Allen and Sarah Wollaston quit the Conservative Party to join the Tiggers

22 Feb – Rudd, David Gauke and Greg Clark jointly pen an article warning that MPs will stop a no-deal Brexit, making clear they are prepared to resign

25 Feb – Corbyn announces that Labour will back a referendum unless MPs vote to support Labour's Brexit plan

27 Feb – Government forced to adopt an amendment tabled by Yvette Cooper to force ministers to offer a vote on a Brexit extension if they did not pass the deal by 12 March

5 Mar – Over dinner in Brussels, the EU team makes clear Cox's proposals are unacceptable

6 Mar – Oliver Letwin and Nick Boles meet Corbyn to discuss their Common Market 2.0 plan

7 Mar – Jonathan Jones, head of the government legal section, tells Cox he thinks the new plan for a joint interpretive instrument does reduce the legal jeopardy of joining the backstop

8–11 Mar – Cox warns six times that the plans do not go far enough for him to change his legal advice. He calls for a unilateral declaration stressing Britain's right to 'terminate' the backstop

11 Mar – May and Steve Barclay fly to Strasbourg to sign deal with the EU. Cox tells her not to sign

12 Mar – Geoffrey Cox's second legal advice says there is still no legal escape from the backstop, sinking May's hopes of winning MV2. In the second meaningful vote, the government loses by 149 votes, the fourth worst defeat in parliamentary history

13 Mar – Croissant Club ministers become the Rebel Alliance as 18 abstain on a motion ruling out no-deal. Julian Smith asks Gauke to resign

14 Mar – Gauke warns that all 18 ministers will leave with him. Barclay proposes a motion on a new Brexit timetable then votes against it himself

16 Mar – The March to Leave departs Sunderland en route to Westminster

18 Mar – Bercow rules that the government cannot hold the third meaningful vote on the same motion. May's team says this sank a deal with the DUP. Graham Brady tells May MPs want her to resign

19 Mar – For a period of around 48 hours, May seriously considers no-deal

20 Mar – May makes people v Parliament speech in Number 10, which enrages MPs

21 Mar – PM flies to Brussels to ask for an extension

21–23 Mar – Pro-deal ministers discuss whether David Lidington should be installed as a caretaker prime minister

24 Mar – May hosts Phillip Lee then a delegation of key MPs at Chequers. Iain Duncan Smith, Jacob Rees-Mogg and Boris Johnson tell her to announce she is standing down if she wants to win MV3

25 Mar – Rees-Mogg tells ERG meeting he will vote for the deal

27 Mar – May tells the 1922 Committee she is prepared to stand down. Johnson tells ERG meeting he will now back May. The DUP say they

will vote against. In the first round of indicative votes all seven forms
of Brexit are voted down

28 Mar – Steve Baker has a wobble and comes close to announcing he
will vote for the deal

29 Mar – In the third meaningful vote, May loses by 49 votes after 34
Tories (six Bresisters and 28 Spartans) vote against her. Senior Tories
hold a secret meeting to discuss whether to call a general election

1 Apr – In the second round of indicative votes, all four propositions –
customs union, Common Market 2.0, a referendum and revoke – are
defeated. A second referendum gets the most votes (280) but the
customs union comes closest to a majority, falling 3 votes short

2 Apr – Cabinet rules out an election and agrees, after interventions
from Cox and Michael Gove, to launch cross-party talks with Labour
instead

3 Apr – May meets Corbyn. Speaker Bercow breaks a tied vote in
favour of the government, preventing a third round of indicative
votes. MPs then vote 312–311 to seize control of the timetable. The
Cooper-Letwin bill ruling out no-deal passes third reading by 313
votes to 312

4 Apr – Cross-party talks begin in earnest

12 Apr – Nigel Farage launches the Brexit Party's European election
campaign

23 Apr – Brady warns May that the 1922 Committee could change its
rules to permit a second vote of no confidence

1 May – Gavin Williamson sacked as defence secretary after a leak
inquiry

2 May – In local elections the Conservatives lose 1,330 councillors and
44 councils. Labour also loses six councils

6 May – In the sixth round of talks, Starmer rejects language which
came straight from a Labour proposal

9 May – With the cross-party talks stalled, senior aides begin to meet in
secret and make more progress

11 May – Brady publicly calls for May to set a date for her resignation

16 May – Boris Johnson says 'of course' he is going to run for the
leadership

17 May – Corbyn announces that the cross-party talks have failed

20 May – Heidi Allen threatens to resign after telling Change UK MPs
they should recommend people vote tactically for other parties

21 May – May tells cabinet that the government would make time for a vote on a referendum

22 May – Andrea Leadsom resigns when it becomes clear the government has gone further than cabinet allowed. May tells her aides she will quit. Allen offers to resign as leader of Change UK after telling Channel 4 she backs tactical voting

23 May – Voting opens in European Parliament elections

24 May – May resigns as Conservative Party leader. Johnson says if he wins the UK will leave on 31 October 'deal or no deal'

26 Mar – The Brexit Party wins the European elections with 30 per cent of the vote. The Tories get 9 per cent, their worst ever result in a national election

4 Jun – ERG MPs meet and agree to back Johnson not Raab. Change UK MPs meet and agree to separate

5 Jun – Johnson is backed as leader by Rishi Sunak, Oliver Dowden and Robert Jenrick

7 Jun – Gove's campaign hit by revelations that he took cocaine

13 Jun – In the first ballot, Johnson gets 114 votes and is guaranteed a place in the run-off

16 Jun – Rory Stewart wins the first debate

18 Jun – In the second ballot, Johnson advances to 126 votes. Gove in third closes the gap to Hunt in second but Stewart leapfrogs Javid and Raab, who is eliminated. But in second debate that night Stewart fails to capitalise

19 Jun – In the third ballot, Stewart is eliminated. Johnson leads with 143 votes and Gove closes to within three of Hunt

20 Jun – In the fourth ballot, Johnson advances to 157, more than half the parliamentary party, and Gove grabs second place. In the fifth ballot, amid claims of chicanery, Hunt is second and earns the right to take on Johnson

21 Jun – Story breaks that police were called to the home of Carrie Symonds in the small hours of the morning after an explosive row with Johnson

24 Jun – Hunt calls Johnson a 'coward' for ducking debates

25 Jun – Johnson says the UK will leave on 31 October 'do or die'

1 Jul – Gove and David Cameron make their peace in meeting at 5 Hertford Street

3 Jul – Hunt's momentum killed by fox hunting gaffe

9 Jul – In a debate, Johnson refuses to back Kim Darroch, the
ambassador to the US, after his cables about Donald Trump were
leaked

10 Jul – *Panorama* reveals devastating details of Labour's handling of
antisemitism

12 Jul – Johnson embarrassed by Andrew Neil over his support for a
GATT XXIV Brexit solution

18 Jul – Philip Hammond rebels for the first time, abstaining on the
Benn-Burt amendment to the Northern Ireland (Executive
Formation) Bill designed to make it difficult for Johnson to prorogue
Parliament to force a no-deal Brexit

23 Jul – Theresa May's final cabinet. Johnson elected Conservative
leader with 66 per cent of the vote

24 Jul – Boris Johnson becomes prime minister

PART ONE

OUT PLAYED

THE BACKSTOP AND BEFORE

July 2016 to December 2017

'The quickest way of ending a war is to lose it'

– *George Orwell*

ORIGINAL SIN

The Joint Report

December 2017

It was probably the bravest decision Theresa May ever made as prime minister. It was also the decision which marked the beginning of the end of her premiership. The prime minister and her closest aide, chief of staff Gavin Barwell, were alone in her study. The dull thump of music from the Downing Street Christmas party upstairs sent a tremor through the walls. Moments earlier May had come off the phone with Arlene Foster, the leader of Northern Ireland's Democratic Unionist Party (DUP), whose ten MPs the Conservative government relied upon for a majority in the House of Commons. Her talk with Foster had not gone well. 'What do you think?' she asked Barwell.

The chief of staff was a cautious figure, but he felt the time had come to grasp the nettle. On the table were plans for a 'backstop' to prevent a hard border being imposed between Northern Ireland and the Republic when the UK finally left the European Union. 'I'm going to give you two answers,' he said. 'If you're asking me what's politically in your interest, I wouldn't do it. I cannot tell you that you're going to have the Conservative Party or the DUP with you if you go and sign this. If you're asking me what I think is in the interest of the country, I think you need to move these negotiations on. We're trapped in this bloody backstop. The only answer is in the future relationship. We've got to find a way to get to that. In the national interest I would go and sign it.'

All who worked for Britain's fifty-fourth prime minister concluded that she was a decent woman whose prime motivation was public service. Barwell knew that framing a decision as in the interests of the country would be decisive. He repeated his warning: 'I have to be honest, you're taking a massive political risk if you do that.'

May had made up her mind; she was going to Brussels. The deal was on. The DUP could take it or leave it. She knew the risks but, in her mind, she was doing the right thing. 'To me, that is Theresa May,' Barwell said.

There was more to it than altruism, of course; it was also an act of political self-preservation. For seventeen months May had been trying to pilot the nation towards a Brexit she had not voted for and, to start with at least, did not fully understand. Six months earlier she had called a general election, hoping to strengthen her hand, and had weakened it. Since June 2017 May had been operating with no majority. Both Parliament and the EU had become more assertive. The Commission had decreed that, for substantive talks to begin on the future relationship, 'sufficient progress' had to be achieved in three areas of the withdrawal agreement – the divorce deal between the two sides.

In September, the prime minister made a speech in Florence agreeing to 'honour commitments' to pay a divorce bill and write the protection of EU citizens into UK law, moves that prompted even Michel Barnier, the EU's chief negotiator, to recommend that the EU27 decree that 'sufficient progress' had been achieved. That just left Northern Ireland. But when the heads of government met at the October European Council in Brussels, the member states rejected Barnier's suggestion. The prime minister, facing cabinet dissent and backbench plotting, needed a win. May's inner circle believed that if she failed to make progress that December, the government would fall. At the time, the details scarcely mattered. May needed a deal or she was finished. Later, the details would matter a very great deal.

In the history of Brexit, the role of Northern Ireland came to be seen as the tail that wagged the dog, a peripheral issue that played a disproportionate role in shaping the final outcome – but in many respects it *was* the dog. After Brexit, the 310-mile-long border between Northern Ireland and the Irish Republic would be the only land border between the UK and the EU. What happened there would have profound implications. The Belfast 'Good Friday' Agreement of 1998, which had brought peace to the province after three decades of paramilitary violence, was made possible by the fact that both countries were in the EU and that for most practical purposes there was no border. 'It's like a Jenga game,' one Tory Northern Ireland secretary said. 'You're removing a fundamental pillar of the agreement.'

With three hundred crossing points it was reputed to be the most porous border anywhere in the EU, with some properties straddling it. There was flourishing cross-border activity, with integrated supply chains operating between North and South, and an all-Ireland economy in sectors like agri-foods. Brexit created 'nightmarish' practical problems if there was any sort of border, a member of the negotiating team recalled. 'Someone taking a pint of milk from the kitchen to the living room' could theoretically have faced checks in their own home. 'You'd have to check wooden coffins to carry them from the church to the graveyard. There would be a ban on taking sausage rolls across the border. You couldn't walk your dog across the border. You would need to show that they've been in quarantine beforehand due to the rabies risk.'

Both sides agreed there could be no 'hard border' after Brexit. What 'hard' meant in practice was the question on which the negotiations turned. For the Irish, the priority was to avoid the creation of border posts, cameras or inspection centres, which could become a target for terrorists or encourage smuggling, a key means of financing terrorism. On the EU side, the priority was to uphold the sanctity of the single market. That meant checks on goods such as farm animals and chemicals that had previously crossed the border freely. Barnier and his team also foresaw a world in which Brexit Britain did a trade deal with Donald Trump's America. Frans Timmermans, a Commission vice chairman, explained, 'Just imagine the United Kingdom [had] an agreement with the United States to import chlorinated chicken without restrictions. This is something most Europeans abhor, they don't want it. But if you don't have a border, chlorinated chicken could come into the EU and go to all parts of the EU without us being able to control it.'[1]

Barnier, who was French and had previously been Commissioner for the single market, was absolutist on this issue. A senior Commission official said, 'It is only 1 per cent of all trade that passes via the Irish border. The real de facto problem is relatively small. But the philosophical problem is big. Because it can be used as de facto participation in the single market.' The EU, too, feared that the tail would wag the dog. They just didn't agree with the UK on which was the tail and which was the dog.

For the EU, the logical way to square this circle was for Northern Ireland to continue following EU rules and regulations. That approach, to the Brexiteers, was a trap to keep Britain in permanent submission to EU directives or inside the European customs union. The other solution, giving Northern Ireland different status from the rest of the UK, would place an effective border in the Irish Sea, cleaving the province from the mainland – something which was unacceptable to the DUP and to many in the European Research Group (ERG) of Brexiteer hardliners.

The Brexiteers favoured a light touch regime that would enable firms trading across the border to join trusted trader schemes and register their cargo in advance by computer, with crates sealed, bar coded and tracked electronically, perhaps in tandem with number plate recognition systems for vehicles – with any regulatory checks conducted away from the border. This was known as 'alternative arrangements'. The British government had also argued, perfectly logically, that the ultimate solution would be found in the future trading arrangements.

Neither the Irish government, nor the Commission was prepared to proceed on the basis of hope. They wanted a guarantee, in black and white, that whatever trade deal was eventually signed, there could never be a hard border. Which is where the 'backstop' came in.

After the setback at October's European Council, Oliver Robbins, May's chief civil service negotiator, and Sabine Weyand, Barnier's deputy, agreed to work on a Joint Report on the three pillars of the withdrawal agreement, to be presented at the December 2017 EU Council. Together they would try to convince the heads of government that sufficient progress had been achieved. In return, May was desperate to get agreement to a two-year 'transition period' to give business time to adapt to the new world after Brexit.

On Wednesday 8 November, a day before the sixth round of Brexit talks, Robbins was handed a Commission document which said to avoid a hard border it would be 'essential' that there be 'no emergence of regulatory divergence' between the North and South in Ireland. Robbins was the model of a modern diplomat: tall, clever, and agreeable to his EU interlocutors. Yet when he saw the paper, he went 'apeshit'. Northern Ireland was now the government's biggest headache. It was to remain so for two years.

The truth is that most politicians and civil servants did not see the issue coming. When former prime ministers Tony Blair and Sir John

Major visited Northern Ireland during the referendum campaign to argue that a Leave vote could damage the peace process, they were largely ignored. Sir Jeremy Heywood, the cabinet secretary, did see the dangers. On 24 June, just hours after the referendum result, he explained to his wife Suzanne the challenges he faced. 'Do you know what the most difficult issue is? … Ireland.' A hard border would 'demolish the Good Friday Agreement,' he said. 'I don't yet see how we will solve it.'

Despite this insight, work on the issue was only sporadic and nearly invisible. Chris Wilkins, May's director of strategy until the summer of 2017, said, 'I don't remember the issue of Ireland being raised in any of the meetings I sat in, and I used to sit in the weekly Brexit strategy meetings.' The assumption in London was that the situation could be resolved through fudge, technology and a blind eye turned to smuggling – the arrangements which kept the peace process on track. A civil service Northern Ireland unit was set up in the Department for Exiting the European Union (DExEU) in February 2017 but consisted only of Brendan Threlfall, a pin sharp official who would play a key role in the drama ahead, and one other person. 'The civil service was as much to blame as politicians,' an official recalled. 'For the first few months no one was interested. A train was coming hard at us, though over the summer the EU was deliberately disguising what they were up to.'

May's political aides say that throughout 2017 Robbins and his team downplayed the likelihood of Northern Ireland being the biggest problem (which was thought to be the money). 'The advice we were consistently getting was that Northern Ireland was not an issue,' one said. Even in mid-November, an adviser recorded in his diary that, 'Olly was telling us Northern Ireland was not going to be the main stumbling block to sufficient progress, which I thought was rubbish. It was an error on his part, not seeing it coming, and not just him, the wider diplomatic network.'

The backstop became a major issue because the Irish government – led by Enda Kenny until he was replaced as prime minister, or Taoiseach, by Leo Varadkar in June 2017 – was determined to make it one. While Whitehall sat idle, the Irish department of foreign affairs prepared a 130-page Brexit strategy document in the two years before the referendum. The day after the vote, rival party leaders met in Dublin and agreed they should present a united front, something never achieved in Westminster. Opposition leader Micheál Martin of Fianna Fáil told the Dáil, 'We all need to be wearing the same jersey.'

The Irish government did, initially, consider a special bilateral deal between Britain and Ireland on agriculture. May flew to Dublin in January 2017, with the goal of getting Kenny to agree the two countries should work together on a frictionless solution for the Irish border. Her Majesty's Revenue and Customs (HMRC) and the Irish Revenue Commissioners (IRC) had already had meetings on the issue. Nick Timothy, May's joint chief of staff until the 2017 election, said, 'While I was in Downing Street and Enda Kenny was the Irish prime minister, there were pretty constructive talks ongoing … where Irish customs officials would work with British customs officials to see what the solutions were to the border. Those solutions were going to be a combination of policy and technology.' David Davis wanted the Irish to agree that 80 per cent of goods moving between the Republic and the North could be excluded from checks using trusted trader apps. He recalled, 'When Enda Kenny was still the Taoiseach, his Head of Customs said to his Senate, "We can maintain an invisible border without any changes." The head of HMRC said the same to the British.'[2] However, on her trip to Dublin, a 'very aggressive' Taoiseach rebuffed May, saying technology was not the answer. 'You can't solve this without the customs union,' Kenny said.

Dublin had been leaned on by Barnier, who visited in the autumn of 2016 with a clear message to stop negotiating directly with Britain. By February 2017, the Commission had produced a confidential note – 'Brexit and the Border between Ireland and the UK' – which said the only way in EU law to accommodate the need for a soft border and Britain's policy of leaving the customs union was to propose no border controls for agriculture and food, leaving Northern Ireland subject to EU law. The note bluntly admitted that such a plan 'could harm the peace process'. Robbins travelled to Brussels and warned, 'You will leave Northern Ireland with no say in the laws governing it. That is tyranny and will be unsustainable.'

Policy wise, there was no real difference between Kenny and Varadkar. Both wanted a backstop. In tone and style, the handover of power made a difference. Gregarious and gay, Varadkar, just thirty-eight when he took power, was the first Irish leader of Indian descent and the figurehead of a new generation of politicians less concerned about good relations with their former colonial masters. A British negotiator said, 'Enda Kenny was better at making the same points in a way that landed more easily to a British ear. Leo Varadkar is not a natural diplomat.' It was not just Varadkar: 'My prime minister and that Taoiseach was a difficult combination.' May and anyone was a difficult combination. Before the publication of one set of British proposals, Varadkar asked May what to expect. She said he would have to wait until it was published, a response regarded as tin-eared in Dublin.[3]

The new Taoiseach was also in a confidence and supply agreement with his main political opponent. 'He would have been complete toast then if he didn't get something that was sufficient for his purposes,' Barwell acknowledged.[4] On 17 November, Varadkar used an EU summit in Gothenburg to warn that he would block progress to phase two of the talks at the December Council meeting unless the UK guaranteed there would be no hard border. 'We want that written down,' he said. As reality dawned, ministerial colleagues remember David Davis 'briefing cabinet that unless we could solve the Irish problem we might have to stay in the EU'. A fellow Brexiteer recalled, 'Everyone went, "Uh?"'

On 30 November, Robbins was presented with the draft of the Joint Report. He flew back to London to see May. The solution devised by Weyand's team was for Northern Ireland to remain for all practical purposes in the customs union, something that would move the customs border to the Irish Sea. May repeatedly attempted to telephone Varadkar, but he refused to take her calls. 'That text was sprung on us,' said Barwell. 'That was incredibly problematic.'[5] Denzil Davidson, another Number 10 adviser, said, 'It was very much a "sign here" process.'[6]

The only way to square the circle was to keep alive the possibility that alternative arrangements or the future trade deal might, eventually, provide a solution which rendered the backstop irrelevant. On Sunday, 3 December, new language was drafted. Paragraph 49 of the Joint Report decreed that, in the event these other solutions to the Northern Ireland border were not forthcoming, the UK would promise to 'maintain full alignment' with the rules of the single market and customs union on issues that concerned Northern Ireland. The British could argue that other solutions would present themselves, while Barnier's team were certain they would not. May called David Davis, the Brexit secretary, and warned him, 'You might have concerns.' She said, 'We've agreed there'll be full alignment between regulations in Northern Ireland and the EU.'

'You can't say that, Prime Minister,' Davis replied. 'It's completely contrary to what you've said. You'll be locking the UK into the European regulatory system. You'll have given away the whole game. That's harmonisation; we're against harmonisation.'

May said, 'Oh, no, no, it's not harmonisation. It's full alignment of outcomes.' This was either disingenuous or self-delusion.

Davis said, 'Are you sure, Prime Minister, the other side sees it that way? The history of diplomacy where two sides agree the same words but mean different things by them is not a very good history. From the Balfour Declaration onwards.'

'But David, we need to make progress,' May said, bustling through.

When he boarded the prime minister's plane at RAF Northolt for the flight to Brussels on the Monday morning, 4 December, Davis was still telling aides, 'I don't know whether I'm going to sign up to this or not.' He was not alone in having last-minute doubts. The prime minister spent the flight growing agitated at the likely reaction of her MPs. In the car on the way to lunch with Jean-Claude Juncker, the Commission president, May said, 'I'm not sure this is going to work.'

Meanwhile, Juncker briefed the European Parliament Brexit team about the deal. The MEPs were surprised May had agreed to the wording on 'full alignment' and questioned Juncker as to whether Downing Street had really signed it off. However, it was not Theresa May who was the problem. No one had secured Arlene Foster's seal of approval.

Davis was walking through the Berlaymont, the Commission headquarters, on his way to lunch when he took a call from Ian Paisley Jr of the DUP: 'This doesn't work, David.'

'Well, you'd better get your boss to ring my boss.'

May and Juncker were eating turbot on the thirteenth floor of the Berlaymont, when the Irish broadcaster RTE revealed that the UK had agreed to 'continued regulatory alignment' in Northern Ireland. Arlene Foster responded, 'We will not accept any form of regulatory divergence which separates Northern Ireland economically or politically from the rest of the United Kingdom.'

Martin Selmayr, Juncker's chief of staff, who was present for what was supposed to be a convivial gathering to celebrate 'sufficient progress', recalled, 'It was just a friendly working lunch, that was the plan. And in the middle of this a phone call came—'

The call was from Julian Smith, the chief whip. 'We have very big problems here,' he told Robbins, who left the room to speak to him. Robbins returned and said, 'Prime Minister, you have to take this.' May took the phone and went pale, physically reeling as if punched, becoming visibly distracted. Selmayr whispered in Juncker's ear, 'I think we'd better leave them alone now.' The president offered May the use of the dining room and took his team to his own office.

May was patched through to Arlene Foster's mobile while Robbins and Davis watched: 'I believe you have some concerns.' An understatement. The conversation lasted more than an hour. Foster recalled later, 'I related to her that what I read in the texts was simply not something that we could sign up to and therefore we would not be supporting her in the House of Commons if that's what she brought back.' May persisted, explaining her reading of the text, cajoling, a plaintive air to her words. It was awkward to watch: a prime minister with her career in the hands of another. The DUP leader did not budge. Foster said, 'I think she was trying to bounce us … We weren't going to be bounced into something that was going to break up the United Kingdom.'

When the call was over, Robbins found Selmayr and said, 'We have to go back and try to sort this out.' Juncker lost his temper with May. His team had made it clear she should not come to Brussels unless she was ready to do a deal. Now he accused her of 'failing even to speak for her own government', adding, 'You can't come here to negotiate if you don't have a mandate.' As May flew home, Selmayr and Juncker pondered whether she would return or whether her party would force her out. 'We were not sure that we would see them again,' a Commission official said.

Who was to blame? One factor was the move, a month earlier, of the chief whip Gavin Williamson to become defence secretary, robbing May of her chief conduit to the DUP. MPs complained that his replacement Julian Smith and his deputy Esther McVey should have man-marked Nigel Dodds and Jeffrey Donaldson, the senior DUP figures in Westminster. 'While Theresa and DD were in Brussels, the whips' office should have been sitting with the DUP, holding their hands,' one said.

By Tuesday a small group of previously loyal MPs began openly discussing whether they should submit letters to the backbench 1922 Committee demanding a vote of no confidence in May's leadership. On 5 December, fifty MPs in the Tory 92 Group gathered for dinner. Philip Davies, the MP for Shipley, 'gave a speech about how crap Theresa May is', calling for a different leader to deliver Brexit. Zac Goldsmith, the former London mayoral candidate, pondered whether to submit a letter of no confidence. 'My four-year-old daughter could do a better job,' he said.

The same day, Downing Street reopened talks with Barnier while Smith anchored talks with the DUP in 9 Downing Street. The dialogue continued into Thursday. May spoke to Varadkar mid-morning while Robbins, Smith and Davis went to and fro with the Commission, the Irish and the DUP. At the centre of this spider's web, unbeknown to the British media who demonised him as the 'Monster of Brussels', was Martin Selmayr, Juncker's right-hand man. Selmayr was seen as an antagonist of the UK but his boss wanted a deal and Selmayr derived almost erotic pleasure from doing deals. He was in close touch with Robbins as well as Varadkar's EU sherpa John Callinan and his ambassador Declan Kelleher.

Robbins secured six changes to the text, the most important of which was a new paragraph 50, inserted on Wednesday, in which the UK pledged that 'no new regulatory barriers' would be imposed between Northern Ireland and the rest of the UK and that the province would enjoy the 'same unfettered access' to the UK internal market. In a classic Euro-fudge, paragraph 50 came close to contradicting paragraph 49. The EU saw it as a promise from London to the DUP, not from Brussels. The British saw it as something the EU had agreed to help deliver. May summoned the DUP to Downing Street and told them, 'You've got some big wins here.' She asked them to secure Arlene Foster's support.

Meanwhile, Gavin Barwell was keeping the senior Brexiteers informed of what was happening. He spoke to Michael Gove, the environment secretary, by phone, while Boris Johnson, the foreign secretary, visited May in 10 Downing Street at 5.30 p.m. on the Thursday. The content of these conversations was to become highly controversial.

The crunch came in two phone calls between May and Foster, the first at 8 p.m., the second three hours later. May argued that the document was not perfect, but it would allow the talks to move to phase two. Foster was still not happy. After an icy exchange she agreed to ring back. The Number 10 Christmas party was by now in full swing. Barwell recalled, 'We were waiting for Arlene to call us back ... and "Come on Eileen" was playing very loudly.' Number 10 staff belted out 'Come on Arlene!'

As one hour of silence from Belfast became two, Barwell held a small meeting of senior staff. 'Give me your thoughts so I can give good advice to the PM,' he said. One by one they said that their prime minister should call the Unionists' bluff even if it imperilled her premiership. One of those present said, 'The DUP respects strength.' In his pivotal heart-to-heart with May, Barwell told her it was in the national interest to go for it.

May phoned David Davis, who was getting into bed. He told her, 'You are the prime minister, you are doing the negotiation, you have to make the call. And if they won't accept it, tell them you're going to do it anyway.'[7]

By 11.30 p.m., the prime minister decided she could not wait any longer and rang Foster again. Thanks to a technical fault, a tired-looking May had to move to her outer office to connect the call. Her officials listened while the PM sat cross-legged and hunched making her argument. Foster said, 'It's not as bad as it was. But I am still not happy with it.'

May replied, 'I appreciate your candour.' Then she made her move. She said, 'I'm prime minister of the United Kingdom and I've now got to make a decision about what's in the best interests of the country. This is about the Union and about people's jobs.' Those listening to the call felt their chests tighten. 'I will travel to Brussels shortly and say what I have to say.' When she put down the phone, May's team erupted in applause.

For civil servants the DUP 'overestimated their own power', discovering that their usual negotiating technique would not work. 'The DUP were used to talks with the British government where it's all about who holds firm the longest. [The EU] was a bigger player, out of the room, that they couldn't control. They weren't really used to that.'

After midnight Julian Smith, who had a camp bed to sleep on, exchanged texts with Timothy Johnston, the DUP's chief executive and chief fixer. The 'mood music' left him hopeful May had made the right decision. Barwell went home at 1 a.m. Other Number 10 staff slept in their offices. Around 2 a.m., two tiny tweaks allowed the DUP to climb down gracefully. By 4.30 a.m., the prime minister was at Brize Norton, boarding a pre-dawn flight to Brussels. At 5 a.m. Smith rang May to tell her Foster would signal that she was not opposing the deal. 'Your instinct was right,' he said. A cabinet minister recalled, 'The issue with the DUP is often they will not want to consent. They're not always going to say, "We're happy". The next day there was a sort of de facto consent.' However, it was never explicit, something which would haunt May for another fifteen months.

* * *

On arrival in Brussels, an elated May breakfasted with Juncker and Barnier. At 6.06 a.m. Selmayr tweeted a picture of white smoke, the signal that a new Pope has been selected. The deal was done. May agreed to the backstop. In exchange, the EU gave her what the most ardent Remainers in her cabinet and big business had demanded, a two-year transition period to help them prepare for Brexit. Selmayr said later, 'That was probably the most important achievement for her, that was her negotiation success. That was something where we compromised.' But at what price? A Number 10 private office official said later, 'It felt huge at the time. Effectively, we were buying transition. To think how much we paid for a transition period. I don't think anybody really knew what we were agreeing to.'

At the press conferences which followed, both Juncker and Donald Tusk, the European Council president, seemed as pleased as May as they announced that 'sufficient progress' had been achieved. The prime minister had survived, but there was little illusion that she had won, a feeling reinforced in a triumphalist press conference by the Taoiseach. 'Varadkar went out of his way to say that alignment and convergence were the same thing,' a senior Tory complained. An Irish diplomat said, 'We couldn't believe the British had accepted the text.'

Nonetheless, the initial reaction to the deal at home was positive. 'She was cheered to the rafters in the House of Commons,' David Lidington recalled. The solution to the Irish border question remained as elusive as a real-life unicorn. A senior UK negotiator joked: 'We all know unicorns don't exist. The question now is whether everyone can agree to make do with horses with shells glued to their foreheads.'

Brexiteers came to see the backstop as an imposition from Europe, something which riled Robbins' civil service team. 'The Joint Report is just a manifestation of the UK government's commitments,' a member of the Europe Unit said. If it was contradictory and confused that was because the government had not made the key decisions. A special adviser added, 'Boris, DD and the DUP agreed to have an Irish backstop.'

What was to stick in the craw of the Brexiteers, however, was that May's inner circle were far from frank about the implications of the deal. 'To the EU "full alignment" meant full regulatory harmonisation,' a member of May's inner circle admitted. 'Full alignment to us was outcome equivalence.' Michael Gove was uneasy but was ultimately won over by this argument peddled by Barwell, Robbins and Robbie Gibb, Downing Street's communications director. Gibb warned fellow Leavers that they should back May or imperil their own project. 'The risk at this point in the political process is that the Remainers in Parliament in our own party will try and stop us delivering Brexit,' he said.

Gibb's advocacy was to damage his reputation with the cabinet Brexiteers. In a meeting in the foreign secretary's office, he took Johnson and his spads, David Frost and Lee Cain, through the plan. One of those present claimed Gibb said, 'I don't understand this myself, but the civil service has said it's needed and that it's a good idea and that's why I think you should back it.' The witness added, 'That cost him a large amount of credibility.' Carrie Symonds, Johnson's girlfriend, branded him 'Robbie Fib'. Gibb even called Dominic Cummings and argued that Heywood 'absolutely guarantees that it doesn't mean' what the Brexiteers feared. Cummings replied, 'Jeremy has guaranteed a lot of things over the years. We've seen this move before. He guarantees ABC, the British government signs on the dotted line and then it turns out that's not what we signed up to at all.' Gove and Johnson were also told that the deal was not legally binding and Britain could get out of it later. Multiple sources say Gibb used the phrase, 'It's just words.' This later looked like sophistry or ignorance. A senior civil servant admitted: 'The text of the Joint Report was argued over as if it was a legal text; it was all about dots and commas.'

When Johnson saw May and Barwell on the 7th, he was armed with legal advice from Iain Macleod, the top lawyer in the Foreign Office, that the backstop would, in Johnson's words, 'make it impossible for the UK to opt for no-deal' since walking away would cut Northern Ireland adrift. Johnson argued with the prime minister and chief of staff 'until I was blue in the face'. He said, 'It's going to make it impossible for us to negotiate freely, because we're ultimately pledging that if we can't sort out certain problems – whose solutions are not wholly in our gift – then we must lose economic control of Northern Ireland.' The foreign secretary's view was that the Joint Report was 'a terrible trap' which was 'prelude to a greater surrender'. He recalled, 'By vowing to keep Northern Ireland in regulatory alignment and the customs union, it was a step towards what I'd been fighting against for six months, which was the UK – entire – remaining in the customs union and the single market.'

In reply, May and Barwell offered the same view as Gibb. 'It's just something we've got to say in order to make progress … It will never be operational.' One of May's EU advisers said, 'We all hoped there were enough ambiguities in the text.' But Johnson later concluded this was 'shameful stuff'. He said, 'I remember being absolutely reassured that this was just a form of words that was necessary to float the negotiations off the rocks. The [backstop] issue [was] allowed to dominate in a way that we were expressly promised would not happen.'[8] One of his aides added, 'Theresa May and Barwell were at best disingenuous and at worst, flat-out lying. We could see Brexit going off the rails. We couldn't work out if it was because the negotiating team didn't know what they were doing or because they did know what they were doing and didn't have the same objectives [as us]. They tried to reassure Boris with magic words.' A Paleosceptic admitted alarm bells should have been ringing louder: 'The Joint Report was a very important moment because the ERG got it wrong. We made a mistake.'

David Davis believed Number 10 was guilty of 'deal-itis'. He said later, 'They signed up to the backstop because they were desperate to make progress. They basically had a loss of nerve.'[9] Of the cabinet Brexiteers Davis was the most concerned but the most loyal. Which alarmed Brussels when he told the BBC's Andrew Marr that Sunday the deal was 'more a statement of intent than it was a legally enforceable thing'. Barnier thundered, 'We will not accept any backtracking from the UK.' An aide admitted later, 'DD lost an awful lot of credit with people in the EU because of that.'

All the focus was on paragraphs 49 and 50 but May's biggest mistake may have been agreeing the language of Clause 43, which allowed the avoidance of a hard border to be defined as ruling out 'any physical infra-structure or related checks and controls'. That would make it all but impossible to put in place technical measures to police trade, even away from the border area. 'No infrastructure meant literally nothing,' said former education secretary Nicky Morgan, who became an expert on the practicalities, 'including eyes in the sky, using your mobile phone to log your details.' A Downing Street aide later concluded, 'Meeting that bar through anything other than a customs union and single market or a backstop was very difficult.'

By the spring of 2018 a narrative had gained momentum that May and her team were deceiving the Brexiteers about their true intentions. A Number 10 adviser claimed cock-up not conspiracy: 'I genuinely think that the building didn't understand exactly what we'd given away in

December 2017.' Denzil Davidson admitted, 'We had a collective failure in government at the time properly to understand the implications for Northern Ireland, for which I must share the guilt. The only guy at the time on our side who really understood the Northern Ireland Brexit problem ... was David Lidington.'[10] Others are unwilling to absolve the prime minister. A senior figure in the government legal department recalled, 'I think May understood. She's a details person. She knew what she was doing.'

Cummings and Vote Leave's legal expert Richard 'Ricardo' Howell told the Brexiteers the deal did not work and they had already lost what they campaigned for in 2016. Had Davis, Johnson, Gove and Liam Fox joined forces and opposed May she might have been forced to change tack or been forced out. But they were divided. Davis remained loyal to the woman who brought him back to frontline politics. He and Fox shared a mutual respect, but Davis and Johnson saw each other as leadership rivals and all three distrusted Gove. 'DD thinks Boris is a charlatan who's only interested in himself,' an aide said. Johnson calculated it was not the right issue on which to take a stand. 'Boris knew it was a disaster, but he thought nobody would understand if he resigned,' a close ally said. At that point the backstop was seen as 'arcane'. Johnson did not want to resign 'over a technicality'.

It was not just the Brexiteers who were uneasy. Denzil Davidson feared the deal would likely lead to Northern Ireland being semi-detached from the rest of the UK. He became the primary advocate of a potential solution. At this point the Joint Report contained three potential Brexit outcomes: alternative arrangements (as yet undefined) at the border, a future trade deal that created a UK-wide solution, or the backstop. Davidson argued that the Joint Report would only become a problem when the political agreement was converted into legal text in the withdrawal treaty. Britain, he argued, should write its own version of the legal text. If it did so there would then have to be a negotiation to consolidate that with the EU's draft. If the UK left the drafting job to Barnier's Commission lawyers, it would be far harder to push the EU negotiators off their own text.

In this campaign Davidson was supported by May's middle-ranking political aides and by Raoul Ruparel, Davis's special adviser who would go on to work in Number 10. Davis trusted Ruparel, a bear of a man who introduced himself to intrigued colleagues with the words, 'Dad Indian, mum Swiss, Irish middle name, born and raised in the UK'. He had as much experience of dealing with Brussels as anyone in DExEU under the rank of director general. While he voted Remain, Ruparel believed that Brexit had to mean leaving both the single market and the customs union.

However, Robbins felt the proposal to draft a legal text impractical. The cabinet was divided and would not decide Britain's end goal for another two months. To write down a legal text in black and white would have meant deciding which of the three outcomes to back. Davidson recalled, 'I suggested at the time that we should work on [a text] but I think officials felt that our politics would not have allowed us to put forward one that was even remotely realistic, and so it was better for the EU to lead the process.'[11] A civil servant blamed the prime minister: 'By writing it down, you would have forced the argument and that was always the problem with May. She was never willing to force the argument.'

Robbins did have another option, which would have been better than waiting for Brussels to dictate terms. An EU adviser suggested, 'Olly could have said, "Our politics is too difficult for us to produce a text, but let's work together on your [EU] text and I can tell you what could eventually work."' That might have led to a less objectionable text.

Instead, the two months after the Joint Report was a missed opportunity. One of those involved said, 'We were never on the front foot.' Another said, 'It is a huge moment, because the whole narrative was dictated by them getting stuff out before us, and us having to work back from their positions. It was terrible negotiating tactics.' The folly of this decision would become evident in February 2018, when the Commission's legal text was published.

The Joint Report was a battle lost because fatalism and survival trumped strategy. As one Downing Street aide recalled, 'Politically the pressure on her to get something done by December was so great that she was willing to consider concessions that she was not willing to consider up until that point. Her confidence had been knocked by the general election.' A senior civil servant agreed: 'She was wobbling very badly. If we had not got sufficient progress before Christmas, I don't think you could have said with any certainty that she would have made it to the new year.'

In doing the deal May had survived the greatest crisis of her premiership to date, but she would navigate the rest of the Brexit process with a policy which had been dictated to her rather than by her. With that she went into battle against her cabinet, the EU and Parliament. Within a week she had suffered her second foundational setback.

THE MONOGRAMMED MUTINEER

The Meaningful Vote

December 2017

Julian Smith faced another difficult conversation with his prime minister. Six days after he had to call Theresa May to tell her she had lost the DUP, the chief whip had to warn her she was on course to lose her first parliamentary vote on Brexit. It was lunchtime on 13 December 2017 and the mood in the whips' office, a warren of rooms off the members' lobby in the House of Commons, was grim. Smith looked around him. His deputy Esther McVey was there, along with his special adviser Simon Burton and Nikki da Costa, the Downing Street head of legislative affairs, the point person between the MPs and Number 10. That morning each whip had phoned their 'flock', the group of around twenty MPs who they both counselled and cajoled. They went through the numbers. The conclusion was stark: the votes were not there.

The situation was acutely embarrassing for 'the chief'. A workaholic who used an easy charm to win over MPs he favoured, Smith was also prone to periods of brooding intensity and some in May's team believed he kept information to himself if it enhanced his standing not to share it. Everyone agreed no one else worked harder to deliver for his prime minister, the dark circles into which his tired eyes sank were testament to that. Smith had held four different posts in the whips' office, but he had only been in the top job for a month. He turned to da Costa, the air seeming to go out of him, and said, 'I need you to back me up. I want to go to the prime minister and say, "We're going to have to take the defeat."'

For months da Costa had been warning that the demands of Remain-backing MPs for a 'meaningful vote' on the final Brexit legislation were a covert attempt to block Britain from ever leaving the EU. She said, 'Okay, you have my backing.' They agreed to meet again at 2 p.m.

The issue of the meaningful vote blew up because of the contradictions in Britain's unwritten constitution. The withdrawal agreement with the EU and any subsequent trade deal would be international treaties. The government, the executive, was solely responsible for negotiating, signing, ratifying, amending and withdrawing from all international treaties, using royal prerogative powers. It was the government that would be bound by the treaty under international law.

Parliament, the legislature, could not block the ratification of a treaty but, since 2010, they could vote to delay the government from ratifying one for twenty-one days, a process that could continue indefinitely (though it had never been used). MPs also had a say if a treaty required legislation to implement it. Usually, such laws would be nodded-through the Commons using an order called a statutory instrument.

Brexit was different from most treaties since it was highly controversial and a referendum had pitched popular direct democracy (where 52 per cent voted to Leave) against parliamentary democracy (where two thirds of MPs wanted to Remain). Consequently, MPs wanted the right to pass judgement on any Brexit deal and some of them wanted to be able to demand a different approach. The government was determined that the executive should make the decisions and that essential primary legislation was passed without being amended.

Into this stand-off stepped the unlikely commander of the rebel forces. Dominic Grieve believed there was an 'enormous error' in the legislation. Clause 9 of the European Union Withdrawal Bill, the legal means by which the UK would leave the European Union, 'gave the government the power to implement the withdrawal agreement without primary legislation,' he explained. Grieve was a constitutional lawyer, a former attorney general no less, with a punctilious belief in things being done properly. He was not a natural leader, nor an orator. His influence came from his command of detail, his legal expertise and a certain saintly intensity, which to David Cameron had smelt of priggish pedantry when he dismissed Grieve as chief law officer in 2014.

Clause 9 of the bill had been written to enable measures 'the minister considers appropriate' to implement the withdrawal agreement 'on or before exit day'. For May and David Davis, arbitrary powers were necessary to ensure that the gargantuan task of turning EU law into British law was completed in time. For their critics the only thing that was gargantuan was the power grab. The clauses were known as 'Henry VIII powers', named after the most dictatorial of England's monarchs. Grieve regarded the government's attempt to push all the Brexit laws through as secondary legislation as inappropriate.

The government was already on the back foot. In November 2016, the High Court had ruled in favour of City fund manager Gina Miller, who had brought a case demanding that Parliament give its approval before the government trigger the process of leaving the EU. The ruling had led the *Daily Mail*, one of the primary Brexit cheerleaders, to brand the judges 'enemies of the people', a bitter foretaste of the divisions which followed.

Following pressure from Keir Starmer, the shadow Brexit secretary, in January 2017, May had announced, 'The government will put the final deal that is agreed between the UK and the EU to a vote in both Houses of Parliament, before it comes into force.' The MPs had their vote. But Starmer believed MPs deserved the same powers over the deal as the European Parliament, which would have to ratify a withdrawal agreement on the EU side. With May's majority obliterated, he sought to make it a 'meaningful vote', where Parliament could not just approve or reject the government's approach, but potentially change it too.

Starmer knew a successful move could not come from the Labour front bench since it would require Conservative MPs to back an amendment. Instead, he worked closely with Grieve, who had been attorney general while Starmer was director of public prosecutions. 'There was a strong element of trust between the two of us,' Starmer said.

On the second weekend in December, as the ink was barely dry on the Joint Report with the EU, Grieve tabled what became Amendment 7 to Clause 9, which stipulated that the Henry VIII powers could only be used once Parliament had passed a 'statute … approving the final terms' of the withdrawal agreement. It explicitly stated that MPs could make any 'provision', including 'modifying this Act'. If Grieve got his way, the government could not enact a Brexit deal unless MPs gave their permission and the MPs could tell them to rethink the details.

Amendment 7's clipped language was rather like its author – low key but quietly revolutionary. It was to make Grieve a folk hero for the liberal Remainer clans with whom he previously had very little in common. At

Oxford he had been a right-wing antagonist of Theresa May and Philip Hammond and helped to throw Damian Green (appropriately, a Tory 'wet') from a bridge into the River Cherwell. Green narrowly avoided being impaled on iron railings.

Grieve was adamant then and afterwards that he was not simply intent on blocking Brexit. He had regarded the referendum result as 'a terrible mess' but, in 2016, felt he should support Theresa May. However, May's speech to the Tory conference in 2016 'depressed' him 'no end' since it signalled a hard Brexit. The government's failure to 'protect the judiciary' from attacks like the *Mail*'s further radicalised him. In the general election campaign, Grieve reconciled himself to the Conservative manifesto pledging to deliver the referendum result because it also promised 'a deep and special relationship' with the EU. After the election, with May propped up by the DUP, he grew concerned that the prime minister was drifting towards placating the hardline Eurosceptics. 'That's when the resistance movement started to coalesce,' a former minister said.

A group of around seventeen Conservatives began to meet, often in Grieve's room, sometimes in the room of Stephen Hammond, a vice chairman of the party, or Heidi Allen, whose office was close to the Commons chamber, a useful location to coordinate before key votes. The inner core also included Nicky Morgan, Anna Soubry, Jonathan Djanogly, Antoinette Sandbach and Bob Neill. 'They were psychotherapy sessions for ex-Remainers,' one participant recalled. In these meetings Grieve told colleagues May 'would like to do a deal which keeps us closely intertwined with the EU' but he had concluded, 'This is never going to work', because the prime minister was in hock to 'ideologically obsessed' Eurosceptics. 'These people are becoming more and more extreme,' he warned. Believing May was retreating from her own manifesto pledge, Grieve no longer felt bound by it either.

In November 2017, May gave in to a demand from Eurosceptics that the time and date of Brexit be written onto 'the face of the bill', meaning that 29 March 2019 was written into the text of the legislation. When Grieve and fourteen others objected, the *Daily Telegraph* branded them 'The Brexit Mutineers' on its front page.[1] Grieve was initially stung by the coverage but, in time, it strengthened the group's resolve.

Nikki da Costa, an intense Brexiteer who spoke at nineteen to the dozen, was an early and vocal harbinger of the threat from what became known as 'the Grieve gang'. 'Nikki had been screaming about it,' a

Number 10 aide said. Her fear, outlined to colleagues, was simple: 'The meaningful vote is designed to create deadlock. It's a Remain tool to create the unholy alliance between the ultra-Remainers and the ultra-Brexiteers to avoid a deal ever being passed.'

As the vote on Amendment 7 approached, Julian Smith called in Grieve and tried to find a compromise that would neuter the rebellion and preserve the government's room to manoeuvre. Grieve suggested that 'one possibility might be to allow statutory instruments to be laid and voted on' by MPs 'but not allow them to be brought into force' until MPs had approved the withdrawal bill. These conversations, to Grieve's surprise, went nowhere. Smith appealed to his pragmatism. 'I've got to unite the whole party here,' the chief whip said. 'I can't give you everything.' Grieve was unmoved. He was no longer prepared to be more reasonable than the Eurosceptics.

Rebel MPs impressed by proximity to power, appeals to loyalty, or those with a reasonable expectation of promotion, were called in to see the prime minister. The whips dealt with those more vulnerable to flattery or threats. May did 'very heartfelt one-to-ones with all the rebels, some of whom she'd known many years,' an aide said. 'She was shaken by the fact that their long-standing relationships didn't seem to count at all.'

On the day of the vote, 13 December, David Davis issued a written ministerial statement clarifying that 'the government has committed to hold a vote on the final deal in Parliament as soon as possible after the negotiations have concluded. This vote will take the form of a resolution in both Houses of Parliament and will cover both the Withdrawal Agreement and the terms for our future relationship.' He had wanted to make this clear earlier but ran up against plans for a 'concession strategy' by the whips. 'We've got to be able to concede that later,' he was told. Davis, a former whip during Maastricht, thought this 'a fucking stupid way to do it', since 'the act of giving concessions creates the appetite for more concessions'. Coming too late, his statement did not assuage the rebels.

At 2 p.m. May's team met to consider what to do. Da Costa ran through the concessions that had been offered to the rebels. They debated the merits of giving in. Da Costa argued the government needed to keep its ability to use the special powers outlined in Clause 9. 'There isn't anything more we can do whilst protecting this red line,' she said. Smith's view from the whips' office was that it was better to fight and lose than to give way. There was a chance of victory, but he was rolling the pitch for defeat. 'There's a chance, Prime Minister, but we should prepare.' The room went quiet. May's team tried to get precise numbers from the chief whip. Smith was evasive. Then May spoke: 'Okay, we'll fight it to the end.' One of those present said, 'There was a decision by the prime minister to take the defeat. There was no alternative.'

Smith had asked for consensus that there should be no more concessions. May had agreed. Yet at the back of his mind, he always believed that if he worked just a little harder a deal could be done.

The debate was bruising for the government. The two sides talked past each other for eight hours, the speakers heavily weighted towards the rebels. Around 2.20 p.m., Grieve got to his feet, exasperated that his Amendment 7 had become a totem in a culture war. 'All rational discourse starts to evaporate,' he said, when opponents claimed its 'underlying purpose is the sabotage of the will of the people, which it most manifestly is not'. He complained about 'people telling one that one is a traitor'. Lifting the lid on his talks with Smith, Grieve expressed despair that the government had not tried to meet him halfway. 'I do want the Government to listen. The opportunity is here for them to accept the amendment.'

Grieve could not disguise his emotions. He responded to an intervention by Jacob Rees-Mogg with a florid denunciation of a no-deal departure from the EU: 'Simply leaving to jump off the top of the tower block is not the best thing to do.' He concluded by baring his teeth at those Brexiteers who saw him as a monogrammed mutineer. 'Apart from on HS2, I do not think that I have ever rebelled against the Government in my twenty and a half years in this House. I do find it quite entertaining that some who criticise me for speaking my mind on this matter are individuals who appear to have exercised the luxury of rebellion on many, many occasions.' After half an hour, Grieve sat down. It was a little before 3 p.m.

At 4.20, Dominic Raab put the government's case. He pointed to the ministerial statement that morning which clarified that the withdrawal bill would only be introduced after Parliament voted to back the deal. Yet Raab continued to insist that Clause 9 would give ministers the 'agility' to implement 'technical' aspects of an exit agreement where ministers were 'squeezed for time'. Raab said the amendment would 'risk materially damaging responsible preparations for exit'. It was nearly 5 p.m. when he offered a political promise in three parts. First, any Henry VIII statutory instruments would be 'affirmative', meaning they had to be voted for by MPs. Second, Raab said they would be published in draft 'as early as possible, to facilitate maximum scrutiny'. Finally, the minister offered a 'concrete assurance' that 'none of the SIs introduced under Clause 9 will come into effect until Parliament has voted on the final deal'. With that, he called for the amendment to be withdrawn. The only problem was that these were verbal, not legally binding promises.

While Julian Smith was trying in vain to get his MPs to back Raab's compromise, his Labour opposite number, Nick Brown, was quietly working on Labour MPs who backed Brexit and might have been tempted to support the government. Brown deployed Jeremy Corbyn to phone Lexiteers like Dennis Skinner, Grahame Morris, Ronnie Campbell and John Mann to convince them that defeating the Tories was a bigger prize. All four voted for Grieve's amendment, enough to make the difference.

At 6.20 p.m., forty minutes before the vote, Nikki da Costa arrived at the whips' office. She found Smith, Davis and Raab, who had stepped out of the chamber, in conversation. 'We're going to tough this out,' Smith said.

'Well, are we going to win?' asked Davis.

'No,' the chief whip admitted.

'Well make the fucking concession,' Davis said. He proposed writing into law that none of the statutory instruments envisaged under Clause 9 could come into force until after Parliament had voted on a final deal. For fifteen or twenty minutes they debated it. Smith thought it worth a try.

Da Costa was horrified, for two reasons. Putting the promise into law was to ensure that the parliamentary vote on the deal would now supercharge the notion of 'meaningful' as it would give Parliament a veto over every step of turning Brexit into reality, placing a minority government at the mercy of the smallest factions of rebel MPs. Not four hours earlier Smith had asked the prime minister to go down fighting rather than give way and May had agreed there would be no further concessions. 'This is a big step to take,' da Costa said. 'You just asked the prime minister to take a decision. She's given her view.' Most importantly, da Costa did not think the concession would be enough to win the vote.

Smith did not see another way. 'No, go and do it,' he said.

'It was very typical of Julian to go back and try and try again,' said one May adviser. Raab returned to the chamber at 6.40 p.m. and told MPs the government would table their own amendment at report stage of the bill, writing into law that the Henry VIII orders 'will not come into force until we have had a meaningful vote in Parliament'.

Furious, da Costa called Gavin Barwell, May's chief of staff. 'We're offering a concession twenty minutes out, and they're not going to buy it,' she warned. 'We know they want blood.'

In keeping with Brexit as concurrent drama and farce, Grieve was not even in the chamber to hear Raab's concession. Five minutes passed. He was alerted and returned. Too irate after a fortnight of futile negotiations to back down, he said: 'It is too late. I am sorry, but you cannot treat the House in this fashion.' To his admirers, Grieve was never more principled. To his critics, there was about him the whiff of martyrdom, of which David Cameron had tired. Julian Smith reflected later, 'This was when that group began to reveal their true colours. We had given a lot, but like Pac-Man they kept coming for more. They just wanted to defeat us.'

At 7 p.m. the chief whip stood grim-faced as the MPs trooped through the division lobbies. The result was close enough that the rebels thought they had lost. Sitting on the opposition front bench, Keir Starmer had prepared two press statements, option A for a win, option B for a loss. 'It was on an absolute knife edge,' he recalled. Yet when the whips assembled before the mace, Downing Street knew they had lost. Labour's Stephen Doughty, a teller for the rebels, read out the result: 'The ayes to right 309, the noes to the left 305.' May's government had lost its first vote on Brexit. Starmer, the hairs now upright on the back of his neck, pressed send on a text to his team: 'Option A'.

When Smith returned from the chamber, he was confronted by da Costa in front of witnesses. 'You can't do that,' she said. 'You cannot ask me to back you with the prime minister and ask her to take a decision and you just override it with no consideration.' Smith had botched his first big test, an experience which was scarring. 'It changed him,' a close observer said. Smith and da Costa's relationship was irreparably damaged. 'From that moment on he stopped talking to Nikki,' the source said.

For Grieve's branch of the Bresistance the first rebellion was a crossing of the Rubicon. There were eleven and a half rebels. As well as Grieve and Soubry, Heidi Allen, Ken Clarke, Jonathan Djanogly, Stephen Hammond, Oliver Heald, Nicky Morgan, Bob Neill, Antoinette Sandbach and Sarah Wollaston all backed the amendment. John Stevenson voted both aye and no, a formal abstention. Hammond was promptly sacked as vice-chair of the Conservative Party. With the bonds of loyalty loosened, it would be difficult to bind them again. 'It has broken the dam,' a Labour whip predicted that night.[2] That evening the rebels gathered in the Pugin room for a much-needed drink. Brexiteers briefed the press that they were quaffing champagne to toast the defeat of their own government. 'That is not true,' one said. 'We only had a glass of wine.' Yet there was a triumphal mood. Nicky Morgan tweeted, 'Tonight Parliament took control of the EU withdrawal process.' Nadine Dorries, the MP for Mid Bedfordshire called for them all to be kicked out of the party, an intervention with future echoes. The Conservative parliamentary party now consisted of two armed camps with a bewildered mass of MPs in the middle seeing both Brexiteers and Remainers radicalised.

To Starmer it was a watershed moment which showed that Labour and the Tory rebels could work together. 'It was the single most important foothold in the whole process,' he said later. 'It was the first time we'd secured a massive victory against the government. It was the first demonstration that there were Tories prepared to work with us.' It was also a moment, Starmer reflected, when May should have pivoted herself. 'At that point she probably should have realised she needed to reach out to the whole house. That didn't happen.'

Eighteen months later May's team saw the events of 13 December 2017 as key. 'For me, the moment her premiership fell was the meaningful vote defeat,' one special adviser said. In the space of a week Downing Street had given MPs veto powers over a future Brexit deal and handed them an issue, in the backstop, which was to give a sizeable number of them incentive to exercise that power. Together these issues dominated the rest of May's premiership. A Number 10 adviser concluded that, for a minority government, 'It was checkmate.'

Neither would have had the same impact if the prime minister had made fewer mistakes in the seventeen months between the referendum and Grieve's big win. To understand the scale of the mess, it is important to understand how she got there.

3

OUT MANOEUVRED
Before the Backstop
June 2016 to December 2017

In Brussels, Brexit did produce one winner. Frans Timmermans, the Commission's vice president had bet Jonathan Hill, the British commissioner, that Leave would win the referendum. Timmermans, a former Dutch foreign minister, had been educated in the UK and understood British politics better than most Eurocrats. If Timmermans was not surprised, he still felt it as 'a very tough punch in the gut'. He, like others, had been urged to stay out of the referendum campaign by David Cameron. Eurocrats felt they had lost the game without even playing.

Most Commission and Council officials could not comprehend that a member state would ever want to leave. In the Commission offices, including those of the president Jean-Claude Juncker, where two British-born officials worked, 'people were in tears'. Denzil Davidson, May's EU adviser who had spent time working in Brussels, said, 'The Brits in the Commission were distraught and very angry. A lot of what they spent their life working for, and what they believed in, were smashed.'[1]

In the EU institutions, there was not just disappointment, there was also fear. 'We knew that this could pose a potentially existential threat to the union,' said one senior EU official.

Officials in Brussels were also prepared. In the two days before the referendum result was announced, Tusk called all twenty-seven other EU leaders to coordinate a response. A former prime minister of Poland, Tusk was the first Eastern European to lead the Council. He combined a strong emotional opposition to Brexit with a belief in representing every EU nation, small as well as large. 'If it happens,' he said, 'it is important that we are united, it is important that we know what to do.'

Tusk shared the text of a statement drawn up by Jeppe Tranholm-Mikkelsen, the senior official in the Council, and Piotr Serafin, Tusk's chief of staff, which he would issue if there was a Leave vote. Just five paragraphs long, it shaped the following three years to a degree which is remarkable. It stated that 'the Union of 27 Member States will continue'. London would consistently underestimate the unity on the other side.

The document dictated the terms of the negotiation: 'We expect the UK to formulate its wishes when it comes to our future relationship.' Immediately the onus was on Britain to decide what it wanted, not for the EU to devise solutions. It was a challenge to which the May government would struggle to rise. The paper continued, 'Any agreement, which will be concluded with the UK as a third country, will have to reflect the interests of both sides and be balanced in terms of rights and obligations.' A lot of pain might have been spared in London if this sentence had been understood. A post-Brexit Britain would be treated not as a trusted member of the club but as a 'third country' outside the union. Britain could not just cling on to the benefits of membership without paying a price. That was what 'rights and obligations' meant.

The third paragraph made clear the EU would dictate the choreography of the negotiation. Negotiations would only begin 'as soon as the UK has notified its intention to leave in accordance with Article 50 of the Treaty'. This was the Lisbon Treaty and Article 50 decreed that once a state had fired the starting gun, a two-year negotiation with Brussels would begin. Lord Kerr, the Briton who had written the clause, did so to make leaving difficult and to give the EU the cards.

That was one reason why the official Vote Leave campaign, run by Dominic Cummings, Michael Gove and Boris Johnson, had made clear during the campaign that they did not wish to use this formal mechanism. 'We will negotiate the terms of a new deal before we start any legal process to leave,' Vote Leave pronounced on its literature. Neither Johnson nor Gove won the leadership election and May had not taken this stance. Yet whoever was in charge, they were now facing an EU bloc that would refuse to talk until they had triggered Article 50. 'You have the principle of no negotiations without notification,' a member of Tusk's team said. 'When we thought that up, we were thinking about the number plates in Washington – "no taxation without representation".'

At 6.22 a.m. in London, the morning after the referendum, with the result not yet certified, Tusk issued his statement. Ivan Rogers, the UK's permanent representative in Brussels, knew Tranholm-Mikkelsen had the document in his top drawer a long time before the referendum and remarked, 'Virtually everything that's happened since, you could derive from the decisions they took in the first few days. They dictated the play … At every stage, the UK has been batting last on a wicket taking a lot of spin.'[2]

The contrast with the civil service across the Channel was stark. David Cameron had banned his cabinet secretary, Jeremy Heywood, from making any preparations for Brexit, on the grounds that he was not contemplating defeat.[3] At an away day in Brussels early in 2016, Sir Nick Macpherson, permanent secretary at the Treasury, argued for contingency planning.[4] Heywood overruled him. He feared plans would leak and affect the referendum result. May's cabinet and officials had to spend months getting up to speed on key issues. Damian Green, who became her deputy, recalled, 'The British state had not done a shred of preparation. The whole machine went on a journey, and part of that journey was to discover problems that hadn't been discussed at the time of the referendum.'[5] A senior EU official was withering about Heywood's failure to prepare: 'It is always the obligation of politicians to say there is no plan B and there is always the obligation on civil servants to make sure that there is one.'

Viewing Brexit as a threat to the existence of the EU led inexorably to a belief that Britain should not be able to gain economic and political advantages from leaving, lest it encourage other member states to follow. François Hollande, the French president until May 2017, watched the results of the referendum with his closest aides in the Élysée Palace. When it became clear that Leave had won, he called a crisis meeting. 'This is the very first time that a country is going to leave the EU, so it's an historic moment,' Hollande said. 'If we want to hand down some lesson here then it's important that there be a price. If it's all win-win to easily withdraw from the EU then that would mean the end of the European project.'[6] Europhiles in London frequently dismissed claims that Britain was punished for leaving as fake news from Brexiteers. But officials in Brussels agree the French government was determined to see Britain lose out and was far from alone. 'At the very beginning, there was in some circles – the French president is a perfect example – this punitive attitude,' a senior Commission official explained. 'If somebody you like or you respect slaps you in the face, you don't say "Thank you." The emotion initially [was]: "Let's slap them back."'

There were three camps on the EU side. The 'punitive school', a senior
EU figure said, 'saw Brexit as an opportunity, as a moment to finally get
rid of the British, even to punish the British'. At the other extreme were
those who 'not only regret Brexit but wanted to undo it'. They included
Donald Tusk but also parts of the German political establishment. 'There
are many Germans in Berlin who would say, "Don't leave us alone with
the French,"' the official said. The third 'bureaucratic-pragmatic' faction
in Brussels thought Brexit 'a mistake' but recognised they had to 'respect
and execute' the result with minimum disruption. In this bracket,
contrary to some British media commentary, was Jean-Claude Juncker
and his right-hand man Martin Selmayr, though neither was above
enjoying Britain's discomfort along the way.

To EU officials it was a given that the process would be painful and
economically damaging. 'If you're disentangling something that's grown
together for over forty years, you're going to kill some of the branches,
some of the roots and that's going to hurt,' a Commission official said.

Fears that the EU project was endangered were heightened by the
growing success of political populists around the world. Hollande, who
faced re-election in 2017, feared Marine Le Pen's Front National, which
wanted to leave the EU. The far right was thriving in Italy, Austria and
the Netherlands. By November 2016 the attention turned to Donald
Trump, who was nearly as enthusiastic about Brexit as he was about
himself. When Trump spoke to Tusk, he taunted the Council president:
'Who's next?'

Hollande was also an influential voice in arguing that the EU should
stick together to stop the British picking off member states one by one, a
view the Commission shared. Selmayr said, 'The most important thing
was to … make sure … all twenty-seven saw eye to eye.'[7] Hollande won
the argument that there should be one EU Brexit negotiator. There was a
brief power struggle between the Council, which represents the member
states, and the Commission, the EU's permanent civil service. The
Commission was a professional negotiating organisation ten times the
size of the Council. Michel Barnier, formerly France's commissioner for
financial affairs, took on the job, but he was kept 'on the leash' by the
member states, who demanded to be in the loop. This would not be like
other negotiations where the Commission delivered a fait accompli to the
capitals. 'It was clear to us that for member states it would be politically
impossible to be presented with something at the end of the day,' a

Council official said. Tusk appointed Belgian Didier Seeuws as his Brexit pointman with national governments. He and Tranholm-Mikkelsen met regularly with Barnier and his deputy Sabine Weyand and sometimes with Selmayr. By creating one point of contact for the UK, the EU removed the prospect of key decisions being taken at summits. Selmayr warned David Lidington, 'There's not going to be the traditional EU late into the night horse trading. It'll be the Commission that your side talks to. We are not going to give your prime minister the chance to try and pick us off.'[8]

Barnier's antagonistic attitude to the British owed much to his Gaullist political roots and to his personal history. In 2005 he had been fired as French foreign minister after his own countrymen voted in a referendum to reject the EU constitution. For Barnier, Brexit was a wholly negative event, not an opportunity to do things differently. 'Everybody will have to pay a price, EU and UK, because there is no added value to Brexit,' he said. 'Brexit is a lose-lose game for everybody.'[9] Emotionally and tactically, it made sense for Brussels to play hardball. To their surprise, the EU found a British government that was slow to understand the game, let alone play it effectively, under the leadership of someone who either did not know or did not like to say how she wanted the game to end.

Theresa May's decision to back the Remain campaign was typical of her – it came after a lengthy period of contemplation and was couched in pragmatism rather than ideology, a response to calculated fears about the impact on the economy and security. As a lukewarm backer of Remain, only her absence was notable in the referendum campaign. Craig Oliver, the director of communications for Britain Stronger in Europe, recalled, 'We felt that at each stage when there was an opportunity for Theresa May to be helpful, she would actually say something that was nuanced and a bit difficult for the Remain campaign.'[10] May's ambivalence also made her a unifying figure (as she doubtless intended) when Cameron's resignation put the leadership up for grabs and Gove and Johnson's falling out rendered them both unelectable. May's stance put her in the mainstream of public opinion, in a world where many voters did not see Brexit in black and white. 'She was pretty Eurosceptic, but on balance was quite uncomfortable about some of the risk,' Nick Timothy said.[11]

The story of the next three years is the story of how May contrived to alienate both Remainers and Brexiteers. Having helped to create two sides, she failed then to pick one.

Her aides and enemies agreed on one thing: that she felt a near-missionary zeal to deliver on the referendum result. Damian Green said, 'The actual details of where we land are less a motivator to her than we have to land somewhere, and that somewhere has to be outside the European Union.'[12] Never before has a prime minister had to make the centrepiece of their programme something they believed to be damaging to the country. The prime minister saw Brexit as a problem to be managed. Many Brexiteers would never forgive her for failing to embrace it as an opportunity to be grasped.

At the start, May did have one strong view, shaped by her time as home secretary. She thought Brexit meant controlling immigration. Chris Wilkins, her director of strategy, said, 'That for her was the issue where for many years the public had been saying one thing, and people in Westminster had been not listening and trying to do something else.' This was reinforced by what one cabinet minister called May's 'Berkshire vicarage element, where she believes that people don't have jobs because they have been taken by immigrants'. The paradox was: controlling immigration was a key driver of Leave votes but not what drove most Brexiteers in Parliament. The Paleosceptics cared about sovereignty, others like Boris Johnson wanted regulatory freedom. It would be MPs May needed to convince to pass her Brexit deal. Gavin Barwell said: 'If you're looking at the political difficulties the country has gone through, that gap between what motivated people to pursue this project over a long period of time, and the arguments that were front and centre in the referendum campaign, is part of the issue.'[13]

Two days before the referendum, Ivan Rogers predicted to Tranholm-Mikkelsen that the close relationship anticipated by most commentators would not materialise: 'If we go out, we'll obviously go a really long way out, mid-Atlantic, and it'll be at most a skinny free trade agreement, because we'll obviously leave the single market and the customs union.' The Dane, the EU official who perhaps best understood Britain, agreed: 'Most of the European elites are not ready for that because they think that that's obvious insanity and you won't do it. But I think you'll have to do it because there's no other way, if it's about free movement, borders, the ECJ and trade policy sovereignty.'[14]

May's initial quest for a clean break was also a function of the fact that, as a Remainer, she felt her first move had to be to convince Leavers she could be trusted to deliver their dream. In so doing she staked out a more hardline position than might have been the case with a Brexiteer prime minister keen to reach out to Remainers.

May also declined to invite in the opposition, to build a consensus. When she took over, Oliver Letwin, the cabinet office minister, had been asked by Cameron to begin Brexit preparations. His main insight was that the issue would become 'extremely politically charged' and to see off the challenge of 'ultra-Remainers' and 'hard Brexiteers' would require a 'solid phalanx of 400-plus members of Parliament who were joined in a single pursuit'. Letwin recalled, 'It became pretty apparent to me at that time that the likelihood of a successful outcome ... was much greater if it was a bipartisan or even tripartisan effort.' He had meetings with opposition politicians. 'The thing that continued to alarm me throughout Theresa's stewardship of the matter, was that ... she took the view it was necessary, if at all possible, to avoid ... cross-party governance.'[15]

Letwin and his insights were swiftly despatched to the backbenches but a cross-party approach was also suggested by Peter Storr, a Home Office official who May appointed to run a new Europe Unit in Number 10. 'It was fairly quickly poo-pooed,' an official said. Yvette Cooper, May's former Home Office shadow, said, 'I did call on her to set up a cross-party commission to oversee the negotiations ... to try and heal the divide between Remain and Leave – that's never been something that she was prepared to do.'[16] Stephen Parkinson, May's political secretary, argued in vain that a role should be found for Labour MP Gisela Stuart, who had worked closely with Johnson and Gove at Vote Leave. Yet Gavin Barwell, later her chief of staff, was probably right to observe that had she, at this stage, tried to 'do some kind of cross-party deal, it would have been catastrophic to her position as party leader'.[17]

If May's approach to Labour was short-sighted, it was also understandable thanks to Jeremy Corbyn. Denzil Davidson said, 'Could overtures have been made to the Labour benches earlier? Yes, I think so. But if you've got a leader of the opposition who is a Kremlin-hugging terrorist cheerleader ... who has been against his country in every dispute, it's quite hard to have a cross-party cooperative relationship on national interests. That shaped the evolution of Brexit.'[18]

The lack of preparatory work in Whitehall meant that May's team pushed through plans, barely scrutinised, to create two new departments: one for exiting the European Union – DExEU, pronounced 'dexy-you' – and a department for international trade (DIT). When May told David

Davis she couldn't decide between department for 'Leaving' or 'Exiting' he said, 'We've got to be the Department for Exiting, then we can call it Department X.' May, he recalled, 'didn't get the joke, she was completely straight-faced'.[19] More importantly, there was probably no need for it at all. The creation of DExEU was 'absolutely ludicrous', Philip Hammond argued. 'A rookie civil service trainee could tell you that that was a stupid idea.'[20] Heywood, the senior mandarin, had thought DIT 'a bit premature' but, to cement his position with May, downplayed his reservations. The department's very existence suggested the UK was preparing to withdraw from the European customs union to pursue an independent trade policy. 'One of the great disasters of this whole process is the creation of DIT,' said a civil servant in May's private office. Duncan McCourt, one of Hammond's spads, phoned Number 10 to ask whether a decision had been taken to leave the customs union. One of May's political aides denied this, but McCourt pointed out that the pledge to sign free trade deals 'is in the press release announcing the creation of the department'. Ivan Rogers forcefully argued that the message had been received in Brussels, a message May refused to believe she was sending, an early example of the cognitive dissonance that marred the negotiations. With hindsight, a senior civil servant said, 'We needed to work out what the government's objectives were and then set something up with a view to delivering that strategy.' Instead, machinery of government changes shaped the policy.

The creation of both departments left officials in the Treasury and the Foreign Office furious and marginalised, a process that also robbed the centre of the expertise of Tom Scholar, the permanent secretary at the Treasury, who had been central to Cameron's renegotiation but was seen as tainted by Eurosceptics.

Vote Leave had refused to say what sort of Brexit they were pursuing because Dominic Cummings concluded that to do so would fracture his carefully constructed coalition. May had to start from scratch. To give herself political cover, she gave three senior Brexiteers key roles. Boris Johnson became foreign secretary; free marketeer Liam Fox took on international trade; and David Davis was given the Brexit department. Nick Timothy recalled, 'Theresa felt that it was important that the people responsible for developing the Brexit policy should be people who really get it, and really mean it. There probably was a calculation, too, that compromise would need to happen at some point and it was important that leading Brexiters were party to those compromises.'[21] Initially, it was ill-judged optimism that dominated the public comments of the 'Three Brexiteers'. Fox predicted a trade deal with the EU would be the 'easiest in history', while Davis said forty trade deals would be in place 'one second after midnight' when the UK left.

DExEU was a Janus-faced mess, a department that was both a participant in devising policy and a referee between others. 'Departments won't take orders from a rival department,' a special adviser said. 'They will only take orders from the centre. You could have easily just done this in the Cabinet Office.' To Rogers it was 'completely bloody obvious' the minister responsible for coordinating a cross-Whitehall response should have been the Chancellor of the Duchy of Lancaster, the senior minister in the Cabinet Office, Damian Green. Heywood told Rogers, 'I tried to sell it to her. She simply wouldn't have it. She hates the Cabinet Office.' Later, JoJo Penn, who rose to be deputy chief of staff, admitted, 'I don't think we ever managed to get that set-up right.'[22]

Destructive ambiguity also governed the role of May's civil service negotiator Oliver Robbins, who combined the post of permanent secretary at DExEU, where he theoretically reported to Davis, with a role as May's personal sherpa. The quick resolution to the Tory leadership election, which was expected to run throughout the summer, also robbed both May and Robbins of the opportunity to get up to speed on the issues. Again, Rogers warned that the split role was 'lunacy', telling Heywood, 'He simply can't do both jobs. The only job that matters is the sherpa job. You're going to have a Chinese walls problem. There are going to be occasions when he's going to have to say things to the prime minister that he never wants to divulge to David Davis. Davis is going to feel marginalised and betrayed by that. You're setting him up to fail.'

Robbins, 'Jeremy's blue-eyed boy', was the model mandarin on the fast track to the very top. While reading Philosophy, Politics and Economics at Hertford College, Oxford, he was known to fellow students as 'Sir Humphrey', the cabinet secretary in Yes Minister. He had already been the prime minister's principal private secretary and was now second permanent secretary in the Home Office, where he had won the respect of May. But Robbins, forty-one at the time of the referendum, did not want the job of negotiating Brexit. When Heywood contacted him two nights before the vote to say, 'In the unlikely event that we vote to leave, I would like you to lead the negotiation with Brussels at official level', Robbins refused: 'The campaign has been so divisive that I'm worried about how it would affect my family.' Heywood, trying to convey an optimism he did not feel, said, 'Well, a lot of the venom will disappear once we're past the vote.'[23]

On the morning of 24 June 2016, Robbins was summoned back to the Cabinet Office and told he had to take the job. 'I don't want my family dragged in,' he repeated. Heywood predicted the Brexiteers would back him: 'You'll be delivering their Brexit.'[24] Robbins was the more gifted clairvoyant.[25]

Davis and May were also ill-matched. A cabinet colleague recalled, 'DD had this very 1980s industrial relations approach to negotiation. You go in and you get someone behind the bike shed, you give them a kicking and then they agree with you.' Davis believed holding back the money Britain owed was the UK's best bargaining chip. Another cabinet minister said, 'David is much more aggressive. The PM is someone who believes in sheer relentlessness, to never walk away from the table.' It might have been better for Britain if the minister in charge of mastering the detail had been the methodical one and the prime minister in charge of delivering the grand strategy under pressure had a more forceful personality.

Davis also believed the civil service, conditioned to minimise risk, only reinforced May's caution. 'They were so afraid of no-deal,' he said. 'If you do an international negotiation … there's always a point of tension where you're uncertain about the outcome. Indeed, you have to design them. Instead, the Whitehall strategy was basically to avoid them all, that was the problem.'[26] He added, 'Whatever she said publicly, there was not enough nerve in Number 10 to even take a small risk of a no-deal outcome.'[27]

May and Davis did initially agree they could win over other EU countries one by one, but in that they were quickly proved wrong. May spent her first weeks in power visiting Paris, Berlin and other capitals but heard the same message everywhere: 'Speak to the Commission.' Selmayr said, 'You can only divide and rule if you have a concept, if you have a plan, if you have a vision of where to go. That was almost shockingly absent in the negotiation on the other side.' Davis confidently predicted that German car manufacturers would persuade Angela Merkel to help. One of May's Europe advisers said, 'It was all bollocks.' In the end, the other twenty-seven EU countries negotiated as one, while the British state behaved as if it was twenty-seven different countries.

The civil service is regarded, not least by itself, as a Rolls-Royce outfit, but its senior figures shared misgivings about the wisdom of Brexit. Davis observed, 'You can count on the fingers of no hands the number of permanent secretaries that voted to Leave.'[28] He added, 'There was a lot of passive resistance. It didn't take the form of refusing to do things, it just took the form of saying, "Yes, sir", and it didn't happen.'[29]

The second issue was that Heywood deliberately built a negotiating team with no experience of the EU. He wanted a 'clean skin' with no baggage and Robbins' professionalism was more attractive to May and Timothy than Rogers, for whom every silver lining was a harbinger of clouds. 'The way that anyone who'd ever worked on the EU was ruled out was just bonkers,' another ambassador said. 'The whole team, not just the chief negotiator, had no EU experience. It was like one of those friends' battalions in the First World War', innocents with little experience, sent off to fight. Rogers recalled, 'Imagine running a financial crisis and saying, "Let's put someone on top of it who is not contaminated by expertise in the financial sector." Absurd.'[30]

The biggest problem of all was that May had no plan for Brexit. No 'one-sentence political objective and instruction' was given to Robbins. George Bridges, DExEU's minister in the Lords, fantasised that 'somewhere in Number 10, a very small, very secret group, [was] putting together an almighty chart, a big plan of how we were going to negotiate and crucially what our overall objectives were. The prime minister – rather like a Bond villain – would be sitting with her white cat on her lap with this big plan behind her.'[31] But he quickly concluded, 'There was no plan. [Brexit was] like playing multi-dimensional chess in the dark, where the rules haven't even been written.'[32]

May said she would provide 'no running commentary' on her plans, an embargo which even extended to her ministers. When Philip Hammond was offered the job of chancellor, he asked her joint chief of staff Fiona Hill how May would approach Brexit. 'She said to me, "Brexit means Brexit." That was it. That was the only discussion we had about it.'[33] Bridges was not even allowed to look at key papers on which he was supposed to answer for the government in the Lords. 'I was learning more from the *Financial Times* ... than I was from papers I was being shown,' he complained.[34]

May also had a personality problem. Brexit required a leader who not only knew where they wanted to go but had the verve and drive to persuade others to follow. The prime minister was pathologically secretive even with those in her inner circle. Her personal style in meetings might politely be described as Sphinx-like. Those less polite found her blank and devoid of conviction. Nor was she someone adept at winning over MPs or her EU counterparts. 'She is on the spectrum, without a doubt,' said a Tory minister with family experience of autism.

May's inner team regarded her as thoughtful and kind. But most Westminster people found her socially awkward, strangely boastful of lacking the bonhomie that greases the wheels in SW1. Craig Oliver, Cameron's communications director, recalled: 'I went for a drink with her at the Goring Hotel. At the end of the first five minutes, I'd used up every conversational gambit I could think of. After ten minutes I was starting to say stupid things in a desperate attempt to keep the conversation going, and after fifteen minutes I was feeling real physical pain because I didn't know how I could exit this politely. In situations where it requires somebody to put somebody at their ease or be bigger than the situation, she seems to struggle.'[35] An aide who was very fond of May said, 'Reserved people make other people feel awkward. They don't mean to, they just do. It is like trying to outstare a cat. It's just how she is.' May's lack of empathy with those she did not know well made it difficult for the PM to put herself in others' shoes, a key attribute for successful negotiators.

As home secretary, May worked methodically through problems and she sanctified Brexit decisions made at similar length. Yvette Cooper, who shadowed her at the Home Office, said, 'She has never felt fleet of foot, never moved quickly if the evidence changes ... She can get very focused on one view in the tramlines and not look up and around.'[36]

The prime minister did have two concepts but they were ones the EU had already rejected. First, she envisaged the negotiation as a rerun of her time as home secretary, when Britain opted out of all EU directives on justice and home affairs and then back into the ones she liked. Fiona Hill told people in Westminster, 'We know what we are doing, we have done this before.' That was why May hired Peter Storr, the lead negotiator on the home affairs directives, to run her Europe Unit. However, as Tusk's original statement made clear, the UK would be treated as a 'third country', as if they had already left. Opt-ins would not be welcome; they would come at a high price. Martin Selmayr recalled, 'I had the feeling that our British counterparts thought it would be a very easy thing to just switch from one side of the border of the European Union to the other side of the border and basically everything stays the same.'[37]

May's second principle was that she wanted a 'bespoke deal' for Britain. The EU thought in terms of the models adopted by other countries. Norway was inside the single market and paid into the EU budget and followed its rules, except on fisheries, agriculture, justice and home affairs. This made it a 'rule taker, not a rule maker'. Switzerland had more than a hundred bilateral deals to access the market but was a member of the European Free Trade Area (EFTA), paying less into the budget than Norway. Canada had struck a free trade deal with the EU after seven years of negotiations which gave it tariff-free access on most goods but not services and sensitive items like chicken and eggs. A no-deal departure from the EU, barely considered at this stage, would mean trading with tariffs imposed by the World Trade Organisation (WTO).

May was interested in none of these models, perhaps logically so, since Norway had to accept freedom of movement, Switzerland's arrangements were cumbersome and constantly being renegotiated and Canada had little access for its service industry. But the prime minister's mistake was not to clearly articulate what she did want in language the EU understood. When Storr, Rogers and Simon Case urged her to look at the third country options, they were given short shrift. 'We are the UK, we are the fifth largest economy!' she said. 'We want a bespoke British deal. We have to get away from the binary thinking of the past.' To the EU, this was arrogant British exceptionalism. May's failure either to talk the EU's language or to play hardball by preparing aggressively for no-deal left her in no man's land. To Brexiteers, this was a failure of negotiating strategy. To Remainers and EU officials, it was an inability to confront the compromises that would be needed.

As the official who had to translate May's wishes into a negotiating argument, Robbins came to see her stance as 'intellectually true but politically false'. He told colleagues May's wish was to design a new relationship from the ground up 'as if a major economy of 70 million people has just popped out of the North Sea', rather than one which was seeking to walk away from four decades of being closely entwined with the EU. A senior civil servant said, 'For a senior politician she was curiously emotionally unintelligent about how the EU sees us.'

These issues all came to a head when May made her first major public intervention on Brexit at the Conservative Party conference at the end of September 2016. Her priority was to reassure her party base she could be trusted. Nick Timothy wrote the line 'Brexit means Brexit', later derided as vacuous. 'It actually meant three different things,' he explained. 'Firstly, that she understood that having been a Remainer when the country voted to leave, she would deliver on that mandate. It was [also] a warning to others – in particular in Parliament who were already show-ing signs of not really accepting the result – that Brexit must mean Brexit. Then, at a third level, that Brexit must meaningfully mean Brexit and couldn't be a kind of shadow membership.'[38]

In her speech, May said, 'There is no such thing as a choice between "soft Brexit" and "hard Brexit". This line of argument – in which "soft Brexit" amounts to some form of continued EU membership and "hard Brexit" is a conscious decision to reject trade with Europe – is simply a false dichotomy … It is not going to be a "Norway model". It's not going to be a "Switzerland model". It is going to be an agreement between an independent, sovereign United Kingdom and the European Union.'

May's most important line was: 'We will invoke Article 50 no later than the end of March next year.' Davis had suggested the March dead-line, believing the Brexiteers would need proof the prime minister was serious about delivering the referendum result. Boris Johnson publicly urged her to 'get on with it'. Paleosceptics like Iain Duncan Smith warned May the party would not stomach a delay. From her officials, though, there was a determined campaign to persuade May not to include the line. When Robbins got wind of the plan he called Rogers, who was quaffing champagne with other EU ambassadors on a Danube river cruise. 'She's about to announce a date for the invocation of Article 50.'

'Fuck!' blurted Rogers. 'That's obviously insane. It reduces her lever-age. It's a completely mad thing to do. We should fight it.' They spoke to Heywood and all three argued that it would be giving away one of Britain's trump cards. A senior civil servant said, 'Jeremy, Ivan and Olly were all giving consistent and coordinated advice that it would be a mistake to invoke Article 50, or even give a timetable for invoking Article 50, until we had secured commitments as to how the process was going to work.' Peter Storr and Denzil Davidson wrote to May arguing that the deadline should be dropped. They were ignored. 'Nick Timothy played a decisive role,' Davidson recalled.[39] When Robbins tried to talk Davis around, the Brexit secretary replied, 'Olly, she's dead unless she tells us when she's going to trigger.'

May thought she had put the EU under time pressure. In fact, she had fired the starting gun at her own foot. 'The clock is ticking' became Barnier's taunting catchphrase. Ivan Rogers said, 'Champagne corks were popping in Brussels and EU capitals when they heard her comments.'[40]

When she took to the stage, most of her cabinet had no idea what she was going to say. Philip Hammond, the chancellor, said, 'I was absolutely horrified by what I was hearing. All I remember thinking was, "There will be a television camera on your face. If you move a muscle, it will be the story on the front page of every newspaper tomorrow."'[41] He said later, 'She dug a twenty-foot-deep hole. From that moment onwards, cupful by cupful of earth at a time, she was trying to fill it in, so she wasn't in such a deep mess. It was a total unmitigated disaster that scarred her prime ministership. I think she only realised later how badly that had constrained her ability to deliver any kind of practical Brexit at all.'[42]

By taking a hard line, May ducked an opportunity to set herself above faction, to speak for the 48 per cent who backed Remain as well as the 52 per cent who voted Leave. One aide concluded two years later: 'Where did it go wrong? Probably the September conference speech.'

In a second speech to conference, three days later, outlining her domestic agenda, May went further, saying she would not 'give up control of immigration all over again' or 'return to the jurisdiction of the European Court of Justice'. Davis thought her focus on immigration was typical 'of what Remainers think Leavers want', not what actually motivated Brexiteers for whom 'the bigger thing was control'. He said, 'I think that was a misjudgement.'[43]

After the speech, Ivan Rogers said to May, 'You've made a decision. This gives me clarity. I can work with this. We're leaving the customs union.'

May, aghast, replied, 'I have agreed to no such thing.'[44]

Officials concluded that the prime minister either did not understand that in order to pursue free trade deals with other countries Britain would have to leave the customs union, or she was not prepared to confront this fact. A minister said, 'The prime minister both wanted all the advantages of a customs union and to have an independent trade policy. She was being told, "You must choose one or the other." Her reaction was, "Give me something with both." Asked to choose, she said: "Both."'

The repercussions were wide-ranging, both at home and abroad. 'When the prime minister set out her red lines, they were so extreme that lots of people who voted to Remain felt they'd been pencilled out of the future of the country,' Keir Starmer, the shadow Brexit secretary, said.[45] The speeches also 'genuinely shocked the EU', a close aide admitted. Jean-Claude Juncker told Rogers, 'I've read her speech three times and it's extraordinary that she should say such things. Why has she done that, before she has even come to Brussels?' At the European Council meeting, a fortnight later, May was pictured alone and friendless in the Council chamber, Britain's isolation made flesh.

'You have no idea how bad this is,' Rogers told Heywood. 'This is a disaster in Brussels and around the capitals. She's put herself in an incredibly weak negotiating position. She's blown herself up, she just doesn't know it yet.' Heywood urged calm, fearful the officials would be banished from the room if they kicked up too much fuss. Rogers later pronounced May's second conference speech, setting out 'unobtainable' red lines she 'patently did not understand', as 'the single daftest speech given by any British prime minister since the war'. He added, 'I really don't think she knew what she was doing, and I don't think Olly knew enough at that stage to give her a viable version of Brexit.'

The EU single market was based on the so-called 'four freedoms' outlined in the Treaty of Rome: freedom of movement for goods, services, capital and people. May, probably rightly, had concluded that immigration was a significant concern to Leave voters and that meant suspending freedom of movement of people. The EU was equally determined that in rejecting one of its pillars, Britain could not continue to enjoy the other three. They seized on comments by Boris Johnson that Britain should try to 'have our cake and eat it', a position mocked in Brussels as 'cakeism' or 'cherry-picking'.

Ivan Rogers' view that May's positioning was 'fucking madness' got back to Number 10 and led to his decision to resign in January 2017. His pessimism grated on May's advisers but also Heywood, who called him 'a man who enjoys discussing the problem more than he enjoys finding a solution'. By the time he quit, Rogers had decided May was finished and faced a long and painful demise. He told his office, 'She won't last another two years.' His departure felt cathartic to May's team, but it denied them the expertise of the official who best understood the rip tides in Brussels. His replacement, Sir Tim Barrow, was a gifted diplomat but 'I don't think his knowledge or reading of the Brussels scene was anything like as good,' a Number 10 aide said.

May set out her formal position in a speech at Lancaster House in London later in January 2017. Calling for 'a new partnership' with the EU, she finally announced that she wanted a 'clean break' by leaving the single market and the customs union, as well as the jurisdiction of the European Court of Justice (ECJ). She committed Britain to maintaining the Common Travel Area with Ireland, an acceptance there could not be a hard border between Northern Ireland and the Republic at Britain's only land border with the EU. It was the least noticed of the important things she said.

May was ambiguous on customs, saying she had not decided whether to seek a 'new customs agreement', become an 'associate member' of the customs union or 'remain a signatory to some elements of it'. Not even her closest aides agreed on what she meant. Nick Timothy said, 'People say that that was an early sign that, really, she wanted to stay in the customs union ... but that was never the intention. It was more a reflection of the fact that ... we were not in a position to propose something concrete at that stage.'[46] For Chris Wilkins the 'deliberate ambiguity' meant 'my expectation was that the place we would end up at the end of the Brexit negotiations was with some form of customs union'.[47]

The Lancaster House speech was greeted with raptures by hard Brexiteers, who thought May had accepted their key arguments on sovereignty. Bill Cash, the arch-Paleosceptic, told fellow Brexiteers, 'Everything's fallen into place.' Nigel Farage called the speech 'brilliant'. Steve Baker, the backbench general who had made David Cameron's life a misery, wrote in his diary that night, 'Amazing speech. Joy abounds.'

May's mistake was not to make clear that this was her opening offer. Instead, it was seen as a canonical text by Brexiteers, every word of which became a standard to which she was to be held, every retreat from which was labelled a betrayal.

At Lancaster House, May also seemed to accept the hard Brexiteers' negotiating strategy. 'While I am sure that a positive agreement can be reached,' she said, 'I am equally clear that no deal for Britain is better than a bad deal for Britain.' The phrase delighted those, like David Davis, who saw negotiation as an exercise in game theory. May had finally threatened to walk away if she did not get what she wanted. However, even Fiona Hill doubted her conviction. 'The words were written by Nick [Timothy], who believed them, but I don't think she ever did,' Hill told Anthony Seldon later. 'To her, it was just a tactic.'[48]

May did little to convince the EU she was serious. Most Brexiteers, and some ministers who voted Remain, like George Bridges, felt they had to prepare seriously for no-deal. 'It was our responsibility and duty to make sure that those words were credible and that we had a plan to back them up,' Bridges said. 'I couldn't see the urgency to do that.'[49]

On 29 March 2017, Tim Barrow delivered into Donald Tusk's hands a letter triggering Article 50. Two years later, Hammond admitted, 'With the benefit of hindsight, I can now see that that was wrong.' Britain should have spent time 'debating with ourselves what kind of Brexit [we] want[ed] … before we triggered the process'.[50]

Triggering Article 50 was a cornerstone of May's future malaise and it united Brussels native Ivan Rogers and Brexiteer-in-chief Dominic Cummings in despair. On the same day, 23 May, Rogers gave a lecture and Cummings wrote a blog which diagnosed the same problems. The Vote Leave director accused the government of having 'irretrievably botched' its preparations. 'Vote Leave said during the referendum that: 1) promising to use the Article 50 process would be stupid and the UK should maintain the possibility of making real preparations to leave while NOT triggering Article 50 and 2) triggering Article 50 quickly … without a plan "would be like putting a gun in your mouth and pulling the trigger".'[51]

May's allies say, perhaps correctly, that delaying was politically impossible. 'We were incredibly conscious that Theresa had campaigned for Remain,' said JoJo Penn. 'There was a trust issue around delivering the outcomes that people had voted for. We were conscious that when Article 50 should be triggered was caught up in that.'[52] Chris Grayling, one of May's most loyal ministers agreed: 'Some in Vote Leave wanted to leave Article 50 for years while we prepared for no-deal. I don't think that was tenable. I think Theresa waited about as long as she credibly could … If she hadn't, it would've looked like the Westminster establishment's just trying to squash the result of the referendum.'[53]

Nonetheless, the next two years unfolded like a chess game between ill-matched players. At every turn, May pondered at length, putting herself under time pressure, before making dubious moves. The EU stuck to its guns and replied quickly, like a grandmaster slapping down the clock button after just a few seconds of thought.

Philip Hammond's next battle was to fight for a transition period after Brexit day to allow business to adapt to a new relationship. He found an ally in Davis, whose priority was that Brexit be completed in good time for the general election due in 2020. The logical conclusion was that May should get a new five-year mandate. 'That would reset the clock,' said a confidant of Davis. 'Two years of Article 50, two years of transition. And then you're out cleanly, a year before the next general election.'

The Tories were more than twenty points ahead of Jeremy Corbyn's Labour. May had every chance of increasing her majority. The two ministers tackled the prime minister together. Unbeknown to Davis and Hammond, May's chiefs of staff had also concluded they needed an election. The government was already struggling to win Commons votes with a majority of 12 and they had not even got to contentious Brexit legislation. May told a stunned cabinet and then the public on 18 April. The decision was welcomed by MPs, the centre-right media and even the European Commission. Selmayr called Robbins to say that Juncker thought it an 'excellent strategic decision' which made a transition period viable.

Juncker's enthusiasm was dented, however, when he and Selmayr went to dinner in 10 Downing Street on 27 April. May's inability to state her ambitions and Davis's bravado both 'raised alarms'. Selmayr said, 'There was no clarity, which shocked us.' On the way home, Juncker said the negotiation was 'never going to work'. Selmayr concluded that 'the other side doesn't know what the negotiation is about even six or seven months after they had started the process'.[54] Relations deteriorated further after Selmayr was accused of briefing a German newspaper that May was 'deluding herself' and Juncker thought she was 'living in another galaxy'. The briefing was actually given by another member of Juncker's staff, but it reflected his and Selmayr's view of the dinner.

In the seven weeks between May's announcement and polling day, disillusionment with the prime minister set in among her campaign team, the media and, finally, the public. The campaign proved a catastrophe for the Conservatives. May was thrust centre-stage in a 'Brexit election' with nothing new to say about Brexit. Gavin Barwell, then an observer, noted that she failed to persuade the public that she needed them to help deliver Brexit. 'In order to get those Leave voters who are not normally Conservatives to vote Conservative, they had to see two years of Brexit being obstructed in Parliament. It wasn't enough to warn them. They had to see all the difficulties actually materialise before they would switch their voting allegiance.'[55] It would be two years before this criterion was met. The Tories lost thirteen seats and fell nine short of a majority.

When the exit poll dropped at 10 p.m. on 8 June, Boris Johnson gasped and said, 'Christ. We've fucked Brexit.' James Slack, May's official spokesman, texted a friend in the media: 'That's Brexit fucked as we know it.' Like Cameron before her, the prime minister had called a nationwide vote to strengthen her hand against Brussels and the rebels on her own benches and, like him, she had failed. Having gone into the election with one problem – increasingly agitated Remainers – May emerged with those rebels emboldened plus a phalanx of Eurosceptics ready to cry 'betrayal' if she backtracked on the Lancaster House blueprint. She was also at the mercy of the Democratic Unionist Party, whose ten votes were needed to give the government a majority.

Even the DUP deal was a chaotic farce. Gavin Williamson was despatched with political aide Alex Dawson to negotiate with Nigel Dodds and Jeffrey Donaldson. He offered a full-blown coalition with a seat in cabinet or a confidence and supply deal. The following day May told him, 'Don't offer them a coalition.' Heywood had told her not to put a strain on the peace process by bringing one party into government. They were fortunate that Arlene Foster chose a confidence and supply agreement.

After the election disaster, a prickly Davis was sensitive to the charge that he had persuaded May to go to the country. 'I told her to call an election,' he told one friend. 'I didn't tell her to run the worst fucking campaign in history.'

The Conservative Party might have been well advised to choose this moment to change leaders. Johnson (accurately) judged that Davis would stand against him if he ran, preventing a coronation. But Philip Hammond, who expected to be fired by May, encouraged Johnson to strike. 'There was a moment when, if we'd both decided that the game was up for her, we could have made a change,' Johnson recalled. 'Philip was definitely in the mood to do that. I thought it would probably be better to allow her to get on and deliver Brexit, because I genuinely believed that she would take us out of the customs union, she would take us out of the single market. I'm afraid, that looks like a terrible mistake.' He was talked out of moving against her, in part, by Gavin Williamson, May's chief whip, who sat him down in the Locarno Room in the Foreign Office and said, 'Now's not your time. You make a move now, you'll take her out, yes, but we'll make sure that you don't win. Bide your time, it's not going to be long, then the throne will be yours.'

One 'sliding doors' question remains: what May would have done with a larger majority? Nick Timothy had pressed for an election to bolster Number 10 against Remainer rebels, but a proper majority could also have inoculated May against revanchist Brexiteers. The loss of both her majority and the sacrificial resignations of her closest aides, Timothy and Hill, left the PM at the mercy of both wings of her party. JoJo Penn recalled, 'There was more than one set of usual suspects, and they wanted opposite things.'[56] The effects were felt in Brussels as well. Gavin Barwell said, 'That result diminished her standing within the Conservative Party, and it also weakened her at the negotiating table ... The EU never really believed that she could get whatever deal they gave her through.'[57]

None of this compelled May to change course, an act of mulish determination that was part admirable, part inexplicable. When Keir Starmer, Labour's Brexit spokesman, saw a missed call on his mobile after the election from Davis, he assumed the Brexit secretary was ringing to invite him to join cross-party talks on a way forward. In fact, 'It was David telling me more about BMWs and how, in the end, the Germans would crack,' Starmer said.[58] 'It would have actually really helped her because she would have had much more authority if Brussels knew that she had a majority in Parliament for whatever she was going to agree.'

Davis told Starmer much later that he had recommended to May that he should sound out Starmer about cross-party talks, but the PM said, 'No.' To some this is the great missed opportunity of May's premiership. Oliver Letwin recalled, 'I did think that it would be absolutely required to have some cross-party agreement to proceed ... She didn't try. My level of anxiety ... increased from considerable to extreme at that point.'[59] As the year went on, Letwin was in the vanguard of MPs who took it upon themselves to seek to forge the cross-party consensus May sought to dodge. The likelihood, though, is that an attempt to reach across the aisle at this point would have succeeded only in ending May's tenure in

Number 10. 'If she had tried to go bipartisan, I think her party would have shot her earlier,' Rogers concluded.

May's new team was more inclined to compromise on Brexit than Timothy and Hill had been. Their replacement as chief of staff was Gavin Barwell, who had been a minister, an MP, a councillor and the party's chief operating officer. 'Gavin had done every role there is,' said one colleague, 'which meant he understood where everyone was coming from.' He had also fought and won a marginal seat, Croydon Central, a subject about which he wrote a 'how to ...' book, yet he was only available because he had just lost. If this caused mirth among some MPs, the statement which was to cause him the most trouble came on the night of the EU referendum after 54 per cent of Croydon voters backed Remain. Barwell tweeted, 'Proud that my hometown and the great city of which it is part rejected the politics of hate and division yesterday.'

Barwell resembled a bookish chipmunk but he was clever, with an endless capacity for work, and was a good boss – a Labrador replacing Rottweilers. 'Gavin was a fundamentally sane person,' a Downing Street official said. 'He made the atmosphere much better in Number 10.' Those who worked under the old regime 'emerged like shell shock survivors' after the election. But some missed the 'clear direction' which Timothy, in particular, had given. 'You knew where you stood, there was a clear strategy,' a spad said. 'After the election, power just dissipated and fragmented to different parts of the building. You had clever people, but all with completely different views and agendas.'

In July, Robbie Gibb was appointed director of communications – the yang to Barwell's yin. Gibb, who had been head of political programming at the BBC, was a Brexiteer with long-standing links to the Tory right. He was a pack animal who joined any team to fight for it. Gibb was one of just four Brexiteers in May's political team, along with deputy press secretary Kirsty Buchanan, Stephen Parkinson and, from September, Nikki da Costa, who joined as head of legislative affairs. 'It was not a strong note in the building,' one said.

The Europe Unit was bolstered by the arrival of Ed de Minckwitz, who formed a double act with Denzil Davidson. De Minckwitz 'understood the politics and what would fly in Parliament,' said a fellow aide. But it was telling that May's Europe advisers had all voted to stay in the EU. 'They were all Remainers,' David Davis recalled. 'That doesn't make them bad people, it just means their perception of what's right and wrong, in terms of delivering Brexit, was different. They were all survivors of the abortive Cameron negotiation … He aimed low and went lower.'[60]

David Davis predicted 'the fight of the summer' over the sequencing of the talks. But when he returned from the campaign trail, May and Robbins had already conceded that the negotiations would proceed in the manner outlined by the EU on the morning of the referendum result. Brussels would only talk about a future trading relationship once the UK settled its bills. Martin Selmayr explained EU thinking: 'It's a divorce. First, you separate the assets … then you see if you can remain close friends afterwards.'[61] Stefaan De Rynck, who advised Barnier, added, 'One of the situations we had to avoid was the financial settlement being the last issue standing.'[62]

In her letter to Tusk when triggering Article 50, May had said the UK wanted to agree the terms of Britain's future relationship 'alongside those of our withdrawal from the EU'. But when the Irish lobbied hard to ensure the Irish border was resolved before the trade talks, Robbins regarded this sequencing as inevitable. May, distracted by the election, did not contest his view. On the morning Barwell walked into Downing Street, four days after the election, he was presented with a briefing pack by Robbins. 'Sequencing was a done deal at that point,' Barwell said.

Davis was furious: 'I had intended … to make two things the battle: money and sequencing. They'd given away sequencing. I found out when I arrived in Brussels.' For several hours he thought to himself, 'How the fuck do we get out of this particular hole?'[63] He ruled out going back to London for a row with May, calculating that it would weaken their position further. Eventually Davis concluded, 'She felt pressurised, unconfident, maybe even insecure after the general election outcome.'[64]

Agreeing to sequencing paved the way for the backstop and contributed to a narrative among Eurosceptics that May was weak, naive and bewitched by Robbins. It came to be seen, along with the triggering of Article 50, as the signal strategic mistake of British Brexit diplomacy.

When the formal talks began, on 19 June 2017, Barnier's team showed themselves just as adept at PR as they were at process. At the first meeting, Barnier and his deputy Sabine Weyand sat down with huge piles of papers. Opposite them was David Davis empty-handed. That image symbolised a British team that was ill-prepared in comparison with its EU rivals. 'It was a set-up,' Davis said later. 'Barnier had a foot-deep heap of papers. It would have taken him a year to read through them all.'[65]

In the first two rounds of talks in June and July, Britain *was* less well prepared and Davis, a political bruiser, palpably uncomfortable along-side Barnier, a political schmoozer, at their joint press conferences. Stewart Jackson, a Brexiteer who lost his seat in the 2017 election and became Davis's chief of staff, said, 'We used to describe them as Barnier's lectern moments: great teeth, great hair, fabulous suit, seamlessly segue-ing from English into French. David didn't always feel comfortable.'[66]

The second frustration for Davis was that broadcast journalists tended to quote Barnier's pronouncements as holy writ, rather than as the posturing of one protagonist, simultaneously dismissing government statements as a mere negotiating position. 'They were totally addicted to listening to what Michel Barnier had to say as though he was some ultimate arbiter of truth,' an aide complained.

In criticising Davis, much of Westminster misunderstood Barnier's role. He was the public face of the negotiations and the liaison with the EU27. In the comically obtuse language of the civil service, he was 'facilitator of the authorising environment'. But the real negotiating was done by Barnier's deputies, Sabine Weyand and Stéphanie Riso. Behind them sat Jean-Claude Juncker and Martin Selmayr, who were in constant touch with member state governments. The most active were Germany, France, Spain, Poland, Belgium, Denmark and the Netherlands, with the Finns and Romanians also engaged. Juncker and Selmayr then held trilateral discussions with Barnier in Juncker's office, where they spoke 'very frankly', before agreeing a common line. A Commission official said, 'Juncker was the boss of all negotiators. Martin was his right hand. Everything that was political, everything that required approval by the college of commissioners, or by the president, went over Martin's desk.'

Robbins was forced to open negotiations not knowing his government's desired destination, still less its bottom lines. 'Olly felt very uncomfortable,' a member of the negotiating team said. 'He was an empty vessel being sent off to Brussels to create a conversation without really having an awful lot to say.' It took until February 2018, eight months after the election, for the cabinet to agree a position.

Senior EU officials concluded – accurately – that Britain was 'winging it'. In 2019, Frans Timmermans, a fan of British culture, compared the

British team to the chaotic weekend warriors of *Dad's Army*: 'We thought, "They are so brilliant they will have in some vault somewhere in Westminster a Harry Potter-type book with all the tricks and all the things in it to do." Then the first time I saw public utterances by David Davis … I thought, "Oh my god, they haven't got a plan." That was really shocking, frankly. It was like Lance Corporal Jones [shouting] "Don't panic, don't panic", running around like idiots.'[67]

Over the summer of 2017 the EU demanded 'sufficient progress' in all three areas of phase one, without specifying what that entailed. One of the teams had created new rules, not revealed them to the opposition and appointed itself referee. Robbins described Barnier's move as, 'You must jump this hurdle, but we will not describe to you how high it is.'

That summer, tensions between Davis and Robbins broke into the open. The Brexit secretary had tired of Robbins commissioning work from DExEU civil servants behind his back in his capacity as the PM's sherpa. 'You had the Olly Robbins department working directly for him,' a DExEU official said. 'They were doing stuff that DD had no idea about. The other parts of the department were left unguided – the stuff that Olly did not care about.' In August, Davis demanded that Robbins be removed as permanent secretary: 'Either he goes, or I go.' May could not afford to lose a cabinet minister. Davis told aides, 'I have won.' It was a Pyrrhic victory. May asked Robbins to stay as chief negotiator and move to a new Europe Unit in the Cabinet Office, where Davis had even less idea what he was up to. 'It was Olly's dream come true,' a Number 10 adviser said. Robbins' deputy at DExEU, Philip Rycroft, was promoted to permanent secretary following an eccentric interview with Davis about the last item on his CV. 'David Davis is the only person who's interviewed me for anything, ever, where the first thing they've said was, "You've done an Ironman triathlon",' he recalled.[68]

A regular fixture in Downing Street before the election, Davis and May drifted apart. Extraordinarily, he did not have the prime minister's mobile phone number.[69] Other ministers tried to push the weakened PM around. Philip Hammond recalled, 'Through this whole period, it felt like trying to run through treacle. She would vacillate – she would move a few paces in the direction of pragmatism then something would happen, or she'd get a delegation led by Jacob Rees-Mogg, and suddenly … she'd give up 90 per cent of the ground. It was like the First World War.'[70]

That autumn, May and Boris Johnson had their most explosive row, a 'knock-down, drag-out fight about the customs union'. Johnson recalled, May's face 'sort of dissolved, it starts writhing and tears sprang from her eyes'. The PM said, 'Why don't you just trust me, Boris?' He said something 'suitably gallant' but later regretted backing off. 'She begged him to back her,' a Johnson aide confirmed. 'She was in floods of tears.' Johnson wrote May several letters 'setting out my deep anxieties'. He said, 'I was trying to point out to her that the economic benefits of Brexit were going to be lost if we went down the route she seemed to be on.'

In September 2017, May made another Brexit speech in Florence. Cabinet Brexiteers pushed for a 'Canada-plus' free trade agreement with more benefits than those enjoyed by the Canadians. In the other camp, Philip Hammond and Amber Rudd pressed for a closer relationship with the EU than outlined at Lancaster House. The Florence speech ruled out the Norway option because it would leave Britain as a rule taker and maintain freedom of movement, but it did not rule out mirroring EU regulations, a score draw for the warring factions in the cabinet. May asked for a two-year transition period and acknowledged the UK would continue to 'honour commitments to the EU budget', a form of words agreed with Sabine Weyand which paved the way for a deal on a divorce bill of £39 billion. Steve Baker, who had been in ecstasies about Lancaster House, wrote in his diary, 'Florence speech seems to capitulate.'

Barnier called the speech 'constructive' but his efforts to get member states to approve 'sufficient progress' in October 2017 were rebuffed, one of several occasions when the member states took a tougher line than the Commission. Emmanuel Macron, the new French president, led the vetoes, something Davis attributed to 'small man syndrome'.[71]

May was damaged goods. Her speech to the Tory conference at the start of October was a frenzy of farce. First, she was consumed with a coughing fit. Then, a comedian interrupted her to present the prime minister with a joke P45. May struggled on, spluttering and croaking, her posture of grim but shambolic defiance a bizarre metaphor for her stewardship of Brexit. Just as she seemed to have rebuilt some credibility, the slogan mounted on the wall behind her began to fall, letter by letter, to the floor.

Two weeks later the prime minister had lunch with Juncker and Selmayr in Brussels. Again, a report appeared in the German press, saying an 'anxious' and 'despondent' May had 'begged for help'. Then, in early December, Juncker's dining room at the Berlaymont was the scene for the third agonising meal, where Robbins took the call announcing that the DUP had pulled the plug on the Joint Report. When Ivan Rogers saw the Joint Report he told friends, 'This can never fly. She's going to need to go for an all-UK backstop. But that delivers a version of Brexit which a majority of her own side hates.' He was right again.

As 2017 closed, Theresa May faced the same choices she had avoided since June 2016. On 15 December, Michel Barnier published a soon-to-be-famous graphic of a staircase, with each British red line taking you to a lower step, descending past Norway, Switzerland, Ukraine and Turkey. It concluded that May's decisions led inexorably to the bottom step, negotiating a free trade deal like Canada or South Korea's. The prime minister was furious at Barnier's attempt to kill a bespoke British solution. 'The staircase was a very clever device,' a Number 10 EU adviser said.

In 2018 May had two options: to pick a step or design her own, win over her cabinet and then strike a deal. The omens of 2017 were not good. At every turn the government had made tactical decisions – triggering Article 50, accepting sequencing and then the backstop – based on what was politically expedient, and fallen into tank traps laid by the EU. 'It was tactics over strategy,' a special adviser said. 'It seemed like a reasonable thing to do at each stage, but when you look back you think, "How the hell did we get here from there?" There was no strategy to keep us on the path.'

Before May sought to forge cabinet unity around a Brexit policy, she tried to change her cabinet, but the reshuffle only succeeded in highlighting how little control the PM had left.

PART TWO

WORKING IT OUT

NEGOTIATING WITH THE CABINET

December 2017 to July 2018

'Success is going from failure to failure without
losing your enthusiasm'

– Winston Churchill

'A genuine leader is not a searcher for consensus
but a moulder of consensus'

– Martin Luther King, Jr

4

CLEAR OUT

'Pestminster' and the Reshuffle

January 2018

Chris Grayling was chairman of the Conservative Party for just twenty-seven seconds. It was long enough to turn Theresa May's reshuffle into a farce. Ever since the debacle of the 2017 party conference, presided over by Patrick McLoughlin, senior Tories expected him to be replaced by Brandon Lewis, the immigration minister, a no-nonsense Essex boy and experienced campaigner. Yet Gavin Barwell helped convince May that Grayling, who had been an effective campaign attack dog in opposition under David Cameron, was the man for the job. On the morning of 8 January 2018, he contacted Conservative campaign headquarters (CCHQ) to tell them. When Grayling appeared in Downing Street at 11.47 a.m., Iain Carter, the party's political director, fired off a tweet: 'Congratulations to Chris Grayling following his appointment as Conservative Party chairman/cabinet reshuffle.'

What Carter did not know was that the Grayling plan had met fierce resistance in Number 10 from spin doctor Robbie Gibb, deputy chief of staff JoJo Penn and from senior staff at CCHQ, including communications director Carrie Symonds. Julian Smith backed Grayling, believing him loyal. But when MPs reacted with fury, the chief whip changed his mind and then May changed hers. At 12.52 p.m. it was announced that Lewis was going to CCHQ after all. As the reshuffle descended into shambles, Paul Richards, a former Labour adviser, declared, 'I think Grayling's time at CCHQ will be seen as a golden age, free from gaffes or blunders.' It was more than could be said for the rest of the day. The changes May had to make, which had important implications for Brexit, were the result of events known in Westminster as the 'Pestminster' scandal.

It took three weeks for the #MeToo movement – sparked by a *New York Times* exposé of movie mogul Harvey Weinstein sexually assaulting actresses – to engulf Westminster. On 26 October, the *Sun* splashed on a report that a WhatsApp group had been set up where victims of SW1's sex pests could name and shame their abusers. The Guido Fawkes website published a redacted spreadsheet labelling MPs 'handsy in taxis' and 'perpetually intoxicated and very inappropriate with women'. Six cabinet ministers were on the list. This was alien terrain for Theresa May, who made a virtue of eating dinner with her husband rather than gossiping in bars. The *Sunday Times* revealed that she received updates from her chief whip, Gavin Williamson, on the peccadilloes of MPs, briefings dubbed 'the ins and outs' by Number 10 staff. As the scandal grew, an exasperated May was repeatedly heard to say, 'Why can't they just do their jobs?'

Things escalated when the *Sun* named Michael Fallon, the defence secretary, as the owner of an errant hand that had been placed, years before, on the knee of Julia Hartley-Brewer, then the political editor of the *Sunday Express*. Now a talkRADIO host the journalist, known as GBH to friends, revealed she had threatened to 'punch him in the face' but regarded the matter as closed. There it might have remained had Jane Merrick not picked up the phone to Gavin Barwell. She told the chief of staff that in 2003 Fallon 'lunged at me' after a lunch. She wrote, 'This was not a farewell peck on the cheek, but a direct lunge at my lips … I shrank away in horror and ran off … I felt humiliated, ashamed.'[1] Barwell said the allegation would be reported only to May, to Fallon 'and the chief whip'. At 7.28 p.m., just two hours later, Fallon resigned.

What happened in those two hours became evident when the *Sun* revealed that Andrea Leadsom had told Number 10 Fallon had made inappropriate comments to her. The twist was that Leadsom had not complained to May. Gavin Williamson had heard gossip and approached her demanding to know what Fallon had done. Leadsom was summoned to speak to May. She too requested anonymity and was promised it. She did not regard it as a resigning offence and said so. 'I do regret that those trivial incidents involving me were dragged into Michael's case,' she wrote later.[2] The only people in the know were May, Fallon and the two

Gavins: Barwell and Williamson. The chief whip always denied that he leaked Leadsom's identity, but Barwell was certain Williamson was behind the story. Fallon was asked whether he could guarantee there would be no other claims against him. Unable to do so, he resigned. 'Gavin killed Fallon,' a fellow cabinet minister said.

Williamson went to see May and demanded the job himself. 'Gavin said, "You owe me",' one of May's advisers recalled. He also issued a threat, that having helped install May, he could also bring her down. One of the PM's inner circle said, 'I heard him say it. I don't know if he said it to her.' Another said, 'He appointed himself.'

The spotlight fell next on Damian Green, an Oxford contemporary of May's. His accuser was Kate Maltby, a thirty-one-year-old journalist. Her parents had known Green at Oxford, where her father was the only known former boyfriend of Ann Widdecombe. Maltby revealed in *The Times* that she met Green, thirty years her senior, at the Archduke restaurant in Waterloo in 2015 and felt 'a fleeting hand against my knee – so brief, it was almost deniable'.[3] Green called the allegations 'deeply hurtful' and said he was consulting libel lawyers. Then, in a kamikaze PR move, allies suggested a tablecloth had brushed Maltby's leg. The Archduke had no tablecloths.

Jeremy Heywood handed the job of investigating Green to Sue Gray, the head of propriety and ethics in Whitehall. She interviewed Maltby at length and found her believable, but the inquiry dragged on for weeks. 'I don't think the prime minister was psychologically up to forcing out someone who was a loyal friend and ally,' an aide said.

Before Gray could publish, May lost another cabinet minister. Priti Patel, the international development secretary, was fired after failing to tell the truth about meetings she held, while on holiday the previous August, with senior figures in the Israeli government. Summoned by May, Patel said she had disclosed all her meetings. Patel was on a trip to Africa when press secretary Paul Harrison took a call saying a story was about to run that she had also met the Israeli prime minister. 'She met Netanyahu,' Harrison told May. 'Obviously that is not what was disclosed to you.'

'Oh, bloody hell,' said May. Patel was ordered home – with political Twitter following her progress on a flight tracker – then fired.

Like Patel, it was the cover up, not the original offence, which finished Green's cabinet career. In 2008 police had raided his Commons office during a leak inquiry. His computers were seized and pornography was found. On 5 November, the *Sunday Times* ran a front-page story based on a statement by Bob Quick, the former assistant commissioner of the Met, who had led the 2008 probe, saying material of 'an extreme nature' was found. Quick had already informed Sue Gray. Green issued a statement in which he stated, 'The police have never suggested to me that improper material was found on my Parliamentary computer.' In fact, Green's lawyers had been told in 2008 and police personally briefed him in 2013.

On 18 December, Gray sent her report to May saying Green had made inaccurate and misleading statements, a breach of the ministerial code of conduct. She called Maltby's account 'plausible'. Green had expected to be cleared and May did not want to sack him, but she had no choice but to cut him loose. It was five days before Christmas.

'Pestminster' reshaped the government and how it dealt with the EU negotiations. Reshuffles ought to be the moment of a prime minister's maximum power, when governments renew themselves publicly. All this one revealed was Theresa May's impotence. Grayling's brief tenure as chairman was just the tip of the iceberg. The prime minister's big plan was to swap Jeremy Hunt, the health secretary, with Greg Clark, the business secretary, a manoeuvre of striking mediocrity even if it had come off. Hunt, however, had told the chief whip he would rather resign than move. He wanted to stay past June, when he was due to become the longest-serving health secretary, until at least July, when the NHS marked its seventieth anniversary – the moment he hoped to announce a historic uplift in the NHS budget. He entered Number 10 wearing an NHS lapel badge and refused to take it off.

'Jeremy, I've decided I want to move you to business,' May declared.

'I totally understand that; it's of course your call,' Hunt replied. 'But I will then step down and leave the cabinet.'

A startled May said immediately, 'Well we wouldn't want you to step down.' Hunt was ushered into a side room where he was visited by Julian Smith and Sue Gray, to see if he was serious. Heywood sounded out NHS managers. Hunt was ushered back in to see May who announced, 'We've decided you can stay.' He left the building having added the words 'and social care' to his title and department. Only his offer to become deputy prime minister was rebuffed.

Clark spent two hours in Downing Street before a very brief audience with May in which he was never even asked to take the health job. When he left at 4.49 p.m. almost nothing had been achieved and the evening news bulletins were just an hour away. One of May's aides recalled: 'It was one of my worst days in the job – pretty humiliating.'

Justine Greening was in Number 10 for nearly three hours, resisting a move from education secretary to the Department for Work and Pensions. First Smith, then Barwell and then Smith again closeted themselves with Greening in a side room and begged her to do as she was asked. Running the benefits system might have seemed a natural fit for a minister interested in social mobility. But Greening told Smith, 'DWP is entirely controlled by the Treasury.' She resigned, her job going to Damian Hinds, a friend of Barwell from the 2010 intake. Number 10 briefed that Greening had been in tears, a claim she rejected later as 'total bollocks'.

Robbie Gibb had wanted the story of the day to be promotions for women and non-white politicians. The day ended with not one new minority ethnic face in the cabinet, while the only person May felt able to sack was a working-class woman in a same-sex relationship.

The appointment with the greatest implications for Brexit was the most senior. In Damian Green's place as deputy prime minister in all but name, May promoted David Lidington, the justice secretary. Lidington had been an effective Europe minister during David Cameron's EU renegotiation, working hard to maintain the trust of Paleosceptics like Bill Cash and Bernard Jenkin. 'Lidders was always her first and only choice,' an aide said. 'He is ridiculously impressive, even if he looks like an over-excited stick insect.' It was an appointment pushed hard by Barwell. He and Lidington were to form a key axis on Brexit. 'Lidders had a large network of Europeans,' said a member of May's political team, 'and the Irish.' He would chair the cabinet committees on preparations to exit. Lidington also joined the main negotiations committee, where Brexit policy was decided. In elevating a more pro-active pro-European than Green, the balance of May's inner circle shifted. 'Let's be honest, David never wanted to leave, he didn't see it as a good thing,' a close ally said. 'He thought we had to respect the wishes of the people, rather than actually embrace Brexit. He did struggle to see where the hardline approach of the ERG was coming from. Maybe at times he didn't try and understand.' Green was a less partisan figure and had also worked closely in opposition with David Davis. Another Brexiteer cabinet minister said, 'I think he was a much more agile and politically sensitive operator than Lidders. I think she lost that.' Lidington would become a key figure in guiding May towards a softer Brexit.

His replacement at justice was a bird of similar grey plumage, David Gauke, a protégé of George Osborne who had come to embody the high-wattage brain power and low-key delivery of the Treasury. He would also become a pivotal player on Brexit.

The prime minister thought about moving or removing Boris Johnson and Philip Hammond but did not have the political capital. To maintain the Brexit balance of the cabinet, May had to shift both or neither.

The reshuffle stored up problems. David Davis let it be known he wanted to leave DExEU. He hoped his protégé Dominic Raab, the housing minister, would succeed him. Davis told May to put Raab in the cabinet. In response she 'curled her lip' with distaste. As the Brexiteer May trusted most, her team did not wish to lose Davis, but they might have been better heeding this early alarm bell. 'He certainly wanted a change of scene,' recalled Robbie Gibb, who later concluded that not listening to Davis's rumblings of discontent was 'a big mistake'. For the next six months Davis was a hand grenade with the pin out, rolling around on the deck of a ship of state foundering in increasingly choppy seas.

A promotion for Brexit minister Steve Baker was also thwarted. 'An official indicated to me that in the January reshuffle in 2018 I was going to be promoted,' he recalled. Baker's hopes were raised further by a story on the front page of the *Daily Telegraph* that he would attend cabinet as the minister for no-deal preparation. Both Baker and Chris Hope, who wrote the article, knew Robbie Gibb was an enthusiast for the idea. Others in May's team thought it unnecessarily provocative and an aide remembered, 'DD did not think that Steve Baker should be made a cabinet minister.'

Instead of promoting one former leader of the European Research Group, in Baker, May brought in his successor, Suella Braverman, as another DExEU minister.[4] This superficially clever attempt to neuter the ERG backfired spectacularly. In a move that ought to have been incompatible with his position as a minister, but reflected his continuing influence with Eurosceptics, Baker met on 13 January with Christopher Montgomery, a savvy, waspish and uncompromising media adviser to the ERG, to decide who should take over the organisation. 'When Suella was promoted to government it was clear that they were trying to kill the ERG,' Baker said. 'Christopher and I agreed that the only way to counter it was to really ramp up the capacity of the European Research Group to be difficult for the government.' Baker and Montgomery planned a media blitz on the ERG's 'red lines', with a high-profile new chairman. 'He and I agreed that we should invite Jacob to do it.'

Jacob was Jacob Rees-Mogg, the MP for North East Somerset, who had emerged as a darling of the Tory faithful and even been talked about as a prospective leader. Possessed of great height and wealth, a languid plummy voice and the appearance of a man born in a double-breasted suit, Rees-Mogg's patrician airs, nonetheless, concealed a willingness to make mischief that was more Lord Flashheart than Lord Snooty.

When Baker called asking him to be chairman, Rees-Mogg – aware of the constitutional incongruity of a minister agitating for the raising of an army against his own government – said he was 'honoured to have been asked by a serving minister'. He agreed to take over. In seeking to de-fang her most dangerous internal critics, May had indirectly contributed to the revival of the ERG as an instrument of her own torture.

Prominent Remainers were also disgruntled not to have their merits recognised. Rory Stewart, who had been widely tipped for the cabinet, was made the minister for prisons outside it. He joined Phillip Lee, the minister for youth justice, a friend of Philip May, in the ranks of the disgruntled. Both would be thorns in May's side over Brexit.

The reshuffle also included two key strategic errors which would haunt May throughout 2018. She promoted a roster of inexperienced new whips, getting several women onto the lowest rung of the frontbench ladder and improving the gender balance of the government. But May had just lost her first Commons vote. Saddling herself with a whips' office without experience or collective memory would prove costly. 'That reshuffle blew another hole in the boat,' a Downing Street spad said.

For good or ill, May had now put in place the team with whom she would fight for the government's version of Brexit. Now all she and her cabinet had to decide was what that policy would be.

COP OUT

Chequers I and the Mansion House Speech

January to March 2018

Had things worked out differently, the most significant ministerial meeting in early 2018 might have been the one that took place in a drab conference room where Downing Street meets Whitehall, shortly after the reshuffle. That was where the ministers in the Department for Exiting the European Union (DExEU) – David Davis, Steve Baker, Robin Walker, the newly appointed Suella Braverman and Martin Callanan, the Lords' minister who had once been leader of the Tory MEPs in Brussels – took their seats one drab January day down one side of a long conference table. Opposite them sat the mandarins, a group of civil service director generals ready to brief them on the crucial choice ahead. 'It resembled a summit,' one of those attending recalled. Soon politicians and civil servants were on opposite sides of the debate as well as the table. 'We were faced with a choice between, on the one hand, a free trade agreement-based Brexit, with a lower degree of mandatory alignment [to EU rules] and potentially lower market access,' one minister said, 'or something like the customs union plus the EEA', membership of the European Economic Area.

The question was: which EU model, which step on Barnier's staircase graphic, was the best jumping off point? Should Britain start with Norwegian-style alignment with EU rules and negotiate down to secure greater freedoms or begin with a Canada-style free trade deal and negotiate upwards to closer ties? To the apparent surprise of the civil servants, Steve Baker recalled, 'We all agreed we should build from a free trade agreement Canada-style rather than take an EEA-lite deal.'[1] His argument was: 'If we were in the Customs Union and the EEA then we would not have left the EU from an economic point of view.' More surprisingly, the ministers who voted to remain, Walker and Callanan, did not disagree. Braverman confirmed, 'We had a unanimous view.'[2] A witness added, 'The officials all looked crestfallen.'

If this had been a normal meeting of departmental ministers, their unanimous recommendation would have been delivered to Downing Street with the expectation that it become government policy. But as Davis, by then, knew all too well, Brexit policy was not being made in the department which carried its name, but in Number 10.

The real decisions were taken in a Wednesday afternoon meeting in May's office, with Gavin Barwell, JoJo Penn, the Europe advisers Denzil Davidson and Ed de Minckwitz, the civil servants Jeremy Heywood and Oliver Robbins, plus May's principal private secretary (initially Simon Case, then Peter Hill) and her private secretary for Europe, Catherine Page. 'I don't want DD or Boris there,' the prime minister decreed and, despite repeated demands that he be admitted, the Brexit secretary was never allowed to attend.[3] Another cabinet minister said, 'She brought with her to Number 10, the culture of the Home Office, with a very tight inner core and the assumption that everybody outside it was the enemy.'

No one really knew what Theresa May wanted including, it seemed, the prime minister herself. Aides, ministers, MPs, EU officials and diplomats who met her all said there was no clear conclusion to meetings. 'My experience of working with her was that she never really had a view on anything,' said a civil servant in May's private office. 'Nor did I see her make a decision. She was entirely reliant on Gavin to interpret her ramblings.' A British ambassador claimed this was not introversion but a weapon. 'I think it is a deliberate thing; she employs silence,' he said. 'She would just sit there and say nothing. What I saw was the most fantastic stubbornness.' To allies like Damian Green, May's guardedness was a skill: 'She was very good at keeping a poker face and not revealing herself.'[4] He added, 'One of her great strengths ... is that she doesn't care, when she and you leave the room, whether you like her or not. That is an incredibly rare quality in a politician.'[5]

To others, though, there was a paralysing diffidence about May. Unlike David Cameron, who encouraged his EU advisers – Jon Cunliffe, Ivan Rogers and Tom Scholar – to disagree in front of him so he could hear different arguments, May was not comfortable with conflict. A special adviser said, 'She will not naturally lead the conversation. She will not naturally say, "This is what has been agreed." There is a lack of clarity and leadership.' Even to close aides, May appeared shy and unconfident. 'She'd come out of her office,' one said. 'It was like school when you approach a group and you're not invited in. I'd always step aside, so she could come in, but she's not somebody that would force herself into these conversations.' It is hard to think of another modern prime minister who lacked the force of personality to make themselves the centre of attention the second they entered a room.

As she had done before, at Lancaster House and Florence, May decided she would make a speech, in March, to outline the government's position to the EU. The cabinet, after eighteen months of division and vacillation, would have to decide. Senior ministers were allowed to make 'Road to Brexit' speeches about what they wanted. The members of the Brexit cabinet committee would then come together at Chequers, the prime minister's country retreat, to thrash out their differences.

On 26 January, Davis gave his speech, calling for an 'implementation period' after Brexit, which he declared a 'bridge to the future', but also the right to diverge from EU rules. Steve Baker dubbed Davis's speech, which offered something to Brexiteers and Remainers, 'Operation Goldilocks' because it imagined a Brexit that was 'neither too hard nor too soft', just as Goldilocks' porridge was neither hot nor cold.

Brexiteers already feared May and her chief negotiator Oliver Robbins were on a different path. 'All the senior officials were briefing that we have to have a high-alignment Brexit, plus something like the customs union,' a minister recalled. This view gathered adherents on 29 January, when the Treasury's economic analysis leaked to BuzzFeed. It made for sobering reading. 'Under a comprehensive free trade agreement with the EU, UK growth would be 5 per cent lower over the next 15 years compared to current forecasts,' the website reported. 'The no-deal scenario, which would see the UK revert to World Trade Organization (WTO) rules, would reduce growth by 8 per cent over that period.' Even the softest option, EEA membership, 'would, in the longer term, still lower growth by 2 per cent'. The article went on, 'Almost every sector of the economy ... would be negatively impacted in all three scenarios ... Every UK region would also be affected negatively.'[6]

Worse for the morale of DExEU ministers, the leak came before the papers had even been shared with ministers. 'Steve [Baker] was bloody furious,' a DExEU source recalled. Davis and Baker did not trust the numbers either. 'They fed what I think are erroneous assumptions into the model and got terrifying answers out,' Baker said. Davis's beef was that the Treasury used a 'proximity model' which assigned what he saw as too much weight to Britain's geographical closeness to the EU and not enough value to doing deals with other global partners. Baker attacked the models from the despatch box, a minister turning openly on the civil service. Privately, he told fellow MPs the government machine had adopted 'a posture of supplication' that would 'keep us so close to the EU so that we can rejoin later'.[7]

The perception that officials were trying to undermine Brexit had frightening implications. In mid-February a padded envelope arrived at the office of Suzanne Heywood, wife of the cabinet secretary, the address a child-like scribble. Inside she found a note ('Remind your fucking husband how the country voted') and a box of matches. She called the police.[8]

Baker possessed the zeal of the convert. 'Casually pro-EU' and even 'pro-euro' in his younger days, he had been radicalised by the passage of the EU constitution, which became the Lisbon Treaty. One of the few British people to read it, he saw the blueprint 'for a new country' rejected by the French and the Dutch and the people of Ireland asked to vote twice until they gave the right answer. 'The sheer, obvious trampling of democracy just sent me through the roof,' he recalled. 'The reason that I got into politics ... was absolute fury that those who rule us, very, very clearly don't ... care how we vote. It is absolutely wrong for state power to be advanced without the consent of the governed.'[9] May's team sought to keep Baker in the tent. 'Denzil Davidson popped in every Tuesday morning at ten o'clock to ultrasound scan Steve Baker's head, thinking they could neutralise him or turn him round,' said one DExEU source.

While some Brexiteers were determined to prove that leaving the EU could be an economic boon to Britain, the more profound divide was between those who thought the economy should come first and those for whom Brexit was about sovereignty. Brexiteers who had spent decades denouncing the EU for putting federalism ahead of capitalism suddenly seemed to believe that the Commission and the twenty-seven other member states would put mutual economic advantage ahead of politics. Boris Johnson and David Davis suggested Britain would get a good deal because the UK was a huge market for Italian Prosecco makers and

German car manufacturers. Frans Timmermans, the Commission vice president, said, 'That is to think that continental Europeans see the EU in the same way as the United Kingdom – as a market ... For Germany the EU is much, much more than a market; it's their destiny; it's not revisiting the horrors of history. So even the car industry itself understands that this is more important than selling cars to the United Kingdom.'[10]

To May's aides and his cabinet colleagues, Johnson's tendency to wish away problems with boosterism was alternately dishonest and naive. 'I lost count of the times I was told, "The EU has a trade surplus with us, so it's in its interest to do a deal",' Gavin Barwell recalled. 'Well, yes, but its primary concern is preserving the integrity of its institutions, particularly the single market and the customs union. What it means by that, although it is normally too polite to say it explicitly, is that there has to be a cost to us leaving.'[11] Philip Hammond said, 'Boris would tend to resort to exhortation to optimism and "If we want it, we can do it." Unfortunately, I don't think that's the answer to a negotiation with the European Union.'[12]

When Barnier came to London to meet Davis on 5 February, his team was determined the Brexit secretary not be upstaged on home soil. Stewart Jackson recounted, 'When Barnier came to Downing Street we actually put him on a chair which was shorter.' While the Frenchman read a prepared script, 'we persuaded David Davis to learn his script by heart. [He] came out looking much more polished and eloquent than Barnier so it was one nil to team Davis.'[13] It was a consolation goal.

In the battle for May's ear, the most outspoken minister for close alignment with the EU was Philip Hammond. The chancellor argued that Brexiteers did not understand that eliminating tariffs was not enough to protect the economy. He argued that friction from regulatory non-tariff barriers would kill off companies reliant on 'just-in-time' supply chains. Hammond told May, 'If you introduce frictions at the border, on components in automotive supply chains, whether or not you impose a tariff on finished cars crossing the border between Europe and the UK, you're going to greatly diminish the attraction of the UK as a place to make cars.' Hammond's view was that even an understanding with the EU to align regulations would still lead to checks at the border. 'It's only if we have a treaty-based obligation to align that we will avoid those checks.' In short, the chancellor believed that only a legally binding commitment to adhere to EU rules would prevent a major economic setback. By contrast,

Hammond thought the silver bullet of some Brexiteers, trade deals with other countries, would only 'produce a very small benefit'.

Between mid-2017 and mid-2018 May absorbed Hammond's argument and concluded that she needed to seek as near frictionless trade as possible. May was loath to admit the economic arguments were moving her because that would have goaded the ERG. It would also have given too much satisfaction to a chancellor she was coming to dislike intensely. Their antagonism extended to May privately ridiculing Hammond for boasting that he regularly switched energy suppliers. 'I use one of the comparison websites,' the chancellor explained. May thought the image of the multi-millionaire hunched over a laptop trying to save a few pounds on electricity ridiculous. She told aides the chancellor was obsessed with 'pounds and pence' to the exclusion of all else. 'That's the difference between him and me.' Despite their personal antagonism, May saw that Hammond had a point. 'The chancellor did solidify in her mind the importance of not introducing friction at the border in the trade of goods,' Barwell recalled. 'Not just at the Northern Ireland–Ireland border, but at the wider UK–EU border.'[14] Hammond's views were echoed by Greg Clark, the business secretary, who was described by one adviser as 'almost in mourning about the result' of the referendum.

Clark chaired a meeting in his office at 9 a.m. every Wednesday with Carolyn Fairburn, director general of the CBI, Britain's biggest business group, plus the heads of the Institute of Directors, the British Chambers of Commerce, the Federation of Small Businesses, the Engineering Employers' Federation and Frances O'Grady, general secretary of the Trades Union Congress (TUC). They impressed on him the reality of just-in-time supply chains. Clark said, 'I'd visited production lines and seen how the parts and the components arrive at one door and within four hours, they're fitted to a car or aircraft wing. I couldn't put it out of my mind. I felt very strongly that the responsibility of the business secretary was to communicate the truth, however inconvenient, to the negotiating team.' May, he recalled, 'started from a position of not being very interested in customs arrangements', but was later persuaded by the manufacturers. A Brexiteer who attended some of Clark's Wednesday meetings said, 'It was basically a Remain therapy session. They all sat around discussing what a total disaster this was for Britain.'

Boris Johnson laid out his very different views in a Valentine's Day speech at the Policy Exchange think tank. The foreign secretary began with a love letter to Remainers experiencing 'grief and alienation', vowing to 'reach out to those who still have anxieties'. Brexit, he said, was 'not some great V-sign from the cliffs of Dover'. A deal on aviation would mean, 'We will continue ever more intensively to go on cheapo flights to stag parties in ancient cities, meet interesting people, fall in love, struggle amiably to learn the European languages whose decline has been a paradoxical feature of EU membership.' It was the most emollient speech he made as a cabinet minister.

It was directed, though, at a woman who was immune to both his charms and his arguments: Theresa May. Laying down his red lines ahead of the Chequers summit, Johnson argued that Brexit had to mean the right to diverge from EU rules if it was to mean anything. 'We would be mad to go through this process of extrication from the EU, and not to take advantage of the economic freedoms it will bring,' he said. He argued that it would be irresponsible of the government not to 'do things differently' in emerging sectors like artificial intelligence, robotics and stem cell research, where entrepreneurs and scientists should have 'the freedom to innovate'. In a scarcely coded attack on May's failure to elucidate what she was trying to achieve, he added, 'It is this government's duty to advocate and explain the mission on which we are now engaged.'

Privately he was withering. When Jacob Rees-Mogg asked Johnson, 'Is it as bad on the inside as it appears from outside?' the foreign secretary replied, 'No, no, no, it's a lot fucking worse.'

Johnson hosted drinks for MPs, but seemed to attendees a lost soul. 'He cut a really lonely figure at this point,' one said. At one gathering, a newly elected MP took him to task for his Q&A answers after the Valentine's Day speech, in which Johnson made an ill-judged joke about sex tourism to Thailand and said Brexit would be good for 'organic carrots'. The female MP asked him, 'Why do you keep self-sabotaging?' She suggested that Michael Gove had done Johnson a favour by ending his 2016 leadership bid: 'I don't think you were really up for it at that stage.' Intrigued, Johnson invited her to lunch. There, she asked him: 'If you think about your autobiography, how far through it do you think you are now?'

Johnson replied, 'A third of the way.' This confirmed the MP's view that the clowning masked still serious ambition. 'I thought there was a sense of destiny with Boris,' she recalled. 'I think he felt it but, at this stage, he didn't know it would come good for him. He was seen as a busted flush. It was the point at which Boris ceased to be loved that he had nothing to lose.' Johnson told friends his dining companion 'scared' him because she could 'see my soul'.

May's attempts to push things towards a softer Brexit led to a showdown with the cabinet Brexiteers ahead of the Chequers meeting. On reading Robbins' draft proposal, David Davis erupted. In attempting to resolve the tension in the Joint Report, the Brexit secretary wanted mutual recognition not alignment with EU rules. Raoul Ruparel, Davis's special adviser, said, 'The wording was moving towards a commitment to align.'[15]

Davis told the prime minister, 'If you try and do that I'm not going to Chequers.' After one foray into Number 10, Davis recounted to his aides, 'I spoke truth to power.' One recalled, 'DD was in a relatively strong position in February.' Davis, Ruparel and Tim Smith, his media spad, launched into a rewriting exercise which went on until 11 p.m. on the 22nd. Davis went in and out of Number 10 for nearly three hours to deliver new drafts to May. The PM could not afford a public split with Davis. The Brexit secretary ensured the divergence mechanism was acceptable to Johnson and Michael Gove, the environment secretary. Ruparel recalled, 'DD was able to water it down, with support of other people in cabinet, so that it wasn't such an upfront commitment to align and was much more about managing divergence where it came in.'[16] At this point, the prime minister was searching for consensus. 'If we disagree it won't go through,' she promised Davis. 'She didn't want to lose him,' an aide said. It was 1 p.m. on the 23rd before Davis was happy and the convoy could leave for Chequers.

The prime minister's country residence, a sixteenth-century manor house at the foot of the Chiltern Hills, looked more like the location for an Agatha Christie drama than a political summit. For the ten cabinet ministers and Number 10 staff who gathered there on 23 February, the outcome was a mystery. 'There was a slight element of Cluedo about it,' said one. The meeting was technically a gathering of the Strategy and Negotiations sub-committee of the cabinet, known in the press as the 'war cabinet', in Whitehall as 'SN' and to several of the participants, who regarded it as sado-masochistic torture, the 'S&M committee'. The membership of SN was balanced between the competing factions: Davis,

Johnson, Gove and Fox represented the Brexiteers. As PPS then chief whip to David Cameron, Williamson kept his views to himself, but as defence secretary he aligned himself with the Brexiteers. Hammond, Lidington, Amber Rudd, Greg Clark and Karen Bradley argued for closer ties to the EU.

The day was orchestrated by May and her aides to create an atmosphere of solidarity and compromise. Ministers' mobile phones were confiscated, forcing colleagues who had spent months briefing against each other to talk. 'During the Oslo peace process the Norwegians got the Arabs and Israelis into an agreeable location in the Norwegian countryside and plied them with smoked salmon,' one minister noted. 'In the same way, if you get a group of Tories in a country house and give them cups of tea and shortbread biscuits, it tends towards harmony.'

Discussions started in the grand hall. To create a Rorke's Drift spirit, the chief whip, Julian Smith, first outlined the forces ranged against them. There was a 'real, real danger' of Tory rebels uniting with Labour to keep Britain in the customs union when the government's trade bill came before the Commons. Davis discussed the ERG. 'The election of Jacob is a sign that they are militarising and have tanks on our lawn,' a colleague said.

Tensions spilled over when Greg Clark gave a presentation on the consequences of divergence for the car industry. 'There are 425,000 jobs at risk in the automotive sector,' he said. Johnson interrupted to say divergence was essential to ensure innovation. Another minister said, 'Greg had his Weetabix. He really roared. Boris was quite taken aback.' May stopped the fight, telling Johnson that he would get to speak first in the next session. 'She was quite tough with Boris.' The exchange unnerved Johnson who had been contemplating resignation. 'For much of the day he thought it was going in totally the wrong direction,' a friend said. 'He thought there might be a long walk home.'

It was 7 p.m., five hours into the gathering, before May finally revealed her hand. The ministers were gathered in the boardroom upstairs. She asked Robbins to outline her plan. Only Davis had any idea what he was about to say. 'She does treat everybody equally,' one cabinet minister joked afterwards. 'She keeps everybody in the dark.' Robbins mapped out a four-point plan in which Britain would demand mutual recognition of standards for goods traded between the UK and the EU; make a public commitment that British standards would remain as high as those of the

EU; pledge to keep rules and regulations 'substantially similar'; but also insist upon the creation of a dispute mechanism to oversee areas where the UK wanted to diverge from EU regulations – with no role for the ECJ.

May explained that trading relations would fall into one of three 'baskets'. The first would include industries, like cars and aerospace, where the UK would remain fully aligned with EU rules and regulations. Clark had got his way on that. The second basket would include the environment and consumer rights where Britain would agree shared goals with the EU but retain the right to achieve them by different means. The final category would cover sectors where the UK wanted to remove itself from the orbit of EU regulation, particularly fisheries and agriculture.

In the key moment of the meeting May turned immediately to Johnson, the most outspoken Brexiteer, and asked his opinion, putting the foreign secretary on the spot. Johnson thought back to his speech nine days earlier. He had demanded the ability to diverge from EU rules. The fourth point was enough for him. Theoretically there could be divergence, even if in practice many sectors would choose not to take advantage. 'It answers the requirement to take back control of our laws,' Johnson said. 'This is something which we can sell to the country and will unite the party.' Seated to the side, James Slack, the prime minister's spokesman, felt the tension drain from his body. 'Until Boris spoke,' he told a friend later, 'I wasn't sure we'd be okay; I wasn't sure that she wouldn't have to resign.'

Next up was Philip Hammond, the most outspoken advocate of close alignment with the EU. 'This is broadly a good paper,' the chancellor said. May visibly relaxed. Her two most awkward ministers were on board. There was even time for levity. Hammond said, 'I was actually quite happy with this until I heard what Boris said. If we both agree with it, there must be something wrong.' Cue laughter, an uncorking of pent-up tension. But Hammond was privately concerned. Recognition and divergence satisfied the two sides of the cabinet, but he doubted it would satisfy the Commission. Nonetheless, the chancellor found time to laugh at himself. When David Lidington made a downbeat point he said, 'I don't want to sound too Eeyore.' Hammond piped up, 'No, that's my job.'

Slack told journalists later it was 'the moment of greatest harmony in the life of the government'. A cabinet minister said, 'It was a script written by Olly Robbins, produced by David Davis and directed by Theresa May – with Boris, as the first viewer, delighted.' Another cabinet minister spoke of 'magic' in the room. It was magic of a sort, but the Chequers concordat was more a conjuring trick than a choice. 'The whole thing was more fudge,' a civil servant said. Even the Brexiteers knew it might be difficult to get the EU to agree to the plan. 'The real problem was going to come when we had to compromise on the compromise,' an official observed. Nevertheless, as they got their ministerial cars home that night most agreed with Michael Gove's view, shared with friends: 'In a not particularly hotly contested field, it was a good day for the government.'

The public relations battle was won by the Brexiteers. When Johnson got his phone back, he called his special adviser Lee Cain, a veteran of the Vote Leave campaign. Cain, softly spoken but with the hard looks of a nightclub bouncer, bald, tattooed and usually sporting a five o'clock shadow, was enjoying a convivial dinner with Paul Stephenson, his boss on Vote Leave, Paul Harrison, May's press secretary, and a group of journalists. When Johnson rang, Cain took the call at the back of the room. It was a brief conversation. Speed not detail was what mattered. Cain hung up and, in full view of Harrison, announced, 'Divergence has won the day.' He WhatsApped journalists and within seconds the phrase was all over social media. It was 10.53 p.m. Cain's briefing, that the Brexiteers had triumphed, was the established view before Robbie Gibb's lines-to-take had got their boots on. There was a reason why Stephenson regarded Cain as the best spin doctor he had hired.

The truth was, but for the intervention of Davis, the proposal put in front of ministers would have accepted that Britain mirror EU rules. Instead, ministers agreed that they would seek the right to diverge in carefully defined areas. To Johnson and Davis, the rot had been stopped and an important principle established. 'We ended with conclusion that regulatory divergence would be possible, that we were definitely coming out of the customs union,' Johnson recalled. Dominic Cummings disagreed, telling a friend Johnson and Gove had 'achieved nothing' and merely 'complicated the surrender'. To some of May's team, including Gavin Barwell, it seemed that a broad direction of travel towards alignment had been modified but not halted. 'That meeting came very close to accepting the common rulebook,' he said. It was an idea that would return later with a vengeance.

Whatever her reservations about the negotiability of the Chequers concordat, May set out to fight for what had been agreed. 'The prime minister and the team were determined to try to negotiate it,' said a senior figure. 'She was up for trying to make it work.' May now had something to say in her fourth big Brexit speech. All she needed was for the EU to agree to the same approach.

The following day Donald Tusk, president of the European Council, dismissed the UK's plan as 'based on pure illusion', complaining that 'It looks like the cake philosophy is still alive.' Leo Varadkar, the Irish prime minister, added, 'It is not possible for UK to be aligned to the EU when it suits and not when it doesn't.'

Before May even got to make her speech, the EU published a draft version of the withdrawal agreement, converting the Joint Report from December 2017 into legal text. It was written quite deliberately to skewer Britain and enshrine the EU's view of paragraphs 49 and 50 in law. When Barnier privately addressed the Brexit Steering Group of the European Parliament, on 10 January, he told the MEPs that by writing the text in the Commission he would force Robbins to 'use ours as a basis for negotiation'.[17] A British negotiator said, 'That was not an act of good faith on their part.' The following month Barnier told MEPs the document would strip out the 'constructive ambiguity' of the Joint Report. 'It is an especially sensitive subject, so we are taking a risk.'[18] His adviser Stefaan De Rynck admitted, 'Our patience was wearing thin with the failure of the UK to come up with proposals, in spite of us having understood that that was what would happen in January or February. We need[ed] to pin down the UK on what we had agreed. We threw in the Northern Irish protocol because we thought it was time to un-fudge the fudge.'[19]

The EU was also motivated by a fear that Britain was dragging its feet on Northern Ireland in a bid to get the same open borders at Calais. 'During phase one, we were very strongly convinced that the UK was trying to use Northern Ireland as a bargaining chip for the future relationship, and we wanted to avoid that at all costs,' De Rynck said.[20] May's team is adamant that, if this was her secret plan, she kept it secret from them.

A week later, on 27 February, the day before the document was published, Barnier bluntly stated that he fully intended it to be incendiary. 'I want to provoke them,' he said. 'I want to force them to give a view on our texts.' These comments are perhaps the clearest 'smoking gun' for those who say the EU set out to punish the UK for Brexit. Not only would the backstop be enshrined in law, it would be enforced in such a way that Northern Ireland would have to 'maintain full alignment' with EU rules, including those governing livestock and agriculture, a sector the SN committee had just identified as one where London wished to diverge from Brussels. To cap it all, Barnier told the MEPs, 'Regulatory alignment alone is not enough – we also need the Union's customs code to apply to Northern Ireland.'[21] It was just as Denzil Davidson and others had feared when they said Britain should write its own legal text.

The final part of Barnier's ambush was to keep Britain in the dark until the last minute. Robbins heard the text was to be released the next morning. He stormed to the Commission to see Sabine Weyand, urging her 'not to publish at all'. When this did not work, he said, 'You could at least share it with us in advance.' Her reply was curt: 'Sorry, no.'[22]

The document, both in content and timing, was a bombshell for May. To avoid a hard border between North and South, Northern Ireland would have to stay in the EU customs union. That created a border between one part of the UK and another. To cap it all, the text landed on a Wednesday morning as May was preparing for Prime Minister's Questions in the Commons. The timing appeared designed to wound. Blindsided and unable to prepare, she had little choice but to denounce it out of hand. 'The draft legal text the Commission have published would, if implemented, undermine the UK common market and threaten the constitutional integrity of the UK by creating a customs and regulatory border down the Irish Sea,' she thundered, anger evident in her voice. 'And no UK prime minister could ever agree to it. I will be making it crystal clear to President Juncker and others that we will never do so.' Arlene Foster denounced the text as 'constitutionally unacceptable'.

In Brussels, Barnier faced questions from the press about whether he was seeking to 'topple' the May government. Realising he had overplayed his hand, the EU's negotiator dissembled: 'I am not trying to provoke or create any shockwaves.' EU officials, in turn, blamed May's blunt rejection of the EU proposal for elevating the backstop into an intractable problem. 'When you turn it into a sovereignty issue, when you weaponise it like that, you cannot compromise afterwards,' one said.

The row laid bare misunderstandings on both sides. On the British side, Brexiteers believed the quest for a political fudge was being thwarted by an excessively legalistic approach from the EU. To EU officials the rules were just the expression of the principles which held their Union together. 'This is not just about wretched bureaucrats who read the treaty before they go to bed, it is about us pursuing our legitimate interests,' a senior EU official said. 'The four freedoms go together. That is not a rule, that is a principle that is key to the contract that constitutes the EU. If we break that, we break the EU. You can't have the rights of Norway and the obligations of Canada, not because we are rules-based or rigid or because we are bureaucrats, but because it would be sowing the seeds of our own destruction.'

The Eurocrats, who saw Brexit as a device for managing the internal politics of the Conservative Party, in turn underestimated the pressures on May. David Lidington, who understood Brussels as well as any minister, said, 'They thought Tories were simply pandering to Ukip or the DUP and never understood that Euroscepticism, a desire for sovereignty, support for the Union were real forces that any political leader and party would have to address.'[23] Lidington, who had been asked by May to handle the Irish government (without telling David Davis), called Simon Coveney, the deputy prime minister who doubled as foreign minister. 'There is no way I or Philip Hammond or any of the more Europhile cabinet members can possibly sign up to something that looks like this,' he said. 'Don't think that this is just Eurosceptics. The Conservative Party thinks about itself as a unionist party.' A senior Commission official admitted it was a dialogue of the deaf: 'There is such an incredible lack of understanding of the continent in London. But I have to be honest, on the continent there are actually very few politicians who get the UK.'

The government deserved criticism for failing to draft their own legal text but the Commission's power play was reckless on an issue, Northern Ireland, which Barnier admitted required sensitivity. It is unimaginable that he went in studs up without the approval of Juncker and Selmayr. Cabinet ministers believed claims that Selmayr had described losing Northern Ireland as 'the price Britain has to pay for Brexit'. He denied both the comment and the sentiment, but Denzil Davidson said, 'I think Martin Selmayr was central to this. [He] thought we had to be hauled to reality because we were dragging our feet. They very unilaterally came up with text … which was framed pretty offensively.'[24] The same week, an EU official, widely believed to be Weyand, told the *FT* that Britain needed 'shock therapy'.[25] A Downing Street adviser said, 'Selmayr was warned by

people who knew Northern Ireland that what he was doing was dangerous. That text was a very serious mistake. You don't unilaterally land
something like that in a live peace process.' It was a classic case of Brussels
choosing a tactical political win over strategic wisdom.

May's big speech, on 2 March, was originally intended to be given in
Newcastle, a city which voted Remain in a region that voted to Leave,
but a historic snowstorm dubbed 'the Beast from the East' forced her to
divert to the Mansion House in central London. The prime minister set
out her plan for 'managed divergence' agreed at Chequers. But that was
included only after cabinet ministers demanded the text be toughened
up to reflect their views. 'I remember, in the run-up to Mansion House,
literally rewriting the speech,' Boris Johnson recalled, 'getting her to
agree changes to the language about divergence.' The foreign secretary,
caught in the same snowstorm on a visit to Budapest, waited anxiously
by a fax machine to see the final text. Only then did he tweet his
approval. Privately, he thought, 'She was trying to bubble gum
everything together.'

The key section of the Mansion House speech began when May said,
'We all need to face up to some hard facts.' To the Remainers she said,
'Our access to each other's markets will be less than it is now.' To the
ERG she warned, 'Even after we have left the jurisdiction of the ECJ, EU
law and the decisions of the ECJ will continue to affect us' and Britain
would not be able to 'enjoy all the benefits without all of the obligations'.
However, May also had a message for Barnier: 'The Commission has
suggested that the only option available to the UK is an "off the shelf"
model. But, at the same time, they have also said that in certain areas
none of the EU's third country agreements would be appropriate … We
will not accept the rights of Canada and the obligations of Norway …
This is a negotiation and neither of us can have exactly what we want.'

Gavin Barwell said, 'The thing I'm most proud of in any of those
speeches is the hard-truth section of the Mansion House speech. I think
it stands the test of time very well.' Yet, the section did not get the notice
speechwriter Keelan Carr expected. 'That was going to be the moment
where we finally stopped riding two different horses and made some
serious decisions,' a Number 10 aide said. 'We expected that hard facts bit
to cause more of a ripple because the ERG never accepted any hard
truths.'

The Mansion House speech was cautiously welcomed at home. But in Brussels, the compromise thrashed out at Chequers was dead on arrival. Barnier attempted to sound positive, tweeting that he welcomed May's 'clarity' about leaving the single market and the customs union and the 'recognition of trade-offs'. But on 7 March, just five days after Mansion House, Donald Tusk published the European Council's response. Making no effort to hide his distaste for Brexit, Tusk announced that Britain's 'pick and mix' approach was 'out of the question'. There was 'no possibility' of pursuing the three baskets approach, with 'exclusive access to the single market for some parts of our economies'. He said, 'The only remaining possible model is a free trade agreement.' Tusk proposed a deal involving zero tariffs and continued EU access to UK fishing waters. But the lugubrious Pole went on, 'This will be the first FTA in history that loosens economic ties, instead of strengthening them.'

In private, Barnier was even more withering. The following day, 8 March, he told MEPs on the Brexit Steering Group that May was guilty of 'double cherry-picking' and declared, 'Mutual recognition does not exist with third countries.'[26] A British official, had they been present, might have argued that no other third country began from a position of total regulatory alignment either, but Barnier's words were further proof that asking the Commission to think beyond what it had done before was an uphill task. The SN committee's plan had flickered briefly, for five days. Tusk had turned off the life support machine.

Barnier's decision to use Northern Ireland as a wedge issue enraged even long-standing pro-Europeans in May's team. With his grey hair, bookish mien and near-surgical attachment to his briefcase, Denzil Davidson, one of the PM's Europe advisers, seemed to Brexiteers more like a civil servant than a political adviser. But when he and Ed de Minckwitz visited Steve Baker for one of their regular chats on 13 March, Davidson's blood was up. A unionist first, he said, 'If they try to annexe Northern Ireland, I would be happy to go for no deal.' Surprised and delighted, Baker responded, 'Hold on to this moment. This is how the Eurosceptics feel all the time: that the whole United Kingdom's been annexed by them [the EU].'

Despite his distaste for the EU's response, Davidson did, however, take on board one piece of advice offered by Guy Verhofstadt, the European Parliament's Brexit coordinator, when he visited Downing Street on 6 March, four days after Mansion House. Verhofstadt argued that May's proposals were lacking 'a concept', an assessment Tim Barrow privately agreed with, saying, 'You cannot be successful if there is first of all not a concept, an architecture of this relationship.'[27] In short, May needed to dress up her asks in a grand theory of UK–EU relations.

The concept Verhofstadt was pushing for was an 'association agreement' with Britain, an established mechanism for managing relationships with non-EU countries. Davidson, realising that more effort had to be made to make the Commission comfortable with a bespoke deal, became an advocate in Whitehall for an association agreement. He was supported by David Davis. The template had been used for deals with Ukraine and Moldova and the countries in the Balkans who were candidates for future EU membership. 'It didn't presuppose any policy outcome,' said another of May's advisers. 'I think Olly ruled it out because it wasn't his idea.' A member of Robbins' team reflected, 'Olly couldn't get beyond the fact that this problem had to be solved by him and him alone.'

On 16 March, Tusk repeated his offer that Britain could have a free trade deal like Canada's, enhanced with side deals. This entered Brexiteer folklore as the moment Brussels offered what Steve Baker and his ERG allies wanted. It was presented as an olive branch that May should have seized. But the fatal flaw in the Tusk proposal was that the offer excluded Northern Ireland, as Robbins quickly ascertained when he attended a briefing by one of Sabine Weyand's team. Robbins interrupted and asked, 'Let me just be clear, this is Great Britain only, isn't it?'

'Yes, this is Great Britain. And we'd have separate arrangements for Northern Ireland.'

Robbins 'got very cross' with Weyand: 'Sabine, this is where it falls down. You know a Conservative and Unionist prime minister can't accept that.' In a second conversation with Weyand by telephone, he said, 'If you're going to write completely dishonest crap like that then we'll have to start doing the same.'

Baker went quickly from thrilled at Tusk's offer to frustrated that he was not allowed to cheerlead for it publicly. References to Tusk's proposal were cut from his public statements, on one occasion by civil servant Catherine Webb – reinforcing Baker's view that officials, not ministers, held the whip hand. 'I explicitly wanted to talk about the good news of Donald Tusk's offer to the UK matching what DExEU ministers had decided a few weeks before,' he said. 'Time and again I had my speeches amended and my instructions to officials overridden by Number 10.' Suella Braverman added, 'I was never allowed to say, "Canada's a good solution" publicly.'[28]

The final legal text of the withdrawal agreement was published on 19 March. Downing Street (and the press at the time) failed to understand the significance of a clause which decreed that the backstop would apply 'unless and until' another solution was found. The government's fatal error that March was to allow the EU to define what a hard border was. The document stated that Britain would 'guarantee' there would be no 'physical infrastructure or related checks and controls' at all in Northern Ireland. This was not just a ban on new infrastructure but implied no monitoring of any sort. The legal text had both made the backstop permanent and weaponised it. A senior cabinet Brexiteer said, 'At every point we allowed an interpretation of what the backstop meant and what our obligation to Ireland was to be defined by either the Irish or the EU.' Dominic Cummings put it more bluntly: 'The government has … aided and abetted bullshit invented by Irish nationalists and Remain campaigners that the Belfast Agreement prevents reasonable customs checks on trade between Northern Ireland and the Republic. Read the agreement. It does no such thing. This has fatally undermined the UK's negotiating position.'

What began as ambiguous in the Joint Report was now set in reinforced concrete. May was to chisel at this edifice for fourteen more months before giving up, defeated.

When she arrived for the European Council, on 22 March, May was greeted by Michel Barnier at the entrance to the Europa building with a kiss on the hand. The member states agreed to an 'implementation period' lasting until 31 December 2020 and to the start of talks on a final deal. Yet on the two major issues – how closely to align with EU rules and customs arrangements – there was no agreement. May's attempt to proffer a fudge between the two wings of her cabinet, 'managed divergence', had been rejected by the EU. The February Chequers meeting had simply delayed the reckoning. 'All we did was kick the can four or five months down the road,' said a Number 10 official who believed May should have forced a 'moment of truth' at Chequers. 'We would have had more time and used up less capital in the intervening months to get to the same place. The PM was determined all the way through to keep the cabinet together. If we are honest, that leads to her making some bad decisions.'

The counterpoint came from a cabinet minister close to May, who said that by insisting on divergence, the Brexiteers were responsible for handing the government a diplomatic defeat. 'The delay could have been avoided by those people being more pragmatic,' the minister said.

What followed was one of the most controversial periods of May's premiership, in which she performed a policy pirouette without sign-off from the Brexiteers in cabinet. The reason she was momentarily strong enough to act unilaterally was that May had spent most of the EU Council meeting and Thursday's dinner successfully persuading her fellow leaders to join Britain in a mass expulsion of Russian spies. The events which led to that moment briefly revised May's authority and showed what sort of prime minister she might have been had Brexit not dominated. These events ensured that she would be around to make the case for her Brexit policy – and that when MPs decided they hated it, they were not prepared to install Jeremy Corbyn in her place.

6

POISON

Salisbury, Syria and Antisemitism

March to August 2018

It was 14 March 2018 when a government led by Jeremy Corbyn became a practical impossibility. That was when the leader of 'her majesty's loyal opposition' got to his feet to respond to a statement by the prime minister about the poisoning, eight days earlier, of Sergei Skripal, a former KGB spy who had worked as a double agent for Britain, and his daughter Yulia. Both had been found foaming at the mouth on a bench in the cathedral city of Salisbury on 4 March. May revealed that the Skripals had been targeted by a Russian-manufactured nerve agent called Novichok. In one of the strangest self-inflicted wounds of the era, Corbyn appeared to place more trust in Vladimir Putin than in the British security services. Minutes later, his senior aide Seumas Milne, who shared Corbyn's world view, compounded his mistake. Together they rendered their party as toxic as the Skripals' front doorknob on which the Novichok had been smeared.

Yulia, thirty-three, was unconscious for three weeks, her father, sixty-six, for more than a month. Samples of the nerve agent were sent to the Defence Science and Technology Laboratory at Porton Down. Amber Rudd, the home secretary, chaired meetings of the Cobra emergency committee. May had deliberately put her higher in the cabinet pecking order than Boris Johnson, so responsibility would fall on a calm head.

Some were more gung-ho. In the first National Security Council (NSC) meeting, 'Gavin [Williamson] wanted to close the Russian Embassy,' an NSC member revealed. A week later, Williamson provided a signature *Thick of It* moment when he said, 'Frankly, Russia should go away and should shut up.' The comment came in a Q&A session after a speech at Rolls-Royce. The plan had been to position Williamson in front of a large engine. 'But when we arrived it looked like a massive dildo,' an aide recalled. The three-ton engine was dragged away.

In a statement to the Commons on 12 March, Theresa May demanded to know whether the attack was Kremlin-sponsored or whether Russia had 'lost control' of the nerve agent. When he got to his feet, Corbyn appeared more concerned about cordial relations with Russia than in condemning the attack: 'We need to continue seeking a robust dialogue with Russia on all the issues ... rather than simply cutting off contact and letting the tensions and divisions get worse.' Labour MPs looked on in horror.

Corbyn and Milne both had form on Russia. The Labour leader had been a regular on RT, the British branch of Russia Today. Milne had defended the 2014 Russian annexation of Crimea from Ukraine as 'defensive', praising Moscow as 'a counterweight to unilateral western power'. The same year he even shared a platform with Putin, at a conference in the Black Sea resort of Sochi. Earlier in Corbyn's leadership, Milne had meddled in a Labour statement about Iran's support for terrorist groups. A colleague remembered him saying, 'If you're referring to Hezbollah, they aren't a terrorist group, they're an army.'

Two days later, 14 March, May announced the expulsion of twenty-three Russian spies masquerading as diplomats 'to dismantle the Russian espionage network in the UK'. It was the biggest round of expulsions for thirty years. She told MPs the 'Russian state was culpable' and guilty of 'an unlawful use of force' against the UK.

Rather than accept this, Corbyn questioned whether the government had made a 'formal request for evidence from the Russian government', then, extraordinarily, suggested Britain give 'a sample of the agent used in the Salisbury attack' to the Russians 'to run their own tests'. This unleashed a wave of condemnation from his own benches. Pat McFadden, a grizzled Blairite who was the nuggety soul of the Labour right, delivered the *coup de grâce*. In his dry Scottish growl, McFadden said, 'Responding with strength and resolve when your country is under threat is an essential component of political leadership. There is a Labour tradition that understands that, and it has been understood by prime ministers of all parties who have stood at that despatch box.'

Milne addressed a huddle of lobby journalists in the lower press gallery directly behind the chamber – routine procedure after PMQs or a big statement. The convention was that his comments would be reported as from a 'Labour spokesman'. What Milne said that day led the press corps to tear up the rules and name him. Milne reiterated the need to send a sample of Novichok to the Russians. Then he suggested the views of the British security services should not be trusted: 'There's a history in relation to WMD and intelligence which is problematic, to put it mildly.' Reporters tried and failed to get Milne to explain what evidence would satisfy Corbyn. 'Do you trust the Kremlin more than MI6?' was met with a silent smile. In John McDonnell's office, his spin doctor James Mills kicked a bin across the office. 'That's fucking going to cost us the election!' he shouted.[1] The shadow chancellor was also agitated. Salisbury would be the first of several issues on which McDonnell felt Corbyn's ideology was an impediment to winning power.

Thanks to intensive diplomatic efforts from May and Johnson (his sole major contribution as foreign secretary), by the end of March twenty-eight other countries had joined the UK in expelling 153 Russian intelligence officers. On 5 September the British authorities would identify the would-be assassins as members of the GRU, Russian military intelligence.

Even Andrew Murray, the ex-communist Corbynite, acknowledged the Skripal poisoning was 'something we got wrong ... We just didn't think the Russian state would be so stupid and brazen to do something like that.' It was the first of three incidents in quick succession which poisoned Corbyn's reputation.

In the small hours of 8 April, news broke of a suspected chemical weapons attack in Douma, the last rebel-held city in the Eastern Ghouta region of Syria. Helicopters dropped barrel bombs full of chlorine on a residential block. Horrifying images of the dead showed them frothing at the mouth.

Bashar al-Assad had used chemical weapons before and had got away with it. In Number 10, chief of staff Gavin Barwell regarded the vote not to authorise military action in 2013, after eight hundred people were killed in a chemical attack in Damascus, as 'the most shameful moment' of his seven years as an MP. David Cameron's failure to get Labour backing for air strikes led Barack Obama to back off too. Assad had crossed a red line and nothing happened.

On 10 April, May spoke to Emmanuel Macron and Donald Trump who were contemplating air strikes. Later the same day, May chaired the NSC, where it was agreed that Britain should act to prevent the normalisation of chemical weapons usage. There were no dissenting voices. May was shown intelligence that 'Syrian military officials coordinated' the attack. 'That was the key bit of intel,' a close aide said.

Trump veered between bellicosity and uncertainty. On 11 April he tweeted: 'Russia vows to shoot down any and all missiles fired at Syria. Get ready Russia, because they will be coming, nice and new and "smart!"' The following day, the president backtracked: 'Could be very soon or not so soon at all!' A cabinet source noted, 'When Trump started tweeting, he hadn't even had his intelligence briefing. He was speaking without having the first clue of what he was talking about.'

Cabinet approved air strikes on 12 April. At 5 p.m. the following day, May signed off on the target list with Williamson and the attorney general, Jeremy Wright. The final go order came at 10 p.m. in a call between Williamson, his US counterpart Jim Mattis and the French defence minister, Florence Parly. Farcically, as Williamson sought to sign off a military strike, a fire alarm went off in the MoD. Then half the call was taken up with Williamson explaining that the British defence attaché in Washington could not join the planned post-raid Pentagon press conference because May needed to be the first Briton to address the public. 'You had this bizarre thing when the three people who were sanctioning a military attack were talking about the formalities of a fucking press conference,' a defence official said. Mattis, who was constantly amused that British ministers also had a parliamentary seat, rang off by saying, 'Gavin, thank you for taking time out of your constituency work.'

At 4 a.m. on Saturday 14 April, four Tornado GR4s from RAF Akrotiri in Cyprus joined US and French air forces in hitting several chemical and biological weapons research and storage facilities. 'Initially, the military plan was for the RAF to drop six missiles and Gavin pushed them to go up to eight,' an MoD source said. 'So, the French air force fired nine [plus another three from ships] – the French being the French.'

May was back in the office by 7 a.m. and addressed the nation at 10 a.m. Some in Number 10 wanted a retrospective Commons vote, but Smith and Williamson, the serving and past chief whips, vetoed that. 'There will be PMs in years to come that will have a great deal to thank her for,' a senior aide said. It was probably the best moment of Theresa May's premiership.

When Corbyn appeared on *The Andrew Marr Show* that Sunday he called for a 'war powers act' to force governments to seek approval from

MPs before launching any military action. 'Where is the legal basis for this?' Corbyn asked. 'Humanitarian intervention is a legally debatable concept. I think Parliament should have a say.' Most who had served in government in a security crisis regarded this as a fatuous stance to prevent any form of foreign intervention.

In the Commons, the following Monday, Corbyn repeated the mistakes of his response to Salisbury. He said that while 'suspicion' pointed 'to the Assad regime', it might have been someone else. Even if Assad was responsible, Corbyn made clear he would not support military action. Once again, his belief that tyrants and enemies deserved the benefit of the doubt put him at odds with his own party. Fourteen Labour MPs backed May.

A combination of Salisbury and Syria had a dramatic effect on the personal standing of May and Corbyn. 'Post-2017 it was the highest her personal ratings went in our private polling,' James Johnson recalled. The events that damaged Corbyn most were not the poison attacks in Salisbury or Douma, but another poison he had allowed to flourish in Labour's own ranks – antisemitism.

At 7 a.m. on Friday 23 March, Luciana Berger was feeding her new baby when she was sent a Facebook post from 2012 by a street artist called Mear One. He complained that Tower Hamlets Council wanted to paint over his latest work, *Freedom of Expression*. Beneath was a comment from Corbyn. 'Why? You are in good company,' he wrote. 'Rockerfeller destroyed Diego Viera's mural because it includes a picture of Lenin.'

Why indeed? The answer ought to have been obvious to Corbyn since the mural depicted hook-nosed bankers playing Monopoly on the backs of the naked and downtrodden. It was an image so blatant that it might have been designed by someone trying to explain to a child what antisemitism looked like – and yet Corbyn either didn't, couldn't or wouldn't see it. His enthusiasm for Palestinian causes meant he had shared platforms with people who were antisemites. Corbyn's own visceral anti-Zionism veered, in modern definitions of antisemitism, close to if not over that line.

Berger tweeted a picture of the mural and announced she had asked the leader's office for an explanation. She heard nothing. The tweet was read by more than a million people. LOTO – the leader of the opposition's office – went into meltdown. Over the next three days they would provide three different statements. In the first, that evening, a spokesman said Corbyn had defended the mural 'on the grounds of freedom of speech' but admitted it was 'offensive' and 'it is right that it was removed'. Berger declared this 'wholly inadequate'. Corbyn then said, 'I sincerely regret that I did not look more closely at the image I was commenting on, the contents of which are deeply disturbing and anti-Semitic.' It took until 25 March before he apologised.

It was too late for the Jewish community. That Sunday 1,500 people rallied in Parliament Square, many carrying placards saying 'Enough is enough' – a minority group protesting against racism in the party which was supposed to speak up for the oppressed. The speakers included Jonathan Goldstein, chairman of the Jewish Leadership Council; Jonathan Arkush, president of the Board of Deputies; and Labour MPs Berger, John Mann and Wes Streeting. Berger said, 'Antisemitism is very real and alive in the Labour Party. It pains me to have to say that today.' When the rally was over, the Labour MPs went back into Parliament for a parliamentary party meeting. Berger gave the same speech to her colleagues but added, 'Anyone sending me private messages of support, text messages, I do not want your sympathy. I don't need your sympathy. This cannot be my fight alone. If you want to do something about it, then this is your fight as well.' There was an instant standing ovation, but Berger became disillusioned by how many of those clapping failed to stand with her in the months ahead.

On 29 March, Christine Shawcroft, a veteran left-winger, resigned as head of the NEC's disputes panel after leaked emails showed she had opposed the suspension of a council candidate who had posted an article on Facebook suggesting the Holocaust was a hoax. Shawcroft claimed, 'This whole row is being stirred up to attack Jeremy, as we all know.'

The 'oldest bigotry' was already a running sore in Labour. Shami Chakrabarti, the human rights activist, conducted a review in 2016 but concluded that antisemitism was not endemic in Labour. The finding did more harm than good for relations with the Jewish community, made worse when Chakrabarti undermined her 'independence' by accepting a shadow cabinet job and a peerage. MPs cried 'whitewash'.

The mural was more serious, since Corbyn himself was implicated. To the rest of the party, it seemed that he did not regard antisemitism as real racism. Adam Langleben of Labour Against Anti-Semitism said, 'Corbyn's world view is shaped by the three Cs: class, colonialism and colour. In his head, Jews are rich, and therefore we're not working class. In his head, Jews are white, so we're not a minority in the same way, and Jews are colonialist. On all three metrics, which are fundamental components of his political identity, Jews are on the wrong side. I think that's what drives his accidental antisemitism.' Langleben told a podcast, 'One senior member of staff in Jeremy Corbyn's office admitted to me that they thought Jeremy Corbyn was an antisemite, but they were going to try and manage it.'[2]

Corbyn spent the first night of Passover, Sunday 3 April, at a Seder dinner with a Jewish group. What might have been an act of reconciliation, turned into a provocation. His hosts were Jewdas, a radical left-wing fringe group, whose members had previously described Israel as 'a steaming pile of sewage which needs to be properly disposed of'. The following day LOTO was forced to agree that Corbyn would meet the Board of Deputies and Jewish Leadership Council.

By the time he did so, on 25 April, Labour had agreed to change its code of conduct for members. Both groups pressed Corbyn to include the full International Holocaust Remembrance Alliance (IHRA) definition of antisemitism. First published in 2005, it had been adopted by thirty-one countries, including the UK in 2016. The definition was uncontroversial, but it came with eleven examples of antisemitism in action. A month after muralgate, Corbyn might have buried the issue by adopting the definition in full. 'That was the view of pretty much everyone apart from Jeremy, Seumas and Karie [Murphy],' an aide said. Instead, LOTO chose to exclude four of the eleven examples, all of which related to Israel. Those in the leadership team who most wanted to win an election regarded Corbyn's stance as absurd, but he believed he would be betraying the Palestinian cause by satisfying the Jewish groups. Payback came in the local elections on 3 May, when Labour lost five seats in the London borough of Barnet as Jewish voters turned to the Conservatives.

Ahead of an NEC meeting on 17 July, the chief rabbi, Ephraim Mirvis, wrote to Labour accusing them of 'unprecedented contempt' for British Jews. The same evening, the Parliamentary Labour Party (PLP) overwhelmingly passed a motion calling for the IHRA's definition to be adopted in full. Corbyn did not even bother to turn up.

The NEC meeting was an angry affair. Tom Watson, the deputy leader, asked, 'Are we serious about winning a general election? If so, we need to grip this issue and close it down.' The NEC adopted the new code of conduct without a vote but decided to consult Jewish groups on how it might be improved. Margaret Hodge, whose parents were Holocaust refugees, was behind the speaker's chair with Gavin Shuker and Ian Austin, when Corbyn returned to the Commons from the NEC meeting. Fury bubbling within her, she said, 'I'm going to tell this guy he's a fucking antisemitic racist.' As she stalked her fellow Islington MP, Hodge promised herself she would not swear. She told Corbyn, 'You've made Labour a hostile environment for Jews. It is not what you say but what you do and by your actions you have shown you are an antisemitic racist.' Shaking with rage she departed, unaware that Austin had already briefed Paul Waugh at the HuffPost, complete with the profanity.[3]

Hodge was suspended from the party. McDonnell demanded the decision be reversed. At a shadow cabinet away day, on 23 July, the shadow chancellor lost his temper at Corbyn's refusal to budge. 'John ended up in a blazing row with Karie and Seumas,' a senior frontbencher said. 'They all start shouting at each other.' The same evening Labour MPs voted unanimously to incorporate the full IHRA definition into their rulebook. Britain's three biggest Jewish newspapers[4] then ran a joint editorial calling Corbyn an 'existential threat to Jewish life'.

The Hodge probe was eventually dropped in early August. On 10 August pictures emerged of Corbyn laying a wreath at a cemetery in Tunis in 2014 to commemorate members of the Palestinian terrorist group Black September, who had slaughtered the Israeli Olympic team at the 1972 Munich games. Corbyn's explanation – which took two days to emerge – was that he had been 'present but not involved'. Two weeks later footage emerged of Corbyn telling Jewish protesters that Zionists 'don't understand English irony'. Jonathan Sacks, the former chief rabbi, called these remarks the most offensive by a British politician since Enoch Powell's Rivers of Blood speech.

When the NEC met on 4 September, there was now a big majority for adopting the IHRA definition and all its examples in full. Yet Corbyn stubbornly refused to give way. The leader read out a page and a half of caveats. It should not 'be regarded as antisemitic to describe Israel, its policies or the circumstances around its foundation as racist because of their discriminatory impact,' he said. The NEC, sick of the opprobrium Corbyn's views had heaped on the party, refused to back him.

In putting warped principle ahead of pragmatism and basic politeness, Corbyn had shown himself totally unsuited to national leadership. Those in other parties who wanted to work with Labour on Brexit – Tory Remainers, Lib Dems and the nationalists – were repulsed by his views and incredulous at his inability to solve a simple political problem. Over the next year there would be moments when a skilled Labour leader could have forged a cross-party alliance. Corbyn, in his response to Salisbury, Syria and antisemitism, had made himself persona non grata.

REVEALED PREFERENCES

The Secret Pivot

April to July 2018

The meeting was a 'horror show', 'awful', 'unpleasant', according to those who were there. With each new outburst from a minister, Theresa May's aides exchanged looks; the sense of her authority leaching away was palpable. When Gavin Barwell saw Gavin Williamson pass a note to Boris Johnson, the chief of staff immediately sensed danger. It was 2 May and the SN cabinet committee was entering its third hour. The prime minister had made a presentation about her preferred customs policy, reading from her own handwritten notes. It was quickly clear that those who preferred the different approach advocated by David Davis were not only determined but organised. James Slack, May's official spokesman, watched like the former journalist he was. Some contributions felt like a performance, as if half the ministers had a script and knew what was coming next, while the others didn't realise they were on stage.

May gave nothing away, imperturbable in the face of the barrage. There were moments when her ability to sit unflinching as humiliation was heaped on humiliation was a blessing not a curse. She absorbed criticism as a black hole absorbs light.

Williamson, the defence secretary, scribbled on a piece of paper every time another of his cabinet colleagues spoke. The day before he had warned May that she would not get her proposal through. He slipped the paper to Johnson. On it was the calculation that six of those who had spoken were opposed to the prime minister's plan. Just five had backed her. The foreign secretary read the note and shot forward in his seat. Voice raised, he interrupted, 'Prime Minister, there's a majority against you!'

May, startled by Johnson's Bunterish behaviour, pushed back, telling him to be quiet, denying his charge. The foreign secretary would not be silenced. 'It's six-five against you!' he said, bouncing in his chair like a toddler who has learned a new word. 'It's six-five against you!'

There were not supposed to be votes in cabinet committees. The views stated had been nuanced, not binary. But Williamson and Johnson had successfully framed the outcome of the meeting, just as 'divergence won the day' had done after Chequers. 'It was a total stitch-up,' said one of May's aides. 'I think they planned it. They bounced the room. It was designed to leak.' Leak it did, of course.

Outmanoeuvred as well as out-gunned, the sense that Downing Street could not orchestrate a meeting was just as damaging as the fact that half of May's senior ministers opposed her.

The road to that crunch SN committee meeting had begun in April, after the EU Council meeting. The prime minister needed answers on regulation and on customs. A member of the negotiating team recalled, 'For the level of access we wanted they were telling us we had to accept greater alignment. Option one is: you accept greater alignment. Option two is: you accept less access. Option three is: you think they are bluffing. I genuinely think DD thought they were bluffing.'

Oliver Robbins convinced May they were not. Before the February Chequers meeting the Europe Unit had drawn up plans for Britain to remain in close alignment with EU rules. At Chequers, and again at Mansion House, May had tried to persuade the EU to accept David Davis's concept of 'equivalence' rather than 'alignment', with Brussels recognising British standards as the equivalent of their own. This had been rejected. Sabine Weyand said to Robbins, 'Not now, not tomorrow, never.'

For May and those around her, it made sense to return to the original idea. One of May's EU advisers said, 'Their rejection convinced her that, on the regulatory side, the only solution was a common rulebook.' Controversially, she and her inner circle decided that the only way to enact this pivot successfully was to do it in secret.

To Brexiteers, the key figure in persuading May to soften her approach was Robbins. In the spring of 2018 the negotiator found himself in the firing line; his personal motives maligned, his management style attacked, his performance as negotiator disparaged. A big man, well over six foot,

Robbins was bespectacled and wore his Jaeger-LeCoultre dress watch discreetly, his intellectual self-confidence less unobtrusively. While he had little EU experience, he brought to the role an imaginative problem-solving mind and a Stakhanovite work ethic, turning in nineteen-hour days and six-and-a-half-day weeks. 'Fucking hell, he put the hours in,' a Number 10 special adviser said. Robbins told friends that for three years he did not have many 'waking moments where I haven't been thinking about Brexit'. Even dinners with his parents quickly turned to the latest news from his day job.

MPs who thought Robbins personally opposed to Brexit pointed to a report in February 2018 which revealed that, as a student, he had been president of the Oxford Reform Club, which supported a federalist EU. Yet even Number 10 aides who disliked his influence said he regarded his job as delivering what his prime minister wanted. Philip Hammond said, 'I think Olly was, by personal instinct, strongly pro-European, but he didn't overplay his hand, and I don't think he allowed his personal prejudices to get in the way of doing what the prime minister asked him.'[1]

Robbins' job had five strands. First, he was the prime minister's personal policy adviser on European issues. Second, he was there to help ministers arrive at good decisions. He told the cabinet, 'It is not my job to tell you whether this is the best deal, or the best compromise on a particular issue. It is absolutely my job to offer my professional judgement on whether this is the best available option.' Third, he sought to help the government achieve support at home for their approach. Fourth, he had to explain British decisions to the rest of the EU. Robbins always placed fifth and last the task for which he was best known, the negotiations, which he described as 'sitting in a windowless room in the Berlaymont building until two in the morning arguing over adjectives'. In three years as chief negotiator, he only spent eight weeks doing the aspect of his job on which he was judged.

Michael Gove regarded Robbins as clever and fair. Robbins, in return, saw Gove as a pragmatist. Liam Fox, Robbins told one confidant, was 'ideological but not to the exclusion of facts'. Of Johnson and Davis he was more dismissive. The feeling was mutual. 'Olly is such a Remainer,' Johnson said. 'He once came to me almost in tears and said how tragic it was to see forty-five years of trust being slowly undone in these Brexit negotiations. I had to say to him, because I spent a long time in Brussels,

"That is not how it works. It is not about trust. It's about national inter-est." The British establishment has reverted to a 1970s lack of self-confidence about this country. It's as if Thatcher never happened. It's just gutless.'

There were also tensions between Robbins and Tim Barrow, Britain's ambassador to the EU, a more debonair and charismatic figure, who made a point of deferring to elected politicians. 'His and Olly's relation-ship was hilarious,' a Davis ally said. 'Olly just hated him. Tim Barrow gets politics and how to handle politicians. Olly doesn't.'

The principal criticism of Robbins – voiced repeatedly by ministers, political aides, fellow civil servants and even members of his own team – was that he was pathologically secretive and used this secrecy to maximise his influence. This was never more evident than between April and July 2018, when May tasked him with drawing up a plan partly behind the backs of her ministers. 'I had reservations about a number of ways Olly did his business,' said one political adviser on Europe. 'Classic civil service tricks like sending the papers in so late that nobody had the chance to provide objective advice on them.' A Downing Street political aide agreed, 'It was a fucking nightmare to get Olly's team to send the papers.' Some Brexiteers saw his secrecy as an underhand way of advanc-ing a secret plan which Robbins kept to himself. If there was a strategy, it was 'in Olly's head'. May's team felt it was more about ego than Robbins running his own foreign policy. 'The biggest problem with him is not that he is Machiavellian, [but that] he is a megalomaniac,' a May adviser said.

A civil servant close to May said in both DExEU and the Cabinet Office, Robbins built 'cliquey' teams in which he relied on a small group 'and the rest were discarded as they become less useful to him'. The offi-cial added, 'The way Olly operated, a lot of people struggled to feel like they were in the club – and that's quite difficult if you're senior; you expect to be trusted.' A special adviser said, 'He was a nightmare to work for. He picked a bunch of favourites. He ran the Europe Unit like a renaissance court.' This official, who voted Remain and sympathised with the 'impossible job' Robbins had, nevertheless concluded, 'I think his way of working is not a million miles away from being completely constitutionally improper. He is a securocrat who has a total paranoia about sharing information.' A senior member of the negotiating team said the only colleague in whom Robbins confided was Kay Withers, with whom he went running in Brussels when he needed to release his frustrations and work out his next moves. 'Olly was his own worst enemy,' the fellow negotiator said. 'Kay was the only one who was allowed into his head.' Fellow civil servants saw these tendencies as a product of Robbins' civil service training. 'We had him from the age of twenty-one,' a senior mandarin said. 'So, if he was not a very good leader of people and he was a bit of an arse and he was massively secretive, it is because all we'd done was reward him for those skills and characteristics.'

Like May, he failed to use the media to further his goals. In the public phases of the negotiations, the Commission leaked and briefed relentlessly after meetings, framing decisions to suit their narrative and ridicule the UK's. Robbins, who loathed public attention, refused to sanction a response and rejected suggestions from colleagues that he engage with a select group of senior journalists so people would understand better what he was attempting to achieve and the difficulties he faced. James Roscoe, an experienced Whitehall comms man who had been the Queen's press secretary, urged Robbins to do so, as did Simon Case. Robbins' response was, 'I'm on the stickiest wicket. Why would I want to get out there and advertise the fact?' Another official said, 'Olly was so against any kind of comms strategy. Every time we'd come out of the negotiations they would brief against us and we would have nothing. Simon was trying to create some kind of narrative.'

The other criticism which stuck was that Robbins focused on what was negotiable in Brussels rather than what was acceptable to the Conservative Party or to a majority in Parliament. Nick Timothy said, 'It's just natural that an official, however talented, will not see things in the same way as a politician. They won't understand the history of division, rancour and distrust inside the Conservative Party when it comes to Brexit.'[2] Robbins won the respect and admiration of his EU counterparts. A senior Council official said, 'Olly is the most impressive civil servant I have ever met.' But Robbins seemed reluctant to pursue ideas which might cause him to lose face with those admirers in Brussels. 'The view would be, "If we do this, we won't look serious" or "This is a silly ask and they'll think less of us",' a Number 10 spad recalled. 'It's definitely a Robbins argument, this feeling that we shouldn't ask for something if it's going to make us look like silly little Englanders.'

Whatever his faults, it was Theresa May who empowered Robbins, handing him far more power than her ministers, trust he repaid by cleverly pursuing her very specific personal priorities. 'She likes working through official channels,' explained Nick Timothy. 'She is slow to trust fellow politicians.'[3] But from the moment May and Robbins accepted the EU's sequencing, they were locked on tramlines set by Brussels – condemned to seeking tactical fixes that prioritised advancing one more step, instead of working out a destination and pursuing a strategy to reach it. Since his job was to deliver May's desires, rather than challenge her approach, Robbins did not stand back and question whether it would have been better to do things differently. One of May's frustrated political advisers said, 'Olly has not taken a strategic view of things. He has been taking a tactical view step by step and ended up in a bad place.'

By April 2018 what Robbins called the prime minister's 'revealed preferences' had crystallised into three firmly held views. The first, clear to her aides by early 2017, was that she wanted any deal to protect jobs. 'She started to hold the view that there are good people who voted for Brexit in the industrial heartlands – Sunderland – who if we pursue an ideological Brexit will lose their jobs.' The second view, which Philip Hammond and Greg Clark had eased her towards prior to the Chequers meeting, was that an agreement must not disrupt supply chains. The third strand – and the most important – was that a deal must preserve the Union. Philip Hammond recalled, 'It was like a light bulb going on, when she understood that the problems over Northern Ireland would inevitably lead to the break-up of the United Kingdom if we were not able to secure an arrangement with the European Union that allowed us to access the Single Market. Once she understood that, Theresa became a fanatical devotee of an ambitious deal with the European Union. Not because it would save the economy, but because it would save the Union.'[4]

May's decision to adopt the common rulebook on regulations paved the way for a battle royal on the second key issue: customs. Members of a customs union buy and sell goods between themselves without tariffs or quotas and charge a 'common external tariff' to countries outside. Consignments are checked coming into the common customs area but can travel freely inside. May had repeatedly pledged not to join the customs union, since doing so would have made it impossible for the UK to pursue free trade deals, perceived by most Brexiteers to be a central benefit of Brexit. That meant forging 'a' customs union, rather than joining 'the' customs union.

To avoid a hard border between Northern Ireland and the Republic, there were three places the customs border could be drawn. First, there was the EU proposal of a special arrangement for Northern Ireland, effectively adding a customs border in the Irish Sea. Second, the whole of the UK could join a customs arrangement with the EU, ensuring the rules were the same in London, Belfast and Dublin. The third solution was to draw the border around the entire British Isles, with Ireland in a customs union with Great Britain and Northern Ireland, separate from the rest of the EU. The latter solution was anathema to the Irish government, since it smacked of colonialism. May did not want a border between Great Britain and Northern Ireland. The ERG would not tolerate membership of a customs union. Tory rebels and Labour would not tolerate anything else.

There were two broad solutions: a structural agreement which negated the need for an intrusive border or a technical solution which meant any checks were digital, electronic and invisible. The first, structural, plan was initially known as 'the hybrid' and had its roots in work done in 2016 by Jeremy Heywood and Jonathan Black, the director of Europe at the Treasury. Black, a former press secretary to George Osborne and private secretary to both Gordon Brown and Alistair Darling, had by 2018 joined Robbins' Europe Unit in the Cabinet Office. Under the 'hybrid option', Britain would leave the customs union but continue to collect tariffs on behalf of the EU at its borders, as if still a member. The UK would forward the revenue to Brussels if the item was re-exported to the EU. If the goods stayed in the UK, the Treasury would retain the revenue.

This was devilishly complex but it removed the need for a customs border between Northern Ireland and the Republic and between Great Britain and Northern Ireland. Heywood found it 'the most intriguing' solution.[5] However, by the time of the 2017 election officials were concerned it would look too like Britain had not left the EU. After the election, when May asked Heywood about the hybrid option, he said, 'HMRC hasn't done much work on it because it would be so difficult politically.' She replied, 'Well, I want it worked up.'[6]

By the spring of 2018, the hybrid had been rebranded the New Customs Partnership (NCP) and it was May's preferred option. One of her closest cabinet colleagues said, 'On customs, she wanted something that would leave the door open for the best of both worlds. We would be able to maintain the benefits of a customs union without actually being in the customs union or the single market.' The NCP was a brilliant piece of imaginative thinking, but its weakness was its innovation, as well as its political practicality. 'It was a total nonsense,' one minister said. Nothing like it had ever been tried anywhere in the world. Nor did it fit neatly into any of the EU's conceptual boxes. 'It suffers from the fact it is not well understood by the EU,' Davis told May.

The Brexit secretary's preferred option, and that of many Brexiteers, was to use technology to make border checks invisible. This was called 'maximum facilitation', or 'Max-Fac', but in Whitehall, where no opportunity was missed to create a confusing alphabet soup, the HSCA, which stood for 'Highly Streamlined Customs Arrangement'. Since much of the cross-border trade in Ireland and between Ireland and the UK was conducted by a small number of firms, Davis imagined 'trusted trader' schemes, combined with bar coding of consignments and number-plate recognition cameras, would smooth things over, with any checks on non-trusted firms conducted in warehouses far from the border. The bizarre ideas floated to track the goods included 'facial recognition for pigs'.[7]

Number 10 aides who remembered the disruption Davis caused the coalition government, watched incredulous as he extolled the virtues of remote surveillance: 'David Davis, a man who resigned from David Cameron's shadow cabinet over civil liberties, because CCTV was too much, saying that in Northern Ireland we should be tracking people's number plates was fucking unbelievable.'

On 24 April, Davis wrote to May in a blistering 1,400-word denunciation of her favoured NCP plan, branding it 'both politically unpalatable and technically deficient'. Had it leaked, the letter would have severely damaged the prime minister. First, Davis warned May that adopting the plan to 'become the EU's tax collector' would be seen 'as a betrayal of the referendum and of the manifesto'. He feared the World Trade Organisation would rule that, legally, it was a customs union. 'It requires the EU to trust us to enforce their border for them. I think this incredibly unlikely to happen.' Davis concluded it would lead to 'an unacceptable level of oversight and alignment' and that 'pursuing it would seriously handicap our ability to deliver on the result of the referendum before the next election'.[8] The letter was ignored.

Davis felt he had to write letters because he was excluded from key decisions. Brexit policy meetings in Number 10, to which he had never been admitted, were slimmed down, with Brexiteers Stephen Parkinson and Nikki da Costa now also excluded. 'Number 10 is a court,' said a Remainer in the political team. 'The way you succeed in a court is by knowing more than other people.' It was a material disadvantage to the Brexiteers to be left out. Davis was not invited to an away day on Europe at Admiralty House on 12 April. 'We had a strong regard for David; he was personally very helpful to the PM,' Barwell said later. 'But there was absolutely no evidence that what he wanted as a solution was going to be negotiable. We needed to think about a policy solution that might work.'[9] Barwell added, 'We were clear we had to try and square DD. But we were also clear that if we brought him in at the start, he would just say, "Don't like it."'

By April, Brexit policy was in the hands of barely a dozen people, none of whom worked in the Department for Exiting the European Union. David Lidington was invited to the key meetings with growing regularity. The only Brexiteer in the room was Robbie Gibb. Those who read Davis's red box notes say he was not sent papers on customs. 'I think DD was probably more sinned against than sinning,' said one. 'He was appointed Brexit secretary to negotiate this thing, or at least provide a political cover for it, and yet was almost permanently excluded from the discussion. It felt at DExEU like you were receiving the policy from on high.' Steve Baker found Downing Street's desire to ignore DExEU fundamentally wrong. 'Around the beginning of March 2018 was the point at which the prime minister diverged from her DExEU ministers. To me it is a constitutional outrage.'

Essentially, May was concerned by the detail of what Robbins thought negotiable while Davis wanted to change the big picture dynamic of the negotiations. 'Fundamentally, DD was trying to negotiate Brexit while pursuing a totally different strategy to that of the PM,' a Davis ally observed. 'His strategy was: "We'll face them down in the endgame." He has a much higher risk appetite than the prime minister.' A May adviser agreed: 'Her assessment was that the kind of cliff-walking exercise he wanted to undertake would not be politically viable.'

The Brexit secretary also believed passionately that Britain would have more leverage if the government made a big, public, effort to prepare for no-deal. He 'wasn't nervous' about no-deal itself 'partly because I thought it would never happen, or if it did happen, it would happen for a month and it would work, or there'd be anarchy', prompting Brussels to deal.[10]

On 10 January, he wrote to May arguing they had 'a duty' to launch 'a clear "no deal" strategy'. On 28 March, Davis wrote again calling for 'an order of magnitude change in the current Whitehall approach to "no deal" preparations', arguing 'It is important we continue to have an option to walk away in March 2019.' Neither had any meaningful effect.

Davis and his aide Raoul Ruparel believed the way to alleviate Brexiteer concerns about the withdrawal agreement was to set out in a white paper what Britain wanted from the final trade deal – turning the political focus from the past towards the future. The Brexit secretary set out his thoughts in a letter to May on 27 March, accusing Robbins of not showing 'the level of ambition necessary'. MPs, Davis warned, 'cannot expect those who supported leaving the EU to agree to signing off on the financial settlement without any idea of what we are gaining for it. Similarly, we cannot expect those who voted to remain in the EU to support formally leaving the EU without a clear idea of where we are headed.' If May adopted the approach recommended by Robbins, he argued, 'We will fail in Parliament, fail in the negotiations and therefore fail to deliver on the result of the referendum.'

Like many of Davis's missives to May, this one accurately identified the Achilles heels of her approach – but he lacked the political clout, allies and deftness of touch in the Whitehall war-games to force a rethink. A concerted campaign to expose her approach and enlist other cabinet Brexiteers would, at the very least, have brought May's premiership to a crunch point earlier and denied both her and the country much of the political agony of the subsequent year.

Increasingly frustrated, Davis wrote an even more apocalyptic letter on 10 April, in which he put the blame for the failure to seize the initiative in the negotiations squarely at May's door. 'It is fundamental to [the] success of the negotiation, and frankly to the survival of the government that we take steps forward,' he wrote. A relationship which had saved May's bacon after the election, just ten months earlier, was falling apart. He warned that unless there was a deal by the end of 2018, 'Parliament will rightly vote down any deal we put in front of them – something which this government would not survive.' Failure by the government to take decisions would mean 'decisions will be taken from us. Either by the Commission or by Parliament.' Davis reiterated that it was 'crucial' to publish 'a detailed white paper' before the EU Council meeting in June to shape the debate. A Davis aide said, 'Olly and others were always pushing back at that.' The problem for Davis was that his proposals had been rejected by the EU and May's team had concluded that the only way forward was closer alignment. The problem for May was that Davis's predictions about the consequences would prove to be lethally prescient.

At this stage, however, Ruparel was concerned that his boss, and many ERG members, were naively clinging to the idea that they could change the policy without changing prime minister. He repeatedly stressed that May's signature on the Joint Report, which pledged that nothing would change in Northern Ireland, made that impossible. 'If you don't change that you can't change anything,' he warned. 'She made these personal commitments. You're saying she has to go back and rip up the Joint Report – and that is something she is never going to do. So long as she is prime minister, she isn't going to change.'

The reason Number 10 kept stalling Davis's plans to publish a white paper authored in DExEU was that, unknown to most of the cabinet, Robbins' Europe Unit in the Cabinet Office was, on May's orders, writing a different plan. From the start of April to the end of June, 'there were two teams writing two different' policies, a special adviser recalled.

Boris Johnson, Michael Gove and Liam Fox were not informed where May and Robbins were heading. 'There were noises off,' said one Brexiteer cabinet minister, 'but I wasn't aware that there was a wholly alternative project being prepared.' Johnson began to grow suspicious that May had sent David Lidington around Europe, in effect, to do Davis's job. The foreign secretary arrived in Madrid on his way to Latin America to discover a British jet on the runway which belonged to Lidington, who was quietly talking to the Spanish. In cabinet, May continued to 'slather DD with praise', a minister recalled – the 'love fest' more 'toe curling' the more out of the loop Davis became. One of Johnson's closest allies said later, 'I've come to the conclusion that she was exceptionally duplicitous.'

May and her team backed the NCP over Max-Fac for three reasons: officials told them the technology would not be ready in time. One cabinet minister said, 'We had a presentation from HMRC and they said it could be done but it would take five to ten years.' Second, they were warned that any infrastructure at all at the Irish border would become the target of dissident republican terrorists. Finally, Robbins told May NCP was negotiable with Brussels and Max-Fac was not.

Several EU advisers are clear that Robbins misled May. Brussels had firmly rejected both plans. In mid-April Robbins, accompanied by Jonathan Black, Brendan Threlfall and Catherine Webb, gave a presentation with Jim Harra of HMRC and Simon Case to the Commission on customs. 'I very explicitly remember getting briefings from Simon Case, coming back from these negotiations in Brussels, saying, "They hate both equally. They think both are rubbish, and both are never going to work",' one adviser said. Peter Foster of the *Telegraph*, one of the best-connected British journalists in Brussels, was briefed by EU officials that they had subjected both plans to a 'systematic and forensic annihilation'.[11] A senior Council official close to Tusk agreed that May's preferred hybrid option was a non-starter: 'We were clear that that couldn't work, this customs idea, we were abundantly clear.'

The key meeting during May's secret pivot came at Admiralty House on Thursday 19 April, following two fruitless weeks of talks with the Commission. The negotiating team admitted they were 'stuck'. Those present included Barwell, Penn, Davidson and de Minckwitz from Number 10; Heywood and Harra from the civil service; Robbins, Black and Threlfall from the negotiating team. 'Olly was candid about the un-negotiability of the hybrid, about the impracticality of both models and about the fact that Max-Fac could not meet the objectives he had been set,' a Number 10 source said. Robbins went further. 'He said the only way really to meet these objectives is with a customs union,' the witness said.

Robbins was right that this was, in negotiation terms, the logical landing ground and one which had a chance of passing in the Commons. Straight after the general election, Davidson had told Barwell, 'If anything, the majority of this Parliament is for a customs union.'[12] But, given her repeated assurances that the UK would be able to strike new trade deals, it was not one May could grasp if she wanted to survive. May told the meeting, 'I can't sell it to the party.' A Number 10 source said, 'Olly was shut down pretty quickly by the PM. It was the last time a customs union was properly explored.'

However, rather than tell May to think again, Robbins implied he could work around the problems and find a tweak. An official in HMRC, which had regarded the NCP plan as unworkable since 2017, said Robbins was 'keeping a corpse warm'.[13] This failure to kill the plan left May clinging to an idea even her own team regarded as delusional. A member of her private office said, 'She drank the Kool-Aid. She believed you could have your cake and eat it on customs in a way that everyone else thought was insane.' Another Downing Street aide said, 'Olly relished trying to solve the unsolvable. Of greater service would have been saying, "No, Prime Minister, this is not going to work."'

Officials in UKRep, Britain's outpost in Brussels, knew May was on a hiding to nothing. They got wind of comments made by Michel Barnier to the Brexit Steering Group of the EU Parliament, just after the Mansion House speech. Barnier 'categorically rejected the idea that the EU would delegate customs controls to the United Kingdom after Brexit, as Mrs May had suggested'.[14] This made sense since the Commission was, at this time, accusing Britain of failing to collect £2.4 billion of duties on goods imported from China, even while a member of the EU. Barnier went further in mid-May telling MEPs, 'Neither proposal is operational and acceptable for us', complaining that 'political capital and energy' was 'being deployed in London' on plans that were non-starters.[15]

Raoul Ruparel, Davis's policy adviser on Europe, warned Denzil Davidson in Downing Street that the prime minister was being given a distorted view of reality. 'Olly was pitching that they liked NCP more,' an EU aide said. 'That was a big part of why she ended up going for it. Raoul warned Number 10 that Olly was giving them skewed readouts.'

A Europe adviser believes Robbins' excess of optimism and lack of candour was damaging: 'It ended up costing her and costing the country because the government invested huge amounts of time, effort and political capital into this thing which most of us who know anything about the EU were telling them was never going to work.' May's covert pursuit of a customs solution which had little chance of success also flowed from her failure to admit to the public or MPs that any likely answer to the backstop would see Britain locked into something which (however it was labelled) would legally be a customs union. Barwell admitted, 'Both the backstop and the NCP are legally a form of customs arrangement. We got ourselves into a position where we didn't feel able to be just blunt.'

On 22 April, three Sunday newspapers carried reports that May was backing the NCP customs plan. One claimed Robbins had told EU officials she would ultimately accept a customs union. Jeremy Heywood told people that he had tried to persuade May to accept a customs union.[16] A member of Robbins' team said later, 'From January, we were doing policy work on associate membership of the customs union.' The story which troubled Number 10 most appeared in the *Mail on Sunday*, which stated that Davis was leading a cabinet revolt and carried an article by David Jones, the former Brexit minister, denouncing the NCP as 'a Byzantine scheme designed first to slow down Brexit and then to strangle it'. He added, 'I speak for many Tory MPs when I say that whatever the consequences, we could never vote for it.'[17] To Downing Street, this was a hit job sanctioned by Davis to whip up ERG opposition to his own prime minister. 'It totally destroyed any trust that Number 10 had in DD,' one of his advisers admitted. A May loyalist labelled it the 'proximate cause' of Davis's resignation ten weeks later. 'That briefing gravely damaged trust. They weren't then able to have the frank conversations they needed to over the next month. They spoke past each other.'

This communication failure meant Davis convinced himself he was winning the argument on the new plan. An EU adviser recalled, 'Theresa was basically saying to him, "Anything other than the common rulebook won't fly as an end solution that gets rid of the backstop." It was also perfectly clear that DD's Max-Fac plan was going down faster than a lead balloon tied to a ton of uranium in the deepest trough in the Pacific Ocean. It wasn't going to work for the EU, it wasn't going to work in Northern Ireland. She was trying to say that, but he didn't hear that clearly enough. He thought she was taking on board messages, when she was saying, "I hear you", rather than "Yes". He didn't listen with the right ears.' A senior civil servant agreed: 'He didn't thump the table and say, "This is outrageous. If you do this, I'm going to go." He thought, "I've made my points and she hasn't said, 'No', so I've won." That's not how she works.'

The prime minister and her Brexit secretary were now interacting like a bad third date, where the man thinks he is on a promise and the woman is wondering why he won't take a hint that she is not interested.

The mistrust worked both ways. Davis's chief of staff Stewart Jackson smelt conspiracy everywhere and was not slow to pick up the phone to journalists. His ire was often directed at Davidson and de Minckwitz, who he saw as the twin sirens helping Robbins to lure May onto the rocks of close alignment with Brussels. Steve Baker eventually called for the duo to be fired. When Baker spoke to Davidson on 21 June, he scrawled in his diary that the Number 10 man was 'wet and cautious'. Such animosity was hugely frustrating to both men, not least because they did try, often in vain, to point out the political difficulties of Robbins' plans only to see themselves excluded from key meetings by the chief negotiator. 'The problem with political advice for Olly is that we would have told him that none of this was deliverable,' one adviser said. 'It really frustrated us that Stewart thought we were in on this conspiracy, because we weren't. I wouldn't have done what I did to myself for two years if I hadn't wanted to leave the European Union, believe me. I wanted to make it work, but they didn't think that we believed enough.'

Just days ahead of the key meeting of the SN committee about the customs policy, Theresa May suffered the loss of another key ally. On 29 April, Amber Rudd, the home secretary, was forced to quit over what became known as the Windrush scandal, in which those who emigrated to Britain in the 1950s in the first post-war wave of Afro-Caribbean migration were deported as a result of the 'hostile environment' policy towards illegal immigrants set up by May when she was home secretary. The Windrush generation had been granted indefinite leave to remain in Britain in 1971 but many lacked the right documentation, in part because the Home Office had destroyed all the landing cards in 2010. Rudd was slow to circle the wagons and poorly served by senior officials, who gave her misleading information. Unwilling to throw civil servants under a bus and unable to vociferously condemn the policy bequeathed to her by her own boss, she fell on her sword.

May's first choice to replace her was Karen Bradley, the Northern Ireland secretary. Barwell and, particularly Robbie Gibb, pushed for Sajid Javid, the communities secretary, sensing that appointing Britain's first non-white home secretary was the only way to quell the incipient race row. May relented, a decision she was quickly to regret. Rudd's resignation left ripples in the Brexit pond. First, it robbed May of a vocal cabinet ally at a crucial time. More importantly, Rudd's departure (and Javid's promotion) changed the membership of the SN committee as it was about to make one of the most important decisions of the year.

When the meeting began in the Cabinet Room on 2 May, sun streaming in through the windows, May set out her reasons for backing the NCP. The next minister to speak was Javid. The new home secretary's participation in the Brexit debate had been tortuous. Javid had bowed to pressure from David Cameron and George Osborne to back the Remain campaign, a decision he announced in a newspaper article which was largely a list of things he disliked about the EU. Any lingering gratitude he might have had for his promotion evaporated in the summer heat. Like Williamson, he was now aligned with the Brexiteers.

Johnson, who was 'chuntering away' in his seat a lot of the time, spoke against the proposal, so too did Davis, Gove and Williamson. The defence secretary, possessed of some of the best political instincts in the cabinet, thought that 'pretending' to leave the EU would finish May and that it would be politically disastrous for the Conservatives to be anything other than the party of Brexit. Fox, instinctively the most loyal Brexiteer, was more couched but, as the minister charged with negotiating trade deals, backing a form of customs union would have been an act of self-re-dundancy. Javid made it six ministers against NCP. May was usually the deciding vote, now she was in a minority in her own war cabinet.

Williamson passed his note to Johnson and the foreign secretary yelled, 'Six-five!' May's aides watched helpless as the initiative was seized from them. Ed de Minckwitz had also been keeping a tally. He had scored it 'three or four in favour of the hybrid, three or four in favour of Max-Fac and three or four on the fence to varying degrees'. Crucially, though, only five had definitely said they would support May. But he told colleagues after the meeting, 'The prime minister would have won a vote', because Julian Smith was also present and could have made it six-six, handing the prime minister the casting vote.

Was it a stitch-up? To a degree. On the Sunday night before the meet-ing, Johnson, Davis, Gove and Fox 'had a couple of drinks' at Carlton House Terrace, the official residence of the foreign secretary. Over crisps and claret raided from the stash set aside for diplomatic receptions, 'We more or less coordinated our approach,' one cabinet minister said.

Cock-up was the handmaiden of conspiracy. Amazingly, May's senior advisers and political aides did not know that Williamson and Javid were going to switch sides. 'We hadn't really got them on board before they went in,' a Downing Street aide who was present recalled. 'The PM's power perception had waned and they seized the moment to score one.'

May's desire not to provoke confrontation was her undoing. After Rudd's resignation David Gauke, the justice secretary, heard through the civil service machine that he would be joining SN, in addition to Javid, to ensure the Brexit balance of the committee was maintained. The appointment did not happen, a staggering oversight. 'We did think about adding him,' a senior aide said. 'But the view was that a change, when it was all so fraught, would be seen as provocative.' The prime minister and her team had failed Lyndon Johnson's first rule of politics: learn to count.

This refusal to play politics as a contact sport, to use the authority of her office to pack the committee, or to force a vote if she thought Williamson's six-five count defective – all in the apparent belief that passivity avoided provocation – was typical of May. 'That was when she lost her authority over the cabinet,' a senior figure in Number 10 opined a year later. 'I don't think she ever recovered it.'

Others think what truly undermined May was what happened next. Having been defeated on what was becoming the central plank of her Brexit plan, the prime minister simply ignored the SN committee and ploughed on regardless with NCP. By 5 May, three days later, it was being reported that the customs partnership idea was 'the only Brexit we're going to get'. A senior Number 10 official said, 'The customs model we ended up with should have been killed off after that cabinet session; it was obvious that if we pursued it the consequences would be pretty strong.' The SN committee never met again. 'That was the last meeting,' a spad said. 'If things didn't go [Number 10's] way they'd just change the game.'

Next time, in order to command a majority, it was announced that the Brexit policy would be signed off by the entire cabinet – where there was a strong 'soft' Brexit majority – at a second Chequers summit.

In the meantime, Downing Street set up two working groups on 11 May with the stated purpose of trying to refine and improve the NCP and Max-Fac plans. Barwell and Robbins structured them so that each contained two opponents of each plan and one supporter. Gove and Fox joined the hybrid group alongside Lidington. Greg Clark and Karen Bradley were put on the Max-Fac group with Davis, its primary advocate. Johnson and Hammond were deliberately excluded from both as too divisive. It was no accident that the more heavyweight group was concerned with the customs partnership. The hope was that Gove, with his political creativity, and Fox, with his concern to make trade deals viable, would refine the proposals so they would be more palatable to Eurosceptics and more likely to work. In the other group, May's hope was that Davis, exposed to the views of the Northern Ireland secretary and Clark channelling the concerns of business, would see that Max-Fac did not work. However, most of those involved in the process over the next seven weeks came to see them as a giant diversionary exercise. Lidington told friends the experience was 'two months of my life I'm never going to get back'. Another cabinet minister called it 'a Potemkin exercise'.

In the customs partnership group, Lidington – May's representative – seemed disengaged, something Gove interpreted as evidence that her team had given up fighting for the hybrid plan. Davis, too, did not realise he was losing the argument on customs. 'There was a lot of bravado but you never got the sense that he was necessarily on top of the detail,' one of May's political team remembered. Another Downing Street aide said, 'It was quite easy to do things round the back of David.' Davis and Stewart Jackson assumed the NCP proposal was dead and that the focus was on making Max-Fac practicable. They were wrong. 'DD was not in the room much with the PM and was unaware of what was going on,' said one ally.

This tendency on the part of Brexit partisans, on both sides, to believe that what they wished to happen was what would happen was one strain of BDS, the 'Brexit Derangement Syndrome' which was becoming a feature of Westminster life. 'Stewart took the view that if you tell enough journalists that something is the case, it becomes true,' a colleague said.

The Brexiteer least fooled by the working groups was the one with the most feral instincts – Boris Johnson. The foreign secretary had been convinced for a year that the Treasury wanted to keep Britain in the customs union and he saw the groups as a feint to achieve that. 'We thought we'd killed the crazy double tariff customs regime,' he said. 'But they kept prising off the coffin lid and it kept re-emerging.' Johnson had, by now, lost all faith in May. 'She has at no stage gone to Brussels and argued for a vision of the future,' he said. 'She has at no stage set out what she thinks should happen. She has asked them what they think should happen, and she has listened to her cabinet, and endlessly split the differ-ence, and she has ended up in an absolutely diabolic position.'

While the customs groups cogitated, Robbins 'forced the pace' of the negotiations, proposing a British version of the backstop in which the whole of the UK would stay in a customs relationship with the EU if no other means was found to prevent a hard border in Ireland. This was not, technically, a proposal to stay in the customs union, since it would only come into force if the final deal failed to find a solution at the Irish border, but to the Brexiteers it looked very like one. To many it was BRINO, 'Brexit in name only'.

The advantage of this approach though was that it turned the balance of risk on its head. Instead of the backstop being a trap for the UK which risked losing Northern Ireland to the EU economic sphere, it meant the backstop could be used by the British government to secure customs access to the EU, not normally granted to a third country.

It was what Michel Barnier had feared for months. When the Frenchman met the Brexit Steering Group in mid-May he complained, 'They try now to expand solutions for Northern Ireland to the whole of the British territories. The British have a strategy that consists in mixing up the issues at stake in Ireland with issues that have to do with the future relationship.'[18] Others in the Commission, including Martin Selmayr, could see the strategic merits of keeping Britain close. Barnier complained that the UK would keep dozens of diplomats in Brussels to lobby the Commission. 'They will be worse than Google,' he said. (The tech giant maintained a huge lobbying operation in Brussels.) Selmayr replied, 'They will not be in the room.' Juncker was prepared to overrule Barnier. Keeping the UK close, with no say in the rules, was preferable to seeing Britain become 'Singapore on Thames' with a deregulated economy and low taxes on the EU's doorstep.

Until that point, the ERG had been comforted by the presence of Steve Baker and Suella Braverman in DExEU. As an ERG grandee put it, 'Most of the time people thought she [May] was useless rather than devious.' Now they concluded the ministers had been 'comprehensively deceived' by the prime minister. On 19 May, Steve Baker wrote a resignation letter and put it in his jacket pocket. On 7 June, the government published their plan for an all-UK backstop, but even as they did so an even worse row on the backstop had led David Davis to threaten to resign for a second time.

The issue this time was how long the backstop would remain in place. At the previous SN meeting, ministers had agreed to support a UK-wide backstop as long as it was temporary. But when the papers, drawn up by Robbins and the Europe Unit, were sent to Davis over the first weekend in May, no end date was written into the document. The Brexit secretary 'went absolutely mental'.

Ministers like David Lidington tried to explain that the backstop was supposed to be an insurance policy for the Irish government; time limiting it would undermine support among the nationalist community. In Number 10, May's team argued that the backstop would die when arrangements were put in place to supplant it, rather than to a fixed timetable. This was not good enough for Davis or most of the ERG. 'There were two problems,' one of his team recalled. 'One is you get stuck in the customs union with the EU. The second is that it screws our negotiations for the next stage because it becomes the starting point.' MPs were soon warning the backstop would become the 'frontstop' for the future trade deal.

On Tuesday 5 June, Downing Street told Davis they would publish the backstop text two days later. The Brexit secretary met Boris Johnson and Liam Fox in the Foreign Office. Davis explained he was not happy with the paper. The next day, the anniversary of D-Day, he made a speech at the Royal United Services Institute. 'The Committee papers on the backstop were leaked as soon as they got sent round that morning,' an aide recalled. 'Straight onto Twitter.' In the Q&A session with journalists, Davis was quizzed about the lack of a time limit and whether he was likely to resign. Throwing fuel on the fire, Davis said, 'That's a question, I think, for the prime minister.' MPs who saw Davis at a Buckingham Palace garden party that evening say he was on the verge of quitting.

Davis and Ruparel drew up a list of changes needed to Robbins' document if he was to stay. There were twelve bullet points but the two key demands were the first and the last. On the backstop Davis insisted it 'needs to be strictly time limited and in our unilateral control'. This was the crux of the row that would engulf Westminster politics for the next year. 'I like to think that we were the first ones to flag the issue that killed us,' a DExEU source said. Davis also demanded that May start 'sharing and sighting ministers on these big decisions earlier on'. He added, 'Ministers currently feel bounced into important decisions.'

Ruparel went to Number 10 to discuss Davis's demands with Barwell. On the Wednesday evening, Davis himself went to see the chief of staff and made clear that he was prepared to resign unless language on a time limit was inserted. Then he met Julian Smith in 9 Downing Street. Davis brought a resignation letter with him. Smith agreed to help.

That evening the Brexit secretary consulted his political advisers. As they were talking, a request came through from Number 10 for Davis to conduct the broadcast media round on the backstop the following day. 'Tell them to fuck off,' he instructed. He asked if he should resign. Jackson advised against it: 'These guys are constantly trying to fuck you around, but we need you here otherwise it's all going to be much worse.' A colleague recalled, 'Raoul was in similar position but without the swear words.' Tim Smith, the third spad who had backed Remain, told Davis, 'If you're going to stay, you need to realise this is not the end of the process. There are going to be many more ways in which the PM goes down a different path. You have to try and get in the room so you can influence decisions. But you have to accept that this is not going to end up looking exactly as you want it, or maybe even at all as you want it.' The special advisers did not know which way he was going to go.

As discussions continued in DExEU, Theresa May was preparing to go to the theatre with her husband – a rare outing for the couple. The prime minister agreed she should invite Davis to Number 10. One of May's team contacted Davis's private office. 'I'm not going,' he said.

At nine the next morning, Thursday 7 June, Davis went to the prime minister's Commons office. Only Barwell was with her. May made warm noises; she wanted to keep Davis if she could. He compared the passage of Brexit to a mountain goat picking its way along a perilous path. He told May that failure to deliver a time-limited backstop would lead to cries of betrayal from Leave voters and a landslide defeat at the next election. He said Robbins' team failed to understand the political implications of what they were peddling. The meeting overran. Stewart Jackson arrived to find the PM's outer office packed with advisers wondering if Davis was quitting. 'Are you worried about your job?' Julian Smith taunted.

'No. Are you worried about yours?' Jackson shot back.

Afterwards, Davis called Johnson and Fox to tell them, 'We need this agreed and if it's not, I'm walking.' One MP advised that, if he resigned, he should hold an impromptu press conference outside Number 10 waving the offending text – a scenario reminiscent of Michael Heseltine's resignation from Margaret Thatcher's cabinet, which ultimately led to her downfall. 'He would have taken her over the cliff with him,' an MP said. But Davis was not yet in the mood to resign.

May also had private conversations with Fox and Johnson. 'Liam was livid and made his feelings known to Number 10,' one official said. 'At one point they were more worried about him than DD.'

After his meeting with May, Johnson rang Davis, who put him on speakerphone so his advisers could listen. 'The meeting was torrid,' Johnson said. He told May her backstop plan was 'intolerable': 'They are talking out of both sides of their mouths. She's trying to lie to us. HMT want the backstop to last for ten years. It's bullshit.'

Davis teased him: 'So did you say you'd resign?'

Johnson shot back, 'I told her I would accept her resignation.'

The exchange was telling. Davis and Johnson could have worked more closely together. Their views of the backstop were indistinguishable. But neither trusted the other. A Davis ally said, 'I think Boris always wanted to work more closely with DD but DD was always wary of being a facilitator for what Boris wanted – which was Boris being prime minister.'

Steve Baker decided if Davis went, so would he. Baker was called to see the chief whip. 'Shred the resignation letter,' Smith said. 'Don't be the one who wrecks Brexit.' Baker thought it was May and Robbins who were doing that. Davis's job was 'dangled' in front of him. 'The idea that I would sell out Brexit, sell out my colleagues in Parliament just to get a promotion and be in the cabinet and sit there ashamed of myself, I was absolutely furious,' said Baker.

At 11.30 a.m. on the Thursday, May presented Davis with revised language, saying the end date for the backstop deal would be 'expected' to be December 2021. There were also verbal commitments to drop the 'student union politics' used to bounce ministers into decisions.

However, when updated SN committee papers were circulated they still failed to reflect all of the concerns in Davis's memo. He told Number 10, 'You have to agree to them in front of everyone.' Another ally said, 'It was agreed that DD would raise the concerns in the SN meeting. The PM would agree with him and say, "We must note those." Then there would be amendments [to the text] and then that would be the government's policy.'

It did not turn out that way. Even close allies say that, in the SN meeting on 7 May, held once more in the 'stiflingly hot' confines of the lower ministerial corridor, Davis failed to deliver a concise rundown of the twelve bullet points. 'He did not quite nail the delivery,' a friendly witness said. 'He talked around them and mentioned some but not all.' One of May's EU advisers agreed: 'He ended up not making a whole load of points he had meant to make. They were extremely vague.' May concluded the meeting with her coded statement: 'We must take on board all of David's considerations.'

The following week it became clear May's team had summarily ignored them. Davis went to see her and said, 'We agreed this last week and we can't do it this way.'

She replied casually, 'I didn't think you cared that much about it.'

An incredulous Davis said, 'You should never confuse courtesy with compliance, Prime Minister. This is the central piece of the argument. We can't work like that. You can't do this.' Davis tracked down the cabinet committee minutes. 'They had no reference to my objections at all. I placed a formal objection to the Cabinet committee meeting minutes, and that, in truth, was the point at which my decision to resign started.'[19]

This was brazen behaviour from May but Davis was guilty too. He had won his verbal victory but not ensured it was written down. In Whitehall, if it's not in the minutes, it did not happen. 'A bit of basic following up could have resolved that,' one official said. Davis 'massively kicked off about it' to Number 10 but failed to get the official record rewritten.

Five days earlier the Brexiteers had ambushed May. In less than a week they had squandered their six-five win. May's relief was also short-lived. A few hours later details leaked of a speech given by Boris Johnson to a private dinner of the Conservative Way Forward group on the Wednesday evening, in which he said Donald Trump might do a better job of negotiating with Brussels than May. The night before, Johnson addressed the ERG for the first time, repeatedly refusing to back May and branding Hammond's Treasury 'the heart of Remain'. Reworking William Hague's line that he wanted to be 'in Europe, not run by Europe', Johnson said the May–Robbins plan would leave Britain 'out of Europe but run by Europe'.

In retrospect, the key part of his Conservative Way Forward speech came when Johnson expressed incredulity that Brexit was being shaped by the Irish border: 'It's beyond belief that we're allowing the tail to wag the dog in this way. We're allowing the whole of our agenda to be dictated by this folly.' This was dismissed at the time as Johnson failing to confront reality. It was actually a signal that if he became prime minister, he would approach things in a very different way. A cabinet minister seated near Johnson recalled him going further during the SN meeting, muttering under his breath, 'Fuck Northern Ireland.' Johnson does not recall this, but a senior cabinet minister agreed: 'Boris made some very dismissive remarks about Northern Ireland.' A Number 10 source said, 'I have heard of a meeting with officials where he said something very similar.'

Davis and Johnson were both entering their final month as cabinet ministers. Had either resigned at the start of June it is possible (though not inevitable) that May would have been close behind. 'DD's departure would have been the first snowball and it would have led to an avalanche,' a former minister said. Yet they did not act, just as they hadn't after the general election, after the party conference debacle, or at the time of the Joint Report. While they prevaricated, the way was clear for Remainers, reversers and even the EU themselves to offer May a different way out.

RULED OUT

Paths Not Taken

June to July 2018

Donald Trump literally made them tremble as they took tea on the terrace of the Manoir Richelieu hotel, a French chateau perched on cliffs overlooking the St Lawrence river. The G7 summit was drawing to a close and the leaders of Europe could still not quite believe what they had seen. They heard and felt the helicopters before they saw them. The crockery shook as the thwump-thwump of the blades cleaved the air. Then the sky was full of menacing black birds as the president's delegation departed for the airport. The summit in Charlevoix, in the Canadian province of Quebec, was one of the more remarkable international gatherings of this or any decade. The G7, a cornerstone of multilateral cooperation since the oil crisis of the 1970s, had been an arena instead for the forty-fifth American president's unilateral policies and singular personality. He had left early to see Kim Jong-Un, the leader of the hermit dictatorship of North Korea. 'To meet the other nice guy,' said one of those on the terrace. 'He flew away in these huge helicopters. If you have seen the movie *Avatar*, they look a little bit like that. Everything was really trembling – the whole building. Everybody was also a bit shaken.'

The summit produced an indelible image of the leaders of Germany, France, Japan and the UK leaning over a stubborn Trump, arms crossed, a contemptuous smile on his lips as he resisted the imprecations of Angela Merkel to change his stance on trade tariffs, climate change and Iran's nuclear programme. Behind closed doors, in the summit room, it was not Merkel who confronted Trump, it was Theresa May, the first foreign leader to visit the Trump White House. 'Theresa gave him what for,' a British witness said. 'She was the only one who stood up to Trump.' In Berlin, an ally of the German chancellor said, 'Merkel was impressed. It was May who was making the European argument.'

Christine Lagarde of the International Monetary Fund was also on the terrace, along with May, Merkel, her EU sherpa Lars-Hendrik Röller and Martin Selmayr, as Trump's helicopters thundered across both the skyline and their world view. As the noise faded away Selmayr spoke: 'My goodness, it's such a tragedy what is happening ...' On all the big issues, Britain was still European. 'It was a romantic moment,' he told colleagues. Seeds sown. 'That was the moment Selmayr decided that they should try to keep the Brits close,' a British negotiator said.

'The leaders of the world saw that Donald Trump really wants to disrupt the global order,' Selmayr recalled later. 'The European leaders were left behind when he took the helicopter and they looked each other in the eyes and also at Theresa May and they thought "At least we all agree with each other, we are the last bastion of the rules-based international system." I think that led to many thinking, "Well if she comes back tomorrow and has thought again [about Brexit], we wouldn't mind."'[1]

On the plane back to Brussels, Selmayr talked to Jean-Claude Juncker. 'Let's see what we can offer the Brits,' he said. 'It's probably totally hopeless, but I will not sit and do nothing.' With the Commission president's permission he worked up a plan for an extraordinary offer to the UK. 'It's totally absurd that the UK leaves,' he said. 'Should we not make a last effort, and also document it somewhere, because somebody in five or six years will tell us, "You stupid idiots. You have missed this opportunity to at least try it."' In great secrecy, Selmayr got some of the Commission's best brains – Clara Martinez Alberola, Paulina Dejmek Hack and Richard Szostak – to work up a two-page 'non paper', a memo that would not be put into general circulation in the Commission, where it would have crossed fifty different desks. What he proposed was a delay.

David Lidington had requested lunch with Selmayr. They met at the Berlaymont, in the same dining room on the thirteenth floor where May and Juncker had lunched the previous December. Lidington reflected on how well the UK and the EU had worked together over Salisbury and climate change. He expressed hope that it was a good sign for future relations. It was the opening Selmayr needed. 'Let's try this as a thought experiment,' he said. 'Why don't we just put all this on ice for five years?'

The world was changing, he argued. 'Brexit was decided at a moment where Putin was not poisoning people, when Mr Trump was not walking away from the rules-based international system and the Iran agreement. So while I respect the vote we need to rethink.'

Selmayr knew that suggesting a cooling off period alone would not be enough, so he dangled a carrot. 'Instead of going for two more years of negotiations, a two-year transition period, why don't we say, "We pause this for five years", but we shift the negotiation to something else. Let's get the UK involved with France and Germany.' Selmayr spoke of the need for Europe's Big Three to work together at a time of American nationalism, African migration and Chinese global activism. Lidington got the impression he was offering to create an 'informal directorate', giving the UK a place in the inner counsels of the EU. 'We need to be working together. Let's see how the dust settles and let's talk about whether we can come to a new deal for Europe.'

The offer was clearly 'serious' as well as tempting to Lidington, a life-long pro-European who was very worried about the geopolitical impact of the UK leaving the EU. 'A new deal' had been precisely what David Cameron wanted when he sought to renegotiate the UK's membership in 2015 and 2016. Selmayr argued it was different this time. 'In the Cameron negotiations there was a problem; Cameron wanted a new treaty in one and a half years,' he said. 'The last treaty took us ten years. But we are in a different situation, and now our next treaty change is closer.'

Selmayr also made the point that some of the key players were different. Emmanuel Macron was more willing to think imaginatively about the future of Europe. The French president was openly talking about the EU, not as a federal superstate but as a series of concentric circles, in which Britain might sit more comfortably in an outer ring. He and Merkel wanted to set up a European Security Council, for which Britain, as a leading military power, would have been a natural fit. 'There is the necessity to clarify relations with the UK, Switzerland and Turkey,' Selmayr said. 'There may be overlapping concentric circles, with close cooperation on security matters, a free trade area, and some countries more integrated. We could negotiate that. We do this for five years. We try to achieve this by the end of the term of the next Commission. Until then we pause Brexit. Then the UK holds another referendum on whether they still want to leave or whether they want to change the European Union.'

That was the offer. Selmayr stressed that it was a private proposition, not a lever in the negotiations. 'If anybody says there is such a paper in circulation, we will deny that it exists,' he said.

Lidington had toiled to make his EU counterparts understand that Britain needed a new relationship. He also thought about the referendum result and his prime minister's belief she had a 'sacred duty' to deliver that result. He spoke, not without reluctance, but sure he did not need to refer this olive branch to Downing Street: 'I appreciate very much what you're saying but we cannot do it. I can tell you that without checking with the prime minister, because we would be crucified in the UK if we did this.' Lidington explained that Britain took a different view on the result of referendums to some countries. 'Practically all of us in Parliament said we were going to accept the result of that referendum whether it went our way or not,' he explained. 'That matters in British democratic politics and I don't think there can be going back on that.'[2]

Selmayr smiled. 'I knew that you would say that, but I want you to remember what I told you …' He phoned Robbins to say what had been discussed. His view was the same as Lidington's: 'It would be great if it happened, but it probably won't.' Lidington sent a note for May's prime ministerial red box but correctly anticipated it would not be taken up.

Was this a historic missed opportunity by the British government? Lidington was right that nothing like Selmayr's plan was politically viable in the UK by the time it was offered. Yet the offer was striking because it was the one moment throughout the process when the EU took a strategic decision and with it the initiative. 'We had to make all the running,' said a cabinet minister. Had the same vision been advanced in 2015, showing Brussels taking Cameron's renegotiation seriously, prepared to enshrine the results in a new treaty, it is much more likely the UK would have voted to stay in June 2016. That can't be certain, since the disillusionment with establishment politics which drove millions of Leave votes would still have been there. But in a campaign of narrow margins, Cameron would have had an easier job selling his renegotiation as a complete rethink, rather than a disappointing exercise in tinkering at the margins.

After Selmayr's offer, a senior Commission official said, 'At least we tried everything. Nobody can say we pushed the UK out.' Yet even diehard Remainers were suspicious of Selmayr's motives. One senior cabinet minister said, 'Selmayr's design was always that we crashed out, had a horrible experience and came crawling back on Europe's terms as a second-class citizen.' The alternative view is that, once passions have receded, the idea of Britain in some sort of orbit just outside, rather than just inside, the EU remains a plausible path for future relations.

It was not just May's political guts at Charlevoix which led to the Commission's offer. It followed a steady drumbeat of pro-EU grandees reaching out to continental power brokers, privately begging them to drag their feet, so those at home who wanted a second referendum could get organised. A succession of delegations to Brussels urged the EU to stand firm on the grounds that May would back down and pursue a softer Brexit. To many Remain voters, these were the acts of elder states-men who wanted the best for their country. Increasingly, Brexiteers would see these interventions as something akin to treason.

On 15 January, Dominic Grieve, fresh from securing the meaningful vote, went to see the Commission, along with fellow Tory Anna Soubry and Labour's Chuka Umunna and Chris Leslie. A member of the delega-tion called it a fact-finding mission, dismissing claims they were there to 'scupper Brexit' as 'complete gibberish'. In a planned forty-five-minute meeting they were briefed by Sabine Weyand on the EU's red lines, but Michel Barnier only turned up for the final fifteen minutes.

However, the UK politicians ensured Barnier understood the power of MPs in a hung Parliament. 'We're not going to behave like some simple rubber-stamping mechanism,' one MP told the Frenchman. 'Parliament is not just a bystander.'[3] Barnier needed no encouragement to play hard-ball with Robbins, but the notion that May would have trouble passing any deal gave him little incentive to offer her major concessions.

On 6 February, Nick Clegg, the former deputy prime minister who began his career working for the European Commission and then served as an MEP, visited the European Parliament in Strasbourg, where he met Guy Verhofstadt. In his public comments, the former Liberal Democrat leader said MPs had a 'democratic duty' to reject whatever deal Theresa May came back with. In private, he begged Verhofstadt to 'find some mechanism to give us time'. He said, 'Out of that chaos emerges fresh new flowers of hope, a re-alignment of British politics, brave leadership of the Labour Party, a new generation.'[4] All these routes to an alternative outcome would be tried, without conspicuous success.

To Commission officials these meetings were futile. Stefaan De Rynck recalled, 'I think all these Remain people who came to visit us came away disappointed, because they didn't get a receptive ear. Being a politician, Barnier was always interested in the chances of British politics changing direction, but it was not up to him to engineer any of that, or even to support any of that. He never did.'[5] That said, one of the best-connected Labour Bresisters said MPs got far more encouragement from the Council and member states than the Commission: 'They would always tell us in private, they were happy for there to be space for a democratic process, for us either to pass a withdrawal agreement bill, have a second referendum or a general election. Quite frankly, they didn't really care which.'

Few tried harder than Sir John Major. On 28 February, the former prime minister gave a speech at Chatham House in which he said, 'The electorate has every right to reconsider their decision … I know of no precedent for any government enacting a policy that will make both our country and our people poorer.' As 2018 went on, Major was regularly in contact with Remain-voting ministers, exhorting them to action, too regularly for some. One spad remembered a call from Major at which their minister snapped, 'What the fuck does he want now?' Major also sent handwritten letters with his latest suggestions. 'His writing is illegible,' an aide said, 'so we would respond with, "You raise many good points …"'

Then, on 15 April, the People's Vote campaign to demand a second referendum was launched at the Electric Ballroom in Camden, London, with Umunna, Soubry, Liberal Democrat Layla Moran and Caroline Lucas from the Green Party. The Remainers suddenly had a focus.

What all branches of the Bresistance wanted was that Parliament should begin exerting itself against the executive. On 16 May, the government suffered its fifteenth defeat in the House of Lords on the EU withdrawal bill. The most significant had occurred four weeks earlier, on 18 April, when peers voted 347–225 to support membership of the customs union. The amendment was written by Lord Kerr, who had drawn up Article 50. Twenty-four Tory peers rebelled. The names supporting the motion were either proof of its wisdom or that the entire establishment was lining up against the referendum result. They included every living former cabinet secretary (Lords Armstrong, Butler, Wilson, Turnbull and O'Donnell); Kerr and his two successors as chief mandarin at the Foreign Office (Lords Jay and Ricketts); the former heads of the BBC, the Metropolitan police, the Treasury and MI5; a former private secretary to the Queen; a former lord chief justice; a former speaker of the Commons; and the astronomer royal.[6] The government's quest to overturn these amendments when the bill returned to the Commons in the second week of June was the next major drama.

Opposition to May was building from all sides of the House. On 12 June, Phillip Lee became the first minister to resign, declaring May's Brexit policies 'detrimental to the people we are elected to serve'. He had been resolved to go for two months. When he and Guto Bebb attended a Downing Street briefing on May's customs plans on 18 April, they were the only ministers who turned up. Gavin Barwell made them tea. But as they left, Lee said to Bebb, 'Well, that isn't going to work. It's going to end in tears.' Bebb agreed. The night before he resigned, Lee dined with Grieve, whose Beaconsfield seat was next door to his Bracknell constituency. Lee had been on the selection board which picked Grieve as a candidate in 1997, over the Brexiteer lawyer Martin Howe, who was now assisting the ERG. It was the last intake of Tory MPs where hardline Euroscepticism was not a requirement to get selected.

'Are you sure?' Grieve asked.

'I can't support this,' Lee replied. 'The whole thing is a mess. I have to do something, I can't stand idly by, mute.' He had seen his own constituency association 'infiltrated' by a 'fascist core' of former BNP supporters.[7] When he quit, Lee announced he was backing a second referendum, only the second Tory to do so after Anna Soubry. To the bemusement of colleagues, supporters appeared in the streets outside Parliament carrying placards bearing his face and the slogan, 'Great British hero'. He insisted they 'just appeared'. In fact, Lee had contacted a Brighton-based PR agency in the spring to ask for help to make his resignation more impactful.

That evening Boris Johnson approached him in the lobby and said, 'You're a Remainer, aren't you?'

'No, we're going to end up with the worst of both worlds,' he said. 'Nobody is going to be happy. That's why I've done it.'[8] Lee thought revoking Brexit would be 'completely undemocratic', but he did not think May had a 'deliverable strategy'. Three weeks later, Johnson quit the cabinet. In his resignation letter he condemned May's deal as 'the worst of both worlds'.

In Downing Street there was fury at Lee's betrayal of a prime minister with whom he had boasted of being friends. One usually mild-mannered aide branded him 'the Godzilla of cunts'. Fearful that Lee was the first of a coordinated wave of ministerial resignations, the whips reacted with ruthless vengeance to deter copycat quitters. They ordered Lee out of his office, consigning him and two researchers to one of the smallest rooms in the Commons. The whips dubbed it 'the cunt cupboard'. They only dropped the punishment when Lee, who still worked part-time as a GP, reminded them that as a doctor he was privy to nearly as many secrets about his colleagues as they were.

Far from starting a wave, the People's Vote failed to capitalise on Lee's resignation to build support for a second referendum in Conservative ranks. 'I resigned into a void,' he said later. 'There was no understanding that we needed to persuade enough of the Tory party to back a second referendum. The People's Vote was all about persuading the Labour Party.'

Lee resigned so he could vote against the government when the EU Withdrawal Bill returned to the Commons that day, 12 June. The key rebel amendment the government wished to overturn had been drawn up by Grieve, though in the Lords it bore the name of Viscount Hailsham, the former cabinet minister Douglas Hogg. It mandated that, in the event of May failing to secure an exit deal, the government 'must follow any direction' given by MPs and peers. This gave Parliament the power to block a deal, then block no-deal, then dictate the government's approach. It took away the threat of a no-deal Brexit – both in talks with Brussels and in trying to persuade MPs to back a deal by threatening no-deal as the alternative. To Eurosceptics it was nothing less than an amendment to block Brexit, a view reinforced by Hailsham telling peers, 'I do not believe in Brexit. I think it is a national calamity.'

To make matters worse for the government, the evening before the vote, Grieve tabled a new amendment (known as Grieve 2) which decreed that Parliament could start issuing orders if no agreement had been reached by 15 February. Nikki da Costa, the Downing Street director of legislative affairs, warned colleagues that if the amendment passed, 'The EU would just sit tight until 15 February. Why negotiate, when they can rely on a remain Parliament to go for the softest possible exit or possibly rule it out altogether?' Hailsham – with Grieve's assistance – was expected to table that same amendment for the Lords debate on Monday 18 June unless the government had successfully done a deal with the rebels before that. The stage was set for a titanic battle.

First, the government had to overturn Hailsham's 'Amendment 19'. On a torrid day in the Commons, David Davis opened the debate saying ministers could not accept anything that undermined the government's negotiating position. May decided to buy time. Robert Buckland, the solicitor general, intervened from the front bench to say there was 'much merit' in part of Grieve's proposal and, 'The Government are willing to engage positively ahead of the Lords stages.'

With voting just minutes away, fourteen rebels were invited to visit the prime minister in her wood-panelled rooms overlooking New Palace Yard. May sought to convince Grieve and the others that she was listening. Grieve sat upright, hands folded in front of him. Others present included Soubry, Nicky Morgan, Justine Greening and Ed Vaizey. 'I took a look around the room,' said one, 'and realised I was stuck in the worst dinner party ever.' May argued that the amendment saying ministers 'must' do as they were told by Parliament would bind her hands. When Soubry began a monologue about 'Brexit and how dreadful it was', May complained about 'those of you who want to reverse the result', triggering another outburst from Soubry. However, the prime minister signalled that she understood their concerns, perhaps would even agree to the broad thrust of their demands, while asking, 'Please don't push this amendment today.' It was not May but Nicky Morgan who swung the room, telling her fellow rebels, 'Now is not the time to push this.' It 'changed the temperature in the room,' an MP said. The government would bring forward an amendment of its own in the Lords on the following Monday, the 18th. The government had three days to finalise the details with Grieve.

Amendment 19 was defeated by 324 votes to 298. May approached Morgan later that evening and said, 'Thank you very much for what you did.' Only two Tory MPs, Soubry and Ken Clarke, broke the whip. Phillip Lee abstained. Having resigned to vote against the government, he felt the armistice 'made me look stupid'. A colleague said, 'Dominic encouraged Phillip to march up the hill and then left him there to be shelled.' It was a futile conclusion to a once-promising career. As the wife of Phineas Finn observes in Trollope's novel *The Prime Minister*, 'Your man with a thin skin, a vehement ambition, a scrupulous conscience and a sanguine desire for rapid improvement, is never a happy, and seldom a fortunate politician.' In Lee's case, it proved apt.

Brexiteers were quick to condemn any accommodation with Grieve. DExEU, on Davis's orders, issued a statement: 'We have not, and will not, agree to the House of Commons binding the Government's hands in the negotiations.' Steve Baker dismissed Grieve's vision out of hand, 'You cannot have 650 MPs conducting the negotiation.'[9]

With power ebbing away, Nikki da Costa devised an audacious plan to seize it back which, had it been adopted, would have changed the course of Brexit. She thought it vital that the government had the ability to use no-deal as a negotiating tool. Prior to 2010, governments had the ability to treat a crunch vote on a key government priority as a vote of confidence. A prime minister could threaten to call a general election if MPs refused to back them. The Fixed-term Parliaments Act, introduced when the coalition took power, removed that threat by mandating that there had to be a specific no-confidence vote – and even that only triggered a fourteen-day period of reflection rather than an immediate election. Da Costa vowed to reclaim the power to threaten an election.

Da Costa's plan, drawn up on the evening of 13 June, proposed that MPs get one 'free hit' when a Brexit deal was put to the meaningful vote. But if the government tabled a second motion, that would become a vote of confidence mandated by the Fixed-term Parliaments Act. Da Costa saw the first vote as a way of reassuring Grieve that MPs could register their concerns about a deal, the second vote as a way of demonstrating to Brexiteers that they would link the government's survival to securing Brexit. The process of reconciling amendments to legislation between the Commons and Lords is known in Westminster as 'ping pong'. Da Costa christened her plan, designed to trump them all, 'King Pong'.

Da Costa remembered an old whips' office adage that 'the person with the piece of paper wins' – the same insight that led the EU to write the legal text. She wrote a memo overnight and presented it in the 8 a.m. meeting for senior staff on Thursday 14th. 'We are going to get defeated,' she said. 'We need to transform the prime minister's hand.' Gavin Barwell said, 'I like it.'

At the main morning meeting with the prime minister which followed at 8.30, da Costa told May, 'We've had to give ground on a vote on the deal but it's really important that we don't give MPs a vote to stop no-deal. The question on my mind has been: "Can you make a meaningful vote a confidence vote?"' She explained her plan. In the event of a second meaningful vote being lost, the government would have fourteen days to return with a plan and seek a majority in the House again. Failing that, the prime minister could call an election.[10] 'It's an aggressive move,' she conceded. 'But Parliament is able to express a clear view on both the deal and a no deal. It is a "meaningful" vote. The government cannot progress to any deal (including a no-deal) without Parliamentary approval, but Parliament cannot direct the government how to conduct negotiations.' The plan also had a built-in bias towards Tory unity. Da Costa's memo concluded, 'When we come to a deal, if it does not satisfy one wing of the party or another, they can express a view but the second time, they have to think long and hard' or risk bringing the government down. May was cautious but not dismissive. 'Let's explore it,' she said.

Julian Smith hated the idea. 'Completely mad', a 'crackpot plan', he told colleagues. The chief whip thought da Costa oblivious of the fact the government had no majority and focused on 'trying to defy gravity'. He glimpsed a future where failure to pass a meaningful vote would bring down the government, with the blame laid at his door. Worse, he could see a situation in which even asking MPs to back the plan would spark an immediate crisis. To Smith the 2017 election had been a 'Kamikaze' operation which left a swathe of MPs with wafer-thin majorities. Asking them to back da Costa's scheme would condemn them to 'certain death' in a snap election. 'Prime Minister, I understand you want to go for this,' he said, 'but I'd like to talk to Oliver Letwin first.'

Letwin, a former cabinet minister and Whitehall Mr-Fix-It for Cameron, was renowned in Parliament for his towering intellect, unmoored by practicality. A studious bustling figure with a professorial air and eccentric dress sense, when shadow home secretary he had once let a burglar into his home in the small hours of the morning, and the man duly made off with his wallet. On another occasion he was caught depositing confidential constituency correspondence in the bins of St James's Park. Tory spin doctors originally worried that Letwin's gaffe had been worse. He was notorious in CCHQ for leaving a ripe smell after visits to the lavatory. When the *Daily Mirror* contacted the press office to say he had been caught 'dumping in St James's Park', they feared he had been caught short in public. Colleagues referred to him as 'the stupidest clever person' in SW1. The chief whip, however, had been using Letwin as an unofficial broker between Tory factions. 'Julian thinks Oliver Letwin is the bee's knees and the cat's whiskers,' a Number 10 official said. 'He treated Oliver like a quasi-minister.' May asked Smith to test the King Pong idea with MPs. The chief whip had a different idea.

Smith had another reason for opposing da Costa. In January she had complained to Barwell that the chief was freezing her out of meetings and decisions on the passage of legislation. By the end of March she had submitted a formal complaint under the ministerial code of conduct accusing Smith of 'a pattern of behaviour' designed to 'intimidate, bully and undermine my ability to do my job'. Da Costa dropped the complaint for fear that the infighting would leak and damage May, but not before relations between two of the key people charged with piloting Brexit legislation through Parliament had irreversibly broken down precisely when they needed to be strong. 'The reason why it's relevant to Brexit is that it degraded the machine,' a Downing Street adviser said.

Smith's views on Brexit also explain his opposition to King Pong. 'He's always struggled to reconcile leaving the EU with what he really thinks is best for the economy and best for the country,' one ally said. Another remembered, 'Julian hated the idea of no-deal.' The idea of weaponising it was anathema to him.

At 9.30 a.m. da Costa went to see David Davis and Raoul Ruparel in 9 Downing Street, home of DExEU, and got their approval for King Pong. She then returned to Number 10 to brief officials on the drafting of the amendment and the media team on how they might sell the idea. Smith went back to his office elsewhere in Number 9 and asked Letwin to come over. When he arrived, Smith handed him da Costa's memo. Letwin studied it, shaking his head. 'No, no no, we can't have this.'

Without Smith even present, Letwin occupied the chief whip's office and began hosting key MPs in the different Brexit camps – Stephen Hammond and Nicky Morgan for the former Remainers, Jacob Rees-Mogg and Owen Paterson from the ERG. 'Oliver wasn't testing the plan,' said a witness. 'He was saying there is this ridiculous plan that people are trying to push but this is mad.' By 11 a.m. da Costa had discovered what was happening. She rushed to Smith's office to find Barwell present as well. Letwin told her, 'The party just doesn't need a general election.' He was writing an alternative amendment. The sight of a backbencher, however august, at the chief whip's desk drafting government legislation while rubbishing an idea the prime minister had asked her team to explore was jarring. Da Costa complained. Barwell threw his hands in the air. 'I don't know how we got here,' he said.

Da Costa found initially supportive MPs turning against her. 'They were worked on by the chief,' another aide said. 'There was an operation to kill it.' One of those involved said, 'The division lobbies were on fire with frustration and fear that Number 10 could be so tin-eared. The appetite for another election battle led by Theresa was about as popular as a cup of cold sick.' Smith actively whipped up the fury, urging MPs to call and text their opposition directly to May's mobile phone. In two meetings that afternoon in the PM's Commons office, he told her King Pong would 'spook the marginals'. Those MPs would rebel 'here and now', he warned. 'You might lose the confidence of the party, Prime Minister.'

Letwin's idea was that in the event of there being no Brexit deal, the government would offer a meaningful vote that would be placed on the order paper 'in neutral terms'. Under House of Commons rules, known as standing orders, a motion tabled in neutral terms could not be amended. This would become hugely important later.

At 1 p.m. Robert Buckland, the solicitor general, met Grieve to discuss a new government amendment. Buckland thought the King Pong plan was a 'nuclear option'. He did not want the presumption in Grieve's amendment that Parliament would dictate the terms of Brexit, but he was prepared to allow wording that would have made the meaningful vote an amendable motion, opening the door to MPs expressing a view on the direction ministers should take. 'It was perfectly obvious it had to be amendable,' Grieve said, 'because otherwise we were simply expressing in neutral terms more views about what the government was doing.' Buckland and Grieve were both QCs and had known each other for two decades. 'This is one option,' Buckland said. 'I'm prepared to sell it, but you've got to understand, she's going to make the choice.'

Grieve left, content, thinking he had a deal, and caught a train to a recording of *Any Questions* in Bangor. He phoned Anna Soubry, Nicky Morgan and Stephen Hammond to tell them what had happened. As Grieve's train chugged West, Buckland began receiving calls from ERG grandees, the Paleosceptics of the Maastricht era – Bill Cash and Bernard Jenkin – and Jacob Rees-Mogg. Jenkin was concerned. 'Why aren't we being consulted?' he texted. The ERGers were pushing a different idea: a 'motion in neutral terms'. They had not moved against May so far because they wanted the withdrawal bill to pass, believing it their guarantee that Brexit would happen on 29 March 2019. For that to be the insurance policy they sought, it had to pass without amendments.

At three that afternoon, Buckland was summoned to Number 10. As he was walking there, Davis phoned and he relayed his discussion with

Grieve. The Brexit secretary was frustrated: 'I'm fed up of giving in all the time, we've got to make a stand.' By the time Buckland got to Number 10 it was clear that Smith's warnings had turned the prime minister against King Pong. 'I think it would be very risky,' Buckland agreed. However, at that point Barwell entered the room and said Buckland could not move forward with his draft amendment either. 'DD doesn't agree with it, and he wants a motion on non-amendable terms,' the chief of staff explained.

The frustration in Number 10 was palpable. 'DD had obviously spoken to the Eurosceptics, picked up this line about non-amendability and decided it was his Hill 60, this is where he's going to fight,' a source said. 'I don't think he had heard of the concept two hours before.'

Buckland had to phone Grieve to tell him their tentative deal was off and that Downing Street was insisting on a non-amendable motion. Grieve, normally a mild-mannered man, was incandescent: 'This is unacceptable. We can't agree this.' Buckland replied, 'There's nothing more I can do.'

The government tabled a new amendment that evening, which ensured that the meaningful vote in both houses would be on a neutral motion. The Commons would simply 'consider' the government's Brexit deal, the Lords would 'take note'. Buckland's view was that it did not matter what the motion was since, if a government could not pass its main business, it would fall anyway. He reminded May that arguably the most important debate of the previous century, in May 1940, which led to the collapse of the Chamberlain government, was on the motion, 'This house adjourns for Whitsun'. Buckland said, 'It doesn't really matter what it says. If the debate is all about confidence in the government, then that's what it is.'

Grieve rushed to help Hailsham retable the Grieve 2 amendment in the Lords. It was 'more or less' the deal Grieve and Buckland had originally agreed, with an amendable motion rather than one in neutral terms. He then took to *Newsnight* to denounce the government. The last thing Buckland did that night was to send Jacob Rees-Mogg's mobile number to Grieve, in the hope that the two sides could talk. Instead, a circular firing squad unleashed volley after volley across the Sunday political programmes. Grieve denounced the motion in neutral terms as 'a slavery clause' which asked MPs to 'sign in blood' that in the event of no-deal, they would follow the government 'over the edge of the cliff' to 'catastrophe'. He added, 'That, I can tell you, I am not prepared to do.' He warned that the rebel Remainers could 'collapse the government'.

On Monday 18 June the Lords passed the Hailsham amendment by 354 votes to 235, a majority of 119. MPs would consider the Lords' amendments on Wednesday 20th. The government had less than two days to strike a new deal.

That evening Julian Smith invited representatives of all the warring factions to a meeting in his office in the Commons. Grieve and Soubry were there from the ranks of the Remain ultras, Stephen Hammond and Nicky Morgan from the more moderate soft Brexit advocates. The ERG was represented by Rees-Mogg and Mark Francois, a pugnacious and emotional Brexiteer, who combined almost pugilistic patriotism with a Latin temperament bequeathed by his Italian-born mother. Buckland and Letwin tossed around ideas with Brandon Lewis as the group shared pizza.

Smith's idea was to expose the two sides to each other, to hear their reasoning unfiltered, to see the emotion of the other side in the raw – to appreciate what as chief whip he had to contend with in trying to keep a bitterly divided party together. 'I think it was engineered by Julian, so that we could understand just how much trouble he was having from Francois and Rees-Mogg,' said one Remainer.

For his side, Grieve said, 'An unamendable motion is meaningless, it doesn't give anybody any chance to put down a marker on what Parliament wants the government to do.' But he also made the point that even an amendable motion could not force the government's hand. 'It's not a mandatory motion, so why is everyone getting so worked up about it?' Briefly, there was a sliver of understanding. Another source who was present said both sides were scared: 'Dominic was petrified of a hard Brexit while Jacob was petrified of a watered-down Brexit in name only.'

Gradually, however, something remarkable – and rare in the history of Brexit – began to happen. A modicum of mutual understanding developed. 'That was an important meeting,' one of those present said. 'The main factions of the party could look each other in the eye, say what they thought to each other frankly, and realise they all had to step back from the edge.' Another MP said, 'It was a pretty extraordinary meeting because I don't think those people had sat in a room and talked like that for years, if ever. There was common purpose.' They agreed to sleep on it.

Nikki da Costa, who had not been invited, arrived as the meeting was winding up. There were sharp exchanges between her and Letwin as she argued for her King Pong plan. 'Why on earth are we killing this?' she asked. 'This is the only opportunity to change the power dynamic. It could get a deal over the line.' Letwin was dismissive: 'Your job is to protect the prime minister. I will prevent a general election at all costs. Why should MPs put their jobs on the line for the prime minister's deal?'

When the group assembled again in the lower whips' office on Tuesday morning, 19 June, it became instantly clear to Grieve that the patterns in the kaleidoscope had shifted. Both Stephen Hammond and Nicky Morgan were getting cold feet about maintaining the rebellion. 'They felt that the party would be broken apart, which is not an entirely unreasonable fear,' an MP said. 'We could have destroyed [May] but we didn't know where we would end up.' Buckland presented a written ministerial statement he was planning to issue in Davis's name, detailing the government's plans. Rees-Mogg made a suggested change to the text. Buckland agreed with him immediately. 'It showed people were thinking in the same terms,' an MP said. 'No one seemed to want to have their finger on the trigger.' It was Julian Smith's finest hour as chief whip.

The statement reassured the rebels that the government 'recognised' MPs could table motions on 'matters of concern' over Brexit and pledged that 'Parliamentary time will be provided for this'. In the debate that followed, Grieve said, 'I am prepared to accept the government's difficulty and support it.' He urged people not to support the Lords amendment (actually his own Grieve 2 amendment), a U-turn which attracted some ridicule. The government won by 319 votes to 303, a majority of 16. Grieve was quickly dubbed 'the grand old Duke of York' for leading his troops up the hill to battle and then down again. 'I didn't want to break the party in two,' he said later. He also believed, like Buckland, that when the moment for a meaningful vote arrived, it would be impossible to stop MPs expressing their views. 'I thought we'd eventually get what we wanted anyway,' he said.

The government had escaped but Nikki da Costa was left with a nagging concern. She and others in Number 10 only got sight of the wording of the written statement an hour before it was due to be published. The source of her angst was the fourth paragraph, which read, 'Under the Standing Orders of the House of Commons it will be for the Speaker to determine whether a motion when it is introduced by the

Government under the European Union (Withdrawal) Bill is or is not in fact cast in neutral terms and hence whether the motion is or is not amendable.'

To Buckland, this was a simple statement of fact, but it failed to spell out that, under the existing standing orders, when a motion is expressed in 'neutral terms' then 'no amendments to it may be tabled'. Instead, the government put all the onus on the speaker. 'That [written ministerial statement] feels like it gives a lot of ground,' da Costa told a colleague. The government's only protection was the standing orders. 'What if they can change the standing orders?' she asked. She had listened to the debate. It was clear that some Bresistance MPs felt John Bercow, the speaker, might help them in future. She felt a 'nagging' fear that Grieve was one step ahead.

By killing off da Costa's plan to turn a meaningful vote into a confidence vote, Smith removed a nuclear deterrent from the prime minister's armoury that she would badly need a few months later. Those, like May, who valued Conservative unity the most concluded she was right to ditch King Pong. Those who thought a clean-break Brexit mattered above all else came to the view that forcing the issue in June 2018 would have produced a government better able to face down the Remain majority in Parliament or her replacement by someone more Eurosceptic.

Whatever its merits, King Pong was an issue that went to the heart of Theresa May's understanding and use of power. This was exactly the kind of procedural hardball the Brexiteers wanted to see. It ought to have been proposed, discussed and decided in a formal strategy meeting, the subject of reasoned debate between the prime minister and her closest aides. Instead, it was advanced as an ad hoc proposal by one aide and killed off in a black op between the chief whip and a former minister who had no authority to make decisions of such gravity. Throughout the Brexit years May focused on what was right in front of her, seeking tactical fixes to survive another day or week; she seldom ever took a step back and asked whether a different approach was needed to her entire strategy.

Julian Smith, by contrast, handled this episode adroitly, marshalling MPs to get what he wanted and then creating conditions for compromise. The Withdrawal Act was passed on the back of the last great rapprochement between Remainers and Brexiteers. But the events of June 2018 were also a key staging post in the radicalisation of Parliament.

The ERG, Davis and Grieve had all seen they could get their way by pushing harder. Even moderates absorbed the merits of militancy.

The third path untrodden was an issue of presentation not policy. On the Sunday before the Lords vote, Theresa May announced that the government planned to give a £20 billion a year 'birthday present' to the NHS, to mark the health service's seventieth anniversary. It was the biggest public services funding announcement in a generation. By 2024, the NHS would be getting an extra £600 million a week, partly funded from a 'Brexit dividend' once the UK stopped making payments to the EU.

There was an opportunity to make the connection with the pledge that had been emblazoned on the side of Vote Leave's bus to spend £350 million a week extra. That was the sum Boris Johnson and Michael Gove said was being paid to Brussels. In reality, it was a gross figure that took no account of money flowing back to the UK. To Remainers it was Leave's foundational lie, but to Brexiteers delivering on that promise would bring political gains.

Johnson had ambushed May during a cabinet meeting in January 2018, demanding an extra £100 million a week for the NHS. 'It showed Boris could still make the traffic stop and politics focus on him,' a Number 10 political adviser said. But the driving force was Jeremy Hunt who had written to May in September 2017 calling for a ten-year plan for the health service. On 7 February, spad Alex Dawson gave a presentation pointing out that the NHS had 90 per cent approval ratings. 'That's the same as the Queen,' he said.

Philip Hammond fought tooth and nail against the handout and, in one meeting, even suggested the NHS was not viable on a long-term basis. 'He indicated rationing was the only way,' said one witness. May peered disapprovingly at the chancellor and said, 'You can't just tell the NHS to stop treating sick people, Philip.' Eventually, with Hunt and Simon Stevens, the NHS chief executive, playing hardball, the Treasury was forced to fund a 3.4 per cent budget increase for five years.

It ought to have been one of the government's great triumphs but it garnered May surprisingly little political capital. 'Hammond was arguing throughout that we must not be seen to be delivering on that bus,' an aide said. A cabinet minister added, 'They did not want Boris to have his £350 million.' This was surely a mistake in presentational terms. But May's animus towards her foreign secretary blinded her to the benefits.

The prime minister's incomprehension that communications was integral to good policy-making revealed someone ill at ease with the basic craft of modern politics. 'She does not think about doing things because you can make a great big public argument,' a supportive but despairing cabinet minister said. Contrast that with Abraham Lincoln, arguably the greatest democratic leader of all, who once remarked, 'With public sentiment, nothing can fail; without it nothing can succeed. Consequently, he who moulds public sentiment, goes deeper than he who enacts statutes or pronounces decisions.'[11] May was too often simply an enactor and pronouncer. That autumn, Number 10 would have to try to sell what, it was already clear, would be an unpopular Brexit deal to a sceptical public and a fractious Parliament. Here, she had failed to capitalise on an announcement that was popular with nine out of ten voters.

May had delivered the biggest domestic measure of her premiership but she had still not finalised her Brexit policy, indeed she had not even told her Brexit-supporting ministers what it was. On Monday morning, 2 July, David Davis turned on the *Today* programme to find that Robbie Gibb had briefed the BBC that May was planning a 'third way' on customs. There were just five days to go until the second Chequers summit and the secretary of state responsible had not even heard of the new plan.

CHEQUERS MATE

The Cabinet Agrees

July 2018

Michael Gove read through the paper which had been prepared for the customs working groups and decided to make a scene. The civil service had prepared red, amber and green ratings – known in Whitehall as 'RAG ratings' – for different aspects of the New Customs Partnership (NCP), favoured by Theresa May and the Max-Fac plan supported by David Davis. Both models were to be judged by three criteria. A cursory glance at the sheet showed that, by selecting those metrics, the NCP was going to receive two green ticks and one red mark; conversely, Max-Fac would get two red marks and one green light. For six weeks he and Liam Fox had been arguing with David Lidington and the officials that the customs partnership, with Britain collecting tariffs for the EU, was bureaucratically unworkable. Now it was clear their arguments had not been heard. 'This is a rigged exercise,' Gove said. 'This is a worthless exercise.'[1] With that he picked up the paper and tore it in two from top to bottom. The room was momentarily stilled. Officials looked stunned. This was both political theatre and an expression of impotence.

It was early evening of Wednesday 27 June, a warm day in a month of blue skies but the sun was setting on the last vestiges of cabinet unity. There were nine days to go until May was planning to assemble her senior ministers at Chequers.

Gove was not alone. Liam Fox was also growing frustrated with Number 10. An official in the department for international trade recalled, 'He started talking about the "shitshow over there" in front of civil servants. He started being more indiscreet.' On the same day Gove was tearing up the customs plan, Conor Burns, Boris Johnson's parliamentary private secretary, was in the upper ministerial corridor. He found Fox camped in his small office. 'We are waiting for the prime minister,' one of Fox's advisers said. At that moment Oliver Robbins walked past. 'Well he's here,' said Burns, deadpan. Robbins gave him a 'sulky look'.

To Gavin Barwell, the customs working group exercise was not a waste of time. From Gove and Fox's objections to the customs partnership would emerge another plan, which incorporated some elements of Max-Fac. 'We took Michael's objections to the hybrid,' he said. 'A few of them were not resolvable. But there were some things you could do something about.' At this point, Gove had no idea a third way was even under discussion. The chief of staff spent the week talking to ministers and their aides. Gove and his special advisers met Barwell and Robbins. 'They were war-gaming who was going to resign,' said an aide.

Top of the list of those expected to quit was Steve Baker. Ten days earlier, on 17 June, he had sat down with Nikki da Costa and drawn up a flowchart on how May's deal might fare in Parliament. Together they concluded that the SNP would vote for 'maximum political difficulty' and that Labour, while public supporters of a soft Brexit, would oppose May's deal. That meant she would have to present something which was acceptable to the Conservative Party. In Tory ranks there were 80 MPs pushing, through the ERG, for a harder Brexit, just 12 demanding a soft Brexit. Their 'decision tree' concluded that May would have more chance if she pivoted to a looser free trade agreement. It was already too late.

The minister May and her team most cared about was Davis. They knew on 13 June that he was likely to resign, twenty-three days before Chequers. That was when Raoul Ruparel, Davis's spad and senior counsellor on Europe, was asked to go to Number 10 for a briefing. He arrived in the terracotta state room on the first floor, to find a welcoming party of Robbins, Barwell and Denzil Davidson. They took him slides showing the shape of the deal the prime minister was planning to present to her cabinet at Chequers. It was the first time anyone on the political side in DExEU had been entrusted with this information.

Ruparel had repeatedly warned Davis that things seemed to be moving in a direction he would not like. The spad took one look at the slides and said, 'DD is never going to back this. He is going to resign.'

Barwell and Davidson asked how they might best 'pitch' the plan to Davis. Ruparel made a few suggestions for tweaks in the presentation. One was a review clause, promising the Brexiteers that if they agreed to the plan for a number of years they would have the chance to forge a new relationship in future. But it felt like fiddling at the margins. Ruparel was in an invidious position. May was pressing ahead with a common rule-book and a customs plan to which Davis was implacably opposed – and yet he was sworn to secrecy and did not feel able to warn his secretary of state. When Davis discovered the position Ruparel had been placed in, he declared it 'constitutionally improper'.

Ruparel said he would try to explain to Davis 'the logic of where we are and why we have got here'. But he added, 'I do not think he will accept it.' Ruparel had written Davis's letters to May pointing out the problems with her chosen path. He did not think the plan would work or get through Parliament. As he walked back to DExEU, he felt for the first time that the government's days were limited. *This is it. It's over.*

On 29 June, with a week to go until Chequers, DExEU was ready with its own version of a white paper. 'By Friday there was a fully worked-up PowerPoint presentation to be given to the cabinet,' a source said. At its heart was a free trade agreement but it remained vague about customs and how to resolve the Irish border. 'It doesn't say what our customs policy should be, which is embarrassing,' a DExEU official said. 'Basically it's an FTA for Great Britain, and Northern Ireland is cut off on its own, which is fine if you think Brexit is more important than the United Kingdom. Maybe it is.' Davis envisaged a situation where EU customs officials could check goods on ferries between Great Britain and Northern Ireland, which might have been practical but looked legally dubious to some.

May's team thought the Davis white paper did not work at all but were losing hope of talking him around. Afterwards some allies claimed the Brexit secretary was kept totally in the dark. This was not true. Barwell said, 'The suggestion that this paper suddenly turned up the day before and came as a complete surprise is a nonsense because he must have had five or six bilaterals with the prime minister over the three or four weeks before Chequers, trying to get the two of them into the same place.'[2] He added, 'The common rulebook had been there since before the first Chequers meeting as the way we might get out of the regulatory bit of the problem.' A civil servant in Number 10 agreed: 'I think DD knew what was going on, he was playing his own game and trying to push the outcome he wanted. Ultimately she listened to Olly rather than DD.' Yet even May loyalists admit the Brexit secretary was blindsided on the 'third way' customs plan, which was still being finalised the weekend before the crunch meeting. 'The gripe on customs is a fairer gripe than the gripe on regulation,' Barwell admitted. Robbie Gibb added, 'He was, in my view, not in the loop enough. But there's a reason for that. He was just not on board with the direction of travel.'

When Stewart Jackson, Davis's chief of staff, heard the BBC report that Downing Street had devised a 'third way' on customs, he called the Brexit secretary. Davis had two meetings lined up with the prime minister. When he got into the office he told his team, 'I don't know what it is. But I'm sure the PM will tell me later. It's a good job I wasn't on the *Today* programme to have to defend it.' They met later that Monday, 2 July. May was at her most opaquely obstructive. She talked Davis through the common rulebook plan. But when he confronted her about the customs report, she said the BBC story was 'a mistake'. Davis told his team May had said, 'They got the wrong end of the stick.' An MP who talked to Davis about the meeting said, 'DD challenged her head on about this third option and she denied any knowledge of it. She denied its existence.'

What May did reveal, Davis did not like. 'This doesn't fly at all,' he said. 'Let me have a go at rewriting it to make it tolerable.'[3] He said later, 'The fundamental problem of the Chequers proposal was that the right to diverge had disappeared.'[4] He added, 'We were signing up to what was delicately called a common rulebook, actually a European rulebook. They were going to write it, we were going to obey it. This is nowhere near taking back control of our laws.'[5]

The following morning, Jonathan Black from Robbins' Europe Unit went to DExEU to brief Davis about the customs plan. It was indeed a hybrid of the customs partnership with elements of the technical solutions he had been pushing as the cornerstone of Max-Fac. 'The idea was to present the customs model that we ended up with as a genuine child of the two models,' a Number 10 official explained. 'It did not survive the contact with sunlight. It became obvious that it was just the old [NCP] model with a few bits and bobs attached to it.'

Afterwards, Davis remained diplomatic. 'The prime minister is a vicar's daughter, so I don't think she told me any lies,' he said. 'Whether it was the whole truth is another matter.'[6] However, every one of Davis's team, who ranged from emotional Remainers to hard Brexiteers, was adamant that the prime minister lied to her Brexit secretary the day before. This twenty-four hours was to rank highly in the list of May's perceived crimes among Brexiteers when word, inevitably, spread of the encounter.

For a prime minister desperate to keep Davis on board, May's actions were inexplicable. However, the subterfuge did buy her time to convince other ministers and helped to prevent Davis peremptorily quitting at the start of the week. A Davis ally said, 'They thought he was going to resign. He was either going to resign before the meeting, in which case the meeting would have been a disaster and they're all fucked. Or he resigns afterwards, in which case they think: "At least we've got the plan out." I'm afraid they were basically right in that calculation.'

At cabinet that day, the truth dawned on the Brexiteers that they had been outmanoeuvred. After the meeting Gove approached Johnson and Davis and said, 'I think we are filt.' When this contribution leaked, one journalist wrote that Gove was so depressed he had 'lapsed into his native Doric'. In fact FILT was an acronym Gove had picked up from Tory grandee Nicholas Soames. It stood for 'Fouquet in Le Touquet'. Obsessively polite, Gove had not wanted to say, 'We're fucked,' but that was what he meant.

On the Tuesday night, while England defeated Colombia in a World Cup penalty shootout, Davis and his advisers gathered in his parliamentary office to discuss whether he would have to resign. Tim Smith said staying might be best for the country. Jackson and Ruparel agreed he would have to go. 'I don't see another option,' Davis said. 'They're pushing something that I cannot defend in public.'

While Davis was contemplating his future, Gove was hosting a party at his home in west London, where members of the cabinet and senior journalists rubbed shoulders while England triumphed. After the game, he played referee as another shootout took place around his kitchen table over what to do about Brexit. Amber Rudd, the former home secretary, urged Gove to back a Norway-style option. Dominic Cummings and Paul Stephenson of Vote Leave pressed him to take a tougher line. Gove threw out leading questions but did not commit.

Tensions escalated further on Wednesday when officials from HM Revenue and Customs went to brief DExEU on what was now grandly called the Facilitated Customs Arrangement (FCA).[7] Barwell told Stewart Jackson that only one special adviser, Ruparel, could attend and he was not invited. 'Bollocks,' Jackson replied. 'It's our meeting, we've invited HMRC and we'll decide who's at our meeting. If you want to come over and throw me out, Gavin, do it.' The briefing did not go well. 'Clearly it had been thrown together,' a DExEU source said. The same day Robbie Gibb went to DExEU to complain to the spads. Jackson told Gibb his customs plan was 'a pig with lipstick on it'.

Gibb replied, 'If you can't support the government get another job.'

'I am supporting the government,' said Jackson. 'I'm supporting our current policy.'

Gibb left 'in a strop' and Jackson went for lunch with Davis at Bellamy's, an upmarket fish restaurant in Mayfair, where he again contemplated resignation.

By that stage, Davis had made his final play. Having received the paperwork on May's plans on Wednesday morning, he and Ruparel wrote a 1,400-word letter back explaining why Davis thought them fatally flawed. It was the most damning of all his missives to May. There were 'fundamental problems' with both the proposals and the prime minister's negotiating strategy. 'The proposal for a common rulebook on goods between the UK and EU essentially means us accepting their rulebook and doing so indefinitely into the future,' he wrote. It was tantamount to membership of the EEA. His second point was that once Britain accepted even 'concepts of EU law', Brussels would insist that the European Court of Justice (ECJ) 'is the only body which can interpret those laws'. He went on, 'I do not see returning control of our laws as a policy choice but as a clear instruction from the British people during the referendum.'

Without greater freedom, Davis argued, there would be 'little chance of other countries wanting to strike free trade agreements with us'. He dismissed the new third way on customs as 'still the New Customs Partnership albeit with some facilitations added on' then repeated his concern that the EU would use the plan to 'push the UK towards the EEA and Customs Union', something he called 'the worst of all worlds – essentially in the EU but with no influence'.

Davis then launched a blistering attack on May's repeated retreats. 'Throughout this process we have been seen to make a series of concessions. Rightly or wrongly, we are perceived in Brussels as saying "no", until we say "yes".' The letter concluded by telling May that her plan 'would breach two fundamental promises we made in our manifesto and which you have reiterated in your series of speeches – to deliver control of our own laws and to deliver a meaningful independent trade policy'. He said she had no choice but to change her entire approach, stick to the demand for divergence made in the Mansion House speech and adopt his white paper. Taking aim at Robbins, he wrote, 'While I understand many people are advising that this is not negotiable, the reality is that we have never truly tested this, particularly with member states. I am of the firm view that the member states will never truly engage with us and push the Commission unless they believe the Commission is putting their interest at risk. All this argues for sticking to our current position and trying to force the member states to engage.' Davis admitted this would lead to a 'point of tension in the negotiations' but he argued it was 'inevitable and it is better to have it sooner rather than later, and on our terms and not theirs'.

At 2 p.m., just an hour after he pressed send, Davis heard from Barwell that May had responded with a 'blanket refusal' to consider his suggestions. Davis thought: *This is not going to deliver what anybody would call Brexit. It will become Brexit in name only. They haven't shifted from a strategy that's bound to fail.*[8]

Julian Smith met forty members of the ERG, who told him May would be 'toast' if she reneged on her previous pledges. The chief whip left some with the impression that he was happy to push the deal through Parliament with Labour votes, telling them, 'If you don't like it, don't vote for it.' Andrew Bridgen, always the first MP to don chain mail, warned that if the red lines set out in her speeches were erased, 'it's going to be very bad personally for the prime minister – probably terminal'.

That afternoon Boris Johnson invited Davis, Gove, Fox, Andrea Leadsom, Chris Grayling, Penny Mordaunt and Esther McVey to his vast rooms in the Foreign Office. Sajid Javid was invited, but did not turn up, apparently not wanting to be seen in seditious company. Johnson wanted to be the centre of the resistance but he was also feeling the heat. The night before a Eurosceptic MP had accosted him in the corridor and warned that if he backed the deal his leadership hopes would be finished. 'He had a look of dead fear in his eyes,' the MP said.

Johnson's instinct was 'Brexit's in danger, what are we going to do about it?' said one witness. He spoke for five minutes, explaining that May's vision at Lancaster House was the right one. 'We need to move her back to that vision. It's vital that we work together.'

Davis spoke about the detail of the deal, which most of the cabinet would not be handed until the following morning, criticising May and Robbins for 'giving away all our key cards'. He said, 'These negotiations will not make progress until we are willing to say "no" to the EU. The only time we've played hardball is with the money and that's the only time we got any success in the entire negotiation.' Leadsom said, 'We're not going to get this through the House' and suggested they go for no-deal instead. Others said Parliament would block it.

Mordaunt and McVey then savaged Robbie Gibb, who had shown them the press release he was planning to issue after the Chequers meeting. 'It sounded good but didn't answer any of the difficult questions,' McVey said. 'To me, it appears that the plan will fall apart the day after it's announced.' She was the 'punchiest' in the room, even suggesting, 'Perhaps we should all resign if this goes through.' Johnson joked that they link hands and leap off Beachy Head. 'We were trying to create a kamikaze squad of people who would hurl themselves in front of the incoming missile,' he recalled. 'We wanted a group of people who would take a bullet for Brexit.' There were no other takers. 'There was a certain amount of, "After you ...",' Johnson said. But the mass resignation (if not mass suicide) might have been the only course of action which would have stopped May in her tracks.

Davis mapped out the possible outcomes at Chequers. 'Either Number 10 wins and we are fucked, we win and the PM is damaged or there is a fudge where nothing is really agreed, which would be the worst outcome.' He predicted that the Brexiteers had a 40 per cent chance of success, which was optimistic in the extreme. Mordaunt and Davis advocated presenting an alternative plan at Chequers. It was agreed that Davis and Ruparel would work something up overnight. They would reconvene the next day.

Not everyone was on board. Grayling, who had chaired May's leadership campaign in 2016, said they should accept her plan. One witness said, 'He looked like one of those villains in a Bond movie who refuses to back the Spectre plan to take over the world and is expecting to be thrown into the shark tank at the end of the meeting.' Grayling left before Gove even arrived and would not return the following day.

Johnson and Gove spoke privately. Gove's instincts were that Davis's white paper would not provide a blueprint to win over the rest of the cabinet. It might be better to stiffen May's terms as much as possible, secure a withdrawal agreement and use the trade negotiations during the transition period to get what the Brexiteers really wanted. 'Let's yield as little as possible but sort it out later,' he said. He described his mood as 'pessimism of the intellect, optimism of the will', the Italian political theorist Antonio Gramsci's warning against both wishful thinking and defeatism.[9] Johnson disagreed, fundamentally. He feared mistakes now would prove irrevocable. 'The problem is, Michael, that we will have agreed to so much that is bad,' Johnson replied. 'It's like setting a broken leg. If you don't set it properly, you can't reset it again. We've got to have an alternative now.'

It was only on Thursday, the day before the Chequers meeting, that most cabinet ministers got to see the proposals. 'We kept it from them because they leak like four thousand colanders knitted together,' said the most lyrical member of the Number 10 comms team.

Backbenchers were still in the dark. At 8.30 a.m. Paleosceptics Bernard Jenkin and Peter Lilley went to see May, who chose sophistry over candour. 'The assurances she gave us gave no hint of what she was about to present to the cabinet,' Jenkin recalled the following year. 'We came out quite reassured.'[10] So reassured that Jenkin told Johnson not to 'rock the boat' and 'stick with the prime minister', an instruction which prompted Johnson to ask an aide, 'What the fuck's happened to Bernard Jenkin?'

One by one ministers were sent the papers or briefed by May, Barwell, Gibb, JoJo Penn and Denzil Davidson. But when Esther McVey asked for legal help to decipher the documents and for a simple chart to explain what accepting the common rulebook would stop Britain doing in free trade deals, her requests were declined. She concluded that May's team did not want her to read and understand the detail. Penny Mordaunt received her papers at 11.30 p.m. She expected small groups to decide issues of national security but on Brexit, which affected the whole government, she thought the way ministers were excluded was detrimental to good governance.

Robbie Gibb told his flock that, as a Brexiteer, he had accepted the compromises as necessary because 'I saw the workings of how we got here.' Far from the conspiracy divined by some ERG members, Gibb said, 'It is necessary to deliver Brexit.' He was convinced nothing more was negotiable. As a comms man, he would come to realise that suddenly confronting ministers with such a view, which he had several months to come to terms with, was a mistake. Downing Street had been secretive because there were so many leaks. Gibb eventually asked himself, 'Given the fact that everybody leaks anyway, should we have just done a weekly update on the record?'

One paper sent to cabinet ministers detailed 'seven Parliamentary locks' on the Brexit process. Nikki da Costa, the head of legislative affairs, had never seen the document still less been asked by Robbins' Europe Unit to contribute to it. She immediately spotted an error in one of the bullet points. 'Why did nobody pass this to me?' she complained, with justification. A colleague said, 'That's how Olly operates.' From her perspective, the paper had been written to make it look like a Parliament with a Remain majority held more of the procedural cards than it did.

Steve Baker refused to be briefed on the plans by Denzil Davidson or Robbie Gibb. 'Steve was sick of them warming him up every week for the next capitulation,' a DExEU source said. On Wednesday he scribbled in his diary that Number 10 was guilty of presiding over 'a shitshow of cowardice and capitulation'. When Gibb finally got hold of him, on Thursday, Baker accused May of 'subterfuge to overturn Brexit'. The chief whip agreed that Baker could lie low for the next three days. Resolved to resign, he would let Chequers play out so he would not embarrass May.

When Johnson saw the papers they were worse than he had expected, 'an absolute great steaming pile of ordure'. He texted Davis, 'Have you seen this stuff? It's blatant treachery.' Davis and his senior aides were sitting in his office when the phone rang. Stewart Jackson recalled, 'He puts it on speaker phone, and it's Boris Johnson, who's just got his pack. He's absolutely going ballistic, he's apoplectic.'[11] Johnson said, 'Have you seen this fucking bollocks, David?'[12]

The cabinet Brexiteers met again in the foreign secretary's office at 5.15 p.m. Johnson made the point that this was only May's opening offer and it was already unacceptable. 'This won't be the end of the story,' he said. 'They will have us over a barrel.' It was a chaotic meeting. 'I never quite saw how bad a chairmanship could be until I saw Boris trying to chair those meetings,' one of those present said. 'It was a stream of consciousness.' Others blamed Davis. While the details were now clear, the Brexit secretary had not produced a rival paper to present at Chequers. 'It wasn't clear what the alternative was around which we could rally,' another cabinet minister recalled. Davis had abandoned plans for an alternative paper after a conversation with Ruparel, who told him that it would be 'an open challenge to the prime minister'. It would have been tantamount to saying, 'Accept our plan or we all walk.'

Leadsom said, 'We are shooting ourselves in the foot if we don't put in counter proposals. We need to present a suitable plan.' But Davis could see that May would be finished if she submitted to such a mutiny: 'She will be humiliated.' He argued they should, instead, seek to modify the worst of it. 'He backed down because at that point, he still thought she was the right person to be PM,' an aide recounted. 'DD is a lone wolf. He just wanted to do what he wanted to do and not the bigger role of getting everyone together and fighting her.' Just as he had in the vital hours after the 2017 election debacle, Davis lacked the killer instinct which might have overthrown the prime minister and changed the history of Brexit. 'DD bottled it,' a Johnson ally said, bluntly.

Gove took the initiative, floating an idea which had come up around his kitchen table on the Tuesday evening. 'Gove said we should cancel transition and join the EEA for a short period of time until we're ready to negotiate a free trade agreement,' one source said. Johnson hated the idea and it did not get traction. But in offering it as a suggestion, Gove was to be distrusted by hardline Brexiteers from that point forward.

While the cabinet was seeing summary documents, Robbins' Europe Unit was crashing out a white paper. 'Everyone thought this was a stitch-up and the white paper had been written in advance by Olly's team,' one of the civil service authors recalled. 'The reality was: four days before Chequers, when that had all been done, we wrote the white paper in four or five days.' Later, some of those involved felt the white paper was counterproductive. 'The EU hated every word of it and used it to beat us with for six months,' an official said. 'I'm not sure it was a hugely successful operation. You'd show up in the Commission and they'd just regurgitate the lines you'd written. Having a fudge written in black and white exposes your inconsistencies.'

May's meeting with Boris Johnson that week was 'as close to a stand-up shouting match as you get,' a civil service witness said. Johnson accused the prime minister of going down 'the wrong path' and suggested she would be 'remembered poorly by history' for flunking such a 'seminal' decision. 'You're taking us to colony status,' he said.

'We'll be able to diverge,' May said indignantly.

'But there will be consequences,' Johnson replied. 'It's quite obvious the penalties for divergence will be draconian, to ensure we never diverge.'

A source said, 'She just started shouting, "You're wrong, you've got to back us on this", and started going on about Ireland. It was a very heated exchange.' It was the last one-to-one meeting Johnson and May ever had.

Johnson was also lobbied by another unlikely source. Two weeks earlier May had reached out to her predecessor David Cameron. They discussed how to survive a leadership coup against her. With May's support, Cameron met Johnson the day before Chequers and 'gave him hell', urging the foreign secretary not to resign and lead an exodus of cabinet Brexiteers. 'Boris has to understand that the vision of Brexit he has peddled is a fantasy,' said a friend of Cameron.

The two Old Etonians had buried the hatchet after Johnson wrote to Cameron not long after the referendum. 'It was a long and rather noble letter,' a friend of Cameron said. 'Boris apologised and said no hard feelings.' Johnson recalled, 'I wrote him a letter thanking him for all the help he'd given me over the years, and what a good job he'd done leading our party.' When they met that Thursday, in a 'weird back garden at the Carlton Club', Johnson teased Cameron, telling him he was the 'godfather of Brexit' and suggesting he 'take credit' for his role. Cameron managed a wry smile. They agreed May's deal was 'the worst of all worlds', but Cameron argued it was the only one which might command a majority in the Commons. He also passed on intelligence he had gleaned directly from May, that if there was a no-confidence vote in her leadership, she would fight on even if she only won 'by one vote'. The two men agreed that a Johnson resignation would achieve little. Adapting his earlier joke, Johnson told Cameron: 'The only alternative to staying is for the Brexiteers to link arms and jump off Beachy Head.' Later he admitted, 'I didn't think at that stage that I was going to have to resign, so I'm afraid I gave him a bum steer. He told them I was safe.' Number 10 staff concluded Johnson was 'a bottler'.

That evening May invited Liam Fox to her Downing Street home for a drink. 'As soon as he went to the flat we knew he'd sell out,' said one Davis aide. The Brexit secretary went for a drink with Gibb but declined another conversation with May. When Barwell suggested he come over, Davis replied, 'There's no point. I know what I want to say tomorrow.'

He told a friend that night, 'Would you want to spend forty-five minutes doing small talk with her?'

Earlier, Davis had called together his ministerial team and taken them into his confidence. 'The proposal they came up with won't work. I will need to resign, but that won't be tomorrow.' Addressing Robin Walker, he said, 'You, have to stay. We need continuity in the department.' Steve Baker instantly volunteered to resign as well. Suella Braverman was agonised. Davis said, 'If you resign, people will think you've got a great point of principle and you've got lots of time to get your career back, but, if you don't resign, no one is going to blame you.'[13]

While all this played out in London, May had also spent the week trying to line up support from key EU allies. On Tuesday she flew to The Hague for a working brunch with Mark Rutte, the Dutch prime minister, who had been Cameron's closest EU ally. She spent most of Thursday in Berlin with Angela Merkel. These meetings would become the focus of Eurosceptic fury that foreign leaders were told May's plans before her own cabinet. 'There was no point in going through all the pain of selling it in the cabinet if it wasn't going to work,' Barwell said.

After a very early morning flight, Rutte took May for a walk around the gardens of his official residence, the Catshuis. When they sat down for food, Rutte turned to his EU sherpa and the senior official at the ministry of foreign affairs, and said, 'This is what the prime minister has described to me.' For the next forty-five minutes they interrogated May, Robbins and Barwell on the plan. When they were done, Rutte turned to the sherpa. May and the half-dozen aides with her watched, butterflies in their stomachs. 'It works,' he said.

The German chancellor's support for the plan was what May craved most. For long periods Merkel had not been engaged with Brexit. 'She thought it was for the Commission, the UK and Ireland to work out,' a British official said. This time it was just May, Robbins and Barwell in a room with Merkel and her EU expert Uwe Corsepius. While Merkel watched, pensive, Corsepius picked over the British plan. He had concerns that it did not take enough account of the service agreements added to the sale of goods. 'If I buy a BMW I'm buying both a car and a servicing package and it's not always so easy to split these things,' he said. He predicted 'detailed questions' from the Commission on how the rulings of the ECJ would be treated. Corsepius was less emphatic than the

Dutch official but he called it a 'significant evolution' that meant he could see a 'landing zone'. He concluded, 'This is definitely a big step forward and it makes me feel much more optimistic.'

On the plane home Barwell allowed himself a quiet moment of satisfaction that they might, finally, have found something that could work. 'It was probably the most optimistic moment in the whole two years,' he said later.

Back at home, Philip Hammond and David Lidington met Simon Coveney, the Irish foreign minister and deputy premier, in a bid to get Dublin on board. The communications team briefed Paul Dacre and Tony Gallagher, the editors of the *Daily Mail* and the *Sun*. May was even rewarded on the Friday with a conciliatory tweet from Michel Barnier, who also made a speech that day offering to compromise if Britain did too: 'I am ready to adapt our offer should the UK red lines change.'

Ministers were told to arrive at Chequers before 10 a.m. for coffee on Friday 6 July. They were banned from bringing their special advisers and, on arrival, they had to hand over their mobile phones. May and her team could not afford any leaks to the media before the meeting was finished.

Several ministers were already irritated on arrival by an inflammatory press briefing that anyone resigning would lose their ministerial car but could make use of business cards for the local taxi firm which had been placed in the hallway. A 'full reshuffle plan' was in place, said the source. 'A select number of ego-driven, leadership-dominated cabinet ministers need to support the PM in the best interests of the UK or their spots will be taken by a talented new generation of MPs who will sweep them away.' This inept intervention did nothing to help May. Robbie Gibb was widely blamed, but the culprit was Julian Smith.

Davis, the one minister confident he would be resigning, sought out the chief whip and said, 'I see the children have taken over the kindergarten, chief.' He said later, 'I was a bit tempted to call up Jacob Rees-Mogg, who has an antique Bentley, and say to him, "Buy yourself a peaked cap, Jacob, and get over here!"'[14] Penny Mordaunt's driver was outraged by the idea he might abandon her. 'Look, girl, you do what you think is right,' he said. 'Whatever happens, we've decided we're driving you home.'

Fortified by coffee and croissants, the ministers gathered in the Hawtrey Room at 10.15 that morning to listen to a series of presentations:

Brandon Lewis, the party chairman, with polling on the damage to the Tory brand caused by disunity and Greg Clark on why May's proposal was best for the car industry. ('What matters to my constituents in Wolverhampton is jobs not the finer points of sovereignty.') It was a softening up exercise. The prime minister seemed in bullish good spirits. When she called on Julian Smith to speak, Boris Johnson groaned, 'Oh God.' May replied, instantly, 'He'll always like that as an introduction.' The chief whip set out the balance of forces in the Commons between five groups: the fervent Remainers, the pragmatic Remainers, the pragmatists, the pragmatic Leavers and the fervent Leavers. Smith warned that if the plan was not agreed the pragmatists would side with the Remainers to amend the upcoming trade bill to force Britain into a customs union.

Oliver Robbins and Tim Barrow set out May's plan. It was Robbins' answer to the exam question which the prime minister had set him: how to find the least economically damaging relationship that also permitted May to regain control of Britain's laws, borders and money, allowing freedom of movement for goods but not people, leaving the single market and the customs union while continuing in a synchronous orbit with both. It was a curate's egg of a contraption, unsatisfactory to hard Brexiteers and Eurocrats alike, but redeemed in part because it was a brilliant civil service attempt to reconcile red lines that were close to mutually contradictory.

What it was, at least, was evidence the prime minister had finally made a choice. Philip Hammond said later, 'The prime minister had understood for a long time that she was going to have to address this tension between the desire to be completely free of EU involvement and the need to protect our economy. At Chequers she came down decisively on the side of the need to protect the UK economy.'[15]

The plan had two key parts: regulatory policy and customs policy. On regulatory policy, there were three elements. Britain would voluntarily choose to follow EU rules on industrial goods and agrifood products. Second, British courts would pay due regard to the relevant ECJ rulings. British courts would decide what the rules meant but in a way that was consistent with the EU's policy. Third, there was a dispute resolution mechanism. The combination of those things would negate the need for regulatory checks on goods at the border between the UK and the EU, including between Northern Ireland and the Republic. The new FCA plan was designed to remove the need for customs checks as well. By removing friction, while remaining outside the customs union, Britain was effectively asking for a common market in goods without the rest of the single market. For years the 'four freedoms' had been a cornerstone of the EU. Theresa May was asking the Commission to sever the link between the movement of goods and people.

As ministers began to respond, it was not the EU's worries that concerned them, but fears of ECJ jurisdiction over large parts of the British economy. It looked to the Brexiteers like the power still lay in Brussels. One of May's political aides agreed: 'She did two pivots in her leadership. One was after the leadership election. She dumped the Remain block of Conservative MPs who supported her, to adopt all the Leave-supporting MPs who had backed Andrea Leadsom, Michael Gove and Boris Johnson. That was shift one. Shift two was Chequers where she switched back to get the Remainers on board.'

May opened the meeting by explaining that the EU was offering three alternatives: the EEA and customs union membership, a free trade agreement (FTA) or no-deal. She said, 'The EEA is unacceptable because you would be respecting free movement. An FTA is constitutionally unacceptable because, under the terms of the backstop, Northern Ireland would be separated from the rest of the UK. And no deal is economically unacceptable.'

As the ministers who had done most to deliver Brexit, and the two most likely to be listened to by the media, Johnson and Gove were seen as the swing votes by Downing Street. Despite one-on-one sessions with May, Barwell and Robbins that week, they still did not know which way the environment secretary would jump. Before the formal talks Gove had urged Barwell to 'acknowledge the disquiet' that some Brexiteers felt and 'show willingness to amend the proposal'.

'We can't do that,' Barwell replied, 'because it's all signed off.'[16]

In the morning session, Johnson was the most agitated, letting rip a 'six-minute moan' of semi-profane invective against the proposal. His defiance had been fortified by a text at 5.15 a.m. from Conor Burns, urging him to feats of Churchillian steadfastness: 'Stay strong today and face down these modern-day Lord and Lady Halifax types. You have huge support and expectation.' With characteristic flourish, Johnson branded the plan 'a big turd' and suggested anyone backing it 'will be polishing a turd'. Gesticulating at Robbie Gibb and the other spin doctors, he added, 'I see there are some expert turd polishers here.' Not expert enough, it transpired. Johnson complained that the customs partnership, which he had wished dead, had 'emerged zombie-like from the coffin'. The shadowing of goods regulations would leave Britain a 'vassal state' and was a violation of the referendum pledge to 'take back control of our laws'.

One of those who watched from the sidelines began to relax. Johnson was not happy, but he had not walked out or dismissed the entire project. Davis, keeping his counsel, looked on, unimpressed. 'I thought it was going to be a huge fight but they had done a good job at pre-cooking it,' an adviser present said. 'Even in the first session Boris was tinkering around the edges and that pissed DD off.'

The 'dress rehearsal' part of the day was not without its levity. David Gauke, the justice secretary, drew a parallel between Sir Tim Barrow, Britain's ambassador to the EU, and England football manager Gareth Southgate: 'We've got to hope that this is a good week for bearded men in waistcoats.' To relieve the tedium, Gauke got his private office to send him notes with the latest football scores.

Philip Hammond took a swipe at May for the way the Brexit talks had been handled. 'We have wasted time during this negotiation,' he said. But May was in no mood to be pushed around. After a ten-minute monologue from the chancellor, May snapped at him, 'Is there a question?'

'No, I'm making a statement,' Hammond replied. May cut him off, saying he had to wait until the cabinet meeting in the afternoon.

Sajid Javid announced he had devised a 'new plan' to save the day, cheekily arguing that since May had sprung 'last-minute ideas' on her cabinet it was fine to bring last-minute ideas of their own. 'His proposal was to have two rules, so [companies] could choose to follow the EU rule or the British rule,' one colleague recalled, using technology to police two different regulatory regimes in Great Britain and Northern Ireland. 'I've just thought of this in the last two hours,' Javid said. Officials duly examined Javid's idea and predictably concluded it was impractical.

Davis was becalmed in the morning, saying only that May's plan was 'a move away from what I had hoped to see'. But the prime minister's aides knew Davis was at his most dangerous when brooding rather than brawling. His true feelings emerged after David Gauke and Damian Hinds walked in on him talking to one of May's team. 'If you think I'm just going to swallow this, don't kid yourselves.' Davis and Julian Smith took a walk around the gardens, the chief whip urging the Brexit secretary to 'complete the task you were given, in the national interest'.

Lunch was a collation of chicken thighs, barbecued to rubber. More than three hours was set aside in the afternoon for a formal cabinet meeting around the dining table in the Grand Parlour upstairs. May opened the proceedings at 1.30 p.m., declaring it, in her understated way, an 'important' moment and said all ministers present would be invited to speak. Outside of decisions to go to war, what followed was arguably the most significant cabinet meeting of the previous quarter century and, in terms of cabinet unity, the most seismic since the Westland crisis in 1986.

The first to speak was David Lidington, May's deputy. He was officially called in order of precedence, but in reality to set the tone. In his unflashy but cerebral way, Lidington set out the balances he felt they needed to strike: 'The government needs to deliver [Brexit] in a way that will be understandable to the average voter, but it is also essential that jobs, supply chains and the flow of inward investment, which are vital to the prosperity of the country, are not disrupted.' He was depicted as an arch-Remainer but ahead of the meeting he had taken to saying, 'We are all Brexiteers now', to stress that he did not wish to overturn the verdict of the referendum. As a former Foreign Office minister, Lidington also made a broader point about 'the state of the world'. The Brexit deal would be struck in an environment where the West was in 'a more fragile state' than he could remember. He regarded the deal as 'ambitious' and 'just about credible', though he admitted there were things he did not like. He backed May's customs plan and the common rulebook, pointing out that many businesses would want to follow the 'existing rules', making the case that 'Parliament would have a lock' and could change its mind later. He said the Withdrawal Act would 'end the primacy of the EU and the direct effect of its laws', pointing out that the ECJ 'would always be arbiter of what people needed to do to comply with EU law and anyone who traded with the EU would be subject to that'. This was not a message the Brexiteers wished to hear, but Lidington reached for their preferred model to make his case, adding, 'as Canada has recently found out'.

He concluded with the point his prime minister regarded as the most decisive – the Brexit impact on the integrity of the United Kingdom. As a former frontbench spokesman on Northern Ireland, Lidington said this meant giving special thought to the concerns of Welsh lamb, Scottish shellfish and Aberdeenshire beef farmers about frictionless trade. 'The political cost of doing damage to those communities cannot be over-stated,' he said. More importantly, a free trade agreement, like Canada's, 'implies border checks on the island of Ireland', which the government had pledged to avoid. The peace process in Northern Ireland was 'very fragile', Lidington warned, with an 'uptick in violence'. He added, 'For the first time since partition in 1921 there is no automatic Unionist majority in the six counties of Northern Ireland.' There was also 'read-across to Scotland' where Nicola Sturgeon was 'creating a catalogue of grievances' and would seize on anything which gave 'special status' to Northern Ireland to strengthen the case for Scottish independence.

Having made the prime minister's case more eloquently than she had, Lidington wound up with an appeal that the cabinet back her. 'The cabi-net has to trust the prime minister to negotiate; making the trade-offs is something that only heads of government can do. Despite the doubts we all have about the proposal, we should all endorse it and give the prime minister the flexibility she needs to go into the negotiations without her hands being tied.'

The Chequers cabinet resembled a court case in reverse. After Lidington concluded the case for the defence, David Davis delivered what amounted to the case for the prosecution. 'I've got fundamental concerns on the content of the paper and the negotiating strategy,' he said. The Brexit secretary stressed that what would be accepted by the country was just as important as what was negotiable with Brussels. 'On customs, and on goods, the paper is not in line with the government's core promises to take back control of its laws and have an independent trade policy. We should be up front that this means the harmonisation of legislation with the EU and being a rule-taker for vast swathes of the economy.' Davis pointed out that there had been twenty-six changes in just five years on the regulation of chemicals alone.

His fundamental objection was that May had now accepted the prin-ciple of 'harmonisation' of rules, ditching his plan for 'outcome equivalence', which the Brexit war cabinet had backed at the first Chequers meeting. Davis argued this would give the whip hand to Brussels, since it was no longer a case of working out if British and EU rules achieved the same ends: 'it will become a straightforward legal question of compliance with the rules, with no wriggle room'. Northern Ireland 'could become the detonator' which blew up the whole deal.

Next, Davis mauled the plans for the ECJ, arguing that harmonisation handed power to the Luxembourg court where equivalence could have been decided by a separate tribunal. 'It is not true to say that the proposal will mean the UK is taking back control of its own laws,' he said. 'If the UK accepts EU laws and concepts, the ECJ is the only accepted interpreter of those laws.' He conceded that May's new customs model was 'an improvement' on her previous new customs partnership, but expressed doubts that the EU would trust Britain to enforce their external border and said they would insist on oversight by the EU's anti-fraud office (OLAF), under ECJ jurisdiction. 'This would be a serious issue for the UK in taking back control of its borders,' Davis warned. 'We would find it very hard to sign trade agreements.' Downing Street was arguing that only 4 per cent of imported goods would be affected but Davis argued that this fraction of the economy was disproportionately important in securing trade deals.

The Brexit secretary concluded with an outspoken attack on May's entire approach to the negotiations, arguing that she should be 'dealing directly with the member states', rather than the Commission. Almost plaintively he said, 'I don't like us being dictated to by the EU. Stop giving ground to the EU and stand up to them. They will take it. We should be telling them what we want, not the other way around.'[17] His words exposed the chasm between him and May in policy, politics and personality.

Lidington's and Davis's contributions together captured the contradictory dilemmas of Brexit for the government. Lidington's analysis was the embodiment of the Remainer approach to the negotiations: sensitive to the economic dangers, realistic about what the other side was prepared to accept, pragmatic about the real-world impact of remaining in the orbit of the Brussels institutions. Davis summed up the Brexiteer case: far more concerned with sovereignty and regulatory freedom than economic peril, hostile to the EU's rules and courts, but also tacitly acknowledging that the Remainers were right about what the EU would negotiate. But rather than accept this, Davis and the Brexiteers wanted to throw the game board in the air and become much more aggressive in pursuit of their goals, to force the Commission out of its comfort zone and fight for their beliefs. In Theresa May, though, they had a prime minister who was prepared to accept the views of Lidington, Barwell and others about what was realistic. She was temperamentally unsuited to prosecuting a hardball strategy in pursuit of a sovereignty-first, deregulatory Brexit in which she did not believe and from which she had been slowly retreating since October 2016. The greater surprise, perhaps, is that it took until the second Chequers meeting for the Brexiteers to realise that was who she was and where she was taking them.

Davis's comments left several of his colleagues around the table wondering if he would resign there and then. It was difficult to see how his opposition to the plan could be reconciled with his position as political negotiator. But while Davis had refused to salute May's flag, he had not planted one of his own. 'We were waiting for the explosion in the afternoon,' a Remain-voting cabinet member said. 'David was very much against the Chequers strategy, but he didn't really offer much of an alternative.'

They watched even more closely as May asked Boris Johnson to speak. To Davis he seemed 'disorganised' and didn't 'really make a very good argument'.[18] Johnson had little good to say for the prime minister's plans. He agreed 'substantially' with the detailed points Davis had made and put forward a broader point disparaging May's quest to align closely with a European Union which he argued was failing. Exasperated, he said, 'The paper treats the EU economic model as if it is one from which no one would wish to dissent … and its regulatory system as something to be welcomed. Both business and the government have fought tooth and nail for many years to stop Brussels legislation … The EU is not a model of economic success.'

May's plan also offended Johnson's martial spirit. 'What this paper does,' he argued, 'is lock the UK into the EU legislative and regulatory framework – but without the capacity to fight. We will have no representation in Brussels, no judge in the ECJ and we will be a rule-taker. This will be difficult to sell politically.' He backed the original Max-Fac plan on customs, suggested a level playing field for EU and non-EU migrants and insisted, 'There should be no further concessions on money.'

With arguably the deftest popular touch in the cabinet, Johnson warned that the public would smell a rat if the prime minister did not level with voters. 'They will see it as a concession and expect the government to explain itself … If the UK's ability to do trade deals is going to be reduced or we are going to remain in the regulatory orbit of the EU, then the government should be up front about that.'

Compared with his outburst before lunch, Johnson's more measured approach in the afternoon gave allies of May room for hope. They detected advice on how to sell something Johnson regarded as unpalatable, rather than outright rejection. Yet there were also clues about what was to come. Johnson's peroration was a *cri de coeur* at the way the promises of the Leave campaign were coming undone and the condescension of Remainers towards Leave voters. 'It's very important not to underestimate people,' he said, 'or to ascribe to them primitive reasons for their views on the EU.' This was a defensive Johnson, still seeking to justify his decision to back Leave, but he also saw himself as the politician with the greatest obligation to deliver on the vote. If Brexit was to break, the blame would be his. 'I am sad about the paper,' he said. 'I fought hard for Brexit and the cabinet seems to be embracing a vision that does not correspond to the self-confident and self-believing view of the UK that I hold.' This was Boris of City Hall, the Boris of Global Britain, the Boris who wanted to present a Churchillian chin to the wider world. 'Committing to that could have captured the public imagination and would be economically advantageous in the long term.' Northern Ireland, he complained, 'has been allowed to spook the government and drive the process'.

Those who listened might have detected the same distaste for small-scale compromise and the emotional need to realise a buccaneering vision of Britain's island story which had led him to break with Cameron's pragmatic but uninspiring EU negotiation two years before. This was not an argument designed to win over a divided cabinet, it would serve instead as an elegy for Johnson's time there.

Johnson later told friends, 'I wish I'd just walked down the drive and given a press conference', or asked, 'Anyone got that taxi number?' to signal that he was resigning. One of May's political advisers is in no doubt that would have 'destroyed the government right there and then'. The aide said, 'It would have been more honest.' Instead, Johnson's contribution left the meeting hanging in the balance. His accusation was plain: May had lost her nerve. Two of the three Brexit beasts had spoken and the prime minister's authority was on the line.

May turned next to Karen Bradley. The Northern Ireland secretary was an arch loyalist and was guaranteed to put May's greatest concern back at the heart of the debate, but she also said she was speaking that day for her constituents who voted to leave. Bradley made the case that, since Britain was starting from a position of totally frictionless trade across the Northern Ireland border with the South, 'adding any degree of friction was therefore unacceptable'. As a member of the Max-Fac working group, she said, 'There was not a single technological solution ... that could deliver' what its supporters claimed. To cap it all, she warned that since the peace process, '40 per cent of dissident Republican activity has taken place at the border' and that any additional infrastructure there would require 'a minimum' of an extra one thousand police officers.

Gavin Williamson spoke briefly, Greg Clark at great length. ('Greg went on about, well, Greg just went on,' an official said.) No one was surprised when Philip Hammond backed the deal, but the chancellor even questioned whether freedom of movement should end for good. He argued that 'preferential mobility' deals could be important leverage in trade deals and even with the EU. He saved his harshest words for a no-deal departure, which would have 'a catastrophic impact on the economy'.

The decisive moment came around 3.15 p.m. when Michael Gove spoke. The environment secretary was 'thoughtful and quiet', a colleague recalled. He said he was 'not joyous' about May's plan and made clear his preference for a Canada-style free trade deal. 'The concessions have all been one way,' he said. He also emphasised that the government should be doing more to prepare for a no-deal Brexit. His main point, though, was to stress that May needed to come clean with voters that the plan was a 'dilution' of her previous position. 'We will not be credible with Europe or the electorate if we don't acknowledge the change,' Gove said. 'In the prime minister's Mansion House speech she said that the UK would adopt substantially similar rules on goods; those rules will now be identical.' Attempting to diverge now would be 'fraught and difficult'. 'Where the UK had hoped to take back control of its laws, we are choosing, for the foreseeable future, not to.' Harmonisation of rules would make free trade deals 'more difficult to negotiate and potentially less attractive to our negotiating partners'. Gove said the customs plan would be 'difficult to negotiate'. But he concluded, 'I am not happy, but I understand why the proposal needed to be made and I will support it.' To those in the room, the molecules in the air subtly shifted. 'That was the moment of change,' a fellow minister said.

Gove's logic was that if he was going to help 'get Brexit over the line' it meant accepting unpalatable compromises, since the alternative was

Parliament intervening to prevent the UK leaving in March 2019. From his perch 'in the belly of the beast' in Defra, Gove believed that trading on WTO terms without a deal would be hugely disruptive. 'By a process of elimination' he had reluctantly concluded that May had the right to put her plan to the EU. If Brussels refused to 'show generosity and flexibility', the government would then be in a better position to tell the public no-deal was the only option. There was also a personal factor. Gove had delivered Brexit only by turning on his friend David Cameron. Afterwards he had torpedoed Boris Johnson's 2016 leadership bid and with it his own. Now he felt he had a responsibility to both Brexit and to the prime minister who had brought him back to try to make it work. He told one friend he was sick of being seen as 'some sort of psychopath'.

Liam Fox, the international trade secretary, concluded, 'The proposal is at the absolute limit of what can be reconciled with the promises the government has made.' He was not happy but, for now at least, he was on board. May had gone out of her way to woo Fox, getting officials to confirm that the plan allowed, at least in theory, the UK to join the trans-Pacific trade partnership. The real reason he did not quit, though, was that Fox thought the deal would fail. Privately he told friends, 'Frankly I don't think the EU will ever agree to it.' An ERG source was more cynical: 'He likes travelling and shaking hands with people in exotic countries; I think he just wanted to stay in the cabinet.'

Of the other notable moments, David Gauke, the justice secretary, warned against threatening no-deal, which he said would be 'holding a pistol to our own head and threatening to pull the trigger, like the sheriff in *Blazing Saddles*'. There was a brief moment of humour when a pack of Haribo Supermix sweets was passed around the table. When they reached Jeremy Hunt, the health secretary, he said, 'I should take those off you, I think.' Few were in the mood for a lesson in healthy living. Chris Grayling came to the prime minister's aid, urging that once agreed, 'if any minister challenges the proposal or brings forward an alternative proposition, that should be seen as a breach of the ministerial code'. He was, in effect, calling on May to fire dissenters. Elsewhere around the table, another cabinet minister thought: *What a cunt.* Liz Truss said she would prefer a free trade deal and divergence.

Of the other Brexiteers, Penny Mordaunt made clear she was 'not happy with where we are' and would back the plan only if there were changes to the language. She said, 'As it is drafted, I cannot support it.' She wanted it to stress the 'damage' the Commission would do to their own side if they did not give Britain a bespoke deal. Mordaunt argued that, by changing the text, May could show she had listened to the Brexiteers, rather than imposed the deal on them.

Esther McVey urged May to 'go out fighting' and maintain the threat of no-deal. She warned that the real 'crunch point' was the vote in Parliament, which she predicted would split the party. Taking on Remainer fears of 'disruption', she argued that Leave voters actually wanted disruption – to the old order. 'This is a working-class movement and people knew it would be bumpy.'

The contribution which raised most eyebrows, however, came from Andrea Leadsom. The leader of the Commons began by saying, 'I hate this. I regard it as breaching the government's red lines and I don't think it's true to the 17.2 million people who voted for Brexit.'

At the side of the room, Paul Harrison, the prime minister's press secretary, turned to his comms colleagues Robbie Gibb and James Slack and said, 'She's going to resign!'

Leadsom went on, 'Most ministers and civil servants have Remainer tendencies and an arrogance that they know better.' The government, she said, was 'on a slippery slope', in danger of becoming 'a vassal state' and 'I'll wager a large sum the chancellor's numbers are wrong'. Yet, after this sustained outburst, she told May, 'I will back you. The public just want us to get on with it.'

Two months earlier, Johnson had yelled 'six-five'. This time there was no need for a count because it was clear May had won. Just seven ministers out of the twenty-seven had spoken against the plans. Summing up, the prime minister said, 'There is a clear majority around the table for accepting the recommendations in the paper and therefore there is collective agreement to it.'

Johnson fought for and won textual changes. The joint statement would be rewritten to stress that Parliament could choose not to incorporate future EU rules into British legislation. Another tweak would prevent British citizens appealing directly to the European Court of Justice. More would be done to prepare for no-deal.

After the carrot, came the stick. The prime minister went on, 'Having reached this agreement the cabinet must unite and be seen to unite behind the proposal. During the EU referendum campaign David

Cameron allowed ministers to advocate positions other than the government's and over the previous two years I have allowed considerable latitude to those who have expressed personal views—' This was a generous description of the concatenation of cabinet chaos over which May had presided, but she now showed she was prepared to put her foot down. 'Everyone must now accept the agreed position and speak with one voice. If the England football team can pull together, then the cabinet can too. Collective responsibility is essential. Every member must commit to moving forward together, to show the EU we are serious and that we will not be divided.'

The message was clear: back the Chequers deal in public and private, or resign. It was 6.45 p.m. The meeting, scheduled for three and a half hours, had taken more than five. Two years and thirteen days (743 days in total) after the EU referendum, her Britannic majesty's government of Great Britain and Northern Ireland finally had a policy on Brexit.

A palpable sense of relief descended as ministers and Downing Street aides hit the pre-dinner drinks (Pol Roger or an elderflower soft drink). Julian Smith felt later that if the mood in the room at that moment 'could have been bottled' much of the unpleasantness that gripped British politics over the following year might have been avoided. As they clinked glasses, Downing Street issued a statement at 7 p.m. which read, 'Today in detailed discussions the Cabinet has agreed our collective position for the future negotiations with the EU. Our proposal will create a UK-EU free trade area which establishes a common rule book for industrial goods and agricultural products …'

There were still awkward moments. Gavin Barwell approached Mordaunt and asked which paragraphs she wanted changed. They went into the next room and were shooed away by a housekeeper because they had mistakenly entered the prime minister's bedroom. Mordaunt pointed out four 'stinkers which make it unacceptable to anyone who wants Brexit'. Barwell said, 'We can't change the wording because it has already been agreed with Merkel.'

'Well, why are we having a meeting then?' Mordaunt snapped. Not only did she not get the changes she wanted, when the minutes emerged, three weeks later, she demanded they be rewritten too since they attributed to her the thoughts of Chris Grayling and the words of Claire Perry. 'They were gratuitously inaccurate,' she said. 'It was appalling.' She was ignored again.

Ministers dined that night on honey and whisky-dipped Scottish salmon, Oxfordshire beef fillet and marmalade bread and butter pudding. There was an end-of-term feel to the exchanges. Davis and Johnson were asked how the deal could best be sold to the public and MPs. Davis stood and, sticking to his divide and rule mantra, told his colleagues to reach out to other member states. 'Over the summer, wherever you are, go and meet your counterparts, sell it to them,' he said. One minister thought to himself: *The danger has passed.*

The most indelible moment, since it was the one that surprised them most, came when Johnson, still seated, offered his thoughts. According to multiple witnesses, he toasted May personally with raised glass and said that while he had come 'feeling really miserable' he was cheered that they had 'agreed on a battle plan'. The phrase everyone remembered was this: 'Now we have a song to sing.' Johnson denies making a toast and claims he was discussing the future of the Foreign Office. Most cabinet ministers took his words as assurance that he was reconciled to the decision. Gove, watching closely, was not so sure. Johnson had already begun muttering over drinks about May's call for collective responsibility: 'She can't ask us to unsay that which we've said.' In his columns and books, he frequently set up a dialectic, an argument with himself. He had done the same when deciding whether to back Brexit, penning two opposing newspaper articles to convince himself he had made the right decision. The conversation in Johnson's head was only just beginning.

May was 'visibly relaxed' and was joined for dinner by her husband, Philip. 'You could almost see the sense of relief that it had got over the line,' a minister said. 'I think she genuinely felt that if she didn't land it then it would be terminal for her.' She drew the dinner to a close at 10.01 p.m., just one minute later than she had promised. 'That Friday night of Chequers everyone was very, very happy,' a senior Downing Street figure recalled. 'There was a great atmosphere. We'd got through it.' Even Michel Barnier issued a warmish tweet, saying the discussion was 'to be welcomed' and, 'I look forward to the White Paper. We will assess the proposals to see if they are workable and realistic.'

The euphoria bordered on hubris. Robbie Gibb circulated, signing up pairings of Brexiteers and Remainers to put their names jointly to op-ed articles for the papers, showing how the cabinet had come together to back the deal. A member of the comms team recalled, 'It was Boris's idea to do a joint op-ed with Hammond', a political buffet plate of chalk and cheese.

Yet, compared with a simple government announcement, for which endless cross-departmental meetings would be held to agree a media plan for the rollout, Downing Street had done no preparation to sell the deal. 'I understand that they didn't want it all leaking, but equally there was no pitch rolling of any description,' said one of those with the task of briefing ministers and MPs on the arguments for the deal.

David Davis was 'clearly unhappy' as he headed home. 'David is some-one who wears his heart on his sleeve,' Barwell said. 'I think he had been surprised that he hadn't got more support and surprised at some of the people that had not backed his position.'[19] As they parted Johnson said to Davis, 'Let's stay in touch over the weekend.' Once in the car Davis gave vent to his true feelings, texting an aide, 'Gove actively backed the paper. Duplicitous shit.'

Davis called Ruparel and signalled that he was minded to resign. Ruparel agreed, telling him, 'If you are going to stay in government, you will then have to sell and own this policy. You can't half-arse it. You are the Brexit Secretary. I don't think you can do that. It's not who you are.' Davis phoned Stewart Jackson and Suella Braverman and told them, 'I'm going, but I'm going to do it in my own time.' He planned to spend Saturday with his family and Sunday with his daughter at the British Grand Prix. He wanted a quiet time without the media frenzy that would surround him if he had already quit.

When Boris Johnson got mobile reception back, he phoned his special advisers, Lee Cain and David Frost. Usually optimistic, he was 'very downbeat' and said, 'I'm going to have to think about what to do next.' At 10.23 p.m. his phone vibrated with a text message from his PPS Conor Burns, a committed Eurosceptic. The intelligence was disturbing. Despite the Number 10 spin, the deal – and May's ban on dissent – was going down very badly on the backbenches. 'When you get this phone back you'll find there is a massive amount of anger and bewilderment among colleagues as to how this has been signed up to,' Burns wrote. 'Her threat that this is now government policy and she won't accept people express-ing their own views anymore is worrying. For three years she has said "no single market or customs union and free trade deals". Let's hope the EU reject it. I and others fear they won't, they will take this as an opening offer and press for more in October. Not a good day.' Johnson called

Burns at around 10.45 p.m. and said, 'We didn't have the bloody numbers.' Burns questioned whether he would be able to stick to the agreed line: 'She's clearly going to enforce this collective responsibility lark. Do you genuinely think you've got the self-restraint and discipline for the next six months to sell this in every utterance you make?' He answered his own question, 'I'm not sure you do.'

With the antennae of a former chief whip, Gavin Williamson was also concerned by what he was hearing from MPs. Late that night he phoned a Westminster friend. 'I think the winds are going to blow now,' he said, dismissing Julian Smith's hope that Labour might come to his aid. 'There is no chance that they will vote for this in a million years,' Williamson warned, prophetically. 'The only way that Labour can unify on this is to vote against the government. If you give any opposition a chance to vote to humiliate a government they'll take it.' Williamson was the shrewdest reader of Parliament in the cabinet. It is intriguing to wonder how differently May might have behaved if he had still been chief whip.

By Saturday morning a sense of peril was beginning to permeate. James Slack asked one journalist that morning, 'Have you got hold of DD?' The Brexit secretary was not taking Number 10's calls, or those of the press. Kirsty Buchanan, who had worked closely with him during the general election campaign, told colleagues, 'When David blusters and shouts he needs to get it out and move on. When he goes very quiet that's when you've got a problem.'

BREXODUS

DD-Day and Bye-Bye Boris (Part I)

July 2018

As Saturday 7 July dawned, the silent signals from David Davis were drowned out by the noise from Eurosceptic backbenchers. MPs were invited in for a briefing in 10 Downing Street. First to speak was Philip Davies, the combative Brexiteer from Shipley, who combined ocean-going truculence with a blunt intelligence: 'Can you stop all this bollocks about "the cabinet agreed"? We all know the cabinet didn't agree, the cabinet were bloody bullied. You got a whole load of bloody Remain members of the cabinet and they bloody outnumbered the Leave ones. We won the bloody referendum, so let's stop this bollocks.' Another MP present said, 'Philip basically tore Gavin Barwell a new one.'

The phones ran hot between key players in the European Research Group (ERG). Jacob Rees-Mogg, Steve Baker and the Paleosceptics on the ERG's steering group had all concluded that the details of the cabinet's plan would mean 'we might lose Brexit'. Collectively they agreed to vote down the plan in the meaningful vote. One said, 'We have to blow up the government one way or another and try to win on penalties.' Baker consulted Davis, Rees-Mogg, Suella Braverman, Stewart Jackson, Christopher Montgomery, Andrea Leadsom and his whip Mark Spencer. Bill Cash called the deal 'unacceptable' but urged Baker to stay so that the DExEU minister in charge of preparing for no-deal was a Brexiteer. However, by the end of the day Baker had concluded he had to quit.

Watching at home, where he was recuperating from cancer treatment, Jeremy Heywood texted May to congratulate her, but he felt downbeat. 'I worry about where we are going,' he told his wife. 'We have a referendum result and we have what our elected MPs want. In the gap between the two, our democracy is ripping itself apart.'[1] In fact, it had barely begun.

In London, Boris Johnson was getting cold feet. At 9 a.m. Lee Cain took a call from Poppy Trowbridge, Philip Hammond's special adviser, explaining that she was emailing him the text of the joint op-ed Downing Street wanted to release in Johnson and the chancellor's name. Trowbridge asked Cain to get Johnson to sign it off. Those who read it felt it was 'deliberately unappetising', a 'loyalty test' which could have been written by Hammond. Johnson replied to Cain, 'Alas, this is a pack of lies.'

In his account, Johnson was at Chevening, the foreign secretary's mansion in Kent, a poignant reminder of what he would have to give up if he resigned. 'It's a beautiful day. I was swimming in the lake.' There he watched two vintage Spitfires in the clear blue sky above him, perhaps a reminder of the resolution of his hero Winston Churchill. 'I'm looking at this unbelievable seventeenth-century Inigo Jones house, easily the most beautiful of all the government residences, thinking, "God. I've got to go. I've got to go. There's nothing else I can do."' Johnson rang Cain and said, 'I can't put my name to this. I think it's a huge mistake and future generations will judge us. I'm going to have to resign because I can't defend this.' Cain urged him to take the weekend to think about it and consult his family. There was peril in both directions. Eurosceptic MPs made clear that he had to quit if he wanted to become leader. Failure to resign, as one pithily put it, would leave Johnson 'as dead as a Bojo'.

On Sunday morning Michael Gove was sent out to bat for the government on *The Andrew Marr Show*. May had done an interview with the *Sunday Times*, in which she urged Brussels to 'get serious' and ditch their 'rigid approach' to negotiations. Gove made the pragmatic case for May's plan: 'I'm a realist and one of the things about politics is you shouldn't make the perfect the enemy of the good.' Yet this was the prime minister's flagship policy, the basis on which her government would fly or founder and May delegated the task of selling it directly to the public. She hated interviews but it was also an abdication of responsibility.

Gove and Johnson spoke on the phone before lunch on Sunday. The foreign secretary was 'clearly unhappy', Gove told friends and aides, but he did not expect Johnson to resign. Johnson recalls Gove urging him not to. Davis was still furious with Gove for not backing him at Chequers, so did not consult the environment secretary about his intentions.

Late morning, Davis called Stewart Jackson from Silverstone: 'Go to London. I'll need to talk to you tonight with Raoul.' Davis asked for a 'briefing pack' with 'lines to take, questions and answers' on how he would handle media questions around a resignation. Jackson phoned Ruparel and they agreed to meet at the Carlton Club, the St James's bastion of high Toryism, that afternoon. Davis decided to give Johnson twelve hours' notice of his intention to resign at midnight. He was determined not to announce it in time to give the papers the chance to make mischief, knowing he would get a slot on the *Today* programme the next morning, where his decision could be 'set in the crystal that I wanted to set it in'. He also assumed that when he resigned, Johnson would do so too. 'If he didn't resign over this, his position in this great debate of the age would be subordinated – so I knew he would have to go.'

What followed remains contested. 'DD called him and said that he was going to resign, and he wanted Boris to resign with him,' a Johnson camp source said. 'He felt like it had more impact to go together and thought that would be the best plan.'

The Davis account is different. 'I won't recount the exact words because they would be very embarrassing to him,' Davis said later. 'But he wasn't enthusiastic about resigning.'[2] In one account of the call which reached Downing Street, Johnson expressed surprise that the Brexit secretary was planning to quit. 'Really, do you have to?' the foreign secretary said. 'Maybe I'll have to go too.' His recollection is that he spoke to Davis and suggested, 'Whatever we do, let's do it together.' Either way, Johnson phoned Cain and Frost around 5.30 p.m. to discuss whether to jump with Davis. 'I'm going to have to go. Is now the right time?' he asked. Both spads thought it ridiculous to resign late at night. 'You don't want to rush your resignation,' Cain said. 'That's the most important thing you can do; you need to set out properly why you're resigning.'

Around 4 p.m. Davis went to 9 Downing Street to see Julian Smith. The Brexit secretary was calm, his mind made up, resistant to the chief whip's charms and pleas. By the time Robbie Gibb got wind there was a problem and arrived in Downing Street it was nearer 5 p.m. He and Davis went back years. Gibb played out the same argument as Michael Gove was using. 'Let's just get Brexit done and worry about part two [the final trade deal] later,' he said. 'We've been forty-six years in this thing. We may not be able to get to exactly where you want to be in one move. Let's just get it done and then no one's going to bring us back.' Davis would not budge.

Smith and Gibb tried an audacious gambit, suggesting that Davis take Johnson's job as foreign secretary. Neither had consulted Theresa May about a move that could have torpedoed her government. 'The PM didn't know,' a source familiar with the conversations said. Davis said 'no'. Improvising, they suggested Johnson could move to the business department. 'You're wasting your time,' said Davis. 'I can't be bribed out of it.' A friend of the Brexit secretary was blunter: 'DD was definitely offered the foreign secretary job and then he turned it down, and then he was offered Andrea Leadsom's job.' Accepting defeat, Gibb persuaded Davis to go over the road for a pint at the Red Lion. It was in the street outside Westminster's best-known watering hole that Charlie Whelan, Gordon Brown's spin doctor, told Tony Blair that his government would not be joining the euro. Now it hosted an encounter between another director of communications and a cabinet minister quitting the government over a prime minister's determination to remain in close orbit with the EU.

At 7 p.m. Davis called Jackson and Ruparel, asking them to go to his friend Andrew Mitchell's in Islington. Mitchell was on characteristically waspish form. 'I knew Barwell when he made the tea in the local government department at Central Office,' he recalled. The four men ate Häagen Dazs ice cream and drank brandy in Mitchell's garden. Tim Smith was not told his boss's intentions because Davis did not want to compromise the young aide in the eyes of Downing Street.

All resignations are highly personal decisions. Davis could not look himself in the mirror and publicly defend the policy. But he later claimed his departure was a calculated attempt to change that policy without him being blamed for ousting the prime minister. He worked out this strategy in a 'think evil session', a technique for planning ahead and assessing what can go wrong, which he had learned in the army. 'I thought there would be an 80 per cent probability – maybe more – that if I went, she would go at some point; not immediately, but at some point,' Davis said. 'So, I thought, how do I deliver the outcome which is as clean as possible and doesn't become highly personalised.'[3] He believed that a leadership challenge, right then, was too unpredictable. 'To throw in a leadership bid at that time would have made it too complicated and make the odds of my preferred outcome possibly less. Imagine, for example, you have a leadership bid and she wins. She's reinforced her deal … The deal itself has to fail, which is what eventually happened.'[4]

Davis's refusal to attack May personally was loyal but, to many others, a bad use of his maximum moment of public power. It was hugely appreciated by Barwell, who said, 'You will not ever hear a word from me against DD. I think he behaved very honourably.'

Around 9.30 p.m. the Downing Street switchboard called Davis. 'The prime minister wants to talk to you.' He put the call on speakerphone. May made a half-hearted effort to get him to reconsider, telling him he was 'part of a historic mission to deliver Brexit', but those listening could tell her heart was not in it. 'It was like someone ringing to say your Hoover bag's ready for collection,' one said. 'It was quite funny in terms of her pathetic lack of humanity and ability to talk about anything.' To allies of Davis, who knew he could have declared the PM 'a broken reed' after the general election, this stuck in the craw. Davis was firm that his mind was made up. 'It was very underwhelming,' the witness said. 'It lasted about two minutes. He was a lot happier having done that.'

Another cabinet minister who was in 9 Downing Street that day remembered the bleak expression of Julian Smith when he put his head around the door to wish him goodnight: 'The chief whip looked the colour of wax.'

As May was talking to Davis, Johnson was talking to Conor Burns, who had been to Number 10's briefing for backbenchers. 'This is hot shit,' he said. 'They've agreed to full alignment on goods. You take back control, in a technical sense, with a promise never to use that control that you've taken back.' This was an effective summary of Eurosceptic concerns about Chequers and it helped to crystallise Johnson's unease.

'It's bollocks, isn't it?' the foreign secretary blurted. 'It's absolute bollocks.' To Burns, he seemed 'really disillusioned'. In that call they discussed resignation for the first time. 'Are you going to go?' the adviser asked. Johnson remained guarded: 'I'm thinking about it.' Burns took him through the implications of resigning and, more importantly, the implications of not doing so. 'When we sign up to a load of rubbish in November, whenever it is, you'll be completely tarnished by that,' he said. 'If you get out now you have the opportunity to resume the campaign for an optimistic, global, free-trading Brexit.'

For the second time in two years Johnson had to decide whether to defy his party leader on a matter of policy towards the EU. For the second time the decision involved risking his position but was laced with a subtext of reward, that to rebel might one day deliver him the party leadership. Johnson spoke to Will Walden, who had helped him through the 2016 decision. 'David's going to resign,' Johnson said. 'I think I've got to go.'

'What's stopping you?'

'How am I going to have any influence in this argument if I don't fight it from within?' There was more: the inconvenience of having to move house. Walden sensed the same hesitation as Johnson had shown in 2016, a reluctance to do the hard yards in the final quarter of the game.

'My understanding from talking to you for the last six months,' Walden said, 'is that you've been trying with May and she's not been listening for ages. You've got no option but to resign – and you might want to think about getting on with it. Davis is going to beat you out of the door.'

'I don't care.'

'You do, because you raised him resigning.'

When it dropped, Davis's resignation came like thunder from a sky which had appeared, to the outside world, to be clearing. His fifty hours of silence misled the media. 'The thing I most enjoyed about DD's resignation,' one of his aides recalled, 'was that the one time where the press weren't going, "DD's got to resign", DD actually resigned.'

Baker waited until Davis had put in his resignation letter and then did the same. If he'd gone first or waited a few hours, the sense of momentum building against May might have been more damaging. 'I don't actually want to bring down the government,' he told fellow MPs.

At 8.30 on Monday morning, Johnson met Cain and his policy adviser David Frost, at his official residence on Carlton House Terrace, along with Ben Gascoigne, his Sancho Panza from City Hall days. On one of the biggest days of his career, the foreign secretary answered the door in a T-shirt and shorts. All three aides had met earlier in a Pret a Manger and agreed among themselves that Johnson should resign. 'He didn't want to walk away,' a close ally said. 'He loved working in the Foreign Office. But I always got the sense that he knew that if he didn't move the dial at Chequers, he'd have to walk.'

The foreign secretary had already ducked one potential resignation, when the government backed a third runway at Heathrow airport, a policy he had vowed as mayor to stop by lying down in front of the bull-dozers. Johnson had arranged for a trip to Afghanistan so he could dodge the vote. 'He felt he couldn't walk out over Heathrow because Brexit was more important,' an aide recalled.

Just as in 2016 when Johnson backed Brexit his path to that decision was not smooth. His decision-making was reminiscent of a cow with seven stomachs that regurgitates as it chews the cud – the pros and cons on each side mulled over and revisited, his decision made and unmade. This process was dismissed by his critics and enemies as cynical political calculation, or indecision. Yet it had served Johnson well in 2016. As they assembled that morning, the foreign secretary's team knew he would follow his gut, but which of the seven would he follow?

Now that Davis had gone, Johnson's instinct was to resign, but he was riddled with doubt. 'Anyone who says these decisions about Brexit are simple is kidding themselves,' he told one friend. 'Everybody is to some extent ambivalent. Everybody is capable of slightly different views.'

Johnson stretched back on a sofa, Cain and Gascoigne opposite, Frost in a chair to his left. He asked them what he should do and how the various scenarios would play out. All three favoured resignation. The politics of the leadership were simple: 'If you back this deal, you lose all the Eurosceptics and the Remainers aren't going to turn around and say, "Oh isn't Boris great, he backed this."' Johnson was always keen, even with close allies, not to give the appearance that ambition was his only motivation. He said, 'This isn't really about politics, it's about what is best for the country.'

Frost, the most cautious, played devil's advocate, wondering if Johnson should delay his departure: 'You could hang on until the autumn. See what happens with the negotiations.' Cain, however, was adamant that he should go immediately, for his own self-preservation. Like Burns, the adviser thought Downing Street would bank Johnson's support, force him to publicly cheerlead for the deal and then abandon him. 'They'll hang it on you and then hang you out to dry,' he said. Cain told friends later it was 'fifty-fifty' whether Johnson would have walked without his intervention.

Johnson went for a shower. He seemed to have made his mind up, but he wanted time to think. The spads, by now, were fielding frantic calls from the Foreign Office. Johnson was due to chair a mini summit. 'Send Alan Duncan,' they said. Washed and dressed, Johnson returned to the sofa. 'Nothing has really changed my mind from where I was when I left Chequers, which is I don't think I can in good grace stay and defend this. I'm going to have to resign. But I want to do this properly …'

Around 10 a.m., Johnson rang Burns. The MP missed the call and when he phoned back he could hear Johnson typing: 'I presume that is your resignation letter.' By now the entire press pack was camped outside, the stutter of the Sky News helicopter audible overhead. Cain's phone was doing St Vitus' dance with calls from journalists. He answered none of them. Will Walden messaged Gascoigne and Frost to say, 'This looks horrendous on television. He's got to get on with it.' At 1.34 p.m., Johnson rang Burns to confirm that he was quitting but swore him to secrecy. 'I don't want to put it out until after the PM has addressed the Commons.' Johnson said he would release the news at 6 p.m.

He had already spoken to Julian Smith. The chief whip did not try to persuade him to stay and had no intention of allowing the timing to be dictated by Johnson. If May gave her statement to MPs and Johnson quit later, all the focus would be on him. If news of his resignation emerged while the PM was on her feet, the prime minister would be tethered prey at the despatch box. The chief wanted the deed done, so that May's statement would be seen as a moment where she steadied the ship.

Smith phoned Johnson and asked, 'When are you going to hand in the letter, Boris?' Johnson vacillated so Smith forced his hand, saying, 'Why don't you speak to the prime minister' and handing the phone to May. She was at her most Thatcherite. 'Are you resigning, Boris?'

Johnson said, 'The cabinet has to have a song to sing, but I won't be able to sing that song.' They spoke for twenty minutes, the prime minister making more effort than Smith to talk Johnson off the ledge: 'It's important you stay in the tent, I think this is the right path for Britain.'

Shortly after May had hung up, Downing Street issued a statement announcing that Johnson had quit. He was still writing his resignation letter. 'That was the intention,' said one of May's inner circle. Number 10 briefed that he had been dithering over whether to go. 'Total crap,' Johnson declared. 'Bollocks,' said a source in the room with him. 'He was very clear.' Cain gave his resignation letter to Laura Kuenssberg to break on the six o'clock news. Cain, Gascoigne, Frost, Johnson and his parliamentary assistant Alice Robinson then huddled round a laptop to watch it on iPlayer. Johnson opened a bottle of red and said, 'Oh well, that's that then.'

Why did he go? Undoubtedly there was calculation, but in the end, Johnson realised he was being asked to take ownership of a Brexit he did not support and, as the pivotal figure in the campaign, that was a position he could not tolerate. Team May saw it differently, of course, depicting him as a self-centred cynic. Barwell contrasted Davis's departure 'over a genuine difference that we respected' with Johnson 'thinking not about the country but about his own narrow position'.[5] Yet Johnson had been just as consistent as Davis in his opposition to close alignment. Refusing to factor in his views was a common myopia among Johnson's enemies. Even if you did not believe them, it made sense to assume he would act on the poses he struck. A Davis ally said, 'I think until quite late Boris didn't want to go, he wanted to remain in the cabinet, he wanted to have influence. But I think history will recall that it was the best thing he ever did.'

In 2020, Johnson would text Davis and acknowledge the Brexit secretary's resignation had made his own possible. Davis confirmed, 'To quote Boris Johnson, if I had not resigned, neither would he. His words to me – and he's right.'[6] Evidence of self-serving ambition? Perhaps, but it would have been very odd if Davis's decision had not been a factor in his own. Johnson's aides dispute that his departure was about the leadership. One said, 'He gets an awful lot of stick for his personal ambitions, but on this issue, hand on heart, to me he acted on a point of principle. His instinct is always delay making a big decision until you absolutely have to, without having the pain. I think he was loath to make such a bold stand, but he eventually realised there was no other way.' A cabinet minister said that whatever Johnson's true beliefs, 'he invested himself in Brexit and had to deliver it'.

This is the key point. Yes, he was equivocal about Brexit before the referendum and he may well not have expected to win, but only stupid or ideologically fossilised politicians exist in a world of certainty. Yes, his embrace of a buccaneering self-confident post-Brexit Britain was not matched by an understanding of how that might realistically be achieved. But, having been front and centre of the campaign, Johnson knew that he owned the referendum result. Delivering on its promise was not just a responsibility he felt keenly, it was also, for him, a political necessity. Like the errant shopper told 'You broke it, so you own it', Johnson owned Brexit and he did not want to own the version of it fashioned by May. Burns said, 'Brexit wouldn't have happened without him, if we'd had a

"Faragist" dominated Leave campaign. It was Boris's charisma, character, personality, celebrity, that gave Leave a hearing for a lot of people. So, he has always felt a sense of moral ownership of the result and it was just gnawing at him that that which he created was just being so diluted.'

To Johnson it was May who had broken faith with her public vows, not him. He concluded that she had deliberately misled the Brexiteers since the Joint Report. 'I think the whole thing was a plot,' he said. 'Having failed to get a majority, Theresa basically became the tool of the establishment, and decided that there was not a majority in the House of Commons for a decisive and clean Brexit, and that her best bet was to shaft the Brexiteers. I think they decided to use the Northern Ireland border issue as the mechanism to trap the whole of the UK in the customs union and the single market and thereby to answer the Treasury's demand for frictionless trade at Dover. All those humdrum questions of Brexit should have been solved with despatch and energy and belief and enthusiasm. They failed to address them for two years and then she folded.'

Together, the twin resignations were May's moment of maximum peril since the 2017 election. Nigel Mills, the Brexiteer MP for Amber Valley, put it best on the ERG WhatsApp group: 'The glittery turd is hitting the fan now.'

Others decided to stay. Chris Grayling had known Theresa May for twenty-five years. He had helped install her as leader. He did not feel he could abandon her now. Penny Mordaunt and Esther McVey were described by government aides as on resignation 'suicide watch' but neither jumped. Mordaunt believed there was a strategy to peel off the Brexiteers and that some needed to stay at the cabinet table. Andrea Leadsom wrote in her memoir, 'I felt a duty, ever since my decision to drop out of the leadership race back in 2016, to support Theresa to remain prime minister so long as she was committed to delivering Brexit.'[7] She saw the resignations of Davis, Johnson and Baker as 'the moment when the desire of some Brexiteers to see Brexit done became an ambition to destabilise the government to get rid of Theresa and do it themselves'.[8]

When they were in government Downing Street had taken very different approaches with Davis and Johnson, the one slathered in praise, hugged close; the other briefed against, assumed to be hostile, pushed away until this became a self-fulfilling prophecy. 'They always kicked

Boris about,' an ally said. 'They always briefed against him. There was a general feeling that he was a busted flush. Strategically, it was a mistake not to bring him in and try to utilise his skills.' After their resignations, Davis was allowed to keep his grand ministerial office. Johnson's staff were told he would have to share a room with Andrew Percy, the Canada trade envoy. Eventually he was given space of his own in One Parliament Street, the decaying and unfashionable building that abuts Portcullis House.

Johnson's public image was of a bold, self-confident character. The day after he quit, some in his team claim he was 'entirely liberated' and 'full of beans'. But on the evening of the day he resigned and again in the weeks ahead, he suffered episodes of profound self-doubt. One who saw him that night said, 'He was miserable as hell.' Another said he endured a 'black dog' depression, 'sitting around in his pants wondering if he's done the right thing'.

Johnson had other worries too. No one had noticed two removal vans leaving Carlton House Terrace after he resigned, turning in opposite directions, carrying his and his wife Marina's belongings to different locations. Unknown to most of Westminster, his marriage was effectively over and divorce proceedings loomed. 'Money is a big issue,' one ally said that week. Johnson quickly signed on the dotted line to revive his column in the *Daily Telegraph*, a contract worth £275,000 a year.

Many in Number 10 were glad to see the back of him. 'He became a focus for opposition to rally round,' one of May's senior advisers said. 'On the upside, he was a bad foreign secretary, who was daily doing damage to Britain's image around the world. He was a deeply unconstructive force in cabinet, and without him you could actually make some progress.'

Theresa May appointed Dominic Raab, the housing minister, as the new Brexit secretary. A former lawyer at the Foreign Office, Raab had entered politics in 2006 as chief of staff in David Davis's parliamentary office. A grammar schoolboy whose father, a refugee from Czechoslovakia, died when he was twelve, Raab was, like many politicians who lose a parent young, a driven man. He was a keen boxer with a command of detail and confidence in his own beliefs, yet some found his focus, and his tendency to hold their gaze longer than necessary, disconcerting. His knowledge of European law, his precision and his uncompromising approach made him, in the eyes of many, a more suitable secretary of state than Davis. He would prove to be a thorn in May's side. But the prime minister needed a convinced Leaver to do the job and Raab was widely seen as the most able minister outside the cabinet. 'We needed to get a decent Brexiteer,' a Number 10 political adviser said. 'Raab, unlike some Brexiteers, was able to sound plausible on media and had been support-ive throughout.'

The price of accepting the job was that he agreed to the Chequers deal as the basis for negotiations with the EU. Raab thought the proposals were at the outer reaches of compatibility with the Tory election mani-festo and that May's early vision at Lancaster House had been 'whittled away', but he believed Brexiteers had a duty to 'step up to the plate' when asked. Robbie Gibb, Julian Smith and Michael Gove all called to encour-age him to take the job. Raab told friends there was 'still enough of Brexit worth fighting for'. Davis told him to do his best to improve May's plan. Like Liam Fox, Raab thought the EU would ultimately reject Chequers, forcing May to pivot to a Canada-plus trade deal position to get a deal through Parliament. He resolved to encourage her in that direction.

There was never warmth between Raab and May's team. 'We didn't have much to do with him,' a May aide recalled. 'There was a certain oddness about him.' They clipped his wings too. That afternoon, Stewart Jackson was drinking in the sunshine outside the Red Lion with Raoul Ruparel and Tim Smith when he was summoned back over the road to DExEU. On Davis's recommendation, Raab asked him to continue as chief of staff. Later, around 4 p.m., Raab texted, 'I'm picking up some static from Number 10.' May's aides wanted to see the back of Jackson, who they blamed for negative media briefings.

To replace Boris Johnson, May turned to Jeremy Hunt, who was keen to move from health, having helped to deliver the NHS funding settle-ment. That did not alter the balance at the top of the cabinet as much as some Brexiteers feared. Hunt had voted to Remain and made comments about a second referendum soon after the first one. But he was now firmly convinced the government needed to deliver on the Leave result or fall, a position stiffened by his ambition to run for the leadership one day. Matt Hancock, the culture secretary, replaced him at health.

* * *

That afternoon May faced the 1922 Committee of Conservative back-benchers to try to sell the Chequers plan. Julian Smith packed the room with loyalists, whose interventions seemed to Johnson's allies to be 'choreographed' to minimise the impact of his resignation. A Brexiteer compared them to 'Soviet meerkats' bobbing up and down. Patrick McLoughlin, the former party chairman, 'told everyone what the period 1992 to 1997 looked like' – the last time divisions over Europe had rendered the Tory party unelectable.

The star turn, though, was Geoffrey Cox, an MP and QC better known for his advocacy at the bar than in the Commons, who had previously only come to the attention of the media when he topped the list of MPs with the highest earnings outside Parliament. Not everyone who listened to his rich baritone had heard him speak before. It was not long, though, before they were listening intently. As if summing up a difficult case, Cox argued that the deal was far from perfect, but as Brexiteers they should accept it as 'the only safe way' to leave the EU. Cox was concerned by the apparent permanence of the backstop. The continuing functions of the European Court of Justice he found 'difficult to swallow'. But his fear was that failure to agree a withdrawal agreement would give time, space and momentum to those MPs who wanted to stop Brexit altogether. In those circumstances, he warned, the '22 would find themselves in the midst of 'a major constitutional crisis' in which the Conservative Party would be 'faced with extinction'.

When he spoke, Cox had no idea about the kernel of an idea forming in Julian Smith's head. Steve Baker insists it was him who had planted it there: 'Geoffrey Cox really ought to be attorney general.' Smith asked Cox to speak to the media after the meeting. The government had found a charismatic advocate for an already embattled position and the resig-nations had afforded May the chance for a small reshuffle. 'We need people who can sell,' Smith said. Cox was in court when Smith rang a little later, asking questions about his views and whether he had any embarrassing skeletons in his closet. He confessed that his only vices were good claret and smoking cigars like a chimney while the jury was out, a habit he had now shaken. In his thirteen years in Parliament it was the first time he had ever been sounded out about a ministerial position. Sensing that he held the cards, Cox played hardball. When he saw Smith in person at 6 p.m. he made clear he would only accept one job and the cabinet rank that came with it: 'I don't want to embarrass the prime minister, really the only role where I can see myself being useful to her and to the government is attorney.' He had decided that if he was offered the more junior post of solicitor general he would turn it down. Cox was at dinner with his wife, Jeanie, when the phone went again at 8.45 p.m. inviting him to see May.

Cox had backed Brexit because he believed Britain's democracy was being stifled by the EU's lack of accountability, that the 'restlessness of the human spirit' needed democratic elections as a 'safety valve' through which people could 'express their right to see fundamental change'. He saw in the EU a distant overlord with no democratic legitimacy whose elites did not really believe in popular democracy. To him, the referendum result was 'an inchoate, profound cry from the volcanic depths of our country', to persuade politicians that 'fundamental change was necessary', a 'geyser bursting from the depths of the earth' to politicians to devise 'imaginative' ways of responding.

Cox had read the draft agreement but in agreeing to do the job, his main priority was to get the prime minister to agree a different structure for decision-making on Brexit. He told May that, under the ministerial code, 'The attorney general must be consulted on any and all matters involving our international legal obligations.' Jeremy Wright, the outgoing attorney general, had played no role in the Brexit policy process. Cox regarded this as 'a mistake' and demanded to be consulted on proposals being made by Oliver Robbins and the Europe Unit – 'and in good time, before steps are taken in the negotiation that might contract international legal obligations'. May agreed he would be involved.

Of all the things that happened in that frantic two days, Davis's resignation had the biggest immediate impact. Johnson's resignation would have the greatest long-term significance. But it was the appointment of Cox that did most to determine Theresa May's fate.

No sooner had the PM seen the back of one populist, pro-Brexit big beast, in the form of Johnson, than she was compelled to welcome another – in the person of Donald Trump. The US president arrived just three days later, on Thursday 12 July. The visit of an American president was usually a career highlight for Downing Street staff, however with Trump it was an ordeal to be endured. He and May could not have been more different and aides who listened to their calls cringed at the staid prime minister trying in vain to work through her talking points in the face of a blizzard of free-wheeling from the president, which veered from his British golf course to his love of Ireland and whatever else entered his head. As one source put it, 'She has no small talk; all he has is small talk.' A British diplomat who watched them together said, 'She works methodically, maybe a bit laboriously through her speaking points. His conversation goes off in all sorts of directions like a roman candle. You never know where he's going to go next. She finds that disconcerting.' May did learn that to make progress with Trump you had to compliment him and her briefers armed her with bullet-point guides of 'six nice things you can say to him'. The diplomat said, 'He will say something expecting something back about how great he is. It's like watching a couple of gorillas groom each other. He leads the conversation and she basically flings compliments back.'

Most acutely, Trump, a fan of Brexit, which he saw as a harbinger of his own election triumph in 2016, bullied May over her failure to get tough with Brussels, starting calls with the taunt, 'Are you out yet?' A bruising business negotiator, he advised May to veto new Commission rules and ignore those the UK disliked. This approach was anathema to a process-driven politician like May.

However, private comments made by Boris Johnson had leaked in which the then foreign secretary admitted to being 'increasingly admiring' of the 'method in his madness', adding, 'Imagine Trump doing Brexit. He'd go in bloody hard. There'd be all sorts of chaos, everyone would think he'd gone mad. But actually you might get somewhere.' Anyone reading that eighteen months later might be forgiven for thinking that Johnson was describing his own handling of Brexit.

To pile on the pressure, Trump's new national security adviser, John Bolton, met at the end of June with members of the ERG, including Iain Duncan Smith, an old friend, to discuss the prospects of an Anglo-American trade deal. Getting such a deal was seen by the Paleosceptics as a litmus test of May's seriousness about Brexit. But it split the cabinet. Michael Gove, the environment secretary, was fiercely opposed to anything that lowered food standards, while Liam Fox, the trade secretary, was open to America winning market access for its chlorine-washed chicken and hormone-injected beef, likely to be key asks from the US agricultural sector.

In the small window between Chequers and Trump's arrival, a sixty-strong delegation of US trade experts flew to the UK and met civil servants in Fox's department to understand the implications of May's approach to the EU. Officials sought to reassure the Americans that they could still do a deal on tariffs, quotas and geographic indicators (meaning the UK could import feta cheese from Wisconsin, not just from Greece as under EU rules). But one of those involved in the talks admitted the common rulebook 'made us look less attractive'.

Word of all this reached Trump. On the Thursday he was guest of honour at a dinner at Blenheim Palace, the birthplace of Winston Churchill, whose chair Trump proudly tweeted he had sat in. For once, he and May became immersed in conversation as they tucked into their Hereford beef fillet. Unknown to the prime minister as she sat down at 7 p.m., her spokesman James Slack had taken a call from Tom Newton-Dunn, the political editor of the *Sun*, who had interviewed Trump the day before as he attended a Nato summit. The president had been explosively undiplomatic. Slack decided to let May enjoy her meal, not wanting to sour her conversation with Trump, whose words were soon online under the headline, 'May has wrecked Brexit ... US deal is off'. Trump rubbished the Chequers plan, saying, 'If they do a deal like that, we would be dealing with the European Union instead of dealing with the UK, so it will probably kill the deal' and 'definitely affect trade with the United States, unfortunately in a negative way'.[9]

If that was unhelpful, Trump's views on May and Boris Johnson were incendiary. He complained of the prime minister, 'I would have done it much differently. I actually told Theresa May how to do it but ... she didn't listen to me', with 'very unfortunate' results. Trump then declared he was 'very saddened' that Johnson had resigned. 'I like him a lot. I have a lot of respect for Boris ... I think he would be a great prime minister. I think he's got what it takes.'[10] The interview – unprecedented in a century of meetings between British and American leaders – was a humiliation for May. Slack, sensibly, played it cool, agreeing with his opposite number in the White House, Sarah Huckabee Sanders, that they absorb the hits, then meet in the morning to repair the damage.

The following day at Sandhurst, home of Britain's royal military academy, Trump lamely claimed the story was 'fake news'. 'I said a lot of nice things about you, Theresa. We've got the tape.' The *Sun* soon put the recording online to show they had quoted the president accurately. (The paper's website also carried pictures of a grinning president holding an England football shirt. Trump might have been less enthusiastic if he'd known the shirt had previously been the property of the picture editor's dog. 'It was washed,' a source explained.)

May and Trump were at Sandhurst because John Bercow, the speaker of the House of Commons, had rejected a plan for Trump to address Parliament, as his predecessor Barack Obama had done. Deploying a trademark combination of activism and pomposity, Bercow declared it was 'an earned honour – and my view is that he has not earned that honour'.

It was the SAS who saved the day. Bursts of automatic gunfire and the sight of black-clad special forces descending from a helicopter to take out a nest of terrorists is not usually a sign of success during a visit by foreign dignitaries, but it was the moment Trump's trip was saved. The president watched enraptured a mock raid on a terrorist camp. 'It had dogs, it had explosions, it had helicopters. It was brilliant,' a Downing Street official said. 'He loved the dogs that take down the terrorists.' In the margins, May had a chance to explain that trade deals were still possible under the Chequers plan.

At the press conference, held at Chequers, Trump was on his best behaviour, praising May as an 'incredible woman' he had got to know 'much better', pledging to 'double, triple, quadruple' trade and declaring their relationship 'the highest level of special'. But even Trump at his most diplomatic could not resist repeating his view that Johnson would 'be a great prime minister', on the grounds that 'he thinks I'm doing a great job ... I *am* doing a great job.' A British spin doctor recalled, 'We were white, hanging on to the chair waiting for it to finish.'

It was left to May to supply the surreal coda. In an interview with Andrew Marr that weekend, she was asked what advice Trump had given her about Brexit. 'He told me I should sue the EU,' she revealed.

In Downing Street, James Johnson's polling showed the damage the week had done. His first survey on Saturday, the day after the Chequers meeting, the reaction from the public was 'very positive'. The effect of Davis and Johnson's departures had an immediate and devastating effect on opinions among Leave voters. Johnson's second poll, on the Tuesday, saw opinion settle where it was to remain, implacably against the deal. 'The moment that DD and Boris's resignations hit the news, people thought "The Brexiteers don't like it and I probably shouldn't like it because I am a Brexiteer too",' Johnson said.

Two weeks after Chequers, Johnson presented the findings to a meeting of the political cabinet. 'There was net support for every aspect of the

Chequers agreement, including with Leave voters,' he said. The only exception to this was that Leave voters didn't like the scale of the divorce bill. Then Johnson presented data from voters who had switched from Tory to Labour. 'The reason was not because of Chequers it was because of division in the Conservative Party,' he recalled. 'The Boris and DD resignations harmed the Tory brand. People were not going off the Tories because of the Chequers plan, they were going off the Tories because it was a shitshow.'

The numbers suggested that if Number 10 could focus on the plan and sell it hard to the public they could ride out the opposition from their own ranks. An equally valid conclusion from the data might have been that the Conservatives were finished unless they could find a Brexit plan the vast majority of their own MPs could support. The policy had caused the shitshow and now the shitshow was killing public support for the policy.

Later, key players in the Brexit process pointed to July 2018 as the pivotal moment. For the first time Theresa May had written down what Brexit she wanted. In so doing she provided a target for everyone else to aim at. 'There was one absolutely pivotal moment where everything changed and that was the Chequers deal,' Labour's Peter Kyle said later. 'It was like a meteor coming out of the sky, obliterating the political landscape. They had got through each week by telling different people slightly different things. Nothing had ever been committed in writing. Brexit was finally defined in writing – and everyone hated it. It was suddenly possible that you'd remain in the EU. It was suddenly possible that Boris Johnson would be prime minister. It was not inconceivable that Jeremy Corbyn could be prime minister. One or both parties could just fall apart and split. These really outlandish political settlements suddenly had a credible pathway.'

The cabinet resignations gave Tory grassroots members and the Brexit-backing newspapers, particularly the *Telegraph*, the cover to oppose a government they ostensibly supported. David Gauke concluded, 'I think there's quite a strong argument to say Theresa was doomed from that point.' For Gavin Barwell and Robbie Gibb, the departure of Davis, in particular, was the moment things began to fall apart. 'His resignation opened up a new flank in the Brexit battle,' Gibb wrote later. 'Until that point, the Government had been defending itself against Remainers … From the Chequers' resignations onwards, it was Brexiteers … Fighting this second flank was to stretch our forces and would, eventually, over-whelm us.'[11] Barwell said, 'We couldn't win a war on two fronts.'

Given Davis's importance, even members of Robbins' team thought keeping him on board should have been a primary goal for Downing Street, rather than a sideshow. 'They needed a Brexiteer who could sell what they were doing,' a senior official said. 'It was a mistake from them not to fight harder.' The way to do so, the civil servant argued, was to press for a more ambitious plan for the future relationship. 'DD could have blown away the withdrawal agreement if they had come to a different track on the future relationship.'

By the start of September, May was facing a hydra-headed political crisis that pitted Downing Street against the ERG rebels, the prime minister's 2017 campaign director, plus Tory donors and campaigners intent on destroying the central policy of her government and then her.

PART THREE

FOUND OUT

NEGOTIATING WITH BRUSSELS

July to November 2018

'The worst of doing one's duty was that it
apparently unfitted one for doing anything else'

– Edith Wharton

'They were in with loads of opt-outs
and now want out with loads of opt-ins'

*– Xavier Bettel, prime minister of Luxembourg,
March 2018*

'What she wants is the softest possible hard Brexit'

*– Alexandre Fasel, Swiss ambassador to the UK,
to the author, 2018*

'CHUCK CHEQUERS!'

July to November 2018

The steering group of the ERG held its first weekly meeting with David Davis present on the Monday after Chequers in the office of Iain Duncan Smith, the former party leader and arch-Paleosceptic. The officers of the ERG – Jacob Rees-Mogg, Steve Baker, Mark Francois, Priti Patel, Anne-Marie Trevelyan, Craig Mackinlay, Charlie Elphicke and John Penrose – met every week in the palatial wood-panelled room on the upper committee corridor. Davis explained how May had authorised a parallel policy over the summer without oversight from the Brexiteers. 'He was clearly very angry and we were wondering, what next?' an MP said.

Then Bernard Jenkin noticed a news alert on his phone. 'Boris has just resigned!' he announced. Duncan Smith leaped from his seat and cheered, arms pumping like a football fan whose team has scored. 'Now we're moving!' he exclaimed. The meeting broke up. As they left, Norman Lamont, the former chancellor, turned to Jenkin and said, 'Boris Johnson is going to be the next prime minister.'

The fight to fulfil that prediction began with a battle to defeat the Chequers plan. Over the weekend, it was reported that ten MPs were ready to submit a letter to the chairman of the 1922 Committee, Sir Graham Brady, demanding a vote of no confidence in Theresa May's leadership. Forty-eight would be needed to trigger a contest. Andrea Jenkyns, who had resigned from the government in May 2018 to fight for a hard Brexit, said, 'If the detail is as bad as we're hearing, then I'm prepared to put a letter in.' MPs phoned Jacob Rees-Mogg, urging him to run for the leadership, but the ERG grandees were not yet ready to call for May's head. 'Jacob's not a man for close bayonet work,' an MP remarked. His hopes rested with the return of Steve Baker: 'In putting Jacob and Steve together they have made a perfect killing machine.'

Baker looked like an accountant, but his born-again Christianity lent his Euroscepticism a proselytising intensity. To his enemies, he was a seventeenth-century figure; as one MP put it, 'He would have apologised before he burned you at the stake.' But Baker was also a backbench organiser of genius, who maintained email, phone and WhatsApp lists of Eurosceptics to instruct his tribe when to defy the government. Under David Cameron and Theresa May, he led Conservatives for Britain and the ERG with cordial fury, delivering a series of Commons defeats. In person he was courteous to colleagues and deferential towards the Maastricht generation. Politically, he was a choirboy with a sideline in serial killing. He now began what he recorded in his diary as a period of 'the most intense political activity'. Like a twenty-something hacker, Baker sat at home, flip flops on his feet, staring at two computer screens, orchestrating chaos. He privately vowed to cause the government 'the maximum amount of pain' to force a rethink.

Baker was convinced May would never get the plan through the Commons. He had drawn up a histogram of Conservative MPs, assigning them a number based on their Brexit views. The 'agnostic centre' of the party were given zero, the most Eurosceptic a five and the most pro-Remain MPs minus five. On this scale Mark Francois and John Redwood scored plus five, Anna Soubry and Antoinette Sandbach, minus five. George Freeman, a vocal Remainer, was minus three, while Robert Buckland was minus two, because 'you can work with him'. This exercise made clear that the centre of gravity of the party was miles from May's conception of Brexit. It was equally clear to Baker that the Tory right would not be able to change the policy or oust May unless the agnostic zeroes accepted the impossibility of getting Chequers through.

This view was shared by a group of young Eurosceptic MPs who were first elected in 2017. On the Monday after Chequers they met in the office of Lee Rowley, the MP for North East Derbyshire. The group included Ben Bradley, Simon Clarke, Robert Courts, Marcus Fysh, Andrew Lewer and Julia Lopez. 'There was a feeling that May could be finished within a fortnight,' one attendee recalled. 'That was our naivety as an intake. We thought: surely it's obvious she's over.'

Two more Brexiteers – Bradley and his fellow vice chairman Maria Caulfield – resigned on the Tuesday after Chequers, egged on by Baker.

Five days later it was the turn of Courts, who replaced David Cameron as MP for Witney. Baker helped him write the tweet in which he quit as a parliamentary private secretary to Foreign Office ministers. Courts wrote, 'I had to think who I wanted to see in the mirror for the rest of my life.' Baker sent the message to MPs on his lists, urging them to retweet it and provide supportive commentary – and to journalists, ensuring the departure of a minor member of the government was magnified into a news event on a quiet Sunday.

Lopez, who won Hornchurch and Upminster, came at Brexit with fresh eyes and from first principles. She considered herself a floating voter during the referendum who only decided to vote Leave in the final fortnight. Cameron's renegotiation convinced her the EU was an institution unwilling to change. Now the EU had rejected the 'half-in half-out' proposals from Britain since the referendum. Britain would have to 'sign up to their rules and regulations but not be a voting member. For me that was fundamentally incompatible with the whole idea of Brexit.' She shared Bradley and Courts' fury at the Chequers plan. 'The contempt it showed to the electorate was just staggering,' she said, 'pretending to deliver Brexit but essentially keeping us to EU rules and laws while conceding more sovereignty than if we'd stayed. I was disgusted and for the first time completely ashamed to be a Conservative. I knew in my heart that it was not only wrong but risked profound consequences for faith in our democracy. This was about one group with a mandate from the largest democratic exercise in our nation's history and an elite trying to stop their will being enacted.'

On the Tuesday after Chequers, Simon Clarke and Colin Clark hosted the first of several 'Clarke and Clark' parties at their shared flat in Marsham Street, where the main subject of discussion was whether to submit letters of no confidence in May. Clarke led the way in drumming up volunteers, though he was later pressured by the whips into publicly withdrawing his own letter. Rowley and Lopez were convinced 'this is bust'. But one MP said, 'Others were in a state of mass denial, able to convince themselves that Chequers was acceptable or broadly deliverable or that actually we just needed to get out and could tie up the details later.'

Later that week, at the request of the ERG's steering group, Baker's strategic planning was supplemented by the creation, in secret, of a team of whips under the command of Mark Francois, with the express goal 'to organise colleagues to vote down the deal'. Francois said, 'We tried jaw-jaw. That failed. So now it's war-war.' The ERG was operating, formally, as a party within a party.

A pint-sized political pugilist, Francois was seen by many MPs as a blunt political instrument who led with his chin and never whispered his views when a loud-hailer was within reach. Shadow Europe minister under David Cameron in opposition, he had experienced his political 'epiphany', like Baker, with the Lisbon treaty. 'We had fourteen nights debating it, night after night and we couldn't change a bloody semicolon,' he fulminated to colleagues. He thought afterwards: *We have to get out of this. We don't run our own country.* When he read the withdrawal agreement, Francois concluded, 'If we sign this we haven't left. Once you sign this, you can't get out, we're fucked forever.' His often emotional broadcast appearances led to him being pigeonholed as the comic relief of the operation. One Downing Street aide fulminated: 'Not having a majority gave rebellious people on both sides of the argument a disproportionate amount of political influence. Mark Francois suddenly became a massively important player, when he shouldn't have been.'

Yet despite his bovine reputation, perhaps to a degree because of it, Francois was to create an operation of subtlety which was successful precisely because it operated under the radar. His intelligence about the voting intentions of MPs proved more accurate than Julian Smith's official whipping operation and was vital in reinforcing the ERG belief that, if they held firm, they could defeat May's deal. 'Mark was very important,' another ERG figure recalled. In David Jones, Laurence Robertson and Charlie Elphicke, he had whips' office veterans. The ERG officers vowed not to use strongarm tactics on their own kind. Baker told colleagues with a smile, 'The ERG does not "whip" colleagues. We merely extend the hand of friendship and support in a systematic way.' Francois was adamant, too, that they not be called whips. Thus, were born 'the Buddies'. The team also included Baker, Simon Clarke, Michael Tomlinson, Anne-Marie Trevelyan and Theresa Villiers. Two others asked Francois not to identify them, even after the event. One said, 'It was a marvellous little quiet team of networkers. It was very effective by virtue of total silence.' While the whips' office was criticised for its aloofness, the Buddies put time and effort into stiffening the resolve of their band of brothers. 'We talked to people day in and day out and listened to them,' one of the Buddies said. 'We heard what they were saying so we were able to help them get over misconceptions and talk to experts and other colleagues to help ease anxieties.'

The first test of the ERG's strength came on 16 July, ten days after the Chequers meeting. The group tabled four amendments to the customs bill. One, designed to undermine May's new Facilitated Customs Arrangement (FCA) plan, forbade the government to collect tariffs for the EU unless Brussels did so for the UK in return. A second amendment ruled out a border in the Irish Sea – intended to prevent the EU's version of the backstop from being agreed. Word circulated that up to 40 rebels were prepared to defy the government. Baker was surprised that Downing Street's expectation management was so poor. The Buddies had 78 rebels lined up.

May's team held crisis talks. It was the prime minister who conjured the solution. She read the amendments very closely. While they were clearly designed to derail Chequers, the precise wording was more limited. Passing a law to ban tariff collection for the EU, unless they reciprocated, was a nuisance measure that might even strengthen her hand in Brussels. The others closed off scenarios that May did not wish to see unfold. She decided to accept the amendments. 'It looked as if we were going to get shot to pieces,' a senior ally said. 'She looked at those ERG amendments, she saw they weren't terminal, she went for them.'

All hell broke loose. Dominic Grieve described the new clauses as 'entirely malevolent' and his group of twelve Bresisters voted against. Disgusted with what he saw as May's capitulation to the ERG, the fiercely pro-Remain Guto Bebb marched to the division lobby, told the whip at the door that he was resigning as minister for defence procurement and joined the rebels in the No lobby. On two of the votes the government scraped home by just three votes.

Bebb sat down with Phillip Lee afterwards to bemoan May's willing-ness to do the ERG's bidding. Both had been old-style Eurosceptics, members of Business for Sterling; now they believed there should be a second referendum. They concluded that MPs on their side needed to get organised. Lee said, 'We realised that there was no coordination and coherence and that we were going to lose unless we became much more organised and much more ruthless in our opposition, and in our campaign to get to a second referendum.' They estimated they could get between thirty and forty Tory backers for it, which might be enough for a cross-party coalition to triumph.

Brexiteers sought to persuade Boris Johnson to use his resignation statement in the Commons on 18 July to 'do a Geoffrey Howe', attacking May to trigger an avalanche of no-confidence letters as Howe had against Margaret Thatcher twenty-eight years earlier. Instead, Johnson made the argument most likely to endear him to fellow Brexiteers – that May's 'vision' in her Lancaster House speech had been undermined by 'a fog of self-doubt' and 'eighteen months of stealthy retreat'. He said, 'We never made it into a negotiating offer. Instead, we dithered. We burned through our negotiating capital. We agreed to hand over a £40 billion exit fee with no discussion of our future economic relationship, we accepted the jurisdiction of the European Court over key aspects of the withdrawal agreement and, worst of all, we allowed the question of the Northern Irish border ... to become so politically charged as to dominate the debate.' The prospect of 'technical solutions', to avoid a hard border, 'became taboo' and 'were never even properly examined', he said.

By Johnson's standards, it was low-key. There were occasional flour-ishes ('volunteering for economic vassalage', and a 'fantastical Heath Robinson customs arrangement') but only at the end did he make his pitch, projecting himself as the optimist: 'It is not too late to save Brexit.' Ministers should spend the next two years making technical preparations in Ireland, 'accelerate' no-deal planning and escape the 'miserable permanent limbo of Chequers' to seize the 'glorious vision of Lancaster House'. He concluded, 'We need to take one decision now before all others, and that is to believe in this country and in what it can do.'

To his critics, this was classic Boris boosterism substituting exhorta-tion for explanation. But for many Brexiteers it was catnip. Johnson had not plunged the knife, he had not triggered a leadership contest, he had not raised his standard. But from that point forward his flagpole was clearly positioned. He remained a divisive figure among MPs, but he had articulated a clear alternative to May's plan and made himself the most likely successor to implement it.

When he spoke, a couple of hours later, Baker delivered a clear warn-ing to May and Robbins: 'The establishment believes that any deal will be voted through by this House and is working on that basis ... I do not believe for a moment that it is true. It will fail.' The two speeches failed to electrify Westminster. Yet the fact that they were made at all was a dark omen for May. The man who did most to popularise Brexit and the MP who had most effectively marshalled the forces of Leave in Parliament were now both free to operate against her.

When the Brexit Steering Group met on Monday 23 July, Baker came with a plan, which he called 'controlled chaos'. As he had when forcing David Cameron to change the referendum question from 'yes-no' to 'remain-leave', the wannabe guerrilla commander turned for inspiration to a book entitled *The Thirty-Three Strategies of War* by Robert Greene. In controlled-chaos strategy, Greene explains, a commander should: 'Decentralise your army, segment into teams, and let go a little to gain mobility. Give your different corps clear missions that fit your strategic goals, then let them accomplish them as they see fit.' Baker put the theory into practice at a meeting of the 'outreach group', a collection of pro-Brexit groups outside Parliament who exchanged information in another of his WhatsApp groups. He outlined how they should try to support each other. 'I call it shoaling,' he said. 'Everybody needs to watch everybody else and see the direction of travel. You're not under my command but when we say things you need to move with us.'

Baker told the steering group that if the ERG's opposition to May's plan was to be taken seriously, they would have to come up with a 'credible' plan of their own to ensure there was no hard border in Northern Ireland, one which worked within the framework of EU law, 'so we can't be accused of going for magic technology or unicorns'. Baker, Duncan Smith, Owen Paterson and Peter Lilley worked on the plans through the summer, with Shanker Singham and Hans Maessen, two trade experts. Baker also suggested Brexiteers start talking about 'exit without a withdrawal agreement' rather than 'no deal', a euphemism which never caught on.

The following evening, 24 July, Rees-Mogg hosted a dinner at his home in Westminster. The guests included Baker, Priti Patel, Maria Caulfield, who had just resigned as a Tory vice chairman, Charlie Elphicke, Mark Francois and Boris Johnson. Over dinner, those who were there say, Johnson devised the slogan 'Chuck Chequers', which was to become the rallying cry and social media hashtag for those opposed to May's deal. Baker had voted for Andrea Leadsom in the 2016 leadership election but her failure to resign over Chequers was a 'deal breaker' for him. As the evening went on, he concluded, 'What we all really want is for Boris to be prime minister and do this job properly.' He said, 'At that dinner with Jacob I saw a new sincerity and authenticity in Boris which I had not seen before – a genuine belief in what we were doing and a genuine willingness to commit. It was a turning point moment for me.'

The new pact was sealed four days later, 28 July, when Baker spent thirty minutes on the phone talking Johnson through the plans for 'shoaling' against Chequers. He wanted reassurance on one point, that if they succeeded, Johnson was prepared to back a no-deal Brexit. Johnson said he was. Baker recalled, 'My direct one-to-one experience of Boris is that he always understood we had to leave the European Union well.'

Rees-Mogg and Baker spoke on 30 July. Both were publicly committed to changing the government's policy, not its leader. But that day Baker said, 'She's not going to chuck Chequers. We can keep asking her to do it, but she won't. The only way to solve this is to create circumstances in which we can change the prime minister.' Rees-Mogg agreed. 'I came to the conclusion, personally, that Boris Johnson was the right answer immediately after he resigned from the cabinet,' he said later. 'There was a lot of chatter about me thinking of standing. It was great fun and I enjoyed it, but I never had an intention of doing it.' By September, they had been joined by Bernard Jenkin, not usually a plotter, who sent a memo to key ERG MPs concluding that May had 'made the Chequers policy inseparable from her continuation in office' and that Tory MPs 'have a duty to choose a new leader and prime minister'.

One of Boris Johnson's political gifts was to leave people with the impression that he agreed with them. He knew there was value in Baker's activities, but he did not want anyone thinking they had got him the job. Very quietly, he began reassembling some of his closest allies. David Frost returned to advise him on the intricacies of the Brexit deal. Johnson was also in regular contact with Dominic Cummings, the campaign director of Vote Leave, and he started speaking regularly to another Vote Leave alumnus, who would come to play a prominent role.

Oliver Lewis, the former research director of the campaign, was one of those characters that Brexit seemed to attract, an intense maverick with more intelligence than social skills, who spoke nearly as fast as he thought. Now in his mid-thirties, Lewis was a self-described 'mad Eurosceptic' and 'lunatic' who had been campaigning against the EU since he first heard about the euro at his Surrey comprehensive school. His access to Westminster had come via Cummings, who had taken a liking to Lewis in 2008 when he did a two-week internship in the office of Michael Gove. Cummings was amused by Lewis's email address which billed him as Sonic the hedgehog hero of console games, to which Lewis bore a slight resemblance. Cummings nicknamed him 'Sonic', a name he still used a decade later when Cummings was best man at Lewis's wedding.

After the referendum Lewis joined Hanbury Strategy, the company founded by Paul Stephenson, the communications director of Vote Leave, and Ameet Gill, a Cameron aide who had been chief strategist for Remain. Lewis was driven to re-engage with politics after watching events around the Grieve and Hailsham amendments in June 2018. Already appalled at the soft Brexit course that May was charting, he told friends, 'The realisation hit me that these guys were going to try and stop the whole thing.' Like many in Vote Leave, he considered Brexit more than just a campaign: the experience of 2016 became part of the fabric of his being. One night in early June he woke up his wife and said, 'There may well be a second referendum and if so, I'm going to have to go and fight in it.' They had only just got married. She agreed, 'if you buy me a new house'. The next day Lewis said he needed his bonus early. They moved in three months later.

Lewis was in contact with Iain Duncan Smith and with Lee Cain, Johnson's special adviser who had stayed on the payroll after his resignation. Johnson called regularly to discuss Brexit on the macro level: where Chequers would lead and the implications of other choices. Lewis's argument was that Brexiteers had been on a glide path to failure ever since they accepted the backstop in December 2017. Johnson sought to get Michael Gove to resign as well. 'There comes a moment when you've got to grip the column of the temple on either side of you, strain your sternocleidomastoid muscles and bring it down,' he said. 'You're the last left in the cabinet able to do that.'

Cummings, meanwhile, believing May's performance would open the door to a Vote Leave prime minister, hired Marc and Ben Warner, his referendum campaign data experts, to build new data models to use in a future general election, or a second Brexit referendum. 'In 2018, we thought: there's a reasonable chance that this whole thing is going to collapse in 2019 and maybe there'll be a chance for us to seize control of Downing Street in the chaos,' he said. 'So, what we should do is ramp up the election models that we started to build in the referendum, so that if we do manage to grab control of Number 10, then we've got a key bit of technology that will be crucial for the election. I went off to some hedge funds and billionaires and said, "Give me half a million quid, and I'll build this secretly. And then we'll have a substantial advantage." We had these models built secretly in the cloud nine months' before the 2019 election.[1]

Initially the most significant of Johnson's old allies to return to the colours was Lynton Crosby, who had helped him win the London mayoral elections of 2008 and 2012 and was widely credited with securing the Tories' majority in 2015. The 'Wizard of Oz' blamed May's 2017 election performance, a campaign he helped to run, for sullying his reputation as a winner. Over the summer of 2018, Crosby despatched a CTF employee, David Canzini, to coordinate pro-Brexit groups campaigning to 'Chuck Chequers'. CTF also employed Stewart Jackson, David Davis's former chief of staff. His contract included four 'milestones': 'Destroy the credibility of Chequers, remove May, get Boris in as leader, win the general election'. Crosby's role as the puppet master of the campaign was revealed by the *Sunday Times* on 2 September.[2] But CTF's involvement was more long-standing. In March 2019, the *Guardian* revealed that staff at CTF had been running Facebook adverts against May on Brexit issues since 'late 2017'. The paper reported, 'The pages were designed to create the impression of a grassroots uprising for a hard exit from the EU and were fronted by supposedly independent pro-Brexit campaigners. However, they were overseen by staff at Crosby's company.'[3] Using Facebook advertising to promote political messages was standard practice on both left and right and the use of 'sock puppet' campaigns had been an issue in Britain for two decades. Nevertheless, anti-Brexit groups found this behaviour sinister. The ultimate source of funding was unclear.

In late July, David Canzini and Steve Baker met and agreed that, among the overlapping pressure groups in the shoal, there should be one that would coordinate engagement with MPs and journalists and act as a 'home' for Boris Johnson. Change Britain, the group which emerged from the ashes of Vote Leave, was rejected since it was regarded as a front for Michael Gove, who neither the ERG nor Johnson's circle trusted. Instead Canzini and Jackson poured resources into Global Britain. 'It meant Boris was free of the ERG and the ERG was free of him and the two could combine to best effect when the time came,' an ERG adviser said. 'For Boris to achieve the quintessence of Boris he couldn't be pigeonholed with the right.' A Johnson adviser said, 'Wisely, he was very cautious about being seen as the king of the Eurosceptics. There were a lot of people who are frankly quite mad in that cohort. He was aware that attaching himself too closely would damage his chances of bringing in more moderate MPs.'

Global Britain employed Ed Barker, a Westminster comms man who had spent two years in Hollywood as a professional saxophone player, going on tour with George Michael.[4] While he was watching the 2015 general election coverage in Caesars Palace in Las Vegas, the exit poll showing a Tory majority caused him to go all in with his chips and pine for a return to Westminster. Barker began writing articles for MPs and helping them with broadcast appearances. As the Brexit wars hotted up in 2018 and 2019, he combined Leave activism with fifty shows a year for the George Michael tribute tour, filing press releases from provincial dressing rooms.

On 1 August, Baker briefed Johnson on his strategy to vote down May's agreement, which he called Operation Renew. Throughout the month, members of the ERG worked on different aspects of policy, some of them with expertise, others by apparently scanning the dustbins of Whitehall for every oddball notion they could find. While Baker was on holiday, Bernard Jenkin assumed responsibility for the document. When Baker returned, at the end of August, he found it was riddled with factual errors and had ballooned to an unwieldy 140 pages. In addition to plans for the Irish border, it called for Britain to set up a permanent 'expeditionary force' to defend the Falkland Islands and suggested billions should be invested in a 'Star Wars' missile defence programme, policies with no discernible link to Brexit. When the document was circulated, Johnson made clear that he would not put his name to it. Rees-Mogg and Baker were already concluding that the document was 'not adequately coherent' – code for an unutterable dog's breakfast – and should not be published. Word reached them that Robbie Gibb, May's spin doctor, was 'gagging' for them to release it. 'He was trying to goad us to publish everything,' an ERG source said. 'Precisely so the government could tear it apart.'

Baker and Rees-Mogg decided the only paper that mattered was the one on the Northern Ireland border. That was launched on 12 September. It recommended a system of checks away from the border, mutual recognition of standards, data sharing and electronic customs pre-clearance to avoid queues. The paper suggested measures could be adopted that were in use at the port of Rotterdam in the Netherlands, where inspections were conducted twenty kilometres from the dockside. It was seen as a grown-up attempt to be constructive, and with a government determined to fight for it, there were elements that could have formed the basis for negotiation, but it contained no silver bullet that May's team, bruised by the rejection of these ideas in Brussels, could pick up and run with.

While Baker believed it was likely that Brexit would have to be delivered by Johnson, he had not entirely abandoned the idea that he might run for the leadership himself. On 18 September, he met Christopher Montgomery at the Carlton Club to discuss what Baker needed to do to put himself in contention: make a wide-ranging speech to stake out his ground and build backbench support. They even discussed a potential slogan: 'A prime minister who says what he believes and does what he says.'

The shoal of anti-Chequers campaigns expanded again on 23 September with the launch of a social media hashtag #StandUp4Brexit to promote a campaign which had been running since July. It was the brainchild of Rachel Ryan, a grassroots Brexiteer who wanted MPs to publicly pledge to 'deliver the Brexit that was promised at Lancaster House and in the Conservative manifesto'. Ryan had been introduced to Baker by a member of his constituency association. He introduced her to Canzini and then worked on drumming up pledges from MPs.

The following day, 24 September, the Institute of Economic Affairs (IEA) think tank released a document called 'Plan A Plus', a fully worked up version of the Donald Tusk plan, which Baker had been pressing for since March. Rees-Mogg called it 'supercalifragilisticexpialidocious Canada'; the MP most associated with nannies quoting cinema's most famous nanny. Johnson liked the plan, but he did not want to front it or to be held accountable for its contents. David Davis appeared at the launch, while Johnson tweeted, 'I think it's a very good piece of work', enough for the *Telegraph* to dub it 'the Boris plan'.

The final piece in the jigsaw, for Baker, was a conversation, on 26 September, with Nigel Dodds of the Democratic Unionist Party. Baker asked for a mutual defence pact, in which the ERG would stand four square with the DUP on the Union if the DUP backed them in resisting Brexit in name only. 'There was no covenant signed in blood,' a source said. 'But we had a mutual expectation.' The DUP's ten MPs bridged a range of opinion on Brexit, from the agnostic through to Sammy Wilson, whose commitment was scarcely less than that of the Paleosceptics. The party within a party had gone into coalition.

After a chaotic August, the forces opposed to May's plans had an effective September. Baker and Canzini had drummed up popular opposition to Brexit as well as solidified the number of MPs prepared to defy the whip and vote it down. They had advanced a plan for the Irish border and, in a bid to maximise their influence, they had a mutual understanding with the DUP. Finally, if May was to fall, there was tacit agreement that they would work to install Boris Johnson in her place.

Worse for May, while all that was playing out in London, and despite the warm words of the Dutch and the Germans prior to the Chequers meeting, her plan was about to be torpedoed by Brussels.

CHEQUERS GOES POP!

Showdown in Salzburg

August to September 2018

The first clue that things were going wrong came when Theresa May broke off from her traditional summer holiday, walking in Switzerland with her husband, to travel to the French Riviera to Fort Brégançon, the official retreat of French presidents since Charles de Gaulle. 'It's quite difficult to fathom where the French system is unless you hear directly from Monsieur Macron,' one of Britain's Brexit negotiators explained. The location was hardly auspicious. When the British came in sight of the Mediterranean outpost in 1793, they were attacked by French revolutionary forces. De Gaulle spent just one night there, complaining he was attacked by mosquitos. On 2 August, May asked Emmanuel Macron for his support over Chequers and her reception was scarcely more satisfactory.

Macron engaged with the issues and even made some constructive suggestions about the proposal and his desire to see Britain locked into a productive relationship with the EU. In the autumn he would advance the idea of a Europe of concentric circles, with the UK in an outer rim. But on the fundamentals of the plan, he said Britain was still trying to retain the advantages of EU membership without the obligations and that it was for the Commission, not him, to negotiate. Divide and rule had failed again.

Oliver Robbins appealed to French practicality. 'If Japan turned up and offered you the kind of relationship we are asking for, you would bite their hands off,' he said. Macron's reply was sharp, emotional, exposing the hurt feelings that still governed the UK–EU relationship. 'He said something like, "But Japan isn't betraying us by leaving",' an official present said. 'That's something that, oddly, most ministers have either not understood or chosen not to understand. That rational interest argument hasn't really worked.' Added to this, a rationalist argument for France involved excluding Britain and stealing business from the City of London.

While Macron was cool towards the plan, Michel Barnier and his chief negotiator Sabine Weyand regarded it with hostility, seeing it as a new device to simultaneously consume and conserve cake. The Commission dismissed May's customs plan. 'On good days, Sabine would accept it was just about intellectually credible, quite possibly even implementable,' a British source said. 'But [she thought], it's just not in the interests of the [European] Union.'

On the day after Chequers, Barnier's team had to be stopped from publishing a PowerPoint presentation detailing what was wrong with the deal. 'That would have killed it immediately,' a senior Council official recalled. 'Theresa May phoned Tusk asking him for assistance.' It was agreed that the EU would 'shut up' until the autumn. Similar efforts to protect May's blushes were launched by Tory Bresisters. On the Wednesday after the meeting, several went for breakfast at the German embassy, where a minister said, 'Chequers is unacceptable.' Nicky Morgan was one of several MPs to advise, 'Don't say that publicly because you will play into the hands of the Brexiteers who want no-deal.'

It was the Irish government's view of the border situation, not the Commission's, which would be decisive. Throughout the summer, the government in Dublin warned fellow member states that May's proposal risked undermining the peace process. A senior cabinet minister said, 'The brilliance of the Irish diplomacy is they went round the whole EU, places like Slovenia, and said, "This is a litmus test as to whether the Commission stands by its small states." The Irish really wanted us to stay in the customs union.'

The subtler officials in Downing Street understood the power of the Irish case, based on emotion, not the practical fudge advocated by the ERG. 'The combination of the peace process, and Ireland and the UK in the single market and the customs union, created a situation where it felt like there wasn't a border, although legally there is,' Barwell said. 'If you're a nationalist, anything which changes that feeling is going to create a problem. It doesn't really matter whether that border is at the border, or inland in a warehouse. To the DUP, anything which changes their feeling that Northern Ireland is a wholly integral part of the United Kingdom is also a problem.'

It was into this environment that Dominic Raab stepped when he became Brexit secretary. Emulating David Davis's habit of presenting his views to May in writing, he set out his assessment of the 'state of play' in a letter to the prime minister dated 16 July. Raab called for the government to get aggressive and 'assert fresh pressure on the EU's tenuous position on Northern Ireland'. The Commission's proposal, which had become known as 'Barnier's backstop', he wrote, 'either requires a border along the Irish Sea or UK membership of the Customs Union'. Raab warned this was a 'direct threat to the territorial integrity of the UK' and raised the spectre of the bloody collapse of Yugoslavia. 'Given recent European history in the Balkans, and present separatist movements within EU states, it is a deeply irresponsible position – at odds with the most basic conceptions of European unity – which we should be making more uncomfortable for the Commission, including publicly.' Raab believed that in the Irish border the EU had found Britain's weak spot and proceeded to 'press on it with full force'. He said later, 'I do think it is both predatory in relation to Northern Ireland and bullying and controlling in relation to the long-term relationship that they would envisage with the UK.'[1]

Raab's first trip to Brussels, on 20 July, was not a success. The Commission marked his arrival by announcing it was stepping up preparations for no-deal. Before that, he faced embarrassment because the translations of the white paper by British officials were full of errors. The Estonian and Finnish version misspelled the names of their own countries and the French translation turned 'principled Brexit' into 'un Brexit verteux', suggesting Brexit was a moral good. A Dutch newspaper said their version read like it was the product of the 'cheapest available' translation software.

In his first exchange with Barnier, the Frenchman treated 'with total scorn' Raab's suggestion that there were mutual wins to be had in a deal. Like Davis before him, the Brexit secretary felt May had to be far more 'resolute and hard-nosed'. Raab said later, 'I think it was a mistake to leave so much of the technical leg work to the team out in Brussels which was not subject to political direction and control on a day-by-day basis.'

Inevitably, civil servants and people working at a technical level, will look at this in a very different way from ministers and politicians.'

In his second meeting with Barnier, on 26 July, Raab got what he thought was a major admission from the EU negotiator, which was to shape his approach for the rest of his time as Brexit secretary. With Robbins at his side, he 'put a marker down', raising the fact that the Article 50 process was, by definition, finite. The backstop could not last indefinitely. He 'hammered home' his point, a witness said, and warned Barnier, 'It won't pass otherwise, I can tell you that.' The Frenchman appeared to accept the validity of this. 'He didn't put up any resistance,' the witness said. Raab left the room highly encouraged, saying to Robbins, 'That was interesting.'

Robbins replied, 'You can't trust what he says in the room.'

'But that's ridiculous. We've got it minuted. You are taking minutes, aren't you?' Raab was staggered to discover that there was no formal record of Robbins' talks with Barnier's Article 50 Task Force. He demanded that officials start taking a written record. Robbins resisted, objecting to Raab's private secretary writing the official record.

When May offered him the job, Raab had accepted on the grounds that he would be positioned in the chain of command between her and the Europe Unit. He thought it 'outrageous' that Robbins, having been effectively fired by Davis from DExEU, had become more powerful. He wanted no advice going to the prime minister without him having the ability to comment on it, no meeting between Robbins and May that he could not attend. But throughout his time as Brexit secretary, he was convinced Robbins was going behind his back and that May was hearing a lopsided version of events. The Brexit secretary decided to write his own accounts of his meetings with Barnier so May, who liked government to operate formally on paper, could get an unfiltered political view of the negotiations. Those copied in felt they were a very conscious effort by Raab to get his position on the record for the history books.

In the first of these memos, sent the following day, 27 July, Raab outlined the point he would return to time and again in Whitehall discussions: 'I made it clear that any backstop would need to be time-limited to avoid indefinite limbo. It was striking that he put up no resistance to that in the negotiation room, and effectively acquiesced that any backstop needed to be short.'

Raab's view was that opening his 'political track' had put a possible solution 'on the table'. But even some allies thought him naive, a victim of the glass half full syndrome which affected many Brexiteers in Brussels, who heard what they wanted to hear. Robbins' overt scepticism damaged relations with a second Brexit secretary.

They were already strained by disagreements over personnel. Raab had attempted to hire Raoul Ruparel but May wanted Davis's Europe adviser in Downing Street and Raab did not want to share an adviser. There was talk of Ruparel sitting with the Europe Unit, but Robbins was not keen to have a political adviser attached to his team. Ruparel was also supposed to start accompanying Robbins to the technical negotiations as the prime minister's political representative but Robbins vetoed the idea. Ruparel eventually joined Denzil Davidson and Ed de Minckwitz in their second-floor office in Number 10. He assumed responsibility for the Northern Ireland issue, alternative arrangements and anything that involved contact with the Brexiteers and the DUP – at this stage, the lion's share of the work. De Minckwitz led on no-deal preparations.

At their first meeting, Raab told Robbins he was 'keen to make the relationship work' but he asked for total candour in return. 'We can't have two tracks, which is where this has been going wrong,' he said. Robbins agreed. Over dinner at Tim Barrow's ambassadorial residence in Brussels, Raab explained: 'I'm committed to making Chequers work, as long as you understand that if it fails, we pivot.' It was not Robbins but the prime minister he had to convince.

DExEU sources say that Raab did not believe Robbins was candid with him and set out to 'test his integrity'. In early August, the Brexit secretary took a week's holiday in France. While he was away, he heard Robbins had scheduled a meeting with May without him, a move his private office regarded as 'outrageous'. Robbins had not reckoned with the single-minded determination of Raab, who demanded the papers be couriered to him at his sister-in-law's home near Versailles. Having read them, he stayed up until 2 a.m. writing a memo to May, in which he identified several political problems with Robbins' proposals.

This missive began, it can only be assumed sarcastically, with the words, 'Thank you to Olly for the very useful note of 6/8, which asks all the right questions' while noting 'the late arrival of the papers'. Raab then warned that a softening of language on customs would 'signal retreat', and that the potential scope of the ECJ's role in settling disputes 'is wrong in principle and damaging in practice'. The draft Future Framework Robbins was proposing seemed to Raab to lack ambition, something he feared would signal to Brussels 'that we are wavering'. 'It needs to be thoroughly reviewed, including ministerially, for political elephant traps.'

Raab began to form the view that Robbins was not just advising May what was negotiable in Brussels but keeping from her relevant political concerns, allowing the negotiations over the withdrawal agreement to 'magnetically pull' the future trade arrangements towards the softest possible Brexit. 'It wasn't sly, it was pretty transparent,' a DExEU source said. 'Large bits of the Northern Ireland stuff were, through the technical groups, cooked up without [Robbins] passing it back to [Raab].'

Any residual trust was destroyed during Raab's third trip to Brussels on 21 August, when his exchanges with Barnier on Northern Ireland led to a full-blown row. The eruption came after Raab sought to highlight an inconsistency in the EU's approach. The Commission, he charged, was trying to tie Britain to a deal which would bind it to EU rules to prevent a hard border on the island of Ireland. But if there was no-deal, Raab said, 'We would never put up a hard border. The government in Dublin has said it will never put up a hard border. Given all the pressures in Spain, the history of the Balkans which isn't the EU's finest hour, are you seriously going to insist in Northern Ireland that a hard border goes up?'

Comparing the possible impact of the EU's exit policy to ethnic cleansing in the former Yugoslavia was one thing but, to Barnier, this was also tantamount to blaming the EU for no-deal. 'There was a degree of Gallic backlash,' a source present recalled. Barnier, his voice icy with fury, stopped Raab and accused him of reneging on the commitments in the Joint Report of December 2017: 'My dear Dominic, your prime minister, Theresa May, never dared to say this to us, never. On the contrary, she has affirmed that United Kingdom understands the problem it is creating by leaving the EU and the single market, and understands its responsibility. The idea that it would be the Europeans' fault, and that it would be up to us to introduce border controls is absolutely unacceptable … If that is the British position you had better say so now, and I shall report to the European Parliament and Council that our discussions have come to a halt – that negotiations have failed.'[2]

Raab retreated but in his memo to May which reached her the next day, he downplayed his own remarks, accusing Barnier of having 'disrupted' the meeting with 'a bad-tempered and prolonged intervention'. After the main meeting, Raab and Barnier met alone for fifteen minutes. The EU negotiator 'mooted variants of Customs Union membership as the ultimate fix on the economic partnership,' Raab informed May. These 'would not fly' he said. He concluded the meeting pointing out that Britain had made concessions and the EU had to 'meet us halfway'. He ended the memo with a warning that there was a high risk of 'bust up' over the Northern Ireland backstop with Barnier 'bristling'.

Raab was the one bristling when British press reports emerged soon afterwards painting him as the berserker. He blamed the leaks on Robbins or his team, surmising that, if they were not directly responsible, the way they had reported back 'through channels' to Downing Street was suspect. The Brexit secretary felt officials should back him up, however uncomfortable it might be in the room. Civil servants thought his approach needlessly confrontational and liable to upset a finely balanced negotiation. Raab saw the leaks as evidence that someone close to Robbins wanted to undermine his credibility with the prime minister. 'That was Olly leaking that to try and then go back to her and say, "Raab is going to screw this all up",' a DExEU source said. 'Fundamentally, [Raab] wanted to control the message she was getting and Olly just went behind his back and undermined that.'

Raab was the subject of other leaks which sought to paint him as a monomaniacal bully or simply to embarrass him. That April it had emerged that his diary secretary at the housing department was selling sex on a sugar daddy website. Interviewed by the *Daily Mirror*, she branded him 'difficult' and 'dismissive of women' but the detail which cut through was her claim, denied by Raab, that he ate the same lunch every day – a chicken Caesar and bacon baguette, superfruit pot and vitamin volcano smoothie from Pret a Manger, a combination soon known in Westminster as 'the Dom Raab special'.

More seriously, Raab called in his permanent secretary demanding the removal of his principal private secretary, Giles Hall, who he had caught reporting back to Robbins. When Raab couldn't find him one day, a colleague said, 'He's over at Number 10.' On Hall's return, Raab asked where he had been and he confessed he was 'with Olly'. When it happened again, Raab demanded his removal. Shortly afterwards, Hall joined Robbins' team. Despite their differences, Raab told Robbins when they first met he would not brief against him and the incident did not become public at the time.

Geoffrey Cox was also determined to change the way government had been operating. During his early weeks as attorney general he absorbed endless briefings from officials, seeking to fully understand the 'wiring' of the withdrawal agreement and how each of its clauses had been arrived at. He concluded that the critical decisions had been taken at the end of 2017. He saw the withdrawal agreement as deeply flawed but also as the only way Brexit might be achieved, a life raft out of the European Union. He could see, too, that the EU had managed to secure binding assurances they would be highly resistant to tearing up. He determined to insert himself into the process of negotiation. Having heard that Brexiteer ministers had not fully understood the obligations they were signing up to in December 2017, he gave himself one overriding objective: the cabinet would never, from that point onwards, 'take a decision in the dark'. He told colleagues he would 'starkly – if necessary, brutally starkly' set out the real legal implications of any step the cabinet was going to take.

Cox demanded to see, in real time, the discussions taking place between Robbins and Barnier's Task Force 50. He discovered that both Number 10 and the Europe Unit had been seeking their own legal advice from government lawyers and the Treasury solicitor, bypassing the attorney general's office. 'When Geoffrey arrived, senior officials told him that the attorney general's office had been simply out of the loop,' a source said. Cox instructed the director general of his office to ensure that Number 10 copied him into emails between Robbins and May. He started receiving diplomatic telegrams – 'diptels' – and insisted Robbins come to see him once a week. He was also added to the SN committee, the Brexit strategy and negotiations war cabinet.

The new prominence of Raab and Cox was pleasing to the small number of Brexiteers in Downing Street, who had felt outnumbered and marginalised. Nikki da Costa and Kirsty Buchanan, the deputy press secretary, had taken to quoting a sketch by the comedy double act Mitchell and Webb in which reality gradually dawns on two SS officers: 'Are we the baddies?' Now it felt like the cavalry had arrived.

By September, Cox and Raab had formed an effective double act. On the 6th, they jointly wrote to May critiquing the draft Future Framework Robbins had drawn up, insisting that it not be shared with the Europeans until the points of contention had been resolved. They complained that Britain's demands on customs and financial services used 'weaker language' than 'in almost every other area'. This, they warned, 'risks signalling that UK proposals are equivocal'. The ministers demanded tougher language on dispute resolution to avoid ECJ 'mission creep'. Robbins' draft suggested that when new common rulebook rules were introduced the EU would simply have to 'inform' the UK. Cox and Raab insisted this was changed to 'consult'. They wrote, 'It is important not just that we are notified of proposed changes, but actually consulted. This is vital to address concern that the UK will become a rule-taker.'

While things became fractious in Brussels, Downing Street launched a concerted effort to sell the Chequers deal at home. Both Gavin Barwell and Robbie Gibb held dinners for Brexiteers in Number 10 but found themselves on the menu. Gibb held a meal on 10 September for a group that included Bernard Jenkin, Philip Davies and Anne-Marie Trevelyan, which sparked a series of hostile briefings. Government sources claimed half the MPs present had been converted to May's cause. 'Ludicrous,' said the Brexiteers, who then claimed Gibb had called Raab a 'fucking nightmare' as they glugged their claret – something he fiercely denied.

An MP who attended a different dinner hosted by Gibb and JoJo Penn recalled, 'The opaque and utterly confusing way in which Gibb tried to explain the plan completely baffled me. I couldn't believe he was tasked with trying to articulate this to voters. Gibb said most voters don't care about the details, they'll appreciate we are delivering them on immigration. I kept asking myself, "Am I insane, or are they insane?" I felt that I was an ordinary person sitting in this place of mass delusion.'

When Barwell hosted another group in the wood-panelled small dining room the following evening, he came under sustained assault from John Redwood, Maria Caulfield, Martin Vickers, Nigel Mills, Tom Pursglove and John Baron. Arch Eurosceptic Peter Bone, who even Steve Baker regarded as a fundamentalist, refused to discuss his views, telling the chief of staff he feared they would be leaked by Downing Street. 'I'm only here for a nice meal,' he said. Andrew Bridgen said trying to peddle the Chequers proposal to a sceptical public would be 'like trying to sell syphilis'.

Barwell cannot have been surprised. Earlier that evening the Tory whips had reported back on an ERG meeting in the Thatcher Room in

Portcullis House, where MPs spoke openly of their desire to oust May. Jacob Rees-Mogg, who usually discouraged overt leadership talk, was absent because an angry mob of Remain campaigners had descended on his family home. Anne Marie Morris revealed she had put in a no-confidence letter. James Duddridge said the Eurosceptics were being 'boiled alive' and should act. Bridgen said letting May fight the next election would be 'like telling a surviving member of the Charge of the Light Brigade, who knows what's in store, to have another go'.

In one 'interminable' discussion with John Redwood, Bernard Jenkin, and Bill Cash, Barwell said, 'If David Cameron had come back from the renegotiation with something like this, you would have bitten his hands off. It's only because you've seen the "Promised Land", and think you can get exactly what you want, that you're now being difficult about this.' This, they denied. 'But I'm certain that, if in 2013 or 2014 they'd been offered something like that, they'd have leapt at it.'[3]

May's main effort to win public backing for Chequers came in an interview with the BBC's Nick Robinson for a *Panorama* special, broadcast on 18 September. Gibb called in favours from his old colleagues at the corporation to secure a prime-time slot. The prime minister's message was that her plan was the only one that could succeed and 'the alternative to that will be not having a deal'. She dismissed the ERG plan: 'You don't solve the issue of no hard border by having a hard border twenty kilometres inside Ireland.' But when it mattered, she was bloodless. Her argument was the same one Margaret Thatcher had deployed when battling for controversial reforms in the early 1980s – TINA (there is no alternative) – but May was unable to sound enthusiastic about her plan, which she genuinely believed was a positive compromise, or deliver any of the certainty or passion for her cause which Britain's first female prime minister had displayed. 'It got wall-to-wall coverage,' said one special adviser, 'but she hadn't worked out how to sound human about why frictionless trade is a thing worth having.'

It was May's best chance to get mainstream public opinion behind her and the prime minister flunked it. Her awkwardness was on display even before the interview. It is usual for politicians and journalists to have an informal chat while the camera and sound crew set up – an opportunity for politicians to win over their interviewer or for the broadcaster to put the subject at their ease. 'Nick tried to engage her, but she just said nothing,' a BBC man in the room said. 'She just stared ahead. It was massively awkward.' Robinson had been briefed by Gibb on the key points May wanted to make but, despite repeated prompting, she failed to land the arguments, such as how a hard Brexit would damage industries like car manufacturing in Tory target seats.

The programme sought to give a behind the scenes insight into May's life, to humanise her for voters. She agreed to be filmed watching quiz shows with husband Philip. However, her Number 10 minders insisted the couple could not watch their favourite, *Pointless*, because of the connotations of the name.

May's attempt to persuade EU member states to get behind her plan was even less successful. Their verdict was to be delivered at a summit in Salzburg on 19 September. In the Commission, at least, an effort was made to assist her. The day before the summit, Barnier suggested his team had a 'new, improved' proposal for the Irish border to tackle British concerns and made clear Brussels did not wish to undermine the constitutional integrity of the UK. The proposals were communicated privately by Task Force 50 officials to Robbins and by Barnier to Raab. Barnier wanted to 'de-dramatise' the backstop issue by ensuring that the checks they envisaged between Northern Ireland and the rest of Great Britain – the East-West border – take place away from the ports of entry. The idea was to make the Northern Ireland only backstop palatable to London. Even EU officials noted that Barnier was 'using the same language the Brits were using in their "maximum facilitation" proposal'.

The plans were not enough for May. With the Conservative Party conference just around the corner, she could not appear weak in the face of a threat to the Union. Barnier's olive branch was waved away.

Before Salzburg, Raab and May drank red wine together in her snug in Number 10. The Brexit secretary said, 'Prime Minister, you must avoid the rock of customs union and the hard place of no-deal. And the way you do it is by standing firm now. We've got to stand firm on the backstop.' He went on, 'If Chequers hits the wall you've got to pivot. I think that there's a 60 per cent chance it will hit the wall.' He felt he was being generous by giving his prime minister a 40 per cent chance of success. His personal view was that it was far lower than that.

May disagreed: 'The prospects of success are much higher than that.'

'Okay,' said Raab. 'However low you think the prospects of failure, we must be ready to pivot.' May's head went down, she could not look him in the eye. Raab told a confidant later, 'She couldn't entertain it.'

On the morning of the summit, May published a thousand-word editorial in the German newspaper *Die Welt*, asking the EU to meet Britain halfway. It argued that both sides needed 'the frictionless movement of goods' and that 'this is not the same thing as partial participation in the Single Market'. Chequers, she claimed, was the only solution that 'could command cross-community support in Northern Ireland'. By contrast, she wrote, the backstop would not 'protect the Belfast/Good Friday Agreement in all its parts' or respect 'the constitutional and economic integrity of the UK'. She concluded, 'To come to a successful conclusion, just as the UK has evolved its position, the EU will need to do the same. Neither side can demand the unacceptable of the other, such as an external customs border between different parts of the United Kingdom.'

Downing Street officials hoped it would be enough to ensure Chequers as the basis for discussion, perhaps even secure warm words. Instead, the hectoring tone, the suggestion it was her way or the highway, had the opposite effect. 'I think what went wrong at Salzburg is communication,' a senior figure in the Commission said. 'She stated her case very bluntly in a German newspaper. It was very harsh, it was very blunt.'

EU chiefs still believed that, with the Chequers plan, May had ignored their warnings about cakeism. Michel Barnier said later, 'Nobody can have one foot inside and one foot outside.'[4] The EU was also wary of the common rulebook. What for purist Brexiteers was a shackle tying Britain to continental rules in perpetuity was, to many member states, a slippery slope leading to Britain, a third country, being treated as an equal partner in the negotiation of future rules.

On the first evening, May was invited to make her case to the other leaders over dinner. Instead of appealing to her peers for help, her presentation was a disaster, combining the stilted awkwardness of *Panorama* with the blunt certainty in *Die Welt* that only she had the viable answer. Worse, May's talking points seemed to have been lifted wholesale from the article rather than used as the basis for a heartfelt and conversational approach. A Commission official said, 'The expectation was she would come to Salzburg and say, "Let's see how we can get out of this in a way that is amicable." Instead of doing that, she just read out the article again, increasing the antagonism.' The official said May displayed 'a lack of understanding of the emotions of others ... She doesn't see things around her.' Frans Timmermans, the Commission vice president, recalled, 'If you want to be successful in a negotiation you need to know the other side's position better than your own position. Negotiating by saying. "I've said this already, I'll keep saying it until you understand it", is not a way you are successful in negotiations.'[5]

May had assumed she would be more likely to get what she wanted from her fellow leaders than from Commission officials. Not for the first time, that would be a miscalculation. Once she had finished, she left the room so that the other leaders could discuss what they had heard. Her brief opportunity to turn opinion had been thrown away.

Jean-Claude Juncker was more sympathetic to May but he was enraged by a British briefing to the media that she was supported by the leaders of Belgium and the Netherlands. Knowing the consequences, he turned to Barnier, who hated May's plan, and said, 'Michel, say what you think about Chequers.' Ten minutes later, one of those in the room said, 'Chequers is dead.' Macron supported Barnier and demanded Britain come up with something acceptable by October. 'The UK must make choices,' the French president said. 'We have to go faster.' He concluded his press conference with an astonishingly undiplomatic attack on the Brexiteers. 'Those who said you can easily do without Europe, that it will all go very well, that it is easy and there will be lots of money, are liars.'

May's ultimate humiliation was delivered by Donald Tusk. Minutes after Macron had torn up the plans to make progress, the prime minister and the Council president held a bilateral meeting. Tusk looked 'ashen-faced' as he arrived to tell her what had happened, ushering May onto the balcony to deliver the news personally. The prime minister returned 'stony-faced and very stern with him,' an aide recalled. In their meeting, May was far from conciliatory. 'She went back on the attack with Tusk,' an EU official said. 'She said nothing conciliatory at all; nothing to suggest ... that she felt that maybe she should adjust. Nothing.'[6] Nonetheless, the head-to-head ended with the Number 10 contingent expecting Tusk to say something 'less warm' but not terminal about the Chequers plan. 'There was nothing in the room to suggest that he was going to blow the whole thing up in the way that he did,' the aide said.

Tusk used his press conference to deliver a public death blow to the Chequers plan. He was blunt to the point of being undiplomatic:

'Everybody shared the view that while there are positive elements in the Chequers proposal, the suggested framework for economic cooperation will not work.' In case that was not clear enough, he added, 'There will be no withdrawal agreement without a solid, operational and legally binding Irish backstop.' He had not told May what he was going to say. One of his senior officials admitted, 'What Tusk said was true, some would say too true. We wanted to be helpful but there are limits to our contribution to the unicorn hunt.'

To add insult to injury, the Council president then publicly mocked the British prime minister, posting a picture on Instagram of the two of them together after lunch, Tusk holding up a plate of small cakes to May. He added the caption, 'A piece of cake perhaps? Sorry, no cherries.' The cake was actually covered in raspberries. Council officials say Martin Selmayr ate them, perhaps to 'destroy the evidence'. The image seemed to be a ritual denunciation of 'cherry-picking' and mocking the idea that Brexit was 'a piece of cake'. To some of May's staff it felt like Tusk was taunting a diabetic with a sugary treat she could not eat. The truth of the matter, a Council official explained, was different: 'The plate with the cake was bought by Tim Barrow. Tim was the first one making jokes about it.' Nonetheless, in declaring that Chequers 'doesn't work', some member states admitted Tusk's hostility had gone further than they expected.

To the EU, May had rejected a lifeline from Barnier, signalled in *Die Welt* that she was not listening to their concerns and, over dinner, that she was no more realistic in private than in public. In many ways it was the signature moment of the entire negotiations: fundamental differences of politics, philosophy and legality exacerbated by May's tone deafness and the strategic willingness of the other leaders to send Britain packing. The prime minister who took two years to decide where she wanted to go still had no tactical awareness of how to get there or the ability to do so.

To May's team, Tusk had spectacularly reneged on an agreement to soft-soap their disagreements. A senior Downing Street official said, 'Tusk behaved badly. She'd had some very good conversations over the summer with a variety of EU leaders about the plan and therefore wasn't expecting that response from the EU.' To Raab it looked like May was 'ambushed'. He said later, 'Some of the way she was treated I think people felt was pretty humiliating. The Chequers proposals were not just criticised in one or other point but dismissed wholesale.'[7] It was a charge

Frans Timmermans rejected: 'Can we please stop this nonsense?' He said later, 'Brexiteers, who will do anything to avoid taking responsibility for what they've done, will try and put the onus on the EU and continue to spin this story of humiliation, which is nonsense. Nobody ever wanted to humiliate anyone least of all Theresa May.'[8]

Humiliated she was, though. May's team was quickly in crisis mode. Raab spoke to the prime minister by phone and urged her not to do a 'big histrionic walkout'. Instead, he pushed his own agenda, telling her, 'But you can now make a "take it or leave it" offer. You can pivot and given the way people have treated you, if you hold yourself with dignity, integrity, as you always do, you will galvanise public support.'

When James Slack prepped May for her own press conference, he said, 'PM, I think the British public are going to expect you to be quite angry about the way he has treated you.'

She regarded him with a blank look of incredulity. 'I am angry!' Another official said, 'She was as furious as I have ever seen her.'

Senior ministers and officials in Downing Street blamed the setback on an intelligence failure by the civil service. Raab was furious, calling it 'unforgivable' that Robbins and Barrow and their teams had left the prime minister so exposed. It reinforced his view that ministers should lead the negotiations. EU officials are explicit that Robbins and Barrow got a clear message. 'The leaders and Barnier were telling the Brits, "This is not going to fly", so they knew before Salzburg,' a Commission official said. A Whitehall source confirmed that Robbins 'warned her in the last week or so that it might not go according to plan'. Critics said his words were 'last-minute arse-covering'. A cabinet minister suggested the problem had begun much earlier: 'Olly's advice that the PM's plan was negotiable was the clincher at Chequers. That seems to be wrong.' Robbins may not have been blunt enough that things might go wrong but it is also true that May and her team never wanted to hear that Chequers would not fly.

The immediate consequence of the Salzburg disaster for May was that she had vocal support from the Eurosceptic press at home. The *Sun* mocked up Tusk and Macron on its front page as gangsters with tommy guns under the headline 'EU Dirty Rats – Euro mobsters ambush'. As her team fled Salzburg, Robbins and Ruparel began working up plans for a speech to the nation the following day.

Back in Downing Street, more radical thoughts were being considered. At least two of May's senior aides, including Stephen Parkinson, her political secretary, concluded that the only way to break the deadlock with Brussels, her party and Parliament would be to call a general election. Parkinson told colleagues that, at the very least, the option needed to be on the table to 'crack the whip hard' at MPs to show them there were consequences if they refused to back Chequers. 'It's a bit like the nuclear deterrent,' he argued. 'You don't have to use it, but people need to know that you have it and you're willing to countenance it.' They began to war-game how the prime minister could position herself to win. 'The idea is that she pivots, strikes a looser deal with Brussels and if she can't get that deal through the Commons, she calls an election and runs as a Eurosceptic,' one Tory said. 'You say to the public, "I told you last time that I needed your help to deliver Brexit, you didn't believe me, but now it really is critical."' The problem with this idea was that May had no intention of pivoting towards the Eurosceptics and when word got around the next morning that she was due to make a speech, ministers were openly horrified that she might subject them to another election.

In fact, the deadlock was such that if May had not already tried and failed to boost her majority in 2017, this might actually have been the perfect time to call an election. The case was far easier to make in September 2018 than it had been in June 2017 that there was no way through the mire without a new mandate. 'The election was called in 2017 when it should have been called in 2018,' a Number 10 adviser said.

On Friday morning, Barwell worked on the draft of the speech by Robbins and Ruparel. May delivered it outside Number 10. From disaster she fashioned a triumph of sorts, demanding 'respect' from Brussels in a manner which bought her time with her party. She spoke with cool rage about the EU plan to put a customs border between mainland Britain and Northern Ireland, saying, 'As I told EU leaders, neither side should demand the unacceptable of the other. We cannot accept anything that threatens the integrity of our Union, just as they cannot accept anything that threatens the integrity of theirs.' Those watching in Brussels believed the second half of this statement contradicted the first. It was precisely the prospect of an all-UK customs arrangement which threatened the single market. But a Downing Street aide said, 'We need them to understand that we can't break up our country and we will walk away rather than overturn the referendum result.'

May concluded by demanding her personal dues. 'Throughout this process, I have treated the EU with nothing but respect,' she said, in her sternest school ma'am voice. 'The UK expects the same. It is not acceptable to simply reject the other side's proposals without a detailed explanation and counter proposals.' This was arguably disingenuous; May knew full well what the EU's objections were. But politically it was her most effective moment of the negotiations, successfully depicting Brussels as both rude and truculent. 'That was her handbag moment,' one aide said.

The reaction in London was rapturous, the newspapers comparing her to both Thatcher and Boudicca. As a consequence, May refilled the well of goodwill in the Conservative Party which had been draining away since Chequers. The curiosity is that despite having seen how effective it was to throw her toys from the pram, May never did so again publicly.

The prime minister's speech cut little ice with Brussels, however. When Barnier addressed the Brexit Steering Group on 25 September. he said May wanted 'half of the customs union and a third of the single market'. Her demand 'is not a backstop, it is a UK-wide solution, and this UK-wide solution is, as easy as pie, cherry picking'.[9] His colleague Stefaan De Rynck added, 'What Chequers tried to do was shift the EU away from its core principles, and that was never going to work. That was made clear to some in the UK delegation. On the common rulebook, mutual recognition and equivalence, Chequers stressed Parliamentary sovereignty to deviate … outside of the Court of Justice … That was always a threat to the Single Market. The glue and trust between EU member states depends on common institutions. The UK wanted a common rulebook but no common institutions.'[10]

Barwell concluded that the domestic drama had prevented May building on the warm words from Merkel and Rutte before Chequers: 'We had to spend two months fighting an internal battle, following the resignations of DD and Boris, when we should have been out selling this thing to the Commission and to the other capitals. By the time we finally got back to talk to them, the Commission had killed it off.'[11]

A senior Commission official said that if May had 'better prepared' the ground, 'Chequers could have been the basis' of a deal. Much of its underlying philosophy would find its way into the eventual withdrawal agreement. In conversations between May and Robbins on the one side and Juncker and Selmayr on the other, the prime minister had signalled that she knew she would not get everything she wanted. The Commission pairing indicated that her plan was something which could be built on with 'some tweaks'. 'Britain wanting a high level of convergence and common standards – they had no problem with that,' said a Commission official. 'That was in line with their philosophy of an orderly divorce. Barnier had a very different view.' But Juncker and Selmayr were prepared to order their lawyers to make it work. 'We have innovative and creative people in the Commission … If you have this agreement in principle where you want to go, we will find a way to write this down. This is what we're good at.'

It was not all May's fault. Tusk had also messed up. At best he had misled her about the reaction of the EU27; at worst he had kicked her when she was already down. Remainers at home also felt that EU leaders were making a strategic error in not trying to accommodate May. A cabinet minister said, 'If she is voted down that's the end of her. This is the thing Europe needs to understand. You lose her, you get Boris. They fucked it up in 2016, they didn't give Cameron nearly enough, and if they do it again, it's their bloody fault.'

Regardless of where the blame lay, May was now deeper in crisis. She had been prepared to stake her premiership on a compromise she believed to be negotiable. To the hardline Eurosceptics, she had given away too much and then still been rebuffed. This generated feelings of contempt towards Brussels and pity towards May. An ERG source said, 'Yet again the prime minister has been able to shoot herself in the foot without our assistance. It's political S&M. It's like every disaster gives her a grisly shudder of pleasure.'

More than two months after Chequers, neither Penny Mordaunt nor Esther McVey had made any public utterance in support of it. Mordaunt was openly drumming up support for a leadership challenge. The next hurdle for May to clear was the Conservative Party conference. As the gathering in Birmingham approached, one Brexiteer said, 'The prime minister has ten days to come up with a new plan and reset Brexit and her leadership, or men in grey suits will be despatched to tell her to go. It's now shit or bust.'

13

OUT OF SIGHT

The Tunnel

September to November 2018

Steve Baker felt nervous excitement; he was planning something big. It was the Tuesday of the Conservative Party conference, 2 October, and the man the papers were now calling 'the Brexit hardman' was due to appear on the *Today* programme, straight after Theresa May. The ERG's most media-savvy member had been booked as if he was the leader of the opposition, which in a sense he was.

Baker thought back to June 2016, eight days before the referendum, when George Osborne had told *Today* that if there was a Leave vote he would immediately have to call an emergency budget to raise taxes and cut spending. Waiting in the wings had been Baker, who denounced it as a 'punishment budget' and announced that fifty-eight Tory MPs were prepared to vote it down. This time, Baker was ready to follow the prime minister's interview with a demand that she resign. This time the figure in his head was forty-eight, the number of letters demanding a no-confidence vote, which he was confident he could trigger. He had warned his list of journalistic contacts that his appearance would be exciting. When he arrived for the interview, BBC staff, expecting fireworks, kept him away from the green room where May was waiting.

Baker listened intently as she spoke. She seemed, to him, hesitant, like a person for whom life was tough. Suddenly, he was seized with enormous sympathy for the prime minister. May was on her home turf, talking about immigration. She landed her lines: freedom of movement would end 'once and for all', her Brexit plan would 'make sure low-skilled immigration is brought down'. Baker found nothing objectionable in this. He had no excuse to call for the prime minister's head. 'I couldn't do it,' he concluded. Senior Eurosceptics all seemed to know she had to go. Nobody wanted to be the one to say, 'Do it now.'

That May was in a dogfight for her survival had been starkly illustrated by the front page of the *Sunday Times* two days earlier. Both May and Boris Johnson had given their big pre-conference interview to the newspaper, which placed them head-to-head on the front under the headline 'Boris Johnson v Theresa May – now it's war'. The paper was scrupulous in giving them the same space but only one could win the battle for the splash headline. The prime minister had to play second fiddle to Johnson, who dismissed the Chequers plan as 'deranged', its customs plan as 'entirely preposterous' and made his pitch as an election-winner.

Pressed on whether a Brexiteer would really get a better deal, Johnson showed a flash of anger. 'Unlike the prime minister I campaigned for Brexit,' he said. 'Unlike the prime minister I fought for this, I believe in it, I think it's the right thing for our country and I think that what is happening now is, alas, not what people were promised in 2016.' His form of words about May was deliciously precise: 'The prime minister said she is going to serve for as long as her party wants her, and I certainly think she should.' He was convinced May had already lost the party. Two days before that, he had filed a four-thousand-word evisceration of the Chequers plan to the *Daily Telegraph*.

Johnson's rhetoric sparked an arms race in hyperbole from potential leadership candidates. In his platform speech that afternoon Jeremy Hunt, his successor as foreign secretary, compared the EU to the Soviet Union. This earned a rebuke from Brussels, with Donald Tusk calling it 'as unwise as it is insulting'. But it also appeared to Eurosceptics to be trying a bit too hard. To Baker it sounded 'tinny and inauthentic'.

On Tuesday, hours after Baker had holstered his revolver, Johnson addressed a 'Chuck Chequers' rally at the conference. He told the rapturous crowds that he was there 'to put some lead in the collective pencil' of a government 'so demoralised and exhausted' it was contemplating submitting 'to foreign rule'. Backing Chequers, he said, would leave Britain 'locked in the tractor beam of Brussels'. He bellowed, 'This is not democracy. This is not what we voted for. This is an outrage', exhorting, 'This is the moment – and there is time – to chuck Chequers' and 'scrap the Commission's constitutionally abominable Northern Ireland backstop'. He concluded, 'If we cheat the electorate

– and Chequers is a cheat – we will escalate the sense of mistrust. We will give credence to those who cry betrayal, and I am afraid we will make it more likely that the ultimate beneficiary of the Chequers deal will be the far right in the form of Ukip.' Johnson was attacked by some MPs, but a supporter noted, 'You only get flak when you're right over the target.'

The media darling of the Tory conference was not Johnson, however, but Geoffrey Cox. The attorney general was wheeled on as a warm-up act for May and proceeded to seduce the grassroots audience with his silky baritone, quickly compared to Mufasa, Disney's Lion King, voiced by James Earl Jones. Eschewing the lectern, Cox wandered the stage, a QC using every trick in the barrister's box to get his audience to accept that some sacrifice might be needed from Brexiteers in order to achieve their 'precious prize'. May was hailed as if Britannia herself. The prime minister, he said, 'will not flinch from her duty and the central mission that the people of this country have set us'. Having pulled his highly Eurosceptic audience close, he whispered the punchline: 'In the real world nothing so valuable is ever gained without sacrifice and compromise.' The goal should not be 'theoretical purity' but solutions 'which work'. He urged activists to accept that the 'nature of negotiation is – with apologies to the Rolling Stones – that you can't always get what you want'.

For his peroration, Cox summoned Milton's seventeenth-century poem *Areopagitica*, to describe his hopes for Brexit Britain: 'Methinks I see in my mind a noble and puissant nation rousing herself like a strong man after sleep, and shaking her invincible locks,' he roared. With a sweep of his arm he finished, 'Ladies and gentlemen, let us seize that prize.' Whether it was the shock of the new, or the power of Cox's oratory, they rose as one as if jolted from their seats by lightning. It was the attorney general's first ever speech from the podium at conference. Even jaded Westminster observers struggled to recall one more memorable from a non-leader. To friends, Cox admitted the prospect of Brexit being lost was a 'shadow in my heart'.

Not even her closest aides knew how May would follow that when she walked on stage shortly afterwards, ABBA's 'Dancing Queen' filling Birmingham's Symphony Hall, and began to dance, robotically, a knowing subversion of the 'Maybot' reputation she had acquired during the general election. Her press secretary Paul Harrison recalled, 'Based on the facial expressions of everybody in the green room, and that includes her husband, it was genuinely a surprise.'[1] The effect was startling and it rather overshadowed the content of her speech, which was most notable, domestically, for a pledge to end the era of austerity in public spending. The prime minister told her party to 'come together', saying, 'If we all go off in different directions in pursuit of our own visions of the perfect Brexit – we risk ending up with no Brexit at all.'

While Downing Street staff told May how well she had done, her cabinet were still on their feet in the Symphony Hall applauding, in several cases behind forced smiles. In the preceding forty-eight hours, over discreet lunches and coffees, the vast majority had confided a desire to see her removed as leader and the timeless backstop ditched.

The other key moment at conference came when the Democratic Unionists signalled for the first time that they were not prepared to support Chequers. Senior figures from the party met the prime minister in her suite at the Hyatt. 'We couldn't get them over the line,' one of those present recalled. An MP who spoke to Nigel Dodds, the leader of the DUP in Westminster, said, 'He was vitriolic about May. He says she doesn't internalise what she is told. She sits there like a wooden tent pole.'

Julian Smith was already contemplating the unthinkable – that the deal would have to be passed with some Labour votes. A Downing Street official said that in October, the chief whip circulated a note 'suggesting that we get into bed with Labour' and offer them a customs union to get on board. Smith was 'pressing Gavin [Barwell] quite hard on it'. Another political adviser said Smith had told Tory donors at conferences, 'The landing zone is a customs union-type arrangement' and that the government needed to 'find a deal for Parliament, rather than for the Conservative Party'. The adviser added, 'He had this very trenchant belief that Labour would come on board, because their constituents would be pushing them, but it just wasn't going to happen in the real world. Labour hate us, more than they hate each other.'

Smith was unusual as a chief whip in that he spent a lot of time in Downing Street rather than in the whips' lair in Parliament. Some allies believed he would have had more chance of winning backing for the deal if he was not seen as part of May's inner circle. 'Chief, you have to have some distance,' one of his advisers warned, 'because you need to be able to tell MPs when it's shit, but with good faith tell your colleagues when it's actually good. But if they know you're as involved in this as you are, they won't trust you anymore.' This advice was ignored.

Rumours of Smith's activities hardened opinion in ERG ranks. In a conference call they openly contemplated voting to bring down their own government by opposing the budget. Steve Baker went on the Conservative MPs' WhatsApp group to accuse May's chief of staff of lying to him: 'The first time this story of reliance on Labour votes went around, Gavin Barwell specifically asked me to reassure colleagues it was not true.' Bernard Jenkin, a veteran of the Maastricht rebellions, wrote: 'Make no mistake, a soft/non-Brexit … put through with Labour support will … remove any sense of obligation among Conservative Brexit-supporting MPs to continue to support the government.'

Things might have gone further. On 10 October, Baker took a call from a Eurosceptic businessman, who told him that a leading haulier was willing to blockade London with his lorries, parking them at motorway exits and bringing the capital to a grinding halt – to highlight opposition to a Chequers-based deal. Baker declined the offer.

The days between the Conservative Party conference, which ended on 3 October, and May's deal with Brussels on 13 November, saw a party undergoing a collective breakdown. The Brexit endgame was supposed to be simple. Oliver Robbins and Sabine Weyand would thrash out the details by the weekend of 13–14 October; fellow EU sherpas would be cut into the talks on Monday 15th; and the cabinet would approve it on the Tuesday; before a dinner for EU leaders in Brussels on Wednesday 17th, a final summit in November and a vote in Parliament to ratify the deal on the 27th. Needless to say, things did not pan out like that.

On 27 September, May's senior team on Europe – Oliver Robbins, Gavin Barwell, JoJo Penn, Robbie Gibb, Julian Smith and Raoul Ruparel – gathered in Barwell's office in Number 10. Robbins set out where things stood on the attempts to negotiate the Facilitated Customs Arrangement and common rulebook. 'He said they would not agree to the FCA and didn't want to dress it up for us,' said one of those present. 'The best hope for something along those lines would be to persuade them it is essentially a customs union for all intents and purposes, but it would just not be called that.' This was a franker assessment than Robbins had imparted before.

May was irked: 'I thought you told me FCA was negotiable and they liked it,' she complained.

Robbins was defensive: 'I am just telling you how it is, don't shoot the messenger!' The common rulebook, he reported, was less clear cut. The Dutch and Irish felt it struck a sensible balance, but the French and Germans were more concerned the plan split the EU's famous four freedoms. They wanted greater protection against British divergence in future from EU rules. 'This was the first time it was explicitly admitted that we wouldn't be able to get anything close to the Chequers proposals in the political declaration or the future relationship,' one aide recalled.

In the late afternoon of Thursday 11 October, May gathered her war cabinet to test their views. The prime minister said almost nothing. One after another, ministers lined up to denounce the deal her team had been trying to negotiate. Sajid Javid, the home secretary, borrowed the vintage US political insult about putting 'lipstick on a pig' and called the plan little better than 'third country status with lipstick on it'. May looked surprised when Jeremy Hunt, the foreign secretary, said he would oppose any deal with no break clause for the backstop, a position endorsed by Javid, Liam Fox, Gavin Williamson and Dominic Raab.

Their views were mild in comparison with Boris Johnson's. In one outburst that October, he compared May to Penelope, the wife of Odysseus in Homer's *Odyssey*. 'She's bloody Penelope! She sits refusing to accept the hand of any suitor until she's finished her tapestry, and every night she unstitches the work of the day, and thereby refuses to take a decision,' he said. 'And she is still not taking a fucking decision about the customs union. All she wants to do is survive in office. She has no other purpose. And she rightly calculates that she can fuck up Brexit and not get blamed, because everybody will blame the Brexiteers rather than her. She thinks that she can style herself as "plucky, battling Theresa", who's been put in this impossible position by a bunch of ideological men who haven't done a damn thing to help her. Actually, what she's really done is fuck the whole thing up from beginning to end.'

Watching from afar, David Davis was more measured but no less damning on the details: 'At the moment we're being faced with a choice between having Northern Ireland as a colony of the Europeans, or the whole country as a colony of the Europeans.'

*   *   *

In Brussels the chief negotiators also found emotions running hot as the European Council on 17 October approached. After the debacle at Salzburg, Robbins and Sabine Weyand had a diplomatic lovers' tiff. 'Olly didn't go to Brussels for a little while,' said a British official. 'Sabine thought he was just in a huff with her.' Robbins was highly disgruntled with the way the EU had behaved and, after fifteen months of intense activity, he was existentially bored with the entire process, ground down by having the same irascible and pointless row. He toured the European capitals instead and in Berlin met Uwe Corsepius, Angela Merkel's chief EU adviser. Corsepius was sympathetic to Robbins. This did not translate into an inch of flexibility on the substance, but the German did not want to see the process collapse. 'Have you seen Sabine recently?' he asked.

'No, I haven't actually.' As he said it, Robbins felt a little guilty.

Corsepius regarded him through his wire-rimmed spectacles. He might have been a therapist. 'Is that because you are angry with her?'

'No, I'm not angry with her, but I'm just conscious that, every time we go, we have the same discussion. Until my ministers tell me I've got a different policy or she hears something different from her masters there is no point ...'

Corsepius spoke softly, one official to another. He knew the difficulties of working to solve the problems of politicians, the duty and burdens that creates. 'There still is a point,' he said. 'If this thing is going to get fixed it's probably going to be the two of you who have to fix it, so there's something to be said for going and seeing her anyway.' As Robbins digested this, Corsepius suggested, 'Why don't you invite her out to dinner and just have a catch-up.'

Robbins swallowed his pride and called Weyand. saying, 'I'm going to come to Brussels this week, why don't we get together?' Over dinner, he suggested it was no bad thing that relations were publicly poor since that might allow them to 'take people by surprise'. He said, 'Why don't I get permission – quietly – to come and settle all the remaining issues in the withdrawal agreement with you, and see if we can do it? If we can, then we might be in a position to surprise the world at the October European Council.' Weyand agreed to give it a go.

There followed an 'incredibly intense' series of talks in the fortnight up to the European Council, working through a range of 'nerdy issues' – the Cyprus protocol, geographical indicators for food, eventually the Northern Ireland Protocol, always the most difficult issue. They made some progress for the first week, enough that on 11 October they entered the Tunnel. This was Brussels terminology for the final push on talks, conducted in utmost secrecy. The deal was that neither side leaked details of the trade-offs being contemplated. It was not in the government's or the Commission's interests to let the member states or the warring Tory factions know where they might compromise; always better to present a done deal and dare people to unpick it.

The Tunnel was not a place, more a state of mind, a mutual determination to reach a landing zone. The talks were conducted in the offices of Task Force 50 in the Berlaymont building, sometimes in the 'one big, awful, conference room', the two sides trying to write a joint text projected onto the wall. The harder and better meetings tended to be in smaller groups with no more than three people on each side, Stéphanie Riso invariably at Sabine Weyand's side, Robbins accompanied by a government lawyer and an official from the relevant department. The 'hardest and best' meetings happened further down the corridor in Weyand's office, just her and Robbins. When he said a concept 'won't fly', she would erupt. 'She's quite irascible, Olly was on the whole not,' said a British source. 'She would lose her temper and literally throw her hands up in the air and say, "What's the fucking point? You lot are all useless."'

It was Robbins who would suggest they all go home and sleep on it. Then he or Weyand would wake and text thoughts on the way ahead. On one occasion, she woke early and went to the office and sent him a lengthy email with a suggested compromise. Another flashpoint was resolved in a café between his hotel and the Berlaymont after they took a stroll in the sun. He told her, 'We could pull stumps now, but you and I are supposed to be the professionals in this. That's not what we're paid to do. I feel we could try this instead …' Weyand calmed down and agreed to find a way forward.

The major sticking point was the same as ever – May's determination that there could not be a customs border between Northern Ireland and Great Britain. Cox called in Robbins and showed him some ideas he had drafted that might give Britain a way out of the backstop. 'Do you think this is deliverable?' he asked. The negotiator considered the paper and replied, 'Yes, Attorney, I think it is.' This proved optimistic. A week later Cox received a 'dismal communication' from Robbins in which he said Task Force 50 had refused to consider the ideas.

On Thursday 11 October, the EU finally made its proposals. The Commission was prepared to include a UK-wide customs deal, like that which May had been asking for, but there was a kicker. This was a pledge to include such an arrangement in the final terms of exit, a promise to create something in future, not a legal description of how it would operate. It became known as 'the backstop to the backstop'.

A British negotiator said, 'We had a quite late night, and angry session with the Commission. We quickly saw that they were basically saying, "We'll work with you to do a UK-wide solution, but the backstop remains."' The EU tried to sweeten the pill. 'They leaned out as far as they possibly could at that stage to help us. They embedded in a legal text a political commitment to delivering further legal text in due course that would establish a UK-wide customs solutions. But it wasn't something that you could operationalise.' Robbins was torn. It was an advance but, he feared, not one that would go far enough for the cabinet. There was a 'gloomy' meeting with Weyand. 'I can't see how this works,' he told her, 'but I will take it back and explain that this is currently as far as you think you can push yourselves.'

An ad hoc group of ministers met in the Cobra rooms, in the basement of the Cabinet Office, so they could hear on a secure line from Robbins in Brussels. Geoffrey Cox had only received the key papers just before the meeting and spent the minutes while the civil servant was outlining the new development to ministers reading them closely. Robbins explained that there was good news and bad news.

Cox was surprised the good news was presented without qualification. For forty minutes he read the papers with growing incredulity, double checking that he wasn't mistaken. When every other minister had spoken, he said, 'Prime Minister, I wonder if you would allow me just to set up a few essential points.' He then proceeded to explain that the legal text showed that Northern Ireland would remain inside the customs union while Britain would not, that Northern Ireland would remain subject to single market regulation in all the areas necessary for free circulation of goods and subject both to the court of justice and to the Commission's jurisdiction, while Britain would not. 'The critical problem here, Prime Minister, is that although in the draft text, there appears to be a commitment to negotiate a UK-wide backstop, it is no more than an unenforceable aspiration. Although the legal text appears to give you the prospect that it will happen, you cannot in law, be it international or domestic, agree to agree. It's a principle that doesn't exist.' As far as Cox was concerned the entire discussion had been built on a fallacy. He said, 'Perhaps Olly could tell me whether I am correct in this analysis.'

There was a pause while the other ministers looked at the giant video screen. Robbins said, 'The attorney has it exactly right.'

Once May understood the situation, she pronounced it 'wholly unacceptable' and sent her lead negotiator back to try again. 'We must have a binding commitment,' she said. Cox called his own lawyers in and very nearly lost his temper with them. 'How on earth could this ever have been presented to the prime minister?' he asked. 'It is viscerally unacceptable.'

To the Brexiteers in the room it was a clarifying incident, both about the value of Cox and of Robbins' reluctance to spell out the full implications of the technical agreements he was negotiating. One cabinet minister present said, 'I think it was because the officials knew that if they spelled it out with clarity, the politicians might say, "We can't do this." And they could see no way other than what they were doing. Their entire posture with the European Union was that we had no choice but to accept these things.'

May asked Robbins to return on Saturday. He met Weyand again that evening. Further ideas, all trying to pull the same trick, followed. They reached Option F before the meeting ended, acrimoniously, around 1.30 a.m. on the Sunday. He said, as politely as he could, 'I will reflect to the prime minister that this is as far as you will take things now, but I have to warn you, my understanding of the British government's position is we cannot do a deal on this basis.'

He reported to May overnight and a conference call followed on the Sunday morning, Robbins down the line from Brussels. May read his submission and said, 'Sadly, you're right, Olly, we can't accept this.' He told her they were no longer in a position to conclude any of the withdrawal agreement at the October European Council. 'It would be a mistake to settle some issues but not this one,' he said. The prime minister reluctantly agreed.

Senior members of the cabinet were growing concerned that Robbins was not pushing hard enough and that political input was needed in the talks. On Sunday, 14 October, Julian Smith formally wrote to May warning that she could 'not cross political red lines set out repeatedly by the

DUP and the Conservative unionists'. The backstop had to be time limited and customs checks between Great Britain and Northern Ireland removed, he wrote. Smith urged the prime minister not to wait for a final deal but to publish details of the gains Britain had made in the negotiation to show momentum, advice that directly contradicted that of Robbins. He then demanded a new negotiating process led by politicians. 'The civil service technical channel was not producing what we need politically.'

At lunchtime that Sunday, Robbins met Weyand and Jeppe Tranholm-Mikkelsen, the senior official in the European Council, at his offices in the Europa building. It was supposed to be a stock take for the 'final heave' towards a deal. Instead, Robbins said, 'I don't think we can do it.' One of the participants remembered it as 'one of the most depressing meetings we've ever had'. Instead of making progress, the two sides discussed how to handle the media fallout from their failure.

Yet, even as the meeting was going on, members of the negotiating team were told to prepare for the arrival of Raab, who was racing to Brussels, apparently to stop his chief negotiator signing up to a deal which was already stopped in its tracks. 'We just don't understand why he's coming,' a member of the EU's Task Force 50 said. 'There's just nothing to discuss. It's over.' Raab had been asked by May to go to Brussels on the Monday but brought forward his visit by twenty-four hours because the exchange of papers made him think that some of what had been agreed by the technical groups crossed red lines that the SN committee had laid down. The backstop provisions were 'a grenade that will go off,' he thought. Raab spoke to May. 'You need to stop this,' he said. 'We can't do this; I won't defend it.'

Before he caught the Eurostar, Raab was met in a station coffee shop, Le Pain Quotidien, by Julian Smith, who bizarrely had raced to St Pancras on a Sunday to 'put some lead in his pencil' to fight for a backstop that was limited, finite and short. 'Just be honest about what you believe,' the chief whip said. 'We need to air this stuff. We need to be seen to have fought for it.' While this was politically true, Smith was egging on a Brexit secretary who was preparing to go way beyond his instructions from May.

Raab's arrival in the Belgian capital bemused the Europeans and irritated the British negotiating team. 'The decisions had already all been taken,' a source said. In the Commission the mood was one of: 'What are we all doing here on our Sunday evening? We've already wasted the rest of our weekend.' It made for a 'bad tempered' encounter. A British negotiator recalled, 'This trip to Brussels was verging on the spiteful towards us. He came to stop us from doing a bad deal. It was a pretty weird episode.'

Raab was convinced Robbins had given away too much. In a memo to May on 12 October, two days earlier, he complained about 'fatal' flaws in the proposals. He accused Robbins' team of accepting a compromise on geographical indicators for food, which he, Liam Fox and Michael Gove 'only agreed on the basis that we could secure a time limit to the back-stop'. The Brexit secretary also criticised a 'lop-sided' arbitration process with Britain facing 'fines' if it failed to comply but with 'no redress' if the EU failed to do so. He reserved his harshest words for the backstop, writing, 'The absence of a time-limit to the UK-wide customs solution is fatal. It leaves the UK subject to a potentially indefinite limbo in the Customs Union. It is indefensible and I cannot support it.'

When Barwell read Raab's note, first thing on the 13th, a concerned chief of staff emailed the Brexit secretary to ask, 'Do you think you or the PM are going to be able to shift them further or do you think this means no-deal? I think you need to set that out given the potential consequences of the latter for the future of the government.' When Raab replied, at 11.12 a.m., he again insisted that Barnier 'recognised – when I pressed – our argument on the finality of the backstop'. Raab suggested making a 'best/ positive final offer' to the EU to show ministers and voters that the UK had done everything possible to avoid no-deal. 'I think a lot of Remainers would be shocked by what the EU is proposing, let alone the public. We need to occupy the moral and diplomatic high ground.'

On arrival in Brussels, David Davis typically spent time with Robbins and other officials at Tim Barrow's residence to get up to speed. 'But Dom very quickly kicked them all out' so he could talk with his special advisers. May had told him to focus on a UK-wide customs solution and some limit to the scope of the backstop. Instead, Raab mapped out a whole list of things he was planning to raise. Even his advisers regarded some of the issues as 'arcane', others as 'a bit pointless'. One said, 'He went down rabbit holes like the dispute mechanism. Olly had obviously told the Commission we wanted to talk about two issues, then Dom went off on these other things.'

In his Sunday evening meeting with Barnier, the Brexit secretary talked about the jurisdiction of the European Court of Justice. He also questioned a demand that Commission officials could launch future investigations into whether Britain was policing the frontiers of the customs area properly. Raab and Barnier clashed over the percentage of agricultural products which would be subject to physical and document checks. 'The default was close to 100 per cent, which is pretty ridiculous,' a Raab ally said. The Brexit secretary said, 'You have lots of agreements with other countries where this is brought down.' A belligerent Barnier hit back: 'Well, maybe we could do that in the future, but for now you have to accept all of these checks.' The tensest exchange came, predictably, on Northern Ireland. May had told Raab explicitly not to press for a unilateral exit mechanism. He did so. 'I don't see how I can sell to the cabinet or the prime minister a limbo in the customs union,' he said.

'Olly had told the two institutions already that we could not proceed,' a British official said. 'Then he watched the secretary of state say that again as if it was news, and raise a whole series of issues he knew were marginal or unauthorised.' A senior Commission official admitted, 'This annoyed us a lot, and it didn't help.'

Robbins bit his tongue in the room, but as they filed out he turned to Raoul Ruparel and asked, 'What the fuck was that?' Later, once they were out of earshot from EU officials, he told Raab, 'Some of that stuff's already been agreed.'

When May held a conference call with Barrow and Robbins that evening, one of her inner circle recalled: 'The PM wasn't happy with it.' Raab told friends she was 'grumpy' when they spoke. 'You went and said more than I said you should say,' the PM complained.

'Yes,' he admitted, 'because you need to recognise we cannot sell this, as I have advised you before. I was quite careful because I was stating the facts; I cannot sell this. I cannot, it's indefensible.'

May and Raab's relationship, never warm, never recovered. 'Trust levels between Dom and Number 10 went down remarkably after that,' a fellow cabinet minister said. 'There was less willingness to trust him with information or activity, more of a tendency to switch back to Olly.' Gavin Barwell disagreed. He saw it as Raab testing the negotiability of his own preferred blueprint for Brexit, a process the chief of staff expected to lead to the secretary of state joining a long line of Brexiteers coming to terms with Number 10's reality. 'I wanted Dom to stay onside,' Barwell said. 'And if him having had the opportunity to test whether what he thought would work, would work, helped do that, then I can tolerate the awkwardness of him advocating something that was not what the prime minister was saying.'

The scales fell from the eyes of senior ministers on the evening of Monday, 15 October, when Andrea Leadsom invited members of the cabinet to meet in her rooms behind the speaker's chair. Leadsom ordered 'hot and spicy' pizzas from a fast-food joint in Pimlico while Geoffrey Cox turned up with two bottles of champagne. Others present included Raab, Michael Gove, Jeremy Hunt, Sajid Javid, Liam Fox, Penny Mordaunt, Chris Grayling, Gavin Williamson, Esther McVey and Liz Truss, who complained to aides the prime minister was 'giving everything' to Brussels. The 'Pizza Club' had been meeting for several weeks and had its own WhatsApp group of the same name.

The star turn was the attorney general, who explained that he wanted to ensure that fellow ministers made all future decisions with 'piercing clarity'. Ever since the Joint Report, he believed there had been 'a want of frank speaking' at the top of government. Cox explained that any withdrawal deal would become a treaty and enjoy an elevated status in international law, which would make it all but impossible to unpick later. The backstop was a trap, he argued, and there would need to be some sort of exit clause for Britain. But he also described May's deal as 'the life raft' which would allow Britain to get out of the EU since it was 'profoundly uncomfortable' for the EU too. 'It is not the trap in which they would wish to contain us because we could make it a very uncomfortable place for them to rest,' he said. Summing up, Cox said, 'It is an acceptable compromise for us to make, provided we get the second leg right.' That meant a political declaration on the future trade arrangements which was closer to a Canada-style deal. The withdrawal agreement was only about fixing the past, the future was still to be defined.

Some ministers felt this was the first time they fully understood what was at stake. Raab tried to explain to his colleagues what was going on with the talks since they were largely in the dark. 'Welcome to my world,' he said, only half in jest. 'There is a basic lack of ministerial oversight.'

The group wanted a tougher line from May. Liam Fox said, 'Our line should be: "We've made you an offer, we're not going any further. We expect you to come to the council in October with a counter-offer." We need to put lots and lots of pressure on.' He did not believe the EU was ever going to agree to Chequers because 'it drives a coach and horses through their red lines on the single market. We think we're being too generous. They think what we're asking for is outrageous cheek. Their counter-offer has to be a souped-up FTA.' The international trade secretary believed that a Canada-style deal would not get through Parliament if it was presented as the Brexiteers getting their way, but there was 'a good chance' it would pass 'if the EU are willing to say it's their preferred option'. He said, 'My advice has been to say nothing. We've made our offer. My route means you have to really hold your nerve. It's a game of chicken.'

The Pizza Club agreed two things that night: they would fight at cabinet for a time limit or exit clause from the backstop and they would demand to see formal legal advice before signing up to any deal. Cautiously, May's demise was also entertained. 'People did say, "In the end we might need someone else to lead the party",' a minister said.

A second, tighter knit group also met from time to time, but details of its discussions did not leak. This brought together Cox and Gove with Raab, Hunt and Javid. This was the moral middle of the cabinet: two Brexiteers open to compromise, two Remain voters who believed the result of the 2016 referendum had to be delivered at all costs, plus the minister responsible for Brexit. After a takeaway in Javid's office, they became the 'Burger Group' on WhatsApp. They also met in Hunt's parliamentary office. 'We were the pragmatists,' recalled one. 'We didn't want the thing to fall over. There was no discussion in there about toppling Theresa.'

At least nine cabinet ministers now wanted May to change tack and four – including the three Brexiteer women: Leadsom, Mordaunt and McVey – were considering whether to resign. All three were told by MPs to quit if they wanted to be leader. The fourth cabinet minister threatening to go was David Mundell, the Scottish secretary. He and Ruth Davidson, leader of the Scottish Tories, were concerned a botched Brexit deal would fuel the case for Scottish independence.

With the balance of power moving against her, May opened the meeting on 16 October with the words, 'This is not a decision-making cabinet.' Cox repeated for the wider cabinet much of what he had said to the Pizza Club. His attempts to explain how the government had got in this predicament since the Joint Report was described by one witness as 'a bit like a builder who comes and says, "You've had the cowboys in here. This is nothing I would have signed off.'" Some detected froideur between May and her attorney general. 'She doesn't want to be mansplained to,' a cabinet minister observed. 'I think the jury rather enjoyed [his performance], but the client was not sure she got what she paid for.'

Gove formed the second spike of the pincer movement. The environment secretary said he would never back any backstop plan until he had been shown 'clear, written, legal advice' on the specific wording. This approach set up Cox as the key arbiter of whether a deal was acceptable to the Brexiteers. It was to be a demand with far-reaching consequences.

Julian Smith finally revealed just how bad the situation was in Parliament. The chief whip told May that she was courting catastrophe if she accepted a backstop with no exit clause: 'I lose one hundred MPs if you do this.' In total, he estimated 150 Tory MPs were planning to vote against her if there was a meaningful vote. May, as usual, gave little away. 'She didn't really say anything,' a minister said. The prime minister's senior aides were stunned by the scale of the looming disaster and furious that Smith had waited so long to come clean about the numbers. After the meeting Barwell lost his temper, administering what was variously described as a 'bollocking' and a 'bucket of shit' to the chief whip. 'Gavin was heard swearing,' an aide said, 'and Gavin Barwell does not swear.'

Smith had previously been telling May and Barwell to get the deal done but as the number of rebels swelled, he joined Raab and the Brexiteers in demanding some sort of exit clause from the backstop. His conversion was too late. Still May did not appear willing to change course. Raab, Fox and others had assumed that when shown the impossibility of success, she would pivot to a Canada plus Brexit. Instead, she was to spend the next eight months in an increasingly desperate game of chicken with Brussels, the ERG and the Remainers, doubling down on her plan in the hope that it would be the last man standing.

The European Council meeting was a disaster for May. The prime minister addressed her fellow leaders for fifteen minutes, urging them to help with 'creative solutions' to the Irish border issue. Her speech was met with a stony silence and no one asked questions. She left for Barrow's residence, where she picked at a fish dinner.

While May cut a forlorn and isolated figure, Angela Merkel, Emmanuel Macron, Charles Michel and Xavier Bettel abandoned their formal dinner and went drinking at the Roy d'Espagne brasserie on Brussels' Grand Place, sinking beers until after 1 a.m. Asked by a tourist how the Brexit talks were going, the German chancellor said, 'Please, it's a wonderful evening – let's not spoil it with that.'[2]

Earlier that week, the ERG leadership agreed they could not be seen to be May's political assassins. Jacob Rees-Mogg told the group's weekly Tuesday evening meeting, 'If you have put a letter in, please take it out. If you are thinking of putting a letter in, please don't.'

However, on 19 October, just three days later, Steve Baker wrote his letter to Graham Brady, accusing the prime minister of taking the country down a 'path to failure' and 'humiliation'. He wrote, 'There seems little point allowing the Captain to continue running the ship towards the rocks … There is objectively no reason to think her exit negotiations will deliver a Brexit worth having. And it is inconceivable she would subsequently lead us to a general election victory.' He kept the letter in his pocket for three days before submitting it, and recalled, 'The period of September through to November was torture. It was absolutely clear to us that the deal wouldn't go through. We were desperate for the agnostic centre to come to its senses, and put their confidence letters in and have a new prime minister but they wouldn't move. We then had a period where people were begging each other to do it.'

Grant Shapps, the former party chairman, had led an effort to oust May a year earlier. One MP who had refused to support his plot in 2017 now approached him, asking him to sign a letter demanding that May go.

Her plight led to a brief re-flourishing of the David Davis for leader campaign. Friends began gauging backbench support for him as caretaker prime minister and whether Boris Johnson would be prepared to stand aside. MPs claimed James Gray, the member for North Wiltshire, was telling them 'Boris is a busted flush and DD could be an interim leader.' Gray denied it. Davis wrote a piece for the *Sunday Times* demanding that the cabinet 'exert their collective authority'. Johnson was some way from the peak of his popularity, but he was not prepared to clear the way for Davis.

Baker was also in regular contact with Mordaunt and Leadsom and from the end of October he and Rees-Mogg began hosting dinners at the ERG chairman's home in Westminster with likely leadership candidates. Michael Gove was their first guest, Mordaunt soon followed. None of these Brexiteers was even, at this point, favourite to succeed May. Javid was the smart money candidate, with Hunt also jockeying for position.

The briefing against the prime minister that weekend was misogynist and borderline psychotic. In a sign of the way Brexit deranged normal discourse, a former minister said, 'The moment is coming when the knife gets heated, stuck in her front and twisted. She'll be dead soon.' A Davis ally said May was entering 'the killing zone'. The PM was due to face the 1922 Committee the following Tuesday, an event likened to a 'show trial'. One Brexiteer suggested she 'bring her own noose'.[3]

Dominic Raab was concerned that not only had Number 10 given up on securing an exit clause from the backstop, Robbins hadn't even properly asked for one. Cox had drawn up two alternatives, known in Whitehall as Option 1 and Option 2. In a memo to May, Robbins wrote, 'Option 1 creates a termination power but does not give the UK a unilateral power to revoke.' Either side could notify the other that there was 'no prospect' of a trade deal and 'trigger' a 'high level conference' to consider the next steps. This mutual consent approach was 'more negotiable', he argued, 'though not straightforward given the EU do not want any termination power'.[4]

Option 2 was 'a unilateral termination power for either party in the event that the future relationship talks have broken down or there has been a fundamental change of circumstances'. This, Robbins suggested, would be 'most difficult' to secure and would spark 'accusations that the UK is reneging on previous commitments'. He also warned that the same mechanism was a double-edged sword that could be 'used as leverage against us' in future trade talks.[5]

Raab wanted to aim high and demand Option 2. His belief, outlined in an email to Barwell on 8 October, was that unless the backstop ended 'by the end of 2022', the government's 'position would be rendered indefensible'.[6] At this point, the chief of staff made clear that May had abandoned hope of securing a time limit. 'We won't be able to secure a cut-off date,' he wrote in reply, 'but Olly feels he and the team are making good progress with a commitment in the Future Framework that the backstop won't come into force.'[7]

Two weeks later, on Saturday 20 October, Raab, along with Cox, Hunt and other ministers, had a conference call with May, Robbins listening in silently. 'We all argue that you've got to go for Option 2,' one minister said. 'The agreement was made that we would put Option 2 to the Commission and it just didn't happen.' The following day, Raab's office emailed a note to Robbins saying any text would need 'a clear exit mechanism' to make it 'acceptable and defensible' politically. The Brexit secretary wrote, 'It could of course be a time limit of say 3/4/6 months. Alternatively, it could be a review mechanism that required both sides to approve, in order for it to continue beyond the review point at say 3/4/6 months.'[8]

Later that day, May's private secretary for Europe, Catherine Page, emailed a draft legal text to be submitted to the EU which reflected 'the preference amongst Ministers to pursue Option 1', the opposite of what Raab thought had been agreed.[9] His office sent a perfunctory two-paragraph response at 5.58 p.m.: 'In the absence of an exit mechanism ... he cannot support this text.'[10]

There was a way of squaring the circle. May and Robbins could have sought a democratic consent mechanism, via which the people of Northern Ireland could have theoretically ended the backstop in future, something that would be much harder for the Commission to decry. Raoul Ruparel and Denzil Davidson both pushed for such a plan. Robbins said the EU would never accept it. 'We need to try to put them under pressure,' Ruparel said. But Robbins was 'never willing to do it,' an aide said. Davidson recalled, 'We wrongly thought that that was not negotiable. We could have been wrong about that.' At this time, perhaps it was not possible, but Boris Johnson would later prove it could be done in different circumstances.

Eurosceptic grandees sought to bypass Downing Street to make their own case to Brussels. On 22 October, Iain Duncan Smith led an ERG delegation to see Barnier and Weyand. He was accompanied by Owen Paterson, David Trimble and trade experts Shanker Singham and Hans Maessen. The group pressed the case for alternative arrangements to prevent a hard Irish border. They were listened to politely and Duncan Smith returned convinced their ideas had been 'positively received'. Cabinet ministers and Downing Street aides who saw the read-out of the meeting insist this was wishful thinking. One Number 10 official said Duncan Smith's optimism was 'just nuts', adding, 'Sabine and Michel mostly machine-gunned what they were saying and then they still come out of it saying it was all fine.' In his memoir, Barnier recalled telling the delegation, 'We will never be able to control the health of cows entering our internal market with drones!'[11] The Frenchman did entertain the idea that technology might have a role to play, but only in future. A Downing Street aide said, 'One of the problems we had with Brexiteers is that they went to see the Commission and the Commission politely said, "Very interesting, but we don't think it works", and because they were not shouting them down, they thought there might be an opening.'

One of May's senior advisers said, 'There is possibly a version of alternative arrangements that works over time. Like the Good Friday Agreement, it requires everyone to take some pain. The Irish on the North/South, the Brits on East/West, the Commission on the integrity of EU law and single market. If everyone takes a little bit of pain then there might be a way through.' The EU was not ready to take any pain, or even risk, when it came to the integrity of the single market. Some aides regarded it as ironic that the Paleosceptics, who had most vocally condemned Brussels' intransigence over the years, were now the most optimistic that the EU would compromise.

Raab thought the Irish held the key. 'The route to unlocking the protocol is in Dublin not Brussels,' he told a friend. The Brexit secretary felt the Commission had 'not been straight with the Irish, since the protocol was presented as a timeless insurance policy but, under Article 50, could not be indefinite'. The problem for Raab was that the minister May had entrusted with relations with the Irish was not him but David Lidington.

On 30 October, Raab had dinner in London with Simon Coveney, the Irish foreign minister and deputy premier. Both men explained the political realities they faced. Coveney rehearsed the need for an insurance policy against no-deal and a hard border. Raab explained the view of government lawyers that Article 50 was by definition a means for winding down an existing membership of the EU, not the basis of a new relationship and that the backstop could be challenged in court in future.

In a note to May the following morning, he added, 'I also explained our political reality in the HoC that, absent a time limit or sunset [clause], any backstop needed to include a mechanism that allowed us to exit, and for this to be something we could control. I walked him through my idea of a review mechanism after say 3/4/6 months, which could only continue beyond a certain point with joint agreement.' Raab thought Coveney 'positive' but the Irish deputy premier wanted the future of the backstop decided by 'joint agreement'. Raab said that 'would not work' but that the UK would consider 'any other political or legal assurances' that could 'make it saleable in Dublin'.[12] He offered to meet him again with a technical team.

The Brexit secretary told May that Coveney's 'nervousness was palpable' that failure to get a deal would lead to a hard border by default and that he 'hadn't shut the door'. The Irishman asked Raab to keep their meeting confidential and Raab left the dinner thinking the Dublin government was 'in the market' for what he had suggested.[13] He also tipped off Jeremy Hunt that Coveney was in town. The Foreign Office had not informed the foreign secretary, who met Coveney for breakfast the next morning to reinforce the same message. Raab and Hunt were then spotted comparing notes over lunch at the Corinthia Hotel on Northumberland Avenue.

The existence of the Raab-Coveney dinner was revealed by Peter Foster in the *Daily Telegraph* on 5 November.[14] His story led on a claim that the Irish were 'stunned' that Raab had 'privately demanded the right to pull Britain out of the backstop after just three months'. The Brexit secretary recalled, 'Simon had asked me to keep our meeting confidential and I respected that. It was then divulged and misrepresented by the Irish *Taoiseach* Leo Varadkar. I didn't think that was a particularly professional or statesmanlike way of resolving a very sensitive aspect of the deal.'[15]

Just as explosive was Foster's revelation that Raab's pitch 'was contradicted by David Lidington, the UK's de facto deputy prime minister, on a visit to Dublin' three days later. Lidington was there for the British-Irish intergovernmental conference. When he asked Coveney how the dinner had gone, the Irish foreign minister said, 'He [Raab] went on about a three-to-six-month time limit on the backstop.' Lidington, politely, made clear that was 'not going to happen' and that Britain stood by what it had agreed in the Joint Report.

Lidington had encouraged Raab to see the Irish, in part, because he wanted the government in Dublin to hear his views directly, so they understood the strength of feeling among Brexiteers. Lidington also wanted Raab to hear the same message he had been receiving: that 'their government would be out in twenty-four hours if they made a serious concession' on the backstop. He felt Raab too readily dismissive of the Irish position, around which there was cross-party unity. 'This story of me somehow blocking an historic breakthrough on time limits, it was never going to be,' he said.

To Raab, Lidington's behaviour was 'unforgiveable' and the episode another opportunity lost. One ally said, 'The problem with Lidington having the dialogue with the Irish and being basically the only person who spoke to them, was a problem, a mistake. We'd never had any Brexiteers talking to the Irish.' To Downing Street it was another example of Brexiteer wishful thinking. Barwell said, 'Coveney very politely explained to Dom why they couldn't do what he wanted them to do. Because he did it very politely – and because Dom didn't want to hear it – Dom didn't hear it. We obviously got feedback via our ambassador in Dublin. It's quite clear that what Dom thinks was said to him was absolutely not said to him.'

A few days later, Raab texted Lidington and asked whether he wanted to talk about 'his campaign to reunite the Conservative party', a prospective leadership candidate seeking to woo his colleagues. It fuelled speculation in May's team that Raab's stance was designed to position him as the choice of hard Brexiteers in the eventual contest to succeed her.

A second footnote: Raab was not wrong to believe that the Irish government was beginning to feel real pressure and was perennially concerned that the EU would sell them down the river. The issue between the UK and the EU was, in effect, whether there should be a customs border in the Irish Sea or between North and South. But there was a third, even more controversial, solution – forcing Ireland into a customs union with Britain and drawing the border all the way around the British Isles. The neo-colonial concept was actively advanced by aides in Emmanuel Macron's office. Ameet Gill, the former head of strategy for both David Cameron and Remain, was doing some work for the French president and he took the idea to Barwell in Number 10. 'It was something they were thinking about in the French system,' a senior government source confirmed. 'They were becoming increasingly grumpy with Varadkar for not setting out what Ireland would do in the event of a no-deal Brexit. They began to punt this idea that you create a customs union of the islands, where we compensate the Irish for the costs that would incur on them.'

The plan would have left Britain facing friction at the Channel ports but it would have negated the need for the backstop. A softer version would have seen Ireland allow some inspections of goods 'between Ireland and the EU26 as a way of getting the EU to agree a softer inspection regime for goods going North-South,' a senior cabinet minister said. EU leaders could see logic in the plan. A senior Commission official admitted, 'It would have been easier for continental Europe to say, "We'll just put the border on the continent and then let Ireland take care of its own problems in a bilateral agreement with the UK."'

The idea did not work for two reasons, one political, one practical. First, Brussels could not be seen to abandon Dublin. Second, as a British negotiator explained, 'We worked out, you had to change the EU treaties, which would have triggered another referendum.'

As November began, Oliver Robbins warned May that, thanks to the timing of EU meetings and a G20 summit in mid-December, there was just a two-week window to secure a deal before Christmas. In a memo to the prime minister dated 2 November, he had some good news. 'The Commission accept that the backstop must be described in operative legal text as temporary in nature.' He had also secured 'clear legal recognition' that the EU would use its 'best endeavours' to agree a 'future deal to supersede it by December 2020' and a 'legal guillotine to ensure that any future deal ended the backstop' provided it negated the need for 'a hard border'. Robbins noted, 'TF50 are concerned they gave away too much here and are attempting to backpedal.'[16]

However, the document was crystal clear that, as Raab feared, 'the Government has committed itself not to seek an arbitrary time limit to the duration of the backstop if bought into force'. Moreover, 'the Withdrawal Agreement, including the Northern Ireland Protocol, does not currently include any termination provision', meaning the UK had no right to leave it in international law. Robbins outlined Option 1 and Option 2 and concluded, 'Our advice is that a unilateral termination mechanism is likely to be rejected in strong terms, and lead to a prolonged hiatus. A termination clause without unilateral mechanism may be negotiable, but will need to be relatively simple if it is to be concluded quickly.'[17] In short, of the two things the Eurosceptics, including the Brexit secretary, needed to support a deal – a time limit or a unilateral exit clause – the government had decided not to demand the first and the official responsible for the negotiations did not think the second was obtainable.

A time limit or an exit clause was never submitted as a formal demand by the British government, but it is not true that Robbins and May never asked for one. Both did so, several times. 'The PM did make that case a couple of times that we did need one and she asked [Olly] to go and make it in both Brussels and Dublin,' a member of the negotiating team said. On 2 November, Robbins held a surreptitious meeting in Dublin airport with John Callinan, Varadkar's Europe adviser, to press the case again for an exit clause. On 5 November, May 'phoned the Taoiseach and asked for it,' one of her Europe advisers said. 'She talked to Juncker about it.' Robbins and Callinan met again the following day in Brussels. Their entreaties made no difference. 'We did ask for it,' a Downing Street adviser said. 'The problem is you get a flat no. Then where do you go?' A senior negotiator opined, 'There is a real difference between exploring an ask, something being collectively agreed and government policy. Establishing a unilateral exit clause to the backstop was never government policy.' The upshot was that May never made sure her party, let alone the public, saw her fighting full-throatedly for something they regarded as vital.

Eurosceptics suspected the Europe Unit sympathised with the EU's belief that a time limit to the backstop was an unreasonable demand. One civil servant said, 'What's the point of designing a backstop for three months? That's not a backstop. You're not going to sign an agreement for three months. No one does that.' The age-old complaint about Robbins' secrecy surfaced again. In Number 10, Nikki da Costa protested to colleagues, 'Olly needs to be stopped from behaving the way he is: saving up advice very late, requiring a decision within hours, bouncing the prime minister.' Denzil Davidson, Ed de Minckwitz, Raoul Ruparel and May's private secretary for Europe, Catherine Page, were all concerned by the chief negotiator's habit of dropping papers late into ministerial red boxes. 'People went to Gavin [Barwell] and said, "It's got to stop."'

More sympathetic cabinet ministers felt Robbins had been crushed by the process. 'He's just a bit shellshocked, I think,' said one. 'The EU wore him down. He's smarter than them but they're more stubborn than him. And the magnetism of what they're about is far more attractive to him than it would be for, say, a Tim Barrow.' Those less sympathetic felt Robbins expected them to bow to his judgement. 'It's a passive aggressive civil servant thing where he'll just keep coming back and he'll think that we'll all blink,' one said. 'Olly would like us to stay in the customs union.'

This belief was reinforced after Raoul Ruparel told colleagues he had been on the patio of Barrow's residence in Brussels with Robbins when the negotiator remarked, 'Oh well, you know, if the EU traps us in a customs union, it's not the worst thing in the world.' This was Robbins at his most unguarded. Economically, he had a point but those Ruparel told saw it as politically naive.

May still thought she had the real solution. 'I told you we needed Chequers,' she informed a minister, 'because that's the only thing that makes all this ridiculous backstop go away.'

To some, the criticisms of Robbins were the well-worn tendency of critics of a leader to blame their wicked aides – a theme in British history from Piers Gaveston and the Despensers to Sir Alan Walters under Margaret Thatcher and Ed Balls, when he worked for Gordon Brown. One special adviser said, 'I think he has been unfairly maligned by a group of Brexiteers who feel they can attack him in a way they can't attack the prime minister.' For his part Robbins loathed the briefing against him. 'He found it profoundly uncomfortable to be even a third-order public figure,' a friend said. It got more than uncomfortable. When Raab first met Robbins in July, the civil servant suggested he was considering resigning because the abuse he was getting was upsetting his family. Several sources say he received death threats. A Brexiteer cabinet minister who saw him speak at an event for the Jo Cox foundation on bullying said Robbins talked frankly about the abuse he received from the public: 'Olly was there, because of some of the things that happened to him. He had a lot of aggro on social media. If he got off a train and someone recognised him, I don't think he was physically assaulted, but he was hounded. He felt he had no right of reply. Olly was only doing what he'd been asked to by his principal, and yet he was hung out to dry.'

On 16 October, Sir Mark Sedwill, the acting cabinet secretary, stepped in, writing a letter to *The Times* in which he denounced those 'sniping' at Robbins, saying they 'should be ashamed of themselves'. He added, 'This has to stop. Civil servants have always trusted that our fellow citizens, whatever their views, know that we are doing our duty to implement the decisions of the governments they elect.'

Robbins was more exposed by the absence from Whitehall of his chief defender Jeremy Heywood. The cabinet secretary worked until nearly the end, only retiring on 24 October, when he was already gravely ill. Eleven days later Heywood died in his sleep at the age of just fifty-six. He passed away believing 'we'll end up with a second referendum'.[18] After his memorial service in Westminster Abbey – at which four prime ministers paid eloquent tributes – May told his widow Suzanne, 'I think people will look back and notice when he stopped.'[19] Brexit had proved intractable even to someone of Heywood's great problem-solving gifts. But those who knew him well say had he been fit he would have forced May into facing reality and making decisions. A fellow civil servant said, 'The worst thing was that he was really ill for a long time. Having a cabinet secretary would have been really handy – and we didn't have one. That was more of a problem than anyone gave credit to.'

It was another of Robbins' key relationships which helped to break the impasse, one he had cultivated with utmost discretion. Since the summer of 2017, Britain's Brexit negotiator had been meeting in secret with Martin Selmayr, the 'monster of the Berlaymont' and the most powerful official in Brussels, to resolve the most intractable issues. They met every three or four weeks, but sometimes three times a week at key moments, at half a dozen discreet locations around the Belgian capital. In scenes reminiscent of a spy movie, the two would talk for four or five hours over dinner at quiet restaurants or the roof of the Sofitel hotel, an area off limits to guests, as well as other 'private locations' away from the city centre. This back channel to Juncker's right-hand man had been explicitly authorised by both May and the Commission president but was unknown to the British public, the media and most of the cabinet. It was, to a degree that has not previously been understood, the engine room of Brexit.

Selmayr's reputation in London was that of an arch-federalist and Anglophobe Machiavelli, the ultimate hate figure for the Brexiteers.[20] But in October and November 2018, his unshakeable belief that he was the best problem solver in Europe worked to Britain's advantage. Robbins and Selmayr, both with a hot streak of intellectual self-regard, shared a mutual respect, the experience of being publicly vilified and a belief that the responsible thing to do was to talk. Someone who was in on the secret said, 'It was a very, very close relationship, and [they] shared this philosophy from the beginning to the end of the negotiations.'

Their conversations always began with a discussion of their families and the books they read, 'not to spoil the evening from the beginning'. The source said, 'Then Olly always set out his plan, his view for the next week. [Martin] told him what [he] thought, honestly, could work ... the hurdles to overcome ... what the views in capitals were.' They swapped draft legal text, which they had scribbled on trains or when they awoke, to test it before showing it to their own sides. This was high-end stuff. 'They didn't discuss the mutual recognition of diplomas,' a Commission source said. 'They discussed the backstop, the sequencing, the transition, the length of the transition, the technique of the transition, the interaction between Article 50 and the withdrawal agreement – the biggest strategic questions. They didn't meddle in paragraph 15 subparagraph 3.'

With Juncker's clearance, Selmayr then told Weyand and Barnier, 'This is how we think this should be going.' For the Frenchman such interference was intolerable. In his memoir, Barnier complained, 'I know that he sees Olly Robbins directly and speaks to him, despite the formal request made by Jean-Claude Juncker in my presence in his office.' He accused Selmayr of 'expressing directly to the British ideas which are his alone and that we have not discussed together'.[21]

Barnier was right to be suspicious since Selmayr provided, under the counter, advice to Robbins on what Barnier was unhappy with in the British proposals and they discussed ways around the obstacles. Relations in the negotiating room between Britain's chief negotiator and Weyand had grown increasingly strained. Commission officials say both she and Barnier had become 'extremely disrespectful' about the British side, frustrated at what they saw as wasted time dealing with both Davis and Raab, increasingly of the view 'they will never get it done on the other side'. Not exposed to such daily frustrations, Selmayr was a calm sounding board.

Barnier and his deputy had been resisting May's calls for an all-UK backstop for months. After Raab's dash to Brussels, the prime minister asked Robbins to remain there and see what could be revived. Following conversations with the Dutch, the Germans, the French and the Irish, the idea developed that some sort of 'British choice' could be embedded in the treaty allowing the UK to choose either an extension of the implementation period or the backstop. Out of that then flourished the realisation that extending the transition period simply meant extending British membership of the customs union, so why not allow a more controlled version of that under Article 50? 'They found that was the lesser of the two evils,' a British negotiator said. The EU also accepted that regulatory checks on goods could take place 'in the market' by

British officials, meaning they could be conducted at factories and shops rather than at the border.

By the end of October, with the help of Juncker, Selmayr and Jeppe Tranholm-Mikkelsen at the Council, the EU finally backed down and allowed the all-UK backstop. Robbins did the heavy lifting while Jonno Evans, May's private secretary for Europe, and Will Burgon, another official, did the legwork on the text. On Wednesday 31st, ambassadors to the EU were briefed by a member of Barnier's team that a 'British backstop' was being worked on. Together Selmayr and Tranholm-Mikkelsen faced down the 'French school of thought' in Brussels, which wanted to punish the UK, and overruled Barnier. 'Selmayr was key in helping us get it over the line,' a member of Robbins' team said. 'Barnier and his team were very hardline. Sabine wanted a very basic FTA with punishing level playing field conditionality. She didn't want anything like the level of market access we got.' Asked later by the BBC's Nick Robinson what his nickname should have been, Selmayr replied, 'Martin the friend of Britain.'[22] That may be stretching the point, but May's team saw the 'monster' as deal-maker not devil. A senior Council official said, 'The member states had a week to agree on a EU-UK-wide customs union. That was something which grew up in the tunnel. From the perspective of civil servants in the capitals, it was completely crazy. But it happened and I think that was a very clear demonstration of the goodwill on our side.'

Securing de facto access to the customs union for the whole of Great Britain, rather than just Northern Ireland, was Robbins' greatest success in the pure art of negotiation. It gave the UK, in customs terms, the benefits of EU membership, without following all the rules of the single market or paying into the budget. Yet it did not come about – despite Barnier's suspicions – because May wanted to leverage the Irish border for wider gain, but because it seemed the only way to secure a deal compatible with her red lines. 'If you plug in all the Theresa May priorities, you get that deal,' a negotiator said. 'There wasn't any particular grand strategy to it.'

However, the analysis of this 'win' was not shared by the Brexiteers, who regarded the ability to do trade deals and a belief in the purity of sovereignty as more important than frictionless trade. May and Robbins' biggest win would be the root cause of her eventual defeat. How to sell the deal was not something the Europe Unit spent any time on. A member of the negotiating team said, 'We'd spent so long focusing on the Commission, we had an enormous blind spot on Parliament. Those of us who were out in Brussels doing the negotiating always felt like there would be a team planning how you were going to pass it in London and that didn't really exist.'

If the withdrawal agreement was labyrinthine in its detailed provisions, the second part of the deal, the political declaration, was an exercise in ambiguity. It offered a range of options that satisfied both Selmayr and the Commission, who dreamed of Britain in close alignment with EU rules in perpetuity, but it allowed Brexiteers to see a future Canada-style deal as an obtainable prize. In essence, May would ask the ERG to swallow temporary customs union membership in exchange for the possibility of more freedom in the future. It would not be enough for the Paleosceptics but, for MPs who wanted one, it was a ladder to climb down.

Even with the deal nearly done, the political flames still licked at the prime minister's ankles. Geoffrey Cox told the cabinet on 23 October that the backstop was 'not the first circle of hell', which in Dante's classic was limbo. But he was blunt: the UK could not force its way out. The only alternatives were no-deal or repudiating the backstop. The attorney general thought the deal the 'lesser evil'. He even despatched his parliamentary private secretary, Alex Burghart, as an emissary to try to win over Steve Baker, a mission which did not meet with success. David Lidington, the only one who had been an MP on Black Wednesday in 1992, the last time a Tory administration had been mortally damaged, warned cabinet to back May or face the same fate.

The lack of a time limit or exit clause prompted several of May's senior ministers to urge her not to sign the deal, warning that the government could collapse. Hunt, Javid and Gove were all vocal at cabinet on 23 October. When the latest draft text was circulated to ministers on the 28th, Raab again complained about changes made by Robbins without his knowledge. He seized on the fact that arbitration was to be used to decide whether a future trade deal was 'adequate to remove the need for an "all weather" backstop'. The Brexit secretary protested, 'That is unacceptable, and I am not aware of any clearance of this position shift with Ministers', saying he had 'serious concerns' about the way Robbins was cutting out the politicians. 'There is no forewarning before papers are sent through on a Sunday with just a few hours to clear. There is cursory explanation of the detail and no opportunity to probe. We are constantly allowing the critical issue (time limit/exit mechanism) to be pushed back, enabling maximum pressure on the UK at the 11th hour of the negotiations. This reinforces my view that negotiations should be completed by Ministers, rather than receiving complex legal text as a *fait accompli* for clearance.'[23]

The following day, Philip Hammond presented his budget. The chancellor billed it as 'a new chapter' in Britain's economic history, opening the spending taps after austerity, with £30 billion for investment in road building and £1 billion for social care. There was a Brexit dimension too. Ministers like Raab wanted Hammond to make the threat of no-deal credible by talking up the 'fiscal firepower' he would deploy in the event the talks collapsed and the deregulated economy that might then flourish on Europe's doorstep, so-called 'Singapore on Thames'. The chancellor saw this dream of a neo-conservative restructuring of the economy, with a hard Brexit and a reduction in the size of the state, as the project of the rich and ideological who were insulated from the economic consequences of their views. Instead, he used the budget to build the case for May's deal, announcing that he would bring forward an increase in tax thresholds, cutting income tax for millions, from 2020 to the spring of 2019, just after Brexit. This would only happen, the chancellor warned, if there was a deal. Without one, 'We would need to look at a different strategy and frankly we'd need to have a new budget.'

Cabinet relationships were now so strained that Hammond took the extraordinary step of banning Liz Truss, the chief secretary to the Treasury, by now an outspoken member of the Pizza Club, from knowing what was in the budget, a punishment which required the cooperation of the permanent secretary Tom Scholar. 'They just put a guillotine down on Truss,' a Treasury official said. 'Liz was not to see any budget documents.' On the Sunday before the budget she was supposed to do the broadcast round, but did not know what Hammond was planning. A civil servant met her for brunch at the Grind café at London Bridge on Saturday morning and, in another scene reminiscent of le Carré, showed her a copy of the budget 'scorecard' which he had smuggled out of the building. A day earlier, Truss was told she would not be doing the closing statement of the budget debates, or the main *Newsnight* interview slot on the day of the budget – by tradition the preserve of the chief secretary. 'She literally broke down in tears, screaming,' a source revealed. 'She was in complete meltdown, saying it was a sexist plot to undermine her.' The experience was scarring for Truss and embedded a deep loathing of Hammond and Scholar, something which would have implications four years later. It also 'radicalised her on Brexit', a friend said and 'triggered' her to consider a leadership run. A week later Boris Johnson urged her to steal a march on the other cabinet ministers and resign. 'There is first mover advantage,' he said. 'No one who stays in the cabinet can become leader.' Johnson wanted a contest but could not be seen to trigger one himself. The self-styled 'Brexity Hezza' quoted Michael Heseltine's dictum that 'he who wields the knife never wears the crown'.

The final run-in to the deal was chaotic. Robbins was forced to agree a last tweak to the political declaration, pledging to 'build on and improve' the customs plan outlined in the withdrawal agreement in the final trade deal. These four words would prove fateful, not least because Weyand revealed their existence to EU ambassadors on the evening of Friday 9 November. Robbins did not tell Raab.

Robbins and Weyand worked through the night on Sunday 11 November, finally pulling stumps at 3 a.m. They were back the following morning to finish off. It was 11.57 a.m. on Monday when Robbins emailed the final text to Downing Street. It contained neither a time limit nor a unilateral escape route from the backstop. He advised May to take the deal because the French were complaining that the Commission had given too much to *Les Rosbifs*. A Number 10 source said. 'The fear was if we didn't go now, they would start to unpick what we had secured.'

Raoul Ruparel stayed up late that night reading the text with growing alarm. At twenty to one in the morning he emailed Gavin Barwell his concerns. 'It is hard for me to see how this text gets support within cabinet,' he warned, since it 'would likely see us locked in a customs union going forward. This is true whether we get a future relationship or if we try to use the termination mechanism. This would be fine if our public position was to be in a customs union.' But it was not. May had repeatedly said leaving the customs union was a red line.[24] Ruparel was concerned that the lack of an exit clause meant the only escape from the backstop would be into an arrangement at least as close to the EU. 'It is hard to see that this protocol is temporary other than in the scenario where we have a future relationship that provides at least as frictionless trade on the island of Ireland.' In effect, the backstop, as the starting point for the future trade deal, was now a 'front stop'. Ruparel seized on the wording that Robbins had accepted the previous week that Britain would 'build on the single customs territory' and warned that it 'will only make this worse'.

As part of the deal, the government had also signed up to 'level playing field' agreements, which meant the UK accepting EU rules on the economy, state aid, climate change, social and environmental issues as well as certain tax rules. Ruparel judged the wording 'ugly' and 'worse than any precedents', including the EU's deals with Turkey and Canada. There would be greater obligations on the UK than Turkey to follow EU rules while still imposing 'significant' frictions in Northern Ireland. 'It is hard to see how the DUP will ever support this,' he predicted. The level playing field 'also destroys our future negotiating position, it becomes the absolute minimum and gives away a huge chunk of leverage'. Ruparel signed off predicting 'chaotic' consequences in cabinet and 'explosive fall out'. He felt paralysed, unsure what to recommend. The following morning, he copied the email to other senior members of May's team. Denzil Davidson responded, endorsing his analysis.

The next day, cabinet ministers were briefed on the details. Mid-afternoon Jeremy Hunt asked to see May alone. She turned up with JoJo Penn, the deputy chief of staff. The foreign secretary had voted Remain, in part because he thought it would be a hassle to leave, but he came to regard it as a 'simple matter of democracy' that the referendum result was properly implemented. If Penn's presence was designed to dissuade frank speaking, it failed. Hunt told his prime minister, 'I want you to succeed. I want this to work for you. I want you to be a long and successful prime minister. But if you go ahead with this deal, it will not get through Parliament, and it will be the end of your premiership.'

Hunt believed the EU was slyly using the backstop to bind Britain into the customs union and bits of the single market, while May, a highly literal politician, too readily accepted it was a temporary measure because the EU said it was. Hunt's experience in business negotiations was that the only way to get a good deal was to push things to the edge, right up until the last day before Christmas if necessary. His memories of watching David Cameron convinced him that May needed to engineer a confrontation. At the Queen's garden party that summer he had told her,

'You need a moment where you've turned down the offer from the Europeans and you come back as tough Theresa. Parliament needs to see that, the country needs to see that.' Now he urged the prime minister to create a 'Maggie Thatcher moment'. They spoke for forty-five minutes, but at the end she appeared spent, saying 'I don't think I can do more.'[25]

Hunt returned to the Foreign Office and, within half an hour, he got a message that there was to be an emergency cabinet meeting to approve the deal the following day. He realised May had already made her mind up before she saw him. Characteristically, she had given nothing away. The decision had been taken, like most of significance were, in the 'small group' meeting in Number 10 that morning.

At this point, ministers think Julian Smith should have staged an intervention by telling her the package would fail to get the support of MPs. 'I think Julian was the problem,' a senior cabinet minister said. 'Theresa needed a chief whip who would say, as I think Gavin [Williamson] would have done, "This will not get through." Theresa never trusts another politician. That meant that in the end she always took Olly Robbins' advice. He was saying to her, "In my judgment, Prime Minister, you will not get a better deal from the European Union." Julian's advice was a loyalist's advice. He would say, "If that's the best deal you can get, we'll have to find a way to get it through Parliament." But he [should have said], "This will not get through Parliament."'

Smith and party chairman Brandon Lewis argued instead that MPs and the grassroots wanted to see their prime minister fight. In Downing Street several officials wanted May to 'kick the table over' just as she had done after Salzburg. They included Nikki da Costa, Stephen Parkinson, Raoul Ruparel and deputy press secretary Kirsty Buchanan. Against this was Robbins' advice that it would achieve nothing. His credo, that officials are there to resolve problems, not play political games, conditioned him to recommend solutions not gestures. 'It would've had to have been a decision by a democratically elected minister to flounce out,' a member of the negotiating team said. 'That was not [Olly's] job. [His] job was to open and sustain a channel of communication.'

May, her instincts reinforced by her PPS Peter Hill and Barwell, who thought theatrics would achieve little, accepted Robbins' advice. The prime minister explained later, 'People have asked me, "Why didn't you tip the table over?" But if you do that constantly, it's like the little girl crying wolf – it ceases to have an effect.'[26] Robbie Gibb said, 'If she felt kicking the table over was the right way of getting the deal, she'd have kicked the table over, trampled it and set fire to it.'

It is hard not to conclude that this was the greatest political error of May's premiership. She was not crying wolf; she had thrown her toys only once before – and that after extreme provocation. If there was one moment when she might have dug in, this was it. That meant engineering one of the 'moments of tension' David Davis had always envisaged as the final act of the negotiations. The prime minister was on the cusp of a deal which would define her but, like David Cameron, she did not exhaust every political tactic to win the concessions she needed. May put the views of civil servants ahead of her senior ministers. 'I think the bit about politics that [Robbins] does not get is the bit about trying,' one of May's frustrated aides said. 'Trying and failing is valuable in itself. That is the point where she should have kicked the table over. Whether it would have worked or not, I don't know, but we certainly should have had the fight. We never ever put them to the test. Thereafter, the die was cast.'

14

SELLOUT?

The Deal

November 2018

Cabinet ministers were still being briefed on the details of the deal when staff in Downing Street realised they had a mountain to climb to get the approval of MPs. At around 5.30 p.m. on Tuesday 13 November the televisions in the Number 10 press office switched to live coverage of the central lobby in the Commons, where the elongated figure of Jacob Rees-Mogg, chairman of the European Research Group (ERG), was standing next to Nigel Dodds, leader of the Democratic Unionist Party (DUP) in Westminster. Together they controlled the votes of more than 80 MPs. Together they denounced May's deal.

The leaders of the ERG decided to take to the airwaves while gathered in the office of Iain Duncan Smith. On this occasion Boris Johnson was present, along with Dodds and Sammy Wilson, the DUP's Brexit spokesman. Details of the deal were leaking. The group had got wind of the government's 'level playing field' commitments to align in certain areas with EU rules. Mark Francois pressed for them to denounce the deal publicly. 'We decided that we couldn't leave this unanswered,' one MP present said. There was risk in not acting too. Failure to respond would hand Downing Street an uncontested win on the evening news. At 5.22 p.m. Steve Baker issued an alert to the journalists on his text message list: 'Group announcement, Central Lobby, now. Sorry for zero notice.'

Addressing a now packed central lobby, Rees-Mogg called on the cabinet to step in. 'If the deal is as in the terms set out and leaked ... then the cabinet should reject it,' he said. 'It isn't a proper Brexit.' Urging ministers to marginalise May, he added, 'We still have cabinet government not prime ministerial government. The PM is *primus inter pares*, not more than that.'[1] Dodds denounced how pledges in December 2017 that there would be no regulatory difference between Northern Ireland and the rest of the UK, unless they were agreed by the Assembly in Belfast, 'seem to have disappeared'. Francois went further: 'What members of the cabinet do over the next twenty-four hours is the most important thing that they do in their lives. They have an opportunity to stand up for their country and defend its destiny.' When they had finished, the group headed to Committee Room 13, which was packed to the rafters, for a full meeting of the ERG's membership. The mood inside was 'absolutely sulphurous'. Others gathered at the V&A Museum, where Crosby Textor, the PR firm behind the 'chuck Chequers' campaign, was having its Christmas party. Boris Johnson held court.

At the same time as the Rees-Mogg/Dodds show of force, another drama was playing out in the Cabinet Room in Number 10. Robbins, accompanied by Sarah Healey, Jonathan Black and other members of the Europe Unit, met May's political advisers to discuss the logistics of selling the deal. At the end, when Gavin Barwell asked if there were questions, Nikki da Costa piped up, 'You're asking the senior team to go out and sell this. You're arranging a reading room for the cabinet. But we need to see the papers too.' Barwell was irritated but agreed. As head of legislative affairs, da Costa would have to help pilot the legislation underpinning the deal, yet she didn't know what was in it.

Da Costa's mood was already dark as a result of a confrontation the day before in a Number 10 stairwell with an official in Robbins' team. She said, 'I'm really worried, I don't think this is going to get through Parliament.' The civil servant replied, 'Don't worry. MPs just haven't swallowed yet what they need to swallow.' To da Costa this was emblematic both of the arrogance of civil servants who thought they knew best and of their naivety about what was politically tenable.

Her worst fears were confirmed when she went upstairs to the policy unit after 6 p.m. to read the text of the deal. Robbins' explainer was refreshingly 'blunt'. Britain was tied to level playing field provisions and the only way out of the backstop was into a customs union. 'Basically, in signing that deal, that was game over. I was shocked,' she said. By 7 p.m. da Costa had located a copy of Geoffrey Cox's legal advice. Barwell had earlier claimed that the attorney general was 'on side', but reading it she wondered, 'How on earth can he be on side?'

Cox first spelled out the basics of the deal. The Northern Ireland Protocol was a 'binding' agreement 'in international law' which 'expressly invoked' the Joint Report of 2017. If that document, as David Davis and others had claimed, was not legally binding when it was written, it was now. It 'comes into force on the conclusion of the transition period, currently scheduled to end on 31 December 2020'. It would remain in place while negotiations continued on a final trade deal and 'unless and until' such a deal was in place that 'avoids a hard border' in Ireland.

Under the backstop the 'UK as a whole (i.e. GB and NI) will form a single customs territory with the EU' for the purposes of applying a common external tariff on goods coming in and out. But Northern Ireland 'remains in the EU's Customs Union, and will apply the whole of the EU's customs' laws, with the European Court continuing to have 'jurisdiction over its compliance with those rules'. In addition, 'Northern Ireland will remain in the EU's Single Market for Goods', and apply 'over 300 different' rules, also under ECJ supervision. Under the level playing field commitments, 'GB will be obliged to observe a range of regulatory obligations in certain areas, such as environmental, labour, social and competition laws.' British, not European, courts would enforce compliance, except in the area of state aid, where breaches would be referred to a Joint Committee.

Most ministers turned first to the next section, where the attorney general spelled out the 'indefinite' nature of the backstop. The protocol was supposed to exist 'only temporarily' but, Cox explained, the 'unless and until' provision meant the backstop would remain in place 'even when negotiations have clearly broken down'. Da Costa read the next sentence with a sick dread. 'Despite statements in the Protocol that it is not intended to be permanent, and the clear intention of the parties that it should be replaced by alternative, permanent arrangements, in international law the Protocol would endure indefinitely until a superseding agreement took its place.' For Brexiteers, this was a devastating legal judgment. Those two words 'endure indefinitely' were the most important written in any government document during Theresa May's time in power.

To cap it all, Cox added, 'I understand that we attempted to negotiate a unilateral termination mechanism … but this was rejected by the EU.' He also noted that a 'clause allowing for mutual termination once it was clear that negotiations had irretrievably broken down' would also have given Britain greater protection. 'I understand that the EU was not prepared to agree to this,' he added.

Da Costa went home to talk to her husband. Next morning, she grabbed Barwell and said she would have to resign. 'The only way out is to the customs union,' she explained. Barwell replied, 'A customs union.' Da Costa wrote a resignation letter to May but assured the chief of staff, 'I want to keep this quiet.' She watched the cabinet meeting then went home for good. Her departure leaked a day later to Guido Fawkes.

Da Costa was not the only one considering their position. Dominic Raab was the first minister to be briefed on the deal but even he only saw the full text on the Monday evening. Earlier that day, he bumped into an MP who asked him, 'What's in this deal?' He replied, 'Don't ask me I'm only the secretary of state for exiting the EU.'

Raab was furious when he saw the concession Robbins had made on the future economic partnership, which called for a trade deal with 'ambitious customs arrangements that build on the single customs territory provided for in the Withdrawal Agreement'. He rang Ruparel, who reinforced his fear that it would lock Britain into permanent alignment with EU rules. 'The language changed to make clear that the backstop will be the starting point for the future relationship,' Raab said later. Worse still, the change had been concealed from him, pretty clearly because he would not have accepted it. The Brexit secretary was also troubled by the scope of the level playing field commitments: 'From social policy to tax policy, a whole new range of obligations that were being imposed at the eleventh hour by the EU.'[2]

For more than two months Raab had been minuting May with his concerns, precisely to avoid the charge of blindsiding the prime minister with objections at the last moment. He had been ignored. When Barwell went to see him in the Commons on Tuesday, Raab told him it would be a 'national humiliation' to accept the terms.[3]

As the details emerged, Boris Johnson took a call from Oliver Lewis, the head of research for Vote Leave. 'It's so much worse than what they're letting on,' he said. Lewis also sought to impress on Johnson the strategic peril for the Brexiteers. 'There is a growing group of MPs who are trying to organise a second referendum. You need to understand where this is going.' Johnson was also in touch with David Frost, now kicking his heels at the London Chamber of Commerce. Frost fed in information from his old contacts on how the deal had, in several important regards, been 'cobbled together' at the last minute and was consequently riddled with 'ambiguities'. Johnson made his way to the central lobby, where he told the waiting journalists the deal was 'utterly unacceptable to anybody who believes in democracy'.

Privately, Johnson's view of May was more vivid: 'No one in history has had such a tenacious grip of the wrong end of the stick. She just hangs on like grim death. She's like some terrier mistakenly mounting a trouser leg. She is a dog barking up the wrong tree, a rat up the wrong drainpipe. And once she's gone there, she won't come down. She won't move.'

Johnson's fury intensified the next morning when *The Times* printed leaked extracts from a diplomatic note of Sabine Weyand's briefing to EU ambassadors the previous Friday. It confirmed the EU believed they had outmanoeuvred the UK. 'We should be in the best negotiation position for the future relationship,' Weyand said. 'This requires the customs union as the basis of the future relationship. They must align their rules but the EU will retain all the controls.'[4] Johnson took to Twitter to say, 'This means super-canada impossible. Cabinet must live up to its responsibilities & stop this deal.' Weyand's note was to become a foundational text in Eurosceptic opposition to the deal, a Zimmermann Telegram for Brexit.

Just after 8 a.m. on Wednesday, Esther McVey was one of the first to arrive at the reading room where ministers could study the documents. She made a note of her concerns and then asked for an audience with the prime minister. The work and pensions secretary thought about the black and white films she used to watch as a child in which romances were doomed because people did not reveal their true feelings until it was too late. May, she could tell, thought she would pass her deal. McVey tried to shock her: 'It is going to be a massive loss.' She went on, 'You have managed to unite Brexiteers against this as well as Remainers against it. You have fundamentally gone against what you said at Lancaster House – that you wouldn't have a halfway house deal, which you yourself had said would be purgatory and undeliverable. This is what you're now doing.'

May looked impassive, and McVey urged her to 'have another Salzburg moment' and fight. She was met by a chilly smile and words of reassurance. The vote would be won, the public would come to understand the deal, the legal advice would be solid, the prime minister claimed. McVey's conscience was clear, but she could see May thought she didn't know what she was talking about.

It was not just Brexiteers who were recoiling at the text. James Brokenshire, the usually moderate housing secretary, turned to a fellow cabinet minister outside the reading room and said, 'What the hell is that? We can't sell that!' A Number 10 aide said, 'If James Brokenshire is saying, "What the fuck?" then you have a serious problem.'

The cabinet meeting which began at 2 p.m. on 14 November 2018 lasted more than five hours. It was also the most heated. May made her pitch: Robbins had secured the best deal that was available, now they needed to support it. She then fielded questions, impressively on top of her brief.

When it was his turn, Raab did not hold back, challenging both the prime minister and Robbins to explain how the tweaks to paragraph 23 had happened, making the customs union the basis of a future deal. Neither provided a straight answer. 'I cannot support this,' Raab said. He argued that Northern Ireland would have 'regulation without representation' and the lack of exit from the backstop was something to which 'no democratic country in history has signed up'. 'It's indefensible in principle,' he concluded. 'I do not believe that Parliament will accept it.'

It was left to Geoffrey Cox to swing the meeting May's way. The attorney general said the plan was an 'ugly sister of a deal'. This was Cox the committed Brexiteer speaking. Cox the lawyer made the point that on the money side Britain had unwaivable obligations. 'There is absolutely no doubt that, deal or no-deal, we would have to pay this money back,' he said. On the backstop, he argued that even if Robbins had secured a unilateral exit device it would not give the UK the right to just leave, only to serve notice and go to arbitration. In essence, at least part of Raab's argument was overdone. Cox also stressed that the withdrawal agreement was a legally binding text that obliged both sides to use 'best endeavours' to reach a final agreement by December 2020. 'That is not a small thing,' he explained. 'It is not some highfalutin piece of language. That is quite literally a legal obligation.'

Cox finished with his political argument, now familiar to many, that the EU and Ireland in particular would not want Britain indefinitely in a backstop that gave competitive advantages to Northern Ireland. 'Look at it in the round,' he said. 'It doesn't work for them.' The 'balance of risks' favoured agreement. May's deal was a 'life raft lashed together with bamboo and oil drums' but one that could traverse 'shark-infested seas'. Once out, they could fight for a better trade agreement. 'We've got the second leg,' he said. 'We may be three-nil down, but we can still win.'

The conversation ebbed and flowed, alternately a supporter then an opponent. Sajid Javid challenged the prime minister's assertion that the deal was the best available. Penny Mordaunt called for a free vote on the legislation (so she could oppose it without resigning). Andrea Leadsom questioned 'whether we are actually leaving' and warned May she would face a vote of no confidence from the ERG if she pressed ahead. By the end of her comments, Leadsom was in tears. Matt Hancock, the health secretary, said he could not guarantee people would not die as a result of a no-deal Brexit, calling the consequences potentially 'fatal'. Liam Fox and Chris Grayling were critical but on board.[5] Jeremy Hunt, like Gavin Williamson, warned that MPs would not back the deal, but the foreign secretary concluded, 'Ultimately, we owe you our loyalty.' The pivot point, again, came when Michael Gove spoke. The environment secretary was 'incredibly eloquent' about the problems with the deal, particularly on the prospect of dynamic alignment with EU regulations, but more so about the perils of no-deal, which would badly affect the farming sector for which he was responsible. He eventually said he would support the deal 'with a heavy heart' because the alternatives were so much worse.

There was a brief silence as more than one minister felt Gove's intervention, so clearly an exploration of heart and soul, would carry the day. The mood was punctured by the tin-eared Philip Hammond, who suddenly asked, 'Can I ask, why are the biscuits down that end of the room?' The moment was lost.

Sitting at the side of the room, Kirsty Buchanan, the deputy press secretary, found the debate passionate and thoughtful but could not shift from her mind the words of Abraham Lincoln: 'A house divided against itself cannot stand.'

The fireworks came at the end. Esther McVey 'aggressively' demanded a formal vote so each minister would have to commit one way or another. She was 'shouted down' by Julian Smith: 'Look, you don't actually have a right to a vote.'

McVey became animated, 'feisty' by her own admission. Afterwards someone briefed that she was 'emotional' and that consideration had been given to calling for security to restrain her. 'Well, unfortunately, guys, I've read up on this and you can have a vote, I said it is obviously the prime minister's discretion but you can have a vote,' she said, adding, 'I've looked it up!'[6] She could not understand why others were not prepared to stand up and be counted, like she was. Mark Sedwill, the cabinet secretary, was deputed to read out the cabinet manual, making clear to McVey the principles of collective cabinet responsibility. 'The rules are quite clear,' he said, politely but firmly. 'There is no vote.'

May concluded the meeting and then explained she was going straight into Downing Street to address the television cameras. Ministers were asked to remain, promised a glass of wine after she had finished. Copies of her statement were handed around the table.

The PM's staff watched, more nervous than usual. Tired and under pressure, she now had to repeat a memorised speech without notes or an autocue, live for the cameras and the nation. What she said ('I firmly believe that the draft Withdrawal Agreement was the best that could be negotiated … The choice before us is clear. This deal … or leave with no deal; or no Brexit at all') was less memorable than how she carried it off without incident, testament to her stoicism and cool under pressure.

'I did breathe a sigh of relief as I turned round and walked back towards the door,' the prime minister told her team. However, her speechwriter, Keelan Carr, later wondered whether he should have written the speech more punchily. 'We should have gone out swinging,' a Number 10 aide said, 'saying, "This is a bloody great deal."' Instead, May's sales pitch was bloodless and acknowledged it was a compromise.

Before the cabinet meeting, Robbie Gibb had asked Raab, 'Are you ready to go to Brussels first thing?' A helicopter was laid on to whisk the Brexit secretary away to sign the deal. Now, as his ministerial colleagues supped warm wine, Raab took Julian Smith aside in an empty room to tell him he intended to resign. The chief whip tried to dissuade him, but Raab's mind was made up. A later conversation with May had no effect either. 'Please can you wait?' Smith asked. Raab agreed to delay his announcement until after the *Today* programme the following morning to allow the prime minister to make her case to the nation.

Just as with Davis, a negotiator said more could have been done to keep Raab: 'I never quite understood why they put their political capital into that sentence about the future relationship building on the customs union. They lost a cabinet minister over one sentence in the political declaration, which was pretty flexible.' This underestimates the problems Raab had with the deal, but the political declaration preserved a number of possible futures and flagging up the customs union as the default landing zone was unnecessary and inflammatory.

When word spread in Number 10 of Raab's decision, it knocked the stuffing from one political adviser. 'I remember being in my office on the evening of that cabinet and thinking, "Just maybe this is going to hang together and be okay." Then a colleague from the press office came in and said, "Dom's resigning tomorrow morning." I genuinely thought there was no possible way we could last beyond December because how can you survive a second Brexit secretary quitting? Turns out the PM's resilience was even beyond my comprehension.'

Even as the cabinet met, the ERG was holding another get together in Duncan Smith's office – their third of five meetings that week. This was the 'tipping point' in the long running conversation about whether and when to move against the prime minister. Jacob Rees-Mogg called for 'the gloves to come off' and compared the Brexit deal to another Tory foreign policy crisis. 'Suez was very difficult for us and we went on to win the next election in 1959,' he said. The implication was clear: that had been after a change of leader. Why do it now? 'Because I have no confidence in her so I should send in my letter of no confidence,' Rees-Mogg said. 'It would be dishonest not to.' Not everyone agreed. Mark Francois, the man with the best feel for the numbers, protested: 'It's too early; we'll lose it at the moment.' Rees-Mogg wrote an open letter to Tory MPs calling the deal 'profoundly undemocratic' and urging them to vote it down. Nadine Dorries described the mood in the tearoom as 'worse than Maastricht'.[7]

The fury was no longer containable, as even some in Downing Street acknowledged. 'They feel they've been deceived,' one of May's political aides admitted. 'There's a despair that we're not making the best of Brexit, that she doesn't really believe in it. And then there's a visceral reaction to what they think has been vagueness and misleading one-on-one meetings.' For more than two years the prime minister had pursued an ambiguous Brexit. Now she had chosen and the people whose views she had rejected would seek to finish her. 'The mistake was trying to ride two horses for too long and she's fallen between the two of them,' the Number 10 aide said. 'The counter-argument to that is that we've got as far as we have because we've ridden two horses for as long as we have.'

Launching a coup attempt was not without risk for the rebels, though. Baker had a list of more than 50 names who he believed had written a letter or were prepared to, but most did not think they would be able to muster more than 70 votes against May. If she won a confidence vote, Tory rules meant the PM could not face another challenge for a year.

Dominic Raab was not even the first minister to resign. That distinction went to Shailesh Vara from the Northern Ireland office, who told May her deal left the UK 'in a halfway house' and wrote, 'We can and must do better than this.' It was the first of seven frontbench resignations on a torrid day for May.

At 9 a.m., Gavin Barwell and Oliver Robbins were in the office of Nick Brown, Labour's chief whip, briefing him on the deal when Brown's aide Luke Sullivan put his head around the door and said, 'Dominic Raab has resigned.' Barwell just said, 'Yep', resignation of a different sort evident in his voice.

In his letter to the prime minister, Raab denounced the deal as 'a very real threat to the integrity of the United Kingdom' and rehearsed his opposition to the 'indefinite backstop' and the way it had become the 'starting point' for a future economic partnership. He said later, 'There was no way I could walk that deal over the line. I couldn't do it as a matter of personal conviction and I couldn't do it for the good of my country.'[8]

His resignation was not a surprise but it still had a huge impact. 'To lose one Brexit secretary was unfortunate,' a fellow minister said. 'To lose two in four months looks like carelessness.' Unlike Davis, Raab provoked fury among some of May's team who believed he had resigned to further his own leadership prospects. 'I think it was just a game from his point of view,' one member of the Number 10 political team said. 'He made sure for months that it was on the record that he objected to X, Y and Z.'

Suella Braverman, another Brexit minister, followed Raab out of government, calling the deal a 'betrayal'. Anne-Marie Trevelyan, who thought May had tried to 'appease the EU', quit as a parliamentary private secretary and Rehman Chishti as a vice chairman of the party.

When Esther McVey announced that she, too, was off, an hour after Raab, officials in the Department for Work and Pensions literally threw a party to celebrate. In her resignation letter she said the deal did not 'honour' the referendum result: 'We have gone from no-deal is better than a bad deal, to any deal is better than no-deal.' For McVey, Brexit was an opportunity to change Britain, to reshape the economy and end the North-South divide. She saw a Remainer Parliament trying to undermine that.

The prime minister was preparing to make a statement to the Commons when Julian Smith rushed into her room to tell her about the latest resignations. May snapped, 'I will not be bullied by these people.' She stood and took questions for hours in the Commons.

The surprise for Raab was that more cabinet ministers did not follow his lead. 'He was fairly burnt by the fact that it was only Esther who went with him,' a close ally said. The two who had longest been on resignation 'suicide watch' were Leadsom and Mordaunt. The leader of the Commons was riddled with angst but was a genuine believer in collective responsibility. Mordaunt flirted with both resignation and a leadership run but neither came to a head. 'She's got one of those personalities where she wants people to come to her,' a colleague said.

Liz Truss came closest. The chief secretary to the Treasury got as far as asking one of her advisers to draft a resignation letter. When Raab and McVey went, 'She was teetering that morning,' a friend recalled. 'She was so close to going.' Two things persuaded Truss to stay: the conviction that Raab had already achieved first mover advantage and a conversation with Michael Gove. 'He brought her back from the brink.'

When May made a statement to the Commons at 10.30 a.m., she faced an unremittingly hostile House. In the three hours the prime minister was on her feet, she took 124 questions. In the chair John Bercow calculated that ninety-six were critical. The speaker had 'never seen such a mauling'. In response, he thought May 'monotonous, unimaginative and robotic' yet 'outwardly unperturbed'. He felt 'embarrassed for her'.[9]

From the Brexiteers the theme was one of betrayal, a seam which Nigel Dodds of the DUP mined as well. Voice guttural and trembling with anger, he said, 'I could stand here today and take the prime minister through the list of promises and pledges that she made to this House, and to us privately, about the future of Northern Ireland … but I fear it would be a waste of time, since she clearly does not listen.'

Later, with May still on her feet giving her statement to Parliament, the DUP's leader Arlene Foster was seen walking towards the prime minister's Commons office. When May received the DUP leadership, after her statement, she had to do the listening as they pronounced the confidence and supply arrangement dead. May was now running a minority government.

By then she had other problems. When Jacob Rees-Mogg got to his feet, he pointed out that she had broken her promises to leave the customs union, maintain the integrity of the UK and leave the jurisdiction of the ECJ. 'As what my right honourable friend says and what my right honourable friend does no longer match, should I not write to my right honourable friend the member for Altrincham and Sale West?', a reference to Sir Graham Brady. There were audible gasps as Rees-Mogg hinted the ERG would seek to force her out.

The plotters broke cover at an ERG meeting in Committee Room 10 at 12.45 p.m., dozens of journalists outside listening at the door. Rees-Mogg said he would submit a letter to Brady calling for a no-confidence vote. This was greeted with the thumping of desks. Boris Johnson was visibly supportive, his ally Conor Burns among the most vociferous table bangers. Johnson had already submitted his own letter. Steve Baker told the meeting: 'We've tried everything to change policy but not the prime minister, but it has not worked. It is too late. We need a new leader.'

Rees-Mogg made his way to St Stephen's entrance of the Commons where the television cameras were set up, a pinstriped giraffe at the centre of a giant rolling maul of journalists firing questions. In a three-year political-media Brexit circus this procession stood out as a high point of absurdist theatre. Baker, a shorter, more energetic Sancho Panza, stood a little behind and to the side. Watching on television Simon Hoare, a close friend of Rees-Mogg but also an arch-Remainer, said, 'It did slightly look like the squire and his under butler trying to make a lunch party out of two bread rolls and a slice of ham.'[10]

Rees-Mogg adopted the demeanour of a hanging judge donning the black cap and addressed the cameras, calling for the removal of the prime minister. He and Baker released their no-confidence letters to the media. Baker called on the journalists while Rees-Mogg intoned with grave seriousness. He ruled himself out of running for leader and named Johnson, Davis, Raab, McVey and Mordaunt as possible successors to

May. The microphones picked up Baker attempting to get him to wind things up. 'Come on, Jacob,' he said. 'I know you love it.' Baker did too, of course.

In the ERG meeting, the MPs agreed that they should unite behind a single candidate if the prime minister fell. At this stage Johnson was not seen as a prohibitive favourite. Davis was expected to back his protégé Raab. Penny Mordaunt phoned MPs to test her support. That evening she went to see May to press the case for a free vote. It was even suggested that Geoffrey Cox was discreetly 'offering himself'. But the leadership crown seldom settles on those who wait to be asked; it has to be grabbed.

In Downing Street, May's aides watched with boiling fury. One called the display 'unbelievably self-indulgent'. At a press conference that evening, May told MPs it was their duty to pass the deal. She had done her job, now it was their turn to do theirs. 'Am I going to see this through? Yes,' she said. She even managed to channel her sporting hero, Geoffrey Boycott, when asked about the glut of resignations. 'You are a cricket fan,' a journalist said. 'How many wickets need to fall in your cabinet before you walk?' May replied, 'Geoffrey Boycott stuck to it. And he got the runs in the end.' It was one of her most effective media appearances: authentic but also quotable.

To those close to her, the previous twenty-four hours had only reinforced their admiration for a dedicated public servant. 'She argued with the knowledge of a sherpa in a meeting for five hours, came out of that, memorised and delivered word-perfect an impassioned defence of the decision that she had taken in the national interest, went back in, worked for a few more hours, went to sleep for probably a handful of very short hours, got up and did it all again.' No one doubted May's dedication. The problem was that for many the deal was proof they were right to doubt her judgement. Some Brexiteers went as far as to doubt her sanity too.

May had called Michael Gove to offer him Raab's job as Brexit secretary shortly before she got to her feet in the Commons, a move one Downing Street official compared to the choice presented by Malcolm Tucker, the foul-mouthed spin doctor from *The Thick of It*: 'Come the fuck in, or fuck the fuck off.' The environment secretary asked to 'think about it'. Privately, he thought: *Oh my God. I don't want to leave Defra. I have concerns about the deal. If someone's going to take over the negotiations, they need to know that they're really taking it over.*

Gove asked to see the prime minister. Around 5 p.m. they met in Number 10 for a 'nice chat' and Gove said he did not think the deal would pass in the Commons and that he would take the job only if he could renegotiate it. May told him he had made a 'perfectly reasonable set of points' but refused. 'This is the course we have set,' she said.

Gove replied, 'I don't think I can really do the job', and told her, 'I will have to consider my position', unleashing another plotline. Their exchange delayed May's press conference by twenty minutes.

Rory Stewart, perhaps thinking there might soon be a vacancy at environment, a job he coveted, took to the airwaves to defend May's deal, a performance that was notable for both its rarity and its oddity. Stewart claimed '80 per cent of people' support the deal, before being forced to admit that he had just invented the number.

Dominic Cummings, the campaign director of Vote Leave, texted a friend in Westminster to say, 'Sometimes nothing happens for years. Sometimes years happen in days.' Still a voice in the wings.

Gove returned home and was lobbied by his special advisers and former Vote Leave staff to resign. Josh Grimstone, Henry Cook and James Starkie all told him he should quit. 'People argued strongly that this isn't what Brexit should be,' said one source present. At the same time Julian Smith was running an energetic interference operation, calling Gove that evening from the pavement outside the Clarence pub on Whitehall and rounding up influential Tories like George Osborne and William Hague to ring him and urge him not to quit. The chief whip texted a friend that night that the government 'would be toast' if Gove jumped too.

With Gove's decision hanging in the balance, his aides phoned Cummings at home in north London and urged him to get a cab to Gove's home in Kensington to convince him to resign. When Cummings arrived, he subjected the environment secretary to a relentless barrage, denouncing the deal and warning about the chaos that lay ahead if he propped up this prime minister. He cited the views of Richard 'Ricardo' Howell, Vote Leave's legal expert, who had told Cummings, 'It's completely atrocious and we have to oppose it.' Cummings predicted the government would get hammered in the meaningful vote and would have to resort to crisis measures. 'Number 10's plan is to encourage a crash in financial markets after losing the first vote in the hope this stampedes MPs into voting for it second time,' he said. 'If that doesn't work, they appear to have no Plan B other than to ask Corbyn to dictate what further concessions are needed.' There would then be 'no cabinet majority' for forcing through a no-deal Brexit.

Cummings painted a bleak political picture but Gove, hunched at times like a cornered animal, still resisted a decision. Unlike Boris Johnson, he believed Britain could secure its exit from the EU, then renegotiate. His wife, the journalist Sarah Vine, came down in favour of staying. His old friends Ed Vaizey and Nick Boles agreed with her. Gove's concern was how it would be seen to sink the career of a third leader after having opposed David Cameron during the referendum campaign and then pulled the plug on Boris Johnson's 2016 leadership campaign. He told Cummings, 'Dominic, in 2016 I went against the whole system and against the establishment and it has cost me friends. It's been a disaster for me. I am not doing that again.' A cabinet colleague said, 'I think Michael knows he would have been responsible for bringing down the government.' Brexiteers never forgave Gove for not helping to blow up May's premiership there and then. 'Michael was far more interested in his personal reputation than what he really believed in,' one of those who did resign complained. The next morning, Gove had breakfast with Jeremy Hunt. They considered resigning together, but both decided instead to stay.

Still needing a Brexit secretary, Julian Smith pushed May to appoint Rishi Sunak, the clever and ambitious young local government minister, whose decision to back Leave in 2016 was seen as a bell-wether moment by David Cameron and George Osborne. Fate had a different path in store for him. Geoffrey Cox was also sounded out, but he did not want to give up his post as attorney general. Instead, May chose health minister Steve Barclay, an unspectacular Brexiteer with prematurely silvered hair. One of May's political advisers likened the role to filling 'dead man's shoes'. 'Like the number three in al-Qaeda taking over. Poor bastard.' Esther McVey's replacement at work and pensions was Amber Rudd, returning to the cabinet after just seven months. Her appointment changed the balance of power in the cabinet. May had picked her side, now she bolstered it.

Raab gave an interview to the *Sunday Times* in which he said May had allowed Britain to be 'blackmailed and bullied' by Brussels and called on the prime minister to show greater 'political will'. Pitching for the top job, he claimed Britain would not be 'frightened of its own shadow' if he was in charge.[11] Two polls that weekend put Labour ahead.

*   *   *

Instead of quitting, Leadsom convened a 'breakfast club' of Brexiteers – which also included Gove, Mordaunt, Fox and Grayling – to work up proposals inside the cabinet to change the deal. Leadsom revived talk of Max-Fac-style technical measures and pushing a 'pay-as-you-go Brexit' in which Britain bought extra time to secure a final deal by paying into the Brussels budget for a few more months. Gove's focus was on improving the political declaration. This effort was greeted with similar ridicule by the ERG. 'They're like something from the Wizard of Oz,' said one Eurosceptic. 'There's Grayling, the man without the heart; Andrea, the one without the brain; and Michael, the cowardly lion who didn't have the nerve to resign.'

The only good news for the prime minister was that, so far, the ERG's coup was turning into a farce. Forty-eight hours after Rees-Mogg and Baker published their letters, the magic figure of forty-eight had yet to be reached. That Sunday, Baker wrote in his diary that he believed fifty-five had been submitted. Still nothing happened. Unbeknown to them the figure had actually hit forty-seven, one short of the trigger point, but not long after it did so some MPs got cold feet and contacted Graham Brady to withdraw their letters. 'The tide ebbed rapidly down the beach. 47 … 46 … 45 … 44,' the chairman of the 1922 wrote later.[12]

On Monday 19th, Iain Duncan Smith and Owen Paterson, two of the most senior members of the ERG, went to Number 10 to see May. Neither had submitted a letter of no confidence, something which angered those who had. 'Jacob and Steve had left the parapet and run screaming towards the enemy,' said a prominent Brexiteer. 'They were looking over their shoulders and the most senior guys were not with them.' As a former leader who had been unseated by his own MPs, and who knew the pain for innocent family, Duncan Smith expressed reluctance to join the coup attempt. Nonetheless, when he and Paterson set off, Baker was under the impression they would emerge from their meeting with May and reluctantly say there needed to be a change of leadership. Baker duly fired off a message to his journalist mailing list and the lobby, some of them not dressed for the cold weather, ran to Whitehall to await their departure.

In an hour-long meeting in Number 10, Duncan Smith discussed how a 'virtual border' could negate the need for a backstop with May, pointing out that he had already discussed it with the EU. 'Barnier can't find a hole in it,' he said. The prime minister knew from Brussels that this was nonsense. The grandees urged her to work language on alternative arrangements into the political declaration, due later that week. She listened intently enough that when they left, neither Duncan Smith nor Paterson said anything to the waiting media. In his own words, Baker looked 'like a prat'. The following day the launch of a pamphlet by Peter Lilley on international trade was overshadowed, to Lilley's fury, by questions to Rees-Mogg comparing the plotters to the hapless Home Guard unit in *Dad's Army*. The ERG chairman said, 'I've always rather admired Captain Mainwaring', and then found himself mocked up as Arthur Lowe's character on the front of the *Evening Standard* (editor, one George Osborne).

The setback led to open season on Baker, who was accused, even by Brexiteers, of urging fellow MPs to put their mobile phones in a microwave during sensitive meetings because it stopped them being bugged. Baker dismissed this as 'childish nonsense', but on one occasion he broke off a call with a journalist because he had detected 'ambient noise changes' on the line which he believed to be evidence of electronic eavesdropping. David Davis, who kept his iPad in a biscuit tin at home – like a microwave, a makeshift 'Faraday case' that can block surveillance – fuelled this sense of paranoia by revealing that he had been repeatedly denied the use of a secure smartphone when he was a cabinet minister. 'I assumed I was being bugged at all times,' he told friends.

Downing Street dismissed the idea that the Brexiteers were under surveillance either by their own side or the Europeans, not least because (under the Wilson convention) it was illegal to spy on MPs without the written permission of the prime minister. In 2019 the author had the opportunity to quiz a senior figure in MI6, the Secret Intelligence Service, about whether the UK spied on its EU counterparts during the Brexit process or whether there was concern that they had done so against the UK. He answered, 'No, all anyone needed to do was read the newspapers.'

The political declaration was finally published on 22 November. It was twenty-six pages long, dwarfed by the 585-page withdrawal agreement. Nothing more eloquently symbolised how two years of political energies had been primarily expended on settling the past, rather than the future of the UK–EU relationship. There, in paragraph 27, were the words the Paleosceptics wanted: 'Facilitative arrangements and technologies will also be considered in developing any alternative arrangements for ensuring the absence of a hard border on the island of Ireland on a permanent footing.' On a cabinet conference call, Chris Grayling said these words would be May's 'saving grace'.

The PM had dinner with Jean-Claude Juncker in Brussels that Wednesday and helped beef up the political declaration herself. Robbins and Weyand had been arguing for weeks over whether Britain's adherence to EU rules might eradicate the need for some checks at the border between the UK and the EU. Weyand was prepared to say alignment might 'mitigate' the necessity for checks. Robbins wanted the possibility that they might 'obviate' them altogether. 'We have to preserve the possibility that our policies and our commitments via our future relationship could ultimately remove the need for checks,' he said. Weyand replied, 'I'm prepared to say anything up to but not including that.' It was the prime minister, an old hand at home affairs negotiations, who devised the solution: alignment and technology 'can lead to a spectrum of different outcomes for administrative processes as well as checks and controls'. Juncker, who had been warned via Selmayr, that May would want to raise the issue, agreed. 'In five minutes we got a lot further than we had done in about a month of Sabine on that issue,' a British negotiator said.

The following day, when two members of Robbins' team went to the Commission to finalise the drafting, Barnier's officials 'were horrified' and went 'completely white' when they saw what Juncker had approved. 'You got Chequers!' one said.

'Yes,' came the reply. At the last moment, the future deal at least 'preserved the space' for the theoretical potential of the frictionless trade, May's goal all along. 'They were completely furious,' a witness said.

The prime minister returned to Brussels for a special summit on 25 November, where the EU approved the deal. Juncker insisted, 'This is the best deal possible. This is the only deal possible.' What he did not say was that this line had been scripted by Downing Street over dinner. A source close to Juncker revealed, 'Mrs May said, "Can you please all say this is the best possible deal, the only deal possible and we will not reopen it." Everybody repeated it, faithfully.' The PM needed MPs to see her deal as the only alternative to no-deal or no Brexit.

The same day she released an open letter to voters calling for people to 'put aside the labels of "leave" or "remain" for good' and 'come together again as one people'. She said, 'To do that we need to get on with Brexit now by getting behind this deal. I will be campaigning with my heart and soul to win that vote.'

PART FOUR

NO WAY OUT

NEGOTIATING WITH PARLIAMENT

November 2018 to May 2019

'People can foresee the future only when it coincides with
their own wishes, and the most grossly obvious facts can
be ignored when they are unwelcome'

– George Orwell

'Never interrupt your enemy when he is making a mistake'

– Napoleon Bonaparte

ZUGZWANG

Selling the Deal

20 November to 6 December 2018

Zugzwang n. *Chess* an obligation to move in one's turn even
when this must be disadvantageous – *The Concise Oxford
Dictionary* (8th edn)

As Theresa May's RAF jet cut through the night sky over the Atlantic en
route to the G20 summit in Argentina, one of the pilots was hunched
over a map at the back of the plane with a ruler and protractor plotting
the aircraft's course. The Voyager had fuel for just fourteen hours, yet the
flight to Buenos Aires usually took fourteen hours and fifteen minutes.
Journalists searching for metaphors for the government's quest to drum
up enough support for the meaningful vote – scheduled for 12 December
– could not believe their luck. The trip, on 29–30 November, was a
distraction from selling the deal to press, public and MPs back home. By
then, a week after the political declaration and two since the withdrawal
agreement was published, most ministers feared the government was
badly short of political fuel and on course for a crash landing. When the
press pack arrived at their hotel in Buenos Aires the Eagles' 'Hotel
California' was playing, the anthem of Brexiteer suspicion about May's
deal. *'You can check-out any time you like/But you can never leave …'*
    Earlier that week at cabinet, on 26 November, ministers had been
given a pep talk by Robbie Gibb, the director of communications, on how
to sell the deal. James Johnson, May's pollster, had been testing versions
of the deal for two weeks before it was signed. 'All of the polling showed
that if you talked about the deal in and of itself people would not be
interested,' he explained. 'If you linked the deal to Theresa May and her

brand, which was "she's fighting for Britain, she tries hard", then approval went up.'

May's team decided the prime minister would have to be front and centre. That was why she had given a press conference on the day of the withdrawal agreement, why she had invoked Geoffrey Boycott. The case for action was reinforced when Johnson got the first figures through after the deal. The public had a 'very negative view' of it, one influenced by Dominic Raab's resignation and the ERG rebellion. May went on a national tour to promote 'her deal'. For a few days it seemed to work. Johnson's focus group respondents started saying, 'It's an impossible task … they should just back her …' He recalled, 'They thought she was being ganged up on by posh men and therefore they became more supportive of the deal.' A cabinet minister observed drily, 'She's running the 2017 general election very well now.'

So well, in fact, that rumour spread that May would offer Jeremy Corbyn an election in exchange for Labour's support in the meaningful vote – a suggestion doubly offensive to the Brexiteers. The claim was so damaging that May, not someone who usually even acknowledged gossip, opened cabinet on 20 November by denying it as 'outrageous and untrue'. Spooked, Downing Street cut short the tour. 'I think it would have been better if we'd just carried it on,' said a political aide. 'If you pick a strategy then stick to it.' One of those who wrote May's lines said, 'The theory was: get the country onside, sell it to the people; that will make it harder for those who are already entrenched to oppose it. But it's not a referendum, it's not an election. Voters haven't got a direct say.'

On 20 November, Gavin Barwell instituted a new 7.30 a.m. meeting in the Cabinet Room, before the usual gatherings of the prime minister's senior aides, which appeared in their electronic diaries as 'winning the meaningful vote'. This was not universally popular; not everyone rose as early as the chief of staff. 'Gavin worked phenomenally hard, but Gavin is an early morning person. He doesn't drink caffeine: no tea, no coffee, just orange squash,' said one of those who valued his sleep and morning stimulants. Barwell, Gibb and Alex Aiken, the civil service director of government communications, set up a 'war room' on the first floor of the Cabinet Office, staffed by thirty people from May's political team and the civil service. They pumped out infographics and videos with bullet-point summaries explaining the deal. Both Barwell and Gibb initially sat in the war room, along with JoJo Penn, policy chief James Marshall and spads

Alex Dawson, Richard Chew, Aidan Corley, Joe Moor and William Vereker. 'Gavin approached it like a campaign, sensibly,' a colleague said.

Dawson and Corley drew up a rebuttal 'battle book' to pass inaccuracies peddled by the Paleosceptics to the communications team and the whips' office. 'It was like fighting a religious war with facts,' one aide recalled. Others understood that, in Brexit, faith was as important as facts. 'I think we tried to apply logic to her arguments in a world where people were looking for more emotion and optimism,' a senior figure said. 'I also think we should have been more honest about the trade-offs. We were trying to sell something that was incredibly complex versus people who were able to make arguments of brutal simplicity.'

Aiken would open the morning meetings with a printed summary of media coverage, with supportive stories in green, neutral ones in yellow and hostile ones in red. At the start there were healthy splashes of green. 'In the end they were all red,' a special adviser recalled. As the weeks went by and the effort seemed ever less effectual, the office became known in Number 10 as the 'panic room' and attendance by senior political staff dwindled. 'It ran for about three weeks,' one war room warrior remembered.

However, there was a disconnect between the public-facing war room and where the actual votes were – in Parliament. 'It felt like a huge waste of energy,' said one senior member of May's political team. 'The only people whose opinion we needed to change were 313 Tory MPs.'

A spad said, 'The team at Number 10 were great people and worked really hard, but had a completely false sense of the outside world. They were convinced they were right and couldn't understand why people didn't think the deal wasn't the best thing since sliced bread. Robbie was incredibly blinkered. We didn't have any comms strategy to sell something enormously complicated. It really was done horrendously.'

There was a case to be made for the deal but, for the most part, it was not made effectively by May or Downing Street. The prime minister had asked for a bespoke deal for Britain and she had got one, despite Barnier's repeated insistence that the UK accept one of the steps on his staircase. Gavin Barwell thought this May's 'single biggest' achievement: 'At the outset, the EU basically said to us, "You can be a third country, completely outside the EU, [with a] standard free trade agreement, or you can be in the single market and there is nothing in between, it's a straight choice.

What we achieved was to get them to accept that there are a range of models and ... it's right that we come up with a bespoke relationship.' The UK got an agreement that bound them closely to the EU on goods and agrifood but more loosely on services.

Senior EU officials also say Britain got a good deal on the divorce bill: £39 billion was far lower than they had hoped or expected Britain would have to pay. Colleagues gave credit to Jonathan Black, the Treasury official who joined the Europe Unit. 'That was one of the great successes,' one of May's EU advisers said. A senior Commission source agreed: 'Mrs May won 15–20 billion euros over time from the European Union. That would be my calculation.'

Brussels had also said the UK could not expect to enjoy the benefits of membership without the obligations. May saw off an attempt to separate Northern Ireland from Britain's customs union and won agreement to an all-UK deal. A senior Downing Street figure said, 'The biggest argument in the negotiations was getting rid of the Northern Ireland-only backstop, and she got zero political credit for winning that.' This gave privileged market access without freedom of movement. 'The backstop Theresa May negotiated with the whole UK was the first time that the EU had ever agreed to split the four freedoms,' said Karen Bradley, the Northern Ireland secretary.

Summing up, one of the British negotiators opined, 'Now everyone focuses on the political declaration and the backstop, but the rest of the withdrawal agreement was actually pretty well negotiated, like the financial settlement. Citizens' rights: pretty good outcome. Governance: literally as good as we could have got. If you look through the vast majority of this frighteningly complicated divorce agreement, actually it was a pretty good deal.' Had May taken a different approach to Brexit from the beginning she could have heralded these negotiating successes as a balanced deal that reflected the 52–48 per cent referendum result, giving Britain economic security and sovereignty in key areas. But the prime minister felt unable to advertise her wins because the more high-profile decisions were objectionable to the Brexiteers.

Some of these were practical successes but ideological problems. 'The quid pro quo was that we'd have to comply with the common rulebook across the whole UK,' Bradley said. For her, this was the 'pragmatic' course of action. 'Businesses told me, "We're going to run one manufacturing production line, not two, and it's going to be compliant with the common rulebook because otherwise we can't sell into Europe." You can have your ideology, you can say you're not going to follow the common rules, but the truth is we all are anyway.'

Robbins had successfully negotiated what May had asked him to negotiate – what the Swiss ambassador described as 'the softest possible hard Brexit'. The deal was as close to that as the UK could get economically, while respecting May's insistence that Britain regain control of immigration. The issue was that she, almost alone, seemed to elevate that combination of priorities. As a prominent Brexiteer put it, 'You've got somebody who doesn't believe in exiting the EU but does believe in controlling migration and security cooperation, so she thinks she's got a good deal because it controls migration and you've got security cooperation. The rest of us, who actually believe in this thing, sense it's a fucking shit deal.' Jeremy Hunt told friends, 'The problem is that she selected a form of Brexit which was supported by Brexit voters but not by Brexit MPs.' It meant May's negotiating successes were political failures.

The same problems were apparent with the political declaration. Robbins, with May's help, secured at least a theoretical version of the frictionless trade she had demanded at Chequers, a textural negotiating win which shocked Barnier's team. By then, however, Chequers had become a byword for sellout. A close colleague of Robbins said, 'There were things we were asked to get and we managed to get them. But it turns out everyone in the UK hates [the deal], so it's a bit tainted.'

The political declaration was quickly dismissed by Brexiteers as a vague, non-binding document, not worth the paper it was written on. This stemmed from a misunderstanding of EU practice, rooted in the differences between British and European legal traditions. 'This is a cultural issue,' said Philip Hammond. 'From the EU's perspective, the political declaration has a lot more force than it feels to people from a common law world, where nothing is binding unless it's actually a signed treaty or contract. In civil law, if the Commission writes you a letter saying that it is intending to do something, that is effectively a binding decision by the Commission. While it's not a treaty, it's absolutely a highly material constraint on their freedom to act.'

As far as the Commission was concerned, granting Britain a transition period to adapt to the future was also something they had not, initially, wished to countenance. 'The very concept of the transition period, or the implementation period as she called it, was a concession,' a senior EU official said. But it was not politically easy to trumpet a delay to the clean break that some wanted. The problem was that judging the deal on whether it involved uncomfortable concessions by Brussels was not the full story. David Cameron had also won changes that made the EU uncomfortable in his 2016 'renegotiation'. Years afterwards, Martin Selmayr still kept in his safe the EU legal opinion which said, 'What you have promised Mr Cameron goes against the treaties.' The results of that negotiation were so quickly dismissed as inadequate by Eurosceptics that the government dropped them from their campaign within days. Seeing what, to Brussels, were awkward concessions thrown in the dustbin before the ink was dry in 2016 was also not an experience liable to encourage generosity from the Commission in 2018.

There were also obvious downsides to the deal from Britain's point of view and if you took the position that absolute sovereignty was the key, a nation's right to choose its own destiny, the level playing field provisions, which dictated British adherence to EU rules, were more than onerous, they were a fundamental abnegation of the purpose and meaning of Brexit. Even some of May's closest aides and senior ministers agreed that the ERG had a point about Britain's inability to escape the backstop. All they wanted was the right to leave a treaty their country had willingly joined. Yes, the practical real-life consequences in Northern Ireland hugely complicated the issue, but the principle was clear and reasonable.

It is legitimate to ask whether these circles could ever be properly squared but May believed in her deal. 'She genuinely thought it was great,' a Number 10 aide said. However, the prime minister was unable to convince either her own party, her own MPs, or the electorate to share that view and she must bear the lion's share of the blame for that. In a historic moment when a supreme political salesperson was needed, the government was run by one of the least able communicators to ascend to the office in modern times. 'She's not an actor,' said a close ally of May. 'She was not prepared to turn the table over and yell, "Right, I'm telling you why it's brilliant." You could never get her to do that. She has an aversion to soft-soaping. She was so frustrating to deal with.' A ministerial aide said, 'All someone else might have needed to do was eke 10 per cent improved relations out of the DUP, 10 per cent out of the EU, 10 per cent out of the ERG, and suddenly you're in the terrain of getting it over the line.'

May had a long-standing distrust of the media, which dated back to her time as Tory chairman when the *Telegraph* accused her of organising against then leader, Iain Duncan Smith. She categorically denied the story and provided an alibi for her activities but the allegation still made the front page. 'She referenced that conversation a couple of times,' one said.

Others questioned the role of Robbie Gibb, the prime minister's director of communications. The balding Brexiteer had a lot at stake, both personally and professionally. A conviction Eurosceptic since Maastricht, he came under heavy fire for supporting the prime minister's plan by MPs who had regarded him as an ally for two decades. At the BBC, where he had been head of political output, Gibb was a programme maker not a journalist, with little experience of the ebb and flow of news and how the course of stories could be altered with a well-timed intervention. He did little to disguise his distaste for a generation of reporters keen to break stories and comment on social media, something which limited his ability to get what he wanted from the print media.

Colleagues credit James Slack, May's official spokesman (probably the most accomplished holder of that role, under the circumstances), with doing most of the heavy lifting with the Fleet Street awkward squad, persuading his old editor, Paul Dacre of the *Mail*, and Tony Gallagher of the *Sun* to give May a fair wind. 'James wasn't the playmaker on Brexit but he was the goalkeeper, sent out every day to defend all the shots fired at him,' a political adviser said. Without Slack, May would have been ten-nil down before she started each morning.

Gibb had his successes, using his BBC contacts to get ERG allies bumped from the *Today* programme in favour of the pro-deal governor of the Bank of England. But colleagues thought his priorities wrong. His job was to focus on the public campaign to explain the deal, but Gibb devoted most of his personal energies to wooing MPs. 'He spent his time trying to do Brexit rather than sell Brexit,' said one. Yet as one of the few Brexiteers in Number 10 it was a fight he felt he had to take on – wining, dining and lobbying the ERG. Gibb believed that unless he could get prominent Brexiteers behind the deal, their dissent would always drown out his national messaging. He explained, 'It was a massive comms priority to get Brexiters back on side. We couldn't deliver Brexit without the MPs. So the main focus of the comms was the MPs.'

He sought to win them over saying, 'I'm the biggest Eurosceptic of them all and I can live with this', arguing that if the MPs had been offered similar rules at the time of Maastricht they would have 'snapped it up'. Gibb's goal was to at least ensure members of the ERG had heard the government's arguments, even if they were not receptive to them. His case was similar to Michael Gove's: 'Let's get Brexit over the line and then we can sort out the bits and pieces later.' A colleague recalled, 'You'd struggle to find anyone who wanted Brexit to happen more than Robbie.' Gibb aggressively disputed claims May's deal was 'not proper Brexit' but was taken aback by the 'level of hostility' from old allies. Some thought his own emotional involvement was detrimental. 'Good comms needs a degree of dispassion,' a friend said.

Gibb drew up a 'grid' of news events to promote the deal, which featured a presentation by Philip Hammond in the first week of December on the likely economic cost of failing to pass a deal. That came after the Bank of England warned that a cliff edge no-deal with no transition would slash GDP by 10.5 per cent over a five-year period and house prices by 30 per cent. They fell by 6.25 per cent and 17 per cent respectively during the 2008 financial crisis. The governor, Mark Carney, said May's deal would leave the economy 3.75 per cent smaller than it would have been if it had continued on pre-2016 trends.

The ERG tore holes in what they saw as a rerun of the 'Project Fear' campaigns from 2016. Steve Baker, who was familiar with the Treasury modelling, claimed the estimates were based on a false premise. It was government policy that, in the event of no-deal, the UK would change nothing at the border, allowing goods to continue to flow tariff-free whatever the EU did on its side. Yet the new analysis was based on the idea that Britain would impose tariffs. Baker told his fellow ERGers, 'If you take a gun and shoot your feet off, you will limp afterwards. The economic analysis includes that fundamentally stupid policy choice.' The Treasury also valued new trade deals at a fraction of what the EU themselves calculated they would be worth.

Instead of creating a virtuous circle, where rising public confidence swayed MPs and built momentum towards a win in the meaningful vote, the opposite happened. MPs undermined the deal and the public began to see it in a more negative light. James Johnson's polls turned sharply. 'By the end of November it was pretty clear the MPs weren't going to vote for it and support for the deal went back down again,' he said.

As a final throw of the dice, Gibb and Dylan Sharpe, the other Number 10 link man with the broadcasters, became enthusiastic supporters of a plan for May to challenge Jeremy Corbyn to a televised debate on Brexit. Johnson liked the idea too but most of Downing Street thought it deranged, even if Corbyn had been willing to go along with it. An attempt to ambush the Labour leader by having May challenge him publicly was scuppered when an exhausted Gibb accidentally emailed his entire grid to the editors of two national newspapers and the surprise was lost. Gibb tried to do a deal with the broadcasters, particularly the BBC, for a 'clean head-to-head' so it would resemble Prime Minister's Questions, where May had the edge on Corbyn. But Labour sought to strike a separate arrangement for a wider debate with ITV which would have pinned May in the crossfire between hardline Eurosceptics and trenchant Remainers. The idea died a death.

May's most effective public performance after the Boycott moment was a fireside chat video for YouTube, but that would not come until three weeks after the deal. By then, she was pushing water uphill politically.

Downing Street, critically, failed to make the case that May's deal was just the first part of the battle, that the trade deal to follow would be more palatable to Eurosceptics. This was a function of the sheer amount of time devoted to the withdrawal agreement in the negotiations and the media over the previous two years, something David Davis likened to a children's football match. 'They all chased the ball and nobody was looking where the goal was,' he told one friend. A different approach over the summer could have seen the prime minister strike a deal with the Eurosceptics: their support for the withdrawal agreement in exchange for handing Brexiteer ministers rather than Robbins control of the next phase, as Davis and Raab demanded.

Bigger still was the absence of what, at the start of the process, had been expected to be the main selling point of Brexit – regaining control of Britain's borders, a central issue in the referendum campaign. When he sat at Gove's dinner table that July, Dominic Cummings had said that however bad the deal was 'as long as you end freedom of movement, you'll be able to declare victory'. Afterwards it was baffling that more effort had not been made to dramatise this 'win'.

When Gavin Barwell joined Downing Street in June 2017 he had been warned by Philip Hammond, 'We are going to have to give in on immigration to get what we want.'[1] By June 2018 EU ambassadors in London were warning that an effort would be made that autumn to force Britain to accept freedom of movement if it wanted any sort of reasonable market access. This did not come to pass but it might have been better for May if there had been a huge public showdown. 'At the beginning of the process everyone said to us, "You will never get tariff-free trade without free movement",' a senior figure in the comms team recalled. 'I sat in a meeting with Merkel where it was made clear to us that it was going to be impossible. Yet, we did get that and without much of a murmur. The problem is that which should have been a major victory of the negotiation was banked early on and then we ended up getting into a fire-fight on the backstop and regulatory alignment. If the final showdown had been free movement, we would have had a better chance. We got stuck in the trenches on something that was incredibly complicated against opponents whose messaging was ruthlessly simple and effective.'

In this scenario, immigration would have instantly become the central cause célèbre for Eurosceptics, pushing the backstop into the background, as well as the overwhelmingly newsworthy issue for the public. May might have been able to split immigration Leavers from those motivated by sovereignty. Instead, she sought to placate and then disappoint the right and, as a political aide put it, 'In the Conservative Party, if you constantly feed the crocodiles then they come for you.' The problem with the backstop was that it was the least satisfactory outcome to those who campaigned for Leave and the least explicable for the public, who took their lead on the small print from Brexiteers with strong views.

James Johnson is in no doubt how important this was. Polls showed a majority of voters backing the end of free movement in every age group, social class and political affiliation. 'I spent two years trying to tell people that immigration still mattered, even though polls showed that it had got less salient,' he said. 'It had only got less salient because people thought Brexit was going to sort it. In my focus groups, especially in places like Warrington and Dudley, it was still coming up with the same level of impact. It was one of the few issues where voters were not willing to give you any leeway. It was a fundamental thing to deliver.'

In early December, May sought to demonstrate how the government had taken back control by publishing a white paper on new immigration rules. But it was delayed after bitter cabinet divisions, to the point where it came too late to help. Sajid Javid was a tougher home secretary than Amber Rudd, but still fought to ditch the commitment, dating from

May's time at the Home Office, to cut net immigration to the 'tens of thousands' annually. Figures that month showed it running at 322,000 a year.

Javid insisted on a low-skilled route in. May, who believed British low-skilled workers were the big losers of globalisation, wanted none. 'That was a pretty big bust-up,' a Number 10 aide said. 'Immigration was always the issue I saw her most energised about. She'd raise her voice in meetings and get into school mistress mode.' On one occasion, Javid told May, 'Immigration creates jobs.' She slapped her hand on the table, becoming Margaret Thatcher: 'No, no, no, no, no!' In a staff meeting, the prime minister said, 'Nobody in cabinet understands the importance of this issue. It used to be me and David Cameron and now it's just me.' Yet her chancellor and others forced her hand. 'Hammond was fantastically tone deaf,' one aide recalled. 'He said something like, "I wouldn't be able to go to my local restaurant if we didn't have a low-skilled route."' When the white paper was circulated, creating a temporary low-skilled route, May wrote on it by hand, 'This is very frustrating. Needless to say I am very unhappy with the way this has progressed.' When she launched the white paper at Heathrow airport on 19 December, Javid was not invited.

The resignations kept coming. Jo Johnson, the uber-Remainer brother of Boris, quit as a transport minister on 9 November, saying the public were being offered the choice of 'no say' in EU rules or a no-deal Brexit that would 'inflict untold damage'. He wrote, 'To present the nation with a choice between ... vassalage and chaos, is a failure of British statecraft on a scale unseen since the Suez crisis.' He said he was united with his brother in 'fraternal dismay' at the state of play.

Sam Gyimah, the universities minister, jumped on 30 November in an article for the *Daily Telegraph*, the seventh minister to quit. May's 'deal in name only' would leave Britain 'worse off' and as 'rule takers', we 'will be losing, not taking control of our national destiny'. This sovereignty argument, usually associated with Brexiteers, was now being thrown at May from the other wing of her party, though Gyimah's conclusion, that there should be a second referendum, was the opposite of the ERG's. He had been shocked in his day job by the Commission's decision to throw Britain out of the Galileo satellite navigation project, a rival/back-up to the US global positioning system (GPS) which powered most map direction apps on smartphones. The UK had invested billions in the scheme since 2003. The encryption technology was built by British-based firms. Gyimah had assumed it was a 'win-win' for the UK to stay, but found to his horror that the project became a pawn in the exit negotiations. He and Robbins were both 'blindsided'. At a conference, Gyimah cornered Elżbieta Bieńkowska, the commissioner responsible for Galileo, and warned that Britain would have little choice but to create an alternative. Her reply shocked him to the core: 'You're out of the club. You decided to leave the club. This is what it means to be out of the club.' Britain, he concluded, was in a 'weak position' and about to give away 'our voice, our veto and our vote'. A Eurosceptic might have reacted with fury at the EU, but Gyimah saw Britain getting 'hammered' in years of negotiations.

With May and Gibb, the government's key salesman was Julian Smith, the chief whip. His job was arguably the hardest. His strategy, to start with at least, was to pass the deal using Conservative and DUP votes, with a handful of Labour 'Lexiteers' like Kate Hoey plugging the gaps left by the dozen Tory hardcore Remainers. No one doubted Smith's industry. He seldom slept and was in the office most weekends. He arranged for technical discussions for MPs with civil servants and special advisers. He assiduously met every group of MPs – the ERG, the DUP, Peter Bone's 'G group' ultras who even Steve Baker called 'the Taliban', Dominic Grieve's Bresistance group. Smith had played squash for Scotland when he was a junior and achieved grade eight on both violin and piano. Like May, he knew that the only way to succeed in life was to work hard and keep trying. 'It was to his great credit that he kept the plates spinning for a lot longer than probably even Gavin Williamson would have done,' said one close ally. But colleagues say he was a less effective 'chief' than Williamson, who never failed to ask an MP about their mum's operation or their children's birthdays, but was also prepared to grab them where it hurt, politically, and squeeze. One who worked with both men said, 'Gavin understood better what makes people tick. Julian was less able to have a transactional conversation about votes. He doesn't like conflict.'

Good whipping was about deploying the right persuader at a wavering MP: 'This person needs to go straight to the prime minister, this person needs to go to the chief, this person is mates with that person, they can put a little bit of pressure on.' Insiders say Smith did not empower his subordinates and sent too many people to May herself. There were two

problems here. First, PMs are supposed to be used where they can finalise a deal, rather than look weak by trying in vain to win over rebel MPs.
Second, as an MP cruelly observed, 'She couldn't sell a cold drink in a hot
desert.' Smith was also controlling. An insider said, 'If he ever found out
that somebody had struck a deal with somebody without his knowledge
– "vote for this and you can get that slip you want, or I'll put in a word
with the chancellor about that thing you want in your constituency" – he
would go nuts and say, "I didn't authorise that."'

Smith used the full force of government patronage. Backbench
Brexiteers were told, 'We need more people in the House of Lords … I
think you'd be a strong voice.' Others had knighthoods and privy councillorships dangled. Yet there was a limit to the efficacy of this approach.
'She can't just offer ninety peerages,' said one Tory. It also backfired.
John Hayes, who had been helping May, was given a knighthood but
when colleagues claimed he had been bought, Hayes declared publicly
that he would vote against the deal. When Michael Fabricant announced
in the Commons tearoom that he would happily support the prime
minister if he was handed the right title and an estate in the Bahamas,
Andrew Bridgen replied, 'Given the prime minister's negotiating skills,
you would probably end up with the entire Caribbean.'

A man of compromise by temperament, the chief was overly optimistic about those whose views were more intractable. 'Julian thought we
wanted a ladder to climb down,' said a senior member of the ERG who
Smith indicated he could get a government job. 'We didn't want a ladder
or jobs, we wanted the policy to change.'

After three weeks of intensive activity, things still looked bleak for the
chief. Yet Smith's reluctance to share his numbers led to groupthink
optimism in Downing Street that things might be all right in the end. A
former Number 10 aide who visited at this time said, 'I was surprised
after speaking to quite a few sensible people that they were still expecting
to win the vote. By then, it seemed to me to be mathematically impossible.'

The number of MPs who could be relied upon to vote for Theresa
May's deal numbered only around 200, half of them on her front bench.
Smith was trying and failing to get Labour MPs who believed in uphold-
ing the referendum result to bolster the numbers. John Mann, the MP for
Bassetlaw, a Nottinghamshire mining seat which voted overwhelmingly
for Leave, was ushered in to see May and suggested more than 30 Labour

MPs were biddable. But by late November just two other opposition members were committed to voting for the deal: Caroline Flint, a former Labour cabinet minister, and Stephen Lloyd, an eccentric Lib Dem. One leading Labour Bresister recalled, 'When the deal came out, Barwell and Lidington had this meeting with loads of Labour backbenchers trying to get us on side. It was really cack-handed. Barwell was banging on about the Northern Ireland Protocol. We said, "We don't have a problem with that; that's not the issue for us." He didn't get that. He had come prepared to have the wrong conversation with us.'

Ranged against May were the ranks of Tory Eurosceptic rebels nudging at this point towards three figures, a handful of Labour leavers, plus a dozen Remainer rebels and several factions of backbench opposition MPs, now coalescing into two camps – those pressing for a second referendum, others pursuing the 'Norway option' of single market membership outside the EU. The Labour front bench was itself divided between customs union membership and a smattering of 'Norwegians'. Growing numbers of both persuasions wanted another referendum. As a cabinet minister rightly observed, 'The PM's deal is everyone's second choice. If we had the single transferable vote she'd win easily. Perhaps she should have a referendum on electoral reform instead.'

May was not a persuader. With late votes prevalent, a woman MP came up with the idea that female Tories should have a 'onesie pyjama party'. The prime minister was invited. 'She was told to schmooze the party,' an attendee recalled. 'It didn't include pyjamas in the end but poor old May turned up and was so socially awkward. I had to make small talk with her and I'm the one who had to keep it going. Her character was fundamentally unsuited to this moment of high diplomacy.'

Julia Lopez, who joined a delegation to Number 10 in early December, described a similar mood, 'It was a very polite but clipped discussion. She asked us to set out our reservations.' Lopez told May the withdrawal agreement was 'deceitful: pretending to be something it's not', adding, 'It will have grave democratic consequences. We have to listen to what people said to us in the referendum.' Lee Rowley, the MP for North East Derbyshire, warned, 'We are treating the voters as fools. The result is that we will lose seats like mine.'

On 10 December, supporters of a People's Vote held a 'day of action' with 130 events around the country, a dry run for the arguments a Remain campaign would run in a new referendum. But even here, MPs were split between those such as Chuka Umunna and Chris Leslie on the Labour benches and Tory Sarah Wollaston – who wanted to table an amendment calling for a second referendum – and those such as campaign chief Tom Baldwin, who wanted to wait until May had lost the meaningful vote. He feared the ultras would 'blow the whole thing' by moving before there was majority support in Parliament for a second referendum.

The challenge for Downing Street was to try to persuade the Brexiteers that the danger of no Brexit was more threatening than the prime minister's deal while convincing those who wanted to rerun 2016 that the prospect of no-deal was worse than her agreement. But, by the time the deal was done, each of these groups was surgically attached to its first choice and believed that the more militant it became, the more likely it was to win. They could not all be right.

Most Bresistance groups knew where they wanted to go but lacked the plan to force the outcome they desired. Crucially, the ERG knew exactly where they wanted to go, had a plan to get there and the requisite determination. Mark Francois, the chief Buddie, told one meeting their 'irreducible core' of votes against the deal was 45, more than enough to guarantee May's defeat. Another 29 were in play. 'We're like a fish bait ball, we're getting smaller and smaller, the whips are picking people off at the edges, but we'll win because it's the people against Parliament now and we are on the side of the people,' he said. 'They're driving a car at a brick wall expecting us to move and I'm not going to move.'

Many of the irreducible core were represented at a party thrown by Jacob Rees-Mogg at his £6 million home in Westminster on 27 November. Over glasses of chilled champagne, conversation focused on when and how to oust May. The ERG gang believed they had a 'lucky escape' in failing to force a vote in October. 'She would probably have won comfortably,' one said. 'Now we're measuring up the coffin.'

Three days later Steve Baker was at the funeral of one of his best friends, when Boris Johnson called and asked, 'What should we do?' Baker said they needed to round up a dozen letter writers to be sure they could trigger a vote of no confidence. Johnson was seeing a steady succession of MPs to make clear he wanted to be leader. One said to him, 'My heart wants it to be you, but my head says you're like an ex-boyfriend all women have, who promises to change and who never does.' He 'looked like death', the MP said. 'Tired and downbeat.'

* * *

The first new challenge came not from Johnson but from Labour. The opposition used a Commons procedure called a 'humble address' to demand that Geoffrey Cox's full legal advice be published, a motion that passed on 13 November.[2] The motion put the government in a terrible position. The attorney general was furious, particularly with Keir Starmer who, as a former chief prosecutor, understood the need for government lawyers to provide ministers with confidential advice. Privately, Starmer acknowledged the point but he also knew if there was a genuine reason why it could not be published – beyond political embarrassment – Cox would have talked to him on Privy Council terms to get him to back off.

Julian Smith, foreseeing a lost cause, urged May to get on the 'front foot' and publish the advice, rather than have it dragged from them. Cox insisted the demand be resisted on principle to prevent a precedent being established. The attorney general won. He would make a statement to Parliament but only release a concise summary of his advice. The chief whip felt that while it was 'technically the right decision', it handed MPs the chance to give the government a bloody nose and reinforced the view that the government was indifferent to Parliament's concerns.

Downing Street's discomfort became more acute on 2 December, when the *Sunday Times* splashed on leaked extracts of Cox's suppressed advice, including the killer line that the backstop 'would endure indefinitely' even if future trade talks collapsed. To make matters worse, the paper reported that his full legal judgment was 'far bleaker' than the summary legal advice he was planning to publish or the speech he was going to make in the Commons. It quoted a cabinet source saying, 'The legal advice is very bad which is why they don't want anyone to see it.'

The following day, Cox released his summary advice and made a bravura speech in the chamber, acknowledging legal issues with backstop, but forcefully making the political argument he had rehearsed at cabinet, that the backstop was an uncomfortable resting place for Brussels and that, on balance, May's deal was an acceptable way of leaving the EU.

Six MPs wrote to John Bercow, the speaker, urging him to hold the government in contempt of Parliament for failing to publish the full advice. The whips believed Bercow had put them up to it. In a statement to the House, the speaker said, 'I am satisfied that there is an arguable case that a contempt has been committed', and promptly announced that there would be a vote first thing the following day. MPs voted by 311 to 293 to hold the government in contempt, the first time that had occurred in British political history. Cox, it was said, shed a tear. Bercow thought ministers guilty of 'disgraceful behaviour in ignoring the express instruction of Parliament'.[3] Andrea Leadsom, the leader of the House, was forced to announce that the full legal advice would be published the following day to inform MPs ahead of the meaningful vote.

The question in Number 10 was whether there was to be a meaningful vote at all. Mouth dry, heart thumping in his chest, Julian Smith told cabinet on 6 December they were on course to lose by 200 votes. Others in May's team could scarcely comprehend what they were hearing. Some had thought the first vote would be lost, then MPs would see sense. But this was a potential catastrophe. Robbins had worked for months to get a deal done; now MPs felt they had 'a free hit' to destroy it. 'We are staring into the abyss,' a source said. 'If the vote is lost then either the government will pivot to a plan B or Parliament will take control.' A campaign to sell the deal, which began by showcasing the virtues of May's Boycottian resilience, was now failing precisely because the fate of the deal was inextricably linked to that of the prime minister. 'This is not a bad deal,' one minister said. 'The problem with this deal is that it is her deal.'

Tory MPs were abandoning ship, Labour MPs refusing to come on board, the speaker flexing his muscles. The stage was set for arguably the greatest parliamentary showdown since the 1640s, certainly since the reform bills of the nineteenth century. It was not obvious how May could win. A chess-playing minister said, 'This is zugzwang. It's a position where you have to move and whatever you do it makes things worse.'

16

NO CONFIDENCE

12 December 2018

Julian Smith had two cards left to play. If MPs would not support the deal in the meaningful vote, due on 12 December, perhaps they would back an amendment that provided extra reassurance. By the evening of Thursday 6 December, the whips' office had drawn up a proposal for a parliamentary lock on the backstop. It could not be a government amendment; Smith needed a backbencher to table it and it was already late on a day when most MPs returned to their constituencies. The vote office in Parliament was about to close. 'No one was around because it was a Thursday evening,' said a senior Tory. 'We were scrabbling around for an MP. It looked as if it could be cleaner or restaurant staff tabling it at one stage.' Eventually, they located Hugo Swire, a former Northern Ireland minister, who was happy to put his name to the amendment.

The amendment gave Parliament a vote on whether to implement the backstop and imposed a 'duty' on the government to agree a future relationship with the EU, or alternative arrangements, within a year of the backstop coming into force. However, even as it was tabled, government lawyers were questioning whether the amendment would make it impossible to ratify the withdrawal agreement with the EU. If the government whipped in support of the Swire amendment they would, in effect, be violating the treaty. When word reached the Commission of what had been cooked up, officials made clear the idea would not work. 'It was discredited before it was even tabled,' a special adviser recalled.

Smith took soundings on the meaningful vote. When he called Bernard Jenkin, the ERG veteran said, 'Why are you letting the prime minister crash the Conservative Party into a brick wall? It's going to be a disaster. She can't possibly get this through. Can't you see that?'

By Saturday 8 December, Smith was firmly of the view they had to pull the meaningful vote because of the scale of defeat which loomed. 'He was convinced that you will lose the government if you lose the vote,' a Downing Street aide said. The same message was sent to May by Gavin Williamson, the former chief whip. Robbie Gibb agreed. Others like Stephen Parkinson lobbied for a Thatcher-style showdown with Brussels, another 'handbag moment'. Graham Brady, the chairman of the 1922 Committee, also went to see the prime minister. 'I thought it was impossible to get a parliamentary majority for the withdrawal agreement with the backstop,' he recalled. 'There was no point in holding a vote on something which was going to be lost by a massive majority.'[1]

May resisted, telling the *Mail on Sunday* she wanted to hold the vote. Her instincts were that holding and losing the vote was an important way of showing the Commission what she was up against. 'She wanted to crack on with it,' a senior source said. But the foundations of the government were collapsing. That Saturday night Will Quince, a Brexiteer parliamentary aide to Williamson, resigned, while Tobias Ellwood, a defence minister, signalled he was ready to back a referendum, warning that the 'sell-by date' on the 2016 vote was about to expire.

Three senior figures told the author that Saturday the vote would be postponed but warned that the official line would not change until Monday. The *Sunday Times* splashed the story. As late as 8.10 a.m. on Monday, Michael Gove told *Today* it was 'definitely, 100 per cent' going to happen. By lunchtime, after a conference call with cabinet ministers, it was pulled, May telling MPs she faced a 'significant' defeat. She vowed to take the concerns of Parliament back to Brussels. Alex Dawson, from the Number 10 political team, said, 'There was a view that it was better to give it a bit more time, see if we can take a bit more heat out of the issue.'[2] Jacob Rees-Mogg was withering: 'The prime minister must either govern or quit.' For another six months she was, in effect, to do neither.

The meaningful vote, designed to settle Brexit once and for all, had been scheduled for 12 December. No one then knew that it would take exactly a year – until the general election of 12 December 2019 – for the issue to be resolved. The delay infuriated John Bercow, who judged the government's behaviour 'bare-faced' and 'shameless'. He wrote, 'In the most staggering show of irresponsibility, [May] was deferring the vote for as long as possible in order to run down the clock', leaving MPs with no-deal or her deal.[3] The umpire was as radicalised by Brexit as the players.

The letters of no confidence flooded in, grave drama injected with farce. One MP sent their parliamentary assistant to surreptitiously slip the letter beneath Graham Brady's door. She returned, saying 'I can't get it under the door.' They went back together. 'We were so incompetent trying to shove it under the door,' the MP said. 'We had to use a knife.'

Brady was walking down the library corridor in the Commons on Tuesday 11 December when he bumped into a colleague, who said: 'I'm really sorry, Graham, I didn't want to do this … but I just can't leave it any longer.' The handover was completed with the discretion and speed of a double agent filling a dead drop. 'A House of Commons envelope travelled from his inside jacket pocket to mine in a matter of seconds,' recalled Brady. The chairman of the '22 knew he now had in his possession the forty-eighth letter calling for a vote of no confidence in the prime minister. 'Unseen, the trigger had been pulled.' Brady had been congratulated on his poker face. 'Any sign that this was a critical moment would have changed the whole dynamic of the process, so I bade the colleague farewell and walked quickly back to my office in Portcullis House.' There he gave the letters a 'final count' and sat down to 'plan the next steps'.[4]

Brady's 'door had barely closed when there was a knock on it,' he said. 'Standing there was a Conservative MP who had submitted a letter to me a couple of weeks before.' The MP said, 'The timing is just bloody awful, I'd like to withdraw my letter.' The count returned to forty-seven. Brady shook his head in disbelief. 'It was too early for a large whisky – or even a small one.' This time, however, there would be no reprieve for May. 'In the afternoon the threshold was crossed again.'[5]

The prime minister's decision to delay the Brexit vote had achieved what Jacob Rees-Mogg and Steve Baker could not a fortnight earlier. Yet it was probably Hobson's choice for May. Brady, probably correctly, concluded, 'I am sure that going ahead and losing the vote by a massive margin would have had exactly the same effect.'[6]

Jenkin was one of several Paleosceptics to submit a letter. 'The final straw,' he recalled, 'was when the vote was pulled, and I thought: If you're the prime minister of a government and your flagship policy has basically collapsed and you daren't even put it in front of the House of Commons, you have effectively lost the ability to govern.'[7]

The Conservative Party's constitution said that Brady was required to inform the leader and arrange a vote as soon as was reasonable. He contacted Downing Street. In Number 10, word spread quickly that the dread moment had arrived. To complicate the issue, May was abroad on a tour of Brussels, The Hague and Berlin, trying to drum up support for tweaks to the Brexit deal. She had only been planning to return for Prime Minister's Questions on the Wednesday, before leaving again for the European Council meeting on Thursday. The senior staff met in the prime minister's office without her. Robbie Gibb made a strong case for moving quickly before the rebels had a chance to build up a head of steam. 'Let's get the whole thing done and dusted within one news cycle, so people would wake up and it's not in the papers,' he said. 'And they go to bed and the next day it's a triumph – hopefully.' Julian Smith strongly agreed.

May's plane was still airborne when the phones of her aides got a signal and their screens lit up with the breaking news that Brady had requested a meeting. The prime minister was whisked off the aircraft and Barwell broke the news to her in the car. 'She was obviously upset,' he recalled. But another aide said, 'She was very sanguine, stoic about it in quite a ballsy way.' May did not seek to reassure her staff but they found her demeanour reassuring. One of them, an English literature student, remembered a line from *Macbeth*: 'I have almost forgot the taste of fears.' On return, they found Gibb 'full of energy'. Barwell said, 'Her mood was transformed from despondency by him and his reaction.'[8]

Brady and May spoke on Tuesday evening. 'She's a tough lady, and I think she took it in a resolute, professional way,' he recalled. Brady half expected a request to delay the vote until after the meeting in Brussels, which could have pushed it to the following Monday. Instead, May was 'keen that we should do it as quickly as it could sensibly be done, which from my point of view made life easier'.[9] To comply with Gibb's desire to limit the news to a single day, 'it was agreed that [Brady] would say something on the *Today* programme' the following morning to confirm the vote, with a press release issued to inform the markets at 7.30 a.m. MPs would have until 4 p.m. to arrange proxy votes if they were away and the ballot itself would take place between 6 p.m. and 8 p.m., with the result announced at 9 p.m. 'I think we'd have been toast if we'd left it to Monday,' a senior member of May's team said later.

In Downing Street, the mood fluctuated between determination, fatalism and fury. 'The Brexiteers, in their pursuit of perfection will deliver themselves no Brexit, a broken union and Corbyn in office by Christmas,' one aide raged. It was gone 10 p.m. when May's campaign team assembled with the prime minister – Gavin Barwell, JoJo Penn, Julian Smith, Robbie Gibb, Stephen Parkinson, along with Mick Davis, the Conservative chief executive, and Brandon Lewis, the party chairman. Unusually, Philip May, the prime minister's 'rock', also sat in on the meeting. He was a quiet but trenchant advocate that she should fight. 'If she had stopped the first time a group of men had told her "No, you can't do this or you shouldn't do that", she wouldn't have been prime minister,' said a (male) aide. 'She wouldn't have been home secretary, she wouldn't have been a Tory MP.' The false alarm a fortnight earlier had enabled Barwell and Smith to plan. They had even considered getting MPs to submit letters to force a vote they believed the ERG could not yet win. Philip May was an advocate of that approach, to spare his wife a protracted period with a Damocletian sword above her head. 'Do we call a vote and just settle this?' he said. They decided to wait.

The vultures circled. Sajid Javid, the home secretary, was 'very active', inviting colleagues to breakfasts. A female MP told colleagues only Amber Rudd could 'unite the party' and women should 'get behind her'. That evening Andrea Leadsom hosted a dinner at her London home. David Davis and Dominic Raab, competitors for the Brexiteer vote, shared a very public glass of red wine in Portcullis House. Davis, channelling Alan Partridge, boasted he had lost a stone and a half for the leadership fight by running: 'I do three or four miles. It's mostly sprinting.' Raab, alone of the frontrunners, admitted he was voting for May to go. Esther McVey also contacted MPs. A Brexiteer remarked, 'Esther is hunger wearing lipstick.'

Number 10 staff were in by 7 a.m. on the day of the vote, Philip May present again in the morning meeting. As the country awoke, a battalion of loyal MPs took to Twitter to express their support for the prime minister. Gibb persuaded the broadcasters to run totalisers on air, a spur to others to get on board. 'We felt pretty confident going into it,' a Downing Street aide said. From mid-morning, JoJo Penn and James Marshall chaired a rolling meeting in the Cabinet Room where every political aide in the building was given a spreadsheet of MPs to ring. Even Richard 'Tricky' Jackson, the head of operations, was drafted in. 'Everyone was calling people they know,' a spad recalled. 'The operation worked brilliantly. Every member of Parliament got more than one phone call from somebody in Number 10.' The numbers were recorded on a whiteboard in Barwell's office. Some thought bringing things 'in house' was the secret to their success. 'That was a rare example of Number 10 properly working well,' one staffer said. 'If they'd done the meaningful vote like that, rather than in the whips' office, it might have been a little bit better.' May saw as many MPs as she could to ask for their support, something she joked about at the start of PMQs: 'Mr Speaker, I will have meetings, possibly many meetings, with ministerial colleagues and others.'

The regicides had their own war room in Iain Duncan Smith's office. May's allies put it around that the Paleosceptics were calling it 'the kill zone', black propaganda which stuck, putting off MPs who had contemplated voting against her.

May was to address the 1922 Committee at 5 p.m. Beforehand, her team held a prep session raising a subject which had been already discussed between Barwell and the prime minister – whether to revisit something she had said after the 2017 election. On that occasion she had told Tory MPs, 'I'll serve you for as long as you want me to.' It was increasingly obvious to the prime minister's most senior aides – Barwell, Penn and Smith to the fore – that MPs no longer wished her to lead them into the next election. Conversations that day made clear May would bolster her position considerably if she said she would not do so. A political adviser said, 'There were quite a lot of people who said, "Look, I don't think we should have a leadership election now, but I don't want you to take this as a vote to mean please stay forever."' Nicky Morgan later admitted she was one. Another Downing Street adviser said, 'Everyone knew in their heart of hearts that she was going to have to commit to standing down.' May was put through her paces by Barwell, Penn, Alex Dawson, her speechwriter Keelan Carr, and her PPS Seema Kennedy. 'How would you answer this question?' May offered an answer. Her aides worked on the wording, pressing her to toughen it up.

May still thought she was the best person to hold the party together, that what mattered was the issue, that walking away would not change the parliamentary arithmetic. But her devotion to public service also made it difficult to resist advisers who were clear that the greatest service she could perform was to accept that her days were numbered. 'She found it very painful and difficult to do,' one of those in the room said. 'I think she understood that she had to do it and I think she wanted to provide herself with as much wiggle room as possible. She sucked it up.'

The prime minister handled herself with dignity when she faced back-benchers in Committee Room 14. There were a few pointed questions but not open hostility. When an ERG MP asked, 'What is your long-term intention after March?' May did not pivot straight to her prepared answer. Perhaps part of her wanted to see if she needed to play that card. The Brexiteer MP Lee Rowley said, 'Stamina is not a policy, Prime Minister.' It was a remark that hit home.

May said, 'In my heart, I would like to lead the party into the next general election', due in 2022, but she added that it was not the will of the party or her colleagues that she did so. 'Therefore, it is not my intention to do so.' As she spoke, the gravity of what May was saying had a visible effect on some MPs.

There was some ambiguity, however. Asked whether she would stand down if there was an election in the next year, May 'mumbled'. She had repeatedly ruled out a snap election. She felt her pledge held good. But she also wanted to preserve some freedom to manoeuvre. Afterwards ERG members questioned whether May was selling a false bill of goods. Rees-Mogg accused her of 'hedging her bets'. 'Intention', he observed, was a classic politician's word, not a categorical promise. Number 10 spin doctors briefed hard that May would not fight the next election but those who did not trust her felt justified in their disbelief. Others saw fresh evidence of her poor communication skills. 'Typical May,' one MP said. 'She tries to deliver a message, but no one can agree what she said.'[10]

It was announced that the whip had been returned to two MPs – Charlie Elphicke and Andrew Griffiths – both under investigation amid claims of sexual misconduct. This news prompted some desk banging. Every vote would count. Others thought it a tawdry manoeuvre at odds with May's claim to embody decency and rectitude. At 5.45 p.m. the end came with the loud banging of desks. At 6 p.m. the ballot box was opened and MPs began filing back into Room 14 to cast their secret ballots on whether to sack their boss, one of the most bizarre rituals in Westminster.

Two younger MPs who had submitted letters went together for moral support, arriving at the same time as the prime minister. 'It was awful,' one said. 'I felt she must hate me. I felt like I couldn't compete with her service, her duty, her resilience, her courage. But those qualities did not make her the right leader.' Gavin Williamson was the last MP to appear, just before the 8 p.m. cut-off. 'I think I'll vote for the prime minister,' he said. The ballot boxes were taken to a nearby room, where Brady and his two vice chairmen, Cheryl Gillan and Charles Walker, counted the votes.

At 9 p.m. they filed back into Room 14, half packed with MPs, the rear with journalists. 'Let us pray,' one MP joked as Brady and the 1922 executive filed in with the grave bearing of a Masonic funeral party. Only the smile on Julian Smith's face gave the game away. Brady read out the result. May got 200 votes, with 117 against her. 'The parliamentary party *does* have confidence in Theresa May,' Brady intoned. MPs leaped to their feet. 'Alan Duncan led this North Korean response,' an ERG MP said. The prime minister's pledge to stand down was, by the chief whip's estimate, worth 40 votes, the difference between a humiliating evening and a fatal one. Smith said it made 'a material difference' to the outcome.

Two of the No voters 'bumped into a group of sycophants' downstairs, one recalled. 'Somebody thrust his arms up and said, "Yes!" Twat. His trade envoyship had been expanded. This little vignette said everything about the depths the government was plumbing.'

Around 9.30 p.m. May gave another of her speeches to the waiting cameras in Downing Street, in time to top the 10 p.m. bulletins. She was 'pleased' to win but acknowledged, 'A significant number of colleagues did cast a vote against me, and I have listened to what they said.' She conceded the onus was on her to deliver: 'I have heard what the House of Commons said about the Northern Ireland backstop and, when I go to the European Council tomorrow, I will be seeking legal and political assurances that will assuage the concerns.'

After May walked back through the black door, she found an atmosphere of rare euphoria. Barwell and Gibb hugged. May and husband Philip got a cheer as they joined the staff for drinks outside the Cabinet Room. She spoke again, acknowledging that all their jobs had been on the line. Philip May put his hand gently on her arm. With characteristic dedication, the PM spent the rest of the evening doing her ministerial red box. 'She was back to work like nothing had happened,' said Gibb.[11]

In winning 200 votes, May had got one more than when she won the Tory leadership in 2016. It represented 63 per cent of the vote. Yet the PM had won less than half of the backbench vote. Her team had hoped the rebel count would be under 100. Margaret Thatcher was mortally wounded when she secured 204 votes in 1990, four more than May, admittedly in a bigger parliamentary party. May had done worse than John Major in 2005 when he secured 218 votes to John Redwood's 89. Jacob Rees-Mogg had a valid historical point when he said that evening, 'This is a terrible result for the prime minister. Under all constitutional norms, she ought to go and see the Queen urgently and resign.' But his churlishness upset even some Brexiteers. 'It totally undermined the case he's been pushing to honour the referendum result,' one rebel observed. 'And there was nastiness to his words that were off-putting.' Rees-Mogg said later, 'I regret doing that, because it lacked grace. When you've lost, you should accept that.'

The greater significance of the 117 figure was that it was close to the number of Tories expected to vote against the Brexit deal. May was safe, for now, but her plan was on life support. 'We knew she was a wounded animal,' one ERG member said. A depressed Bernard Jenkin phoned Barry Legg, chairman of the Bruges Group, who tried to cheer him up: 'It's a very good result,' Legg said, with the perspective of distance. 'It means the next leader of the Conservative Party is going to be a Eurosceptic.'

The papers that night were split, the *Daily Mail* ('Now let her get on with the job!') backing May, while the Tory *Sun* ('Time to call it a May') joined the Labour-supporting *Mirror* ('It's lame duck for Christmas') in condemning her. It was the *Daily Telegraph* which captured what most MPs were now asking: 'A vote to Remain, but when will she Leave?'

May, like Thatcher, had been lucky in her enemies. In forcing a vote, the ERG leadership had miscalculated the mood of the party. According to party rules, as they were understood by MPs, they had given May a year in which she could rule unchallenged. Eurosceptics privately questioned Rees-Mogg and Baker's handling of events. 'She's in for another year,' an ERG member said, 'and another year will shatter the Tory party.' Yet the ERG chairman did give a hint about what his support would cost. Asked if there was 'no prospect' of him ever supporting her EU withdrawal plan, Rees-Mogg said, 'If she can take the backstop out, there are bits of the withdrawal agreement I don't like, but I'm willing to compromise.' Earlier that evening, the prime minister had also met Arlene Foster and Nigel Dodds of the DUP. Afterwards Foster said, 'We emphasised that tinkering around the edges would not work. We were not seeking assurances or promises. We wanted fundamental legal text changes.'

17

'NEBULOUS' NEGOTIATIONS

December 2018 to January 2019

Theresa May's expression was that of a church warden catching the local troublemaker scrumping apples in a graveyard – weary, indignant but unsurprised at the turn of events. It was 14 December, two days after the no-confidence vote. Jean-Claude Juncker, the Commission president, wore a look of offended innocence, May the uniform of a home counties spinster: hair a helmet of grey above a floral brown jacket that could have carpeted a curry house, a necklace of silver spheres big enough to mine the Channel. She had returned to Brussels seeking legally binding assurances to bolster her case at home. Instead, she was confronted by quotes from Juncker, denouncing her approach to Brexit as 'nebulous'.

When May spied him in the Council chamber she moved in for the kill. 'What did you call me? You called me nebulous.' Juncker denied it. 'Yes, you did!' May's aides had asked for a 'handbag moment' and here it was. Mark Rutte, the Dutch prime minister, made a beeline for the confrontation, an aggressive peacemaker. All too often in the talks May had been pictured in this same room alone and isolated, separated by both personality and circumstances from the other leaders. Now, she was the national embodiment of a nation's indignation.

At his press conference later, Juncker attempted to clarify that he used 'nebulous' to mean 'foggy', a comment on Parliament's Brexit debates rather than the prime minister herself. Yet many at home shared the frustration in Brussels at the government's vague approach. Juncker's nebulous comments were a distraction from May's real problem – the refusal of EU leaders to go along with a stage-managed rescue effort by senior EU officials to help the prime minister.

After May pulled the meaningful vote, Oliver Robbins returned to Brussels for secret meetings with Martin Selmayr and Piotr Serafin, one of Donald Tusk's top officials. Together they discussed the text of a communiqué to beef up the withdrawal agreement. The leaders of the member states would be asked to sign off on a document stating that the backstop was 'undesirable' and that if it did come into force, it would only last for a 'short' period. The key sentence for May was that the EU would say they were 'ready to examine whether any further assurance can be provided' in future. The idea discussed by Robbins and Selmayr was that the two sides would return in January to negotiate a 'joint interpretative instrument', a legally binding addition to the Northern Ireland Protocol that would explain how it should be interpreted.

Copies of the communiqué had been circulated among EU ambassadors on the Wednesday, even as May was fighting for her political life at home. When British officials saw a final draft on the Thursday they were satisfied. Over dinner that night, May explained that the legal device she hoped to use was the same as that the EU had deployed to persuade the Belgian region of Wallonia to accept the EU's trade deal with Canada, after it had rejected the agreement in a referendum.

The problem with May's argument was two-fold. First, the EU had gone the extra mile to help two member states. The UK was asking for the same assistance when it was about to become a third country. The prime minister also caused irritation by suggesting in her presentation that 'we are at the beginning of a negotiation' as if the deal, which had taken months to negotiate, was being unpicked just four weeks later. A senior EU official recalled, 'People said, "But Theresa, last time you said this was the best deal possible, now you come back and ask for more."'

The second problem became evident when May left the room. Officials like Selmayr were dedicated to solving problems. EU leaders were politicians to their fingertips; they could smell the stench of decay around May. Many of them read the English papers. They did not believe, even if they did what was asked of them, that it would make the difference. An EU diplomat said, 'Everyone is following UK politics, they just don't believe that she can get [the deal] through.'

The leaders removed the key sentence about 'future reassurance'. As ever, Emmanuel Macron and Leo Varadkar were key voices. But the most telling intervention came from Denmark's leader Lars Løkke Rasmussen, who said May had not even bothered to try to work cross-party to find a solution at home, as the Danish government had after the Maastricht Treaty was rejected in a referendum in 1992. He said, 'When my government had such a situation, before we went back to the other EU member states and bothered them, we spoke to our opposition, even though we also don't have tradition of speaking to them. We are very British in this sense.' Juncker's midnight press conference made things worse. 'We would like ... for our UK friends to set out their expectations because this debate is sometimes nebulous and imprecise and I would like clarifications.' His intervention angered Tusk's aides and confused Robbins, who had been explaining them all week through the Selmayr back channel.

May won some cosmetic reassurances. Tusk issued a statement that the backstop was 'intended as an insurance policy' against a hard border and that the EU would 'work speedily' to conclude a new trade deal 'so that the backstop will not need to be triggered'. If it was, the communiqué read, 'it would apply temporarily'.

In her press conference, May denied that her pledge to MPs to secure 'legal and political assurances' was dead but few were fooled. Tusk admitted, 'We have to exclude any kind of reopening our negotiations on the withdrawal agreement.' Simon Coveney explained Ireland's opposition to a time limit: 'We can't sign up to that approach, because if we do, it's not a backstop at all.'[1] Julian Smith felt the member states missed a real opportunity to put the Brexit story on a different path. 'The EU chose not to be more flexible,' he said. 'Maybe they saw the parliamentary arithmetic [and concluded] if they squeezed down on the Conservative Party they'd eventually get what they wanted. But I think everybody needs to look at how they conducted themselves during this period.'[2]

While May had invested her political future in finding a legal solution with the EU, her senior aides were beginning to wonder if the only way through was to attach a confirmatory second referendum to her deal in order to win Labour votes. On Tuesday 11 December, the day the no-confidence vote was triggered, David Lidington held a confidential meeting with Labour MPs including Stephen Doughty, Chuka Umunna, Chris Bryant, Ben Bradshaw, Chris Leslie and Angela Smith to discuss how a People's Vote would work in practice. May met a similar cast list of MPs around the same time. One said, 'We went through all of the pros and cons.' May responded, 'I just think a second referendum is wrong.'

Doughty spoke for the others: 'Yes, but if you can't get a majority for your deal, it might be the only way through this.'

The prime minister raised her second objection: 'If we have a second referendum, it will be problematic for the Union.'

An MP present recalled, 'We were saying, "No, the biggest damage you're going to do to the Union is carrying on this particular course of action." She was just hyper cautious about everything', her manner a combination of 'indecisiveness and stubbornness'.

The thought of another referendum left Lidington 'queasy'. He struggled to see how it could provide a result decisive enough to stifle the clamour for a third. But it was his job to test the arguments. His officials in the Cabinet Office were already exploring the practicalities. It is unclear if the prime minister ever authorised this work. 'I needed to be in a position, whether I was at the despatch box or advising the PM, if you are drawn into the practicalities of a referendum then this is how long it would take, this is the legislative process,' he recalled.

It was more complicated than some MPs believed. Each referendum required a separate Act of Parliament. The question, the length and spending caps of a campaign were all regulated by the Electoral Commission. Lidington, who was Europe minister under David Cameron, had piloted the 2016 referendum bill through the Commons and knew that had taken thirteen months to pass the legislation.

Even if May changed tack, there would be a row about what question voters would be asked. Downing Street would need to pitch May's deal versus no-deal, while supporters of a People's Vote would insist on the choice of May's deal versus remaining in the EU. Options were explored for a two-question referendum. Lidington's view was that voters would have first had to be asked to choose between leave and remain with a second question asking them, in the event of a leave win, whether they prefer the existing deal or no-deal.

It might merely have been contingency planning, but Lidington nonetheless left the Labour MPs with the impression that he would support a confirmatory public vote if that was the only way to win backing for May's deal. He later admitted this was the case. 'What I did start to think about, particularly when we got to the turn of the year, if we were in deadlock, then is there a way out? It was very clear that more of their party was moving towards a referendum. I had certainly come to the view that I would rather have that than a chaotic crash out.'

He was not alone. On 19 December, Amber Rudd became the first cabinet minister to break cover, telling ITV's Robert Peston there was a 'plausible argument' for 'taking it back to the people again' if Parliament could not reach a majority view on the way forward. Perhaps more significantly Gavin Barwell told a cabinet minister that holding a second referendum might be 'the only way forward'. A colleague said later, 'It was discussed in senior team meetings.'

Personally, Barwell 'hated the idea' and mused with friends that, if there was to be another referendum, he would like to remove himself from the country for the duration. But it was also true that on 'several' occasions the chief of staff said to May, 'Although I don't like it and I wouldn't want it, I have to be honest with you and tell you, you could get a majority for your deal if you conceded a second referendum.'

On each occasion May gave him a withering look. 'You know I don't want that,' she said.

Barwell replied, 'Fine, but I have to keep reminding you that there is a way out of this.'

In the Commons that week the prime minister told MPs, 'Another vote would do irreparable damage to the integrity of our politics, because it would say to millions who trusted in democracy that our democracy does not deliver.' She was particularly incensed that Tony Blair emerged on Thursday 14th to give an interview and make a speech arguing that the EU would be more likely to help her if they knew another referendum was on the way. She called it 'an insult to the office he once held' and insisted, 'I have never lost sight of my duty, and that is to deliver on the referendum result.'

May had another reason, beyond her Brexit mission, for opposing a second EU referendum. If it became established that a first referendum was an emotional, in-principle, vote and there could be a second to work out the constitutional detail, that could be dangerous for the future of the Union, allowing the SNP to stage another independence referendum in Scotland without having to spell out what it would mean in practice. 'That's her real fear,' a close aide said. 'That you're establishing a very dangerous precedent.'

Not everyone believed May's opposition to a referendum was definitive. As 2018 ended, the prime minister consulted her predecessor, David Cameron. He told friends she was a 'servant of the Commons' and would back a second referendum if MPs voted for it.

Those who knew her better felt she would never change her mind. Philip May told an MP that she would never do anything that went against her party and her association members in Maidenhead in particular. 'For her the Conservative Party came first before anything,' the MP said. 'If doing something meant upsetting her association members, she wouldn't do it.' That, in effect, gave veto powers to elderly home counties grassroots members, conservative with both a large and small 'C', but these were the people among whom May was most comfortable for a reason. Barwell said, 'We had MPs queuing up saying to us, "I'll vote for your deal if just put a referendum in." But she does what she thinks is the right thing even though it's politically quite painful and unpleasant.'

Most of the cabinet remained unpersuaded. Jeremy Hunt warned, 'It would be dangerous for the fabric of democracy if Britain didn't leave the EU on March 29.' The debate in cabinet that week was over a different process to ascertain the balance of opinion in the Commons. On a conference call before the no-confidence vote, Damian Hinds, the education secretary, raised the idea of 'indicative votes' to test support for May's deal, no-deal and a referendum. He was supported by Lidington, Rudd, Hammond, Gauke and Clark, as well as Karen Bradley and David Mundell. Labour veteran Frank Field suggested a backbench business debate could be used to hold the votes. On the cabinet call Lidington said there would need to be 'some sort of cathartic moment where people can vote for their perfect Brexit'.

For the time being, every group was clinging to its perfect version of Brexit and showed no sign of compromising – something that was also true of Theresa May. As Christmas approached, she embraced none of these ideas and tried again to win concessions from Brussels.

She began the process on 18 December – six days after the no-confidence vote and four since the European Council had torpedoed her chosen Plan B – by inviting Jacob Rees-Mogg and nine other MPs to peace talks in Downing Street. Those present included backbench shop steward Sir Graham Brady and key figures in the different party factions: Bresisters like Vicky Ford and Guto Bebb, who supported a second referendum; pro-deal pragmatists Nicky Morgan, Oliver Letwin and Simon Hart of the Brexit Delivery Group; plus ERG members Alister Jack and Bernard Jenkin.

Awkwardly genteel exchanges between May and Rees-Mogg, reminiscent of a vicarage discussion of liturgical differences, were the main event. The ERG chairman expressed gratitude for the invite: 'Even the policeman on the door looked surprised', and then joked that the media coverage of the coup had not been positive. 'If you thought your coverage was bad over the past couple of days, imagine what it's been like for me over the past two years,' May said, wearily. She then pulled Rees-Mogg's leg about his European affiliations, pointing out that as a practising Catholic, his allegiance was to Rome. 'Only in matters spiritual, Prime Minister,' he replied.

May said she wanted to put the events of the previous week behind her. 'She appealed to us as long-standing Conservatives to come together and find a way through,' one MP said. Rees-Mogg and Jenkin were notably conciliatory, suggesting that they could still back the deal if May could get greater legal clarity on the backstop. She reiterated that there could be no legal changes to the withdrawal agreement but said she was still fighting for the EU to make its support for the UK's territorial integrity more explicit.[3] The meaningful vote would now take place in the week of 14 January.

After his Number 10 visit, Rees-Mogg attended an ERG meeting and made clear that if the DUP got on board with the government, he would find it difficult to continue to oppose it. Another MP present said, 'This gave me a feeling of deep, deep unease that I found hard to shake. I feared there was going to be a fudge with some legal concession from the EU presented as a great climbdown on their part. I thought, if Jacob backs the deal, it's going to make me look like a complete loon if I still oppose it.'

Serious cracks were also beginning to show in May's inner circle. Julian Smith's relationship with Barwell became fractious and the 'winning the meaningful vote' meetings became dominated by their mutual sniping. A Number 10 aide said, 'Those 7.30 a.m. meetings turned into Gavin and Julian having quite catty arguments with each other around the cabinet table and not much being progressed because of that tension.'

Barwell regarded Smith as one of his closest friends in politics. They had once been in the whips' office together. No one, in his view, worked harder for May. The chief was a hero. But Barwell liked a clear decision-making process and grew increasingly weary of Smith's tendency not to give clear advice about what should be done. A witness said, 'Julian would say, "On the one hand we need to take this path and on the other we need to do this …" Gavin would huff a bit and say, "What's your recommendation?" We wouldn't get a clear answer.' Another Number 10 aide said, 'I never once saw a firm recommendation from the chief on what to do, particularly on Brexit.' The chief of staff and the chief whip were temperamentally poles-apart too. Another member of the political team said, 'Gavin likes to think these things through properly. Julian would be slightly frantic the entire time.' On one occasion they had a blazing row in a corridor in Parliament. 'It was not a pleasant conversation,' an MP witness recalled. 'They were like a couple of stags facing each other.'

Where Smith did have a clear view, it was unwelcome. The chief wanted another Salzburg-style showdown and repeatedly suggested May travel to Brussels and other European capitals during the Christmas holidays to speak to Juncker and other leaders. 'What I need are dinners with Juncker, bottles of wine, trips to all over Europe,' he said. 'When was the last time prime ministers or ministers stayed an extra night in a European capital to just go and have a meal, go and have a beer, go and have some human interaction?' On another occasion he said, 'I would have had the prime minister going to Brussels, sitting in the Hotel Ibis and waiting at the local bar and trying to see who walked past.' To say that this was not May's style is an understatement.

Barwell understood that it was Smith's job to feed in demands from MPs, but he regarded much of what the chief suggested as unrealistic. 'That has literally zero chance of success,' Barwell would say. Most European leaders would be nowhere near Brussels at Christmas, let alone the Hotel Ibis. Smith wanted May to be seen to be doing things 'because it will reassure colleagues' even when they would bear no fruit. Other aides were more protective of May's time and keen for her not to be associated with things that were doomed to fail. The chief whip's view remained that the solution to the Brexit conundrum would not come from technical negotiations but through a diplomatic and political effort. He wanted to see cabinet ministers visit their counterparts. 'If you're told to fuck off by then at least you've seen that they're being difficult,' he argued. The chief became, in the words of one senior figure, 'a stuck record' demanding more effort, lobbying May, writing her letters.

Smith put his money where his mouth was, spending most days on the telephone trying to win over MPs. On Christmas Day and Boxing Day he

made calls to several Labour members in Leave seats who he hoped
would back May's deal. He urged Jon Cruddas and Lindsay Hoyle to get
the trade unions on board. He rang Nigel Dodds on New Year's Eve; he
pounded the phones of Tory rebels. In footballing parlance, Smith
wanted to leave it all on the pitch, to feel he had tried everything to drum
up votes for the deal. In a phrase he used frequently, by pulling the meaningful vote, the government had 'pulled off the park'. But there was little
point in the delay if they did not use the time to improve things.

Robbins returned to Brussels on Wednesday 19 December and was met
with a cold shoulder by EU officials. They had worked to improve the
offer and rather than use it, as they had expected, for a last-minute vote
before Christmas, May had banked the communiqué and demanded
more. 'When Olly went over, the reaction was pretty cold. People were
saying, "Frankly, you're lucky we're even taking your calls",' a British
negotiator recalled. A senior EU official confirmed, 'The five points given
in December were given on the assumption that Mrs May said, "I need
them now." Then she didn't bring it to the house before Christmas
because she knew she would lose again. And that pissed off quite a
number of people.'
    Disillusionment with the British government had become widespread.
Donald Tusk, always the most emotional anti-Brexiteer in Brussels, was
now a fully-fledged advocate of a second referendum. 'Tusk had given up
on Mrs May,' an EU official said. Robbins found the door of Piotr Serafin,
Tusk's gatekeeper, closed to him. 'Piotr didn't receive him,' the official
said. A senior figure in the Council explained: 'It was increasingly clear
to us that Theresa May was damaged goods. Nobody really believed that
she could deliver. The Commission kept coming up with new ideas,
adding a little bit here and adding a little bit there; they were more keen
on finding new victories for Theresa May. We, frankly, didn't believe that
it would work, and there were limits to how much we should prostitute
ourselves. We did engage in the end, but we didn't do it with much
conviction.'
    May attempted some Christmas diplomacy but made a diplomatic
faux pas by calling Juncker on 24 December. Britain marks Christmas on
the 25th but in most of Europe the big day is Christmas Eve. Martin
Selmayr was literally sitting under his Christmas tree, celebrating with
his family, when the phone went. It was Juncker. 'I have to take this,' he

said. 'It's the president.' Selmayr's wife, wearily familiar with such intrusions, replied, 'I am sure it is Brexit.'

Juncker told Selmayr about May's call. 'You have to meet Olly in the next five days.'

'Are you serious? Okay, I'll do it.'

Selmayr and Robbins met between Christmas and New Year. 'Before she calls the vote, she needs something else,' Robbins said. He asked for help. 'I think I am persona non grata, even in Berlin. I can't even speak to Paris.' Selmayr could not move the capitals, but he could get Juncker to help. The simplest thing to do was to have the Commission president write a letter. Selmayr also offered to help involve the Council. Jeppe Tranholm-Mikkelsen, its director general, was a pragmatist who wanted to get the deal done. Eventually Tranholm-Mikkelsen persuaded Tusk to get involved. Juncker and Tusk would jointly sign a letter to May.

Robbins thought it might garner a few votes, and there was virtue in being seen to keep trying, but he knew it was not enough. 'Martin, I'll tell you honestly,' he said. 'We are making this effort, you are sacrificing your Christmas and it will still not work. It may bring us a bit closer, but there will need to be another step.' EU officials say Robbins had first warned that the meaningful vote would be lost in October, when the negotiations over the withdrawal agreement were in their final stages. 'I am not sure the prime minister knows that,' he said. 'She has to believe it will work, but I think we have to factor in the likelihood that this will fail.'

Since that time, he had opened a dialogue with Selmayr about how they might build on the original deal. The German was highly sceptical that the treaty could be reopened. Fortunately, EU history was scattered with addendums, declarations and interpretive documents, most famously to secure Dutch accession to the Maastricht Treaty by guaranteeing that Dutch citizens would not have to join a European army.

They also began quietly preparing for the likely areas of negotiation in a trade deal, so the talks could begin straight after the withdrawal agreement was ratified. 'We started doing the scoping, setting up our teams,' a senior EU source said.

Robbins and Selmayr met again on 2 January and mapped out possible future gambits. They envisaged a return to the idea of a joint interpretative instrument, the device rejected by the EU leaders two weeks earlier. Robbins suggested that they also began discussing how an extension to the transition period could be orchestrated, since the deadline at the end of March was approaching fast. Had that become public it would have set off a political firestorm for May with the Eurosceptics. A senior EU official said, 'Mrs May is a politician, and every politician has to believe in the next step otherwise you are not credible. Therefore, you don't want to listen to what happens after that. Your advisers have to prepare for the next step, because you cannot.' Selmayr and Tranholm-Mikkelsen met on 5 January so the German could get the Council to prepare. 'We knew there would have to be an extension,' a senior EU source confirmed.

The Juncker-Tusk letter was published on 14 January, the day before the meaningful vote. It was not legally binding but it had more force in European law than was widely understood in London. 'European Council conclusions have a legal value in the Union,' the letter stated. 'The commission can confirm that, just like the United Kingdom, the European Union does not wish to see the backstop enter into force,' they wrote. 'Were it to do so, it would represent a suboptimal trading arrangement for both sides.' This, to a degree, answered the charge of the ERG that the withdrawal agreement was totally one-sided. Juncker smuggled in the language which was ditched from the December communiqué by the leaders. If Britain did enter the backstop, 'the commission is committed to providing the necessary political impetus and resources to help achieve the objective of making this period as short as possible'. He offered a 'high level conference' to monitor progress 'at least every six months'.

Juncker and Tusk also wrote that once there was a trade deal, 'Should national ratifications be pending … the Commission is ready to propose provisional application of relevant parts of the future relationship.' That meant the deal would come into force before all twenty-seven member states had approved it, an attempt to answer the charge of some Brexiteers that countries ill-disposed to Britain could delay things for years if it suited them to trap the UK in the backstop.

In devising the trade deal, 'the Commission is determined to give priority … to the discussion of proposals that might replace the backstop with alternative arrangements'. This went some way to allaying the concerns of Brexiteers that a customs union was the only basis for a final agreement, though its tepid wording meant it was unlikely to satisfy those who saw technology as the centrepiece of any deal.

Brexiteers were quick to pick holes in the letter. Martin Howe, a QC who had been quietly advising the ERG, wrote in the *Telegraph* that nothing in the letter would cause a change in the attorney general's legal advice. He concluded May was 'only seeking to change the perception of [the deal] without changing the substance'. Since presentation is the essence of good politics, the letter had merit, not least because it showed that the EU, within its own red lines, was trying to be accommodating. But for those who had a principled legal-constitutional view about sovereignty, as many Leave voters did, it was never going to be enough.

Theresa May had the best version of the deal that Brussels was prepared to give her. Now it would have to be tested in Parliament in the long-awaited meaningful vote. Yet in the five weeks that had elapsed since the prime minister pulled the vote, political focus had shifted in a dramatic way from an agreement to the consequences of no-deal. That in turn was to have profound implications for the battle in Parliament.

18

YELLOWHAMMERED

A Brief History of No-Deal

January to December 2018

On 18 December the cabinet met and agreed that preparing for a no-deal Brexit would be the 'principal operational focus' of the government, with other domestic priorities ditched. The week before, Theresa May's fellow EU leaders had rejected her hopes of a legally binding add-on to the withdrawal agreement. The prime minister had now to seriously contemplate the possibility that she would not be able to win parliamentary approval. The cabinet had effectively pulled the emergency cord.

Twenty-three months had gone by since May proclaimed that 'no deal is better than a bad deal'. In nearly two years this was the first time that preparing for no-deal had been the government's top priority. When the decision was signed off, there were just 101 days until the UK was due to leave the European Union. A cabinet Brexiteer said, 'If you talk the talk you've got to walk the walk and we should have been demonstrably showing we were ready for no-deal.'

Nothing in the Brexit process provided a Rorschach test of where you stood more quickly than a politician's or voter's attitude to no-deal. To some (but actually very few) hardcore Brexiteers, it was the best outcome, a clean break to go it alone. To most parliamentary Brexiteers preparations for no-deal were doubly virtuous: a vital device for leverage in the negotiations, to convince the EU that Britain was ready to walk away from the talks if the terms were unacceptable, but also a possible outcome that it was responsible for a government to prepare for. However, for other ministers – soft Brexiteers and many of those who voted Remain – no-deal prep was a costly distraction or, worse, a self-fulfilling prophecy which would condemn Britain to economic ruin. The cabinet reflected these divisions, with a running battle between ministers who wanted to prepare and those who believed every penny spent on no-deal was a waste of money and that the more that work revealed the risks, the more implausible it was that it should ever be allowed.

Even the decision to make no-deal prep the 'principal operational focus' of the government was a compromise hammered out by David Lidington between those who wanted no-deal planning to be the 'central planning assumption' of the government and Remainers who only wanted contingency planning as a last resort. It was agreed in the cabinet meeting that ministers on the frontline would gather on 2 January, under the chairmanship of Steve Barclay, the Brexit secretary, to 'turbocharge' the preparations.

May appeared to side with those taking a tougher line at cabinet. It was usually her style to call ministers from different camps alternately. On this occasion, 'she called the people who were more in favour of the managed no-deal first, the likes of Andrea [Leadsom], Penny [Mordaunt], Chris Grayling, Steve Barclay,' a source said. 'It was quite a long time before you had Amber Rudd and David Gauke.' But May did not sanction daily no-deal meetings of the Cobra emergency committee, something demanded by Sajid Javid and Liz Truss. 'They were arguing that if you don't have the daily drumbeat of Cobra, then Whitehall sits on its backside not doing anything,' one of those present said.

Until this point, officials can be forgiven for not prioritising no-deal planning – they hardly had a strong lead from ministers. This was only the second cabinet meeting that was dominated by the subject. The first had been on 13 September, just before the disastrous Salzburg summit, when ministers argued for three and a half hours. The 'must prepare' faction was backed, perhaps counter-intuitively, by senior civil servants Mark Sedwill and Helen MacNamara. Sedwill told a meeting of permanent secretaries, 'You do have to be ready for this.' A senior colleague recalled Sedwill's concern that his fellow mandarins blithely assumed no-deal would never happen: 'He had to ram the machine really, really hard.'

The cabinet secretary and his de facto deputy, MacNamara, also pressed May to acknowledge that the real choice was between a customs union and no-deal – and that persuading people to accept the former would require them to face the reality of the latter. A senior civil servant said, 'Mark and Helen's approach was: "Would you like to go with option A or option B. Make a choice." She needed to choose and she needed to make other people choose. "If the other choice is no-deal, could we have a plan for that please?"'

By the autumn of 2018, May's team had spent a year actively suppressing discussion of work the government had done to prepare for no-deal. As a minister for Brexit between June 2017 and July 2018, Steve Baker demanded a 'no deal moment', to publicise the planning. In doing so, he discovered just how junior a junior minister can be. From October 2017, he found it 'a matter of acute frustration' that the media believed that the work was not being done. 'I was not only trying to get it done but I wanted us to start getting information out there to equip businesses.' Baker wanted to publish a plan containing 'milestones' spelling out what needed to happen and when in each department: what contracts needed to be agreed, who needed to be hired. 'It requires the prime minister and the cabinet to press the button to say implement no-deal plans,' he said. 'You can't do it as a junior minister. Number 10 kept pushing it back.' At this point, May was pressing Brussels to agree to the implementation period to reassure businesses. Stressing no-deal prep would have cut across that narrative.

Davis, but more usually Baker, chaired an inter-ministerial group (IMG) on Brexit preparations, both for a deal and no-deal scenarios. A DExEU adviser said, 'The IMG actually took more decisions on no-deal than the cabinet. I constantly sat there reading the papers thinking, "It's amazing this doesn't routinely leak every week in the way that the cabinet does."' But even when good work was going on, such as in Defra, where a functioning IT system had been set up to handle animal and plant health imports, no press releases were written. It was not until Chequers, in July 2018, that the decision was taken to talk about domestic preparedness.

The sclerotic pace with which the cabinet decided Britain's Brexit policy also hampered no-deal preparation. Without a decision on what rights would be granted to EU citizens in the UK, or how customs arrangements would work, it was difficult to get systems in place. 'The fundamental policy choices have to be made before you start delivering,' said Baker. Second, ministers found themselves unable to approach third parties to work with them until the basic decisions had been taken. To Brexiteers like Baker, May was rejecting a key lever in the negotiations.

'We should have been showing the EU that we were willing to go, come what may, but they did not want to do it.'

Baker also proposed that Britain gather evidence of the likely effect of no-deal on individual EU countries, in the hope that they lobbied the Commission to agree a better deal for Britain. Ireland, in particular, would have been a big loser if Britain slashed food tariffs for Argentinian or New Zealand meat products. This information was never deployed. Baker said, 'The fundamental problem was that the negotiators wanted to seem friendly and accommodating in the hope that the EU would be nice to us.'

Early in 2018, Davis began agitating to talk to business. On 30 January, he wrote to May, demanding more 'effort and investment across government'. Three months later, not much had happened. On 28 March, he condemned the 'delays and risk aversion' in Whitehall. 'The current position allows us neither to build business confidence in the implementation period or allow us to keep contingency plans genuinely viable,' he warned. He called for 'an order of magnitude change in the current Whitehall approach to "no deal" preparations and a very significant communications campaign … Without such preparations the EU will know we don't have any ability to walk away from a bad deal.'

By the end of March, Baker was 'tearing his hair out' and ready to resign over May's refusal to either prepare properly or to talk about no-deal publicly. In a blog post on 23 May, Dominic Cummings wrote about the failure of the civil service system to prepare: 'This process should have started BEFORE triggering A50 but the government has irretrievably botched this.' He said some ministers, including Philip Hammond, 'understand this and are happy' but accused others of remaining in blissful ignorance where they 'prefer not to think about it'. He wrote, 'It will be trashed in the history books as the pre-1914 cabinet has been for its failure to discuss what its military alliance with France actually meant until after it was too late', concluding, pithily, 'The state has made no preparations to leave and plans to make no preparations to leave even after leaving.'

Brexiteers were fond of saying Britain would prosper when freed from the shackles of EU regulation but were less adept at identifying these opportunities. When he was Brexit secretary Davis set up 'Project After' to work out what Britain might do differently once the obligation to follow EU rules was lifted. The project 'fizzled out', because it became clear that the biggest potential gains were 'political hot potatoes'. A DExEU official said, 'The problem with it was the commitments we had given as a government to not allow any standards – environment, consumer, health and safety – to drop. Once you rule this stuff out, you don't have that much to play with. Europe's most costly regulations are always the environment and social employment. Anything you did in that area would have blown things up, so it was put out of bounds.' This left the relatively trivial. An EU adviser said, 'You end up in a long conversation, as I did with Steve Baker, about why his motorbike isn't allowed to be as noisy as he wants it to be because of some German widget, or you are talking about why your hair dryer doesn't blow hard enough or your Hoover doesn't suck hard enough', both areas where Brussels imposed restrictions.

After the Chequers summit in July, the Brexiteers insisted on doing more to publicly prepare for no-deal, one of their prizes for signing up to the common rulebook and May's customs plans. Dominic Raab, the new Brexit secretary, used the summer to release a series of 'technical notices' on the risks in each sector and how the government was planning to mitigate them. The first batch came on 23 August, alongside a speech from Raab, the majority on 12 September and the rest at the end of that month. In a letter to May on 6 August, Raab called for a cabinet discussion covering 'risks', 'readiness', 'mitigations', the 'countervailing opportunities' in taxes, trade and immigration. He also outlined plans for a 'proposed public narrative', which would seek to emphasise areas where 'risks cannot be removed or mitigated because of action or obstruction by the EU'. In short: blame Brussels.

The technical notices contained much eye-opening detail, not least that the NHS had stockpiling capacity for just six weeks. Some of May's aides regarded the technical notes as displacement activity for Brexiteers, rather than a serious exercise. 'It became the thing to talk about because they did not want to talk about Chequers,' one of the PM's Europe advisers said. Another member of May's political team was even more withering: 'No-deal stuff from the Brexiteers was performative. It was a way of burnishing your Brexiteer credentials without actually meaning anything.' Nevertheless, DExEU's permanent secretary Philip Rycroft was proud of his team for this and the papers which went to cabinet. 'Dominic Raab … was not a believer in the risks of no-deal,' he said, but his officials produced 'an honest account of the impact of no deal ... It was pretty unadorned advice.'[1]

To most of May's team, no-deal was not an end state, it was a holding operation. The way you mitigated no-deal in crucial industries like aviation was to strike mini deals. In their eyes, once you had a handful of those it got to the point where you might as well just have a full deal to start with. Downing Street aides thought Brexiteers who believed they could leave with no-deal and then negotiate a trade deal were seriously misguided. 'The ultimate problem is that you would be back in the same place with the EU,' one of May's Europe advisers said. 'They will insist on the backstop again. You would not get the implementation period because they would say that we can't do that outside of Article 50. They will say, "We will have the financial settlement and the backstop. Then we can have the free trade agreement." That is how they would play it.' In essence, Downing Street believed the price the EU would want Britain to pay would be the same as just doing a deal up front.

Raab got the no-deal cabinet meeting he wanted on 13 September. Ministers sat through a briefing by Mark Carney, the governor of the Bank of England, on the worst-case scenario for the economy. Among the lowlights: GDP falling, employment down, inflation of 6 per cent and a 35 per cent crash in house prices. May asked icily: 'Is this what you think will happen or what might happen?' Carney, all tan and smiles, said he was 'always careful' not to make predictions. May did not look impressed. She knew the Brexiteers would see this as another example of 'Project Fear'. The prime minister said, 'I used to work for the Bank of England and I don't totally believe all these figures.' Her irritation was shared by a Brexiteer minister present: 'It wasn't in fact what could happen, it was, "If there were a collision of this, this, this and this, then this would be your worst outcome", but that did not need to be the case had you done preparations in advance.'

Just as May sought to reconcile hard and soft approaches to trade, customs and goods regulations, so too had she to walk a fine line on no-deal, never letting it come to the boil. 'They would never take a policy decision to go for no-deal because if you had done that then the cabinet would have exploded,' an adviser said. 'Some would have walked.'

In the September cabinet, Philip Hammond, the chancellor, suggested there would need to be a fiscal stimulus in the event of no-deal. But he was overshadowed by Sajid Javid, the home secretary, who called for tax

cuts, the deregulation of workers' rights, the scrapping of auto-enrol-
ment into pension schemes and some environmental regulations. Not to
be outdone, Andrea Leadsom proposed Second World War-style 'Brexit
bonds', while Chris Grayling suggested a 'Brexit bonus'. A source said,
'He wants to give everyone in Britain £200. There was a lot of eye-rolling
at that.' More than two years after the referendum the political thinking
about no-deal had barely progressed beyond an 'imagineering' session
from one of Stewart Pearson's 'thought camps' in the television satire,
The Thick of It.

Most of what leaked were horror stories in key sectors. On 3 June, the
Sunday Times splashed with details of how officials were planning to
cope with shortages of food, fuel and medicines, in the event of no-deal.
Davis's team were furious. Tim Smith, his media spad, had to respond
while on a stag do at Headingley. Afterwards, Stewart Jackson texted the
journalist to say, 'I won't help you again as long as I have a hole in my
arse.' The journalist encouraged Jackson to seek medical attention.

MPs were shocked when the story was not denied but these were
indeed scenarios being looked at by civil servants in the Cabinet Office.
The story was only scratching the surface. The contingency plans had
been drawn up as part of a process called Operation Yellowhammer, led
by national security planners on the Civil Contingencies Secretariat. A
full version of Yellowhammer would be published in the *Sunday Times*
in August 2019, but most of the work was done under the May government.

The full document added fears of a three-month meltdown at Britain's
ports, with up to 85 per cent of lorries 'not ready' for French customs and
delays of two and a half days that could 'affect fuel distribution' in
London and the south-east of England, and traffic only returning to 50 to
70 per cent of normal levels after that. The papers predicted a hard
border with Ireland, sparking protests, road blockages and 'direct action',
code for terrorist attacks on border checkpoints. Medical supplies would
'be vulnerable to severe extended delay' as three out of four drugs came
in through the Channel ports. In the worst-case scenario Yellowhammer
warned that people could face a 'restricted diet'. A senior civil servant
said, 'Once you've done the planning, you think: "Holy fuck!"'

Officials felt it their duty to highlight every possible risk 'so that it can
never be said that ministers weren't fully informed', one minister
recalled. A senior civil servant compared the active pursuit of no-deal to

'pulling the pin out of a hand grenade and then holding it next to your own head'. This irritated Brexiteers who felt some concerns were exaggerated. A cabinet minister said, 'The assumptions that would be put up to you by Whitehall civil servants were astonishingly pessimistic. They weren't just reasonable worst-case scenarios, they were kamikaze worst-case scenarios.' It was the dangers, not the plan to deal with them, which tended to leak. In some cases the remedy was just as eye-catching as the problem. When the government started buying up most of the spare fridge capacity in the country to stockpile medicines, Matt Hancock, the health secretary, was dubbed 'the fridge magnate'.[2]

Despite some carping, Brexiteers had nothing but praise for the civil servant in charge of no-deal planning in DExEU, Tom Shinner, who enjoyed a reputation for hard and effective work. Where Robbins divided opinion, Shinner was regarded, by Remainers and Leavers alike, as the supreme public servant of the Brexit process.

To some cabinet ministers, the meetings on no-deal were among the most distressingly surreal they ever attended. After her return to cabinet, Amber Rudd was particularly vocal. She complained the government was 'normalising extraordinary expense and extraordinary behaviour', pointing out that £1.5 billion, the cost of no-deal to that point, was the same as the cost of ending the freeze on the uprating of benefits. Brexit, she argued, should not get 'a blank cheque'.

It was not just the Remainers, though. As environment secretary Michael Gove was running one of the departments most acutely exposed to no-deal, since it would be farmers who were most vulnerable to tariffs imposed by the EU, or to cheap food imports from countries like the US, Australia and New Zealand. In a reference to *The Matrix*, Gove told colleagues he had 'taken the no-deal pill' and seen a dystopian future.[3] Another colleague said, 'Michael was literally lying awake at night worrying about no-deal.'

When Gove decided to support May's deal that November, one of the decisive factors was a Yellowhammer briefing he had received suggesting the UK could run out of clean drinking water within days because the chemicals used in water purification were imported from the continent and were too volatile to stockpile. Yellowhammer warned that if water plants ran out of chemicals, they 'would probably need to stop the water supply to all their customers – potentially millions of people' who would 'immediately face a shortage of drinking water and inability to flush toilets, cook, wash clothes or keep themselves clean'. A leading Remainer, with close links to officials working on no-deal, reflected, 'A couple of years ago, what was the big hoo-ha? Who eats a bacon sandwich the wrong way. Now it's "We might have no water". It's a different world.'

To some Brexiteers this was proof that Remainers preferred to fetish-ise the worst case rather than minimise the risks. Penny Mordaunt thought it fundamentally dishonest for them to say, as Hammond and others did, that 'no one voted for no-deal'. Leave voters voted for Brexit, she argued. 'People understand why you're trying to avoid no-deal,' she told cabinet. 'But you can't go out and say that people didn't vote for no-deal, because the bulk of Leave voters will say, Actually, I think you'll find, though, although it's not our preferred option, we did.'" Other Brexiteers were provocatively blasé. A cabinet minister recalled a conver-sation with Liz Truss. 'I said to her, "Are you concerned for the economy, for no-deal?" "No," she said, "bring it on."' Jeremy Hunt, one of the cabi-net's Brexit swing voters, was less blunt but no less determined. 'His view was that no-deal is suboptimal, and it would be really bumpy,' a source close to Hunt said. 'But if that is literally the only way of doing it, we do have to just get on with it. He genuinely felt quite upset at the way some people in the cabinet were undermining the negotiating position by making a song and dance about how we couldn't leave with no-deal and it was going to be catastrophic.'

At the end of October, Raab and Lidington had 'a proper row' in a ministerial committee on plans for no-deal. The Borders Delivery Group, which Lidington oversaw, had drawn up papers on likely delays at the Channel ports and the consequent reduction in trade, warning that HGV checks on the French side would take ten minutes per lorry. Raab erupted, pointing out that the French themselves had said they would only take an average of two minutes each. 'It's disgraceful and cannot be backed up,' he said. Lidington replied, tepidly, 'We will be clear about what the worst-case scenario covers and doesn't cover.' After he resigned, Raab pointed out that there were two inspection cabins for heavy goods vehicles at Calais. Even extending the inspection time from two to ten minutes, 'the difference between having zero impact at the border and very substantial disruption is eight extra cabins at Calais to deal with the heavy goods'.

* * *

Theresa May boards an early morning flight to Brussels in December 2017 to sign the Joint Report. The deal created the Northern Ireland backstop, a political agony she was never able to escape. Behind her is Richard 'Tricky' Jackson, her director of operations.

May with Jean-Claude Juncker in 2016. The Commission president was depicted by the media as a drunken federalist fanatic, but behind the scenes he did much to help May.

The crunch lunch with May and Juncker's top teams, which was disrupted by the DUP pulling the plug. David Davis and Michel Barnier got all the attention, but the key alliance was Oliver Robbins and Martin Selmayr.

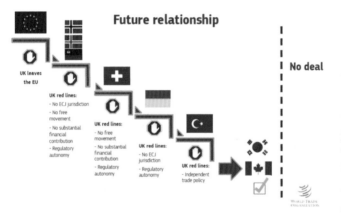

Future relationship

UK leaves
the EU

UK red lines:
- No ECJ jurisdiction
- No free movement
- No substantial financial contribution
- Regulatory autonomy

UK red lines:
- No free movement
- No substantial financial contribution
- Regulatory autonomy

UK red lines:
- No ECJ jurisdiction
- Regulatory autonomy

UK red lines:
- Independent trade policy

No deal

WORLD TRADE ORGANISATION

Barnier's notorious 'staircase' graphic explaining why May's red lines took her towards a simple trade deal like Canada or South Korea.

It was not until the first Chequers meeting in February 2018 (*above right*) that the cabinet even decided what it wanted. At the second Chequers meeting in July 2018 (*right*) May pushed through a compromise proposal that led to the resignations of Davis and Boris Johnson.

(*Top*) Martin Selmayr: the power behind Juncker who met Robbins in secret to move negotiations along.

(*Left*) Attorney general Geoffrey Cox added an eloquent baritone to the Brexiteer band, but his legal advice in March 2019 sank May.

(*Bottom*) John Bercow, the Commons speaker, saw himself as a cheerleader for Parliament, but he changed the rules to help the Bresistance.

The Task Force 50 negotiating team. Barnier was the front man but the heavy lifting was done by Sabine Weyand (*left*) and Stéphanie Riso (*right*).

May confronts Juncker after he called her position 'nebulous'.

Gavin Barwell, May's chief of staff (*above*), brought calm but not victory to Number 10. Oliver Letwin (*above right*) and Dominic Grieve (*right*) were the twin tacticians of the Bresistance in Parliament.

Jacob Rees-Mogg and Steve Baker (*below*) made the ERG an effective fighting force, but when they moved against May they didn't have the numbers.

May dancing onstage to ABBA's 'Dancing Queen' at the Conservative Party annual conference in Birmingham.

Boris Johnson celebrating victory in the leadership election a year after his resignation as foreign secretary.

Lidington was very far from public enemy number one for the Brexiteers. Throughout 2018, they blamed the Treasury in general, and the chancellor specifically, for no-deal preparations having such low priority. 'Philip Hammond particularly did not want to do any preparations,' said one cabinet Brexiteer. A permanent secretary added, 'There's no doubt that Philip Hammond did slow stuff down and was not prepared to give clear instructions, for example, to say to HMRC, "Assume we're going to have a border, even if it's not an outcome that we want."' The chancellor stopped DExEU sending out letters to tens of thousands of small businesses telling them to prepare for a no-deal Brexit. Hammond explained, 'We didn't want to send business a message that we're going to crash out of the EU and see businesses relocating, taking jobs out of the United Kingdom.'[4] This approach was contested by Davis, Raab, McVey and Leadsom, with Fox and Gove as swing voters who could see the potential pitfalls. May sided with Hammond. Davis complained, 'She should have appointed a Brexiteer foreign secretary, which she did, and a Brexiteer chancellor, which she didn't. The whole process would have been a hell of a lot simpler.'[5]

Hammond regarded one of his signal achievements around Brexit as 'stopping business voting with its feet' and writing off UK plc. He felt the prospect of no-deal had to be downplayed to keep Japanese motor manufacturers in Britain. David Gauke said, 'If you are a multinational business, no-deal prep means moving things out of this country. No wonder that Philip and Greg [Clark] weren't saying, "For God's sake, why haven't you closed this car plant? You need to prepare!" In financial services, it's moving assets and teams out of the country.' In the SN committee on negotiations and EU-XTP, the cabinet sub-committee on preparations, Hammond repeatedly argued that highly public no-deal prep would cause economic damage. He recalled, 'We did not want HSBC to move more people to Paris, for example. But if we sent them a message saying you need to prepare for no-deal, as the most likely outcome, that's exactly what they would have done. It wasn't the prime minister, it wasn't me; the committee took decisions repeatedly, to defer the point where we would make no-deal the central scenario.'

To Hammond, it was also a simple truth that the British government did not control its own destiny in the event of no-deal: 'Many of the levers were in the hands of private businesses and many of them were in the hands of the EU27. We could prepare to ensure that goods flowed freely into the UK through Dover. We had no way of ensuring that goods flow freely out through Calais, because that was entirely in the hands of the French. They can dial that up and dial that down – for commercial reasons, for national reasons, for political reasons – and we had no control over it. Just as the Spanish for years have dialled up or dialled down the length of the queues at the border going into Gibraltar.'

For Davis, the Treasury's foot-dragging undermined May's negotiating position. 'In any negotiation you've got to be able to walk away. I've got to be able to say to you, "If this doesn't work, we'll leave anyway" and you've got to believe it. And for you to believe, I've got to believe it.'[6] Hammond's refusenik stance came under sustained attack from Steve Barclay, when he took over as Brexit secretary in November 2018. His view was that government needed to start using its bully pulpit to persuade businesses to spend their own money on extra warehouse capacity. A month later no-deal became a central priority of the government.

Because he was regarded, not without reason, as gaffe-prone and inept at the art of public-facing politics, Hammond's effectiveness as a Whitehall turf warrior was underestimated by his colleagues. One of May's EU advisers noted, 'He seemed to go out of his way to irritate people that he disagreed with, including, on a number of occasions, the prime minister,' but added, 'He was probably the best briefed of all the ministers.' Robbins told colleagues Hammond was 'crafty' at getting what he wanted but also despaired that sensible points he made were undermined by him 'overdoing' the Eeyore act. The cantankerous relationship between May and Hammond meant the chancellor's influence ebbed and flowed. 'He was quite near last in the list of people that she would pick up the phone to consult,' a senior civil servant said. In meetings, Hammond was so patronising 'he just didn't know when he was winning'. The mandarin said, 'It is not enough for him to win, he has to be right. As a result, one in three times, he has thrown it away.' Some thought Hammond principled about avoiding no-deal, others that his primary motivation was truculence. A Number 10 Europe adviser said, 'He is the type of person that, if you give him a mile, he will still take the extra inch just because he has to.'

The Treasury's stubbornness on no-deal was not just a consequence of Hammond's personality, but also of its institutional desire to stop ministers from spending. As Dominic Cummings put it, 'The Treasury argues, with a logic that is both contemptible and reasonable in the comical circumstances, that given the actual outcome of the negotiations will be abject surrender, it is pointless wasting more money to prepare for a policy that has no future and therefore even the Potemkin preparations now underway should be abandoned.'

Hammond's defence against the accusation of needless foot-dragging was that he supplied a budget of £4.2 billion for no-deal prep and departments did not spend their allocation. 'They were telling the media that the reason we were not prepared was because "that mean old bastard Hammond won't give us any more money". We allocated billions of pounds and they weren't spending it.' Some ministers were not prepared to make cuts in other programmes to fund no-deal prep. 'There weren't enough skilled security-cleared civil servants to do the jobs that needed doing,' Hammond added. Eventually the Cabinet Office moved officials from international development and education, which had very little Brexit business, to those like Defra and transport that did.

Hammond had an ally in Greg Clark, the business secretary, perhaps the most militantly anti-Brexit cabinet minister. Clark had a reputation in Whitehall as a man who struggled to make decisions but he seemed to take even longer over those which involved preparing for Brexit, or no-deal in particular. That autumn, his department needed to get eight different computer systems off the ground to deal with various aspects of Brexit. 'He wouldn't give the order,' a cabinet source said. A readiness review of BEIS, the business department, in May 2018 gave red traffic light ratings to the department in every single area.

May's refusal to dramatise no-deal preparations and the Whitehall war about no-deal spending confirmed the view in Brussels that she had zero intention of leaving the European Union with no-deal. 'We did not suspect that Britain wasn't ready,' a senior EU official said. 'We knew Britain wasn't ready.' In the spring of 2019, Martin Selmayr said, 'We have seen what has been prepared on our side of the border for a hard Brexit. We don't see the same level of preparation on the other side of the border.'[7] Asked whether he thought British negotiators would ever choose no-deal, Michel Barnier said, 'No', he 'never' heard May privately issue such a threat. 'We've never been impressed by such a threat.'[8]

Some ministers thought this a misreading of where things might end up. Liam Fox said in the autumn of 2018 that it was 'fifty-fifty at best'.

Another cabinet minister said, 'I don't think they ever really thought we were serious about walking away and actually it became an increasingly likely outcome.' Views on this were mixed in Brussels. One of Selmayr's Commission colleagues admitted he was privately less confident: 'He may say that on TV, but he sent his deputy secretary general to twenty-seven countries with a team of people to make sure everybody was ready for no-deal. The poor colleague who hadn't seen her kids for two months, I think, would certainly disagree.' Nonetheless, the EU prepared for no-deal, in part, because they feared an 'accidental no deal'. 'We prepared for it so that it doesn't happen,' Selmayr said.

Brussels was not above using no-deal to play hardball in the talks. In Raab's discussions with Barnier on 6 September, two months before the withdrawal agreement was signed, the Frenchman said that in a no-deal scenario, Britain should not expect any side deals, even on aviation.[9] When the Commission published its no-deal plans on 19 December, a month after the deal, they included provisions to keep aeroplanes flying between the UK and the EU for a year.

The Irish government published their own no-deal plans on the same day. The 131-page document warned of a severe impact on Irish ports, shipping, travel and security. The Commission was clear there would have to be customs checks between the Republic and Northern Ireland but Simon Coveney admitted, 'We don't have a contingency plan to avoid border infrastructure in this document.' In short, Ireland was prepared for no-deal, except on the one issue that was fundamental. For Brexiteers, this offered hope, since it suggested that in the event of no-deal, the pressure would shift to a stand-off between the EU and Ireland. At some point, Varadkar might want to help secure a deal.

Whether or not Brussels and the EU27 believed May would ever go for no-deal, the 18 December cabinet meeting gave the green light to preparations which made the prospect seem simultaneously real, frightening and ridiculous. Ministers signed off plans to conduct exercises at the border to see if ports and airports could cope. This included deliberately creating a huge lorry tailback in Kent, with HGVs encouraged to gather at Manston airport, one of the overspill sites for waiting freight, before clogging the roads to Dover. Tom Peck, the waspish sketchwriter of the *Independent*, branded it a 'demented pantomime' and a piece of 'national performance art', his rage compounded by getting stuck in a real traffic jam as he made his way to watch the fake traffic jam.[10]

Some of May's aides were happy to highlight the risks to persuade MPs to support her withdrawal agreement. A major figure in the aviation industry approached Number 10 and pointed out that airports were prepared for no-deal. The businessman said, 'We could say all this publicly to put the public's minds at rest.' May's aide replied, 'No, thank you, we need no-deal to look as bad as possible.' Chris Grayling observed, 'The whole machine around the Cabinet Office and Number 10 was geared towards frightening MPs into backing the deal. It was convenient to them if no-deal plans looked like they were not in the best of shape because it was designed to try and encourage MPs to vote for the deal.'[11]

By then, the ultimate Whitehall no-deal row was building to a head, one which came to symbolise how Brexit had apparently descended down an absurdist sinkhole. This was Grayling's decision to offer £14 million to a ferry company which owned no ferries.

The root cause of the problem was that the supply of food and medicines was overly dependent on a few key 'pinch points', notably the Calais-Dover link, through which 2.5 million heavy goods vehicles passed each year. In October, Dominic Raab threw his weight behind efforts by Grayling to get money from Hammond to diversify trade routes, spreading the risk to Folkestone, Harwich, Hull and other ports of entry, expanding links to Rotterdam, Zeebrugge and Ostend. That meant installing computer systems to process freight, setting aside warehouse and car parking space and installing the heavy equipment to operate roll-on-roll-off ferries for goods transported by lorry. He and Grayling ran into resistance from the Treasury and from the Borders Delivery Group.

On 8 November, Raab gave a presentation at a trade conference explaining that the risks could be mitigated to prevent the food shortages predicted by Operation Yellowhammer. Only 10 per cent of food came in through Dover. Unfortunately for the Brexit secretary, no one remembered that because he also admitted, 'I hadn't quite understood the full extent of this, but if you look at the UK and if you look at how we trade in goods, we are particularly reliant on the Dover-Calais crossing.' The minister in charge of Brexit discovering that Britain was an island became a leitmotif of Leavers who didn't understand the reality of what they campaigned for – though in context Raab's words had not caused mirth in the room.

Transport links would be key to weathering no-deal. Several ministers said privately they had done 'all we can' in their departments to ameliorate the worst effects of no-deal, but they were reliant on imports. 'We are ready,' one said. 'Everything will be fine as long as Chris Grayling's transport system works … Fuck!'

From Grayling's point of view, he was one of the few ministers working flat out on no-deal. 'Of course, the brown stuff landed on my head rather than elsewhere because I was the person doing it.' To him, being able to walk away from talks was 'negotiation 101', a position he tried in vain to persuade May to adopt. Remembering that Hammond had been the second cabinet minister, after Gove, to suggest publicly that he might vote for Brexit, was an ironic memory for the transport secretary as he faced a chancellor who was now 'Remain central' doing 'his utmost' to thwart him. On aviation, Grayling quietly had effective talks with member states to ensure that the planes would keep flying. 'The system defaults to permits,' he said, 'so the EU did not have the legal power to say a plane cannot fly from London to Madrid as long as the Spanish government said, "We're happy that a British Airways and Iberia plane lands at Madrid." Likewise, with haulage, there were a number of legacy agreements that were legally still in place, so we were conducting informal talks.' Grayling changed the system so that international driving permits were issued by post offices, rather than by post from the AA. Which just left ferry capacity.[12]

The specific cause of the crisis was a change in the no-deal risk assessment in early October. Until that point the government had been working on an assumption that there would be six weeks' delay at the ports before things settled down. Now analysts calculated the disruption could last as long as six months. This was a problem for the NHS, which had the capacity (despite Hancock's fridge-buying) to stockpile medicines for just six weeks. Grayling told a cabinet sub-committee meeting, 'We should look at whether we can book capacity, so we can guarantee to get stuff in after that.' The Department for Transport examined rail freight but quickly concluded that ferry capacity for HGVs was what was needed. Grayling's team ascertained they could secure an option to reserve some capacity for the Department of Health to use for around £50 million. The message from the ferry industry was that a decision was needed by mid-November because that was the time of year that ferries for the spring got booked up. Failure to act would mean no available capacity on 29 March 2019.

DfT secured enough capacity from the Dutch firm DFDS and Brittany ferries from France to handle the NHS's requirements, running nearly 4,000 more lorries a week via Plymouth, Poole and Portsmouth. It was a third deal with a new British firm called Seaborne Freight, designed to create some reserve capacity, which blew up in Grayling's face. They were to be paid £13.8 million to run a service between Ramsgate and Ostend in Belgium. Seaborne Freight was backed by Arklow, an Irish shipping firm, who were the ones securing the ships. 'We gave the little start-up a contingent contract whereby they would receive no money unless they got the service up and running,' Grayling said. 'And given the fact they were backed by Ireland's biggest shipping company, we judged that was a prudent risk to take with taxpayers' money, because we weren't spending any.'[13] But the revelation that he was proposing to hand nearly £14 million to a ferry firm with no trading history, which had never run a ferry service and did not own any ferries was more proof, to some, of the insanity of no-deal. It was more complicated than that, of course, since much of the transport sector leased its vehicles and ships.

In the Treasury, Hammond thought the plan 'completely, barking, raving mad' and a total waste of money. He argued that it was simply 'paying ferry operators to do what they would have done anyway', delivering capacity they would have 'delivered anyway'. But the chancellor's view took no account of the political need for Hancock to be able to say there was a dedicated supply route for shipments of medicines. Grayling insisted they move fast. Hammond demanded that the DfT fill in an extensive document on the business case for the plan. Another cabinet minister sympathetic to the transport secretary said, 'Phil kept coming back with, "I am very happy to pay this money but first I have 150 questions." DfT should have got their act together earlier but there was not much goodwill there.' By 12 November a one-hundred-page document was handed over which had to go to accounting officers.

Hammond said, 'Some of the things that I was invited to support in the name of preparing for no deal were just ludicrous gestures. The chartering of ferries that didn't exist springs to mind. This was pure gesture politics.'[14] Some in Number 10, hardly a hotbed of Hammond fans, agreed. 'I don't think DfT can lay all their problems at HMT's door because Grayling has fucked so many things up,' a Downing Street aide said.

On 14 November, an exasperated Grayling wrote to Hammond: 'If we delay at all there is a very high chance that ferry operators and ports will be unable to provide the services. My strong view is therefore that we need to … either make a firm choice to proceed or decide this is undesirable or undeliverable.' He added, 'Indecision is effectively a decision not to proceed.' Nine days later, Grayling was still waiting and the cost was rising because shipping companies could see the government was desperate. Instead of buying an option, officials were told they had to guarantee pre-purchase of a percentage of the tickets. The permanent secretary at the Department of Health contacted his opposite number to say, 'We have to have this.' David Lidington, May's peacemaker, intervened to tell Hammond to get a move on. It still took an entire week after that, until 30 December, for Hammond to give the go-ahead. 'The Treasury were farting around for weeks,' a transport source said.

It was Grayling, however, who paid the political price. Labour, who usually branded the transport secretary 'failing Grayling' in their press releases, went a step further, proclaiming him 'the worst secretary of state ever'. It also emerged that Ramsgate port would have to be dredged, having not operated a ferry service since 2013. Arklow booked two vessels into dry dock to be repainted in Seaborne Freight colours, but in February 2019, the Irish firm pulled out, apparently unwilling to be at the centre of a political controversy. The contract was scrapped.

The episode was not the most important in the history of Brexit, but it came to symbolise several of its essential strands – the Brexiteer minister trying to prepare; the Treasury seeking to thwart; the solution: cobbled together; the reaction: rage and ridicule. It unfolded as senior backbenchers concluded that if the government could not be trusted to do what was in the national interest, it was time Parliament seized control of the process.

ERSKINE MAYHEM

Parliament Seizes Control

September 2018 to January 2019

John Bercow tapped his finger on the piece of paper on his desk. 'This is very interesting,' he said. In his nine years in the chair, Bercow had been a champion of the backbenches, but this was a step further, the most controversial thing he had contemplated – yet it had appeal. It was an audacious challenge to the executive, also to a party which he had once represented as an MP, but from which he was now estranged. He tapped the paper again. 'This is an important issue.'

In front of him stood Dominic Grieve, tall, rail thin and sinuous where Bercow was built of gristle and attitude. The former attorney general and unofficial commander of the Bresistance in Parliament had been summoned to discuss an amendment he wanted to table, which the Commons clerks did not think was in order. Grieve's goal was nothing less than to upend centuries of precedent in the rules of the House and create an opening for Parliament to take back control of Brexit. Bercow, jaw thrust defiantly at the world, said, 'I will give instruction that it should be placed on the order paper and I will reflect overnight.'

Brexit was often described as a constitutional upheaval, but the real revolution got the green light there. It was 9 January, six days before the meaningful vote.

The plan was the most important to emerge from the collective energy and competitive instincts of rival Bresistance groups who had formed in opposition to the government and the ERG. Parliament increasingly resembled a series of armed camps with their own command structures and councils of war.

The high command of the ERG, the original party within a party, met in Iain Duncan Smith's room at 10.30 a.m. on a Monday, a meeting called the Brexit Outreach Group. The steering group of Steve Baker and the senior Paleosceptics then gathered at 2 p.m. to discuss strategy for the week. The officers of the ERG met at 5 p.m. on Tuesday before a meeting of the full membership, both MPs and peers, at 6 p.m.

If there was a command centre for the Bresisters it was a WhatsApp group set up in great secrecy in the autumn of 2018 called 'Trains and Buses'. Between November that year and March 2019, its members arguably did more to shape the Brexit process than the cabinet. The name came from the presence in the group of several former transport frontbenchers: Justine Greening and Jo Johnson from the Tories, Labour's Mary Creagh and Tom Brake from the Liberal Democrats. Its innocuous title allowed its members to check their phones in public without arousing suspicion. 'Any time Anna Soubry was having conversations in the corridor, and was overheard, she would switch to talking about trains and buses,' a Labour MP said. 'She'd say, "The trains have been appalling lately. I'm going to see the secretary of state for transport."' The group became the clearing house to coordinate support for motions and amendments on Brexit legislation. The other members included Caroline Lucas, the only Green Party MP; Phillip Lee and Guto Bebb, the two Tory ministers who had resigned over Brexit; other Conservatives like Soubry; and Labour's Ben Bradshaw, Chris Bryant and Stephen Doughty, a former whip who became a key convener of the group. Like the ERG's 'Buddies', Doughty and Bebb's whipping operation was renowned by MPs as better than Julian Smith's. 'A lot of the parliamentary activity at the end of 2018 into 2019 was Trains and Buses,' one member said. 'No one ever knew. It worked and it didn't leak. We understood the reality within Parliament better than the other side.' Jo Swinson, the leading Lib Dem, ran a similar group called 'Secret Squirrels'. That included Keir Starmer, Labour's Brexit spokesman, and even some Conservative ministers.

Dominic Grieve had his own WhatsApp group for the dozen Tory Bresisters. By the summer of 2018, the former attorney general had become convinced that Brexit was a binary business. 'You either want virtually no relationship [with the EU] because you wish to be free of all constraints,' he said. 'Or you accept regulatory constraints, in which case, I'm afraid, it starts to call into question what the point [of Brexit] is.'

Grieve decided there needed to be a new referendum, one in which he would vote to reverse the result. 'For me, the tipping point was watching the party tear itself apart, watching what happened over Chequers. That's when I thought it was never going to work.'

To the Brexiteers, Grieve was hell-bent on stopping Brexit at any cost. He saw it differently, saying, 'Did I feel Brexit was a disaster? Yes. But the only way in which I ever contemplated stopping Brexit was a referendum. Having offered the first referendum, you could only reverse it with a second referendum. I was absolutely clear about that.' Other MPs think Grieve was not honest with himself. A Bresister, who ended up voting for May's deal, declared it 'just rubbish' for Grieve to say he didn't aim to stop Brexit. 'It became explicit in 2018,' the MP said. 'I remember him saying, "The people may not have thought again, but I've thought again and I can't let this through."'

Tory Bresisters spanned a spectrum from revokers and referendum supporters to very soft Brexiteers. Grieve was at the harder end of the spectrum, along with Soubry, Ken Clarke, Heidi Allen, Antoinette Sandbach and Sarah Wollaston. Those prepared to consider a démarche with Downing Street included Stephen Hammond, Nicky Morgan, Damian Green and Nicholas Soames. This less militant group called themselves 'Team 2019' and then the 'Conservative Group for Europe'. They met on Monday evenings, with a second meeting with MPs and peers on Tuesday evenings and a briefing from external experts on Wednesdays.

Another group, 'the Breakfast Club', included Remain-inclined ministers (David Gauke, Greg Clark, Alistair Burt, Jo Johnson, Margot James and Richard Harrington). They met on Tuesday mornings at the Caxton Grill in Westminster. Their view was that they had a duty to support May but if her deal was rejected by Parliament, 'all bets are off'. Each of the Tory factions looked to the 'Gang of Five' in cabinet – Philip Hammond, Rudd, Gauke and Clark, who caucused together, plus David Lidington. He had the most power but, as May's de facto deputy, was also the most loyal. This group wanted a soft Brexit and opposed no-deal.

The bulk of Labour MPs were, by now, supporters of the People's Vote campaign for a second referendum. In Tory ranks, Phillip Lee and Guto Bebb drew up a list of 66 colleagues they thought might back a referendum and quietly lobbied them. Shortly before Christmas, they set up the Right to Vote, to give a Conservative slant to the pro-referendum campaign. Lee recalled, 'The strategy of Right to Vote was: get the referendum, run the Conservative wing of the Remain campaign, during which we were going to attract new members for the Tory party, win the Remain campaign, then have a Tory leadership election in which Remain voters who'd become activists then voted. We thought that was the only way of saving the Tory party from becoming an English nationalist party.' All of these goals proved elusive.

The pressures on potential recruits were heavy. 'I spoke to a typical Tory MP, a good friend and he was 100 per cent supportive privately,' Lee said. 'His association was full of absolute headbangers. He'd moved his family to the constituency in order to secure the seat. His wife sat him down and said, "You can't do what you think is right. You made me move here, we have children in schools, you are not losing your seat." There were a number of people in positions like that.'[1]

Initially, the biggest rivals to the People's Voters were the 'Norwegians', a group driven by Cameroon ex-housing minister Nick Boles and Oliver Letwin. In August 2018, Boles concluded, 'The government is buggering up Brexit.' He had been berated by Nicky Morgan in July when he, Letwin and Amber Rudd declined to join a rebellion. 'When are you guys going to do anything?' Morgan complained. 'If you say that you want a soft Brexit, you've actually got to vote for it.' That got Boles thinking. Over what would he stand and fight?

The idea he worked up with Letwin was that Britain could temporarily join the European Economic Area (EEA), which comprised EU countries and three that were inside the single market but outside the EU: Norway, Iceland and Liechtenstein. Boles also suggested joining the European Free Trade Area (EFTA), which was the three non-EU EEA nations plus Switzerland, inside the single market but outside the EEA. The strength of the plan was that, as a place for Britain to wait while it negotiated a trade deal, it negated the need for the backstop and got Britain technically out of the EU on time. Boles also argued that it would give Britain back control of its fishing waters much sooner, which was potentially attractive to Brexiteers.

The downsides were numerous, not the least of which was the complexity of explaining it to MPs and the public. Both the EEA and EFTA were small groups of small countries; British membership would totally unbalance them. An EU official said, 'It would be like an elephant jumping into a bath. All the bathwater comes out. After a few years the elephant gets out and there is no water left.' Iceland's ambassador went on *Newsnight* to support the plan, but as a campaigner admitted, 'The Norwegians fucking hate it.' Single market membership also meant the retention of freedom of movement, a non-starter for many Tories, including the prime minister. Boles highlighted rules which let Norway suspend freedom of movement in extreme circumstances. But it was not intended for general use and Brussels had rejected an 'emergency brake' on immigration when it was requested by David Cameron.

Boles first pitched the idea at the ERG, selling it as a safe haven for the UK before a pivot to a Canadian-style free trade deal. He called it 'Common Market 2.0' since many Brexiteers wished the EU had never evolved from the economic community the UK joined in 1972. However, ERGers feared Norway Plus meant Britain would never shake off the shackles of Brussels. On the other side, People's Vote spin doctors attacked the plan as a gateway drug to a hard Brexit. 'You think you're on a weekend trip to Oslo,' one expressive soul warned, 'and we'll end up in the frozen wastes of Canada in our underpants bleeding from the arse.' In June 2018, 76 Labour MPs backed an amendment calling on Britain to join the EEA. But when that failed, dozens of those MPs concluded that the only way forward was to back the People's Vote instead.

Boles did build support among Labour MPs who were opposed to a referendum. Former frontbenchers Stephen Kinnock and Lucy Powell became key collaborators. Veteran contrarian Frank Field signed up in October. Boles tried to persuade cabinet ministers that if they presented May with a fait accompli – Norway plus immigration controls – Powell and Kinnock could deliver enough Labour votes to win in the Commons. But despite the presence of serious people, Norway Plus never got the traction its advocates thought it deserved. MPs were suspicious of Boles, seeing his activities as a front operation for his friend Michael Gove, who was still distrusted by many. Told that Gove was working on a solution in case May's deal was rejected, one cabinet minister wryly remarked, 'Will the solution be "Michael Gove", by any chance?'

By Christmas 2018, however, Boles and Letwin's other project was taking off in a big way. Unlike Grieve, they both thought that the 2016 referendum result had to be delivered. Boles concluded that the only way to get the ERG to support a deal was to take no-deal off the table.

* * *

Boles first remembered the way Labour had used the parliamentary device of a 'humble address' to force David Davis to release the government's contingency plans for Brexit. On 3 September, Boles and Letwin went to see David Natzler, the clerk of the House and a long-standing friend of Letwin. 'We need to find a method for Parliament to assert its will,' Boles explained to the clerk. 'Could we use a humble address?'

Natzler said, 'No. The humble address is a cunning thing but all it can do is require the government to publish papers, it's not a general tool for getting them to do things.' No amount of backbench motions or opposition day debates would do the job.

The genesis of the idea came – with supreme irony – from two prominent Brexiteers: Bernard Jenkin and Jacob Rees-Mogg. Jenkin chaired the public administration and constitutional affairs select committee, which published a paper on Brexit legislation. The point which leaped out at Boles was Jenkin's assertion that 'only a statute can change a statute'. Jenkin argued that the Article 50 bill set the date for Brexit as the 29 March 2019, now embedded in the withdrawal agreement. He intended this statement as proof of the immutability of the date. To Boles it was a roadmap to changing it. They would have to change the law. The problem was that governments control business in the Commons. Standing Order 14 of the rules of the House stated, 'Government business shall have precedence at every sitting.' It had been in place since Charles Stewart Parnell's campaign of obstructionism for Irish nationalism in the 1880s.

The solution came to Boles in conversation with Rees-Mogg, who was an expert on Commons procedure.[2] Boles was in the habit of sitting next to the ERG chairman so he could pick his brain. One day in September, Boles asked about the status of standing orders. Were they embedded in a centuries-old act of Parliament? Rees-Mogg looked 'rather horrified' at Boles' ignorance. Genially, he explained, 'The point about standing orders is that the House runs itself. The House can change any standing order by a simple majority.'

It was a 'lightbulb moment' for Boles. He discussed the plan with Letwin, who talked about it with Grieve. All three were thinking along the same lines. Following chats with the clerks, Grieve had concluded: 'While the UK constitution exists in a large number of places as a written text, its machinery is entirely contained in the standing orders.' If they could suspend Standing Order 14 or amend the business of the House, they could pass a law to prevent no-deal and override the legislation dictating the Brexit date as 29 March. For that they would need help from the speaker.

Oliver Letwin's evolution into rebel in chief was a curious transformation for a figure who seemed to embody the establishment: Eton and Oxford, All Souls, Cameron's fixer, Julian Smith's helper, a man of many parts wrapped in tweed or violently colourful cords. Having spent years in the Cabinet Office, his finger in every government pie, Letwin still had key contacts at the top of the civil service. 'He had his own sources of information that the consequences of leaving on 29 March with no-deal would be catastrophic,' another grandee recalled. 'He decided it was his absolute duty to try to stop it.'

Decisive for Letwin was his experience of working on civil contingencies under the coalition government. 'When one thing is going really wrong, the state can just about manage,' he said. 'When two things are going really wrong, if you're lucky. But if seventeen things, of which ten you didn't predict, are all going really wrong at the same time, you just have no idea of where it ends up and what is certain is that the state can't manage. It's just too complex.' John Bercow recalled, 'He had come to the conclusion that a no deal Brexit would be a calamity.'[3]

Letwin had also concluded that Theresa May had lost control of events. 'By that time … almost everything that was happening to her was happening in a way that she didn't want and wasn't planning,' he said. Letwin saw 'this juggernaut heading to a great big brick wall' culminating in 'the cataclysmic choice between two evils, not leaving or leaving without a deal'. He said, 'The party and the government had got themselves into a position where they weren't going to be able to deliver a reasonable solution.' With time running out, he concluded that to break the deadlock, 'I couldn't see any way of doing that other than by opening it up to some kind of cross-party discussion within Parliament.'[4]

Letwin wanted to hear the other side's view. On 27 November he took the unusual step of turning up to an ERG steering group meeting to hear from the leadership of the hard Brexiteers. It was not a meeting of minds. 'He just despaired of us being prepared [for no-deal] on which he was wrong,' a senior ERG official said.

Letwin's alliance with Boles was an example of how Brexit made for strange bedfellows. Letwin was a hunched intense man, with a huge intellect, and a twittering lilt to his speech, who would not have been out of place in a university common room. Boles was a tall and languid character, more practical than academic, who sometimes got highly emotional about the personal business of politics. He became, to the media and to other MPs, Letwin's representative on earth. Having not known each other particularly well beforehand, from September 2018 until the following March they met every day Parliament was sitting, often eating lunch or dinner together, and spoke on the phone three times a day, including over the weekend. 'We agreed that we both wanted a deal but we absolutely would not accept no-deal,' Boles recalled.

A few weeks after their first meeting, in late September, Letwin and Boles went to see Natzler in his rooms at the back of the speaker's chair. 'Can we change standing orders in order to be able to get some time to pass a bill?' Natzler's eyes lit up. It was another lightbulb moment for Boles. Just as with civil servants, to get the best from the clerks you had to ask the right question. It was not their role to push ideas, but asked to make an MP's idea work, many could be innovative in working around a problem. Natzler sent them to see Colin Lee, another senior clerk, whose office was on the public bill corridor. Soon Letwin and Boles were regulars in Lee's office. Boles, who had a great ability to focus, cleared his diary of everything but Brexit meetings. If he had to vote, he did so, but he did not attend debates; nothing could distract from the mission.

While the People's Vote/Trains and Buses faction disagreed with the Norway Plus crowd and those advocating membership of the customs union, they all found common cause in wanting to stop no-deal. A 'No to No Deal' WhatsApp group inevitably sprouted with around twenty members, half of whom were also in 'Trains and Buses'. An omnibus group of the senior players in each Bresistance camp then began meeting in Hilary Benn's office. 'When we came back in January, it was obvious to all of us that the deal was going nowhere and that the ERG would destroy it,' Grieve said. Letwin and Boles found common cause with Labour's Yvette Cooper, Hilary Benn and Jack Dromey, the latter of whom also formed a cross-party alliance with former Tory cabinet minister Caroline Spelman. Ken Clarke, another natural ally, was baffled by this flurry of activity: 'There were so many different factions who wanted me to go to their plotting meetings, but I didn't know where they were or when they were on. I wasn't on WhatsApp, so everybody forgot to tell me when it was on.'[5] Stephen Doughty said, 'There was this extraordinary cooperation that had never been seen before between people who have very different views on lots of different things.'

Grieve and Letwin were solicitous of each other, but MPs viewed them as friendly rivals. Another former cabinet minister recalled, 'Oliver and Dominic were having a great rivalry at that point over who could come up with the most contorted notions to attract the support of the speaker to stop no-deal.' For the next nine months, however, they have a good case to be considered among the most influential backbenchers in recent parliamentary history. While Theresa May had seemingly taken a geological age to devise a plan, secure a deal and failed then to sell it, the rebels had a firm goal and a means of reaching it.

On 7 January Boles and Letwin briefed Yvette Cooper, on neutral ground in Nicky Morgan's office in Portcullis House. They would introduce an amendment to suspend the standing orders and make time for the introduction of a bill to prevent no-deal. They needed a Labour co-sponsor. Cooper agreed. The bill would force the government to seek an extension from Brussels, delaying Brexit until after 29 March, if May's deal was voted down. The conversations broadened out to include Morgan, Hilary Benn and Norman Lamb of the Lib Dems.

Delay did not prevent no-deal, it merely deferred it. The EU might say no to an extension. Even if one was granted, the government might not use the time effectively. That raised the question of whether the legislation should have its own backstop – a clause requiring the government to revoke Brexit if it was not given an extension. Cooper 'was up for it,' said one of those involved, 'but we concluded that it was politically impossible.' There was no way of attracting the Tory votes they would need if there was even a theoretical chance of the referendum result being overturned. Instead, they decided alternatives to May's deal should be debated by the Commons and put to 'indicative votes' in the House. 'You needed to have some organisation that had some innate authority within Parliament' to suggest the alternatives. They chose the Liaison Committee, a select committee made up of the chairmen of the other select committees. The benefit of this idea was that each member was an elected chairman, there was a good cross-party mix and the membership included both Bill Cash and Bernard Jenkin so there was a cross-section of opinion on Brexit. 'We talked ourselves into thinking it was quite a good idea,' said one MP. No one bothered to tell the Liaison Committee.

The following day, 8 January, Cooper and Morgan joined forces with an amendment to the Finance Bill, to limit the government's ability to fund no-deal. The Cooper-Morgan amendment passed by 303–296, a signal of intent. It was the first government defeat on a finance bill since 1978. Twenty Tory MPs voted for the amendment.

A steady drumbeat against no-deal could also be heard inside government. On the same day, Richard Harrington, a business minister, said he was prepared to resign to prevent a no-deal Brexit. Amber Rudd told cabinet, 'History will take a dim view of a cabinet that presses ahead with no-deal. We need to reach across the House and find a majority.' She backed indicative votes as well. Michael Gove made the point that a lot of MPs waiting for their perfect outcome (on both sides) were likely to be disappointed. 'Like fifty-year-olds at the end of the disco, who have turned down all other offers and are waiting for Scarlett Johansson to come along.'[6] David Gauke added, 'They're waiting for Scarlett on a unicorn.'[7]

May continued to choose not to choose. A Downing Street official insisted that week that she would end up backing a second referendum because she had personally told them she would never go for no-deal. Another Number 10 staffer equally solemnly predicted she would go for no-deal because she had personally assured them she would 'never support a referendum'.

Late in the afternoon of 8 January the government tabled its business motion for the meaningful vote and the debate surrounding it. If they had hoped the late hour would prevent amendments, they were to be disappointed.

Section 13 of the European Union (Withdrawal) Act 2018 specified that the government come to the House within twenty-one days of defeat in a meaningful vote to explain the next steps, after which a motion 'in neutral terms' would be put before MPs. Standing Order 24B stated that where a motion is in neutral terms, 'no amendments to it may be tabled'. In December, Grieve succeeded in passing an amendment suspending the operation of Standing Order 24B in relation to Section 13 of the Withdrawal Act, so MPs could intervene if there was no prospect of a deal. However, this only let MPs pass a motion outlining their wishes, it would not be a law. To change the law they would need to control the business of the House themselves.

The government's business motion stated that future changes to the timetable could only be made by 'a minister of the crown' and 'the question on any such motion shall be put forthwith'. This gave the government the ability to vary the date of the meaningful vote, but the key word was the last one. According to *Erskine May*, the bible of parliamentary procedure, when questions were put 'forthwith' the speaker was required to do so 'without debate and usually without the possibility of amendment'. The government thought it was impossible to amend a business motion on Brexit. In this they had acted 'with some advice from the clerks', Bercow admitted.[8] In other words, Julian Smith and Andrea Leadsom, the chief whip and leader of the Commons, thought it was impossible precisely because that was what the clerks had told them the rules said. But the rules of the game were about to change.

That evening, Grieve tabled an amendment which would force the government to come to the House within three days of a defeat on the meaningful vote, rather than twenty-one. It was a smokescreen. What he was really seeking to do was to get the speaker to rewrite the meaning of 'forthwith' so that MPs could vote to seize control of parliamentary business themselves. If they could do so, they could then pass a bill outlawing no-deal, like the one Letwin, Boles and co. were working on. Grieve took his amendment to the table office behind the speaker's chair. The clerk at the table office refused to accept the amendment. 'This is not in order,' he said. 'It can't be tabled.'

Grieve replied, 'I think the standing order is open to interpretation.' He insisted it was shown to Natzler. Grieve went to the tearoom. Ten minutes later a messenger came to see him and said the answer was still, 'No.'

Peter Bone, the arch-Brexiteer, also visited the table office that night with an amendment of his own. He was also refused. ('Peter Bone never came to see me about it,' Bercow said later, 'so I didn't know about it and he was prepared to accept the clerk's word.')

The senior clerk on duty, Philippa Helme, went to see Bercow. 'Mr Grieve has submitted an amendment to the business motion. Obviously, it can't be selected because it's a motion forthwith.'

Bercow replied, 'I'm not so sure about that.'

'Well, that's certainly very, very strong convention, Mr Speaker,' said Helme, 'but you may wish to allow it to appear on the order paper or to prohibit it. I'd like to take your guidance.'

Bercow was already thinking of selecting the amendment. 'You should let it appear on the paper. I'll consider it overnight.' He then called Grieve and asked to see him. A Labour MP saw Grieve entering the speaker's house after dark. Bercow was about to make the second of three key interventions on Brexit.

The first, six years earlier, put Bercow at odds with precedent and with the speaker's clerks, to the great delight of the Paleosceptics. He allowed an amendment to the Queen's speech from Brexiteer John Baron, expressing regret that the government had not included a referendum on EU membership. More than 100 Conservatives rebelled, convincing David Cameron that he would have to call a referendum.

Bercow's action was inadvertently one of the handmaidens of Brexit, an outcome he deplored. The speaker believed the decision to call the vote to be a 'major failure of statecraft' by Cameron.[9] Bercow's 'personal view' was that Brexit was 'a great mistake'.[10] He saw the campaign and its supporters as 'racist'.[11] Bercow found the May government's vague definition of Brexit 'utterly pathetic'.[12] When the prime minister lost her majority, in June 2017, the speaker thought it 'mind-boggling' she did not change her approach, describing the PM as 'quite extraordinarily politically unimaginative'.[13] MPs did not have to wait until after he had retired to learn Bercow's views. Speaking to students at the University of Reading just months after the referendum, he admitted, 'Personally, I voted to Remain.' A family car, parked in the precincts of the Palace of Westminster, was conspicuously adorned with a sticker emblazoned with 'Bollocks to Brexit', his wife Sally's vehicle, the speaker insisted.

Some former colleagues saw Bercow's marriage as the key to his political journey from the pro-apartheid Tory Monday club to a socially liberal moderniser. 'The problem with John is that he discovered sexual intercourse and the Labour Party at the same time,' one remarked. Bercow was a loner, a nuisance to his own side even as a frontbencher. Having failed to crack Tory politics, he set his eyes on the speakership and openly courted Labour MPs. The son of a Jewish taxi driver, he faced unpleasant abuse about his origins, his race and his height. These attributes attracted Westminster's cod psychologists who saw a short man with a plate of triple-cooked chips on his shoulder, a grievance against his own party and a determination to make his mark.

*   *   *

When Grieve arrived in the speaker's house, Bercow said, 'I'm personally sympathetic to this. I've been advised against it, but I think it's orderly. It's a convention, not a rule.'

Grieve put on his lawyer's hat and explained to the speaker all the reasons why he should not accept the amendment. 'This is controversial,' he admitted.

'I know it's controversial,' replied Bercow. 'I will make up my own mind.'[14] In truth, it was already made up.

Grieve would later be insistent that Bercow had no prior knowledge of his plan. His view, as a lawyer, was that 'you don't suborn the judge'. He said, 'I never had a conversation with Bercow in which we were saying, "This is how we're going to stop no deal", or "This is how we're going to get a second referendum." This was about process.'

However, it is the case that Bercow had been warned that something was brewing in the Bresistance by Chris Leslie, with whom he played tennis. 'Chris Leslie would often keep me informed about things that were going on,' he recalled. Leslie 'was always very proper', Bercow insisted. But to Brexiteers, the unfolding of these events late at night smacked of conspiracy, or at the very least a chummy connivance in upending Brexit.

There was no doubt in Grieve's mind that Bercow knew his purpose was to take control of the order paper. Had the government's motion read 'forthwith without amendments' there would have been no wriggle room. But Bercow and Grieve both felt it was not clear cut. 'You shouldn't be entirely bound by what's happened before,' Bercow said, 'because if you are, nothing ever changes. I also felt that people who were in a minority should nevertheless have a chance to be heard.'

When the amendment appeared on the order paper, Bernard Jenkin appealed to Bercow: 'I've heard that you're going to allow this amendment. Please don't do this. It would be a terrible mistake.' The plea fell on deaf ears.

The clerks were no constraint either. When Bercow met Natzler and his team the next morning, there was a row. 'There is an amendment now, Mr Speaker, but obviously you won't select it,' Natzler said.

'No, I do intend to select it.'

The clerk studied the floor, not looking Bercow in the eye. Silence. Natzler took a short intake of breath. He said, 'But, Mr Speaker, you can't. You're not serious?'

'I'm absolutely serious, yes.'

'No, no, but you can't select an amendment to a forthwith motion.'

'Where does it say in the Standing Orders that I can't?'

To the speaker, Natzler seemed 'ashen-faced and as shaken as if he had just learned of an appalling tragedy'. The clerk 'looked up openmouthed and stared' at Bercow 'in disbelief',[15] then said, 'It's not in the Standing Orders, Mr Speaker, but it's a convention.'

'Well, it may be a convention, David, but it isn't an unbreakable rule.'

'*Erskine May* is very clear on this matter. It would be unprecedented, no speaker has ever, to my knowledge, selected an amendment to a forthwith motion.'[16]

Bercow was dismissive, totally sure of himself, 'Well, that may very well be the case, David, but we're in uncharted waters. The government is deliberately holding a gun to the House's head and part of the role of the speaker is to make rulings. New precedents can be created.'

In Bercow's public accounts of the meeting, Natzler did not like it, but accepted Bercow's mind was made up. 'You'd better put your tin hat on,' he said. 'There will be a considerable row.'

'Well, I'm not bothered about that!'

Others present say Bercow ordered the clerks not to make a written note of their objections. 'I don't want to listen to your advice and I don't want to read your advice,' he said, in this account. They say the meeting ended with Bercow storming out, saying, 'I'll do what I want.' That, to his critics, was the essence of the decision. Bercow had convinced himself, apparently sincerely, that what he was doing was right, but those who watched him in action that morning believe the reason he did it was because it was what he wanted to do, a less secure foundation on which to build a constitutionally transformative ruling. 'I never lost a wink of sleep over that subsequently,' he recalled later.[17]

Asked by the author if he relished the controversy, Bercow admitted, 'Yes. I think so. Was I looking for a fight? No. Did I relish doing the dirty on the government? That's not true. But did I quite like the idea of defending my corner? Did I relish that? Yes, to be honest.'

Bercow's other accounts of the incident, in his memoirs and interviews to promote the book, leave little doubt that his decision was coloured by his visceral loathing of Brexit: 'The notion that a minority government should be free to exert unfettered control as part of a scandalous time-wasting plot was absurd,' he wrote. 'That such a plot was intended to blackmail the House to accept a deal it didn't want, or else suffer the indescribable calamity of a cliff-edge Brexit, was not merely ridiculous. It was disgusting and obscene.'[18] These are not the words of someone who cared if he was seen as partial.

Explaining himself later, Bercow said, 'I certainly never saw it as part of my role to get Brexit done, or to help the government to get Brexit done. In my own defence, I would say I didn't think it was part of my role to try to stop the government getting Brexit done either. I genuinely did believe that it was my job to try to facilitate the House to have its say and indeed, for that matter, to have its way. I said I was standing for speaker in order to empower Parliament and I did just that. Some people will agree with decisions I made and other people will disagree with them, but I plead guilty to doing what it said on the tin. They were made honestly. They weren't made for effect. They weren't made for show. They weren't made for some sort of grandstanding. They were honest decisions.'

Views of Bercow's ruling that morning came to define whether someone saw him as a good or bad speaker. What it ensured beyond doubt was that he was one of the most consequential and one of the half-dozen most significant figures in directing the course of British politics in 2019.

At 11 a.m., Bercow's office rang Grieve's office in the Commons to tell him the speaker was going to allow the amendment. Bercow announced his intention to the Commons when the sitting began. Julian Smith marched to the chair and confronted him, shaking with fury and banging his fist on the table to the speaker's right. 'Julian, please don't bang the table like that,' Bercow said, words forced through a rictus of false politeness. 'First of all, it's rather discourteous and, secondly, it's a threat to the wood. You mustn't behave like that; I'm not having it.'

Smith told him the decision was 'totally out of order' and was 'throwing centuries of precedent in the bin'. He said, 'You will not dictate what happens here!'

Bercow already had. He replied, 'I'm not trying to dictate what happens in this place, I am seeking to facilitate the House in making the decision that it wants to make. I think it's perfectly orderly. If you don't like this amendment, my advice to you is to whip your colleagues to vote against it, and we'll see what happens.'[19] When the chief whip pressed his case, a furious Bercow accused Smith of trying to 'bully' him.

After Prime Minister's Questions, May left the chamber without so much as a glance at the chair, the customary polite nod abandoned to a blank stare of rage. Even Gavin Barwell, who described himself later as 'softer on the speaker' than other Mayites, was unimpressed. 'What he did was unilaterally make a ruling that tore up the rules,' the chief of staff said. 'If the House wanted to do that, it would've been much better if he'd granted some time, in a general debate, for a motion on House business, where the House could have formally changed its rules to say that that was okay. Just putting it through by edict, I thought, was very bad.'[20]

Bercow was bombarded for an hour with points of order from incandescent Conservatives, orchestrated in part by the whips. Bercow said his interpretation of 'forthwith' was 'that there can be no debate' but not that no amendment could be voted on. When Mark Francois put to him that only a minister could move a motion, Bercow said, "Tis so. We are not treating here of a motion but of an amendment to a motion.' Francois replied, 'That's ridiculous', and accused Bercow of 'utter sophistry'.

Andrea Leadsom, tipped off about Bercow's row with the clerks, demanded that the speaker publish the advice he had received, something he regarded as a 'stunning display of hypocrisy' after the government's approach to the attorney general's legal advice. Unable to say the clerks supported him, Bercow said merely that he had discussed the issue with Natzler. 'I have made an honest judgement.' Yet he seemed not to have contemplated the implications of his ruling, saying he would have to 'reflect' on whether it would establish a precedent for the future.

Another Brexiteer watching from the backbenches felt sick. 'It was horrible to watch as Bercow effectively said that he is the law,' the MP recalled. 'It made me fear that, if this kind of behaviour continues, nobody will feel it is worth respecting institutions of authority any longer as they hold no legitimacy. I remember feeling frightened.' Even Tory Remainers voiced concern. Simon Hoare warned that the 'dignity of the office of speaker' was in question, adding, 'I think we are – I say this with sadness – in pretty choppy and dangerous waters at the time in our nation's affairs when, frankly, we can least afford it.'

Bercow did receive support, mostly from Labour MPs. Luciana Berger made the pertinent observation that Tory Brexiteers 'who have often advocated our taking back control' in Parliament were 'now doing the complete opposite'. Afterwards Jeremy Corbyn, who hoped the chaos would lead to a general election, approached the speaker and said, 'That was great, John. Well done.'

Throughout it all, Grieve sat silently. His amendment passed by 308 votes to 297 with the backing of seventeen Conservative MPs.[21]

Afterwards, Bercow's critics, including Paleosceptics like Bill Cash, privately accused him of setting up government by Parliament, rather than government through Parliament. In doing what he could to ensure Parliament 'have its way', Bercow made it inevitable that MPs (three quarters of whom backed Remain) would be at odds with the public. Jacob Rees-Mogg, hitherto an admirer of Bercow, was horrified: 'I think he made a grave mistake and it's damaged his reputation irrecoverably. It's a great pity because a lot of what he did was very important and improved the standing of Parliament. I thought he was an historically important speaker who went badly wrong in his last year by allowing it to become apparent that his own political opinions were affecting his judgement. I think that was completely improper and upset the balance of the constitution.' Robbie Gibb called Bercow's role in the Brexit battles 'nothing short of shameful'.[22] Baroness Boothroyd, the former speaker, was overheard telling a Tory MP that Bercow's actions were 'disgusting' and an 'absolute and utter disgrace'.

It was not just Brexiteers who were uneasy. A female MP who voted Remain said, 'I think he probably was biased to the rebels. He became a bit of an anarchist really.' Even revealing his support for Remain was an unprecedented move. Professor Vernon Bogdanor said, 'He's the first speaker, I think, ever to have expressed a view on a controversial public issue, and I think that's tainted his speakership. His procedural judgments may be right or wrong, but they've been tainted by the fact that people think they're influenced by political opinions. The speaker should be neutral, like the Queen.'

Whatever Bercow's intentions, he was still in the job because prominent Remain campaigners believed he would be of use to them. On 2 May 2018 the speaker was accused of bullying members of House of Commons staff, launching verbal 'tirades' and smashing his mobile phone for effect. Bercow denied all the claims but would be found guilty four years later. But the view among leading Bresisters at the time was that Brexit was more important than bullying. This was made explicit by Margaret Beckett, the former acting leader of the Labour Party, whose previous judgement calls included ensuring that Jeremy Corbyn made the ballot for the Labour leadership contest in 2015 (a move she later described as 'moronic'). Beckett said, 'We are going to embark on this huge constitutional experiment in which there may be a key role for the speaker.' Brexit might be the 'most difficult decision' in 'hundreds of years'. She concluded, 'Yes, it trumps bad behaviour.'

This is not to say that Bercow conspired with the rebels. All he needed to do, given the balance of views among MPs, was to make clear that he would always give Parliament the opportunity to express its views. But by revelling in his rulings, Bercow stoked the heated feelings he was quick to condemn when they boiled over in his chamber.

The full implications of what the rebels were up to emerged the following weekend when the *Sunday Times* splashed with details of the Boles-Letwin plan to seize control of Commons business to outlaw no-deal. The headline was derived from a Downing Street official who called it 'a very British coup', after the novel and television series devised by former Labour minister Chris Mullin, a framing that enraged the rebels.

The version of events peddled by the government that weekend had it that Julian Smith had overheard MPs discussing the plan in the members' cloakroom on the evening of Thursday 10 January. Boles and others were convinced that news had actually reached the chief whip via Letwin. 'Oliver told Julian to be helpful,' one source said. 'We did at one point have to insist, "stop briefing the chief whip" literally everything that we were doing.' Even a whips' office source said later that the cloakroom story was 'nonsense' and that 'Oliver would just have told him, he's very straightforward.' In this account, Letwin claimed, 'We are doing you a favour', arguing that the gambit would help persuade the ERG to vote for the deal since they would now fear no-deal would be taken off the table. Letwin left with the impression that the chief whip, while not encouraging the rebels, was prepared to turn a blind eye, partly out of his own aversion to no-deal, partly because he did hope it would sway ERG votes. 'Julian was very sincere in his belief that no-deal would be disastrous for the country,' a source close to the chief whip recalled.

When the story broke, on Sunday 13th, Boles and others blamed Smith for leaking the whole thing, something they saw as a betrayal of Letwin. Smith always insisted the cloakroom story was accurate. Certainly, it assisted in cloaking proceedings under the Victorian Gothic battlements with an air of subterfuge that was helpful to the government.

On the Friday afternoon the author was passed a legal assessment commissioned by Smith and presented to the prime minister at 2.15 p.m. that day. It warned that the Boles-Letwin plan to 'secure time in the chamber such that their business would take precedence over any government business' would be 'a clear and present danger to all government business'. The legal opinion concluded, 'Without control of the order paper, the government has no control over the House of Commons and the Parliamentary business and legislation necessary to progress government policies. The government would lose its ability to govern.' An ERG adviser said later, 'We really are in "burning files in piles in 1940" territory if the government can't control the business of the House.'

Flushed out, Boles confirmed, 'We have a mechanism which will give Parliament control of the Brexit negotiations and ensure we do not leave the EU without a deal on 29 March.' He said he would unveil the details the following Tuesday. It confirmed fears the Brexiteers had harboured for three months that Bercow was prepared to put his hand on the scale. On 19 October a former member of the cabinet revealed that the SNP had told him, 'Bercow has already decided to effectively suspend standing orders.'

Boles had been due to speak on the Monday to Sarah Wollaston, the chairman of the Liaison Committee, about the idea of handing control of Brexit to them. But that morning the *Daily Mail* splashed on that detail of the plan before he had tipped off Wollaston. The paper condemned it as 'Brexit by committee' and a 'constitutional outrage' and pointed out that Bresisters outnumbered Brexiteers on the committee by twenty-seven to nine. At 9.08 a.m. Boles tweeted, 'If the government can't govern, Parliament must.' But the leaks, two days running, blew up the initial Boles-Letwin plan on the launch pad. When the Liaison Committee met that afternoon, they decided they wanted nothing to do with it. But Bercow's bombshell intervention had showed that backbenchers could take control when they had a proposal which could unite the Bresistance factions. Boles was right about one thing: Brexit was about Parliament taking back control. Now it was to do that in the most spectacular way.

20

WIPEOUT

MV1

15 to 18 January 2019

'The first iron law of politics is that
its practitioners need to learn to count'

– Lyndon B. Johnson

When Number 10 staff assembled to listen to the historian Sir Anthony Seldon on the morning of Friday 18 January, they gravitated to a yellowing piece of paper retrieved from the National Archives. Scrawled in pencil was a map of the defensive positions at the mission station at Rorke's Drift in Natal, where 139 British soldiers held out against four thousand Zulu warriors, an encounter immortalised in the 1964 film. May's embattled aides, outnumbered and under attack from all sides, drew strength from one of the most improbable victories in British history. The heroics at Rorke's Drift in 1879, of course, came after one of the most humiliating setbacks in military history, when 1,300 redcoats were slaughtered at the Battle of Isandlwana. The Downing Street team contemplated the events of three days earlier which had delivered the greatest defeat for a sitting government in the history of the House of Commons.

In the five weeks since the meaningful vote had been delayed, very little had changed. Julian Smith and his team of whips hoped to shift the DUP and all but the most irreconcilable members of the ERG, without which they could not contemplate significant support from the Labour benches. The DUP, recognising their power, were unmoved by the hard-won promises in the Juncker-Tusk letter. Karen Bradley, the Northern Ireland secretary concluded, 'They're neither Conservatives or supporters of the Conservative Party; some of my colleagues failed to appreciate that.' She saw them not as unionists but as 'Ulster nationalists' prone to putting 'short-term tactics over long-term strategy'.[1]

The prime minister launched a charm offensive, inviting every Conservative MP to drinks receptions in Downing Street on 7 and 9 January. MPs found the idea that their votes could be bought with warm white wine more offensive than charming. May saw Labour MPs who Smith thought biddable and even phoned union leaders Len McCluskey of Unite and Tim Roache of the GMB to discuss possible concessions on workers' rights. The prime minister scored one personal success when she called Edward Leigh while he was at church, the Sunday before the vote. Leigh told a friend, 'Poor old duck, I felt the only thing I could do was to support her. I hope my ERG colleagues won't hate me.' Others found May's approach excruciating. 'Switchboard came through and then there was total silence and then this "hello",' another MP recounted. 'It was the PM but I had to lead the conversation. She was very worried about Northern Ireland but it was just horrendously embarrassing.'

The pressure on the rebels felt suffocating in its intensity. 'At times I felt completely trapped,' Julia Lopez recalled. 'The physicality of that place and the pack mentality means that, once pressure is applied, people don't want to be outside the pack. People didn't want the social pressure of not being with the rest of the tribe. People will just fold so that they are with the pack.' She asked herself whether she was now a 'zealot' and concluded it was the Bresisters who were out of step with the country and in a state of 'political denial'. 'All I wanted to do was see a democratic result through and honour the promises made in the manifesto,' she said. 'The fact I was seen as radical for wishing to do so tells you how far we had come down a strange and dark path.'

Colleagues thought Julian Smith's efforts, while near manic in their intensity, were not well targeted. 'The data was too closely held,' a Number 10 aide complained. 'There was never a meeting to go through the spreadsheets and the grids of who was winnable and how to win them. Without data you can't really do a campaign.' Some MPs who might have been winnable said afterwards that they were never even contacted by their whip. An MP said, 'I was told by a whip that they were ordered to only go after the pliable and the buyable.' There was criticism of some younger whips, Jo Churchill and Wendy Morton among them, for 'lecturing people who have been here for twenty years'. Each whip was supposed to do a ring round of their flock – twenty to twenty-four MPs each – every weekend. 'That would take twelve hours,' one said, 'and often the same again to write it all up, but I know some of my colleagues were less diligent about picking up the phone and did things by text.' A senior political adviser to the prime minister said, 'It was an inexperienced and poorly armed whips' office.'

May's inner circle knew the meaningful vote was going to be a massacre. Before the 8.30 a.m. meeting, Smith told the prime minister they were on course to lose by more than 200 votes. She was impassive, the depth of her pain unknowable. She did not think they could delay again. 'We realised we had to eat our greens,' a senior figure recalled.

Last-minute efforts to switch votes were not helped by the leak, in Brussels, of the Commission's briefing to member states on the November deal. This said Barnier's team got 'almost everything' they wanted and that 'what the UK has accepted in terms of the Level Playing Field has never been adopted in an FTA before. It's without precedent when it comes to dynamic alignment, dispute settlement and the possibility to issue autonomous measures in case of non-compliance. Moreover, the outline of the political declaration makes it explicit that the future Level Playing Field must build on these Level Playing Field aspects.'[2]

Emotions boiled over. Nick Boles' constituency chairman received more than a hundred letters from members demanding his removal as MP. Boles also received a death threat from a Brexit supporter. The week before, Anna Soubry had endured shouts of 'Anna Soubry is a Nazi' as she was interviewed on College Green, across the road from the Commons. She was then shouted at and jostled by protesters as she tried to re-enter Parliament. On the other side, Desmond Swain, a Brexiteer, urged May to suspend Parliament altogether until April to 'guarantee Brexit'.

On the morning of the 15th, the day of the vote, the prime minister was distracted, giving her aides and the cabinet little idea about what she would do when she lost. May was not ready to abandon her deal and pivot. 'It's the only option,' she said.[3]

At cabinet, Amber Rudd, Greg Clark, David Gauke and Claire Perry joined forces to pile pressure on May to open talks with moderate Labour

MPs. Jeremy Hunt, Sajid Javid, Brandon Lewis, Liz Truss and Gavin Williamson – the swing voters – plus Liam Fox, opposed the idea. If the government was to survive, they thought May had to find a course that was acceptable to her own party. Rudd continued to insist that no-deal should be taken off the table, or Parliament – via Letwin and Boles – would do so anyway. 'Rather than being led, we should do the leading,' she said.[4]

Another rambunctious courtroom-style performance from Geoffrey Cox at the despatch box did nothing to win over waverers. The attorney general (watched from the public gallery by Wham's Andrew Ridgeley) told MPs that if they failed to support May's deal they would condemn the country to no-deal. This, he predicted, would have voters asking, 'What are you playing at? You are not children in the playground.' Dominic Grieve turned Cox's tradecraft against him: 'Entertaining as it was … it filled me with a slight sense of gloom to see that the government had got to such a pass that it had to rely on the skills of a criminal defence advocate to get it out of its difficulties.'[5]

Bercow called four amendments, among them one from Sir Edward Leigh, which stated that the 'Northern Ireland backstop is temporary' and demanded that 'if the backstop doesn't end by the close of 2021, this will be treated as a fundamental change of circumstances and would terminate the Withdrawal Treaty on 1 January 2022'. Another Brexiteer effort, tabled by John Baron, would give the UK 'the right to terminate the Northern Ireland backstop without the agreement of the EU'. Hugo Swire's amendment, cooked up by Julian Smith to create a parliamentary lock on the backstop, was not called. It had not attracted enough support. 'It flopped so badly it wasn't even good enough to get onto the catwalk,' a minister said. Another gambit had failed.

Quietly, the Tory whips urged MPs to support the Leigh and Baron amendments so that the prime minister could show Brussels the strength of feeling about a sunset clause on the backstop. Leigh was trying to be helpful. Smith had delivered privy councillorships to him and two other grandees, while standing outside a Pret a Manger just before Christmas. The Pret a Manger list was not to deliver as hoped.

While MPs debated inside, the crowds outside in Parliament Square were a carnival of British eccentricity overlaid with an air of menace. A Remain protester brandishing a 'Bollocks to Brexit' banner was chased by Leavers whose slogan was 'Stop the Brexit betrayal'. It was one of those days when history's hand felt heavy, everyone convinced they were choosing the righteous path at a key crossroads for the country. Both Brexiteers and Bresisters felt they could achieve their preferred outcome. They could not both win, but they would both ensure that May lost.

The ERG turned their troops out in force. The day before the vote Syed Kamall, a Tory MEP, called Steve Baker and said, 'They think that she's finished in Europe, if she loses by 50.' Baker replied, 'She's not going to lose by 50, she's going to lose by some multiple of 50. Right now, I'm not absolutely sure whether it'll be three, four or five times that.' On the day Mark Francois, chief of the Buddies whipping system, wrote down his predictions, an upper, middle and lower estimate of the scale of the government defeat. The central number was 217 votes. 'Provided Labour didn't crumble,' he said, 'we knew the government would be walloped.' Julian Smith predicted 426 votes against the government. The impetus to rebel was reinforced; there would be safety in numbers for those who wanted to register their objections. 'Once everyone knows you're going down, you're going to go down badly,' Barwell recalled.[6]

The ERG – Rees-Mogg, Baker and Francois, plus Cash, Jenkin, Paterson and Redwood – twice went to see the chief whip. They found him 'surprisingly upbeat'. Smith asked them what they wanted. 'A free trade deal like Canada's.' The chief whip argued that they could get that from the political declaration: 'Wait for stage two, don't bring the government down.'

They also saw May, who became 'really irritated' by their willingness to trade on World Trade Organisation terms (the no-deal scenario) when what they really wanted was a free trade agreement. An 'exasperated' May, strain evident in her voice, asked, 'How could you possibly be happy with WTO rules when you want FTA rules?' An MP said, 'We wanted an independent country that makes its own laws with a normal, democratic process. The prime minister was focused on economic outcomes.' This was a blunt admission that sovereignty trumped wealth; further evidence that Leavers and Remainers were talking at cross purposes, that it was impossible to put a material value on sovereignty. Some Brexiteers like Baker also believed they could achieve many of the benefits of an FTA by unilaterally cutting tariffs and liberalising the economy. May was 'not on that territory' at all.

There was one straw for the prime minister to cling to in the hurricane. Rees-Mogg also had a private conversation with Smith that day which gave the chief hope that the ERG chairman might one day want a ladder to climb down. 'I think if you've been brought up the Eton way, when someone in authority in your own party asks you to do something, you like to say "yes",' an ERG colleague said. 'Jacob was getting to the point where he wanted to be more helpful. He was very worried the Boles plan could work.' For the moment that was not going to affect his vote.

May could not even keep her payroll vote together. The night before, Gareth Johnson, an assistant whip, resigned to oppose the deal. That afternoon Craig Tracey, a PPS to Penny Mordaunt, resigned, alongside Eddie Hughes, the parliamentary bag carrier for Steve Barclay. Tom Pursglove also quit as a Tory vice chairman to vote against the deal.

Theresa May concluded her speech to MPs, 'With my whole heart I call on this house to discharge that responsibility and I commend this motion to the House.' As the House divided, it was soon clear the government was facing obliteration. The loyalists traipsed desultorily through a quiet Yes lobby. In the packed No lobby, Debbie Abrahams, a Labour MP, captured the chaos in a protocol-defying picture, revealing strange bedfellows rammed together – Iain Duncan Smith, king of the Paleosceptics, sharing a joke with uber-Remainer Tim Farron of the Lib Dems, both tucked in behind Yvette Cooper of the grandee rebels; Graham Brady cheek by jowl with Labour's Vernon Coaker.[7]

Contemplating her first ever rebel vote, Julia Lopez arrived at Westminster tube that morning to be greeted by military old boys collecting money for a veterans' charity. She was handed a bookmark which read, 'Freedom is the sure possession of those alone who have the courage to defend it.' It played on her mind through the day. When the chief whip called at 5.30 p.m., she ignored him; her mind was made up. The rebels from the 2017 intake walked to the No lobby together. As they did so, loyalist Richard Graham remarked, 'Look at them all, heading into the same lobby as Jeremy Corbyn.' Lopez felt strangely unmoved. It was an act of rebellion she had long anticipated. She saw David Evennett and Scott Mann, fanatics neither, and concluded she was in good company.

In the whips' office, Smith's team waited, eyes glued to their WhatsApp group. 'We knew roughly who of ours were going through the lobby,' one said. However, there were so many rebels the whips on the ground could not keep up. They would have to wait for the final number.

In the chamber, the tellers gathered at the despatch box, the government front bench ashen-faced. John Bercow, with the intonation of a hanging judge, repeated the numbers, 'The Ayes to Right, 202. The Noes to the Left, 432.' A majority of 230. It was the single largest government defeat on record. Despite John Mann's promises, just three Labour MPs backed the government. In the whips' office one of those present said to himself, 'Oh fuck, it has happened.' He recalled, 'It's one of those things where you're right but you were seriously hoping you were wrong. You think, "Shit, what is going to happen now? How does she cling on from this?"'

Robbie Gibb referred to it as a 'King Canute situation', May unable to resist the inevitable tide against her. The whips' office had underestimated the number of MPs against them by six. Damian Green, still a May loyalist, recalled, 'We had all vaguely assumed that quite a lot of people would abstain, and in fact literally nobody did. If you are a member of Parliament it's a bit feeble not to take sides on that kind of vote.'[8]

The prime minister got to her feet and made a statement as a point of order. 'The House has spoken and the government will listen,' she said, even less colour than usual in her bloodless cheeks. 'It is clear that the House does not support this deal, but tonight's vote tells us nothing about what it does support.' This was true but hardly struck the note of humility many MPs wanted to hear. There was no warmth towards those she needed to win over. A former cabinet minister said: 'I thought she'd read out the wrong version.' Marina Hyde, the writer who best captured the comic absurdity of the Brexit years, said May 'rose to the occasion like a replicant Anglepoise lamp'.[9] In the chair, Bercow could not believe May's 'sullen defiance'. He wrote later, 'Given the enormity of her defeat, the rejection of what she had negotiated over two years with the EU, it would be reasonable to expect a prime minister, either immediately or very soon, to resign … It was as if she thought that Parliament had misbehaved and needed to learn to do as it was told.'[10]

May did offer to hold talks with Tory MPs, the DUP and 'senior Parliamentarians' from other parties in the days ahead. But her spin doctors told journalists her red lines remained intact and the UK must retain an independent trade policy – something which precluded membership of a customs union. The only concession was to describe these as 'principles' rather than immutable goals, but the message was clear: May's was an offer to talk about how people might agree to agree with her. The offer did not extend to the leader of the opposition. Jeremy Corbyn needed to be clear what he wanted from Brexit before they would sit down with him. Corbyn's response was to say he would not speak to May unless she first ruled out a no-deal Brexit. He had not put such preconditions on talks with Hamas, Hezbollah and the IRA when he was a backbench advocate of reconciliation. Yvette Cooper, who was invited, said talks without the Labour leader were 'ludicrous and unworkable'. Nicola Sturgeon added, 'If none of the PM's red lines change, what progress can she possibly make?'

In her approach to the deal and now in her response to the deal, May's mulish refusal to bend united both sides against her. Nick Boles took to Twitter that night to say people should 'be in no doubt' that May was 'the architect of tonight's defeat'. He said, 'She has approached the Brexit negotiation as if she commanded a majority of 150 in the Commons. She has conducted the argument as if this was a party political matter rather than a question of profound national importance of legitimate concern to all MPs. This must now change. The prime minister has tried to dictate terms to Parliament. She must now accept that Parliament will set the terms of Brexit and it is her job as head of government to deliver them.'

Some cabinet Brexiteers were furious with the ERG for inflicting such a humiliation. Andrea Leadsom warned some that they had 'scuppered Brexit', telling one friend, 'If you had any sense you would not have inflicted a defeat of that size because it suggests to the EU that we are never going to leave and it makes them much less likely to change their position. It humiliated the PM.' She also feared it would embolden her nemesis, Speaker Bercow. Steve Baker was concerned too, that the result would embolden the Bresistance. Even before the vote, he said to Bernard Jenkin, 'I hope we haven't overdone this.'

When the ERG met the following day, the mood was upbeat, but there was also a recognition that the meaningful vote had been only the opening battle and that divisions were opening up between the purists prepared to countenance no-deal – Mark Francois, John Redwood, Bill Cash and Will Wragg – and those who felt there might need to be compromise to prevent no Brexit. Baker spoke about his love of sky-diving: 'You're plummeting to earth. The ground is getting closer and closer and closer and it's in that moment, before the parachute kicks in, that you understand what you're really made of. These coming weeks are going to be tough, and it's then you're going to find out who you are.'

May's instinct was, in Churchill's phrase, to keep buggering on. 'I've just got to get on with it,' she told her aides in Downing Street. The prime minister's resilience never ceased to surprise even long-standing aides like Alex Dawson, who had worked with her at the Home Office: 'I don't know where anyone would get that from. One of the features of being prime minister is that you're not given much time to stew on things, you've got to always keep pressing on.'[11]

The six-week delay from mid-December and Robbins' work to secure the letter from Juncker and Tusk had failed. 'The numbers barely changed,' Julian Smith recalled. 'We gained a few and lost a few.' Afterwards some senior figures concluded it would have been better to go ahead with the meaningful vote in December. 'I think pulling the vote was a mistake,' one of May's Europe advisers said. 'It did not change the outcome. You needed to take that loss and then work through. If we could have got that process done a bit earlier, it might have worked a bit better.' A source close to Smith said, 'It was a wasted six weeks.'

Others surmised later that May should have pulled the meaningful vote again in January and replaced it with a series of indicative votes to identify something which could command a majority. A civil servant said, 'There was a push to say, "Don't go into a meaningful vote process where MPs could have a cost-free vote against the motion." They should have been told to say what their plan was.' Philip Hammond said, 'Theresa May made her last big strategic mistake in pushing to a vote. There's something about Theresa that sees the romantic notion of charging into the valley even though you know you're going down to certain defeat. She sometimes confused stubbornness with heroism.' He believed she should have 'conserved her powder', made a 'tactical withdrawal' and 'sought to look at ways of engaging parts of the opposition'.[12]

The disaster of 15 January would be known in Westminster as 'MV1'. May's team had suffered their Isandlwana. They prayed they could make a stand like the defenders of Rorke's Drift at MV2. Yet the more fatalistic among them focused on another document Seldon had brought from the National Archives – a letter written in invisible ink by Henry Garnett, a Jesuit priest who had become embroiled in the Gunpowder Plot. He was hung, drawn and quartered.

In the short term, though, a relief column appeared from two unlikely sources: Jeremy Corbyn and Michael Gove.

A WAY OUT?

The Malthouse Compromise

17 to 28 January 2019

On Thursday 17 January, the leader of the opposition finally tabled a formal vote of no confidence in the government. Labour activists had been demanding Jeremy Corbyn act ever since May's crushing defeat in the meaningful vote two days earlier. Corbyn's team bowed to the pressure from the Twitterati. Experienced hands, including Labour's chief whip Nick Brown, judged it a mistake. 'He thought it was a bit nuts,' said one confidant. The government was on the run but even those who voted against May's deal were not going to vote to eject her now.

The tactical mistake was elevated to a rout by an inspired idea from Julian Smith, who suggested that Michael Gove make the closing speech for the government. May did not trust Gove, but the chief whip argued that he was her team's best debater and now was not a moment for faint hearts. Gavin Barwell approached Gove.

The day was one of fake theatricals, the result never really in doubt. Corbyn went through the motions on May's Brexit mistakes: 'Two years of chaos and failure', 'a national embarrassment', 'shambles', before concluding, 'This government cannot govern and cannot command the support of Parliament on the most important issue facing our country. Every previous prime minister in this situation would have resigned and called an election.' May rejected a general election as 'the worst thing we could do', arguing 'it would deepen division when we need unity, it would bring chaos when we need certainty, and it would bring delay when we need to move forward'. Both leaders were forgettable.

When Mark Spencer, Steve Baker's long-suffering whip, asked him whether he would be in the 'correct lobby on the confidence vote', Baker had some fun, texting back: 'We are voting "aye", right?' Spencer eventually saw the funny side. On the day, Baker presented himself twenty minutes early at the No lobby, a dutiful government foot soldier for the first time in three years.

Gove rose at the despatch box just before 7 p.m., a wry smile playing on his lips as he regarded his prey, the snaggle-toothed leader of her majesty's opposition. What followed was a bravura blast of sound and fury which eviscerated Corbyn and united the Tory benches in a near delirious catharsis. Armed only with a few bullet points plus notes jotted during the debate, the environment secretary teased Tom Watson, Labour's deputy leader, who was squashed awkwardly next to Corbyn, noting that Watson had not once mentioned Corbyn in his closing speech. Gove made only one ritual reference to 'the prime minister's inspirational leadership', before a five-minute dismantling of Corbyn's record on national security, tying together the three episodes which had poisoned the Labour leader's reputation: Salisbury, Syria and antisemitism. 'In fighting fascism, he was present but not involved,' Gove crowed, throwing Corbyn's explanation for the Black September wreath-laying back at him. The Labour benches, initially quiescent, rose to a crescendo of fury. Gove shouted into the gale: 'If he will not stand up for this country when the critical national security questions are being asked, how can we possibly expect him to stand up for us in European negotiations? ... We cannot have confidence in him to lead. We have confidence in this Government!' As he sat down, the Conservative benches were a forest of waved order papers. May patted Gove on the back. The speech transformed the morale of a party drifting towards manic depression, reminding Tory MPs that, even now, more united them than divided them and that the stakes were high on Brexit, since they might let in a foe they regarded as a genuine menace.

With the DUP's support, May got 325 votes to 306 for the opposition.

As Gove also intended, his performance catapulted him back into contention as a credible leadership candidate. A cabinet colleague remarked acidly, 'I notice he chose to attack Corbyn rather than defend the PM.' But in Downing Street they were grateful. On the Labour benches it confirmed many in the view that their leader was guiding his party to disaster. Elsewhere in the House, Gove's punishment beating reinforced the conviction that Corbyn could not be a rallying point for opposition to the government on Brexit. Afterwards, May's aides had a 'jolly' gathering in the foyer of Number 10, supping red wine from a stash of bottles put aside by Stephen Parkinson.

On Monday 21st, May tabled a 'neutral motion', acknowledging that MPs had voted a week earlier to force her to explain her next steps. The most significant amendment to this was that tabled by Yvette Cooper and Nick Boles, giving MPs the right to seize control of the Commons agenda. There was talk that twenty ministers were demanding a free vote. The same request had been issued to May by Andrew Mitchell, a former chief whip, on Thursday 17th. He suggested that would make it easier to attract Labour votes, just as a previous Tory prime minister had done over European issues. 'Ted Heath was finally persuaded in 1973 to lift the whip, which allowed Roy Jenkins to bring over sixty people,' he said.

To its critics the Cooper-Boles amendment was a radical departure from constitutional norms, but Dominic Grieve had actually stepped back from an even more revolutionary plan, which would have seen Parliament propose and pass legislation to hold a new referendum. The complication was that a referendum is an expensive business and would have required a 'money resolution' of the House. Cooper-Boles did not require spending beyond the established threshold of £250,000. Grieve went to see the clerks to discuss the idea. They told him the rule, set out in Standing Order 48, was that money couldn't be spent 'unless recommended from the crown', which in practice meant the government.

'Can we change that?' he asked.

The clerk looked at him in what Grieve was to describe as 'a very clerky way', and replied, 'Well, yes, but you do understand that this order has been in the House of Commons standing orders since 1713 and is in fact a reflection of a royal prerogative right. In its current form, it goes back to the restoration of Charles II in 1660. The last time Parliament did this was when it set up its own government during the civil war by committee with the king in Oxford.' In essence, Grieve could try to change the rules, but to do so would be a revolutionary act by Parliament on a par with the declaration of the English civil war, which would have been open to legal challenge by the government. Grieve baulked at becoming a pin-striped Oliver Cromwell. Another senior Bresister said, 'Dominic, although he knew how to do it, would not do it because he said it didn't feel right and it would open the doors to all sorts of things that could be used against governments in the future. There was self-restraint, even in all this constitutional innovation. Quite often he'd say, "There is a way you can do this, but it would be the end of the British constitution."'

May's team war-gamed their own options for a way forward. The civil service pressed hard to set up formal cross-party talks, not something, at this stage, that was supported by the political team. 'There was a whacko note from officials that going completely cross-party might move things on,' said one of those who opposed a deal with Labour. 'We pushed back on that.'

Outreach to a limited number of opposition MPs was led by David Lidington and Michael Gove. They targeted minor party leaders and select committee chairmen. The talks did not go well. The two cabinet ministers failed to identify enough Labour MPs who might back May's deal, in part because they were not empowered to do a deal. 'We didn't know what her bottom lines were,' said one. 'It's like being asked to bid for something, not knowing whether you can offer £5,000 or £50,000.' Labour MPs also found the Tories naive. 'They didn't have a sense of the state of thinking in the PLP,' one said. Internally, Gavin Barwell advanced the case that permanent membership of the customs union was the compromise which could win a majority in the Commons. But Lidington and Gove were not given licence by May to press this option and they returned from their conversations with Labour MPs unconvinced that even this would get the votes. Those who might have backed a customs union, even in the spring of 2018, were now backing a second referendum.

It was an option that May's Europe advisers, Ed de Minckwitz and Denzil Davidson, were now prepared to contemplate. They wrote May their 'most candid note' ever. It detailed how she still had a 'mandate for Brexit' but, thanks to Parliament, no mandate for her deal. They met May in her Downing Street office in the week of the meaningful vote, when the scale of the looming defeat was clear. De Minckwitz did not want another referendum, but he argued that the prime minister should use the power of her office and 'get a public mandate for her deal'. He believed it was the only thing which could save the Conservative Party. No-deal would split the party. Allowing Parliament to block Brexit would be 'absolutely toxic'. A source said, 'Ed hated the idea of a referendum, but he determined that her premiership was going to end, that it was likely to end without her delivering Brexit and if she wanted to deliver Brexit, that was the best chance she had – to ask the country to vote for *her* Brexit.'

He and Davidson offered a way of selling the idea to voters. One said, 'She could have said, "Politicians are blocking Brexit, we've let you down. We cannot as a Parliament solve this for you. I the PM am talking to you the people to ask you to give me the mandate to solve this problem. I think this is the right Brexit, it protects your jobs, it protects your security."' All the polling evidence suggested that when May levelled with the public it resonated well with voters. The memo also talked about the customs union, but both aides realised even the words were now toxic.

May stuck to her guns: 'That's not something we are going to do.' But those who were there say this was not immediate. She had 'let the idea percolate'. The conversation was one of the few occasions when May was forced to confront a range of unpalatable choices. 'For the first time in a very long time she let herself think about what would happen if she couldn't bring herself to do it,' one of those present recalled.

De Minckwitz and Davidson looked down the path, as advisers should. They saw looming failure and sought a way to change course. That was not May's way. 'She's totally opposite,' one said. 'While there is still a path forward she will go until she hits that wall. She won't choose to make a diversion because she sees something three steps ahead.' Heroic or stubborn, it was bad politics.

Some ministers were not averse to getting voters to break the deadlock, but, like Jeremy Hunt, wanted a general election rather than a referendum. Yet this wasn't really an option either for May. 'She literally just won a no-confidence vote saying she won't fight the next election and that she won't call a snap election,' a senior Tory pointed out.

Allies thought, in extremis, she would have to accept Barwell's approach. 'She will accept a customs union but only by Parliament forcing it on her,' one said. This was certainly the view of the ERG, who saw little difference between May's deal and a full-blown customs union in any case. One ERGer dismissed Liam Fox, Andrea Leadsom and other cabinet Brexiteers who were vocally opposed to a customs union: 'Newsflash: you've literally already signed up for it.'

In opposing a referendum, May sided with Julian Smith and Brandon Lewis, the party chairman, who warned that a second vote would terminally split the Tory party. Peril to her party was always a persuasive argument for May. 'The thing that she cares about most is the Conservative Party,' said one friend. 'She doesn't have kids. She's spent her life having dinners and lunches with party members.' The party was May's family. However, a strong leader might have taken all but the ERG hardcore and much of the nation with her. May was not only opposed to a referendum as a point of principle, she was also temperamentally incapable of such a bold gambit and lacked the political skills to carry it off. Ultimately, she chose to drive headfirst into the wall.

Internationally there was stasis. On the evening of Thursday 17 January and the morning of 18 January, May spoke to Merkel, Rutter, Juncker and Tusk, continuing to insist the UK would leave on 29 March and repeating her previous demands. 'That didn't go down very well,' a Tory source admitted.

There was talk of converting the backstop into a separate bilateral treaty between Britain and Ireland. This might have satisfied the DUP and the ERG, but would have been political suicide for Leo Varadkar, who held cross-party unity in Ireland together with an uncompromising stance. 'He's dead if he moves,' said one who discussed the idea with Dublin.

Influenced by her husband Philip, who believed that talking to Labour would sink the Tory party, May worked on her own MPs, inviting groups into Number 10. To Brexiteers she seemed immovable. 'She looked unfazed,' said one. 'She'd just racked up the biggest defeat of all time. I would look like shit. She just looked blank. I think May just has one mode, which is stubbornness. I think she thought, "I can grind these buggers down." She had the clock and she was going to just wait until we gave in, essentially.'

The prime minister eventually decided to invite members of the ERG and pragmatic Remainers to Chequers, hoping that a third summit at the country retreat would achieve the unity which had eluded her at the first two. She did so, significantly, without her chief whip. 'It was her showing she could just get on with things,' a Downing Street source said.

Over Sunday lunch on 20 January, lubricated with 'a nice burgundy', May consulted Jacob Rees-Mogg, Steve Baker, her old friend Damian Green and Nicky Morgan, who had also shown a willingness to compromise. Rees-Mogg and Morgan had been at Oxford together. May was 'the most relaxed I had seen her in a long time,' said one MP. She showed Rees-Mogg Oliver Cromwell's life mask which resides in a drawer in the upstairs gallery.

However, her guests saw a prime minister who still did not understand where the Brexiteers were coming from. 'We were talking about border security and having French border guards stationed in the UK,' the MP remembered. May dismissed the idea as 'unacceptable', only for Steve Baker to interject, 'I don't mind that.'

'Pardon, what did you say?' a confused May said.

Baker explained, 'The point is if we, the UK, have taken the decision to allow French border guards on our territory, we've taken the decision.' The MP said, 'At that point, the penny dropped. She didn't understand what was important to them.'

Morgan asked Rees-Mogg and Baker directly, 'Do you actually want to hold the party together?' Both swore they did. Another participant recalled, 'She [May] asked us to go away and come up with something that we can all agree on.'

The goodwill engendered at Chequers III immediately fed into a similar initiative by Kit Malthouse, the housing minister, who had previously served as a deputy mayor to Boris Johnson in London. Malthouse, fifty-two, had voted Leave but was a bridge builder. He did not believe the hardliners would be able to force no-deal and he had seen May's Chequers agreement as a way of preventing chaos.

Earlier that week, Malthouse was on the phone to Daniel Moylan, who had run transport in the capital for Johnson. 'It's all falling apart. No one is talking to anybody,' he complained. 'People are sitting at separate tables in the tearoom. We are heading for a catastrophic split.' Moylan suggested, 'Why don't you do something about it?' Malthouse wasn't sure. As a pro-deal Leaver he thought most of his colleagues had 'a special place in hell for me'. But with the cabinet 'sitting on their arses', it would not hurt to try. With Moylan's help he summarised the problem: Remainers were worried about *no*-deal, Leavers were worried about *the* deal, which created a tradeable position.

Malthouse had been on the Treasury select committee with Rees-Mogg, Baker, Morgan and Stephen Hammond, which created mutual understanding that could be exploited. The day after Chequers III, he approached Rees-Mogg and Morgan. Rees-Mogg recruited Robert Buckland. Malthouse invited them to come to his office, Room 34 on the lower ministerial corridor, for a chat. The most elusive was Baker, who failed to respond to Malthouse's texts. The housing minister physically chased him around the Parliamentary estate, missing him by two minutes at the Treasury committee and then again at Baker's office. In the end he was cornered and agreed to attend.

They met that Monday 21 January, in conditions of deep secrecy. Malthouse began with his fears: 'The Party's heading for a catastrophic split. That will result in a defeat in the next general election, the possibility of a Corbyn government and Brexit possibly evaporating completely.' Everyone accepted his premise. To sweeten the pill, Malthouse 'always had this vast bowl of assorted chocolates'. It was full of Quality Street and Chocolate Oranges Malthouse had 'confiscated from my children at Christmas'. He recalled, 'They were slightly over their sell-by-date by then but it's a tradition in my family to give Chocolate Oranges so they ended up with something like six each.' His children's loss was the Conservative Party's gain. The MPs dug in enthusiastically. In the Chocolate Orange summit, Malthouse tentatively suggested that they strike a mutually agreeable two-stage agreement. Most importantly, 'We remade the friendship,' Malthouse recounted. Sealing their new alliance in the now customary fashion, they set up a WhatsApp group called 'Room 34'.

Over the next eight days there were further gatherings, the group dodging in and out of other meetings. Sometimes they were all there, sometimes just a few of them, but Malthouse ensured both wings of the party were always present. He cajoled each side with individual messages and calls, occasionally meeting one-on-one to ensure everyone was happy. He told a friend later, 'It was a proper Israeli-Palestinian-style negotiation. You needed to talk separately, you needed to build trust.' His mission: what could Remain give to Leave on no-deal so that Leave could support Remain on getting a deal?

The most active Brexiteer was Baker, who saw an opportunity to win support for an idea he had been developing for a managed no-deal, something he christened 'clean managed Brexit'. Between the first and second meeting, on the Tuesday, Baker sent an outline of his 'better deal' plan, complete with links and a legal text. The natural landing place for the two sides when discussing a better Northern Ireland Protocol was

better use of technology to minimise border checks: alternative arrangements. By Wednesday 23rd they had the outline of a deal.

Under the scheme, the EU would be offered a choice between two variants of the withdrawal agreement: Plan A and Plan B, two ends of what
Malthouse dubbed a 'dumbbell deal'. Plan A was basically the old
Max-Fac alternative to the backstop, with a free trade deal and 'proven
solutions' to avoid border checks. Under this approach, the transition
period would also be extended for another year until the end of December
2021 to allow more time to agree a trade deal.

    Plan B was basically Steve Baker's idea for a managed no-deal exit,
which would extend the transition until December 2021 to give both
sides time to prepare for Britain to leave on WTO terms. In the meantime, the EU would allow Britain to have a transition period (which was
only supposed to be available in the event of a deal) in exchange for the
UK continuing to make its usual financial contributions to Brussels and
continuing to recognise the rights of EU citizens living in Britain – essentially 'pay as you go' membership of the EU. Malthouse said, 'We got the
dynamic of the negotiation wrong, in that we were the ones who were
being given hard choices, not the other way around. The power of
Malthouse was that Plan A and Plan B put the choice back in the EU's
court. It said, "Here you are, two deals. We'll take either. You choose."'

    Plan A had already been rejected by the EU and Plan B contained
elements that were unacceptable to them, but joining them up was, at
least, evidence that both wings of the party were trying to think crea-
tively. Two unicorns had, in effect, been roped together. The question
was whether May would saddle up and attempt to ride this new contraption.

    Winning over the ERG was relatively straightforward since Baker and
Rees-Mogg were trusted to deliver something acceptable. On Thursday
24th, having deliberately kept him out of the room until the deal was
done, they both saw Iain Duncan Smith to get him on side. Morgan and
Buckland had a harder time since the Remainers were a less coherent
group and opinions diverged more widely. Buckland ran the idea past
David Lidington. Stephen Hammond talked to other ministers. 'They
were more nervous than the Brexiteers,' one recalled.

    The same day, Morgan approached Number 10 and said they wished
to see May. Malthouse was out of town on a ministerial visit so Morgan,

Hammond, Baker and Rees-Mogg went in at 2 p.m. The prime minister, accompanied by Julian Smith and JoJo Penn, appeared 'blindsided'. One MP said, 'Steve said what we had come up with and she was furious. She told him it was all impractical and wrong.' She was 'genuinely cross' that the Chequers lunch had borne fruit distasteful to her. 'We were not meant to come up with a new scheme. We were meant to have gone away and decided that what she had proposed in the first place was marvellous. Kit deserves a huge amount of credit for this because with any sensible, imaginative prime minister, it was a way out.' Another witness said, 'Theresa May's response to anything that wasn't her deal was, "I'm not interested, you should be backing me and not the other way around."'

The gang met in Room 34 that evening. Since he was a sitting minister, Stephen Hammond had become 'queasy' about working with Rees-Mogg and Baker, so Morgan recruited Damian Green to replace him. Still nothing had leaked and they widened the circle of trust to include Simon Hart, leader of the Brexit Delivery Group, a large group of centrist backbenchers who mostly voted to remain but believed Brexit had to be delivered. Malthouse, Baker and Buckland then went together to see the chief whip. Smith was enthusiastic. He had devised a plan of his own to unite the party and the two schemes were not incompatible. 'I'll set the wheels in motion,' he said.

The next day, Friday 25th, Lidington told Morgan the government was looking at the plans and urged her not to go public yet. The Malthouse group spent the weekend holding conference calls with MPs to 'cascade' the idea through the party just as Smith's whips were doing their weekend ring around. 'We should plough our own furrow,' said Morgan. She wanted a groundswell of support, not one dictated from above. 'The best thing would be for people to tell the whips that they like the plan.' From different wings of the party Remainer Nicholas Soames and Leaver Kemi Badenoch came on board. Baker, a one-man secretariat, produced a 'lines to take' document to explain the plan. Malthouse spoke to Gavin Barwell. By Sunday, Tobias Ellwood and Richard Harrington were encouraging. Michael Gove was supportive and agreed to talk to Nick Boles. Matt Hancock texted saying he would 'proselytise in cabinet'. At 9 p.m. the Malthousers had another conference call and agreed to draw up draft amendments to table. Buckland spoke to Geoffrey Cox, the attorney general, to let him know the plan.

*   *   *

Julian Smith's plan to bring the party together was an amendment stating that Parliament would approve May's deal with Brussels, subject to replacing the backstop 'with alternative arrangements to avoid a hard border'. The approach was designed to demonstrate to Brussels the circumstances in which May could secure the necessary support, but it was necessarily vague. The idea had come from a strategy memo written by Raoul Ruparel to Gavin Barwell. 'I wrote an email about the few things we could do and one of them was try and pass an amendment like this to get the party on side,' Ruparel said. 'To bring people together but also show the EU that there was a majority for something.' He would have liked it to be more specific to give May a greater mandate but Smith wanted something broad to maximise votes.

The chief approached Mark Harper, a former chief whip who he thought could be an honest broker, asking him to front the amendment but Harper 'didn't want to get his hands dirty,' a source recalled. 'He bottled it.' Graham Brady, chairman of the 1922 Committee, was more enthusiastic, 'gagging for it', in fact. The shop steward of the backbenches put his name to what became known as 'the Brady amendment'. A senior Tory said, 'Graham was served it on a plate and got a huge amount of publicity out of it.' Taking its place alongside Cooper-Boles, various Grieve amendments and the Benn Act, the Brady amendment was one of a series of legislative efforts which followed the tradition in American politics of labelling initiatives after congressional sponsors, rather than their substance. 'There was a snowball effect where everyone wanted an amendment or a plan,' one of May's senior political aides moaned later.

On Monday 28th, armed with amendments which had been written with the help of the clerks, the Malthouse group saw the prime minister again. She acted as if the initiative was a challenge to her authority. To Baker, her face was a 'glare of rage' and in that instant the bizarre thought occurred to him: *She's got nuclear weapons!* When she spoke May was coldly noncommittal: 'We'll look at it, but it's a question of what is negotiable with the EU.'

Malthouse pushed. 'The party wants specifics now, Prime Minister, and this is a specific proposal.'

She replied, 'We'll think about it and take it away.'

* * *

The ERG met at 4.15 p.m. that day, 28 January, in the Wilson Room to discuss whether to back the Brady amendment or not. Rees-Mogg, Baker and Francois all thought it a trap.

May faced the 1922 Committee soon afterwards. It was clear she was at the end of her rope with the parliamentary party. Brady, presiding over the meeting in Parliament, could see something had to give: 'She is dogged … She will fight her corner until it can't possibly be defended. She'd reached that point … There needed to be a new position.'[1] Smith could see it too. He passed May a handwritten note saying she should commit the government to whipping support for the Brady amendment. The prime minister knew such a move would lay her open to criticism, perhaps even ridicule, in Brussels but the government needed a win. After a few minutes' delay, she made the commitment. The Brady amendment was now effectively the government's amendment.

Adopting it was consistent with James Johnson's polling. In his monthly meeting with May, Number 10's pollster revealed voters were now 'actively ambivalent' about the substance of the deal. 'They just want the thing done,' he said. Attitudes were also changing in Europe. On the plus side for May, fewer people believed that prolonging the process would cause Britain to reconsider and stay in the EU. A cabinet minister said, 'Last year there was a belief, especially in the Élysée, that "Let's just hold on and they could have a second referendum and change their minds and stay." I don't think that is where they are now.' On the downside for May, key power brokers in Brussels were less likely to give her concessions because they thought she was finished.

To the Brexiteers, at the back of the room, May commanded only around a third of the party, a cheering section gathered at the front. Her decision to whip the Brady amendment felt staged. 'The sycophants cheered,' one said. 'She really was the most appalling actor.' Boris Johnson intervened but his contribution was not focused and it descended into a pantomime of shouted comments by both Johnson and May. 'Unlike you, Boris, I don't give up,' she glared.

Julia Lopez, whose back was against the rear wall, bristled and thought of two conversations she had that weekend. The first had been with Simon Clarke, who had imparted details of the Malthouse deal to her. The second came at a Holocaust Memorial Day service, where an elderly Jewish man had confided in her how he had conquered a fear of public speaking, one she shared. 'It's the message that is important, not the self,' he said. Lopez put up her hand and was called to speak, her heart beating like a jackhammer. 'What is happening to our party is sad, but what's happening to our country is even sadder.' Heads turned, all eyes on her now. 'Yesterday, I was told about a plan where both Remainers and Brexiteers had come together with an idea on the route forward that could unite the party. I just want to ask you, Prime Minister, why are you not taking up that plan?' Lopez didn't hear May's response, blood thumping in her ears, adrenaline coursing through her body. Some colleagues patted her on the back. Baker sent her a message full of happy emojis. Later, Nicky Morgan texted to thank her. An MP close to May also congratulated her and asked to meet to explain what had happened. 'The civil service – Olly Robbins – dismissed the idea, as has Barwell,' the MP explained. 'Others supported the plan and the PM seemed receptive.' This was generous to May.

Lopez went for dinner at Jacob Rees-Mogg's house, a stone's throw from Parliament, where Boris Johnson was setting out his leadership stall twice a week to groups of ten MPs. Simon Clarke did the inviting and groups of MPs were plied with beef or veal, decent red wine, plus Rees-Mogg's preferred puddings – 'chocolatey things with lots of cream'. Johnson, seeking to impress, did not drink. As leader he would talk more about policing and low taxes and pitched himself as an enthusiastic and effective campaigner. Rees-Mogg also asked the MPs for advice about what to do about the Brady amendment. Lopez suggested, 'Let's make our support conditional on her putting into place the Malthouse strategy.' When the MPs returned to the House for a late vote, she ran into Steve Barclay, the Brexit secretary, who left her with the impression that May had not told him about her conversations with the Malthouse team.

Suddenly that evening, Nicky Morgan put the details of the Malthouse plan into the main Conservative MPs' WhatsApp group. She said it 'provides for exit from the EU on time with a new backstop, which would be acceptable indefinitely, but which incentivises us all to reach a new future relationship. It ensures there is no need for a hard border with Ireland.' Within minutes the plan had leaked to the media. Seated in the members' lobby, Malthouse, Baker and Buckland found their phones buzzing. 'This is going crazy,' said Malthouse. 'What are we going to call it?' They tried 'The Room 34 Proposals'. Baker, with a flourish, christened it 'The Malthouse Compromise', which conveyed a certain grandeur. He tweeted it out. 'It took off,' Malthouse recalled. 'I became a GCSE politics question overnight.'

On the day, the steering group of ERG met and agreed that they would only vote for the unity amendment if Downing Street embraced the Malthouse model. By noon Jacob Rees-Mogg had communicated this view to the chief whip. When May opened the debate for the government, she took a question from Nicky Morgan about Malthouse and called it 'a serious proposal that we are engaging with sincerely and positively'. In the final speech from the government benches, Steve Barclay said, 'We will take forward the spirit of goodwill on which it builds, as part of reaching the common ground the House needs.'

John Bercow accepted seven amendments. Those tabled by the Labour front bench and the SNP were defeated easily. A bid by Dominic Grieve to force 'indicative votes' went down by 321 votes to 301. An amendment by Rachel Reeves to delay Brexit if there was no-deal also failed. Yvette Cooper's amendment, promoting the Cooper-Boles bill, which had been hotly tipped to pass when first announced, also failed, by 321 votes to 298. Despite Bercow controversially clearing the way for the amendment, the proposal was a victim of its specifics. When Boles' The European Union (Withdrawal) (No. 2) Bill had been presented as a private member's bill on 15 January, it contained a nine-month delay, until 31 December 2019 – too long for Brexiteers and not long enough for Remainers. Cooper's amendment offered the same date. Six days later a modified version, The European Union (Withdrawal) (No. 3) Bill was introduced by Cooper. It required the government to seek an extension, but let ministers decide its length. The constitutional revolution would have to wait.

Two amendments did pass. The first was a broad-brush rejection of no-deal, tabled by Tory Caroline Spelman and Labour's Jack Dromey, which won 318–310, in part because it made no specific provisions.

The final vote that night was for the Brady amendment. For the only time in the period between the Chequers deal and her departure from Number 10, May's MPs marched, nearly united, into the same division lobby. The air of relief was palpable. Simon Hart, head of the Brexit Delivery Group, and Mark Francois of the ERG, old friends who had barely been speaking, embraced in the lobby. 'The sense in the division lobby when Brady delivered his victory was fantastic,' a minister said. 'It was like some heady nightclub.' A Number 10 adviser said, 'It was the most significant time that the chief whip got the say on EU policy over Olly Robbins. We need a win. Let's get it done. Boom. Done.' Malthouse ran into Iain Martin, a political columnist with *The Times* who had voted to Leave. 'God, you've saved Brexit!' he exclaimed.

But even at the point of victory Julian Smith wondered if it was a false dawn. He said later, 'By pretending the marriage was not on the rocks, you then ended up prolonging the agony a bit.'

Pro-dealers thought Morgan and Buckland were human shields for what was essentially an ERG scheme. Anna Soubry, who had once been best friends with Morgan, was scathing: 'This scheme backed by Jacob Rees-Mogg is a recipe for the no-deal Brexit that the hard Brexiters have always craved.' The Bresisters were shocked when Morgan, one of the first opponents of May's approach, voted against the Cooper amendment. Fellow MPs heard Soubry 'snarl' at her in the chamber, complaining about her 'new friends'. Boles deleted Morgan from his WhatsApp groups, an act both futile and symbolic. A Malthouser who had known Boles for years hit back, 'Nick's view of compromise seemed to be that you were compromising if you agreed with him – anything else was not a compromise.' Critics played the woman as well as the ball. 'Nicky just panicked,' a Labour Bresister said. 'She became universally disliked because she took part in all the rebellions, all the conversations and then took the silver shilling and reneged.' Those, like Morgan, who prized their pragmatism, found themselves ostracised by both camps.

There was initially cabinet support for the Malthouse Compromise, with even Amber Rudd prepared to countenance the plan. 'The only person who definitely wasn't enthusiastic was Hammond,' a Malthouser recalled. 'But Hammond wasn't enthusiastic about anything.' However, the PM's inner circle thought it would never be accepted by Brussels. Barwell said, 'Those of us who understood the policy positions were clear that what was being asked for was never going to be achievable.'[2] JoJo Penn agreed: 'I don't think we experienced, at any stage, an indication from the Commission or the negotiators that it would be a possible negotiated outcome.'[3] A minister said, 'We spent ages unpicking [it].'

The death knell of the Malthouse Compromise in Whitehall would be sounded in a memo written to May by Raoul Ruparel on 13 February, copied to twenty-two senior Number 10 staff. It was written after officials held three two-hour sessions with the rebels. It detailed four problems. Malthouse 'required a change in interpretation of the Joint Report' so that

Britain ditched the agreement that there be 'no physical infrastructure or related checks and controls' in Ireland and commit only not to have them 'at the border'. This is perhaps what May should have agreed in December 2017, but it was not what she had signed up to. Second, the proposals 'require significant changes to EU and international law' that made it unlikely the EU would agree. On agrifoods, Malthouse required the EU to 'do away entirely' with border inspection posts. Third, the paper said that, even if the EU accepted these changes, there 'are still questions about whether they are practical and could be implemented in reality', with every farmer on the island of Ireland required to 'make declarations for all their movements of animal products'. Fourth, the rebels wanted small- and medium-sized businesses exempted from customs declarations, something the EU had rejected in November. 'The EU's opposition to the concept of an exemption [was] not practical but ideological/theological around the integrity of the single market,' wrote Ruparel, who also detailed how the plan would change the 'way of life' in Northern Ireland and have 'potential security implications'. Officials from the Police Service of Northern Ireland and Border Force were brought in to make this argument, but the rebels were 'quite dismissive' of the threats of violence since Owen Paterson and Theresa Villiers, both former Northern Ireland secretaries, told them the 'concerns are overblown'.[4]

The paper recommended that the government continue discussions with the rebels, not to make their plans work, but to expose them to the problems so they backed down. Ruparel advised 'keeping Plan A alive' (alternative arrangements) so the 'EU can demonstrate that Plan A does not work now but can do in the future'. Second, he said the government should pursue 'discussions with the group on Plan B' (Baker's no-deal proposal) 'to demonstrate the difficulties of it'.

In the end it was not enough that the two wings of the Conservative Party came to an agreement. That might have been sufficient in 2016, 2017 or even 2018. But two months into 2019 May was locked in four-dimensional chess with the factions in Westminster and Brussels. A Number 10 political aide said, 'You need[ed] to get Jean-Claude Juncker, Angela Merkel, Emmanuel Macron, Donald Tusk, Jacob Rees-Mogg, Andrew Bridgen, Bob Neill, Lisa Nandy, Gareth Snell and Nicky Morgan to all agree the best way for the UK.'

The Malthouse Compromise ended up being a political gesture rather than a negotiating breakthrough. Yet it perfectly encapsulated a key theme of the Brexit process: presented with a political stick to wield (however imperfect), May's punctiliousness prevented her from picking it up. 'She didn't want there to be a perception that there were any other options,' a Malthouser reflected. 'It was her deal, or doom.' The prime minister could well have been right that, in January and February 2019, with her authority shot, the proposal was not something the EU would accept. But it is also true that some of what was proposed in the Malthouse Compromise would form the basis of border arrangements by 2022 – and she did not try.

By 27 February, each of the Malthouse group would conclude the prime minister needed to go. One complained. 'We were begging her to just lead where her party wishes to go – and she wouldn't.' May was locked in a stand-off with backbench rebels, a battle she was ill-prepared to win. As Baker said to Malthouse that month, 'If you're in a Mexican stand-off you need to be sure you're the maddest Mexican.'

By then, MPs in the Labour Party who were equally disgruntled by their leader had concluded they needed to jump ship altogether.

WALK OUT

Labour, Brexit and the Breakaway

January 2018 to 25 February 2019

Since it began with a former vicar, it was fitting that the final preparations were made in a church on a Sunday. It was 17 February when seven Labour MPs gathered in a meeting room at St Martin in the Fields, Charing Cross. Gavin Shuker, a man of the cloth before he became the MP for Luton South, was their spiritual leader, the prophet who had shown them the way. Before them was a 'statement of independence' announcing their departure from the Labour Party, to be unveiled the next morning. They hoped it would emulate the Limehouse declaration of 1981 in which the Gang of Four – Roy Jenkins, David Owen, Shirley Williams and Bill Rodgers – gave birth to the SDP. It was simultaneously self-excommunication from a church they no longer believed in and a faith-based leap into a future they hoped could offer something better. To a significant degree it was a cleavage created by Brexit.

It was the silence of Chuka Umunna, who most outsiders perceived as the leading force in the gang, which gave them away. Not one normally to take a Trappist vow with the media, the former shadow business secretary ignored journalists bombarding him with text messages. Kevin Schofield, who most of the Labour right had on speed dial, tweeted, 'Been trying Chuka for hours and no response. Ominous.'

At 8 a.m. the next day, journalists received an email asking them to assemble at 10 a.m. for an announcement by Labour MPs on 'the future of British politics'. When the lobby assembled, seven orange stools stood empty. The door opened and through it walked Shuker, Luciana Berger, Chris Leslie, Mike Gapes, Angela Smith, Ann Coffey and Umunna.

The timing had been defined by the imminence of Berger giving birth. She was the moral core of the group and the most photogenic – a victim of racist abuse from antisemites in Labour ranks. She spoke first: 'I have become embarrassed and ashamed to remain in the Labour Party. I cannot remain in a party that I have today come to the sickening conclusion is institutionally antisemitic.'

Chris Leslie, with Shuker the driving force of the split, made the other central argument: 'In all conscience, we can no longer knock on doors and support a government led by Jeremy Corbyn or the team around him. The evidence of Labour's betrayal on Europe is now visible for all to see.'

The seven were the inner core, but there had been many fellow travellers who fell away, one MP put it, like the outer layers of a nest of 'Russian dolls'. Between thirty and forty moderate Labour MPs had begun gathering every three or four months in 2016 over 'gorgeous' shepherd's pie in the Covent Garden home of Waheed Alli, a Labour peer and TV entrepreneur, to discuss the state of the party under Corbyn. Having failed to keep Labour out of the clutches of the hard left, they regarded themselves as the 'grown-ups': Margaret and Siobhain McDonagh (close friends with Alli), Leslie, Michael Dugher, John Spellar, Yvette Cooper, Ian Austin, Ian Murray, Margaret Hodge, Graham Jones, Joan Ryan, Rushanara Ali and Kevin Barron. The first gathering was on Alli's birthday, so naturally their WhatsApp group was called 'The Birthday Club'. Angela Smith had to download the app so she could join the discussion. Others were soon invited, among them Mike Gapes, the MP for Ilford South. It swelled to as many as eighty MPs.

They soon fell into two broad camps. 'There was a group who were completely fed up and others who thought, "We can change it, we can moderate him, we can change his position",' one MP recalled. 'Everybody thought he was a disaster – the question was how you deal with it. There were lots of people venting but nothing was happening.'

The first phase came to a head after the referendum result in June 2016. Smith sat at her kitchen table in Sheffield feeling 'very raw', the Birthday Club group 'buzzing red hot' with anger at a leader who had made himself invisible in the campaign. For her and others it was a day that 'seared the soul' and changed everything. When Corbyn immediately and blithely called for the triggering of Article 50, pro-Remainers in the shadow cabinet launched a coup against him.[1] Hodge and Ann Coffey triggered a no-confidence vote in Corbyn and 172 MPs voted for him to go. The Labour leader refused to move, saying he had a mandate from the party membership. 'The Marxist left doesn't care about Parliament or Parliamentary democracy,' a leading rebel said. 'Any other leader would have resigned, but not Corbyn because there was a bigger prize for them, and that was control of the party.'

Corbyn's attitude to Europe was also a problem for the rebels. In the 1980s and 1990s, he had viewed the EU as a capitalist club conspiring against the international worker and had joined the Tory Paleosceptics in voting against every treaty change in Brussels. Andrew Fisher explained, 'He didn't like the neo-liberal trajectory of the EU, as he saw it, and the movement away from the social Europe of Jacques Delors … But he also recognised that it was important to have … European-wide international standards, on things like environmental protections, consumer protections and workers' rights.'[2] Corbyn always denied voting to Leave, but he was supported by Seumas Milne, who never denied doing so. Other key allies, such as Karie Murphy in his private office, and Ian Lavery and Jon Trickett in the shadow cabinet, were concerned that adopting the pro-EU and eventually pro-second-referendum position of the mass membership of the party would alienate Leave voters in what became known as the 'red wall' seats of the North and Midlands. There, immigration was a potent issue, but in London, where most of the leadership cut their teeth, Remain had romped to victory and Labour was an internationalist party. Whoever was Labour leader would have faced an awkward balancing act. When Corbyn whipped his party to vote in favour of triggering Article 50 in March 2017, 49 Labour MPs defied him.[3]

The rebels assumed that the 2017 election would be the end of Corbyn and his brand of politics. The night before polling day, fifty Labour moderates held a conference call to discuss private polling which showed that Corbyn was on course to lose between 50 and 70 seats. They hoped and assumed the electorate would solve their problem for them. When the exit poll dropped at 10 p.m. their illusions were shattered.

Shuker realised almost immediately that he would not make it to the end of the Parliament as a Labour MP. He was just thirty-five. Luciana Berger was feeding her four-week-old child when the poll dropped.

'You've got to be fucking kidding me,' she said. Riding a wave of youthful hysteria, 'magic grandad' had gained 30 seats and was just a few thousand votes in a handful of seats from forcing Theresa May's government to its knees.[4] The Corbynistas declared that they had 'won' the election, even though Labour was 55 seats behind the Conservatives.

By the summer of 2017, Shuker realised that quitting was not good enough. He needed to create an alternative. 'Anyone can walk off the pitch, but if you've got some chips you might as well put them in,' he said. The first person he approached was Leslie, a Brownite bruiser with a serpent's tongue where the leadership was concerned, who existed in a state of mutual detestation with the Corbynites. Leslie, who had briefly been shadow chancellor between the 2015 election and Corbyn's election, regarded the leader's leftism as a menace to the economy. To Shuker, it was the culture of the hard left, with its believers and heretics and its incipient antisemitism which was the problem. In August, they met for lunch at Luton Hoo, a Georgian hotel in Shuker's seat. 'We talked and came to the conclusion that even if Plan A is "stay and you fight", you need a "red team" somewhere working out what a Plan B looks like,' Shuker said. They resolved, together, to find like-minded colleagues and go on a journey together.

Throughout the rest of 2017, Shuker arranged a series of coffees with seventy-five colleagues he thought might be open to joining him. Some were too emotionally committed to Labour; others were on the same journey he was. One of those who felt he had nothing to lose was Gapes, a foreign affairs committee veteran who regarded Corbyn's approach to international affairs as close to treasonous. 'In 2015 I'd got so stressed about the Labour Party I'd had major heart problems,' he said. 'I had a ruptured aneurysm and I was in hospital for two months. I was very lucky to survive. It focused my mind. I decided that every day mattered and I wasn't going to prevaricate.'

Many of those in the Birthday Club, such as Yvette Cooper and Alison McGovern, chair of the Blairite pressure group Progress, were anti-Corbyn but felt they had to stay and fight. Others looked at the arrival of Jennie Formby – the former political director of Unite and mother of Len McCluskey's child – as general secretary of the Labour Party in April 2018, as proof the Corbynites had a vice-like grip on the party machinery. Chuka Umunna told colleagues, 'It is irretrievable. In the 1980s, the hard left never got the leadership, they never got the NEC [the party's ruling committee], the unions were instrumental in keeping things sensible. Now, they've got the leadership, they've got the NEC, they've got the unions and technology has enabled Momentum [the pro-Corbyn pressure group] to organise much more effectively than Militant ever could.'

On Brexit, Corbyn deserved credit for keeping the show on the road. Since the referendum, he had maintained a position of constructive ambiguity, while the more potent divisions, up to the end of 2017, were to be found in the Conservative Party. An aide who spent a lot of time on the road with him said he regularly met angry Remain voters on trains. 'He would talk about "the biggest ever democratic exercise", and it not being easy with Labour representing the most Leave and the most Remain places: "We're not going to bring people together by ignoring the result."' Engaging with the public, Corbyn was in his element.

But in 2018 his MPs were no longer content with constructive ambiguity and the leader found himself unable to control, contain – or even, it seemed at times, to understand – the emotions Brexit had unleashed in his party. When attention switched to Westminster, Corbyn hated what the aide called 'tortured Parliamentary manoeuvring'.

Labour's 2017 election manifesto pledged to leave the single market and customs union and declared, 'freedom of movement will end'. In August that year Keir Starmer, the shadow Brexit secretary, committed Labour to staying in the customs union and single market for the two-year transition period which would begin on Brexit day. But Labour had no policy on what the final trading relationship should look like, the biggest political issue of the day.

It was not a cause which animated Corbyn. Milne, his closest aide, regarded the politics of Brexit as a 'culture war' issue got up by the Tories to distract the workers from the class struggle. A close ally of Milne explained, 'Brexit was a signifier that was used to bring together a very large coalition of disparate forces behind the leadership of the right and the ruling forces in society. The Leave identity and the Remain identity were not really to do with the EU, even if Leave wrapped itself in the flag and stuck two fingers up across the Channel. We needed a new set of signifiers that could bring together our coalition.' Labour's battle over Brexit became one between factions who wanted to woo traditional Labour voters who had adopted the Leave identity versus those who thought the party should just embrace the Remain identity, with Corbyn's inner circle seeking to avoid a decision and focus on their own issues instead.

Andrew Fisher, Corbyn's head of strategy, later concluded that his team learned the wrong lessons from their surprise success in the 2017 election. 'I think our miscalculation, if I'm being honest, at that point, was thinking "Labour are ahead in quite a few of the polls. This is how we've done it: we've talked about ending austerity, spoken about public services, social security, housing, all these bread-and-butter issues. Stick to that and don't talk about Brexit. That's where we build our support." What we should have done is looked further ahead and gone, "What's going to become the defining issue?" The lesson we'd drawn, incorrectly … was, "Don't talk about Brexit, talk about the other stuff. That's where Labour goes up in the polls".'[5]

By January 2018 Shuker had identified around twenty MPs who might be open to a split. They joined a much tighter WhatsApp group called 'Mainstream', the logo of which was 'Bb' for 'Plan B'.[6] On 17 January, a Wednesday, the group met at Fair Oak Farm, a bed and breakfast property in Sussex. Shuker thought getting them out of London for an overnight trip would be good for secrecy but also a means of making everyone complicit. Alongside Shuker, Leslie, Umunna, Berger, Gapes and Smith were: Heidi Alexander; Ian Austin, a former spin doctor for Gordon Brown; Ann Coffey; Liz Kendall, briefly a leadership candidate in 2015; John Woodcock, who had also spun for Brown; and Phil Wilson, who had succeeded Blair as the MP for Sedgefield.

They sat around a farmhouse table and Shuker, acting as the group's pastor-confessor, guided the discussion. That first night they had a local chef, which left people wondering if he was 'safe'. After that, Shuker cooked as well. His chicken and chicory was remembered fondly. There would be three visits, in January, March and May, with around fifteen of the twenty at each one. Shuker approached the meetings as therapy sessions, asking people what they wanted and what they feared. There were some tears as the participants discussed their alienation from a party which to many was a second family. Shuker coaxed confessions that bred mutual trust. When dinner was done, they drank. Heavily.

The second meeting, on 21 March, came a week after Corbyn and Milne's disastrous handling of the Skripal affair. Concern about national security – a particular bugbear of Gapes and Austin – reinforced the collective concern about Labour's Brexit policy and Berger's disgust at growing antisemitism as the three foundational objections to Corbyn. 'We discussed if there was to be a split what would happen? How would we organise ourselves? What would we do? When would be the best timing?' one of those present recalled. 'There were clear divisions about the way forward,' another MP said. 'There were those who thought that any split away from the Labour Party was doomed to fail, and there were those who were absolutely up for it.'

Two days later, the row over Corbyn's support for the antisemitic mural blew up. It was the moment when Berger resolved to leave. 'I'm done,' she told Shuker – and him alone. Understanding that Berger was the moral core of his group, he urged her to wait until 'we have as many people around you as possible'.[7] Another of the key rebels said, 'There's something quite special about Luciana.'

Gradually, Shuker moved more colleagues from 'ifs' to 'whens'. By the time of the third trip to Fair Oak Farm on 23 May he fed the attendees barbecued burgers and asked them to say if they were in or not. A small group would work up a more concrete plan: Shuker, Leslie, Umunna, Berger and Smith. They became known as the 'I-Group', for 'irreconcilables'. They moved their communications to the more secure Signal app. Getting firm commitments was difficult. 'Ian Murray was in, then he was out, then he was in,' one of the core team recalled, 'all over the place, wavering.'

While Shuker tried to move MPs towards a breakaway, Keir Starmer was trying to move Labour's Brexit policy towards something palatable to the party's MPs. Starmer disliked Brexit but did not begin as a Bresister. 'The day after the referendum I spent, before they went to school, some time with my young kids, and just thought: *What kind of world are you going to grow up in?* I was really worried about tolerance and looking inward, but I felt that we had to accept the result.'[8] However, by mid-2018, he could see that Corbyn's position could not hold. 'It became clear to some of us, Keir in particular, that we needed to be clear about what the end game would be, after transition,' a shadow cabinet member said. Both John McDonnell and Diane Abbott shared his view that Labour needed a policy.

At this point, both Starmer and his aides were adamant he did not back a referendum. A leading supporter of the People's Vote complained,

'He never believed in it, he didn't think you could convince the country.' Some in LOTO did not believe Starmer, seeing the six tests[9] he had devised in early 2017 to determine whether Labour would back a deal as being designed to fail and take Labour to a Remain position. Starmer had seized on a comment by David Davis that the government's deal would end up giving Britain 'exactly the same' benefits as EU membership. Having first condemned this as a flight of fantasy from Brexiteers, Starmer adopted it as the first requirement the government had to satisfy, a hurdle he knew it would be impossible to clear. That was clever opposition. 'It was really just teasing their contradictions, more than having our own policy,' Andrew Fisher observed.[10] The more acute criticism, from shadow cabinet ministers in Leave seats, was that Starmer's were London-centric tests. Demanding the 'exact same benefits' of EU market membership (test two) and 'defend rights' for workers (test four) were hardly catnip to voters in seats where people felt the market and the EU had left them behind. In one meeting Jon Trickett erupted, 'We want everything we've got now! That's fine if you live in bloody Camden or Islington. There are 35,000 fucking graduates in your seat, and 9,000 in mine. We're not interested in the status quo. We want to get rid of it!'[11]

Starmer concluded that the end state answer was a customs union. At the end of 2017 and again in early 2018, the shadow Brexit secretary visited Brussels and met members of the EU's Task Force 50 negotiating team, including Sabine Weyand. This was done with the approval of David Davis, then the Brexit secretary. 'My intention is not to undermine the government's negotiations,' Starmer explained. 'I'm not trying parallel negotiations, but I do need to know the position of the commission on certain things.' Davis helped set up the initial meetings.

In Brussels, Starmer said, 'I'm not interested in the Turkey-style customs union. I'm talking about something much more dynamic and forward-looking than that.' He returned with a clear view from the Commission that a customs union was something they were prepared to negotiate and that when he 'surfaced' the idea Brussels would not shoot it down as they had done some of the government's ideas.

While Starmer was working on this plan, Fisher, who was more pro-European than Milne, was working on a Brexit speech for Corbyn, which he was due to deliver towards the end of February 2018. He called it 'Jeremy's plan'. The first draft committed to leaving the single market and customs union, allowing the UK to do trade deals of its own, but demanded that Britain get special access to European markets. Crucially, for the hard left, it would allow Britain to pursue new state aid rules, which would clear the way for renationalisations or huge state intervention in industry. Much of it read like it had been dictated by Milne.

On 12 February, Corbyn presented the plan as a fait accompli to the shadow cabinet's Brexit sub-committee. This was supposed to be 'Jeremy's plan' but it was evident to everyone in the room that the leader had not even a passing familiarity with it. 'Jeremy was reading whatever script was in front of him, I don't know that he knew what was in the paper,' one of those present said.

Unfortunately for Milne, Starmer had seen the text, despite efforts to keep it from him. It had been leaked by Mark Simpson, a LOTO aide who had been meeting Starmer and his team in secret for some time, and had printed him a copy before the meeting.[12] Starmer immediately suspected a Milne plot to blindside him. A source said, 'They tried to bounce Keir.' The shadow Brexit secretary, usually preternaturally calm, erupted in a show of theatrical fury: 'I'm not having this! I'm not working in this way!' He thought it a dishonourable way to behave. Starmer said, 'I'm simply not accepting a paper put before us at the beginning of a meeting.'

The meeting broke up without conclusion but McDonnell and Corbyn, shocked at Starmer's vehemence, and concerned he might resign, directed Fisher to have another go. Starmer worked the affair to his advantage, securing agreement that, in future, only his aides would be permitted to join the sub-committee. On 18 February, he went to Labour's National Policy Forum in Leeds, where a new policy was agreed – Labour would join 'a' customs union after Brexit. A day later, the sub-committee met again and rubber-stamped the policy. It was a significant victory for Starmer.

There was still a week until Corbyn's speech, however. In a measure of Milne's influence (and the farce that gripped Corbyn's LOTO) Starmer and McDonnell assumed Milne would try to excise 'customs union' from Corbyn's text at the last moment. 'It was all very tense because Seumas always has the last go at Jeremy's speeches, and although we'd agreed a position on the customs union the question was whether they were going to row back,' a source said. On Sunday 24th, Corbyn practised his speech on the biggest public policy issue of the day in his constituency office to protect him from the meddling of his own chief adviser.

Starmer was due on Andrew Marr's show that morning. Not knowing whether 'customs union' would make the final cut, he turned the screws, announcing that a customs union had the 'unanimous support' of the shadow cabinet – news to most of its members, who had not even discussed the issue. The new treaty would 'do the work of the customs union, that's the intention,' he said. Having been bounced, Starmer showed he could do some bouncing. Later that day, Milne and James Schneider briefed Monday's newspapers with bits of the speech they liked – Labour's desire to boost British manufacturing – failing to mention the customs union.

Fisher's speech, however, was what Starmer wanted when Corbyn delivered it in Coventry on 26 February. 'We have long argued that a customs union is a viable option for the final deal,' the leader said, 'so Labour would seek to negotiate a new, comprehensive UK-EU customs union to ensure that there are no tariffs with Europe, and to help avoid any need for a hard border in Northern Ireland.' When the words 'customs union' passed Corbyn's lips, Starmer's aide Ben Nunn and their mole Mark Simpson silently pumped their fists at the back of the hall.[13] To Fisher, the episode was barely controversial. 'The industrial trade unions – the GMB, Unite, and people who represent workers in manufacturing and industry – were saying to us, "We need to be in a customs union, otherwise this is going to cost our jobs." CBI and Make UK were lobbying us to say they wanted a customs union. If the unions are saying it and businesses are saying it, why wouldn't we say it?'[14]

The decision to back a customs union was far more popular than some in LOTO had anticipated. Businesses contacted Labour saying they supported the plan, which was emblematic of a desire for a close economic relationship with Brussels. To Starmer's surprise, Corbyn stuck to the script thereafter. 'Jeremy was reluctant on the customs union,' a source in Starmer's camp said, 'but having got there he embraced it and championed it. Some people say Jeremy will never move his positions, but it isn't actually true.'

Starmer also deserved credit, tactically, for focusing on an issue which was not just a dividing line between Labour and the Tories, but would also become a faultline between different factions of Conservatives. 'Keir looked around that corner,' an aide said, 'and thought: This is going to become the dividing line – and it did.' The contrast with Theresa May, refusing to think several steps ahead, was telling.

Starmer was also encouraged that, for the first time, he had been able to work closely with John McDonnell, whose views on Europe were different from those of Milne and Corbyn. McDonnell passionately wanted to win power and believed he needed to be pragmatic on Brexit, as he had been on antisemitism. If he won, McDonnell also wanted to boost manufacturing in the neglected regions of the country. 'If you really want to do regional investment the last thing you want to do is come out of the customs union which is going to put a lot of strain on manufacturing,' a fellow shadow cabinet member said.

Labour now had a credible policy, but it was still not the one that the rebel MPs and most of their members wanted; it still meant leaving the EU. But efforts by Labour MPs to press the government towards a soft Brexit or no Brexit were a failure. On 14 June 2018, 74 Labour MPs defied a three-line whip to vote in favour of a Norway-style Brexit inside the European Economic Area. On 30 June, an amendment tabled to the Queen's Speech by Chuka Umunna, calling on Theresa May to keep Britain in the single market and customs union, secured 101 votes, including those of 49 Labour rebels, but was soundly defeated. On 17 July, just before the summer recess, an attempt by Labour to amend the Trade Bill to force the government to negotiate a customs union failed after five pro-Brexit Labour MPs – Kate Hoey, John Mann, Frank Field, Graham Stringer and Kelvin Hopkins – voted with the government.

Labour MPs began to shift their support to the People's Vote campaign instead. 'The moment the prospect of a second referendum appeared,' Hilary Benn, one of the leading Bresisters, recalled, 'colleagues on the Labour benches who previously had said, "Single Market and a customs union, that's what we want", discarded that because they thought there might be a possibility of the British people changing their minds.'[15]

The most difficult thing for the splitters to decide was when to break away. Not everyone was prepared to wait. On 18 July 2018 John Woodcock, the MP for Barrow and Furness, announced he was leaving Labour to sit as an independent. Woodcock declared Corbyn 'unfit' for office, arguing that he 'would pose a clear risk to UK national security as prime minister'.

The pressure on the breakaway group grew on 7 August, when David Maddox of the *Daily Express* scooped the centre-left papers and revealed the visits to Fair Oak Farm.[16] Maddox had a lot of detail: 'The group would catch the 7.18 p.m. train from Waterloo East on a Thursday evening to Stonegate before taking a seven-minute taxi ride' to Fair Oak Farm. The story quoted an MP who attended though it suggested there had been two, not three, meetings and that Stephen Kinnock – who was not a member – had been present. Some suspected that an MP who had not decided to defect was trying to kill the enterprise. The finger of suspicion was pointed at Ian Austin, a close associate of Tom Watson.

Two weeks later, on 25 August, Mike Gapes let rip in the wider Birthday Club WhatsApp group about Corbyn – the day a video emerged of the leader saying Zionists 'don't understand English irony'. 'I am not prepared to support the racist antisemite. Period. It's over for me,' Gapes wrote. All that remained, was 'the timing of my announcement'. Within hours, Lucy Fisher at *The Times* had been sent his comment.[17] It was the first time the Birthday Club had leaked. Shuker contacted Gapes and pleaded with him: 'Please don't go on your own.'

That summer, however, Shuker's group was not the only one mobilising. The I-Group would find itself in competition both with rival efforts to start a new party and with a determined and unlikely group of Labour counter-revolutionaries.

The axis which posed the greatest threat to Shuker's plans was an unlikely alliance between once mortal enemies: Peter Mandelson and Tom Watson. Watson and Austin had been instrumental in the Brownite Curry House Plot in 2006, which forced Tony Blair to name the date of his departure as Labour leader. Yet on a sunny evening in July 2018, they both attended a barbecue in the garden of Mandelson's London mansion. The 'Prince of Darkness' held court, Watson opposite, surrounded by young MPs who hated Corbyn but did not want to join Shuker's separatist outfit: Alison McGovern, Wes Streeting and Anna Turley from the Remain ranks of the party; Gloria De Piero, Ruth Smeeth and Austin from seats which voted to Leave. Mandelson had once sacked Watson from a senior role in the 1997 general election campaign. Watson responded with an atavistic hatred of Blairites. But by the middle of 2018 he was a changed man. Having been diagnosed with Type 2 diabetes a year earlier, he shed seven stone, and with it his appetite for political malice.

Mandelson believed no breakaway could succeed without Watson. They agreed to work together to keep a core of the party alive from which

Labour could rebuild. That meant scuppering the breakaway. He even sent Watson to see Blair to settle their differences. But by September Blair had concluded that Labour was finished. He saw Watson as the person best placed to lead a breakaway, not the man to stop it.

Blair also received the I-Group MPs, including Umunna and Leslie. When he heard their plan, he did nothing to dissuade them. On 3 January, the former prime minister had written a 2,300-word essay on his website, warning that Labour risked becoming 'the handmaiden of Brexit'. By September he was privately penning an article, which he intended to give to *The Times*, arguing that the centre-left needed a complete rethink. He circulated it to former aides, who unanimously told him his message and timing was wrong – and even if it wasn't, he was the wrong messenger.

Blair pulled the article but chose to record a podcast with the BBC's Nick Robinson. 'This is a different Labour Party,' he said. 'The question is: can it be taken back? That's a pretty open question.' He said the public would not 'tolerate' an election choice between Corbyn and Boris Johnson adding, 'I don't know what will happen, I don't know how it will happen, but I just don't believe that people will find that, in the country as a whole, to be an acceptable choice … Something will fill that vacuum.'[18]

Mandelson was furious, his old boss appeared to be encouraging Labour MPs to jump ship. Those contemplating a split did not think it helpful, either, to be seen as cover for a Blairite revival. The same conclusion had been drawn by Jonathan Powell, Blair's former chief of staff, who was quietly working on separate plans for a new party, along with Emily Benn, the granddaughter of Tony Benn. Powell regarded it as the kiss of death if Blair ended up fronting this new outfit. He hoped, instead, to work up a party infrastructure into which a mass of defectors from Labour could slot once they had walked out.

Powell's was not the only start-up operation. Simon Franks, the founder of LoveFilm, also spent much of 2018 seeking to drum up support for a new party, but his project never went anywhere. What all these groups had in common was that they were pushing an anti-Brexit, socially liberal, centrist economics agenda. For many voters who felt disenfranchised by the aftermath of Brexit there was a gap in the market for a new party. The problem was, there was no real market in that particular gap. Polls showed that the real opportunity was for a party which backed higher state spending but, unlike Corbyn's Labour, was also patriotic, pro-Brexit and socially conservative. A LOTO aide said, 'Any focus group you go to in any part of the country, people are a combination of left economically and right socially. That's where the gaping gap is.' As 2019 went on it became a Boris Johnson-shaped hole in the market.

The Lib Dems were also trying to woo defectors, in particular Chuka Umunna, who had a good relationship with the party leader, from his time shadowing Vince Cable as business secretary in the coalition years. In spring 2018, Jo Swinson also had lunch with Umunna in the Blue Boar. She tried to dissuade him from starting a new party. 'Have you not underestimated how hard it is to do something new?' she asked. She knew how difficult it was to make a breakthrough against the two main parties. In Edinburgh, she talked to Ian Murray. Swinson also had a chat over tea and biscuits with Anna Soubry.

The Labour Party conference in Liverpool was a watershed moment. Before it, Gavin Shuker had lost a vote of confidence in his local party. During it, Luciana Berger had to be accompanied by police to protect her from a baying mob of hard left protesters as she made her way in and out of the secure area, despite being in the city she represented in Parliament. When Emily Thornberry, the shadow foreign secretary, addressed the conference, she was greeted with a mass of waved Palestinian flags. Thornberry, gutsily under the circumstances, gave her party some home truths: 'There are sickening individuals on the fringes of our movement who use our legitimate support for Palestine as a cloak and a cover for their despicable hatred of Jewish people and their desire to see Israel destroyed ... They must be kicked out of our party.'

The main event, however, was the Brexit debate, which would decide Labour's policy. In the weeks before the gathering in Liverpool those who wanted a second Brexit referendum or a more definitive statement from Corbyn had been plotting to push him where he was reluctant to go. LOTO had schemed to prevent an explicitly pro-EU position being adopted.

In one corner was the People's Vote campaign, which had become a refugee camp for Blair, Brown and Miliband-era Labour officials who believed in a referendum or wanted to fight Corbyn, or were just looking for gainful employment. Guided by Mandelson and Alastair Campbell, day-to-day operations were in the hands of James McGrory, a former Lib Dem spin doctor who had been chief spokesman for the Remain campaign, and Tom Baldwin who graduated from Campbell's favourite journalist to Miliband's director of communications. In May they had been joined by John Stolliday and Patrick Heneghan, both senior figures from Labour HQ in election campaigns past. 'It was a job creation scheme for disaffected centrists,' one of the recruits admitted.

The People's Vote was regarded by the Labour leader's closest aides as an anti-Corbyn front. In one meeting in LOTO, Karie Murphy repeatedly jabbed her finger into Tom Baldwin's chest and asked, 'Who the fuck are you and what are you doing?'[19] Andrew Fisher, who found the campaign 'irritating', recalled, 'They were very much from the New Labour wing of the Labour Party. It seemed like, instead of trying to convince the public, they were trying to lobby the Labour Party. If you wanted to … say the people should have the final say on whatever deal comes forward, then actually, you need to make that argument to people who voted Leave. It always struck me that there was either something malicious or something incompetent about it. If it was trying to create a wedge within the Labour Party, then it was pretty effective.'[20]

Umunna and Chris Leslie from the I-Group and Alison McGovern from Mandelson and Watson's counter-revolutionaries worked with Stolliday to write a People's Vote motion. To disguise its origins and not deter those who saw the People's Vote as Umunna's personal plaything, they couched their call for a referendum as 'a public vote'. Heneghan, who knew the grassroots best, got to work persuading hundreds of constituency Labour parties (CLPs) to submit pro-referendum motions to the conference committee.

At the same time, the left-wing pro-EU group Another Europe is Possible, which backed Corbyn, had also grown tired of the leadership's obfuscation and were pushing their own motion. In the Brexit sub-committee, Diane Abbott was openly campaigning for a second referendum, while John McDonnell was beginning to waver. Ian Lavery and Jon Trickett dug in against one. 'In 2017, the Labour Party had taken a discussion on Brexit off the floor of party conference,' a shadow cabinet member recalled. 'And during the course of 2018, members were making it pretty clear they weren't going to be prepared to let that happen again.'

Over the summer Starmer had visited Campbell's home in Hampstead and sought to convince him Brexit could not and should not be stopped.

'I don't know why you're doing this,' he said. 'We've had the referendum. You know you can't stop this. It's got to happen.'[21] But by September Starmer was arguing that the leadership needed to 'evolve' its stance to reflect the hardening position among members and supporters.

As he prepared the ground, Starmer came to the view that the activities of Umunna and Leslie were counterproductive to their pro-referendum cause. A lot of the membership, while virulently anti-Brexit, was still passionately pro-Corbyn, a duality neatly captured by T-shirts emblazoned with 'love Corbyn, hate Brexit', ubiquitous at conference that year. Fisher said Starmer 'couldn't stand' Chuka Umunna and 'expressed frustrations' at the way he was being 'jostled' by back-benchers. 'I think that made Keir uncomfortable and made him tense.'[22] But the weight of numbers in the PLP backing the People's Vote was a factor for Starmer, who had one eye on the leadership. 'Keir is a creature of the establishment,' Fisher said later. 'He doesn't take the view that what matters is what members think, what matters is whether the majority of the PLP thinks something … That's what Keir does; he takes the path of least resistance within the Parliamentary Labour Party, with the people he thinks are important.'[23]

When the Trades Union Congress (TUC) met in Manchester on 9 September they agreed a motion that, after voting against a Tory Brexit deal, Labour should first seek a general election and, if that failed, 'a popular vote on the terms of Brexit'. It was a fudge designed to please those who wanted a referendum, with just enough wriggle room for those who felt Labour had to deliver Brexit.

On arrival in Liverpool on Saturday 23 September the People's Vote held a rally at the city's Pier Head showcasing the most left-wing voices they had. These included Manuel Cortes, the Transport Salaried Staffs' Association (TSSA) boss who had been the first union leader to back Corbyn, and Everton football legend Peter Reid, enjoying a second life as a Tory-baiter on Twitter. The event was so well attended it stopped the traffic.

Backroom deals at Labour conferences are done in the 'compositing' meeting, where hundreds of motions proposed by CLPs are merged into one to be voted on in the conference hall. Ahead of the meeting on the Sunday evening, Starmer read every one of the hundreds of motions submitted. Despite agreeing their compromise, none of the big unions was prepared to put their name to it. Amy Jackson, Corbyn's political secretary, called in a favour from the tiny and virulently Eurosceptic Bakers' Union. Despite their views on the EU, the Bakers agreed to put forward a motion for Corbyn. Starmer also met Cortes in secret, explaining where he wanted the composite motion to land – nodding towards a referendum but just short of explicit. Cortes agreed to help.

Three hundred delegates tramped into a faceless meeting room in the ACC conference centre at 6.30 p.m. It would be nearly seven hours before there was a conclusion. Starmer had the advantage. Two of his aides – Ben Nunn and Chris Ward – were in the room along with Mark Simpson, while Stolliday of the People's Vote was forced to operate from outside, rallying the Remainers with WhatsApp messages. Starmer also had Cortes as the tip of his spear. TSSA staff acting like hired muscle handed copies of the desired motion to everyone entering the meeting. Speaking first, Cortes made clear he was not leaving unless he was happy.

It was a fractious affair. Realising he had been used by LOTO to promote a softening of Labour's line on Brexit, Ian Hodson of the Bakers' Union stormed in shouting, 'The bakers must be heard!' He was promptly thrown out since, under Labour rules, only those present at the start of the meeting were permitted. Also evicted was Richard Corbett, the hyper-Remainer who led Labour MEPs, whose zeal was regarded as an impediment to compromise. Corbyn was also told he was not welcome.

Starmer worked quietly to try to build trust with those in the room, arguing that Labour needed a 'roadmap' towards a referendum but could not jump straight there. 'We need a staged approach,' he said. 'I know a lot of you want to press on more quickly, but give us the space to be able to react depending on what happens when we see the deal. Don't go hard on a second referendum, keep it as an option so that we can make the appropriate decisions at the appropriate time.' After two hours, he sensed that he had the trust of the room and that people did not want to split the party. Many who wanted to go further and faster still didn't want to embarrass Corbyn. Watching from the wings, Starmer's aide Ben Nunn thought for the first time: *If he can negotiate with this lot, maybe we could do a deal with the EU.*

Cortes built support for an even vaguer form of words, designed to satisfy all shades of opinion. Labour would keep 'all options on the table – including a public vote'. In endless questioning, the different options for a referendum were discussed. Starmer was clear that the working assumption had to be that Remain would be an option on the ballot paper. That did not make the final wording, but it was openly discussed. Stephen Doughty was among the Remainers in the room who realised it was the best they could get. It was still 'progress', he told colleagues. 'We can't let the perfect be the enemy of the good. We have to keep giving people hope.' Unanimity was required. By 1 a.m., one Europhile held out. Everyone decided the solo voice of dissent should be ignored.

No sooner had the harmonious fudge been achieved, John McDonnell blew it up. Asked on *Today* about Labour's new stance, the shadow chancellor said the 'public vote' should be a referendum on the deal, not one with Remain on the ballot paper which might cancel Brexit altogether. 'If we are going to respect the last referendum, it will be about the deal,' he said. Friends said McDonnell did not intend to be incendiary and was badly briefed, but it appeared to People's Voters like calculated sabotage.

McDonnell's intervention left Starmer fuming. Having corralled three hundred people to an agreed position just hours before by asking them to trust him, the shadow Brexit secretary saw himself as the moral guardian of the agreement. He could not, in turn, breach their trust. McDonnell's freelancing emboldened Starmer to go off-piste when he addressed conference. A week earlier he had met a friend for lunch who told him 'to show some guts' and make clear 'that Remain is an option'. Now he resolved to do just that. As he reached the end of his speech, Starmer's eyes moved from the teleprompter to the notes in front of him. 'It's right that Parliament has the first say,' he said, 'but if we need to break the impasse our options must include campaigning for a public vote and nobody is ruling out Remain as an option.'

There was a moment of perfect silence then the hall erupted in clapping, cheering and a standing ovation. The thunderous look on Karie Murphy's face in the front row said eloquently what LOTO thought of Starmer's improvisation. Amy Jackson texted Andrew Fisher, 'What the fuck?' Within eleven minutes the Tory press office had clipped a video of Starmer's peroration for Twitter: 'CONFIRMED Labour will not respect the result of the referendum #Lab18.' Jackson chased Starmer backstage waving her phone in his face. 'Look at what you've just done!' she screamed. In a side room Starmer, voice rising in both pitch and volume, defended himself: 'John said Remain won't be on the ballot. I had to correct it. What did you want me to do?'

Starmer considered it a matter of personal integrity. He told one Westminster confidant, 'I wasn't going to let them [the compositing delegates] think that I had stitched them up on the Sunday night.' Starmer, usually a cautious politician, had seized the day. Having spent months arguing with the People's Voters about the validity of cancelling the referendum, he was immediately anointed as standard bearer of the Labour Remain cause. Later, at a conference party, young advisers chanted 'all-op-tions-on-the-table' to the tune of the White Stripes' 'Seven Nation Army', the melody which had once been used for 'Oh-Jer-em-ee-Cor-byn'.[24] Starmer had stolen not just Corbyn's clothes but his song as well.

When the leader used his conference speech to offer Theresa May a compromise, offering to vote for a 'sensible' Brexit (a customs union with added workers' rights), he was largely ignored. It was Starmer's plan which the party gripped as it left Liverpool, one which would, more or less, survive contact with events for the next four months, a period in which the Tories descended into civil war.

To Shuker's secessionists, Starmer was hardly a study in courage. It had taken him most of a year to get to the conclusion they had reached in January 2018. It was too little, too late. One of the I-Group said, 'There was a lot said and written about bravery and courage. Keir put a few words in his speech about Brexit that weren't cleared by Seumas. Wow. Luciana was turning up every day with a police escort.' Three days after conference, Chris Leslie's CLP passed a vote of no confidence in him.

The timing of their departure was defined by Brexit. Shuker concluded their argument to leave would be stronger if they stuck around to fight their corner on Brexit, but this put them at the mercy of events. He saw a six-month window, opening in October 2018 up until the hard deadline of 29 March 2019, the date Britain was due to leave the European Union. Brexit also held some potential defectors back. 'People didn't want to leave because they didn't want to be accused of undermining the People's Vote coalition in Parliament and that slowed things up,' one MP said.

Shuker spent sixty hours a week planning everything which needed to be in place for a successful breakaway – what he called 'go/no go' issues – making sure they had a bank account and that the legal, financial and regulatory issues with the Electoral Commission watchdog were all dealt with correctly. Bluntly, they were not ready in the autumn of 2018.

Shuker said, 'I was always pushing for as long as possible. It was like trying to build a runway while the plane is taxiing down it.'[25]

LOTO was fearful of a split, but John McDonnell was alone among Corbyn's high command who sought to do anything to prevent one. The damage of the SDP breakaway was seared into McDonnell, who had lost Hampstead and Highgate in the 1983 general election to the Tories by 3,370 votes while the SDP candidate got 11,030. As he had over antisemitism, McDonnell preferred sugar to salt in his approach to the rebels. On 1 September, he played peacemaker in the *New Statesman*. 'Talk to us,' he wrote. 'We've got an open door … I'm worried and I'm saddened.'

On Brexit, he also softened. He had been suspicious of the People's Vote when it was first established as a lifeboat for Labour enemies of Corbynism. But on 22 November, McDonnell met Baldwin and Campbell in the shadow chancellor's Commons office – a meeting revealed to the irritation of both sides by the *Sunday Times* three days later. Baldwin explained that the People's Vote high command believed the only way they could get a referendum was with Labour backing.

McDonnell was shown polling, paid for by the TSSA, revealing that Labour voters overwhelmingly supported a second referendum and that six out of ten would be upset if the party enabled Brexit. It found that Labour would get a lower vote share in every seat if it had a pro-Brexit policy than if it adopted an anti-Brexit position. A Labour adviser said, 'John went white as a sheet when he saw it.' The People's Vote polling became controversial. Those who wanted Labour to back a referendum argued the party had to pivot to win the Remain vote. 'It showed that it didn't matter how far you went towards backing Brexit, we would lose a whole bunch of seats in Leave areas because 2017 Labour voters in those constituencies would not vote for someone who supports Brexit. But if we stayed on the fence, we would also lose seats in London and the South to the Lib Dems.' A People's Vote official said, 'We did very effectively show that Labour had far more to lose from the Remain side than from a Leave side.'

On the other side of the argument, Milne, Schneider and Carl Shoben, the head of strategy, dismissed the results as 'push polling', designed to elicit the answer the People's Vote campaign and the TSSA's leadership wanted. A senior Corbynite said, 'They put loads of money into polling because they thought all they had to do was to show people who voted to

Leave that they were wrong and they would obediently change their minds. That was never going to work.' Another said, 'In places like Hackney, Islington and Kentish Town we had majorities of 40,000. We should have been prepared to see slippage of votes to the Greens and the Lib Dems so they were cut to 20,000 so we could hold on to [Leave] seats in the North, the Midlands and Wales.'

Baldwin and Starmer also began having covert meetings in an upstairs room at Cafe Renoir, but the shadow Brexit secretary seemed more committed, at this stage, to negotiating a Brexit deal than a referendum.

None of these characters was moving quickly enough for Umunna or the other members of the I-Group. On 18 November, Corbyn told Sky News's Sophy Ridge another referendum was only 'an option for the future … not an option for today'.

On 10 January 2019, five days before the first meaningful vote, Corbyn gave a speech in Wakefield explaining why Labour would oppose May's deal. Days before, in LOTO, he launched into an impassioned monologue on his desire to bring the country together, which was incorporated into his text, making this the most personal of Corbyn's Brexit speeches. 'If you're living in Tottenham you may well have voted to Remain. You've got high bills, rising debts. You're in insecure work. You struggle to make your wages stretch and you may be on universal credit and forced to access food banks. You're up against it. If you're living in Mansfield, you are more likely to have voted to Leave. You've got high bills, rising debts, you're in insecure work, you struggle to make your wages stretch and you may be on universal credit and forced to access food banks. You're up against it. But you're not against each other.' This was authentic Corbyn, but it was also proof, for the rebels, that he did not want to pick sides by backing a referendum.

In MV1 every Labour MP bar three voted against the deal, helping inflict the worst parliamentary defeat in history. Corbyn's motion of no confidence the following day failed. He refused ever louder entreaties from Labour MPs to back the People's Vote. Starmer warned him that unless he secured a general election, he had only three options: do a deal with the Tories on a customs union, an option, Starmer said, 'that means we own Brexit as well'; second, back a new referendum; or, third, allow a no-deal Brexit. 'I want to be really clear,' he said gravely. 'I did not sign up for that.' The shadow Brexit secretary paused. 'I. Did. Not. Sign. Up. For. That.'

This was an uncomfortable place for Corbyn. Baldwin briefed the press, 'Labour's strategy seems to have been to let Brexit happen without getting the blame, but Labour now knows that Brexit will only happen if they vote for it.'

On 29 January, Corbyn agreed to meet May, not the signal of intent the splitters wanted. On 11 February, Angela Smith, one of the I-Group, tried to intervene on Corbyn in the Commons to challenge him to back a referendum. He ignored her, prompting Julian Smith, the Tory chief whip, to hold up a handwritten sign saying, 'ANGELA WANTS TO ASK ABOUT A SECOND REFERENDUM.' It didn't matter. The splitters had already decided they were leaving Labour in a week's time.

To prepare the group, psychologically, for what would be a defining moment of their lives, Shuker brought in Maggie Ellis, a psychotherapist he had known for twenty years, who coached FTSE 100 executives. 'We had lots of sessions with this therapist about dealing with change, and culture,' one MP said. Luciana Berger and Angela Smith were particularly keen to use the sessions to foster a different, more mutually supportive culture in their new enterprise.

Chris Leslie's wife, Nicola Murphy, came in to work on the practical details of the departure, recruiting people to help secure a venue and office space, to do the PR and comms. She was, in effect, beginning to put in place the rudimentary infrastructure of a new party.

This difference between a movement and a party became the key fault-line in the group, particularly between its founding fathers Shuker and Leslie. Early in January 2019, six weeks before they launched, Shuker told Leslie and Umunna he did not think they should race to become a party. 'It's going to be eighteen months before we're in a position to fight a seat,' he said. 'You've got to build the infrastructure; the moment you're a political party you're judged as a political party.' Shuker saw the launch, in his head, as like the race to the moon. Fair Oak Farm had been the Mercury phase of the space race, the launch would be Gemini, the programme by which the US learned the rudiments of space travel. Only when they were ready would they reach the Apollo phase and shoot for the moon by becoming a political party.

Leslie, a machine politician, thought this timetable unrealistic. The political media was impatient. 'They want to know what the next thing is,' he said. The only way to build momentum, to show you were serious, was to fight and win seats in elections. Shuker snapped: 'Your fear and inadequacy will end up screwing this.'

That same month, Shuker met Blair to get his opinion. Again, the former PM did nothing to dissuade the rebels and even gave them advice. Blair's view was that antisemitism was a good reason to be furious with Labour, maybe even to leave it, but it was not itself a positive flag to rally around. He advised them to set out a basic set of policy principles.

Mandelson, getting wind of what was afoot, confronted Umunna and asked if he had 'something planned'. Umunna lied and Mandelson told him he would be better joining the Lib Dems than starting something new. Umunna laughed vigorously. Four months later, he would be a Lib Dem.

Shortly before the launch, Ian Murray announced that he was out. He didn't want to gift his Edinburgh South seat to the Corbynites. Others refused to jump for personal reasons. Time after time, MPs told Shuker they agreed with his analysis but added, 'I've only got three years left on my mortgage.' One told Berger, 'My mum doesn't want me to do it.'

The final decision to go was driven by Berger's pregnancy, which meant announcing by mid-February. 'I knew I couldn't go into my maternity leave still in the Labour Party,' she said. 'Whether I was joined by others or not, I was going to leave come what may.' When the Commons recess dates were reset, Shuker said, 'We have a ten-day window where we will be the story.' D-Day was fixed for 18 February. It was now an open secret what was going on. The five dined together in the members area of the Commons canteen, inviting speculation about their intentions. On 3 February, the *Observer* revealed on its front page, 'at least six MPs have been drawing up plans to resign the whip and leave the party soon'.[26] The paper's political editor, Toby Helm, had been seen lunching with Angela Smith a few days earlier.

In LOTO, they realised it would be Berger who gave the enterprise credibility. The departure of Labour's most prominent Jewish MP would be highly damaging. Privately, McDonnell believed seventy Labour MPs might jump ship. Pressure from LOTO saw a no-confidence motion against Berger, by her Liverpool Wavertree CLP, withdrawn. Stephen Doughty, a key figure in the Bresistance but also a counter-revolutionary, went to see McDonnell. 'John, I know we are from different parts of Labour, but we don't want this to fall apart.' The shadow chancellor agreed to talk to Remain-supporting MPs to say he agreed that Labour's Brexit position was not right either: 'Things are going to change.'

The night before the launch, at Nicola Murphy's suggestion, they held a dress rehearsal, swapping draft speeches and checking their 'statement of independence', Blair's idea, which outlined the political offer: a market economy, a rules-based global order and, most importantly, Remain. 'We all wanted to know what others would say,' Gapes recalled. 'We worked out the order. We didn't want it to be too long.'

The seven separatists gathered again at 7 a.m. Just before 10 a.m., they emailed letters of resignation to Corbyn and Nick Brown, the Labour chief whip. Led by Berger, they then walked out to face the press, their appearance greeted by an artillery barrage from the waiting cameras.

'My name is Luciana Berger and I am the Labour—' she began. Cue nervous laughter. 'I am the member of Parliament for Liverpool Wavertree. This morning, we have all now resigned from the Labour Party.' She explained, 'We will all sit in Parliament as a new independent group of MPs.' Chris Leslie was next. They could not campaign for Corbyn, he said, because 'the evidence of Labour's betrayal on Europe is now visible for all to see – offering to actually enable this government's Brexit, constantly holding back from allowing the public a final say ... no movement towards a People's Vote.' Angela Smith and Ann Coffey talked in highly personal terms about how Labour had helped them get on in life. Shuker challenged Corbyn's anti-Western world view. Gapes picked up this theme: 'I am furious that the Labour leadership is complicit in facilitating Brexit, which will cause great economic, social and political damage to our country ... A Corbyn Labour government would threaten our national security and international alliances.'

Umunna was 'the closer', delivering the invitation to voters: 'If you are sick and tired of politics as usual, guess what? So are we ... If you want an alternative, please help us build it. The bottom line is this – politics is broken, it doesn't have to be this way. Let's change it.'

The lobby always needs a shorthand nickname, so 'The Independent Group' was quickly abbreviated to TIG and its members to the 'Tiggers', lending them a mischievous and dynamic air.

* * *

When Shuker came off stage, the first person he called was Tom Watson. He wanted the deputy leader to get off the fence. Watson, who did not have Shuker's number in his phone, missed the call. He then sat down with Philip Collins, a *Times* columnist, Pat McFadden and his spin doctor Sarah Coombes to craft a response. This, Watson recorded in his Commons office, refusing to condemn the splittists: 'This is a sad day for all of us. I think our colleagues have come to a premature conclusion. But this is a moment for regret and reflection, not for a mood of anger.' He warned there were likely to be other defectors. Then he revealed the lifeboat he and Mandelson had devised for the moderates. Watson would set up a new group within Labour to 'develop policies' from the 'social democratic and democratic socialist traditions' of the party. The Corbynites had emerged from the Campaign Group of socialist MPs. Watson now planned his own caucus to fight deselections and advance policy interests. The deputy leader of the Labour Party was setting up a party within a party.

Team Corbyn reacted with fury to the defections, demanding that the Tiggers face by-elections. They sent Ian Lavery, the party chairman, to address the PLP. Lavery said he was 'disappointed' with the MPs and rounded on the claim that Labour was antisemitic. 'I wouldn't be a member if it was!' he thundered. Lavery's bombast was greeted with dismay and led a succession of Jewish MPs – Ruth Smeeth, Louise Ellman and Margaret Hodge – to condemn the party's response, while saying they would not join TIG. Ellman said, 'It was appalling. He [Lavery] showed no understanding of the enormity of what is going on.'

In another catastrophe for Corbynite communications, it emerged the same day that Derek Hatton, the Militant former deputy mayor of Liverpool, expelled from Labour in 1986, had been readmitted. Since he was denounced by Neil Kinnock at the 1985 party conference for sending redundancy notices to council workers in taxis, Hatton had been a byword for 'loony-lefty' largesse.

The following day Joan Ryan, the MP for Enfield North who had been chair of Labour Friends of Israel (LFI) since 2015, joined the exodus. She had not been part of the plot at all but previously had conversations with both Leslie and Berger about her disillusionment. 'I knew people wanted to go but I didn't know who they were,' she recalled. Like them, she did not see how she could ask the electorate to vote for Corbyn again. She told her husband, 'I can't let them think that I think in any way he's fit to be prime minister or that it's safe to vote Labour.'

For her, Brexit was a major issue, but she would have been happy to stay and fight for a second referendum had it not been for the antisemitism she witnessed. Ryan was not Jewish, but she received vile abuse. One person on social media threatened to hang her from a tree. Letters were sent to her office calling her a 'Jew whore' and wishing her 'back in the ovens'. Dead rats, an antisemitic trope, were left on her doorstep. 'To find that your own party which should be the very bulwark against racism is actually the perpetrator is quite shocking,' she said.

Ryan had shared a coffee with a circumspect Berger in Portcullis House a week earlier. 'I spend a lot of time thinking about whether to leave,' she admitted, adding, 'If you do leave, and I get the impression you might, anything I can do to support you, I will do.' She could not bear to see a young Jewish woman driven out of the party and not stand in solidarity with her.

Ryan called Henry Zeffman of *The Times* and agreed to meet him at 5 p.m. on the Tuesday. The deal was that he would not post the interview before 10 p.m. Zeffman rang at 9.30 p.m. saying the article was ready. She took a deep breath and said, 'Okay.' Ryan alerted Chris Leslie, who sent her the statement of values and asked, 'Do you want to join us?' She agreed. Now there were eight. They contacted Martha Kearney of the *Today* programme and Radio 4 sent a radio car the next morning; they had never done that for Ryan before. At PMQs she sat with the independent group. By then there were eleven.

On Wednesday morning, 20 February, not long before Theresa May did battle with Corbyn, three Conservative MPs – Anna Soubry, Sarah Wollaston and Heidi Allen – announced they were resigning to join the independent group. They all shared similar views to the Labour defectors on Brexit, though each had been wooed by Umunna and Leslie rather than Shuker, something which would have implications later. The trio all opposed the rightward shift of the Tory party and backed a second referendum.

Allen, the MP for South Cambridgeshire, had already put the government's nose out of joint by opposing cuts to welfare payments. Sarah Wollaston wasn't a tribal Tory either. A working GP, she had been selected in an open primary and went on to become chair of the health select committee. But it was the EU referendum campaign which had scarred her. Originally a Leave backer, Wollaston had been horrified by Vote Leave's bus pledge that Brexit would lead to an extra £350 million for the NHS. She refused to board the bus or write articles saying Brexit would be good for the health service. Two weeks before the referendum she went on *Newsnight* and announced she was changing sides. When Umunna appeared in her office in the autumn of 2018, they compared notes about how 'rubbish' things were. 'This isn't what I signed up to when I became an MP,' she said. 'I thought people would be more competent and put the country first.' Umunna pitched the idea: 'We can do something different.'

Soubry was the highest profile Conservative catch. A former *This Morning* television presenter and barrister, she had charisma to burn and a no-nonsense speaking style which appealed to journalists and voters. Made a minister in 2012, she served in government until David Cameron's departure four years later, latterly as a business minister attending cabinet, a role which reinforced her opposition to Brexit.

Others did not come. Phillip Lee was put under huge pressure to join the breakaway. He and Chris Leslie were close friends; their children went to nursery together. Lee kept telling Leslie, 'It's the wrong time. A new political party is not going to work until Brexit is resolved, either way.' He ended up blaming the split for retarding the quest for Tories to back the People's Vote: 'They took the wind out of our sails. I desperately tried to persuade them not to do it then. It took a lot of money away from us as well, just as we were getting some momentum.'[27] Dominic Grieve was totally at odds with the government's main policy but he was constitutionally a Conservative. Soubry knew he would not come, but she gave Grieve a few hours' notice of her intentions. 'I thought it was never going to work,' he said later. 'I thought she was making a mistake. I thought we had more clout inside the party than outside of it.' Nick Boles felt the same.

That morning, Soubry, Allen and Wollaston met in Allen's office, just above the Commons chamber next to the public gallery. There they finalised a press release and pre-wrote tweets announcing their departures. 'The right wing, the hardline, anti-EU awkward squad that have destroyed every leader for the last forty years are now running the Conservative party from top to tail,' they said. Allen couldn't wait to go public, feeling relieved and excited, sick of compromising her values.

After PMQs, the eight ex-Labour MPs left the chamber and went to Leslie's office, where the three Tory converts were waiting. They shared a cup of tea and sandwiches and, in some cases, started to get to know each other. Then, at 1.30 p.m., they went across Parliament Square to the Institute of Civil Engineers in One Great George Street, where the Tory trio held their press conference. Soubry denounced May for pandering to the ERG while ignoring 'mainstream Conservatives' and called on those 'who share one-nation values' to join them.

On 22 February, Ian Austin, the MP for Dudley North, became the ninth MP to leave Labour, though he decided not to join the Tiggers. He told his local paper there was a 'culture of extremism, antisemitism and intolerance' in Labour and added, 'I could never ask local people to make Jeremy Corbyn prime minister.' The trickiest part of his day was getting his old boss Gordon Brown off the phone when he tried, too late, to talk Austin out of it. Austin diverted him by mentioning Ed Miliband, a subject he knew would send Brown into a lengthy vituperative monologue.

It seemed, momentarily, like the group had a chance of achieving a breakthrough. They needed to generate the momentum that makes people feel they are missing out if they don't join. Shuker lost a stone in weight in the first week as he worked round the clock to try to get others to sign up. Luciana Berger had two weeks and a day before her second child was born. 'It was the busiest two weeks of my life,' she said. She did *This Morning* with Soubry and Andrew Marr with Allen. She was the cover girl in *The Times' Magazine*. 'My baby was so calm, I think because he was rocked around so much, because I was running around, literally.'

On 26 February, the eleven Tiggers went out for dinner together to a branch of Nando's on Victoria Street, an everyman restaurant relatable to voters. Umunna duly tweeted a photo which excited much comment and kept them in the news. By then, however, the counter-revolution in the Labour Party was in full swing.

Ever since the party conference, Starmer, Watson and, increasingly, McDonnell had been keen to get to stage three of the policy agreed there: backing a referendum. At a shadow cabinet meeting in the final week of November, Watson had joined forces with Starmer to demand that, if and when May lost the meaningful vote, the party would call a no-confidence motion in the government and, if that failed to force an election, Labour would move swiftly to back a new referendum. During a twenty-minute discussion – the first of any substance in the shadow cabinet on Brexit 'for months' – Watson said, 'We need a process in place by which we take these decisions very quickly.' Starmer agreed, saying the party would need to 'move through the gears quickly'. McDonnell, like Corbyn, sat 'largely silent'. He did not want to be seen to be collaborating with Watson, by now an existential enemy of the Corbynites, but he was happy to let the decision go where he had always expected it would.

Opposition to the plan came from Ian Lavery, Labour's election campaign coordinator, who warned that backing a new referendum could cost Labour thousands of votes in marginal seats which voted Leave in 2016. He was backed by Trickett. Karie Murphy, Corbyn's gatekeeper, told colleagues there would be a second referendum 'over my dead body'.

As the issue blew up, it prompted fresh covert meddling from Seumas Milne. A colleague recalled, 'This was where you see Seumas's fingerprints, because rather than unpick the conference policy, because he can't, he inserts lots of steps – that we have to secure an alternative deal, that a public vote would only be held on certain deals, not other deals.' Milne was a passive-aggressive operator, more effective at killing other people's plans than in devising his own. He watched in meetings, before intervening afterwards to block outcomes he disliked. Attempts to pin him down in advance usually failed. Colleagues found this maddening. 'Everyone knows that a decision isn't really a decision, or a position isn't really a position, unless Seumas is happy with it,' one said. 'If Seumas actually ruled with an iron fist then he would be in charge – and then he would be accountable. All these profiles of him as this Machiavellian fixer and puppet master completely missed the mark, because he didn't translate any of the power he had into outcomes. That left a massive vacuum.'

Corbyn had very little room for manoeuvre and even less interest in Brexit. Starmer vowed to fill the vacuum. On 23 January, he gave a speech to the Fabian Society conference seeking to neutralise Milne by simplifying the choice. 'There are, in reality, just two remaining options,' he explained. 'Instructing the government to negotiate a close economic relationship with the EU ... Secondly, as our conference motion sets out, the option of a public vote.' A source familiar with Starmer's thinking said, 'What [he] was trying to do was clear away the argument that there were all sorts of things that we could do, and narrow it down to two.'

The battle between Starmer and Milne was not over, though. On 6 February, Corbyn wrote to May outlining his conditions for backing a Brexit deal (a 'permanent' customs union, close to the single market, 'dynamic alignment on rights and protections', UK participation in EU agencies, and agreements on security including the European arrest warrant). Starmer drafted the letter, downgrading Corbynite rejection of state aid rules, a process his allies called 'de-unicorning'. However, a reference to a public vote was edited out by Milne. Starmer agreed to this, as long as LOTO talked about a referendum when they gave the letter to the media. This deal was ignored.[28]

When the seven Tiggers jumped, Starmer was worried. He told aides he feared a 'critical mass' of deserters could be reached which would permanently damage Labour and with it his prospects of leading a credible party one day. He pressed Corbyn to finally resolve the Brexit issue or risk a second wave of defections. Caroline Flint, cynical about his motives, said, 'What started to emerge was discussion about who would be the next leader. To achieve that you would have to be a second referendum supporter, because the majority of our members are. That drove the position of leading figures.'[29]

On 25 February, a week after the split, Corbyn chaired a three-hour meeting in one of the riverside rooms in LOTO's complex of offices in Norman Shaw South. Starmer, McDonnell, Abbott, Trickett, Barry Gardiner and Shami Chakrabarti were all present. Corbyn was due to address the PLP later that day. He needed something to say.

Five days earlier he had met Labour backbenchers Peter Kyle and Phil Wilson, who had drawn up an amendment which would see MPs back May's deal if she submitted it to a confirmatory referendum. Kyle was the slick and TV-friendly MP for uber-Remainer Hove, Wilson a salt-of-the-earth former whip who in 2007 had succeeded Tony Blair in Leave-voting Sedgefield. Together they had become an Odd Couple partnership, like Letwin and Boles, dedicated to finding policy solutions acceptable to their very different constituents. Kyle was a member of Trains and Buses and had been to Norway to enquire about their relations with the EU. 'I'd been receiving a lot of death threats,' he said. 'We were talking about where they were coming from, what was driving them, trying to understand what was doing this to our politics. We sat down together for two

or three days. We came up with this idea of a confirmatory referendum.'
Their concept was to force both Brexiteers and Bresisters to compromise.
Remainers would have to vote for a Brexit deal, Leavers would have to
accept that the public would have the right to rubber-stamp it.

They first took the idea to Alan Campbell, Labour's deputy chief whip,
one of the shrewdest readers of opinion in the Commons. Afterwards he
sat in silence for a while and then said, 'I can't really criticise the proposition.' Campbell asked questions but Kyle and Wilson had been through
everything. They tried others. 'Some people hated it, but they couldn't
kill it,' Kyle said. 'Two things were happening in Parliament at the time;
people would have a bold idea and it got killed straight away, because
there was a fatal flaw in the idea. Or everybody loved an idea because it
was utopian and undeliverable like the Malthouse compromise. Our
proposition was within the reality of the UK landscape and the European
one.' Starmer wanted to know what the referendum question would be?
'It has to be the deal versus the status quo,' Kyle said. 'And the status quo
is Remain.' Starmer urged them to talk to Corbyn.

They went into LOTO on 20 February, two days after the Tiggers'
breakaway. McDonnell and Milne were there. Kyle and Wilson explained
the idea. Kyle said, 'This is the only way we can see of the party staying
united through this.' Until this point, initiatives for a referendum had
been vehicles for attacks on Corbyn. Kyle and Wilson respectfully
suggested it was a solution which would help the leadership. This was a
relief to Starmer since previous efforts, led by Leslie and Umunna, to
move Corbyn towards a referendum had been seen as a plot to remove
him.

Kyle and Wilson also went to see John Bercow to ask his advice. 'There
was never a sense of, "This needs to happen and I'm going to be on your
side", or "You need to speak to these people",' Kyle recalled. 'There was
simply none of it.' The pair, not thinking themselves grand enough, had
asked Margaret Beckett to table the amendment for them. Bercow
snapped, 'I think everyone's just had enough of the great and the good.
We just need people standing up and making sincere arguments about
sincere propositions. Just do it yourselves.'

When they reconvened in the tearoom, Wilson would offer Kyle a
drink, then 'turn his accent up to ten' and growl, 'I'm not ordering a
peppermint fucking tea.'

*   *   *

In the shadow cabinet meeting on 25 February, a week after the split, Starmer and Abbott argued that Labour needed to be able to offer its voters hope of a referendum in some circumstances. Gradually, Barry Gardiner, the shadow international trade secretary, and Shami Chakrabarti, who had both arrived unpersuaded, changed sides, leaving Trickett as the lone voice against. Milne was shocked. 'Seumas looked shaken, to be honest,' said one shadow minister.[30] Later that afternoon, Corbyn announced Labour would back a second referendum – unless MPs voted for Labour's version of the Brexit plan. The Tiggers had spent a year as Labour MPs trying to get their party to back a referendum. It took them just a week as independents to achieve the same goal.

Addressing the PLP, Corbyn said, 'In line with our conference policy, we are committed to also putting forward or supporting an amendment in favour of a public vote to prevent a damaging Tory Brexit being forced on the country.' In a briefing note for MPs, LOTO said 'any referendum would need to have a credible leave option and remain' but that 'Labour would not countenance supporting no-deal as an option'. The run-off would be between May's deal and Remain. This made it more likely that voters would back Remain. 'We hit a bit of a wheeze with this argument that we might have a public vote on a bad Tory deal but not on anything else,' a Starmer source said.

A furious John Mann warned Corbyn the decision 'will stop you being prime minister'. Emily Thornberry, throwing all previous caution to the wind, promptly announced on *Channel 4 News* that both she and Corbyn would campaign in that referendum to remain in the EU.

At the next shadow cabinet meeting, Trickett found support from Lavery, Richard Burgon and Rebecca Long-Bailey, who felt the decision had been taken behind their backs and presented as a fait accompli – but the genie would not go back in the bottle.

Labour backing a referendum had seemed to be the most likely outcome for months, but it had not always been the case. A less stubborn Tory prime minister could have enlisted several dozen Labour MPs for single market membership and hundreds for customs union membership, but the process had radicalised Labour MPs no less than their Tory counterparts. 'As the government screwed this up more and more,' a shadow cabinet minister recalled, 'people went past the moment of close economic relationships into the territory of a second referendum.'

The combination of the referendum policy and Tom Watson's rear-guard action halted the Tiggers in their tracks. 'Tom stopped thirty to forty people quitting,' a senior backbencher said. 'There was a point when things could really have unravelled.' When his Future Britain Group met for the first time on 11 March, around 150 MPs gathered in Committee Room 14 – a decent measure of the scale of what might have been if things had unfolded differently. 'I feel so aggrieved that he kept all those people in the Labour Party,' one of the Tiggers recalled. 'If we just had a few more, we might have made a difference.' The original hope had been that a second wave of Labour MPs would join the exodus a week later, a second Tigger said. 'There were eleven to twelve MPs who had said they were going to come and a number of Labour peers as well. People were scared of doing it and Tom gave them a way out.' Berger was particularly aggrieved that colleagues who had attended her wedding let her down. A third MP said, 'You realise that a lot of people are very timid. A lot of people were waiting to see whether the bandwagon had left the station before they got on it. All these people, Keir included, sat there supporting the naked emperor. It was morally reprehensible.'

Their mission stalled, the Tiggers began to fight among themselves.

THE GAUKEWARD SQUAD

From Croissant Club to Rebel Alliance

5 to 26 February 2019

Villandry, an upscale brunch restaurant on Waterloo Place, a block from the Athenaeum Club, was less than a mile from the Commons. But SW1 was, literally, a small world. Venture past the end of Whitehall and you could meet in relative privacy. It was there, after the Chequers summit in July 2018, that Amber Rudd, a self-styled 'organiser of people', began meeting Greg Clark and David Gauke for breakfast, sometimes joined by other ministers who had voted Remain. When Philip Hammond got wind of the meetings, he was too bashful to ask why he had been excluded and approached Rudd to say, 'I think we should have a group and meet regularly.' An amused Rudd teased: 'Do you want to join us then, Philip?' After just two trips to Villandry, the chancellor decided the world was not small enough: 'This is insane. There are all these ministerial cars parked outside. There are staff, people could see us walking across the park or driving here. Why don't we start meeting in the Commons?'

They switched to Hammond's office on the ministerial corridor. 'It wasn't that I was the leader of the group,' he recalled. 'It was simply that I had the biggest office. When I became chancellor, I refused to move from the foreign secretary's office which is by far the best, apart from the prime minister's. I just stayed put and shoved Boris into the chancellor's pokey little office.' On 14 November 2018 Hammond hosted a meeting of the five minus David Lidington at which they agreed they could not serve in a government that was pushing for no-deal. They dined on soft pastries. One of Hammond's aides christened them 'the Croissant Club', which simultaneously suggested continental credentials and metropolitan sensibilities. Only later, when they finally turned against May, would they become 'the Rebel Alliance'.

The group met for breakfast every Tuesday before cabinet. Rudd's experience in the private sector convinced her that the way to influence a board meeting was to meet people privately beforehand to get their view and try to persuade them of hers. Cabinet was a board meeting for senior ministers. Their goal, one attendee explained, was to 'keep the prime minister on course, to focus on a deal rather than being pulled off course by the no-dealers and the hardline Brexiteers'. Rudd could see, too, that they would only have clout if they stuck together, just as the ERG did.

On occasion they invited Gavin Barwell, the Downing Street chief of staff, to join them, so he could report back on their views. Sometimes he asked to impart information from May. Barwell also saw the Pizza Club and the ERG in this way. Numbers swelled to ten ministers but the core group remained Rudd, Gauke, Clark and Hammond. David Lidington, close in his views to the Croissant Club but May's right-hand man, was necessarily semi-detached.

Hammond had two Brexit priorities. The first was to persuade Theresa May to back a transition period, a goal he had accomplished by the middle of 2017. The second was to prevent a no-deal departure. 'I think he decided quite early on that he was going to make himself the anti-Brexit hero,' a senior civil servant said, 'and his story will be told ten years hence.' Hammond later confirmed, 'I was far more interested in securing what I thought was the right kind of Brexit than protecting my own political career.'[1] As another former Treasury minister, Gauke was also preoccupied with the potential economic hazards of no-deal. He was a militant pragmatist who had begun his career as a hardline Eurosceptic, but as one colleague put it, 'Like Hammond, he's a convert through reality.'

During her six months away from the cabinet the Croissant Club missed Rudd's organisational drive. When she returned, she had a choice to make. Both Nick Boles and Oliver Letwin were discreetly encouraging her to go for the party leadership in the contest expected to follow the fall of May. The pro-dealers wanted a figurehead of their own to take on the Brexiteers. Nicky Morgan, Damian Green, Margot James and Nicholas Soames all sounded her out. Rudd put together a leadership team who began communicating via a WhatsApp group called 'Sunlight' in the summer of 2017. During her time on the backbenches, David Cameron's former Number 10 aides Sir Craig Oliver and Adam Atashzai began discreetly advising her. The group met at Rudd's house in Hammersmith or the home of Kate Fall, Cameron's deputy chief of staff. A new and expanded WhatsApp group named after Rudd's street began in November 2018. Oliver Letwin and Stephen Hammond became members, along with her former special adviser Mo Hussein.

Rudd had a choice to make. To mount a serious challenge for the leadership she would need to attract pragmatic Remainers who believed the 2016 vote should be respected and some moderate Brexiteer support. But her time in cabinet, listening to the dire warnings, had given her the firm conviction that her top political priority had to be to stop no-deal. Over dinner with her closest supporters that December, she chose her path. A senior MP said, 'She made an active choice: "I'm not going to be leader of the Conservative Party and prime minister, I'm going to do this."'

The decision was influenced by Rudd's growing conviction that May did not know what she wanted, that the prime minister was liable to agree with the last pressure group to sit on her. Rudd resolved that the Croissant Clubbers be just as aggressive in stating their wishes as the ERG, telling her colleagues, 'Good behaviour has to go out of the window.'

Rudd's determination to fight no-deal was crystallised by the cabinet meeting on 15 January, the day of the first meaningful vote. Andrea Leadsom warned there might be no Brexit. Rudd pressed for indicative votes but Hunt spoke against. Gove suggested talking to Labour. In her diary, Rudd noted, 'Cabinet is just as bad as the MPs. They criticised all the options but won't support anything else.'

After the vote she invited like-minded colleagues to Hammond's office. The attendees joined a WhatsApp group called 'January 15th'. When Rudd arrived Hammond told her, 'This is your group, you speak.' Seeing the MPs assembled, she urged them to 'keep calm' and thought that, in the absence of other leadership, she should step up. The following day the group met again under her chairmanship. There were thirty MPs present, including five members of the cabinet.

On 24 January Rudd was interviewed on *Newsnight* and asked three times whether she was prepared to resign to vote with the rebels to stop no-deal. She failed to deny the proposition, telling the programme she was 'committed to making sure we avoid no-deal', which she described as 'the worst possible outcome'. When her special adviser Jason Stein was sent the audio he hit the roof. The following day Rudd was interviewed by George Parker, the political editor of the *Financial Times*, for the paper's Lunch with the FT feature, in a piece that was not due to be published for eight days. 'It's quite prominent,' a nervous Parker said. 'We can't give it to a backbencher. Are you still going to be in the cabinet?' Rudd and Stein did not know what to tell him.

The problem for the Croissant Club was that May continued to keep them in the dark. On 7 February they sent the prime minister a letter expressing their huge concerns about no-deal. It was signed by Rudd, Clark and Gauke, but they had also managed to get the backing of Damian Hinds, David Mundell and Claire Perry. Julian Smith sent a furious text message to Rudd to say the letter was 'appalling'. Later that day he rang, urging them not to go public, not something they had ever intended. 'We were trying to make some noise,' Rudd recalled. 'Theresa May was only influenced by who was making the noise.'

Had May been honest with them she might have admitted that a trip to Northern Ireland just two days earlier had convinced her that she could not back no-deal. Characteristically, she kept this information to herself.

The visit emerged from a diplomatic disaster. The prime minister's decision to whip in favour of the Brady amendment, which called for 'replacing' the backstop, had sparked fury in Dublin. Simon Coveney, the Irish foreign minister, cancelled a dinner with Karen Bradley, the Northern Ireland secretary, who was summoned to the Ministry for Foreign Affairs for a dressing down about Britain's colonial attitude.

Bradley had been 'shocked' to be appointed Northern Ireland secretary in the January 2018 reshuffle. The shock was quickly reciprocated in Ulster when she admitted, in September 2018, 'I didn't understand things like when elections are fought in Northern Ireland – people who are nationalists don't vote for unionist parties and vice versa.'

Bradley 'implored' May to go to Belfast to make a speech settling nerves. 'It was clear to me that we had to find a way to explain to people why the Brady amendment had happened because it was a real threat to the Union,' she remembered. 'There was a genuine threat that people would start to turn away from the UK.'

May did so, risking the ire of the ERG by pledging that there was 'no question' of leaving the EU without some 'insurance policy for the future' like the backstop. She said technology could 'play a part' in a rewriting of the withdrawal agreement but she did not embrace alternative arrangements in the way her party wanted.

The prime minister had a meeting at Queen's University with representatives of civic society, business groups and trade unions, spending fifteen minutes at each table. She then visited a nationalist community centre in North Belfast. May was most affected, however, by a private meeting at Stormont House with people who had been involved in the peace process, one Protestant and four moderate Catholics. They warned that their support for the Union was being undermined by Brexit, the prospect of no-deal and the 'unfair leverage' of the DUP's confidence and supply deal with the government. These were people 'absolutely terrified' about the return of a hard border. Bradley recalled, 'They were very powerful in the testimony they gave about how important being allowed to continue to live your life in the way you have for twenty years since the Good Friday Agreement was to the nationalist community – for their ability to manage community relations. People were really, really agitated at the idea of border posts going up.'

One of those present told May, 'Twenty years ago, when I was my children's age, I looked at the Republic and it was economically far poorer than the UK and socially more conservative. Now I look at a Republic that is economically much closer to the UK. It's certainly more socially liberal than Northern Ireland. For my children, the politics of Ireland is not about old-fashioned Republicanism.' Gavin Barwell recalled, 'They all spoke incredibly powerfully about the combination of the lack of devolved government and the fear of a no-deal Brexit.'[2] He added, 'I think her instinctive unionism, which is deep and has been there throughout her political career, was very strongly reinforced by that visit and led to a determination to find a solution that addressed the concerns of those people.'[3] David Lidington said, 'What she could see was that moderate nationalists, upon whose consent the Union relies, were shifting away and contemplating a united Ireland.' This message from middle-class Catholics was reinforced by May's conversations with Sylvia Hermon, the independent unionist MP, who highlighted similar concerns among Protestants. 'Hermon was describing how a section of liberal unionist opinion was moving away from unionism,' a Number 10 adviser recounted. 'That really worried Theresa May.'

May was also concerned there could be a knock-on effect in Scotland. She had been far more invested in the result of the Scottish independence referendum in 2014 than in the EU referendum campaign. A Downing Street adviser recalled, 'She felt very strongly and she wanted to go up and campaign and make speeches in that one.'

On her return from Belfast, it became definitively clear the Union was May's top priority. 'The PM talked about the likelihood of a border poll,' one said. To another aide, the Belfast trip was the moment that 'explains why we got to where we got to'. A senior civil servant agreed: 'It really shook her how fragile it felt over there. She is a unionist to the tips of her fingers and you could tell it left a real imprint on her.'

Three days later, on 8 February, May had dinner with Leo Varadkar at Farmleigh House in Dublin. Barwell judged it the 'best engagement' between the two leaders. The chief of staff had gone over a few days earlier for dinner with Brian Murphy, his Irish counterpart. Both were frustrated with previous interactions between their leaders; they wanted to coordinate in advance, two zoo keepers trying to get less than amorous pandas to mate. May also took Robbins and Peter Hill with her. Varadkar was accompanied by John Callinan, Robbins' main contact, and Martin Fraser, the secretary general of the department of the Taoiseach. May and Varadkar had some time alone and talked frankly about the political pressures they were under. The dinner was drama free. Both left with greater understanding of the other.

The final clincher for May was advice from officials that if Britain left the EU without a deal, there would have to be direct rule of Northern Ireland from Whitehall, a situation liable to make Belfast combust. Karen Bradley warned May that worse would follow. 'It was absolutely clear to me that if you went down the full direct rule route that would be the end of the United Kingdom,' she recalled. All government decisions would have had to be taken by orders in council, not even debated on the floor of the Commons. 'I just felt that you would very, very quickly see all the parties in Northern Ireland turn against the UK government.'

None of this, however, was evident to the Croissant Club ministers. On 13 February, Lidington called Rudd to warn her that the ERG were 'kicking off' and demanding a meeting with May. He suggested the Croissant Clubbers do the same. When the January 15th group met Lidington, they departed just as nervous about no-deal. They became 'alarmed' when he reached for a copy of Hansard to check what the prime minister had said about no-deal. 'None of us left the meeting feeling like he had a plan,' said one cabinet minister. 'He was sympathetic, but he didn't know what was going on either. Theresa was operating in complete isolation.' The situation was becoming more acute since May intended, at this point, to hold a second meaningful vote within a fortnight.

The catalyst for action came on 14 February when the ERG flexed its muscles, abstaining on a procedural motion, condemning May to defeat. On the same day, the government was forced to accede to a demand by Anna Soubry for the publication of cabinet papers on the threat of no-deal. One of May's chief lieutenants blamed the Croissant Club: 'Rudd informed Soubry that there were some scary no-deal papers in cabinet.' The vote was irrelevant, but it contributed to the feeling that May was powerless in the face of ERG truculence.

The following morning Rudd had breakfast with Geordie Greig, the editor of the *Daily Mail* and also an opponent of no-deal, who encouraged her to write an article. Rudd, 'on fire with anger', penned an explosive thousand-word piece denouncing the ERG as a party within a party and sent it to her special adviser. Jason Stein was a man happiest swinging an axe in the heat of political battle, but the piece gave even him 'a heart attack'. He toned it down. Even so the watered-down version labelled the ERG a 'gang of MPs within the Conservative party' engaged in 'guerrilla tactics against the prime minister'. The text went on, 'We must not allow the ideological purity of the ERG to stop us delivering on a negotiated settlement that is the best way to leave the EU.' Rudd compared preparations for no-deal to putting on a seat belt but noted, 'Just because you put on a seatbelt ... doesn't mean you should intend to crash the car.' The article concluded, 'If they succeed the voters will never forgive them, & I suspect the country won't either.'

Stein told Rudd she had to show the piece to Downing Street. 'For fuck's sake!' she complained. She emailed the piece to Robbie Gibb at 11.50 a.m. A panicked Paul Harrison, the press secretary, replied thirty-five minutes later, begging her not to publish: 'I know you feel strongly about this – and the PM was really disappointed last night too – but I am afraid we are going to have to ask you not to submit this piece please. I don't dispute the facts, by the way ... but it will be inflammatory and position the PM uncomfortably in having to take a side.' Privately,

Harrison was furious, telling colleagues it was 'outrageous because it was unnecessary'.

At 1.08 p.m. Rudd backed off, but signalled that she would not remain silent. That very morning, she revealed, broadcasters doorstepping her had encouraged her to 'describe the ERG as traitors'. She noted, 'I am blessed with daily opportunities to put my view out.' The same day Margot James told Channel 4 she would leave the government if there was no deal, proof that others were prepared to put their heads further above the parapet.

February 19th was the day the hardcore of the ERG started referring to themselves as The Spartans, after the small force who fought to the death at Thermopylae.[4] The Croissant Club felt they needed to arm themselves with something more threatening than flaky pastries.

On the 21st Gauke and Clark met Rudd in her office in the Department for Work and Pensions. The three of them agreed they were prepared to resign to vote for anything which would stop no-deal. 'They were the iron triangle,' an MP said, 'Amber led that team and kept them strong in cabinet and in conversations with the prime minister.' Rudd knew from recent experience that backbench life was bleak. 'We only have this influence because we are on the inside,' she said. 'Once you are on the outside, it is a wilderness. You are Damian Green. It is brutal.' But after all the meetings and coded interventions, the anonymous quotes, it was time to do something. Greg Clark suggested they write a joint article to put a marker down. 'We saw this as a prelude to resigning,' said one signatory. The gloves were off. The Croissant Club had become the Rebel Alliance.

Clark was an unlikely figure to take up arms, a cerebral soul who had been the party's head of policy under Iain Duncan Smith and Michael Howard, but whose experience as business secretary had radicalised him on the risks of no-deal. Another pro-dealer, who had known Clark for twenty years, said, 'My great criticism has always been that he's hyper-cautious. He sure as hell redeemed himself in this episode. He was properly brave, out there, really willing to fight for things.'

The same was true of others who would once have been labelled wets – Alistair Burt, Richard Benyon, Richard Harrington and Nicholas Soames – collegiate figures, who had tired of losing to the 'take-no-prisoners' approach of the Tory right and decided that if they could not beat them, they should join them in forming their own awkward squad.

Journalists, always vulnerable to the lure of a pun, dubbed the rebels the 'Gaukeward Squad'.

At 1 p.m. on Monday 18 February, Rudd, Gauke, Clark and David Mundell, the Scottish secretary, saw the prime minister. They met beforehand in Dover House, Mundell's office, to agree their approach. Rudd said, 'Don't fill the pauses. The only time you have a chance of getting the prime minister to say what she thinks is if you sit out her silence.' Nonetheless, it was another unsatisfactory encounter with the enigmatic May. Rudd asked the key question: 'What will you do if you get to the end of March and we haven't got a deal?' The PM erupted. 'Amber, why do you keep asking me that?' she snapped, before changing the subject. 'It was really frustrating,' another minister said. 'We came out none the wiser.' Clark recalled, 'We said that we were very concerned about the possibility of no-deal and could she assure us personally that she not only understood but shared our intention to avoid no-deal? Because she wasn't prepared to give us that assurance we thought we had to say something in public. We came away really worried.'

At 3.30 p.m. a group of around twenty junior ministers went in and repeated the same message about avoiding no-deal. Barwell recalled, 'I constantly had people on both sides saying to me, "What was she going to do on no-deal?" She used to get frustrated by both sides trying to co-opt her onto their side of the argument. I said to both sides, consistently, "I do not believe the prime minister is going to do no-deal on 29th March." That was always my view.' But if it was May's view, she wasn't saying, a tactic and a temperamental tendency which were to cost her dearly.

If May was still not prepared to show her hand, she was reaching the point of personal despair about her predicament. 'Sometimes I think there's a route through,' she told her advisers. 'And sometimes I just think, I don't know how we're going to get through this.' May did not show her emotions. It was spoken matter-of-factly, but was 'uncharacteristically revealing' to those who witnessed this *cri de coeur*.

The next morning, at eight, a wider group of ministers, known as the Union Group, met in Hammond's office. The four who had seen May reported back to others including Bradley and James Brokenshire. Rudd was beginning to conclude that May's shiftiness meant she was prepared to go for no-deal. 'She was telling everyone else different things,' Rudd remembered. 'She was allowing the ERG to assume she was with them.

She was sticking to her clear conscience of not misleading people by not saying anything.'

Gauke wrote the article. The first draft was directly aimed at the government and called explicitly for a delay to Brexit. 'If there is no breakthrough in the next few days the government will only have one responsible course of action to take – to seek to extend Article 50 and delay our date of departure,' it said. 'Crashing out of the European Union on 29 March would be a disaster for our economy, national security and the integrity of the United Kingdom. It is not an outcome that a responsible government should accept. And if the government fails to intervene, Parliament would be right to do so.'

After discussion they agreed to tone it down. Gauke rewrote the piece and shared it with Clark and Rudd, who was in Amsterdam with her new boyfriend. The focus was changed to make the ERG the target, rather than the government. The new final paragraph said, 'It is time that many of our Conservative Parliamentary colleagues in the ERG recognised that Parliament will stop a disastrous no-deal Brexit on 29 March. If that happens, they will have no one to blame but themselves for delaying Brexit.' Gauke was the cabinet's 'unicorn slayer'. He had little time for the fudges and 'pretend outcomes' in which MPs did not have to face tough choices. The ERG would not support the deal while no-deal was an option. May would not take it off the table to placate the ERG. Gauke wanted to be clear that Parliament would take it off the table.

After the tweaks, it was still too much for David Mundell, who declined to sign, and for Philip Hammond. The chancellor's calculation was that, in tandem with Lidington, he would be more effective working on the inside than 'throwing my toys out of the pram'. When Hammond wanted to suggest something political he would write May a memo, typing and emailing it directly to the PM himself without copying in his private office officials or his special advisers. On this occasion, the chancellor was used as an intermediary, sending the article to Gavin Barwell in Number 10, implying the piece would not be published if there were fresh assurances about no-deal. Gauke had approved the move, but Rudd and Stein were furious. 'It nearly fucked the whole thing,' said a source. 'Having blocked the op-ed the week before there was no way we were going to show it to them.' However, by the time Julian Smith was told about the article, it had been sent to the *Mail*. Smith was 'infuriated', feeling Number 10 had failed to crush the initiative, effectively giving tacit approval to something that would cause him whipping problems.

The article went up on 22 February, a Friday evening, and was quickly the lead item on both the 10 O'clock News and *Newsnight*. The *Mail* billed it as a direct challenge to May, which the authors had troubled to ensure it was not. 'The softer version still blew the bloody doors off,' Gauke recalled. 'Robbie was furious with us, as was Julian.' Rudd was still in Amsterdam when the storm broke, her romantic weekend disturbed by repeated calls from the chief whip. She did not ring back until the following day. The group knew Smith agreed with them about no-deal but he hated not being in control.

The reaction of the ERG and the rest of the cabinet to the group's threat to vote to delay Brexit was incendiary. Five cabinet colleagues told the *Sunday Times* that Rudd should be sacked.[5] Brexiteers and cabinet pragmatists like Jeremy Hunt believed taking no-deal off the table would reduce the government's leverage in negotiations with Brussels. Rudd listened carefully to this view, but she was also friends with entrepreneurs, including William Kendall who revitalised the Green & Black's chocolate firm. He told her, 'I would never threaten something that would do me more damage than my opponent.' An ERG member told Rudd, 'The price of democracy is more important than the value to the economy.' To her, the economy had to come first.

The reaction of the Bresisters was that the arrival of the Rebel Alliance was better late than never but might be 'too late' to be decisive. Nicky Morgan told them, 'You are so late to this party if you want to influence things.'

That weekend, the prime minister addressed the National Conservative Convention outside Oxford and insisted, 'We must not, and I will not, frustrate what was the largest democratic exercise in this country's history.' She then flew to Sharm el Sheikh, for meetings on Brexit in the margins of an EU summit with Arab leaders. There, she announced that the second meaningful vote had been delayed until 12 March. Fruitless and dispiriting encounters with Donald Tusk, Angela Merkel, Mark Rutte, Leo Varadkar and Jean-Claude Juncker followed, in which she was repeatedly offered and declined an extension to Article 50 beyond the 29 March deadline. Robbins had a private dinner with Martin Selmayr.

To EU officials and MPs, May was just playing for time, running down the clock in the hope that the threat of no-deal would get people to back her deal. 'I think any extension isn't addressing the issue,' she said as the summit ended. However, pressed by journalists, she refused to say if she would fire ministers who voted to avoid no-deal and delay Brexit.

On 25 February, Rudd took a call from a friend in Number 10 who did not think May had done enough to rule out no-deal. She knew the ERG were getting similar reassurances to the Rebel Alliance. It was time to 'reach into our arsenal'. Twenty-three ministers met that evening. Richard Harrington and Margot James, both more outspoken than their cabinet counterparts, had jointly written another article with Claire Perry. Rudd rang Stein and said, 'Do you think you can get the op-ed in the *Mail*?' The paper ended up splashing on their broadside on the Tuesday morning under the headline, '15 MINISTERS IN THREAT TO QUIT'.

In a Number 10 meeting that morning, James Slack, May's official spokesman, read out comments by John Mann about Labour backing a second referendum, comparing Jeremy Corbyn's change of heart to 'Nick Clegg when he reneged on his pledge on tuition fees'. May, with waspish speed, remarked, 'What? You get a two hundred grand salary and a nice house on the west coast of America.'

This sparked laughter but cabinet was an angry affair. May, so often a black hole of concealed emotion, was visibly furious at the challenge presented by the two Rebel Alliance articles. Her demeanour gave other ministers carte blanche to attack. Liz Truss, with the zeal of the convert, branded Rudd, Gauke and Clark 'kamikaze cabinet ministers'. Andrea Leadsom was 'audibly furious'. Brandon Lewis, Damian Hinds, James Brokenshire and Julian Smith all criticised the trio, though the chief whip tempered his view by saying he understood the honesty of their motives. Brexiteers acknowledged the dangers of no-deal but warned that delivering no Brexit would be far worse.

That evening, May met Leave-supporting junior ministers and her temper had barely cooled. She was at pains to stress that she opposed a lengthy extension to Article 50 because it 'would be seen as a betrayal' by the public. Asked what would happen if Robbins told her a short extension was not negotiable, she snapped, 'I don't just do what Olly Robbins tells me to!'[6] For those familiar with the extent of Robbins' influence, the 'just' in that sentence was doing a lot of heavy lifting.

One minister conspicuous by his silence in cabinet was the one now most pivotal to events, Geoffrey Cox. The attorney general sat out the exchanges and left before the end. When Michael Gove asked May which way she would whip on a vote between no-deal and an extension, she gave no answer. Stuck between the ERG and the Rebel Alliance, two now equally determined groups, May had only one escape route. For several weeks Cox had been travelling to Brussels to try to secure just that.

COX'S CODPIECE

The Legal Advice and MV2

18 February to 12 March 2019

The weather on 12 March was chill and damp, the kind of day which begins overcast and gradually sinks into your bones. The thunderclap that cut through Westminster a little after 11 a.m. came not from the skies, but the pen of the attorney general, Geoffrey Cox. It was the morning of the second meaningful vote, already 'MV2', and dozens of votes on Theresa May's deal hung in the balance.

In his December legal advice, Cox had ruled that the Northern Ireland backstop 'would endure indefinitely until a superseding agreement takes its place'. Since then, he had been engaged in intensive discussions with Brussels to secure further legal assurances, a political fig leaf to enable MPs to back the deal. It became known as 'Cox's codpiece'.[1]

Ministers, MPs and journalists scanned through Cox's text. There were nineteen paragraphs. As they read, morale rose: improvements had been made to the text, more protections were in place, politically it was a more watertight deal. Paragraph 19 delivered the bolt of lightning which left the Conservative Party on fire. Two phrases leaped from the page: 'The legal risk remains unchanged … no internationally lawful means of exiting the protocol's arrangements'. One political editor tweeted, 'Game over.'[2]

The prime minister learned the bad news much earlier. Cox had sat up all night writing and sent his paper to the prime minister at 5.30 a.m. For many of her closest aides, this was the moment that sank Theresa May's hopes of passing a Brexit deal and with it her premiership. With inelegant but apposite imagery, a former political adviser remarked that morning, 'Cox took off the codpiece and fucked her.'

It was a compelling narrative which provoked in several of May's team a deep and abiding hatred of Cox. Why could he not have gilded the lily, presented his views in a more politically palatable form? Who cared about his legal reputation in the face of the collapse of the government? Did he not realise that a lawyer ought to give his client what she wanted? If the advice was disastrous, to spring it on 10 Downing Street unawares was treacherous too. But this was not the full story. Far from springing his decision on May and her inner circle, Cox had on six separate occasions in the preceding days warned the prime minister that her plans did not go far enough and that he, consequently, could not change his legal advice. Given the seismic impact that refusal was to have, it is one of the greatest mysteries of May's enigmatic premiership that she chose to ignore him.

Cox said, 'A myth has grown up that I sprang a bombshell on Number 10 on the morning of the 12th of March, after the prime minister had returned from Strasbourg. That is so far wide of the mark that it is really laughable. As a barrister, I would never let my client be shocked, knowing what was at stake, by not having warned that client repeatedly, in detail, probably over-painstaking detail, about what the nature of my advice was likely to be. The prime minister and the chief of staff knew exactly what I was going to say, in my opinion, days before she signed the joint instrument, an instrument which I urged her not to sign.'

Since early February, the attorney general had been a member of May's inner circle, attending the 8.30 a.m. meetings of key figures, who by now included David Lidington, Steve Barclay – the Brexit secretary – Julian Smith, Gavin Barwell, the cabinet secretary Mark Sedwill and Oliver Robbins. Philip Hammond was sometimes admitted. The chief whip was keen to have a Brexiteer, rather than the uber-Remainer Lidington, 'upfront' in the government's effort to improve and sell the deal. He urged May to use Cox. In mid-February they decided the attorney general should go to Brussels to try to secure a legally binding addendum to the deal which would allow him to reassure MPs that the backstop was temporary. Since Cox was to be marking the government's homework, it seemed logical to get him to write the essay too. Recent weeks had seen the government try to convince Parliament in order to convince the EU. Now the game was to convince the EU in order to convince Parliament.

When it was announced that Cox was to go into battle with the
Europeans, journalists seized on a tweet he had published on 1 February
showing a painting of the Duke of Wellington, whose greatest victory
had been on a battlefield in Belgium.[3] The prime minister asked Robbins
whether there was a chance of the EU agreeing to a legal tweak. He said,
'Prime Minister, on a scale of, say, eight, I think they're at six and we're
at three. There's a gap between us.' But as a witness put it, 'Robbins
wasn't telling her it was impossible.' To Cox and his allies, this ambiguity
raised expectations that were hard to meet in the negotiating room.

Cox was accompanied by Steve Barclay. When the Brexit secretary was
appointed, in November 2018, Barwell said his job was not to negotiate
the withdrawal agreement: 'You are here to prepare for no-deal and then
phase two.' Yet, when phase one dragged into the new year, there was
pressure from the Brexiteers to involve one of their own. 'He wanted to
be more involved because he did not have much to do,' a Downing Street
official recalled. Tall and broad, with the stature of a rugby second row,
Barclay had shown political courage in 2016, when he was the only
member of David Cameron's whips' office to back Brexit. To Barclay, it
was a simple equation that 'you have to be able to change those who
make decisions on your behalf'. This had led to lonely days keeping his
head down while colleagues 'slagged off' those voting Leave. He expected
to be out of a job afterwards and was prepared to sacrifice his career.
Smart and keen, he was regarded by pro-dealers in the cabinet as 'the
sensible face of the Brexiteers'. He was promoted quickly from DExEU
whip to secretary of state after the departure of Dominic Raab. To May's
inner circle, Barclay was a breath of fresh air after the passive-aggressive
warfare of Raab and Davis. 'He would try and find solutions,' said one
fellow Brexiteer. Like Gove, Fox and Cox, Barclay believed it was better
to get out of Europe even if the deal was not perfect.

Cox, crucially, had a different approach to both May and Barclay. 'She
felt we should aim quite high but be reasonable about our expectations,'
said a senior figure. 'We probably weren't going to get our first bid. Cox,
strategically, felt we needed to choose something that we thought was
just about reasonable and then pursue it with absolute ferocity.' Barclay
agreed with the prime minister that there should be a lead option and a
fallback position. He wanted a time limit on the backstop or a unilateral
exit clause. 'The question is: what will get through Parliament?' he said.
A time limit was 'easy to communicate'. Barclay had seen some EU lead-

ers, notably the Poles, talking about a five-year time limit. He felt it 'a lot cleaner' than the complicated legal procedure the attorney general was contemplating. Cox stuck to his guns. 'We just undermine ourselves if we look like we're all over the place and falling back all the time,' the attorney general said. He thought Barclay's wish list impossible to deliver without reopening the withdrawal agreement. May was persuaded that Cox was right. 'We went in with the lowest offer,' a minister said. 'That's what was agreed by the PM: we'll go in with a low pitch.'

Cox spent July and August 2018, his first two months in post, immersing himself in the detail of the backstop agreement. He feared the damage had been done in the Joint Report of December 2017 and when May accepted the legally binding text the following April. Getting what the Tory party needed, a means of exit for the UK, would need a fundamental change in approach from Brussels. 'A backstop is a 100 per cent or whole of life insurance policy,' he told fellow ministers. 'If you put a term on it, or a unilateral exit right, it becomes something different. What we were seeking was a manifest change of principle.' Privately, Cox confided to May his fear it was 'not possible' to deliver. But when the prime minister continued to publicly predict that she would secure changes to the backstop, Cox assumed she had been given some private encouragement. 'I went [to Brussels] wondering what I didn't know,' he told friends later. 'I assumed the prime minister knew something I didn't.' He quickly learned that was a false assumption.

For three weeks the attorney general worked up a proposal which he called 'a fire escape to the backstop'. Cox sought advice from some of Britain's leading experts in EU law, including Prof Sir Alan Dashwood QC – who had run the legal secretariat of the European Court of Justice in the late 1970s and was by now Emeritus Professor of European Law at Cambridge – and Prof Vaughan Lowe, Emeritus Chichele Professor of Public International Law at Oxford. Cox recalled, 'I drafted something that I thought was the least threatening to the European Union, which could be characterised as a modest modification, leaving intact the bulk of the protection of the backstop while providing a fire escape. In other words, not an exit you could use routinely, or just at your will. But I still doubted personally whether, without a major political reset, it could work.' Cox sought to make his plan both acceptable to the EU and 'the minimum necessary to change my opinion'.

Barclay adopted Cox's fire escape analogy and explained to colleagues, 'There was an exit to the building, but it was on the fifth floor, you had to climb various stairs, you had to work out which room it was in, climb over the bed, and then there was a ladder down.'

Without a fallback position, Cox was relying on Barnier and Weyand seeing things the same way as he did. Even his own legal advisers doubted they would. 'They told him what he was proposing didn't work,' a member of the negotiating team said, 'but he refused to listen.' Without EU agreement, Cox could not substantively change his legal advice.

The first challenge was to get anyone to see Cox. Throughout January Robbins and his team fought to get both the Commission and the Council to engage. 'Why are you all still coming out here?' EU officials asked. 'This deal is closed.' Donald Tusk, the Council president, was particularly truculent. 'It was incredibly painful,' said a member of Robbins' team. 'Day and night arguing with people to have a meeting with Olly.' Even May 'was quite exasperated'. So much so that she said to Robbins, 'Perhaps I should just be a bit more Trumpian.'

Robbins' stock at home was not improved by events on the evening of 11 February, when he was overheard in a Brussels bar disparaging MPs and suggesting that they and May would have to just accept the basics of the deal already on offer.

Angus Walker of ITV was doing a live broadcast for *News at Ten* outside EU ambassador Tim Barrow's residence in Brussels when he saw Robbins depart in a cab. When Walker returned to his hotel, the Sofitel, the bar was being refurbished so he went to the section of the breakfast room carved out for drinks and found Robbins there talking to two other British officials. The area was small. Walker had little choice but to sit within earshot. Signalling in vain to his cameraman, who seemed clueless about Robbins' identity, to take a picture, Walker sat with his back to the other group and began to make notes on his phone.

Robbins was 'shooting the breeze', his tone 'conspiratorial', showing off to the other officials, even 'slagging off' the late Jeremy Heywood, his mentor, saying he disagreed with the 'hagiography' of Heywood. Walker's contemporaneous note records Robbins as saying the former cabinet secretary 'had a loose relationship with the truth'. ITV decided not to reveal this when they ran the story. Also omitted were Robbins' dismissive references to the independent arbitrator which would police the deal. He seemed resigned that Britain would not be treated fairly by the EU and would have to rely on 'Mexican judges' to save the day. Robbins also did an impersonation of Cox, describing him as 'an extraordinary character' and then mocked his verbosity: 'I said to the chancellor I had an hour with Cox and he said, "Did you get a chance to speak?"' Robbins' colleagues laughed. He predicted the PM would 'give [Cox] a peerage' – pause – 'once we've paid off the Mexicans'.

There was plenty for ITV to broadcast about Brexit. Walker listened as Robbins explained that Britain had 'agreed' the backstop was a 'bridge', acknowledging the thing the Brexiteers most feared, that a customs union would become the basis for future negotiations in the trade deal to follow. Robbins suggested Britain would 'agree' that 'the protocol is necessary'. This had Walker's news antennae buzzing. The chief negotiator suggested that a likely outcome would see Britain given a twenty-one-month extension, anathema to the ERG. 'If they don't vote for the deal then then the extension is a long one,' Robbins said. To Walker, it sounded like a tactic to scare MPs into backing May's deal.

Robbins and his friends criticised MPs, their tone 'dismissive and mocking'. Walker's notes record the negotiator saying, 'Imagine you're dealing with children and have to make them choose.' One of his colleagues compared MPs to his own children, who he told, 'You can be well behaved and get Harry Potter stickers.' Walker knew that in the UKRep offices in Brussels, there were wartime posters on the wall saying 'loose lips sink ships', urging staff to be careful what they said in public, and not to let strangers see their phone or laptop screens. Yet here was the senior negotiator, one with a close knowledge of intelligence, speaking frankly in the presence of a stranger. 'Despite someone else coming into the room, he didn't break stride,' Walker said later. 'God knows what he'd said before I came in. Anyone could go into that bar, you didn't have to be a resident.'

Once Downing Street realised Walker had no recording, they tried to rubbish the story, but it was consistent with other people's experience of Robbins. An EU adviser who attended the morning meetings in Number 10 said, 'He was pretty scathing about MPs. He would say, "What don't they understand?" That's not something you should say if you're a civil servant. He's a very bright person and the caricatures of him doing his own thing are not fair. But he did not have a high regard for members of Parliament in general and certainly not for the ERG – but those are the people that are the difference between his success and failure. His attitude was, "This is the deal; they just need to come round and vote for us.'"

Like Raab, Steve Barclay found Robbins secretive and unaccountable. In their first meeting he reached out to the chief negotiator and said there had to be 'one version of the truth between the department and Number 10', putting an end to the turf wars of the past. Robbins simply replied, 'I work for the prime minister.' Barclay thought him 'deaf' to MPs.

Geoffrey Cox visited the Berlaymont four times, the first time on Monday 18 February. It set the tone for a difficult set of negotiations. When the attorney general arrived in Brussels, Michel Barnier felt he ought to roll out the red carpet, descending from his thirteenth-floor office to meet Cox on his arrival. The AG stretched out his arms and, looking around at the buildings that line the Schuman boulevard, he said, 'God, I haven't been to Brussels for forty years.' To Barnier, ignorance of the heart of the European Union was a curious thing to boast about. 'It was emotionally tone deaf,' a witness recalled.

What followed coloured Cox's view in the same way. When Barnier walked into the building he kissed several of the British officials waiting by the door. The sense of the negotiating teams as twin participants in a joint enterprise, rather than adversaries, was sealed in Cox's mind.

An attempt by Barclay to break the ice with Barnier was also thwarted by the civil service. It was traditional to take a gift when meeting for the first time. 'England had just played France in the rugby, so we took him a signed match ball,' a political aide recollected. 'We were banned from giving it to him because they thought it would create a diplomatic incident.' A week earlier, England had beaten France 44–8 at Twickenham. 'We were told by Tim Barrow and Olly Robbins, we were not to be giving him that ball, so the ball was confiscated. It was absolutely ridiculous.' This souvenir of political failure was kept in DExEU's private office.

When they sat down to talk, Cox explained, 'I'm coming here on behalf of Parliament and the government, to enable Parliament to know, that in the last resort, there is a way out of the backstop. I call it a fire escape.' The Commission was, at first, cautious. 'They did not say we were out of court,' one of the British team recalled. But that changed when Cox outlined proposals which included the concept that the exit mechanism could be triggered after a minimum period. 'We asked for a unilateral right [to leave], and a term clause, but they were dead against that,' a British source said.

Over a 'relatively pleasant' dinner at the residence of Sir Tim Barrow, Cox's view that he was presenting the bare minimum which was reasonable was met with scepticism, but not hostility, by the Europeans. 'For arguably two and a half years, they have seen the British government take a whole series of, what they regard, as completely fanciful positions,' a member of the British team said. Allies say Robbins had explored some of the same ideas with Weyand the previous October and November and been rebuffed. 'We'd sort of tried all this,' said one.

Robbins also felt that Cox was trying to negotiate something he had already secured. The withdrawal agreement enshrined in law that the backstop should be temporary. Commission officials were confused. A British negotiator characterised their view thus: 'What you're asking for you've already got. And if you want something other than what you've already got, clearly there's something behind this that we don't understand and that makes us suspicious.' The attorney general, of course, wanted something more politically explicit about how and when the backstop might end, but Task Force 50 wondered if Cox was seeking a stalemate that could be used as a *casus belli* for no-deal.

It did not take Cox long, in turn, to become suspicious of Robbins. The AG quickly realised he was 'not the owner of the relationships' and that arriving once or twice a week would make it difficult to intrude upon the well-established interactions between Robbins and Weyand. Despite probing him in detail before each round of talks, Cox did not truly know what Robbins had said to the Commission before he arrived, nor how the key issues were handled after he departed.

Cox, like David Davis before him, also felt the negotiations under Robbins lacked the narrative theatrics he had perfected as a barrister. 'You have to take your interlocutor on a journey,' he said. 'And that journey will involve highs, lows, emotional moments. A negotiation requires a sort of collective psychology that develops in the negotiation, one side striving to achieve not mastery, but moral advantage over the other. And it is sometimes necessary for those discussions to be abrasive, confrontational and difficult, because otherwise, each party won't understand where the other party's bottom line is, they will not discover where the visceral boundaries of an acceptable negotiation are.' In short, Cox did not think the cosy politeness, epitomised by the kisses at the door, was conducive to effective negotiating. No politician who cared about the Union, he thought, could ever have negotiated the backstop. When he returned to London he told cabinet colleagues, 'We needed a negotiating process where we could have a bloody row! It's only by having a row that your negotiator on the other side realises he's gone too far.'

In the negotiating room, Cox's flamboyant style created its own problems. In London, the attorney general's mellifluous tones and old-fashioned courtroom grandeur had made him an unlikely political hit. Cox looked the EU team in the eye and declared, 'I have never lost a trial in court with any jury.'[4] Yet he had never met a jury like this one. It is difficult to conjure a figure less likely to appeal to Weyand, a blunt German trade negotiator with a severe bob and a fetish for detail. Cox's penchant for referring to his Commission interlocutors as 'my dear Michel' or 'my dear Sabine' was grating to Weyand. A ministerial colleague said, 'She found it patronising. Geoffrey is an acquired taste, particularly if you're a woman.' Cox denied calling the women 'my dear' but admitted using '*ma chère* Sabine' and '*ma chère* Stéphanie'. Witnesses say that Riso, usually the warmer of the two, was more annoyed, Weyand more amused than irritated. 'I've had worse than this,' she told one British official.

Cox saw 'poisonous' briefings about his demeanour as an effort by the Commission to undermine the credibility of his proposals. Barclay thought him professional and smart in his presentation. Yet some British officials cringed, finding Cox a figure from 'a 1950s parody'. 'It was pretty awful,' one female British official recalled.

More seriously, Cox and Barclay's approach suggested they had misread where the real power lay in the room. 'I think both Cox and Barclay thought that what they had to do was establish a deep political relationship with Michel Barnier and that would unlock the process,' said a British diplomat. While Barnier was the front man, Weyand and Riso were the real negotiators. Yet when Cox was asked a question by one of them, he addressed his answer to Barnier. 'I found it uncomfortable,' a British official said. 'There was an edge of cultural sexism to everything he said. In the first couple of meetings, he immediately and instinctively marginalised the two senior women.'

Cox's position as both a minister and a lawyer also presented unique problems. Barnier was used to meeting ministers and then leaving Robbins, Weyand and Riso to fight over the legalese. The Frenchman, also a lawyer by training, was slightly horrified when Cox appeared to want to negotiate directly with him. Cox would say, 'What we need is a lawyer-to-lawyer conversation.' Barnier's reluctance to engage in anything more than exaggerated bonhomie 'was frustrating' to Cox and Barclay, according to those who watched their interactions. 'They started, privately, to blame Barnier, [saying], "He's got no grip. He's not really in charge of this. What's the point?"'

For the Commission, Cox's demands were matters of high political principle rather than technical detail. But having a minister, who was followed off the Eurostar by the television cameras, negotiating text with EU legal service officials, young and clever but without huge authority, made Commission chiefs uncomfortable. 'There was a massive reluctance on the Brussels side to put any of their legal officials in that highly politicised position,' a member of Robbins' team said.

Once into the weeds, there was then an awkward contrast between Cox, who made debating points and built an argument, like a good barrister ('Sabine, I know that you worry about this in the dark watches of the night'), and Commission officials like Thomas Liefländer, continental solicitors poring over the treaties ('I don't understand how this works in article X'). A senior British official said, 'Geoffrey's rhetorical balloons kept being punctured. And he just got frustrated because he thought he was there to win the debate and they thought they were there to explore whether he had a new legal point. And, in their view, he didn't.'

This was perplexing to Cox, who felt his own role in deciding whether the deal would pass muster in Westminster gave him a unique position. 'Geoffrey thought his trump card was to turn up in Brussels and explain, "You need to talk to me because I am the man who must change his legal advice for this to all fly",' a British official explained. Instead, the response of senior EU negotiators was, 'It sounds like Theresa May should get herself a new lawyer.' A senior official in the Council said, 'We thought it was more about trying to keep him happy, giving him a role.'

In the second meeting, on 20 February, Cox presented written proposals. Sabine Weyand and her team were able to study the documents but at the end of the meeting, British officials gathered up all the copies. This prompted Weyand, or her staff, to brief the media that the attorney general had made no formal proposal. 'It wasn't true that we hadn't brought concrete proposals,' a British negotiator said. 'But it's true we took the documents back, because we didn't want them being leaked.'

The attorney general's view was that, as written, Britain could only escape if the EU was provably guilty of 'bad faith' when future trade talks broke down. The problem arose if bad faith could not be proved and the talks simply ran into the sand. It was that conundrum which his plan was designed to solve. 'Geoffrey's view was that grounds for exit should be that the talks had not prospered,' a senior British official said. 'He wanted the burden of proof to be on the EU, effectively, to prove that we had behaved badly and that the talks had failed for that reason. If the two sides just honourably disagreed, that was then a route out of the backstop.' Cox explained: 'The test was, have negotiations irrevocably broken down? In order to be able to prove that, you would have to show that there had been a genuine and sustained set of negotiations, in which your side, claiming the right to terminate, had participated in sincerely. That was the test I proposed, and it was well underpinned by international jurisprudence. All of the expert advice that the civil service gave was that these proposals were wholly reasonable.' Unless the EU could prove the UK had acted in bad faith, the default position would be that Britain could leave the backstop. As he was to say later, 'The key thing is the onus would be on them to prove we can't leave.'[5] The problem was that the EU would only countenance an exit from the backstop if it was proven *they* had acted in bad faith. In the first session, the Commission team raised no objection to the formulation. 'They wrote it down,' a British negotiator said. 'Geoffrey sketched out that it required an adjustment of principle. They didn't say no.' But as time went on, 'They put implausible objection after implausible objection in the way.'

After only two sessions, Cox and Barclay were demoralised. In Downing Street, a civil servant said, 'Cox and Barclay: it was Laurel and Hardy. It was very, very funny to watch them trot off to Brussels extremely confident and come back tail between their legs, each claiming the Commission were the toughest negotiators on the planet.' A member of Robbins' team added, 'They found the process quite miserable, as we had done for two years.'

This led to a rare moment of impish humour from Theresa May when she travelled to Brussels on 20 February for a meeting with Jean-Claude Juncker. Beforehand, the prime minister and Robbins were in the library of Tim Barrow's residence when one of the private secretaries passed on the news that Cox had said he would not be travelling the following day to continue the talks. 'They threw a hissy fit about coming out because the Commission were mean to them,' one of those present said. May, with a rare twinkle, said, 'Well, let's see about that.' When the prime minister met Juncker, she told the Commission president she needed legally binding changes to the backstop. She also announced to the television cameras, 'I'm absolutely delighted that Geoffrey Cox will be here tomorrow to continue this discussion.' A member of the delegation said it was 'nice to see a tiny bit of prime ministerial mischief for once'.

One of May's closest aides recalled, 'One of the things that I found amusing about the whole process was the offstage voices saying, "What we need is someone tougher to do these negotiations." Then, strangely, when other people were exposed to it they didn't find it such an enjoyable process. Whoever you sent, it turned out the EU position was fairly consistent.'

This became evident as the negotiations entered week two. Deciding whether trade talks had irrevocably broken down would require an independent arbitrator. Cox proposed that the tribunal agreed under the withdrawal agreement should refer the issue to the International Court of Justice. Weyand and Riso objected, saying that this would give a tribunal the right to decide questions affecting the single market, the preserve of the European Court of Justice. Cox argued that the question of whether the talks had been exhausted was not a point of EU law. 'It's a question of fact that the International Court of Justice often decides in connection with other treaties,' he said.

In the second week the EU team raised a new hurdle. Weyand asked a simple question – if mediation and arbitration had taken place and Britain was to be released from the backstop: 'What then?' At this point, the EU wanted guarantees that the open border in Northern Ireland would be upheld. Cox sketched out what he called a 'mini backstop', filed in an annexe, specifying the things Britain would unilaterally promise to do to ensure the border remained open. This would mean a British commitment to regulatory participation in the single market for the phytosanitary sector. To Cox this was 'a fraction' of the compliance required by the backstop.

Robbins was surprised when Barnier, initially, seemed 'seduced' by the idea. 'We should take the time to look at it,' the Frenchman said. He was immediately discouraged by Riso and Weyand, who snapped at Barnier, '*Non!*' A British source said, 'She was utterly unprepared to consider the slightest adjustment. This rigid, Task Force 50 legalistic approach meant that they simply didn't have the scope or the mandate to contemplate the level of the change that was required.'

The Commission team mapped out their position, that the 'bare minimum' needed, in such circumstances, was the annexes to the Northern Ireland Protocol. Bluntly, they were happy with a mini backstop as long as it contained everything in the original backstop. 'It was the "day after" question that we found it hard to answer,' a British negotiator said.

This was tough for Cox. One of May's senior aides said, 'He felt that he had deliberately calibrated an offer in an attempt to give them something they could give, and they weren't prepared in his mind to meet him halfway.' A former cabinet minister said, 'Geoffrey has always been able to persuade judges and juries with facts and logic but he discovered that isn't how things work in Brussels.' Some think Task Force 50 resented the entire process, as well as disagreeing on the details. 'Cox completely underestimated the level of anger from Brussels that they were being pushed into renegotiating the backstop, which was a mechanism entirely of the UK's own making,' said a source close to the negotiations.

Senior civil servants could see that it was not in the strategic interests of the Commission to compromise to the degree Cox wanted. 'Frankly, they didn't need to compromise,' said a civil servant in Number 10. 'From where they sat, every version led to a softer Brexit. Their calculation was that things could only get better for them, not worse.'

The nadir was reached on 26 February as Weyand chaired a meeting with Cox in which the attorney general pointed out that the backstop was supposed to be temporary and that refusing to give Britain a way out of it risked breaching the human rights of citizens in Northern Ireland, arguing that the European convention protects the rights of people to vote in order to choose their legislature. Weyand briefed a meeting of member state ambassadors, 'The attorney general said there was a risk of violating the ECHR. He said a lot of surprising things this week.'

Cox became suspicious that Robbins was conducting his own parallel discussions, working up an alternative. A political adviser said, 'Olly Robbins had decided a long time before that the idea that Geoffrey was working on was not going to be acceptable to Barnier and Weyand. In the margins of the meetings that Geoffrey and Steve had in Brussels, Olly was working with them on something – and that was what we got.'

Barclay became convinced the talks were going nowhere. 'Steve worked out pretty quickly that for the other side this was about high political prin-

ciple and not about legal drafting,' a senior official said. 'I think he gave up
on it quite early. He decided, and eventually Geoffrey agreed with him,
that the only way this was going to get solved was if the prime minister
threw her toys out of the pram at European Council level.'

Barclay also believed the EU had been encouraged by senior former
UK politicians urging the Commission to stand firm. Sources in both
Paris and London said Tony Blair was privately lobbying Emmanuel
Macron, the French president. 'He's saying, "You've got to hold firm and
then we'll end up staying",' a source close to Macron said. Chris Grayling
was one of many Brexiteers incensed: 'I think it was shocking, the degree
to which people in and around Parliament, senior political figures on the
Remain side, were in constant dialogue with the EU, saying, "Play hardball. They will cave in."'[6]

As the talks turned sour in Brussels, back in London the stakes were
rising. On 1 March, Julian Smith wrote to the prime minister warning
that if changes to the backstop were only 'cosmetic' there was no way the
government could rely on DUP votes in the second meaningful vote. Cox
was 'in constant discussion with the DUP', primarily with Nigel Dodds,
the group's leader in Westminster, also an able lawyer, and less frequently
with Arlene Foster in Belfast. 'They knew the nature of the proposals he
was making,' an ally said. When he visited Northern Ireland, Cox gave
key figures in the DUP dinner. He pledged to Dodds: 'I'll tell you the
truth.' In return, Dodds made clear the DUP wanted a time limit but
would accept a 'bottom line' of exiting the backstop if trade talks had
broken down. The attorney general shared the evolving drafts with the
DUP, highly confidential papers not shown to other ministers. 'They
honoured it to the letter,' the ally said. 'There were no leaks.'

If the DUP got the Rolls-Royce treatment from Cox, they were treated
as second-class citizens by the rest of Whitehall. On the civil service side
there was resistance to involving the DUP in discussions because, constitutionally, they were not formal coalition partners. 'The whole operation,
both politically and on the civil service side, has treated the DUP like we
have to do a deal with them but we'd rather not,' a special adviser said,
adding, 'They haven't got to know them as people, put an arm round
their shoulders, understood what makes them tick, so for them it was
always very easy to have a transactional relationship.'

* * *

Theresa May finally survived a big Commons vote on Brexit on 27 February. She only did so, however, by adopting an amendment put down by Yvette Cooper. The day before, the prime minister told MPs she would hold the second meaningful vote on 12 March. Cooper decided to hold her to it. Her amendment stated that, if there was no deal concluded by 12 March, the government would offer MPs a vote on whether to seek an extension from Brussels. It was not a fight the government needed or could win. With their support, the motion passed by 502 votes to 20.

It came on a day of chaos. Alberto Costa, a parliamentary private secretary, was sacked for proposing an amendment saying the citizens' rights part of the withdrawal agreement should be implemented even if there was no-deal – then the government adopted it without a vote anyway. In another vote, Chris Grayling, the transport secretary, went into the wrong division lobby.

Yet there was a glimmer of hope for Downing Street in the small size of the main rebellion. The twenty rebels included Brexiteer ultras, such as Peter Bone and Christopher Chope, but none of the ERG leadership. 'Those twenty will vote against the deal even if it comes back with a cure for cancer,' one ministerial aide observed. The motion had been expected to be nodded through. When the rebels yelled 'No!', forcing a division, even Mark Francois, the ERG chief whip, was seen mouthing, 'What the fuck?' He, Rees-Mogg and Baker all abstained. Optimists in Number 10 wondered if this could become habit-forming. Rees-Mogg, in particular, was beginning to have serious concerns that voting down the deal might lead to Brexit being reversed. On *Today* that morning he publicly shifted from scrapping the backstop altogether to a position where an 'appendix' saying it would end 'in the lifetime of a Parliament' would be enough.

His anxiety was fuelled by the existence of the Cooper-Letwin bill which replaced Cooper-Boles as the mechanism through which rebel MPs would seize control of the Commons agenda to force the government to delay Brexit and prevent no-deal. The first part of the plan, the business of the House motion, allowing them to override government control of the timetable, had been meticulously crafted. 'It had to be designed to prevent Nikki da Costa, Jacob Rees-Mogg, Steve Baker and Bill Cash from filibustering it,' a leading Bresister said. 'Devising that was an incredibly complicated piece of work which Oliver [Letwin] did.' Boles, who sat near Rees-Mogg on the green benches, was told by the ERG chairman, 'It's very well drafted.' Boles thought he and Baker looked 'rattled'. Bill Cash told Boles, 'It's a thoroughly bad business, we'll live to regret this.'

The ERG had helped defeat Cooper-Boles but the Paleosceptics, who thought themselves the masters of procedural tricks since Maastricht, realised they had a fight on their hands from opponents who were not only clever, but increasingly well organised and uncompromising. Robert Buckland told Baker: 'I have sucked up two and a half years of crap, you have got to start sucking it up from your end.'

Theresa May and Julian Smith were now engaged in a concerted effort to win the support of Labour MPs. The prime minister met a delegation on 12 February at the instigation of John Mann, who was telling Smith he could deliver up to thirty votes for the government from seats that voted heavily for Brexit. Mann was accompanied by Caroline Flint, a minister under Blair and Brown who represented Don Valley, and Gareth Snell, the MP for Stoke-on-Trent Central. Snell had won a by-election in the heavily Leave seat two years earlier, following the departure from Westminster of Tristram Hunt, despite penning a derogatory poem about Brexit: 'Soft Brexit, Hard Brexit, Massive pile of Shit. Sloppy Brexit, Messy Brexit. Quit, Quit, Quit.' After receiving dire warnings on the doorstep, Snell now believed Brexit had to be delivered or Labour would face the vengeance of the electorate. Sarah Champion, Labour MP for Rotherham, was another who said she might be prepared to vote for the deal. But she made clear she wanted to be sure it would make a difference. 'She said it would feel crap to be in those division lobbies seeing you've not got enough numbers and you're surrounded by Conservative MPs,' a Tory source said. The MPs told May they needed legislation binding the government to stick to EU standards on workers' rights if they were to support her.

Julian Smith had little else to cling to but remained sceptical about Mann's numbers. 'Why the hell should these Labour MPs be part of a Tory suicide pact when we weren't getting the numbers,' he told aides. 'What was the point of them going over the top?' The same message was delivered to Smith by Stephen Doughty, the Bresistance whip, who told him Mann would never get the numbers he was promising. Nick Brown's aides regarded Mann as 'one of our best whips' because most Labour MPs were actively repelled by his blandishments. A rebel MP explained, 'John Mann repeatedly fibbed throughout the process, and it became a running joke. We told [Smith] again and again that [Mann] couldn't deliver. They were told it by the [Labour] whips. They carried on talking with them.'

There were also tensions between the different factions of Labour MPs. Flint became increasingly irritated with Lisa Nandy, the MP for Wigan, who repeatedly made warm noises about the need to complete Brexit, which 64 per cent of her constituents had supported. Nandy, who fancied a tilt at the leadership one day, seemed ultimately more interested in parading her credentials than in backing the deal. 'Lisa wanted to raise her profile in terms of the Labour Party,' a minister said.

To help Smith, the Conservative Party chairman, Brandon Lewis, put Tory funds into a campaign to put pressure on Labour MPs deemed possible switchers. 'Brandon was incredibly helpful on assisting in a semi-dark campaign focusing on drilling Leave Labour seats with reminders that their constituents had voted to Leave,' one of May's team said. Flint, meanwhile, was running a Respect the Result campaign out of her parliamentary office, which had similar aims.

The biggest prize on the left, though, was not Mann or Flint but Len McCluskey, boss of Britain's biggest union, and Labour's biggest paymaster, Unite. Greg Clark, the business secretary, was in touch with McCluskey. In return for guarantees on workers' rights, they wanted Unite to protect Labour MPs in Leave-voting seats. 'What we were trying to do was get McCluskey to say to the ninety to one hundred Unite MPs: "You're not going to get turned over at reselection if you vote for this agreement."'

However, May's team did not feel they had full visibility on these conversations. 'Greg was consistently pretty secretive about his discussions with McCluskey,' one member of the inner circle said. 'You had this massive prize if you could turn McCluskey. But Greg was not straightforward to work with.'

In a similar vein, Julian Smith hoped the Lexiteers in Corbyn's office – Seumas Milne and Karie Murphy – would give tacit consent to a rebellion. 'That could have unlocked quite a lot,' he said. A Downing Street official said, 'McCluskey was by far the most amenable of all the unions to the idea that there was a deal to be done. When you had Unison and the GMB saying that they will never trust a Tory, McCluskey was in a space of "there might be something to be done here". He thought it was in Corbyn's interest to get Brexit done and then Corbyn can get back to talking about austerity.' Andrew Murray had concluded the same thing, telling LOTO colleagues: 'Why are we working so hard to stop Labour people rebelling? We should just let them do it.' In the end, neither LOTO nor Unite was prepared to give the deal their blessing.

Nearly a month later, on 8 March, May gave a speech in Grimsby, outlining the proposed deal for Labour Leavers, a package of measures on workers' rights. Downing Street's coup was to line up the two MPs from the city to introduce her: Tory Martin Vickers and Labour's Melanie Onn, one of those the chief had been most assiduously wooing. The following weekend, May called between twenty and thirty Labour MPs asking for their support. Many seemed keen; a decent number indicated they would vote for the deal. Most were not telling the truth.

It was not just May who was trying to come to an arrangement with MPs across the aisle. Two days before her speech, on 6 March, Nick Boles and Oliver Letwin met Jeremy Corbyn and his key aides after PMQs to try to get the Labour leadership to back their Norway Plus plan. They were accompanied by Lucy Powell and Stephen Kinnock, the driving forces for Common Market 2.0 on the Labour benches.

This was a surreal experience for the Tories. Boles had previously only spoken to Corbyn once in his life, on a train to Birmingham for the Tory party conference in 2008 and the Labour leader had not once acknowledged him in Parliament since. To Boles' surprise, Corbyn vividly remembered their conversation about football. The meeting was in the leader of the opposition's office, where Letwin explained he had 'practically lived' for five years prior to 2010. He explained the advantages of single market membership, touching on his closeness to Margaret Thatcher: 'She created it and she always understood what it involved and why it was good for Britain.' It was an eccentric way of wooing the hard left.

Corbyn, who was accompanied by press aide James Schneider and Andrew Fisher, his head of policy, 'asked better questions than I ever thought likely', Boles told friends later. Kinnock, deploying a more Corbyn-friendly argument than Letwin, argued that Norway did more state aid spending than any other nation in the EU or the EEA. Behind the scenes, Powell had been working on Corbyn's team, to the irritation of Keir Starmer, the party's Brexit spokesman, who was not invited. Two weeks earlier, Corbyn's team had also tried to block Starmer from accompanying the leader on a trip to Brussels, Karie Murphy suggesting Richard Burgon travel with him instead. In the end, they both went.[7]

The most insightful questions came from Fisher, but when he spoke, Boles reminded himself that Fisher regarded him as an implacable class enemy: 'I just felt he was measuring me up for the guillotine.'

Despite the incongruity of the occasion, the two sides came to an understanding of how you could reconcile the Conservative desire for eventual freedom on trade policy, not in a customs union, with the Labour desire for a permanent customs union. Both sides could agree to disagree in the short term to deliver Brexit, since the customs arrange-ment in the short term would look a lot like *the* customs union. The two sides could then campaign for different outcomes in a general election. Boles and Letwin decided not to brief journalists and were encouraged when positive accounts of their exchanges were relayed by LOTO to Heather Stewart at the *Guardian* and Pippa Crerar at the *Mirror*.

This effort did not deter Letwin from his many other attempts to avoid no-deal. He was liaising with the Grieve group, the ministerial group and others in the Norway group, as well as Downing Street and the chief whip. 'I don't know how he managed it,' a friend said. 'He spoke to them all every weekend and most days in between. He was speaking to Philip [Hammond] several times a day and Lidders several times a day.'

Suspicious that the government might be able to contrive a compromise which would bring together Letwin's various groups with Labour to pass the deal, the ERG decided to set up a legal audit of their own – a 'Star Chamber' based on the medieval model, to interrogate Cox's conclusions and ensure they were legally watertight, rather than politically motivated. The panel, led by Bill Cash, included eight qualified lawyers, seven of them MPs – Tories Suella Braverman, Robert Courts, David Jones, Dominic Raab, Michael Tomlinson and Nigel Dodds of the DUP – plus Martin Howe QC, nephew of Geoffrey Howe and arguably the most prominent Brexiteer barrister. Cash told Number 10 the Star Chamber would require two days to deliver its verdict, a notion given the shortest of shrift which exposed the fact that some Paleosceptics knew rather more about EU law than they did about politics in the age of twenty-four-hour news.

This enterprise spooked Cox, who disliked the implication that he was not independent. He responded by inviting Dan Hodges, the political columnist for the *Mail on Sunday*, to visit him in his rooms, off central lobby in the Commons. Hodges was smuggled in to ensure he was not seen by officials, and was there when Cox 'burst into his office, scarf trailing behind him, with the urgency of a Battle of Britain pilot returning from a mission, but already hungry for the next sortie'. The attorney general leaned forward on his chair and said, 'I will not change my opinion unless I'm sure there is no legal risk of us being indefinitely detained in the backstop. I am putting my hand on my heart. I will not change my opinion unless we have a text that shows the risk has been eliminated.' In case Hodges had not got the message, he boomed, 'There will be no fudge!'[8]

If anyone in Downing Street was of the view that Cox would cut his cloth to assist the prime minister, he sought to disabuse them of this notion, telling Hodges, 'I have been a barrister for thirty-six years, and a senior politician for seven months. My professional reputation is far more important to me than my reputation as a politician.'[9] It was a function of Cox's political inexperience that he chose to impart this message to a Sunday journalist on a Monday, six days before he could publish a word of it. In the meantime, Cox returned to Brussels.

For a week Downing Street and the attorney general had been locked in a debate about whether he should publicise his proposal to Brussels. Cox wanted to break cover. He told Robbins, 'If the Commission aren't going to accept my proposal, we should just publish it anyway, and appeal to the twenty-seven.' He was supported by Barclay, but the suggestion alarmed both David Lidington and Julian Smith. Their view was, 'Where does the government go if, five minutes after we publish it, the Commission, the Irish, Paris, and Berlin, reject it outright?' MV2 would be lost before Cox had even put pen to yellow legal paper. Smith said, 'How do we get people to vote for the deal if we're saying that we have tried to amend it and failed?' Another wit declared, with scatological force, 'If this goes wrong we're going to stage a protest outside his office yelling, "Cox out."'

The crunch came on Tuesday 5 March, which Cox spent locked in talks with Sabine Weyand. As Raab had before him, the attorney general got the impression Barnier was more open to doing a deal. In private, Cox referred to Weyand as 'Cerberus, the watchdog at the gateway to Hades, waiting to pounce on any doctrinal impurity'. That evening the

British team had dinner with Barnier, Weyand and Riso. Barnier asked Cox, 'What would it take to work on this idea of yours?' The Frenchman had the habit, whenever he had an idea of his own, of looking immediately at Riso and Weyand for approval. Neither offered encouragement. 'Their heads were down and they shrugged in a non-committal fashion,' a witness said. It was painfully clear that Task Force 50 had little intention of working proactively on the proposals. 'Neither of them were prepared to take the issue forward.' After the meal, Weyand angrily confronted Robbins: 'You're going to publish these proposals, and you're going to blame us for not accepting them.'

The following morning, 6 March, Cox talked to Tim Barrow. 'You realise what they're going to try to do to your proposals?' Barrow said. 'They're going to try to poison the well and kill them off. Because Weyand is frightened that you will publish them and you will escalate it to Merkel and the heads of government, and it will be seen that your proposals are perfectly reasonable.' The ambassador warned Cox that Weyand would get the EU machine to brief the details in a way that would 'mischaracterise' them. 'And that is exactly what she did,' a British source said. Rather than frame their own proposal for public consumption, it was Task Force 50 which leaked first, painting Cox's original plan as another unicorn from London. His earlier claim that the backstop risked infringing human rights was also leaked, in a way designed to make the attorney general look ridiculous. 'The reason why the proposals were briefed against is because they were reasonable,' said Cox. 'With that modest modification, the whole continent of Europe could have moved on.' The problem was that what Cox viewed as modest was seen in Brussels as a fundamental challenge to the integrity of the EU.

Still in Brussels, the attorney general held a video conference with May that morning of 6 March, the night after the desultory dinner. Robbins and Barrow were present. In London, Gavin Barwell, David Lidington and May's PPS Peter Hill were all listening. The discussion centred on a paper composed by Robbins overnight which began 'Weyand is starting to prepare for the blame game.'

Robbins' paper – the product of his solo talks in the margins – proposed two options: building down from Cox's plan or building up from the Commission's position. He warned, 'If we carry on trying to take the Attorney's proposition and rub what they see as the rough edges off it, there is a risk it ends up being completely neutered. It might be a better course to take what they have been prepared to offer and push it upwards.' The meeting concluded by giving Robbins authority to see how far he could get the Commission to improve their offer.

As he listened, Cox judged that the plan only represented a tinkering around the edges. 'Prime Minister, these options that Olly is putting forward are no doubt very useful, but they cannot change my opinion on the fundamental questions affecting the backstop,' he said. The analogy he chose was of a rocket in an orbit too low to reach its landing ground. 'What is proposed here will have a trajectory that falls well before where it would need to be to change my opinion,' he said. May and her most senior officials ought to have known from that point on – six days before Cox was to deliver his verdict – what it would be. 'What is proposed in this paper is no longer the mission you have set me,' he added.

The attorney general left Brussels and stepped back from the frontline, leaving the talks to Robbins. On Thursday evening, 7 March, as he always tried to do, Cox departed Westminster and returned to his constituency in West Devon. To some of May's team he was absenting himself from the scene of the crime. A more political attorney general might have remained in London, on hand over the weekend to help in person. A more political prime minister might have demanded that he did so. But for Cox it was simply his routine and, with his primary role exhausted, one he wanted to stick to. He would tell May on five further occasions that she was barking up the wrong tree.

Robbins found things heavy going on Wednesday, Thursday and Friday, his diary stuffed with coffees with Weyand, a sure sign that these were difficult days. 'When things got really bad, Olly would have to take her out of the Commission building to see if that improved things,' a colleague said. 'I remember it as one of the grimmest times. London was really unsure what they wanted to do, and we were just trying to fight for as much as we could.' Another described the British negotiators as 'dispirited' and 'ground down'. Robbins had a mandate but no ability to say what would change the legal advice. Weyand grew frustrated. 'Tell me what the hurdle is that we have to jump here,' she said. The Commission could not understand how Cox's legal advice had become so totemic. A British official opined, 'Everyone in Brussels said, "What are you doing? You're outsourcing an immensely political question and set of parameters to a lawyer. It just doesn't make sense."'

Robbins had some help from Selmayr who believed, since they had come so far, that they should try to salvage a deal. But Barnier was sceptical. An EU official said, 'Barnier had the view – it turned out that this was the right view – that this was as far as we could go and if Mrs May cannot deliver that, we have to save all our ammunition for the new prime minister.' Barwell recalled a conversation with a senior EU official: 'I was saying, "If you just give us X, I think we can do this", and he, basically, said, "If I believed you and thought you could actually get this through, then maybe there are some things we could give you. But I don't believe that, and so we're literally throwing stuff away."'[10] A member of the negotiating team added, 'They fundamentally didn't believe May could deliver, so they weren't going to offer anything.'

Cox's original concept had been that the UK and EU would sign a 'joint interpretative instrument' spelling out how the backstop would be changed. By Friday evening, Robbins had the basis of something he could at least put to May. He talked it through with the prime minister, telling her, 'It's our judgement that this is the best we can do.'

May spoke to both Cox and Barclay. The attorney general was in his study in Devon when the call came through from the Downing Street switchboard. In the two days since he had left Brussels, Robbins and Weyand had negotiated a draft joint interpretive instrument (JII) designed to provide assurances on the backstop. Cox was unimpressed, telling May, 'Prime Minister, I sought to install a fire escape for the backstop, limited and useable in an emergency, and testable against well-known legal tests. What they're offering us here are more assurances from the head of the fire brigade, that there will never be a fire. They're offering to put more fire prevention measures in. But if you ask what happens if the fire breaks out, the householder wants to know can he get out.'

The joint instrument had, in effect, strengthened the basis of Cox's original political judgement that the EU would not want to be trapped in the backstop any more than Britain, but without changing the underlying legal facts. Cox was blunt. 'This simply isn't enough, Prime Minister,' he said. 'I must warn you so you understand, it cannot make the difference.'

May, with her hopes of passing the agreement, her personal credibility and perhaps her premiership hanging on the attorney general's judgement, made no attempt to talk him around. Instead, Downing Street experienced frustrated rage trying to track down Cox, or get through on a poor phone line. 'He was in fucking Devon all the time,' one of May's team recalled. 'We were chasing around him like a dog on heat, it was hugely frustrating.' During the most important European diplomatic negotiations since the 1970s, Cox busied himself with constituency commitments far from phone and internet connectivity. Eventually, the chief whip snapped and raged, 'Can the British civil service not send a unit to fucking Devon to make sure he can be contacted?'

While Smith ranted about Cox's absence, he was also negotiating with the power brokers in the ERG. On Friday 8th he asked Steve Baker to see him in 9 Downing Street. The deal he was prepared to make was stark: the votes of the ERG in exchange for May's resignation. Baker came in from Aylesbury for the meeting. He knew Rees-Mogg might back the government, but Baker was not inclined to back down. After a long conversation with the chief whip on Cox's proposals, he demanded a 'codpiece' plus a clear statement from May that she would resign. 'We have to be convinced and she has to deliver,' he told Smith. It was not just May's head he wanted on a spike. There had to be a 'restructured team' for the negotiations. Translation: no more Oliver Robbins.

Baker saw Iain Duncan Smith and spent thirty minutes on the phone to Cox. He also spoke to Owen Paterson, who talked of the 17.4 million voters who backed Leave and urged him not to give way. 'We honour them by winning, not by dying in a ditch,' Paterson said. Priti Patel was similarly robust. On Saturday the 9th, Baker called the chief whip back and made clear that a 'fig leaf' deal would not be enough. 'Yes, people are flexible, I would say willing to be reasonable,' he said. 'But they are looking for substantial change, not a ladder to climb down.'

Duncan Smith saw May that afternoon in Downing Street. The prime minister was downbeat. She acknowledged that the backstop 'gives up our leverage'. For months May was damned for not acknowledging her predicament. When word spread among senior Eurosceptics that she was finally conceding their point, it was no less frustrating.

On Saturday 9 March, May rang Cox again from Chequers. He repeated his concerns. The attorney general realised he had no record of the advice he was giving the prime minister at a pivotal moment. He reached for a digital voice recorder and began to tape his side of the phone call. 'Prime Minister, I must warn you, again, that this joint interpretive instrument simply cannot affect the judgement I make,' he said. 'There's no way out of the backstop should talks break down.' The attorney general acknowledged that 'useful improvements' were being made. 'But it makes no difference to my advice.'

Cox offered his proposed solution: 'A unilateral declaration might float.' He had already told Barwell that Britain should make its own statement setting out how the UK viewed the backstop. He explained, 'I will draft a unilateral declaration, which will have force in international law, which will set out how the British interpret the backstop. If the union does not object to that, we can say to Parliament that that interpretation will carry legal weight.' That, Cox was clear, 'would enable me to make a change in my advice'.

At 5 p.m. that Saturday there was a ministerial conference call which lasted for several hours. May, Smith, Lidington, Barclay and Cox went over what Robbins had secured and what the attorney general now wanted. The chief whip messaged others on the call to stress, 'We need to focus on what Geoffrey wants', that being the purpose of the exercise. 'We've got to get his minimum.' Smith urged May to get Robbins to pursue the kind of language which would enable the legal advice to change, including the possibility that there could be 'termination' of the backstop.

In Brussels, Martin Selmayr returned to the fray. 'Sabine was extremely rough with Robbins. She was extremely fed up and she didn't believe in this process any more,' a Commission source said. Robbins emerged from one session with Weyand on the Saturday afternoon looking like a man who had 'gone several times through some kind of uncomfortable relationship'. Selmayr, by contrast, had instructions from Juncker to help. At 8 p.m. he invited Robbins for a gin and tonic and for forty-five minutes they talked about nothing serious. Then Britain's negotiator showed him the latest iteration of the document and outlined what he still needed. Over dinner, Selmayr signalled that on some things he could help, on others, not. Robbins secured at least one significant change in language. 'I can sell this to the prime minister to get Mr Cox on board,' he said. It was now midnight.

They still needed Weyand, downbeat with disillusionment, exhaustion and flu, to approve the changes. Selmayr had asked her to remain on standby. He called and said, 'Sabine we are done now. Can you come and say if you can also live with it?' She arrived and was 'really grumpy', a source said. 'It was midnight, she had the flu and she thought it was a waste of her time.' 'If this is what you want and this is what Martin can live with, I can live with it,' she said. 'But I don't believe in this process.'

Juncker usually spent his weekends in Luxembourg but he had gone to Brussels. Robbins spoke to May and they agreed she would meet Juncker there on Sunday evening.

The unilateral declaration Cox presented to Downing Street on Sunday said a lot of the things he had originally wanted the joint instrument to say. It stated that 'If the backstop became de facto permanent, because talks had irredeemably broken down, in those circumstances, the UK would consider itself free to initiate procedures for termination of the backstop.' The document was passed to Robbins' Europe Unit and Cox did not see it again until the Monday morning. The challenge, as the negotiator explained to May, was this: 'It would only have legal force if the other side had not objected to it.' A British delegate said, 'We went through a frustrating couple of days, explaining that if we were to make such a declaration, the other side would denounce it, and then it has no legal value, so you're worse off than you were before when there was a certain amount of ambiguity about whether we had this right.'

Once again, communication was not aided by Cox's absence from Westminster. A fellow minister said, 'They couldn't get hold of him at all on the Sunday. They were tearing their bloody hair out.'

In another conference call with ministers on Sunday morning, May concluded, 'with a degree of reluctance', that what Robbins had achieved so far did not go far enough. There was further 'umming and ahhing' lasting several hours. Her instinctive position was, 'I don't think we're going to do better and we've got to give it a go.' But she was 'talked down' and decided, 'Maybe this doesn't work and is not good enough.'

At 6.30 p.m., the prime minister phoned Juncker and told him, 'I'm not drawing stumps, but I don't think this is enough for me right now.' The Commission president suggested she travel to Strasbourg on Monday morning instead, as long as the final document was agreed by 11.30 a.m., the time by which he needed to leave Brussels. 'But what I am not going to do, Theresa, I am not sitting in Strasbourg together with you and doing a negotiation. I am not ready to do that.'

At home, May's attorney general and her Brexit secretary were telling her to do just that. 'Barclay and Cox consistently urged her to fight,' a senior source said. 'They begged, pleaded with her.' An official explained, 'The alternative that was put forward at that time specifically by the AG was that she just needed to go to the Council and have it out with them.'

Cox told May, 'Prime Minister, you will go to the House, this will be seen as a defeat for you. It will be rubbished as a damp squib. And we have to fight that, we have to escalate this.'

May did not believe this would work and showed her displeasure. 'There were one or two flashes of anger that weekend,' a senior official recalled. 'She said to both of them, "You think I can go and sit outside a room of twenty-seven shouting through the keyhole, asking for more on the Northern Irish backstop. That's not how it works." She thought it was nuts. I think she had a feeling that she was being stitched up again. [Cox and Barclay] found it all a bit difficult, and now they said it was over to her again. The one thing they were definitely not arguing for, strikingly, that weekend was an opportunity to have another go themselves.'

The chances of progress were also damaged by the publication, in the middle of these sensitive negotiations, of Cox's six-day-old interview in the *Mail on Sunday*. The incendiary part was a line he had inserted to placate hardline Eurosceptics: 'If we did secure an arbitration mechanism, it could be triggered on the very first day we entered the backstop. That's because the transition period would have already given two years for completion of negotiations.'

'That horrified Weyand's team,' a fellow cabinet minister said. 'Cox didn't seem to be acting in good faith.' A British negotiator agreed: 'The key thing that affected the Commission was that we could trigger this on day one. It was at a completely critical moment.'

The other problem, throughout Sunday and Monday, officials in both Downing Street and the Europe Unit agree, was that Cox kept changing his mind. 'From the start, the bar that we had to cross for the infamous legal advice to be changed, kept moving around,' a member of Robbins' team said. 'There was a lot of frustration from the PM down.' Another said, 'He seemed torn between wishing to be the great Geoffrey Cox QC, a lawyer of the highest integrity, and the great Geoffrey Cox MP, the saviour of the Brexit process. In each telephone conversation, you got a different Geoffrey Cox.'

The mood in Number 10 that Monday morning was bleak. 'There was just a dreadfully defeatist atmosphere,' a source close to Robbins said. 'No one really knew what to do next.' Around noon, the prime minister called Cox, who was being driven by his wife to Exeter station for the return to London, to inform him that she was heading off to Strasbourg to do the deal. Barclay, who was travelling with May, texted Cox the latest draft of the unilateral declaration. The attorney general was horrified. It had changed beyond recognition. His draft had included the line that Britain reserved the right to 'terminate' the backstop if it became de facto permanent. The word 'terminate' was gone. 'This isn't what I drafted, he told Barclay. 'It has been drained of effective meaning.'

The attorney general felt what remained had no practical effect in law, that it was not worth the paper it was written on. In short, a text designed explicitly and entirely to give the attorney general a reason to change his legal advice no longer satisfied its sole purpose. 'Prime Minister, you can't sign,' Cox told May. 'If it's without the UD in the form I've drafted, it won't change my opinion.'

Later, May and Robbins were on the way to the airport when Cox called to speak to Barwell. 'You must warn the prime minister that the current draft of the unilateral declaration, and the joint statement won't change my opinion.' More than that, Cox had soured on the universal declaration. A witness said, 'Even as we were heading to the airport, the message came that the unilateral declaration, which he had initially insisted on, he had helped draft, that we had row after row with the Commission about, as we're in the car on the way to the airport, he then said, "Oh, just abandon it. It's not worth it."' As they got on the plane, May was incredulous. 'What is he going on about?' she asked. 'How can it possibly do any harm, and it might do some good.'

Cox also contacted Julian Smith to warn, 'The unilateral declaration will become a false hope that will distract from the real truth.' Raoul Ruparel predicted, 'Cox will kill us.'

When May's plane landed in Strasbourg, the attorney general appeared to have shifted position again. Instead of ditching the unilateral declaration, he wanted it tweaked. 'By the time we got off the plane again it was, "Well actually, he'd like a few words added",' an official said. 'I think the attorney had a really hard job to do. But he was all over the place.' Another official added, 'You just can't run an international negotiation on the basis of changing your mind every five minutes.' Robbins called Selmayr, who was in the car with Juncker heading to Strasbourg but, in a classic Brexit twist, the mobile phone reception was terrible and the key words disappeared into the ether. Juncker's car had to pull over.

As the day went on, Barclay relayed two new drafts to Cox but they did not satisfy him. In a text message to the Brexit secretary, sent at 6.01 p.m., he said, 'It gets worse. The draft universal declaration has now been drained of effective legal meaning by textual changes.' Cox was concerned that officials were giving the prime minister false hope. 'She must be told,' he instructed Barclay. When he and Barclay spoke by phone, he told the Brexit secretary, 'Steve, this will not do. You must tell her not to sign. You must re-install the language that I have drafted, otherwise it will not enable me to change my advice.' He also spoke to Barwell, telling him. 'You must warn the prime minister that the current draft of the UD won't change my opinion.' The chief of staff said he would put this information to May. Cox texted Barclay again at 8.02 p.m., London time: 'Only a clear reference to termination in the unilateral declaration would do.'

In Strasbourg, the British and EU-Irish negotiating teams were shuttling between two rooms. Selmayr thought it 'very odd' that Cox had not travelled with May. 'The key guy was not in the room,' an EU source said.

The key room was now in Dublin, rather than Strasbourg. Cox's demands could not be met unless the Irish government gave way, something they were showing little sign of doing. The concern in Dublin was that the Commission was going to give away too much. Juncker had agonised conversations with Varadkar, who had delayed a visit to Washington. 'They were really worried,' a British official recalled. 'They thought the Commission was trying to help us too much. The most difficult discussions that evening were between Martin Selmayr and John Callinan.' In several phone calls, the Commission secretary general sought to reassure Callinan, Varadkar's Europe adviser, about why they were fine to proceed with the tweaks to the protocol. At one point Varadkar took the phone and spoke directly to Selmayr. 'I'm a lawyer, I don't like this,' he said. In Strasbourg, May sat mutely observing as Robbins and Selmayr, sitting opposite each other, scribbled new language, Barclay and Barnier making suggestions. 'The British press is pretty negative about Juncker and Selmayr,' Barwell recalled. 'But to the extent that anyone helped us at any point in this process, it was the two of them. Martin at one point went out and had two or three conversations with the Irish to tell them to play the game and be more helpful.'

Juncker had a stake in the success of the talks. He did not want his presidency to end with no-deal. Selmayr's motives, perceived from London, were more about hastening the process of British departure 'because it was taking up time and energy that should be going elsewhere'.

The Irish rejected Cox's demands for robust language. Barclay asked the attorney general, 'Could we live with the word disapplication?' instead of 'terminate'. Cox replied, 'It depends on the context. It's impossible to advise without it, but frankly I doubt it.' Around 8.30 p.m. Barclay sent through the latest draft wording, which talked about the 'measures that would ultimately lead to the disapplication of obligations, under the protocol'. He added, 'Irish object to the word "end" or "termination".'

Cox and Barclay argued with May and Barwell that they should 'escalate' the issue to the heads of government, primarily Angela Merkel. British governments had a long history of placing false faith in the willingness of the German chancellor to intervene, but this was the crunch moment. It would have made sense to bring all possible pressure to bear on the Irish and the Commission.

When the group in Strasbourg thought they had a solution, Selmayr left the room and emailed it to Callinan. May was, by now, determined to give a press conference, either announcing that there was a deal or that she would appeal to the other heads of government. Varadkar urged caution, then delivered the immortal line, 'I have to consult my attorney general.' It triggered May. A witness said, 'Mrs May was really angry.' Juncker noted, 'You really cannot criticise, because the only reason we are sitting here is because of your attorney general.' The Taoiseach summoned his AG, Séamus Woulfe, to give him legal advice. With Simon Coveney and Paschal Donohoe, the finance minister, the fate of the deal effectively hung on a kitchen cabinet gathering in Dublin.

Juncker then asked May, 'If we are going to do this, will your attorney general give a positive recommendation?' She replied, 'I hope so, but I don't know. He is independent.'

In fact, Cox was clear the new draft was not enough. 'Sorry, won't work,' he told Barclay. Cox spelled out his bottom line: 'It must be enough to say they've not objected to a clear statement of our right to terminate when the talks have broken down. That text doesn't do it.' Barclay took his mobile phone and showed Theresa May the screen so that she could read Cox's message herself. He informed Cox, 'I have notified the PM.' The attorney general signed off, 'Tell them it's not enough and there's no point in signing now. We need help in getting this across.'

While the Irish deliberated, David Lidington was on his feet at the despatch box in the Commons. The government had pledged to give a statement to MPs on the state of the negotiations before the close of play that day. The deadline was 10 p.m. Lidington had very little idea what was going on in Strasbourg. At 9.30 p.m. in London, Julian Smith was trying to lay the motion in concert with officials from the private office. 'The private office was going mental,' said one of those in Strasbourg. At 9.40 p.m., Lidington complained, 'I need to know what is going on.' He was presented with a draft and told, 'We have agreed these three things. You can mention the first one and the second one but not the third.' When he rose to his feet, his speech still contained square brackets around the questionable material.

Juncker called Varadkar and was met with a wall of indecision: 'I'm not sure. I've got to think about it.' Barwell was ready to throw in the towel: 'We're not going to be able to do this tonight now.' Selmayr, increasingly frustrated, tried to remain upbeat: 'I think we're still going to get there, but I think, Olly, you and I have to stay here, and we'll see if we can get it sorted out by ten o'clock tomorrow morning.' Then Varadkar called back demanding three new amendments to the text. 'We rejected two of them and we accepted one,' a source in the room said, 'because it was merging two paragraphs. This is one of the weird untold stories in this negotiation. It was the Commission and the British government who rejected, together, the Irish attempts to change our text.'

The session took its toll, however. Throughout their four hours together, Juncker chain-smoked strong continental cigarettes, despite EU rules banning smoking in offices. One aide branded him a 'rude prick' but May was too polite to complain. The smoke played havoc with her throat, reducing her voice to a strangled croak. She developed a streaming cold – not what the PM needed ahead of a divisive week in Parliament.

In Westminster, Lidington was auditioning for the role of England opener, dead-batting every question with variations of: 'The talks are still going on' and 'I don't want to pre-empt what my honourable friend will say.' Further along the front bench Matt Hancock was heard to comment, 'He's winging it.' Lidington was passed a note informing him that May would be making a public statement at 10.45 p.m.

May signed the agreement without any of the language Cox had demanded. Barclay sent a final resigned text: 'Well, it's now been agreed.' Selmayr told the room, 'It's a good deal.' Barclay thought to himself: *You're kidding yourself, this ain't going through.* He could see May and Barwell wanted to believe it. He felt like the only realist in the room.

Why did May sign? One cabinet minister said, 'I don't think she felt she had any choice. She was being advised by the Europe Unit that this was all she was ever going to get.' Cox and others who knew what had happened were bemused by her fatalistic approach. One said, 'It was almost like a doctor saying to a patient, "Don't do what you're doing now, because it's going to kill you", and watching the patient consciously and knowingly do what the doctor told them not to do.'

To May, even small wins, which had been sweated over, were worth fighting for. 'She wanted to put across the fact that this wasn't a PR exercise,' a close adviser said. 'Going back to get these changes was a meaningful thing. It hadn't been a cake walk, it hadn't been the case that the EU said, "We will sign whatever you want." She'd achieved something substantial.' Barwell knew the deal wasn't 'a game changer' but he and May thought the new wording was 'of value'. New language on alternative arrangements might impress Eurosceptics. Improvements in the representation for Northern Ireland could be sold to the DUP. 'All of those second order things have got, understandably, a bit lost, but it was a package she thought she could sell,' a negotiator said. 'She genuinely thought, based on some of the legal advice that she'd seen, that the package agreed in Strasbourg shifted the dial.'

To Barclay, who had a better read on Cox, the Strasbourg visit was a failure. The agreement was designed to persuade Parliament to back the deal and to persuade Parliament you needed to persuade Cox. He could see there was some legal value in the document but, if there was no political value, the enterprise was futile. 'This won't change the legal advice, and without a change in legal advice it won't fly,' he warned May. To him, the solution was too obviously one cooked up by the old axis of Robbins and the Brussels bureaucrats, who did not understand Parliament. 'I wouldn't have signed in Strasbourg, I'd have walked,' Barclay told a friend later. 'Once she'd signed that, you can't then go back again. The whole bloody thing is to get the vote through Parliament. That's your test. Everything else is candy floss.'

At 11 p.m., Geoffrey Cox received the final documents from Number 10. He was asked to deliver his legal opinion the following morning. Julian Smith had spent much of the evening trying to get hold of the attorney general, who had gone to dinner with his wife at Shepherd's restaurant in Westminster. 'We didn't really have sight of what was about to happen,' the chief whip recalled. Cox first had intensive discussions with his team and then sat down in his flat and worked until 5.25 a.m. But he did not work entirely alone. Senior government sources say he took advice from a pro-Brexit lawyer outside government around 2 a.m. Cox said later, 'I sat up till five o'clock that morning, writing exactly what I had been saying since the previous Wednesday I would have to say.'

Cox's legal opinion offered some encouragement but came with a devastating sting in the tail.[11] He began by agreeing that the joint interpretive instrument had 'binding legal effect' under the Vienna Convention on the Law of Treaties (paragraph 2) and that it put the pledges made in Juncker and Tusk's January letter 'into a legally binding form' which would 'facilitate the effective enforcement of the UK's rights' if it wanted to leave the backstop (paragraph 4). Cox said the unilateral declaration by the UK also had 'legal status' (paragraph 3).

He then examined the specifics. If the EU was guilty of a 'systematic refusal' to consider British proposals or treat the negotiation of a trade deal to replace the Northern Ireland Protocol as a 'priority', it would be easier to escape (paragraph 5). The EU would be obliged to 'immediately' establish a 'negotiating track' to replace the customs and regulation elements of the protocol with 'alternative arrangements' and 'technologies' (paragraph 6). These 'represent materially new legal obligations and commitments', Cox wrote, which 'make time of the essence in replacing the backstop'. If Britain kept up an 'urgent pace' in negotiations, the EU 'could not fail to match it' without 'breaching' the terms of the deal (paragraph 7). If Britain could show 'a pattern of unjustified delay by the EU' in a bid to keep the backstop 'indefinitely' it would have a '*prima facie* case of breach' to take to the arbitration panel, which could let Britain 'unilaterally' suspend 'all or parts of the Protocol, including the backstop'. This Cox called 'another welcome clarification' (paragraph 9). Prolonged suspension of the protocol would make it 'arguable that the

United Kingdom could secure the termination' of the backstop (paragraph 10).

Turning to the unilateral declaration, it stated that the protocol was designed to 'apply only temporarily' (paragraph 11) and asserted Britain's right to 'disapply the provisions of the Protocol' if no subsequent trade agreement was signed (paragraph 12). By not objecting to the declaration, the EU confirmed Cox's view of the legal position (paragraph 13). He stated, 'There is no doubt, in my view', that the new documents 'provide a substantive and binding reinforcement of the legal rights available to the United Kingdom' if the EU was guilty of bad faith (paragraph 14).

Those in May's team reading the legal advice to this point found their hopes rising. Cox made clear the changes 'reduce the risk that the United Kingdom could be indefinitely and involuntarily detained within the Protocol's provisions' (paragraph 17). The attorney general said he was 'strongly of the view' that the correct 'political judgment' was that it was now 'highly unlikely' that the backstop would not be replaced (paragraph 18). There, many in government believed, Cox might have left it.

Instead, he wrote a nineteenth paragraph, fifty-two more words – a political death warrant for his prime minister: 'However, the legal risk remains unchanged', where trade talks remained deadlocked because of 'intractable differences'. The attorney general concluded that, in those circumstances, the UK would have 'no internationally lawful means of exiting the Protocol's arrangements, save by agreement'.

The prime minister was in her study with her chief whip when the document came through. May was not one for demonstrative shows of emotion, but her posture at that moment was that of a cancer patient being given a terminal diagnosis, stoic but floored. Smith was more prosaic, swearing briefly but emphatically about the attorney general. He told friends later that it was 'a very difficult moment' and they were both 'gobsmacked'. A civil servant said May 'was furious, and quite rightly'.

At 8.30 a.m. Robert Buckland, the solicitor general, saw the advice. When he reached paragraph 19, he mouthed, 'Oh shit.' Buckland was the longest serving law officer. To him, there were times when you were a lawyer-politician and times when you needed to be a politician-lawyer. He didn't think it unethical to write advice that was for public consumption in a manner that acknowledged the politics of a situation. Cox, he could see, had put his legal reputation first. Buckland was later to joke with Barwell and Smith, 'Theresa picked the wrong attorney general.'

The chief whip's immediate reaction was that paragraph 19 did not need to be there. When the dust had settled, his considered view was that the whole exercise of elevating Cox's legal advice to holy writ had been a mistake. 'The tragedy of that whole issue was that we got contorted with the legal advice, rather than treating this as a political problem which would be resolved politically anyway,' he said.

In the press team, Paul Harrison and James Slack speed-read the document. Reaching the end, Slack said, 'Right, we're fucked. Go home.' Robbie Gibb appeared. 'What can we do with this?' he asked. They all knew it could not be spun. Word quickly spread through Number 10. 'There was shock in Downing Street,' said one political aide. 'It is very rare that you have a collective building feeling, because you are squirrelled away in separate rooms. But it was almost a collective gasp.'

The cabinet was in session when the advice was published. In the room, Cox stressed his political argument, leaving colleagues with the impression that everything was fine. 'We were all quite buoyed by it,' Greg Clark recalled. 'I remember getting my phone back and seeing messages saying Geoffrey had vetoed the chances of the deal going through and I was mystified. During the time we were in cabinet, the outside world was viewing this final paragraph and regarding it, correctly, as being fatal.' Oliver Robbins also only saw the legal advice when it was published. Until the final paragraph he thought: *This is pretty good.* Then, the gut punch. In Brussels, Stefaan De Rynck of the Commission read it and thought Cox 'politically very clumsy' to present his case in such a 'blunt' fashion when the deal was 'substantially different' from the original backstop.

Aides branded Cox 'politically naive' and 'arrogant' because he had not presented his view in a way more likely to help his client, the prime minister. 'Why put the last line like that?' one of May's EU advisers said. 'It seemed like he was deliberately drawing attention to it.' A cabinet minister who spent time in Number 10 that morning said, 'Geoffrey Cox had made a fortune out of advising the dodgiest offshore locations and jurisdictions. What would make him so prissy about squaring this?'

Some believed Cox had personal motives. 'Because he didn't get what he wanted in his mini-renegotiation, he was always a bit damning of what was achieved [in Strasbourg] and never really thought there was much in it,' a Downing Street civil servant noted. Others thought Cox desperate to demonstrate he was not another Peter Goldsmith, the attorney general before the Iraq War, who was leaned on to change his advice on the legality of war. 'It was a Goldsmith moment,' a senior figure said. 'Geoffrey wanted to be the big player. But when it came to the moment of "we go to war or not", he just held back because then it becomes his fault. Just as Iraq became Goldsmith's fault, because he had said it was fine.'

The remarkable thing is not that Cox fought off political arm-twisting to change his view, but that he came under almost no pressure at all to do so. In the moment of her political career's maximum crisis, May adopted a stance of fatalistic passivity. 'Not once did she ever seek to change Geoffrey's opinion,' a source said.

However, Cox was not the only lawyer inside and outside Whitehall with views. Jonathan Jones, the head of the government legal service, was among several government lawyers who felt she had achieved more in her renegotiation than Cox did. The Europe Unit under Robbins had regularly consulted Jones, the Treasury solicitor, on matters of law, a habit which Cox deplored. Jones, in turn, indicated that he would like to be the one writing the legal advice. In the days before May went to Strasbourg, he concluded that the additional text the Commission was prepared to grant would give Britain a practical way out of the backstop that might well succeed if it went to court. One of those who read his papers revealed, 'He signed specifically off on a couple of paragraphs which said that, in his view, the package achieved in Strasbourg materially changed the dynamics around termination of the backstop. And he'd be comfortable saying it gave us a good arguable case of termination should the talks not prosper.' Jones told Robbins, 'What you and the team have done, Olly, is generate a good argument that we can deploy should we ever be in that situation.'

This was not just Jones's view. Daniel Denman, the director of the Cabinet Office's European law division and senior lawyer in DExEU, and Cathy Adams, legal director of the government legal department, also thought there was merit in the new deal, and that view was even shared by the lawyers in the attorney general's own office. The views were also sought of 'other barristers' outside government, experts with greater knowledge of European law than Cox – and they agreed with Jones. 'The legal service got the best people we could think of on EU and treaty law,' a senior civil servant said. 'They said [the new deal] ended the Brussels trap. You cannot totally eliminate legal risk, but it very significantly reduces it to the extent that it's minimal. Their argument was it materially changed the legal position. If Cox had written the letter with their opinions, it would probably have worked.' A member of Robbins' team added, 'It was a source of some frustration to us that that was a very well-qualified view from a bunch of senior international public lawyers.'

To be clear, that is different from saying that Jones believed there was a legally watertight exit, which is what the hardcore of Brexiteers wanted. Cox and Jones had a meeting in the attorney general's room on the Thursday before May went to Strasbourg. There was no heated disagreement, but a demonstrable difference of emphasis. 'I agree, Attorney,' he told Cox, according to an account Cox shared with close associates. 'But there are marginal gains.'

Cox replied, 'Jonathan, I think you're right, there are marginal improvements. But they don't address the question of what happens if we can't prove bad faith.' A Cox ally said, 'Jonathan may have thought that there might have been marginally more usefulness in some of the text of the joint instrument and the declaration than Geoffrey thought.'

Nonetheless, the belief that the deal had legal merit was included in documents which were sent to Downing Street. That informed the more upbeat mood in Number 10 on the Sunday and May's ultimate decision to sign on the dotted line in Strasbourg. 'They felt it was stronger than Geoffrey,' a senior Number 10 official said. 'They gave greater weight to it than he did in his opinion.'

A fellow cabinet minister said, 'In this situation, quite a lot of ministers would have made sure they were reflecting everything that was coming through the system. Cox thought his job as attorney general was to come up with his own pure thoughts. He was pretty determined to play his own flute.' Far from adapting the official view or even acknowledging the collective view of the government legal service, Cox chose to write his legal advice from scratch. The fact that he had deviated in important ways from the views of the most senior figure in the government legal service would have been political dynamite if it had become public at the time. The views of Jones and others show there were different ways to present the legal advice – and that Cox chose perhaps the least politically helpful to May. Jones privately said he would have written the legal advice differently, conveying that there was 'something to play for' and, in an 'untested' area of law, 'the tone' was vital. 'My punch-line would have been different,' he told colleagues.

If Cox had wanted to be more helpful to May he could have placed a less bluntly worded version of paragraph 19 in the middle of the document and instead built to a conclusion which stressed the gains that had been made and his political judgement that the UK would not be stuck in the backstop in perpetuity and the view of the Treasury solicitor that it was now arguable in court. A cabinet minister said, 'I genuinely think he didn't understand the consequences of his actions or the linguistic options available to keep his legal integrity and still help the deal get over the line.'[12] A civil servant in May's private office added, 'He could have written paragraph 19 in 150 ways and 149 of them would have worked. It was insanity. Just a few words different and we wouldn't be having this conversation. It was astonishing.'

Publication of Jones's and the independent QCs' alternative legal opinions would have given MPs who wanted a ladder to climb down some political cover. That would have undermined Cox and probably prompted his resignation. But, if the communications and political team had understood where Cox was heading, they could have leaked the rival legal conclusions to the media. That might not have changed Cox's mind but would have forced him to acknowledge Jones's views in his final letter.

Instead, May and her senior political aides appear not to have told the communications team in Downing Street what they were expecting from Cox. The people who would have to sell the deal to MPs and the public had no time to prepare a defensive comms plan. Worse, their ignorance meant Downing Street actively encouraged a narrative that Cox might yet save May's bacon, which only heightened the damage done when he did the opposite. With more time, the Number 10 press team could have created a frequently asked questions-style guide to the legal advice, emphasising the gains made. This could have been distributed to every MP and lobby journalist. 'Because he hadn't written the bloody thing until the morning, nobody had time,' another minister said. 'That was the problem.'

This would not have been enough for the hardliners, but it might have helped those looking for an excuse to back the government. Barwell recalled, 'If you ignore the Spartans and the ultras, our MPs were basically saying two things to us: "You've got to get the DUP on side" and "You've got to give me a fig leaf to say: 'This has changed.'"' Jacob came very close to voting with us the second time.' Not only that. Dominic Grieve told May he might be prepared to back the deal if she was close. May's team believed the same was true of some Labour MPs. Barwell added, 'They were basically saying to us: "We'll only vote for the deal if you'll look us in the face and say our votes take us over the line.'

Another Number 10 official said, 'There were a whole load of people who were looking for a pretty flimsy ladder to climb down. We were almost there but for Geoffrey. He was the only lawyer in the universe who did not seem to understand that you are paid by the client; you should deliver what a client wants.' A cabinet minister put it more succinctly: 'In future, just get somebody who's shit at the law.'

We know that Cox was open to greater political pragmatism, precisely because that is what he gave MPs when he delivered his Commons statement at 12.30 p.m. 'Last night in Strasbourg, the prime minister secured legally binding changes that strengthen and improve the withdrawal agreement and the political declaration,' he proclaimed. He repeated his view that the legal risk was 'unchanged', but said that 'matters of law' can only 'inform what is essentially a political decision that each of us must make', whether 'in the light of these improvements' Britain 'should now enter into those arrangements'. Cox's answer was an emphatic 'Yes' and the adversarial exchanges in the chamber positioned him as a defender of May's deal.

When Bill Cash claimed the law should trump politics, Cox disagreed: 'I have taken the political judgment that this withdrawal agreement needs to be supported.' Even on the law, Cox went further than in his formal opinion, telling MPs there was 'a clear pathway to termination' of the backstop. In another answer he said, 'The law is a question of judgment, and it is always blended with political considerations … The preponderance of the two form a single judgment. It is my judgment … that this risk is a calculated one, but one that we can now take.' His formal legal opinion, however, had made that highly unlikely.

May's team found Cox's performance highly frustrating. Barwell said, 'If he hadn't written the letter, I think the statement to the House on its own would have carried the day.' The chief of staff agreed with Cox that the deal 'made the backstop as popular as a bucket of cold sick to both sides … That backstop had tariff-free access to the single market, with virtually no level-playing-field provisions and no deal on fishing.'[13] Proof that the EU was not comfortable with such an arrangement would come too late for Theresa May, when Boris Johnson and his chief negotiator David Frost fought with the Commission over exactly these things in 2020.

The dozen or so most senior Eurosceptics met on the morning of the 12th in Iain Duncan Smith's room. They debated what it would take from Cox to get them to vote for the deal. 'We were all actually desperate to make the misery end,' one said. Jacob Rees-Mogg reflected later, 'Lots of us were getting very worried that it was either Mrs May's Brexit, or no Brexit at all. I think, if the ladder had been provided, people would have been falling off the ladder to get down it fast enough.'

The conversation was in full flow when a late arrival brought in the legal advice and drew their attention to paragraph 19. 'We moved from a meeting of Tory MPs fretting over this decision, tortured by it,' the MP said. 'Everyone threw their hands in the air, stood up and said, "That's it, it's all over", and walked out the room. We were voting against.' Bernard Jenkin thought Cox's statement 'astonishingly honest'.

At 1.15 p.m. the ERG Star Chamber issued its own verdict, saying the new assurances 'do not deliver legally binding changes' to the withdrawal agreement or the protocol, the government's promise after the Brady amendment. 'They do not provide any exit mechanism from the Protocol which is under the UK's control.'

At a full ERG meeting in the Jubilee Room, Bernard Jenkin made a heartfelt speech about his formative experience in politics. 'I only ever abstained on the second reading of the Maastricht Treaty,' he said, 'and I've never been proud of that abstention. I should've voted against it. And whatever you do will live with you. I've had to live with that ever since.' His contribution stiffened the resolve of his colleagues.

When May got to her feet to present her case to the Commons, she took several sips of water but her voice still cracked immediately. Heckled from the Labour benches, she attempted bravado: 'You should hear Jean-Claude Juncker's voice as a result of our exchanges.' But her vocal cords were broken reeds. One minister wondered why she failed to challenge Juncker: 'If she can't even get someone to stop smoking, she's hardly going to get anything more from them.'

Unknown to MPs, a doctor had been called and the House of Commons authorities were so concerned about May's health that the serjeant at arms drew up a plan to evacuate her. 'They were so worried about her collapsing that they put a protocol in place,' a source said. 'They had a plan if she fainted to get her out of there.'

No such mercy was in evidence when the PM addressed the 1922 Committee meeting later that afternoon. 'MP after MP read out the same line, paragraph 19,' a whip said. As he left the meeting, Steve Baker saw Stephen Parkinson, May's political director, and said, 'She's got to go.'

Just as he had before she signed the November deal, Jeremy Hunt went to see May to try to convince her not to put the agreement to a vote. 'He pleaded with her not to do a deal on this basis,' an aide said. 'That it wouldn't get through the House. That it would be a disaster for her. His view was: to get a deal you do have to be prepared to walk away, and to be treated like a strong country you have to act like a strong country.'

It was a day of high emotion. When the chief whip was summoned to see the prime minister in her Commons office, Smith kept May waiting for forty minutes. When he finally arrived, with an aide in tow, the PM was with Peter Hill and JoJo Penn. 'Chief, where are we with the DUP?' May slapped the table, an unusual show of frustration. 'Have you had the conversation?' she snapped. A whips' office source recalled, 'He hadn't done it because he knew what they were going to say.' For a prime minister whose job was now palpably on the line, this was not good enough. 'She exploded at him,' a witness recounted. 'She was thoroughly pissed off and her voice was emotional. She had a real go at him.'

The failure to hold the DUP close and consult them about the negotiations was evidence May's team had forgotten the lessons of the original backstop negotiations. As in December 2017, there was the artificial drama of a plane on standby as the deadline approached, the race to Europe, the last-minute negotiations and the attempt to bounce the DUP and Tory MPs into backing a questionable deal. 'Both in December 2017 and then that Strasbourg weekend we didn't say, "Shall we just ring Arlene and Nigel and see what they think?"' a political aide said. At 2.09 p.m., Arlene Foster tweeted that the DUP would vote against the government.

Always uncomfortable when asked for numbers, Smith admitted he was still expecting 60 to 70 rebels. 'How can you be at this number, you were at this number last week,' May complained.

The perception that she could no longer command her cabinet or fight the EU convinced David Davis, her former Brexit secretary, that May was no longer capable of delivering a no-deal Brexit, which left her with no leverage. He resolved to back the deal, both as the least bad option and to help others: 'There were about twenty-five youngsters who wanted to support the prime minister. One or two of them said to me, "If you vote for it. That gives us cover." It was just me being nice to some people.'[14] Others who switched their votes included Graham Brady, Nadine Dorries, Greg Hands, Nigel Evans, Ben Bradley and Tracey Crouch. Steve Double spoke for them all when he declared, 'It may be the best turd we've got.'[15]

At 7 p.m. MPs voted. Hannah Bardell of the SNP tweeted a picture from a 'rammed' No lobby.[16] The prime minister's agony was extended until 7.22 p.m. when it was announced that the government had lost by 149 votes. In the nearly two months since MV1, the number of Tory rebels had been cut from 118 to 75. Once again, just three Labour MPs backed the deal – John Mann, Caroline Flint and Kevin Barron. It was the fourth largest defeat for a sitting government in parliamentary history.

May got to her feet and promised a vote the following day on a no-deal Brexit, but warned, 'Voting against leaving without a deal and for an extension does not solve the problems we face. The EU will want to know what use we mean to make of such an extension. This House will have to answer that question. Does it wish to revoke article 50? Does it want to hold a second referendum? Or does it want to leave with a deal but not this deal? ... Thanks to the decision the House has made this evening they must now be faced.'

When the PM returned to her wood-panelled Commons office, 'she was pretty down'. To many, this was the worst night of her premiership. 'She thought it was all over,' an aide said. Some claim May was in tears that night. The front pages of both *The Times* and the *Telegraph* were emblazoned with a stark picture of May, being driven away from the Commons, her eyes red rimmed and damp, her mouth a grim slit of livid red lipstick, the strain of humiliation etched deep in her face.

At cabinet the next morning, Julian Smith made his anger with Cox clear. 'He felt quite let down,' an ally said. 'He was instrumental in bringing Geoffrey into the cabinet, so I think that weighed on him quite heavily.' Matt Hancock, the health secretary, also 'had a go at' Cox.

For weeks Cox had attended the 8.30 a.m. strategy meetings in Downing Street. Extraordinarily, he continued to turn up, a decision scarcely believable to some of May's aides. Days later, in the margins of the meeting, the attorney general offered an apology: 'Prime Minister, I'm sorry this has had the effect it's had.'

May replied, 'No, Geoffrey, you had to do it. You had to say what you felt was right.' As epitaphs for the May premiership go, there could be worse. In the moment of her defeat, the prime minister maintained the proprieties of her post. Yet hers was the stiff upper lip of a First World War company commander at the end of the opening day on the Somme thanking the general for the order to walk slowly towards the enemy guns.

Others were less reconciled. Barwell said, 'If the AG's written advice second time round had been as combative as his performance in the House of Commons the next day, instead of losing by 150 we would've lost by 50. And then you're close. If you get the margin down, then the third attempt suddenly becomes viable.'

Afterwards, Cox insisted he could not have gilded the lily: 'I would have no respectability if I blurred, altered or massaged my opinion for political considerations. It is vital to the institution of my office that people have confidence that the attorney general will not alter his opinion for political considerations.'

ABSTENTION REBELLION
The Rebel Alliance Strikes Again
13 March 2019

To one minister in the division lobby on the evening of 13 March 2019, the day after MV2, it was a 'scene from an opera', the leading lady cornered and facing her final aria before expiring. Theresa May was surrounded by a gaggle of pro-deal cabinet ministers imploring her to listen. 'She was in the corner looking pained,' the minister said. One after another, they told May they could not support the government's position on no-deal. 'We need the freedom to abstain. We need a decision.'

May, no aria left in her, thanks to the assault on her throat by Jean-Claude Juncker's cigarettes, seemed defeated, events both fast moving and farcical. She croaked, 'You don't know the pressure I'm under.' It was a rare glimpse behind the mask of May's public inscrutability. It so shocked the ministers that they gave her space. 'I backed away because it looked like we were ganging up on her,' one said. 'I'm always conscious of the body language. It was all a bit fraught.'

That was the first division of the night in what turned out to be another historically bizarre day in Parliament.

At 8.30 a.m., David Cameron, the man who had triggered the Brexit epoch, was doorstepped outside his west London home and gave a rare insight into his thinking. 'Obviously what needs to happen next is to rule out no-deal, that would be a disaster for our country and to seek an extension,' he said, before rounding on the Eurosceptics who would not back May. 'What happened last night is that some people who have always wanted Brexit have voted against it again. This is exasperating for the prime minister and I think she should feel free to look at other alternatives for partnership deals in order to solve this problem.'

On a day when everyone with a view on Brexit appeared to speak, Michel Barnier warned the 'risk of no-deal has never been higher' but said the EU could only offer an extension when they knew what the UK government intended to do with the extra time. In a briefing to EU ambassadors, Sabine Weyand tartly observed that anyone voting for no-deal was 'like the Titanic voting for the iceberg to get out of the way'.

May weathered Prime Minister's Questions, her voice, like her government, croaking as she battled a lacklustre Jeremy Corbyn, who failed to summon the kind of enthusiasm for Labour's Brexit plan that he evinced when discussing Venezuelan workers' rights.

Then, at 12.30 p.m., Philip Hammond delivered his spring statement on the state of the nation's finances. With May's deal apparently dead in the water, the chancellor used the statement to nail his colours to the mast of preventing a no-deal departure. He opened by saying MV2 had left 'a cloud of uncertainty hanging over our economy'. Hammond said that if there was a deal, there would be a 'deal dividend' in the form of 'an end to austerity', which would allow him to release some of the £27 billion Brexit 'headroom' he had built into the public finances to boost public spending, capital investment and cut taxes. By contrast, the chancellor warned, 'Leaving with no-deal would mean significant disruption in the short- and medium-term and a smaller, less prosperous economy in the long-term ... Higher unemployment; lower wages; higher prices in the shops. That is not what the British people voted for in June 2016.' Hammond concluded, 'The idea that there is some simple, readily available, fix that can be deployed to avoid the consequences of a no-deal Brexit is, I am afraid, just wrong.' Brexiteers were furious that Hammond had used a government statement to threaten rather than reassure. Other colleagues admired the chancellor for belatedly discovering some political 'game'.

In line with what the prime minister had promised the week before, the government tabled a motion allowing MPs to vote on whether the UK could leave without a deal. It was worded in such a way that it ruled out no-deal on 29 March, but kept the idea on the table in the long run. The speaker selected two amendments, one of which was the last knockings of the Malthouse Compromise, tabled by Damian Green. The other was an amendment tabled by Caroline Spelman and Jack Dromey, which sought to 'reject' no-deal forever.

At cabinet that morning, there was a row when May indicated the government would whip against all the amendments. Hammond pressed her to find a cross-party consensus, code for a customs union. Gavin Williamson, Chris Grayling, Andrea Leadsom, Sajid Javid and Liam Fox all suggested it would be unwise to oppose the Malthouse amendment, the one thing that had brought the party together. Williamson declared the plan to whip hard 'daft' and 'not clever'.

Ken Clarke visited the whips' office mid-morning and was told MPs would have to oppose the Spelman-Dromey no-deal forever amendment. He passed on the news. This presented the pro-dealers in the cabinet with a dilemma. They did not want to oppose the amendment ruling out no-deal. The chief whip insisted ministers were bound by collective responsibility. 'The Spelman motion was really unhelpful,' a cabinet minister said.

Throughout the early part of March, the Rebel Alliance grew in conviction that, if circumstances like this arose, they might have to resign. As business secretary, Greg Clark worried that as 29 March approached, he would be needed to help companies cope, making it difficult to walk away at that point. 'He felt that if he resigned a few days before we left without a deal, that he would have been deserting his post,' a fellow cabinet minister said. Amber Rudd, having experienced the futility of life on the backbenches, urged caution: 'Once you're out, you're out.' But Clark was beginning to think they could not stop no-deal. 'I have to go some weeks in advance and not leave it till the very end,' he said.

Even ministers who had no intention of resigning were keen that their colleagues dug in. Michael Gove knew better than most what no-deal would mean. After cabinet in early March, he approached Rudd and said, 'Amber, you are so brave. Good luck.' She was also approached by Alun Cairns, the Welsh secretary whose constituency was very pro-Leave. He said, 'I don't want no-deal, but I'm relying on people like you to stop it.'

Rudd privately told friends and backbench colleagues that while the government had done as much as it could, under the circumstances, to prepare for no-deal, 'It's still going to be absolute shit.' Rudd found it disturbingly surreal to be sitting in civil contingencies meetings in which plans were made to move more police to Kent to deal with expected riots. 'We were behaving as though we were going to war,' she said later.

When the main debate opened, at 3.30 p.m., it was Gove who led for the government, not May, symbolically voiceless in a moment when she needed to be at her most persuasive. The government was on a collision course with chaos. If the amendment passed, it would change the main motion, which would mean that instead of backing the motion, the government would then have to oppose it, putting the pro-dealers in another bind. 'This was a day that was cock-up after cock-up,' David Gauke recalled. 'We spotted quite early on in the day that if the Spelman motion wins we don't get to the motion that we want, which was a way of voting against no-deal. If the Spelman motion won, what are we supposed to do? Defeat this Spelman motion which actually we agree with?'

Gauke contacted Oliver Letwin at lunchtime and pointed out what was likely to happen. Letwin and Nick Boles agreed and convened a meeting with Spelman and Dromey behind the speaker's chair. 'It puts us in an impossible position,' Gauke explained, pointing out that what would have been an overwhelming parliamentary majority against no-deal on 29 March, if the government motion had been allowed to stand, would be lost and instead there would be a dogfight about whether to rule out no-deal forever. 'Letwin was going around very red-faced because he'd realised what he'd done,' another minister said.

At 3.30 p.m., Buckland told Chris Pincher, the deputy chief whip, that Spelman would pass. 'I want to abstain' on the final vote, he said. Pincher agreed the government would lose on Spelman. 'Your best hope is for there to be no division called.' Buckland then spoke to Philip Hammond and said, 'You've got to help us.' The chancellor agreed to press for a free vote.

By 3.40 p.m., seeing that the government would not allow a free vote, Spelman announced that she would no longer table her amendment. There was briefly a reprieve for the pro-dealers. However, egged on by other Remainers like Heidi Allen of the Independent Group, Yvette Cooper, who had also signed the amendment, said she would move it instead. Letwin tried to persuade her to drop it, but Cooper would not budge. 'We thought we had a deal,' one minister said. 'Then it was all blown up by Yvette.' As a Labour MP, Cooper had an interest not just in Brexit policy but in fomenting what one minister called 'a shitshow in government'. If that was her goal, it was conspicuously successful.

That afternoon fifteen ministers were ushered in to see the prime minister in her Commons office. Anne Milton, a minister of state at education, looked her in the eye and said, 'Are you clear that if this vote goes through and we abstain you will have to sack thirty to forty ministers?' As a former deputy chief whip, Milton's threat was credible. It would be easy to dismiss one or two ministers; no prime minister could credibly sack a third of their front bench. May, as usual, made no decision on the hoof. On their way out, Milton turned to one of the prime minister's senior aides and reiterated, 'We will do it. This is going to happen.'

At 6.15 p.m., forty-five minutes before the votes began, there was a cabinet meeting around the grand polished table in the prime minister's Commons office. As it began, Greg Clark said, 'Can we resolve what's happening with the whipping tonight? Because if the amendment goes through then what happens then?' May was dismissive. 'Take it up with the chief whip,' she said.

As the meeting wound up, Clark tried again and got no answer. The pro-dealers turned on Smith. 'We will defeat that amendment,' Smith said. 'If the motion is amended, we will oppose it.' Rudd, Clark and Philip Hammond protested but it was still unclear to them what the plan was as the meeting broke up just before 7 p.m. so they could go to vote. 'There was just a flurry of confusion and she just left,' Rudd recalled.

As they were leaving, text messages started arriving from the whips' office, telling Tory MPs they were on a three-line whip if the motion was amended. Rudd met Letwin as she approached the chamber. 'We are very confused about what to do here,' she said. 'I'm not sure what the right thing is.' Letwin replied, 'Don't oppose the government. This isn't the moment.'

At 7.18 p.m. MPs voted for the (still named) Spelman amendment by 312 votes to 308. Nine Tories backed it: Guto Bebb, Ken Clarke, Justine Greening, Dominic Grieve, Sam Gyimah, Phillip Lee, Antoinette Sandbach, Spelman herself and Ed Vaizey. The motion was not binding on the government but was a clear statement of intent that MPs wanted an extension and would not tolerate no-deal. One pro-dealer joked of Grieve: 'He wants a one-thousand-year extension.'

In the division lobby during the vote on Spelman, the pro-dealers – including Buckland, Alistair Burt and Tobias Ellwood – surrounded May. 'We can't vote against this amended motion. We need the freedom to abstain.' May gave nothing away. 'We need a decision!' The prime minister cracked. 'She started waving her hands and her face sort of elongated,' said one witness. Then the admission of the stress she was under: 'You don't know the pressure I'm under.' They backed away.

At 7.35 p.m. the Commons rejected the Malthouse amendment by 374 votes to 164. The concept which had united the Tory party for, it seemed, the life cycle of the mayfly, had now split it down the middle again. Just 149 Conservatives, including 14 ministers, backed the motion. The prime minister abstained.

Julian Smith now faced one of the signature crises of his time as chief whip. The cabinet meeting had been chaos, with no clear line from May, but it was not government policy to rule out no-deal forever, a stance which would have torpedoed Brexiteer support. Therefore, he decided, Conservative MPs should vote against the amended motion, even though, technically, that was now the government motion. Smith's supporters say Greg Clark and the others did know what the whip was. 'It was made clear. It was not a decision they liked,' one ally said. 'We've got the texts to prove it.'

Smith's problem was that May's other senior aides were now convinced the pro-dealers had replaced the ERG as the immediate threat to the government. Barwell told Andrew Bowie, one of May's parliamentary private secretaries, that he should let some MPs know they could abstain. 'There was a panic,' a senior source said. 'There was a discussion where Gavin said to Bowie, "You'd better let some of these people off."' Simon Hoare, the uber Remainer who represented West Dorset, was one he tipped off. Another was Sarah Newton, a minister of state at the Department of Health. Unknown to Bowie, Newton had already voted for the Spelman amendment and had decided to resign anyway. She confided to friends, 'I was told to resign if I couldn't look my constituents in the eye, so I resigned.' Another rebel added, 'At the last minute we were allowed to abstain. Explicitly. That came though literally as the division bells rung.' A Downing Street aide admitted, 'There was a tacit acceptance that some people might be able to go missing.' When he found out, Smith was furious, his authority liquefied by Number 10.

As news spread 'like wildfire' that Bowie was telling people they could abstain, members of the pro-deal group exchanged a pre-arranged message on their WhatsApp groups: 'Tally-ho'. The author saw one sent by Tobias Ellwood, but those present say 'various authors' issued the call to arms. Rudd used her January 15th group to say, 'I have decided to abstain. Meet down in Anne Milton's room.'

For the second time that day, Milton became the centre of attention. She was an interesting figure in the Brexit wars, difficult to categorise. Milton voted Remain but hated the tag 'Remainer'. She thought countries were better off working together, but two years on the European Health Council, where member states read out pointless, pre-prepared speeches and decisions took an age, meant she understood why people voted to Leave. She backed May's deal as a moderate managed route to Brexit and was totally opposed to a second referendum. Her room on the lower ministerial corridor now provided a safe bolthole from prying eyes. 'You don't want to be lurking around while the whips are trying to shove you through the lobby,' one cabinet minister said. Slowly people arrived, looking around to see what company they were in: Rudd, Gauke, Clark, Claire Perry, Stephen Hammond were all there, ministers and parliamentary private secretaries huddled together in silence, awaiting the explosions upstairs. There was gallows humour about whether they would have to resign or face the sack. Slowly the mood evolved into a twelve-step support programme, everyone egging on the others: 'Well, I'm abstaining, if you're abstaining.'

'Well, if you're abstaining, I'm abstaining.'

The most conspicuous absentee was Philip Hammond. When the chancellor was caught by the TV cameras milling around, Rudd and others began shouting at the television: 'Come on, Phil!' Instead of joining them in the foxhole, Hammond put a consoling arm around Rory Stewart and Steve Brine and they all voted in accordance with the three-line whip. Hammond had a difficult relationship with May fuelled by pettiness that governs a marriage after the love has evaporated. Yet one senior official recalled, 'Hammond walked into the prime minister's office and had a tetchy discussion with her about how awful it was that he was being asked to vote in favour of keeping open no-deal. Then he and Lidington, grey-faced, dutifully walked through the right lobby. There was an element of respect in her for the fact that he did, on the whole, keep his disagreements between them and do what the government asked of him.'

Another of those who did not make it to Milton's room was the rebel bugler Ellwood. When the division bell rang, journalists in the press gallery watched as he went toe to toe with Pincher on the floor of the House. The whips' office enforcer tried forcefully to persuade him to vote against the motion. Ellwood refused. Lip readers concluded he had said, 'Don't whip me on this, otherwise I'll resign.'

Robert Buckland took a call from James Brokenshire, an old friend who had remained an ultra-loyalist. 'For God's sake, come and vote,' he said. 'You must vote with us tonight.' Buckland replied, 'I just can't do this. I've had no opportunity to vote against no-deal.' He decided to see Brokenshire in person to explain himself, but by the time he reached the division lobbies, the doors were shut. He had abstained, along with twelve other Conservatives, David Mundell and Claire Perry raising the cabinet count to five. Mundell explained, 'The House made its view clear by agreeing the Spelman amendment, I didn't think it was right for me to oppose that.'[1]

On that third and final vote May lost by a much bigger margin, MPs voting in favour of the amended motion, ruling out no-deal, by 321 to 278. In the long history of Brexit there were few more surreal evenings than 13 March 2019. Tom Peck, the *Independent*'s sketchwriter, described it as 'a madness to echo down the ages'. He wrote, 'Theresa May planned to defeat herself, then decided not to defeat herself by defeating herself, then lost. To herself.'[2]

The Commons had voted against no-deal, but without legislation, the UK was still due to leave the EU on 29 March. The European Commission also issued a statement: 'It is not enough to take no deal off the table – you have to agree to a deal.' May stood at the despatch box at 7.52 p.m. and explained that the government would table a motion the following day which would set a new deadline to agree a deal, the following Wednesday, 20 March. If MPs backed the deal, the government would 'seek a short, limited, technical extension of Article 50'. But if May lost again, she said there would have to be 'a much longer extension' and that 'would undoubtedly require the United Kingdom to hold European Parliament elections in May 2019'. The prime minister concluded, 'I do not think that would be the right outcome. But the house needs to face up to the consequences of the decisions it has taken.' The strategy outlined by Robbins in the Sofitel bar was unfolding as predicted.

Yvette Cooper hit back later that evening, demanding 'indicative votes': 'The prime minister has refused to consult or build consensus, and refused to allow votes on other Brexit options. If the prime minister won't sort this out and build some consensus on the way forward then Parliament will need to instead.'

If MV2 had been May's team against the world, a moment of miserable solidarity, Stephen Parkinson, her political secretary, told friends later the abstention rebellion was 'the worst night' because it was a 'close and unexpected and unnecessary defeat', which pitched members of her team against each other. The cabinet meeting had been a shambles, the whipping arrangements confused until it was too late, Barwell's intervention with Bowie a catastrophic blow to Smith's authority as chief whip, a smoke signal which both fuelled the rebellion and simultaneously made it impossible to discipline. 'In that confusion we couldn't sack cabinet ministers for doing something they've been told to do from Number 10,' a Downing Street source said.

Afterwards, in May's office, the inner team were exhausted and tense, Smith furiously pacing. 'How has this happened?' the prime minister asked. Members of the ERG were already in uproar that the abstainers had not all been fired. 'That was a bleak night,' one of those present recalled.

Smith's team went into open revolt against May's failure to fire the rebels. 'The whips' office went mental,' one of those present recounted. 'If Julian had walked, the entire team would have walked with him,' a whip confided to a Number 10 official two days later. The anger was compounded when Barwell decided to visit the whips' office to thank them for their efforts. He was met with glares and silence. Several turned their backs on him. Barwell and Smith conferred in the chief's office. Smith told him the decision to deploy Bowie was 'appalling'. Voices were raised. They were joined by Smith's special adviser Simon Burton, JoJo Penn and Stephen Parkinson. 'Parky' also wanted sackings. 'You get power by asserting it,' he said. 'If you don't assert it, you definitely don't have it, so you've got to sack someone now.' Penn thought adding to the number of rebels on the backbenches would be a mistake.

In truth, Smith himself had missed a trick. As Pincher had hinted earlier in the day, the best way to avoid the damaging abstentions was to avoid the vote altogether. Once the Spelman/Cooper amendment had passed, it was not in Cooper's interests to press for a vote on the amended motion. Pulling that vote would have enraged the ERG, since it would have allowed the no-deal amendment to stand, but it would have avoided the farce of a government voting against the (amended) motion it had tabled and the damaging sight of frontbenchers defying a three-line whip. 'Who moved the bloody division on the amended motion?' a ministerial rebel said, incredulous. 'The chief whip. Shocking.'

When David Gauke got home, he took a call from Julian Smith. 'They're going berserk,' the chief explained. 'I'm under such pressure.' Gauke took the hint. 'If the prime minister wants me to resign, I'll resign,' he said. Smith did not respond directly, he certainly didn't say that was May's wish. Gauke felt the chief was freelancing.

After midnight Pincher rang Buckland, their most difficult conversation in a thirty-year friendship. The deputy chief whip indicated the solicitor general should expect to lose his job. 'You know the consequences,' he said. Buckland replied, 'I do, but I told you I'd have to abstain. The wrong call was made. It should have been a free vote.'

The following morning, Smith summoned Gauke to his office in 9 Downing Street. It was an amiable game of chicken. 'Look, there's fury about this,' the chief whip said. 'We can't let all of you go.' Some thirteen frontbenchers had abstained. 'But I've spoken to the prime minister and it would be helpful if you could resign.' Smith's view was that Gauke had coordinated the article in the *Daily Mail*. He also felt the justice secretary was an honourable man who could be asked to do the right thing. 'The chief wanted a controlled explosion,' one of Gauke's fellow rebels said.

Gauke replied, 'Fine. I'm happy to do that. But I think you'll find that if I go, others may go as well. But I can see the case for one sacrificial lamb and I'm prepared to do that.' He added that he wanted to speak to Rudd and Clark to persuade them to stay. When Gauke had phoned Rudd the night before and signalled that he was prepared to walk the plank, she told him, 'You're mad. Whatever you do, don't agree to anything in there. Come out and tell us.'

After his meeting with Smith, Gauke, Rudd and Clark met in Clark's parliamentary office. 'Julian's under enormous pressure,' Gauke said. 'There's a rebellion in the whips' office. They want me to go and I can see the case for that.' They called Philip Hammond, who had already been on the *Today* programme saying there would be no resignations. Hammond phoned Downing Street and was told by Barwell that they did want

Gauke's head. Gauke said it would be best if he quit so the others could stay, but Clark was having none of it. 'If you go and I don't go then it makes me look really bad,' he said. 'So, if you go, I will go as well.' Rudd said the same thing. They called Mundell, who agreed he would also resign.

A second meeting was convened in the lower ministerial corridor with the wider group: Buckland, Burt, Ellwood and Milton among them. The other rebels were outraged, none more so than Buckland, who felt that, constitutionally, as lord chancellor, Gauke could only be fired directly by the prime minister. Burt said, 'I'm planning on retiring in a month or so anyway. Let me go. The rest of you stay to keep the show on the road.' Others feared Burt would look like a martyr. They also wanted to stick together. The meeting came to resemble the scene in the Kirk Douglas epic. 'We all said, "I am Spartacus",' Rudd recalled.

The cabinet ministers returned to Clark's room and Gauke phoned Smith: 'Julian, I'm here with Greg and Amber.' There was an audible groan from the chief whip. 'I've tried,' Gauke continued. 'I'm happy to resign, but you should know that the others will go as well. There will be thirteen of us.'

The chief whip, said, 'Okay, thanks,' then hung up. Gauke was safe.

The emergency cabinet meeting on 14 March was compared to a 'punishment beating' by one attendee as ministers lined up to tear strips off Rudd, Gauke, Clark and Mundell. Steve Barclay, the Brexit secretary, 'went nuts', and even the mild-mannered James Brokenshire 'tore into us'. Gauke found his mind drifting, the waves of attacks a haze. Clark sought to defend himself, criticising the 'unclear whipping'. One critic said he began to 'babble' that he had not understood the arrangements. Clark said later, 'You should resign if you can't support the policy of the government. But we were strongly in support of the policy of the government, which was to leave with a deal. We didn't feel the whipping decision was in accordance with the policy.'

Julian Smith had had enough. He was the kind of Englishman more comfortable repressing his emotions, but they burst to the surface. 'The chief was very upset,' a cabinet minister said. 'He got up and walked out. I thought he was going to hit Greg on the way past.' Instead, Smith snapped as he passed Clark, 'Don't lie! Read your text messages, Greg!' Smith stormed out and went to sit in the Downing Street garden to calm down. He was 'gutted' by the result and felt like he wanted to resign. 'I made a bit of a tit of myself,' he admitted later to an aide.

May sat with 'a face like thunder' as she too unleashed months of pent-up frustration, speaking emotionally about the need for collective responsibility. The abstainers shifted uncomfortably in their chairs. 'It was cold fury,' a witness recalled. To the surprise of Rudd, Gauke, Clark and Mundell, they were not the only ones in her sights. The prime minister let rip at everyone who had shown disloyalty, denouncing those around the table who had briefed against her and leaked cabinet discussions – a clear majority of those now intensely studying the grain in the cabinet table. 'She broadened it, which was helpful,' an abstainer said. 'It wasn't just the four of us being told off.' As she finished, the prime minister gave her most penetrating stare and declared, 'After this is over, I'll need to look at ways of reasserting discipline.' For many present, the sight of a prime minister with no authority left talking about retribution was reminiscent of Adolf Hitler at the end of the film *Downfall*. 'She was moving imaginary armies in her head,' said a minister. 'It felt like Götterdämmerung.' Others saw the meeting as a much-needed letting off of steam. 'If it was meant to be cathartic, it worked,' a minister said. But little changed; by the time most ministers had returned to their own offices, May's denunciation of leakers had already leaked. Julian Smith said later, 'I think this was the leakiest cabinet in British political history.'

At the end of the meeting Gauke leaned across to May and said, 'I said to Julian earlier, if you want me to resign, I will do. The difficulty is if I go, the others feel that they must go as well.' May, back to her impenetrable self, was non-committal: 'Okay, understood.' Gauke repeated the message to Barwell who said, 'I thought that's where we would end up.'

For the Rebel Alliance ministers abstaining showed that people historically seen as reasonable were prepared to fight as hard as the ERG for what they believed. One said, 'It was about us kicking back and saying, "Don't push us too far otherwise we'll bring the whole bloody house down."' Yet the effect of Downing Street turning a blind eye was to make it less likely that the ERG backed May's deal in the third meaningful vote now planned for the following week. 'The rage at the way Remainer ministers defied the whip and were not sacked is worse than anything I've seen,' said an ERG member. Mark Francois told *Sky News*, 'Collective responsibility has disintegrated. You might as well tell the whips to pack up and go home. The government is barely in office.' He signed off with the characteristic statement, 'I was in the army. I was trained not to lose.' The sense of Westminster morphing into a bad sitcom was reinforced.

There was one further, farcical twist. The following day, Steve Barclay, the Brexit secretary, got to his feet to close the debate for the government and urge MPs to back a motion outlining May's new Brexit timetable. 'It is time to put forward an extension that is realistic,' he concluded just before 5 p.m. 'I commend the Government motion to the House.'

At 6.08 p.m., when the House divided, the Brexit secretary voted against his own government, against the very motion he had proposed and urged other MPs to back. Barclay, who personally did not want an extension at all, explained to his local TV station, 'We need a deal. We've got to get that over the line, but if we don't have a deal, then we should leave with no-deal. That's always been my position.'[3]

Barclay was not alone. Another seven cabinet ministers and a total of 188 Tory MPs voted against the government. When Francois walked into the No lobby to join the rebels, he found most of the whips' office, including Pincher, voting No as well – apparently in protest that the cabinet abstainers had not been sacked. Julian Smith abstained. Francois, a former whip, approached one of them and said, 'Are you boys trying to make a point?'

'Might be, might not.'

A minister said, 'The most ridiculous thing I've seen is the Brexit secretary voting against his own bloody motion. That was absurd.'

There were, however, three slices of good news for May. An amendment demanding a new referendum only secured 85 votes, with Labour telling its MPs to abstain because the leadership of both the party and the People's Vote campaign judged the timing to be wrong. Indeed, it was Jeremy Corbyn who lost frontbenchers that day, with Ruth Smeeth resigning to back the motion and another four – Yvonne Fovargue, Emma Lewell-Buck, Justin Madders and Stephanie Peacock – agreeing to quit afterwards. Labour's own amendment, demanding indicative votes, went down by 16 votes.

A second attempt by the cross-party Bresistance group to grab control of the Commons timetable – an amendment proposed by Hilary Benn – also failed, by the wafer-thin margin of two votes. The last time this gambit had been tried, the Bresisters' proposed nine-month delay to Brexit had cost the group votes. This time there was no time limit at all.

This pleased Labour MPs like Benn, Stephen Doughty, Alison McGovern and Liz Kendall and others like Grieve and Anna Soubry, who all favoured another referendum. But when Lucy Powell, a leading light in the Norway camp, heard what was proposed, she told Boles, 'This is a fucking disaster; you haven't put a cap on the extension.' Powell proposed an amendment to Benn's amendment to impose a deadline at the end of June, but that failed by three votes. The result was that Labour MPs in Brexity seats, such as Gareth Snell and Gloria De Piero, were unable to support Benn. 'They wanted either for it to be limited to three months or, otherwise, for the government to impose it on them, or the EU to impose it on them,' the MP said. The abstention rebellion showed the potential strength of those wanting a soft Brexit if they enjoyed cabinet backing. The votes the following day revealed that those trying to stop a hard Brexit or no-deal were still dangerously divided.

It was Theresa May, though, who bore the deepest scars of the week. MV2 on 12 March had all but destroyed the central policy and purpose of her government. The insurrection by the pro-dealers a day later obliterated the last remaining vestiges of the prime minister's authority. Cabinet collective responsibility, a gossamer-thin pretence for nearly a year, spontaneously combusted in the division lobbies that night.

Alberto Costa had been sacked as a PPS for putting down an amendment which wasn't government policy, but May failed to discipline ministers who had defied a three-line whip. 'That was a turning point because then there was a lot of bad blood in the parliamentary party afterwards,' a senior member of May's political team said. Brandon Lewis, the party chairman, told friends later, 'That was the point at which it all fell to pieces from a party discipline point of view.' Julian Smith agreed: 'Pragmatism, the key feature of the Conservative Party's survival over many decades, the key feature that is required in a hung Parliament, was lost by too many members of Parliament.'

While her ministers scented weakness, May's reputation for weathering circumstances which would have brutalised others actually made her popular with the public. After MV2, James Johnson sent a memo to Gavin Barwell and JoJo Penn on the results of his freshest polling. It showed that positive views of May were up. Battling on in the face of adversity was 'core to the brand', he wrote.

On Friday 15 March there was even a meeting in Number 10 at which Downing Street aides wrote a grid for the run-in to Brexit day on 29

March in case they won MV3. EU citizens and businesses were to be invited to Number 10. May would visit a Remain seat and a Leave seat in the hope of bringing the country together. 'There was an event pencilled in the Number 10 garden to welcome our exit,' one aide said. 'There was a big bust-up over whether to ring Big Ben or not – some people saying we have to do this to show what a patriotic moment it is and others saying it will encourage protesters.' In the same meeting they signed off on 'a new chapter for Britain', a narrative penned by James Johnson of what the rest of the May premiership would look like ('a fair chance to go where you want in life'). It was never needed.

May was bleeding out, politically, but still determined to lead her troops into the final battle for MV3. That weekend, the prime minister privately warned Brexiteers they had to back her or risk Parliament imposing an indefinite delay that would mean never leaving the EU. Number 10 aides leaked advice from civil servants, which read, 'Once the UK has taken part in the EU elections there is no limit to the number of extensions of Article 50 the UK can ask for or be required to ask for by Parliament.' May also issued a statement calling 'the idea of the British people going to the polls to elect MEPs three years after voting to leave the EU' a 'potent symbol of Parliament's collective political failure'.

Privately, senior Eurosceptics, including Rees-Mogg, were keen to get on board. The ERG chairman publicly declared, 'I'm not the immovable object facing the irresistible force.' Matthew Elliott, one of the architects of the Leave campaign, urged MPs to get behind May, writing in the *Sunday Times*, 'If MPs vote down the withdrawal agreement for a third time this week, Brexit probably won't happen.' Iain Duncan Smith, who had been prepared to vote yes on MV2 if Cox's legal advice had been different, told friends that Eurosceptics should 'jump together' if the DUP supported the deal. Steve Baker felt under great strain and told friends trying to keep the ERG together was like 'herding tigers'. He wrote in his diary on Friday 15 March, 'Jacob softening. Capitulation brewing. The ways begin to part.'

The same day, Nigel Dodds of the DUP met both Lidington and Philip Hammond to discuss plans to offer legislation including a 'Stormont lock' clause in the withdrawal agreement and implementation bill to ensure EU rules on Northern Ireland would be adopted in the rest of the UK or rejected in both. The DUP called their demands 'legislation not remuneration' but Dodds also wanted a cut in air passenger duty (lower in the Republic than Northern Ireland) and ministers admitted they would need to find another £1 billion for Northern Ireland after the deal passed. 'There are probably a billion reasons why they are going to get on board,' a minister said. 'But that won't happen until after the deal passes. We can't have a bribe looking like a bribe, can we?'

As the week of MV3 began there were real hopes of a breakthrough. The only problem was that, in focusing on the ERG and the DUP, Downing Street had forgotten about another key player in the drama, the Rt Hon John Bercow MP, speaker of the House of Commons.

THE QUEEN SACRIFICE

MV3

18 to 29 March 2019

At 3.33 p.m. on Monday 18 March John Bercow got to his feet and announced that he wished to make a statement. He had not alerted Andrea Leadsom, the leader of the Commons, or any other ministers, to what he planned to say. Bercow paused, escalating the drama, the canopy above the speaker's chair dwarfing him. The chair bears several Latin inscriptions, one of which reads, 'The hand that deals justly is a sweet-smelling ointment.' Within minutes Bercow had kicked up a stink.

In a lengthy disquisition on parliamentary history, Bercow quoted from *Erskine May*, the bible of parliamentary procedure, which stated, 'A motion or an amendment which is the same, in substance, as a question which has been decided during a session may not be brought forward again during that same session.' He then ruled that there could be no new meaningful vote unless the motion was substantively different. 'What the Government cannot legitimately do is to resubmit to the House the same proposition or substantially the same proposition as that of last week, which was rejected by 149 votes.'

There followed a tsunami of points of order. This time, the Brexiteers – who had been enraged by Bercow's January ruling allowing backbenchers to seize control of the timetable – lined up to praise the speaker. Jacob Rees-Mogg purred, 'Dare I say that there is more joy in heaven over one sinner who repented than over the ninety-nine who are not in need of repentance?'

Both Chris Bryant, Labour's most knowledgeable parliamentary proceduralist, and Angela Eagle had put the issue on Bercow's radar a week earlier, asking questions about whether it was right to keep bringing back the same issue. Bercow began to read newspaper reports which suggested the government would keep trying. 'I saw briefings, "If we have to bring it back 25, 26, 30 times, we will until we get the right result." And I thought: *I don't like this*. It looked to me like trying to bully the House into deciding what it doesn't want to decide.' This was reinforced for Bercow when a veteran Brexiteer told the speaker about young MPs 'in tears' after 'being browbeaten by the whips' and told their career would be over and they would be 'lucky to stand again' unless they voted for MV2.

Bercow again acted in defiance of his clerks. A week earlier he had commissioned John Benger, who had replaced David Natzler, to examine the rules. Benger gave the work to Colin Lee, who he considered the best proceduralist in his team. When Benger presented it, he declared, 'It's an absolutely first-class piece of work.' The paper detailed the precedents for denying a fresh vote on an issue that was substantively the same, citing twelve examples of when a speaker had mentioned the convention from 1604 to 1920, the last time it had been used. The absence of speaker intervention since 1920 was attributed not to the discontinuation of the convention but to general compliance with it. However, the paper made clear that no speaker had ever actually used it against a government, only against backbenchers repetitively introducing the same bill, and argued that it would be wrong to invoke it now as it would be too controversial when Parliament was trying to reach a view on the government's central policy. When Natzler gave evidence to the Exiting the European Union select committee the previous October, he produced the same answer. 'I do not think the procedures of the House are designed to obstruct the necessary business of government in that way in such a crucial thing,' Natzler said.[1]

When he had finished reading, Bercow summoned Benger and said, 'I'm afraid, John, I don't share your view. I don't think it's a particularly good paper at all.' He explained, 'It's not that the convention doesn't apply to governments, it's just that they have not fallen foul of it.'

The clerk was cool, irritated. 'You're saying that because you don't like the conclusion.'

'I don't think it's grounded in principle,' Bercow said. 'It seems to be a pragmatic argument about my safety or the image of the speaker or the speaker's office. I don't really think that's a matter for the clerks.' Bercow consulted his long-standing aide Tim Hames, a former journalist, and his wife Sally before taking his decision, He did not tell Benger.

To Julian Smith, the common denominator of the rulings was that they thwarted the government and its pursuit of Brexit. The chief whip watched the ruling on a television in his office, then marched to the speaker's chair, where a heated exchange took place in which Smith accused Bercow of perpetrating 'a constitutional outrage'. In Downing Street, the prime minister was 'genuinely enraged'.

To his critics, it seemed wilfully perverse of Bercow to cite precedent so emphatically when, on the matter of whether backbenchers could initiate legislation or control the timetable to pass those bills, the speaker had been a dedicated innovator. One cabinet minister said, 'It was very serious interference indeed. He pulled the rug from under us. That's a pretty big decision when the government was trying to deliver on 17-plus million people's votes, and on its core manifesto commitment. It was pretty dodgy.' One of May's senior advisers said, 'When the history of this is written, the importance of Bercow's unpredictable, ungovernable attitude is hard to overestimate. Parliament became the crucible of the whole thing. The speaker has untrammelled power. He's not answerable to anybody. It was hugely, hugely significant.'

The immediate effect of Bercow's ruling was to torpedo the deal which Downing Street had been working on with the DUP. 'We were just about to get the DUP to come to us,' Barwell said. 'We weren't going to get anything else out of the EU so the conclusion we'd come to is we needed to do some things domestically that made the backstop tolerable to the DUP. There was a document that was ready to publish.' The plan had been to release the pledges that Number 10 was prepared to put into domestic legislation on that Monday evening.

May had agreed that if Northern Ireland was forced to align with the EU then Great Britain would also align on those issues to ensure there was no difference in rules within the UK. This was a major concession and one the government would have written into the Withdrawal Bill. The DUP was also 'offered a sub-committee of the cabinet', a minister revealed. 'The cabinet secretary was very worried about it, but it would have allowed them to produce a paper on any government policy and submit that to the cabinet,' an extraordinary concession for a party which was not in coalition. 'There was also cash,' another official recalled. 'The DUP had an awful lot offered to them.' These pledges were reinforced by a lunch in the Treasury between the chancellor and DUP representatives. 'Philip offering lunch was always a shock,' a cabinet colleague joked.

Jeffrey Donaldson had been pushing the idea of a Northern Ireland economic zone 'looking at the backstop as an economic zone to face both ways'. The civil servant said, 'We were into announcement choreography. Then the Bercow statement popped up and it was gone – dead.'

The speaker's ruling was not the DUP's only reason for refusing to back the deal. They had also spoken to leading Brexiteers and potential Tory leadership candidates Boris Johnson and Dominic Raab and found both less committed to Northern Ireland than they had hoped and expected, raising questions about whether a deal they signed with May would be torn up by her successor. 'That spooked them,' one of May's EU advisers said. With the DUP's support went the chance to win over more Tories and Labour MPs in Leave seats.

The most serious charge, levelled by another member of May's senior team, is that it was Bercow's specific intention to sink this nascent deal with the DUP. 'We were moving towards a positive situation with many of the people that we needed to get over the line, including the DUP,' the source said. 'I think he was aware of that and he took a conscious decision to stop any vote which delivered on the referendum result that week. In my view, he blocked a vote which had a very, very good chance of getting over the line.' Bercow denied this, insisting he was neutral and only ever sought to facilitate the will of Parliament.

Theresa May did not wear her heart on her sleeve, but after she had left government, she would accuse Bercow of an 'abuse of power' and make clear she saw his rulings as a 'key' reason for her political failure. 'What I find most shocking about John Bercow's approach is that the speaker's role is to uphold democracy,' she would write. 'Yet here was a speaker who, it seemed to me, was deliberately using his power in a way that favoured those who wanted to overturn the democratic will of the people.'[2]

Bercow saw in these complaints the grievance of the football fan for the referee: 'People always agree if the referee makes the decision they want. They say, "I have always thought that referee's got very good eyesight, very acute judgement. It was definitely a penalty." Or, alternatively, "Oh, absolute disgrace, the referee got it wrong." When you take a collection of decisions, people bank the ones that suit them and complain when they get the decisions they don't like.'

May's inner circle was so shellshocked by Bercow's ruling that they allowed a setback to become a crisis. Constitutional experts, including

Robert Buckland, the solicitor general, quickly suggested ways to circumvent the ruling – but in Downing Street there was panic. Momentum was lost. 'It was something we could have ignored,' a cabinet minister said. 'But we chose to be spooked by it.' The most obvious way forward would have been to prorogue Parliament for a few days, creating a new session in which the meaningful vote could be reintroduced. Dominic Raab pushed that solution. This would have been seen as procedural trickery and May hardly had time to spare, but a short prorogation would almost certainly have worked. This, though, was not Theresa May's style. A Downing Street political aide said, 'She is not wired that way. It is too irresponsible. Can you imagine the constitutional outrage? Can you imagine getting caught up in the courts? The other side would cry foul from here to all eternity.' It is hardly spoiling the story to note here that another prime minister was to take a different view.

That evening May received Graham Brady, chairman of the 1922 Committee, the most senior of the fabled 'men in grey suits'. Brady told the prime minister he had been contacted by a large number of MPs who wanted her to resign. He did not proffer an opinion, acting as a neutral conduit, but senior MPs said he was 'at the end of his chain'. The sulphurous mood on the backbenches was not news to the prime minister. Over the preceding weekend she had called MPs, including Bob Stewart, the former British forces commander in Bosnia, to ask for his support. 'The deal is no good,' he told her.

Shorn even of the limited powers of persuasion she had exhibited over the previous three years, May could only reply, 'Well I think it is.'

Stewart rebuffed her in kind: 'Well I don't.'

Richard Drax, the MP for South Dorset and owner of the longest wall in England, told her bluntly that she should stand down. An MP in whom Drax confided said, 'Richard told her to resign. She just went quiet. It was as if no one had ever said it to her directly before.'

At that time and in the years since, it became accepted that Theresa May never seriously contemplated going for no-deal, particularly not after her January trip to Northern Ireland. The truth, however, is that for around forty-eight hours that week the prime minister, out loud, seriously contemplated the prospect.

It was first raised in the morning pre-meeting on Tuesday 19 March in May's study upstairs, what used to be Margaret Thatcher's office. A senior figure was explicit that May, wearily but firmly, said, 'You know, maybe we do just have to go for no-deal.' An official present said, 'That was her testing it with herself.' A political aide added, 'She was seriously considering it.' Philip Hammond chipped in, 'I don't think that's a good idea', and gave his reasons. He and Mark Sedwill, the cabinet secretary, 'went very grey'. One source said, 'She was ruminating rather than giving a strategic direction.' Attendees noted the presence of Stephen Parkinson, May's political secretary, a Brexiteer who had often complained about being omitted from her inner counsels. 'Parky' believed no-deal was a negotiating weapon and had also floated the idea that the prime minister could, as a final throw of the dice, fight a general election on the question of 'my deal or no-deal'. Another aide recalled, 'Suddenly, Parky was invited to every senior meeting. The PM had heard him make that argument. I think it was her who wanted him there.' Parkinson was supported by Robbie Gibb. 'I remember thinking: we are going to do this,' another participant said. May had not ruled out the idea by the time the meeting finished. 'It was unusually candid from her.' As they left, Raoul Ruparel and Denzil Davidson quietly expressed surprise about 'how close she was'. Another spad recalled, 'The buzz went around the building that it was on the cards.'

May was also 'pretty hardcore' about no-deal in cabinet that morning, a senior civil servant remembered. 'The boss's tone was more robust and more no-deal than at any point. That reflected her frustration at the speaker and how angry and let down the public were going to be when we did not leave on 29 March.'

Without a deal, May would have to go to the European Council meeting in Brussels two days later and request an extension to Article 50, delaying Brexit. The prime minister had said on more than a hundred occasions in public that the UK would leave on 29 March. But the question was no longer whether there was a delay, only whether it should be short or long. David Gauke and the pro-dealers feared a short deadline and a no-deal Brexit and pressed for a long extension. Gauke told the prime minister, 'If you rule out a long extension, your deal is dead because the pressure will be off the ERG.'

Those who favoured a no-deal Brexit, including Steve Barclay, Gavin Williamson and Liz Truss, argued for a short extension. They were backed by Brandon Lewis, who said a long extension, which

would entail fighting the European elections, would cause 'indescribable pain for the party'. Andrea Leadsom agreed but made her views
clear only late in the meeting. 'It was like she had forgotten to say the
stuff that she was going to brief that she had said,' a colleague
remarked. Liam Fox, the international trade secretary, argued that
May should switch the jeopardy in her Brexit policy from the ERG to
Labour MPs by turning her argument from 'my deal or no Brexit' to
'my deal or no-deal'.

Senior civil servants in cabinet were shocked not only that no-deal was
suddenly an option, but also at the reasons given. One said, 'All around
the table, they said, "If the choice is the Conservative Party staying
together and no-deal or the Conservative Party fracture and an extension, the national interest is in the Conservative Party staying together."
It was one of those moments when you realise that you've been compla-
cent about ideology in politics. They really believe it was the Conservative
Party that made Britain great. They had internalised this mythology.'
When the cabinet minutes were written, the civil servant responsible
made a point of including the observation that ministers had equated the
national interest with that of the Tory party. When JoJo Penn spotted
this, May was furious and demanded it be changed. The mandarins
refused.

It was not just the civil servants in uproar. Penny Mordaunt took a
mental note of the numbers as ministers spoke. The Brexiteers demanding a short extension were joined by pragmatic Remainers like Damian
Hinds. 'Most were in favour of a short extension,' Mordaunt said later,
'but that is not what happened.' While others spoke, May had spent most
of the meeting sitting like a 'nodding dog', another witness remarked.
But she then overrode the consensus view, saying, 'A short extension
would be challenging given the risk of no-deal. We cannot do anything
which provides any incentive not to vote for the deal.' Within twenty-four hours she had abandoned that position and driven another nail
into her political coffin.

The possibility of no-deal was also encouraged by James Johnson's
polling. In his red box notes for the prime minister in February and
several times in March, he noted that the public was warming to the idea.
Johnson confided to colleagues that he was 'more up for it' now, but that
view was not shared by political colleagues like Keelan Carr, the speechwriter, Denzil Davidson or Ed de Minckwitz. 'You suddenly saw the

anti-Brexit colleagues get a bit stressed that they were going to be part of a no-deal Number 10,' one aide recalled.

On Tuesday evening, the Brexiteers and advocates of a short extension gathered for Pizza Club in Leadsom's office. The host, Fox and Grayling all suggested they might resign if May asked Brussels for a long extension. Javid agreed there needed to be a pivot. 'Andrea was particularly gung-ho,' another witness remembered. Their views were passed to the chief whip.

Julian Smith was already receiving intelligence of an ERG meeting the same evening that had turned into a 'bloodbath' for May, with only three speakers out of twenty failing to call for her head. Henry Bellingham suggested that MPs sign a letter calling for May to quit, with the hope of securing the backing of 158 signatories, more than half the party. Under Tory rules May could not be challenged until December, but others suggested Brady should run a non-binding indicative vote on the leadership. At the furthest extreme, it was suggested that up to fifteen Tory MPs were prepared to vote with Labour in a no-confidence motion to bring down the government if May pursued a long-term extension.

On Wednesday 20 March, May performed the first of two dramatic U-turns that week, bowing to pressure from the Brexiteers and the Pizza Club. At the lobby briefing that morning Downing Street revealed that May would only ask for a short extension until 30 June. The PM then used Prime Minister's Questions to disclose that she had written that morning to Donald Tusk informing him that the UK wanted an extension until the end of June and that she would bring forward a third meaningful vote. 'As prime minister, I am not prepared to delay Brexit any further than 30 June,' she said.

May's allies say she was not just bullied into the change. 'In her gut she did not think the public would stomach a long extension,' one said. The pro-dealers were blindsided. 'I was furious,' a cabinet minister said. 'She seemed to be surrendering to no-deal.' Usually a byword for calm, the minister sent his most intemperate message to Laura Kuenssberg: 'Weak, weak, weak. Her most craven surrender to the hardliners yet.'

By that afternoon the prospect of no-deal had energised the cabinet. Gavin Williamson told his team that he believed the prime minister would do it. He walked into Downing Street the following morning expecting it to be government policy. A close aide said, 'For forty-eight hours the PM was on the verge of shifting towards no-deal. She was quite close to saying that if we can't get out by 30 June, that's it.'

The idea energised the pro-dealers even more so. That same afternoon, 20 March, ministers digested the news of May's volte-face as they sat in a no-deal planning meeting. Greg Clark expressed concern that ministers would face censure for allowing no-deal to go ahead. He asked Mark Sedwill 'whether allowing no-deal would be breaking the ministerial code because we know how bad it might be'. He and other ministers were concerned that a future public inquiry into the government's stewardship of Brexit could find that they put the interests of the party before those of the country – a fear reinforced by the fact that this was written in black and white in the cabinet minutes. Another minister said, 'We were sitting there contemplating the length of queues and the size of the riots and the shortages of medicines and when we might deploy the army and the prime minister has just put no-deal back on the table. There was visceral anger.' Clark had to be 'talked down from the ledge' by Amber Rudd, who again regaled him with the miseries of life on the backbenches.

May's position eroded quickly that Wednesday. A meeting with opposition leaders to try to find a cross-party way forward descended into farce when Jeremy Corbyn walked out rather than share a room with the defector Chuka Umunna of the Independent Group.

May also had a fruitless meeting with Boris Johnson. Asked what she was planning to do to change her approach to Brexit, she replied that she would make changes to the Brexit department, an apparent attempt to dangle the prospect of Johnson returning to the cabinet during the second phase of the negotiations. He did not bite. Instead, he pressed May repeatedly to rule out standing again in a general election. She stonily repeated her pledge not to run again in 2022 but on three separate occasions did not rule out calling a snap election in a desperate last throw of the dice to save her own skin. There was 'no shouting', but Johnson left and told fellow MPs that May was 'delusional' about the prospects of getting her deal through.

As evening drew in, the PM met twenty Eurosceptics who had reluctantly switched to backing her Brexit deal on the second meaningful vote. She found that only a handful were still prepared to support her. Nigel Evans, Philip Davies, Maria Caulfield and Ben Bradley all made clear that they thought May should resign. Bradley said she was the wrong person to lead the second phase of talks. 'The key factor is not the deal but what happens afterwards,' he said. 'We don't have trust in you, Prime Minister, to have the right plans to get a better long-term relationship. The only way it is likely to get through is if you agree to leave in the summer.'

May replied, 'Hmmm.'

Evans recalled, 'We went in and said how exasperated we all were. I said that it's a failure if we do not leave on 29 March, and it would be her failure. She has now fudged it so often ... that when she came to the despatch box at PMQs and said, "We are leaving on 30 June and that's my final date," I laughed.'[3]

That meeting meant that May missed the 8.15 p.m. planned start of a televised statement her team had persuaded her to give directly to the voters, over the heads of Parliament. In retrospect, she would have been better to miss it altogether. Having decided to focus on Labour MPs, with the 'my deal or no-deal' approach, she dutifully read out a speech insulting them instead. 'Two years on, MPs have been unable to agree a way to implement the UK's withdrawal,' she said. 'As a result, we will now not leave on time with a deal on 29 March. This delay is a matter of great personal regret for me. And of this I am absolutely sure: you the public have had enough. You are tired of the infighting. You are tired of the political games and the arcane procedural rows.' To the voters she declared, 'I am on your side.'

An early draft of the speech included an apology from the prime minister. 'The word "sorry" got taken out,' an aide recalled. 'We didn't want the headline to be "Theresa May says sorry, she messed up".'

May's address was one of the most disastrous four minutes of her premiership, a populist attempt to pit people against Parliament which ill-suited her political brand and which became emblematic of the collective exhaustion of a Downing Street operation that could no longer think straight. Barwell was seen in Parliament's Portcullis House shortly after the broadcast. 'He looked like he was expecting people to come up to him and congratulate him,' one MP said. 'And quite quickly he was surrounded by MPs saying: "What on earth have you done?"'

Barwell came to see the speech as 'one of the worst mistakes we made'. He recalled, 'It was a classic example of what happens when you're in a bunker, suffering from groupthink.' The finger of blame was pointed at

Gibb, but many of May's senior aides and the entire communications team were involved. James Slack, the official spokesman, normally the most level-headed person in the building, helped write the speech. James Johnson was also in the room and the central message of public anger at parliamentary paralysis was grounded in his polling. 'We had to explain to voters why we weren't leaving on 29 March,' said one of those present. 'There were lots of people in that room, there was no one guilty man.' One of the guilty men admitted, 'We didn't sense check it against the mood in Parliament. For reasons of cock-up we did not get it to Julian in time for him to say what the MPs would make of it – and by the time Julian had decided he did not like it, it was too late.'

The chief whip was furious when he saw the speech. He phoned the chief of staff and said, 'What have you just done?'

'It was really good, wasn't it?'

'No, you're idiots,' Smith replied. 'These are the people we've got to get to vote for the thing, and you've just told the country they're clowns.' A colleague said that week, 'The chief and Barwell are no longer speaking to each other.'

Robbins and the Europe Unit protested about the speech and May's political advisers on the EU, including Raoul Ruparel, could not understand why the strategy of forcing the ERG to confront the risk of no Brexit had changed to threatening moderates with no-deal again. 'It just pissed everyone off,' an aide said. 'We had a strategy and we were peeling off the harder Brexiteers.' A usually loyalist MP from the 2017 intake said, 'Just as it appeared like the ERG were beginning to fold, at that precise moment she does this. It was breathtakingly stupid.'

The reaction was swift and brutal. Lisa Nandy, a Labour MP who Julian Smith had been wooing for months, branded the speech 'disgraceful'. Others warned that May would have blood on her hands if her 'Parliament v the people' theme led to violence. This was a time when MPs were having panic alarms fitted in their homes because of the level of abuse they were getting on social media. 'Unlike her, we don't all have police protection officers wandering around with us,' said one Eurosceptic. 'We are alone on train platforms.'

The speech convinced some that May had finally snapped after two years of pressure, the like of which most prime ministers have never experienced. They believe her state of mind was in the worst place it had been since the immediate aftermath of the 2017 election.[4] Insiders talked of a 'bunker mentality' and 'screaming matches' in Downing Street, where the prime minister was seen in floods of tears. 'Everyone by that point had got so tired, so worn down,' a May loyalist said. One MP said, 'I've got a friend who is a psychiatrist who says she has all the symptoms of mental illness. She's delusional.' An aide confirmed, 'She's always quite a solitary figure but in moments like this that solitude becomes even more self-reflective. She is quite emotional about what has been going on.' Another explained, 'Her decisions are now being made on an emotional response to Parliament's actions. For years she has been trying to make decisions rationally, to a fault. People beg for her to show some emotion. But Bercow and the parliamentary votes are the last straw. She's through with Parliament and is reacting emotionally or irrationally.'

In this maelstrom of emotion, Philip May, the husband she called 'my rock', was urging the prime minister to fight on. A Number 10 official said that week, 'It's just the two of them who will have those conversations. He's still urging her to see through the Brexit she has promised.' His support was not wholly welcomed by all of her team. A ministerial aide complained, 'At this stage in proceedings Denis Thatcher was saying, "Time's up, old girl, time to call it a day."' A senior figure in the ERG compared the Conservative Party to the character played by James Caan in the Stephen King film in which an author is strapped to a bed and mutilated by his biggest fan. 'She's like Kathy Bates in *Misery*. She loves us so much that she's holding us captive and she's breaking every bone in our bodies. She is breaking us all with her devotion to duty.'

The clear signal that May was now actively contemplating no-deal persuaded her predecessor to stage an intervention. David Cameron had slunk away after the referendum to lick his wounds. Now he wrote a heartfelt piece warning of the dangers of no-deal. Cameron got as far as emailing the article to Martin Ivens, the editor of the *Sunday Times*. His views were simple, according to a cabinet minister in whom he confided: 'He wants Brexit to be a success for two reasons. He wants this country to prosper. He doesn't want it screwed up. And the second thing is he doesn't want people to say for the rest of his life, "This is all your fault."'

In private moments, Cameron did admit the lingering pain he felt. Robert Harris, a political columnist before he began a lucrative career writing thrillers, found himself seated next to Cameron at a fiftieth birthday party in the Cotswolds. 'As the afternoon went on, he got redder and redder and drank more and more and kept sloping off for fags,' Harris recalled. But as he drank, Cameron became franker. He thought May had 'behaved crazily' by 'choosing a side' and 'she'd had a moment after the referendum when she should have tried to pull everything together'. Harris suggested that the economy had been poised, post-austerity, to take off before Brexit came along. Cameron said, sadly, 'Yes, that's my agony every day.' The writer asked him what he thought would happen next and Cameron said, 'Oh, it's going to be Boris.'

On Thursday 21 March, May flew to Brussels to formally ask for the extension to 30 June. She started by stiffly reading out the letter she had sent Donald Tusk. In two hours of questioning, she refused to say what she would do if she lost the third meaningful vote. Perhaps she didn't know herself. 'The only thing that came through with clarity was her lack of a plan,' another prime minister said.[5]

When May left the room, Tusk presented the others with a proposal in a sealed envelope: Britain was to be offered a short extension until 22 May on condition that the deal was approved the following week. If not, EU leaders would meet again to decide the terms of a longer extension or prepare for no-deal. The timetable promptly leaked and the attempt to fix the summit conclusions imploded. Britain had few friends in the room. The Danes and Leo Varadkar, fearful of an accidental no-deal, said May should be given the 30 June date she wanted. But other leaders were concerned she had set a trap that would make it look like the EU had pushed the UK into no-deal. Jean-Claude Juncker said, 'We don't want to be the one who kicks out the British.'

The final compromise was thrashed out at 9 p.m. after the formal meeting had broken up, in a huddle of ten people, Merkel and a jacket-less Macron at the centre with Belgium's Charles Michel.[6] The new Brexit deadline would be 12 April. If Parliament passed the deal before then, there would be a short extension to 22 May to ensure the passage of the necessary legislation, but if the deal went down there would be no-deal or a much longer extension.

While this was going on, May and her closest aides were forced to wait in the drab British delegation room. It was an experience Barwell found humiliating. He said, 'The thing that upset me most is I've had to go over there and sit with the PM when she asked for an extension. She made her pitch and was then told to leave the room and sit outside for four or five hours while other people decided this country's fate.' May found the stress of it all overwhelming. 'I am told she was in tears at various points during the day,' one MP said.

While May was in Brussels, her cabinet openly contemplated removing her. On Thursday afternoon, the pro-dealers met in Philip Hammond's office. One idea floated was that either the chancellor or David Lidington should visit the prime minister to tell her the game was up. Greg Clark saw Hammond as a possible 'clean skin' who could wield the knife since he 'doesn't want to be leader'. Hammond's view, relayed to a fellow cabinet minister, was, 'There will come a time when she can't go on', but he did not yet wish to be the agent of May's defenestration.

An idea that attracted more support was to replace May with a caretaker prime minister in the form of Lidington, her deputy in all but name and someone with no leadership ambitions of his own. 'Lidders was certainly not pushing it,' another cabinet minister said, 'but the wheels were falling off at this point, and there was a sense of "What the hell do we do now?" It did come up in that meeting. Everyone knows David's got integrity and he's very competent and also has no big personal ambitions.' The ministers discussed May's loss of authority. Clark went further, questioning the prime minister's judgement and faculties. 'The meeting began with a sense of "has she lost it?",' one of those present recalled. May's apparent pivot to no-deal seemed 'out of character'.

Lidington was not prepared to stand against May, but the pro-dealers believed he was the one person she would have been persuaded to make way for. After the gathering, an effort was made to phone around and gauge the views of the rest of the cabinet. Around half were enthusiastic, but those with leadership ambitions were reticent about endorsing a rival.

On Saturday 23rd, the author got wind of the proposal and telephoned eleven cabinet ministers. Every one of them called back – a unique journalistic experience – with all of them saying May needed to go and six backing the Lidington play. One called May 'erratic' and said, 'Her judgement has started to go haywire.' Surprisingly, Sajid Javid, the home secretary, at that stage the bookies' favourite to be the next leader, signalled he was prepared to stand aside for Lidington as long as he agreed not to stand in a future leadership election. Jeremy Hunt, the other cabinet frontrunner, however, resisted on the grounds that

Lidington would work with Labour to take Britain into a permanent customs union.

The plan died for three reasons. The first was that it was naive to think ministers could engineer an uncontested succession to someone seen as an arch-Remainer. Even if the cabinet agreed, Boris Johnson was waiting in the wings. The second was that May began to change her tune on no-deal and by Friday had softened her position again, removing the danger as the pro-dealers saw it. 'She seemed to be backing away from it,' one said. Representations from Hammond and Lidington and May's fears for the Union helped change her mind again. The third was that age-old driver of politics: ambition. When Michael Gove got wind of the idea, he was swift to dismiss it. Privately, however, his allies phoned journalists to explain that he had a leadership campaign ready to go and that Mel Stride, a Treasury minister, had been hosting dinners on his behalf to drum up support. It looked like Gove had heard of a plot to install a caretaker prime minister and concluded that if there was to be an interim leader it ought to be him. But as a cabinet colleague put it, 'The thing with Michael is, if you put him as a caretaker, you'd never get the keys off him.'

What everyone agreed on, however, was that May needed to go. She had used secrecy and stubbornness to survive but her every decision now sparked consequences she could not control. Most importantly, the whips, the Praetorian Guard for any leader, had lost confidence in her. MPs claimed just one member of the whips' office, Mike Freer, wanted May to stay. Their *omerta* broke and journalists were briefed on an astonishing challenge to the PM's authority two weeks earlier, when a senior whip, Paul Maynard, told May to her face that she should resign because she was 'betraying Brexit' and 'destroying our party'. The entire whips' office had been to see the prime minister to listen to a pitch on her plans for the domestic agenda. Maynard, who voted Leave, said, 'I've heard enough. When I was told that we would have to come over and talk to you I began to cry. I said, "I don't want to go over and talk to that woman any more. She's betrayed Brexit, she's destroying our party. I want her gone."'

May replied, 'I'm sorry you feel that way.'

Maynard said he hadn't finished and 'continued to give her both barrels', a witness said. 'I've never seen anything like it. She has lost all authority in the party and is totally deluded about her ability to govern.'

When his colleagues backed up Maynard, the witness said, 'It was like *Murder on the Orient Express*', where each character plunges in the knife.

In the run-up to MV2, the whips began using May's unpopularity as a bargaining chip, asking MPs if they would back the deal if she agreed to resign. By the weekend of 24 March, her most senior aides concluded it was the only card she had left to play. It was a view shared by one of her oldest friends in politics: Phillip Lee, who had resigned the year before and now backed a referendum. Lee had lived in May's constituency, he had been a member of her association, the Mays had attended his wedding. He had repeatedly sought to contact the prime minister to say, 'Your deal isn't going to pass.' Finally, the PM invited him to Chequers that Sunday.

Unlike some who visited Chequers that day, Lee did not leak that he was seeing the prime minister. They talked for an hour in the morning. He told her, 'Look, you're not going to get this through, and I'm worried you're going to get defenestrated in the process. You might not think it, but I've always been on your side. You're going to lose and we're going to end up with a Brexit that none of us wants.' Lee made the case that the only way she could get her deal through was by accepting a referendum: 'There are seventy to eighty Labour MPs who are prepared to support you against the Labour whip if you propose a second referendum.'[7]

'I was never told that,' May said. But she made clear she could not support a second referendum, something she believed would break the Tory party.

'Well, the Tory party's going to break anyway,' Lee predicted. 'What side you want to win?' He urged her to think of her legacy and whether she wanted to hand Conservatism over to the ERG tendency. 'You have to decide what you want to bequeath. The party is going in this direction. I don't want that, it's not the party I joined. If you keep persisting with trying to get your deal through, you'll get removed and then we'll get … we know who we're going to get.'

As the conversation came to a close, May admitted, 'I am this afternoon meeting with ERG people.'

'Yes, I know.'

'How do you know?' she asked, betraying surprise.

'It's all over the media,' Lee explained. May gave him a look, pained. 'They leak like a sieve,' he added. 'They're liars, don't trust them. No one knows I'm here, but I know that Iain Duncan Smith is turning up in his Morgan sportscar at 2 p.m.'[8]

Steve Baker was at church when Julian Smith phoned and said he could go to Chequers if he was willing to negotiate. He had already had a call from Chris Heaton-Harris, a former chairman of the ERG, about whether his vote was in play and had been to see Smith on Friday, when the prospect of May quitting was made explicit. Baker made the point that he needed the deal to materially change as well. 'I was very clear that I thought we should have both, because you can't expect a new leader to negotiate within unacceptable parameters,' he recalled later. Baker spoke to Rees-Mogg and together they sounded out Iain Duncan Smith. They decided it was 'something we should explore'.

Those present at Chequers included three likely leadership contenders, each of whom had resigned from her cabinet: Boris Johnson, David Davis and Dominic Raab. Duncan Smith arrived wearing a cravat in his open-topped sportscar, putting some in mind of Toad of Toad Hall. Rees-Mogg, somewhat eccentrically, arrived at one of the key meetings of the moment with his fifteen-year-old son, Peter, who was given a guided tour of the house. 'It felt like an Agatha Christie murder mystery,' a Number 10 aide said. 'The country house, there's a man in a cravat, there's a small child in a cricketing jacket ...'

Downing Street also invited Michael Gove and key figures from the moderate wing of the Bresistance who were prepared to share a room with the Brexiteers: Alistair Burt and Damian Green. Gove, along with May, Smith and Barwell, was designated a 'persuader' to seek a grand bargain with a group who had begun telling people they were the 'grand wizards' of the ERG – a peculiar moniker to adopt given its echoes of the Ku Klux Klan. They began with common ground. May asked, 'Do we all agree there is an existential threat to the Conservative Party, here?' Murmurs of support. 'Do we all agree there is a responsibility on all of us to find a way out of it?' A chorus of consent. The prime minister warned that the alternative to her deal was no Brexit. Then Smith 'laid it all on'.

The MPs liked that they were being treated as the party elders. 'It was a little bit sort of Council of Elrond,' said an attendee, referencing the grand meeting in *The Lord of the Rings* between the three free races of men, elves and dwarves to determine the fate of the one true ring.

Gandalf in this imagining was Michael Gove, who was, in the words of a May aide, 'the star of that meeting: the best I've ever seen him, absolutely brilliant'. The former Vote Leave frontman began by saying, 'I know how you feel. I feel the same, but here are some facts. Interrupt me when I'm wrong.' He then began a methodical working through of what might happen next if the deal did not pass. 'The speaker will do this and this …' His case was that MPs would vote to control the business of the House the following day and would then hold indicative votes in which Parliament would back a softer Brexit or a second referendum. A witness said, 'Boris interrupted him a couple times and we went through the arguments in a lot of detail', but May's team could see that Gove was hitting home.

Barwell joined the tag team and told the ERG faction, 'We've tried selling you the intellectual arguments, but you don't buy them.' Gove saw doubts and said, 'I'm going to read you some predictions Theresa May has made in the past and let's have a look at whether she was right or not.' Gove then read out sections of her speeches which had proved prophetic.

In the main discussion, between 3 p.m. and 5 p.m., around the large 'cabinet' dining table upstairs, Boris Johnson talked obliquely about needing 'a new negotiating team' and a different approach in the second phase, code for a different prime minister running things. May looked blankly at him. Johnson told aides, 'She is amazingly impervious. I tried to deliver the lethal bullet but my elephant gun failed.' Having coordinated their approach in advance, both Duncan Smith and Rees-Mogg 'made clear that she should go', politely but in terms that could not have been misunderstood by the prime minister.

Watching from the sidelines, Barwell, Smith and Stephen Parkinson realised the game was up. 'The body language of Gavin, the chief and Parky all said they knew it,' one of those present recalled. May's team were not just fighting for their boss. 'Their fundamental fear was the collapse of the party and of the government,' said one of the MPs.

Baker, perhaps unsurprisingly, was the most 'strident'. 'Steve Baker just lost his shit,' said an official present. 'Completely lost the plot, telling the PM she was "ruining the project", ruining his beautiful Brexit. He was evangelical, purist, and just unbelievably angry about the fact he thought she had fucked it up so badly. He was exasperated about everybody else, yelling, "You're idiots, all of you." It was hilarious.'

Alistair Burt followed Baker, opening with a deadpan, 'That's very interesting, Steve, thanks very much for your contribution', then delivered an eloquent demand for mutual understanding. 'You're asking us to understand how strongly you feel about this,' he said. 'I've believed in the European Union all my political career and fought for Remain. But I accept the result. We should leave the European Union. That is not an easy thing for me to do. But I accept it and I will vote for it. But you have to understand that there are limits to that. And I will not vote for a no-deal Brexit. And I will oppose a government that tries to do that. We have to find something that you can vote for and I can vote for. You've got to understand me as well.'

Slowly the mood changed. A grand bargain began to feel possible. On the table was what chess players would call a 'Queen sacrifice', in which the MPs would vote for the withdrawal agreement at MV3 in exchange for a pledge from the prime minister to resign and hand over the negotiating of a long-term deal to her successor. One colleague said, 'Boris was keen because she was going.'

Rees-Mogg spoke to Barwell and JoJo Penn. In an 'apologetic' fashion he made clear that he thought an offer to go would boost the yes vote. Later he had an audience with May to reinforce that view. This was done in a courtly fashion: 'I tried to get you removed and I lost. And I accept that I lost,' Rees-Mogg told May. 'The rules say you won and you've got twelve months. And if after twelve months, the situation hasn't improved, then we have a right to come back again. But we don't have a right now to say to you, "You've got to go". But I also have to be honest with you; I do believe that if you said this it would increase the number of people that would be prepared to vote in the way that you want them to vote.'

The key intervention was that of Duncan Smith, who had maintained an erratic on-off friendship with May and, despite his regular personal fury, stopped short of calling for her head publicly. After making oblique comments to the group, he had a separate face-to-face meeting with the prime minister in a side room in which he delivered the message that she must resign if she wanted to pass her deal. Allies say that May demanded to know, in return, whether Duncan Smith could deliver the necessary votes to get the deal over the line. The former leader said he could. Boris Johnson recalled, 'Wing Commander IDS, DFC and bar, loaded all his bomb bays and went out over Bremen ...'

Afterwards Baker consulted key allies: Shanker Singham, Simon Clarke, Sammy Wilson and Mark Francois, who remained 'firm'. Christopher Montgomery told him, 'The deal hasn't changed.' But even Baker was desperate to reach what he saw, in quasi-religious terms, as the Brexit 'promised land' of 'a free country'. To him, the 'tantalising glimpse' of a new prime minister negotiating the future was tempting. Barwell told friends, 'We thought we might have got Steve.'

The following day, Monday 25 March, was eventful, but not at cabinet, where not one minister talked about their desire for the prime minister to be replaced. A supporter of Boris Johnson dismissed them as 'jellyfish in grey suits'.[9] May had further conversations with Duncan Smith. Both repeated their pledges: her to stand down, him to deliver the votes. 'She thought long and hard about it,' a close political aide said. 'It was a big decision and a tough one, not least because as party chairman she had stuck by IDS in some pretty dark days for him.'

At the ERG meeting, in the Boothroyd Room in Portcullis House, Rees-Mogg – who had been telling friends, 'I'm like a deck chair, I want to collapse' – came out for the deal, arguing: 'If we don't take it, we might lose everything.' Bill Cash and Mark Francois led the counterargument: 'Don't kid yourselves. We know what the Withdrawal Agreement says. Once this becomes law, we'll never get out of it. We'll be trapped in the backstop forever.' Their position was bolstered by private canvassing information which showed their views were in lockstep with those of Leave voters. 'That gave us great confidence that we were in touch with the mainstream of society,' Jenkin said. He changed the name of the Spartans' WhatsApp group to 'The Real Mainstream'. Asked what the ERG chairman wanted in exchange for his support, a government source said, 'He wants Brexit. That's all.' Steve Baker's diary entry that day read, 'Great disaster'. When the two discussed his decision, Rees-Mogg said he believed in a nineteenth-century-style anarchy between nation states, in which Britain might sign and then break the treaty. On MV1, the ERG had been joined by dozens of other Tory MPs in opposing the deal. On MV2, they peeled away, leaving ERG loyalists. Now, as MV3 loomed, the ERG itself was split. Francois said, 'This wasn't blue on blue, this was dark blue on dark blue' action.

The EU chose the same day to ramp up the pressure, releasing details of its preparations for no-deal. What they did not reveal, but what diplomats privately admitted, was that, in the event of no-deal, they would not be able to impose checks at the border between Northern Ireland and the Republic. 'Instead, they've said they would have to do extra checks at border points into the Republic,' one government source revealed, a move likely to provoke fury and fear in Dublin that Ireland would effectively become part of a UK customs union.

The real drama occurred later, at 10.15 p.m. that evening, when the Commons voted, at the third time of asking, to hand control of the timetable to backbenchers, an amendment tabled by Oliver Letwin. The motion proposed that the House run a series of indicative votes on Wednesday 27th, before the government could table a new meaningful vote. Bercow's ruling in January had now borne fruit. The motion passed by 329 votes to 302. Alistair Burt, Richard Harrington and Steve Brine all resigned as ministers in order to join the 29 Tory rebels. In what seemed to be a cosmic joke, the split of votes was 52:48, the golden ratio which seemed to run like a thread through modern politics.

Sir Bill Cash, the arch-Paleosceptic, warned that the Commons was on course for 'a constitutional revolution'. Brexiteer David Davis used a point of order to complain that Letwin had installed himself as a jobbing prime minister. 'How can he be held to account?' he asked.

When Theresa May swept into Committee Room 14 at 5.05 p.m. on Wednesday 27 March for the 1922 Committee meeting, the room was packed with three hundred Tory MPs sweating in the heat. One compared it to 'the tube carriage into hell'.[10] Word had gone around about what was happening and the herd gathered like animals at the watering hole. David Davis sat on the floor. Boris Johnson stood at the back. David Gauke squeezed into an air gap by the door. Penny Mordaunt, who arrived late, was forced to listen at the keyhole with the lobby journalists.[11]

In the same room where Margaret Thatcher's fate was sealed twenty-nine years earlier, the prime minister offered to lay down her career to save her deal. When she spoke, there was solemn but expectant silence. 'I don't tour the bars and engage in gossip,' she said. 'But I do make time to speak to colleagues, and I have a great team in the whips' office. I also have two excellent PPSs. I have heard very clearly the mood of the parliamentary party. I know there is a desire for a new approach – and new leadership – in the second phase of the Brexit negotiations. I won't stand in the way of that.' The prime minister went on, 'I know some people are worried that if you vote for the Withdrawal Agreement, I will take that as a mandate to rush on into phase two without the debate we need to have. I won't – I hear what you are saying. But we need to get the deal through and deliver Brexit.' If that was not clear enough, May concluded, 'I am prepared to leave this job earlier than I intended in order to do what is right for our country and our party. I ask everyone in this room to back the deal so we can complete our historic duty: to deliver on the decision of the British people and leave the European Union with a smooth and orderly exit.'[12]

May spoke for twenty minutes from notes, the atmosphere emotionally charged. As is often the way with prime ministers, nothing became her so much as the manner of her departure. Several MPs said it was the best speech May had given to the '22. Her words reduced some to tears, including Victoria Atkins. Nick Hurd, a Home Office minister, was also seen welling up.

More importantly, the grand bargain appeared to be working. James Gray and Richard Bacon, who had both voted against the deal in the first two meaningful votes, stood up to tell May they would now vote Yes. Others begged their colleagues to follow suit. Those filing into the corridor afterwards who said they would now, with heavy hearts, back her, included Conor Burns, Simon Clarke, Shailesh Vara and Pauline Latham. 'Perhaps a bad deal is the least bad choice,' Vara said.[13] To the Spartans, this was a 'baying mob' assailing them. May had not given a date for her departure, but her aides texted MPs that she would leave on 22 May, if the withdrawal agreement passed.

James Johnson was running a focus group in Hastings when the participants started getting push notifications on their phones that May was offering to resign. 'The response was genuinely quite moving,' he said. 'Their reaction was, "She's put duty above party for the final time" and "God, how much more is this lady willing to give." That was a real example of the privilege of being out there with real voters when this stuff is happening that you are intimately involved in it.'

Back in Number 10, May's political aides gathered for wine and crisps outside the Cabinet Room (watched by busts of Disraeli and Wilberforce, a portrait of Pitt the Younger, and a Lego model of the PM making her first speech outside Number 10). 'There were not many jokes, but there was a nice atmosphere,' one said. 'It was not too glum, considering.'

May explained what she had said to the '22 and thanked everyone for their support. Barwell said she had 'put the country's best interests first, which is characteristic of her and the reason we're all proud to work for you'. Then Philip gave her a hug. They stayed and chatted for forty minutes.

MPs left the 1922 meeting to head to the chamber where the indicative votes were taking place in the 'No' division lobby. Letwin had set this up as a paper exercise so none of the options had an unfair advantage by being called first. MPs had to simply tick the boxes of the options they were prepared to support. Managed no-deal was on the ballot paper, but the other seven were all softer versions of Brexit than Theresa May's deal: Common market 2.0, membership of the EEA and EFTA, the customs union, Labour's deal, a second referendum, a two-year standstill and, finally, outright revoke of Article 50.

The most determined Brexiteers left the '22 to attend a highly charged ERG meeting, with the group split down the middle by Rees-Mogg's decision to vote for the deal. David Jones, a former DExEU minister, gave an emotive speech quoting Tacitus on the Romans' battles with the Britons, imploring MPs to stand firm. Classicists in the room looked perplexed, Boris Johnson included, and one shouted, 'But they all got annihilated.'[14]

Johnson chose this moment to confirm that he too was going to vote for the deal. He felt like Ephialtes, who sold out the Spartans at Thermopylae, waking up 'two or three mornings in a row feeling physically sick'. But he concluded that May was capable of 'driving the coach off the cliff' in the direction of a referendum. As the leading Brexiteer candidate for the leadership, he was under huge pressure to provide statesmanlike support in the interests of party unity. If he was to win significant backing from the moderate wing of the party, this was the moment to retreat. In the ERG meeting, however, few were impressed. One MP described his speech as 'more Chamberlain than Churchill' and added, 'Jacob and Boris have destroyed themselves on the first day of the leadership campaign.' Johnson sat at the back of the room, quieter than usual.

Baker was 'depressed', an emotion which hardened into rage when he contemplated the prospect of MPs in another part of the building endorsing an outcome that, he believed, would make a mockery of the referendum result. He got to his feet and delivered a highly emotional speech, which so moved Mark Francois that he got Baker to write it down later so he could hang it on his office wall:

'I am consumed by a ferocious rage … after that pantomime of syco-phancy and bullying next door … I resolved that I would vote against this deal however often it was presented, come what may, if it meant the fall of the Government and the destruction of the Conservative Party. If I think of the worthless, ignorant cowards and knaves in the House today, voting for things they do not understand, which would surrender our right to govern ourselves, I would tear this building down and bull-doze the rubble into the river. God help me, I would. But I know that if we do this, if we insist and we take this all the way, we might find ourselves standing in the rubble of our Party and our constitution and our Government and our country. I am so filled with rage that we should have been deliberately put in this place by people whose addiction to power without accountability has led them to place before this country a choice between Remain or Brexit in Name Only. I confess to you I do not know what to do.' Baker, his voice cracking with emotion, reflected on the U-turn of his friend Rees-Mogg, his promises to Francois to stand firm and the looming threat of Corbyn. 'By God this will cost me dear, if in the end, because of the consequences of a communist governing this country I have to vote for this deal. I may yet resign the whip in fury rather than be part of this.'

When he had finished, Baker looked emotionally spent. 'He was hugged by Jacob Rees-Mogg and others at the top table,' said one of those present, who observed, 'We are not a hugging group.' At least one MP was in tears.

That night, Julia Lopez could not sleep at all, in something close to panic about Rees-Mogg's decision. Among the 2017 intake holdouts, Simon Clarke and Robert Courts had both folded. Lopez and Suella Braverman found support in the other's determination to fight. Ranil Jayawardena and Marcus Fysh were also standing firm. Lee Rowley examined the numbers and couldn't see how May could win. Lopez felt deeply that she couldn't vote for something she thought was wrong, a realisation which gave her a profound sense of calm.

*　*　*

When Bercow announced the results of the indicative votes, at 10 p.m. that same evening, all eight options were voted down, most by large margins. As the *Guardian*'s splash headline pithily put it, 'Parliament finally has its say: No. No. No. No. No. No. No. No.'

The pattern of voting was revealing, nonetheless. The option which came closest to success was a customs union, proposed by Ken Clarke, which lost 264 to 272. The Kyle-Wilson second referendum plan, tabled by Margaret Beckett, went down by 268 to 295. However, both options secured more votes than May's deal had in MV2 (242). The second referendum option lost by 27 votes after 27 Labour MPs voted against. At the one extreme, 160 MPs voted for no-deal (including Labour Party chair Ian Lavery) and 184 for revoke, or no Brexit. That number included 111 Labour MPs. Two Tory ministers – Mark Field and Alan Duncan – backed revoke. Nick Boles' Common Market 2.0 plan was defeated by 95 votes. Ken Clarke, one of the few who was prepared to support almost any form of softer Brexit, even voted for Labour's plan. Michael Deacon, the *Telegraph*'s sketchwriter, tweeted: 'In summary: the Commons has now overwhelmingly rejected every single type of Brexit, and no Brexit. Theresa May must now simultaneously stay and resign.'[15]

'I may have been unique,' Oliver Letwin said. 'I literally voted for everything. Any solution that could achieve a majority seemed to me better than any solution that didn't achieve a majority. I thought one might provide a basis for the Government and the Opposition to sit down and try and implement that … but other people were very picky. There were still people who thought if they voted against everything, they could get a second referendum. There were people who thought if they voted against everything, they could get a no-deal Brexit.'[16] The Bresistance was bitterly divided, prompting a stand-up row between People's Voter Stephen Doughty and Lucy Powell, the whip for Common Market 2.0.[17]

A similarly frustrated Peter Kyle said, 'There was always a very decisive majority in the House of Commons for something. Both the front benches refused to allow the Commons to express it. Even on the indicative votes, the cabinet couldn't vote.' He added, 'I was just voting for anything other than a hard Brexit.'

The results created more trouble for Jeremy Corbyn than Theresa May. Labour MPs were whipped to vote for a second referendum, a customs union and Labour's own plan. But in addition to the 27 referendum rebels, three members of the shadow cabinet – Ian Lavery, Jon Trickett and Andrew Gwynne – also refused to back a People's Vote, abstaining on that option. Lavery and Trickett went to see Corbyn the next morning to offer their resignations. 'We love you, but we think we should fuck off,' Trickett explained. Corbyn, decisive as ever, said he would call them the following day. 'Well, we don't want to,' said Lavery, accepting the olive branch. 'How can he keep us?' Trickett interjected. He did, though.[18]

Speaker Bercow was frustrated that his constitutional innovation had failed to provide an answer. Before the exercise he had suggested (but not advocated) to Letwin that he devise an 'exhaustive ballot' mechanism to ensure the options were eventually narrowed down to one winner. 'Otherwise, isn't there a danger that it ends up like the House of Lords votes with Jack Straw in 2007, where every option was voted down?' Letwin's view was that the government would not tolerate a process that was binding and that a transferable vote system would not identify a solution which could sustain a majority through the dozens of votes needed to pass legislation. 'I personally think they made a mistake there,' Bercow said later. 'They could either have ended up with an agreement and a soft Brexit, or an agreement and a referendum. One of them would have got a majority.'

The quote which opens this book by Otto von Bismarck, one of the supreme political operators in European history, that politics is the 'art of the possible' is justly famous. Almost no one knows the line which comes next: that it is the art of 'the attainable – the art of the next best'. Had most MPs digested the lesson that second best can be a win, the story of Brexit would have been very different. Instead, the speaker found his pro-Remain friends dug into separate foxholes, unwilling to join forces. 'Lucy Powell and Ken Clarke would never have accepted a referendum. Chris Leslie wouldn't accept a customs union,' he said. The ERG and the DUP were no less entrenched. Julian Smith agreed: 'Large groups of MPs [were] prepared to gamble that they could force the outcome they wanted – a harder Brexit or another referendum or a general election – rather than backing Theresa May's deal.'[19]

If May's resignation offer was the main drama of the day, with the indicative votes a farcical sideshow, arguably the most important moment came when May returned to Downing Street and took a call from Arlene

Foster, the leader of the DUP. A civil servant listening in described it as 'pretty gruelling' since Foster gave May 'a bit of hope' before dashing it. 'We're really grateful for all the work your team has done, and the offers you've made, and the reassurances given, but unfortunately we've discussed it and we can't do it,' Foster said. The ear-witness said, 'It was a five-minute conversation and only in the final minute does it become clear that they aren't going to vote for it. It was pretty brutal for the PM. You could hear the awfulness of it dawning on her. The most emotional I've heard her was after the calls with Arlene,' on MV2 and MV3. May closed her office door and shut herself away. There were tears as she contemplated her fate. 'She was pretty emotional, but privately,' an aide said. Foster's decision, repeated later to *Sky News*, was a hammer blow to May's chances of victory.

The DUP had turned saying 'No' into performance art, but arguably no group in Parliament put tactical truculence to worse use than they did. By snubbing a Northern Ireland-friendly solution to Brexit on the grounds that it damaged the Union, they only ensured that what followed would be a prime minister more intent on a hard Brexit than protecting the Union. They made perfect the enemy of Bismarck's 'next best'. A member of Robbins' team said, 'The DUP made a massive mistake. The ERG and the DUP were only aligned for a short period where their interests coincided. We knew that couldn't last and thought the DUP would understand that. We thought the DUP would move because it was the best they were going to get. On the Joint Report they said "no" then "yes" and we assumed they would do that again.'

There is evidence that, while not wanting to be seen to endorse the deal, the DUP was happy to see it pass. Jacob Rees-Mogg told colleagues they were 'not sorry' he had voted Yes in MV3. 'I think they would have liked it done, but without their fingerprints on it,' he told a friend. 'They were very, very relaxed about my supporting it.'

May's team studied potential nuclear options for winning MV3. One proposition written on a Number 10 whiteboard, discussed and rejected, was to threaten Tory MPs with the sack unless they backed the deal. In that scenario, one of May's closest aides recalled, the whips would say, 'If we lose this vote there'll be a general election, and if you haven't voted for the deal, you will not be a Conservative candidate at that election.' The prime minister baulked at the proposal since her inner circle believed it would 'break the Conservative Party'. It was another card left on the table that would be picked up by her successor.

Another gambit discussed was to offer a free vote to Tory MPs on the deal. One MP who advocated this approach said, 'If Theresa May had stood at the despatch box and made a statesmanlike speech, which she's quite good at, and said, "This is bigger than any political party. I'm going to allow our party to have a free vote", then I think the pressure on the Labour Party would have been quite great to do the same.' That could have given between 20 and 50 Labour MPs in Leave seats cover to support the government. The problem was, a free vote would remove any pressure on the ERG to support her, costing votes on the other side of the ledger.

There were moments that week when the party seemed to be fracturing. On Monday evening MPs watched a screaming match between Mark Francois and whip Craig Whittaker. The mild-mannered schools minister Nick Gibb and arch-Eurosceptic Bill Cash also had a heated exchange in the tearoom.

On the night of the indicative votes, Bercow repeated his view that the government should not table a substantially similar motion to MV2 – and that they 'should not seek to circumvent my ruling by means of tabling either a notwithstanding motion or a paving motion'. Bercow haters were quick to spot that he had authorised Letwin's motion to take control of the Commons timetable, which stated 'notwithstanding the practice of the House …' To critics, this stank of double standards.

David Lidington and Geoffrey Cox went to visit Bercow in the speaker's house. His usual points of contact, the chief whip and leader of the House, were barely on speaking terms with Bercow. Cox 'lathered on' the soft soap with Bercow, telling him, 'I hope you'll understand, sir, we have the highest regard for your office. We take your rulings with the utmost solemnity.'

They could prorogue Parliament or try to repeal the legislation mandating a meaningful vote (not that such a bill would have passed). But the speaker offered two other options. 'You can change the wording and separate the withdrawal agreement from the political declaration, and make the motion about one or the other,' he said. 'The other thing you could do would be to proceed with the withdrawal bill, and if you can get a second reading that effectively becomes the meaningful vote.' Bercow could see Cox was uncomfortable about bringing forward the bill.

The trump card available to every prime minister before David Cameron, that of turning the meaningful vote into a confidence issue and threatening an election, had been removed by the Fixed-term Parliaments Act of 2010 and the abandonment of Nikki da Costa's King Pong plan. Bernard Jenkin concluded the Act was having an 'absolutely horrific' effect. 'It actually made the government less accountable,' he said. 'The prime minister could never use the confidence mechanism to assert her authority, and yet the House of Commons would carry on wounding and wounding and wounding but not killing.'

May's team decided to separate the withdrawal agreement, which Labour in essence supported, from the political declaration, where different end state visions clashed. MPs would only be asked to vote on the withdrawal agreement. A senior Number 10 figure recalled, 'It came out of the wording of the EU Council decision, which said, "If the UK has approved the withdrawal agreement ..." So we thought, "We don't need to get the deal through to do that." We just needed to get the withdrawal agreement.' It would be the final parliamentary showdown of May's premiership.

On 28 March, Steve Baker cracked. After a slew of lobbying, he decided he would have to support the government. Rees-Mogg's conversion was telling, along with those of Johnson, Duncan Smith and David Davis. Dominic Raab was wobbling. These were people he admired and trusted. Their message was similar: 'We've just got to get out, Steve.'

Baker was a born again Christian and, sitting in Rees-Mogg's office, he briefly experienced a moment of bliss as he decided to join the ERG chairman in backing the deal. He knew in his heart that it was the bliss of the suicide pact, the moment when you give up, the bliss of abandonment. Together, they walked down the corridor to see Nigel Dodds, to tell the DUP man that they were going to have to let him down and vote for the deal. They got as far as knocking on the door, but Dodds was not in. A (non) sliding doors moment.

When Baker told Mark Spencer, his whip, 'I am defeated. I'll have to vote for it', Spencer looked like he might weep with joy. Baker took himself to the Commons library and began writing a piece for ConservativeHome explaining his reasons.

Three encounters had a profound effect on him. He ran into Suella Braverman, his successor as ERG chairman. She had also been asked to vote Yes by the whip. When she refused, Spencer said, 'You'd better go and have a word with Steve. He'll tell you what to do.'

Baker explained his intentions and immediately felt like a distant person to his friend. 'I'm going to vote against it!' she insisted. Braverman felt shocked. 'Let's go and have a chat.' At the far end of the library, the quietest corner, she confronted a man who seemed 'broken'. She said, 'You can't do this. This is crazy.'

Baker stepped outside the library to take a call and met Julia Lopez and Marcus Fysh, Brexiteers from the 2017 intake. To Baker, Lopez seemed to recoil. In his memory, her face 'contorted in horror and disgust'. Lopez was concerned. Baker seemed to be a broken man. Later, she felt compelled to seek him out in the library. She found him on the phone between the library and the tearoom. Her look was 'pleading' not disgusted. She begged him not to send the article. 'You don't need to make a decision until tomorrow afternoon. If you send it and you change your mind there will be no going back.'

Baker explained that he had responsibility for influencing votes in the ERG. 'I can't be responsible for letting a communist into Downing Street.'

Lopez replied, 'Don't take on that burden. Everyone still holding out has strong minds and made their own decisions to get to that point, despite the enormous pressure.'

Baker's call was from Christopher Montgomery, who was due to appear on *Newsnight* that evening. 'Monty, I know you're going to be disappointed, but I'm looking at all these others voting for it, and I just don't see how I can hold out,' Baker explained. Montgomery suggested they talk. Baker thanked Lopez and rode his motorbike to Pimlico where he and Montgomery sat in a square together discussing the wording of the treaty. Montgomery argued that backing it was a more certain disaster than Baker taking his chances with a No vote. He declared May 'finished anyway' and said she should not be rewarded for saying she would resign. 'You won't be able to live with yourself if you vote for it,' he said. Baker felt 'awful'. Montgomery also planted the seed that, if Baker held firm, the crown of standing up for Brexit would pass from Rees-Mogg to him.

Baker also spoke to Julian Lewis, a long-standing Eurosceptic who made his name in Conservative circles in the early 1980s exposing the pro-Soviet views of the hard left. With Baker wavering, Lewis compared the ERG's plight to that of Churchill during the 'darkest hour' of 1940, when Britain stood alone against the Nazis. On that occasion, even honourable ministers felt they had no option but to seek peace with Hitler, putting the preservation of their country and its empire ahead of fighting on against insurmountable odds. To the ERG's opponents this resort to wartime imagery was a ridiculous throwback, dressing up seventy-year-old sentimentality and truculence as principle, but it was one that was persuasive to its adherents. Lewis said, 'You don't win by surrendering to what you know to be wrong. Even if you cannot see beyond the fog, you resist in the hope of eventual aid.'

It was the final injection of resolve that Baker needed. At 9.15 p.m. he texted Lopez to say, 'I'm voting against. Your look of horror told me all I needed to know.'

She replied, 'You don't need to box yourself in by writing and saying things. Make the decision only when you need to make it. The only duty you have is to the country not to us.' She recalled later, 'Everyone was going through their own emotional cycle and we all peaked and troughed at different times. We were able to pull one another up when one of us was down. It needs to be understood how awful it was.'

Much of the history of Brexit is farcical and amusing, the analysis ignorant and facile, the insults exchanged glib, but these were MPs burdened with making decisions they could not truly know were the right ones, aware that they would live with the consequences, politically and psychologically, for the rest of their days.

When Braverman spoke again to Spencer, he asked about her conversation with Baker. She replied, 'I spoke to Steve and Steve has changed his mind.'

Friday 29 March was supposed to be the day Britain left the European Union. In Downing Street, they began the day hoping against hope that the symbolism of the vote would focus minds among those who had backed Brexit. Robbie Gibb rang Julian Smith to ask his perennial question, 'Have you got any switchers for me?' Gibb wanted the names of MPs he could pass to the media to demonstrate momentum for the deal. While Gibb's persuasion operation was not equal to the moment, even that morning the Eurosceptic press – the *Mail*, *Sun*, *Telegraph* and *Express* – all urged MPs to back the deal. Tory MPs were switching, but perhaps not enough of them. Others had simply to be rounded up, more difficult on a Friday. Andrew Percy, the MP for Brigg and Goole, was supposed to be best man at a friend's wedding. May wrote the newlyweds a letter to apologise for his absence.

The most high-profile convert on the day was Dominic Raab, who managed to irritate fellow ERGers with his defection and May's team with the caveated way in which he endorsed the deal. 'I will vote for the motion … to achieve two essential outcomes: stave off a longer extension and prevent European elections in May,' Raab said. But he reserved his position, saying it did not mean he would definitely back the government when it sought to ratify the exit package.

The whips gave the rest of the ERG a cynical loophole. 'They told MPs that if they really wanted a hard Brexit there was a way: vote for the deal and then, when the government introduced the withdrawal bill to Parliament, vote it down,' an ERGer recalled. 'Then you get no-deal.'

Baker refused a request that Steve Barclay, the Brexit secretary, address the group. 'He's not a member,' Baker replied. Instead, Chris Heaton-Harris, the former chairman of the ERG, as well as the man who replaced Baker as a DExEU minister, turned up at the ERG's plenary meeting in the grand committee room. Heaton-Harris admonished those assembled, saying half-jokingly, 'The ERG was in a good state when I left it. Look at what you've become!' He then repeated the case for the reversal strategy. Baker regarded this as 'silly bollocks'. Most were unconvinced. 'We don't trust that once we voted for the deal, there'll be enough people to stop the bill,' an MP said.

Mark Francois recounted that his father a year before his death, when Francois was just thirteen, had given him a copy of Rudyard Kipling's poem 'If …' 'He told me if I was ever anxious or uncertain, and he was not around to offer advice, then I should read the poem again and it would help me decide what to do,' Francois said.[20] He read the first verse:

If you can keep your head,
When all about you are losing theirs and blaming it on you
If you can trust yourself when all men doubt you,
But make allowance for their doubting too …

'This is a very good summary of the situation in which we now find ourselves,' said Francois. 'We have to trust ourselves. The Withdrawal Agreement is still the same as it has always been. We have voted against it twice, we should be consistent.' He concluded, 'Don't just save your country, but set it free.'[21]

Lee Rowley spoke for many when he said, 'When I first read this, I thought it was shit, but I've been told that because I'm in a marginal seat, I have to vote for it if I'm going to survive. Well, I still think it's shit and I'm not voting for it.'

The most electrifying moment came at the end when Michael (now Lord) Spicer, who had created the ERG twenty-six years before, asked to speak. Spicer was seventy-six and dying of Parkinson's disease. His voice was a breathless whisper. MPs leaned forward, straining to hear what he was saying. The situation was 'even more difficult' than for the Maastricht rebels, he said. The ERG had been 'vilified' by colleagues 'but you were right all along'. Spicer concluded, 'If you do vote for this withdrawal agreement, we will effectively be trapped in the European Union forever and everything that everyone in this room has fought for, some of you for most of your adult lives, will come to nought. I realise I am asking a great deal of all of you, but please, please do not give in.'[22]

The Spartans were going to fight.

Those who held out were seen, even by most of the centre-right commentariat, as unbending ideologues. But their votes were not just the result of their beliefs, but of a perspicacious analysis of how events would play out. Egged on by advisers Christopher Howarth and Christopher Montgomery, the Paleosceptics rejected all the arguments for compromise: that Brexit might be lost if there was a referendum to reverse it ('We knew that wasn't going to happen because it would take six months to set up a referendum – and we thought Remain was better than the deal anyway'); that there would have to be an EU election ('That's not a threat to us. We don't care about European elections because we want to leave the European Union'); that it would cause irreparable harm to the Conservative Party ('Theresa May will be defeated, then she'll have to resign'). Nor did they believe, as some cabinet Brexiteers did, that they could leave the EU and then renegotiate the treaty. Opposition to this view was stoked by the suspicion that it was the position of Dominic Cummings, who the Paleosceptics believed had unfairly been given the credit for winning the referendum, over the Maastricht generation's thirty-year campaign against the EU.

Bernard Jenkin, as well as Francois, argued that if May was to win MV3 she would renege on her pledge to stand down. 'Don't ever imagine

she's going to go,' Jenkin said. 'She will be vindicated. It will be her agreement, and it will go through and we will be toast.' They also concluded
that supporting the deal would mean Farage's new Brexit Party would
'take us to pieces'. Jenkin, who found the growing isolation of the
Spartans before MV3 'very lonely', said, 'What we knew was, if we voted
for this agreement, we were dead.' Only by holding firm, they believed,
would they get a prime minister prepared to enact the Brexit they wanted.
'We looked through all the options and game-planned it to the end,' a
Spartan strategist said. 'We knew what we were doing.'

Afterwards this viewpoint became holy writ among the Spartans, the
gospel written by Howarth for *The Critic* magazine, edited by
Montgomery. Howarth said, 'Our group of MPs voted against it and that
meant Labour didn't vote for it, which meant the May deal collapsed.
That led to the prime minister resigning and led to Boris Johnson
winning the election. I think we can take some credit for the Tory majority in 2019.' Was this teleological certainty justified? Events sanctified the
Spartan world view, but it was still a gamble. At the crunch moment, it
was not shared by senior figures like Rees-Mogg and Duncan Smith.

One uncertainty the ERG could not control was the actions of the
Labour Party. 'The greatest mistake the Labour Party ever made was not
backing Theresa May's deal,' Jenkin said. 'Corbyn would have split his
party, but it would've gone through and the Conservative Party would've
been smashed to pieces.' Francois had a more nuanced view than
Howarth: 'We had a very clear-eyed rationale for doing what we were
doing. My sheet anchor was the belief that because the British people
voted to leave the European Union, one way or the other, they would
force us to comply with their will. Our job was to hold out until the
people had a chance to decide the issue. Was it a risk? Of course it was.
We all agreed that, if the Labour Party did a flip flop, we'd had it. But we
really believed that they wouldn't, and in the end we were right.'

Outside Parliament, the streets were again a throng of competing protesters, a medieval charivari of noise, fun and menace. A huge pro-Brexit
march descended on the square, the sun was out and the strains of 'God
Save the Queen' danced in the air. A Brexiteer MP, who went to look,
said, 'We felt weirdly happy and optimistic. But as we got closer, we saw
a separate crowd gravitating to a screen and stage on which [far-right
agitator] Tommy Robinson was speaking. It made me feel sick to the

stomach. This is what Parliament is doing to this country, making people feel that that man has validity. People tried to make us out to be wackos.'

Nicky Morgan and Lisa Nandy did a UK in a Changing Europe event in the QEII Centre. As they walked back both were recognised and verbally abused by people outside the Red Lion pub, who yelled, 'Traitors!' 'It captured for me how crazy the situation was, that two female MPs couldn't walk across Whitehall without being abused in broad daylight,' Morgan said. 'Fearing for your personal safety because of a referendum on Europe – this is bonkers.'

Downing Street worked hard on pro-dealers and Bresisters, particularly former ministers. A hardcore of six were set to join the Spartans in opposing the deal: Dominic Grieve, Guto Bebb, Justine Greening, Jo Johnson, Phillip Lee and Sam Gyimah. 'Sam and Jo Johnson were the most receptive,' a Number 10 source said, but they were not persuaded.

Number 10 was still seeking Labour votes too. At 1.30 p.m., an hour before the meaningful vote, ten Labour MPs were in May's parliamentary office 'sounding like they were going to vote for us', a close ally recalled. This was the culmination of months of work by John Mann and Caroline Flint. Others present included Gareth Snell, Melanie Onn, Sarah Champion, Rosie Cooper, Emma Lewell-Buck and Ivan Lewis. They signalled that they might be prepared to vote with the government once to get the deal across the line, but that was not good enough. 'You're going to be doing it thirty or forty times as the bill goes through,' a Number 10 official admitted. Onn was in tears because she was under such pressure from her Leave-voting constituents in Grimsby and from the Labour whips' office. 'She was getting so much abuse from her constituents,' a witness said.

Nick Brown, Labour's chief whip, had been clever, refusing to answer questions about whether people would be stripped of the whip rebelling on Brexit votes. Instead, he told MPs, 'I will deal with the disciplinary issue in the round at the end of the process.' That gave him room to manoeuvre but also left MPs with a sword of Damocles over their heads. Brown had far more power than Julian Smith. 'Nick Brown signed every MP's nomination form, so they were scared witless about breaking the whip,' Smith explained. 'We literally had Labour MPs in tears. Their whips saw opposing the Withdrawal Agreement as a way of destabilising and tipping over the government. I think historians will identify that desire to trump delivering on what people had voted for, a very bad call.'

Snell had joined forces with Lisa Nandy and, aided and abetted by Smith, proposed an amendment which would have prevented the government doing a trade deal until MPs had approved the negotiating mandate. The speaker did not allow amendments so Geoffrey Cox assured Snell from the despatch box that the government would abide by the terms of the deal. Onn said she wanted something in writing. Smith had a paper drawn up and his special adviser, Lilah Howson-Smith, ran around Parliament to find Onn, who was drinking in the Strangers' Bar with Flint. Just twenty minutes before the vote, she pressed it into Onn's hand. Flint recalled, 'We did get guarantees on employment rights and environmental protections as well as agreement on Parliament's role in shaping the trade negotiations in the next phase. I think [the prime minister] pretty much ticked every single box that Labour was asking for.'[23]

Barwell had also met prominent figures like Ed Miliband and Hilary Benn, trying in vain to convince them that they should support the government because they did not disagree with the withdrawal agreement. 'You either want a closer future relationship, or you want a second referendum,' he said. 'But if you vote for this motion today, we get a longer extension, so we're not up against this cliff edge in two weeks' time. The House will then have to come to a conclusion about the Political Declaration, and about a second referendum. You're not letting us do our version of Brexit by voting for the Withdrawal Agreement.'[24] He also tried to persuade Labour MPs to get in a room with wavering Tories and the DUP, so they could 'all agree to jump together'. All to no avail.

During the debate, May's team watched, some of them still daring to hope. 'There were two glorious hours where I thought we were going to do this, because Boris came out and said he would vote for it,' said one. 'We knew at that point that we were going to get Dom [Raab]. There really felt like there was a sense of momentum. Then Arlene [Foster] comes on the TV and says, "Sorry but no deal." It was so deflating – probably my worst moment.' As Priti Patel spoke, clearly emotional, Paul Harrison turned to James Slack and said, 'I think she's coming with us.'

Slack replied, 'I think the exact opposite.'

Patel voted with the Spartans.

Baker had reserved a room on the committee corridor for the Spartans. One by one those voting No peered around the door and entered. Lopez, who did not think of herself and her 2017 intake peers as Spartans at all, was relieved to see Jayawardena and Rowley already there. 'Every time someone walked into the room there was applause,' an MP said. Eventually there were twenty-eight. Lopez said, 'There were people in that twenty-eight who were always hardcore Brexiteers, who were ideological about it. It was the live or die issue. That's just not where I was. I became profoundly concerned about the impact on our democracy.' As they sat there, the text messages still came. Lopez got one from Liz Truss, which read, 'Would be great if you could back the vote this afternoon. I know difficult – but I believe it will give us a bridge to the future.' She replied, 'Thanks, Liz. I fear it gives us a tunnel into a hole.'

When the division bell rang, many MPs felt they were about to cast the most significant vote of their parliamentary careers. Baker told Rees-Mogg as they went their separate ways, 'My most contented moments have been when I agreed with you.' Baker found himself in the No lobby with twenty-seven other Spartans, Redwood and Cash among them. *It's just like the good old days.* As they walked in to cast their votes, Francois said to him, 'I think there are enough.' The ERG 'Buddies', who had conducted their own soundings with Labour MPs, were confident the Labour Leave-seat MPs would not break for May.

In the Yes lobby, loyalists and those who had changed their votes to support the deal looked around anxiously. A sizeable number of people had switched. The converts queuing up included diehard Brexiteers like Charlie Elphicke, Michael Fabricant and Richard Drax, plus former ministers Michael Fallon, Mark Harper, Esther McVey, Grant Shapps, Anne-Marie Trevelyan (an ERG Buddy) and John Whittingdale, as well as the high-profile public converts: Rees-Mogg, Duncan Smith, Johnson and Raab. Some were very late to change their minds. Journalists watching from above the chamber saw Royston Smith contemplate the floor and the heavens for a long time before heading reluctantly into the Yes lobby. There one MP texted a friend in the media, 'Not enough Labour.'

When the result was read out, May's deal had secured 286 votes but there were 344 against her. Some 43 MPs who had not backed her at MV2 had voted Yes at MV3, but just two of them – Jim Fitzpatrick and Rosie Cooper – were Labour. In the three meaningful votes, the size of the government defeat had reduced from 230 to 149 and now 58, but progress was not enough for May. Of the ten MPs who had met the PM, just two voted for the deal: John Mann and Caroline Flint. Gareth Snell began the day saying he would vote for the deal, then that he would abstain, before, finally, voting against. Melanie Onn, despite the government's written pledge, also voted No.

The prime minister stood and made a point of order. 'The implications of the House's decision are grave,' she said. May referred twice to leaving the EU in an 'orderly' fashion, suggesting she would pursue an extension rather than no-deal. She referred to a second round of indicative votes due to take place on the following Monday, but pointed out bitterly, 'Of course, all of the options will require the withdrawal agreement.' She added, 'I fear we are reaching the limits of this process in this House. This House has rejected no-deal. It has rejected no Brexit. On Wednesday it rejected all the variations of the deal on the table. And today it has rejected approving the withdrawal agreement alone and continuing a process on the future.' To many, that sounded like a threat to call a general election.

May cut a bleak figure after her defeat. As she left the chamber she was comforted by Nicky Morgan. The prime minister managed to mutter, 'Well at least there were more on my side this time.'

Afterwards, in the prime minister's Commons office, May was 'very sharp' about how her offer to resign had failed to produce the votes that Iain Duncan Smith had promised. 'There weren't tears,' said one senior aide. 'It was just exasperation.' May raised her arms as she had in the 'nothing has changed' press conference during the 2017 election campaign, 'She was incredulous,' a close ally said. 'There was a moment when she just put her head in her hands. What more could she do?' Julian Smith found himself in the firing line. May snapped at him, 'You asked me to trade my job to get the deal through!' Smith, in turn, was furious with Duncan Smith for failing to deliver the votes, telling others it was 'a slapdash effort'. A close ally noted, 'A lot was drunk.'

The big beast Brexiteers brought few colleagues with them. Johnson and Raab made no effort to lobby other Spartans. 'Boris didn't lift a finger,' said a fellow MP. 'It suited him to look like he was doing the right thing and that Theresa still lost.'

Barwell initially thought the progress meant an attempt at MV4 was possible, but it soon became clear that the mood had changed. After

MV2, there were MPs telling Downing Street, 'I was nearly there, don't give up.' But after MV3 none of the 34 Tory rebels gave off those signals. James Slack told friends later, 'For me, her premiership finished at that point because she had done everything she could.'

The aftermath of MV3 produced fresh drama. Richard Drax, who had supported May, took to his feet in the Commons the following Monday and made a point of order recanting his vote and calling for May's resignation unless she could guarantee to take the UK out of the EU on 12 April. 'I feel utterly ashamed of myself,' he told MPs. 'I made the wrong call.' Drax had been told by his whip that his vote would be the difference between May winning and losing by one vote.

In the second round of indicative votes, all four propositions (customs union, Common Market 2.0, a referendum and revoke) failed. Labour, also split down the middle, had not even managed to concoct an amendment that both LOTO and Starmer could support. Once again, the customs union came closest to success, falling three votes short. Ken Clarke's motion would have succeeded if the Liberal Democrats and the Independent Group backed the motion, but both parties refused to endorse any form of soft Brexit – another moment when MPs defied Bismarck's dictum. The SNP also abstained. The referendum got the most votes, 280, but fell 13 votes short, largely because forty Labour MPs voted against or abstained.

'The customs union option would have won, if the people who wanted a People's Vote had voted for it, instead of either voting against it or abstaining,' Andrew Fisher said. 'A customs union alone wouldn't have been everything we would have wanted, but it would have scuppered the Tories and ... put Theresa May in an impossible position ... I found it very frustrating.'[25]

Common Market 2.0, having secured the official backing of Labour and the SNP, did much better than before (gaining 261 votes), but still lost by a majority of 21. The cause was not assisted by George Freeman, one of its leading advocates, missing the vote because he was either reading a magazine or asleep in the library, depending on the explanation you preferred. Boles felt utterly deflated. He had tried to find an acceptable compromise but the bad feeling between the Norway MPs and the People's Voters was profound. Boles thought people ought to want the least damaging options, but he felt advocates of a referendum wanted the chance to be up against the worst options. No-deal was their favoured opponent. Boles suggested to them, 'Listen, vote for Common Market 2.0 and then vote it should be put to a referendum, I won't support you, but if you can win a majority, it's much better to have a referendum on that than not having one at all.' They were not persuaded.

The disarray in Bresistance ranks contrasted starkly with the unity of purpose among hard Brexiteers. 'It was a classic prisoner's dilemma situation,' Stephen Doughty said. 'You have one group of people, the Brexiteers, with a very clear agenda and a very clear way forward. They were able to operate as one coherent whole. It was always going to be a very, very long stretch for anybody on the other side to achieve anything, because of the number of individuals and the number of competing agendas.'

Having seen his efforts of the last few months come to naught, Boles got to his feet in the chamber and said, 'I accept I have failed. I have failed chiefly because my party refuses to compromise.' He announced he was resigning from the Conservative Party and would sit as an independent. Boles considered himself one of the rational people in the Commons, but at that moment, he, like so many others through the Brexit years, was consumed by pure emotion.

In Downing Street, the anger was directed primarily at Labour, who had voted down a withdrawal agreement they essentially supported. 'The third attempt is the one I'm most angry about,' Barwell reflected. 'First and second time around, I don't agree with them, but I can see why people took a different view to us. The third time round, in my opinion, Parliament made a terrible decision. The truth is about 500 out of the 650 MPs in the House of Commons supported the withdrawal agreement.' The opposition's stance infuriated Robbie Gibb, who could not get the media interested in Corbyn's breach of his manifesto pledge in 2017 to deliver on the referendum result. 'The media, particularly broadcasters, were not holding Labour to account,' he recalled. 'They were obsessed by the internal battle between those that wanted a second referendum and those that didn't. But the elephant in the room was that Labour was not supporting their manifesto and Brexit.'

The Tories later calculated that there were thirty-seven occasions when Labour MPs 'voted against delivering Brexit'. Labour's argument was that backing the withdrawal agreement without the political declaration would lead to a 'blind Brexit'. A senior Number 10 official said, 'It was just bollocks. All they would have done is signal to the EU that the withdrawal agreement bit of the deal was acceptable to Parliament. They could still have argued for a referendum.' Defending his corner later, Keir Starmer said, 'To vote through a deal which you think is the wrong deal isn't respecting the referendum result it is setting up the future to fail so I don't think there was an obligation.'[26]

Gibb and May were both exasperated with the Brexiteers as well. Reflecting on what had gone wrong, the prime minister said, 'I had assumed mistakenly that the tough bit of the negotiation was with the EU, that Parliament would accept the vote of the British people and just want to get it done, that people who'd spent their lives campaigning for Brexit would vote to get us out on 29 March. But they didn't.'[27] Gibb wrote later, 'I'd always worried that Brexit would be stopped in Parliament by those who claimed to accept the EU referendum result in public even as in private they sought to undermine it. What I'd never thought, not even in my wildest nightmares, was that the people who would stop Brexit would be the Brexiteers themselves.'[28]

Was there a way May could have won? Some of her team believe they should have decoupled the withdrawal agreement from the political declaration sooner. 'We should have made people understand earlier that they could have a really cool fight about phase two if we could just get phase one out of the way,' an aide said. This had arguably been a failing since the time of Chequers. A second, linked, insight was that May was paying the price for delaying the first meaningful vote before Christmas, a six-week period which meant the third vote pressed up against the March deadline. With a little more time, a special adviser observed, 'we could have hopefully moved the conversation on to talk about the future'.

Had May announced that the Brexiteers could handle the future trade deal, it might have halved the number of Spartans. 'That would have given us a real shout, I think,' a Downing Street aide said. Instead, MV3 'felt like the moment to me that we were fucked'. May now had twelve days before she would have to ask Brussels for another extension. She had offered her own head on a spike and still failed. Boris Johnson joked with his supporters, 'Theresa fell on her sword – and missed.'

Barwell and Julian Smith war-gamed the best possible outcome if there was a fourth meaningful vote. They could just about envisage a scenario in which they won by two or three votes. But to pass the Brexit legislation they would need to hold the coalition together. 'I don't see a route to a secure majority,' Barwell said.

There were only two options left: do a deal with Labour or call a general election.

OUT OF THE QUESTION

Election Time?

29 March to 3 April 2019

Within minutes of the result of the third meaningful vote, a little after 2.30 p.m. on 29 March, an alert began pinging on the phones of a select few of Theresa May's closest aides. It was a diary invite to a meeting in Number 10 at 4 p.m. 'There was a padlock on the diary,' one official recalled, something which signalled that this was a very secret meeting indeed. In Downing Street, a large number of people usually have access to shared diaries. But only those on the invite list would even know it was taking place. It was described simply as 'political meeting'. A source recalled, 'This was TV box set stuff.'

Gavin Barwell, the chief of staff and his deputy, JoJo Penn, were there, along with May's political secretary Stephen Parkinson, policy chief James Marshall and pollster James Johnson. Anyone chancing across the meeting, though, would have guessed what they were talking about when they saw Brandon Lewis and Sir Mick Davis, the Tory party chairman and chief executive, and Darren Mott, the director of campaigning.

Mott was one of those unsung heroes of Tory politics, a fixture of party backrooms for three decades but anonymous to the public and press. The nearest he had come to public attention had been on election night in 2017 when he collapsed and vomited as the exit poll presaged disaster. On 29 March, Mott was smuggled into Number 10 by the rear entrance on Horse Guards Parade, but he was spotted by someone who had not been invited to the meeting, who said, 'There is no other reason Darren would be in Downing Street unless they were talking about a general election.' One of those in the meeting agreed, 'You know it's big when he is in through the bins entrance. He hadn't been in since April 2017.'

Barwell opened the meeting and made clear that an election had to be a serious option: 'It could be our way out of this.' He wanted to give May an informed choice. 'We need to think about whether we want to do this and present a recommendation to political cabinet.' The chief of staff asked Lewis, Davis, Mott and Johnson to present a considered opinion to the prime minister on Monday. 'We need to know how feasible an election is. Is it winnable?'

The mood in the room was one of nervous tension. Some of those present appeared to like the idea of running an election. 'Brandon was a bit up for it,' a source said. 'Gavin was a bit up for it. James looked excited by the idea.' The proposal was not as wild as it might have seemed. The Conservatives had taken the lead in national opinion polls in February and, while that had changed, even May's defeat in MV2 had not torpedoed their standing. One of those in the circle of trust said, 'That 29 March discussion was not "go and tell cabinet this is a bad idea". There was a very realistic possibility we'd come back on Monday and say, "We think we can win it." We were in serious-crazy mode.'

May's communications director Robbie Gibb and Parkinson both favoured a general election. While Barwell entertained the idea, he was more closely aligned with David Lidington, who was pressing for a cross-party deal for a soft Brexit.

That Sunday the Rebel Alliance pro-dealers – Amber Rudd, David Gauke and Greg Clark – used a conference call with May to press the prime minister to accept whichever softer Brexit option ended up securing a majority in the House in a third set of indicative votes the following Wednesday. They made clear that they would resign if she opted for no-deal at the next deadline, 12 April. The Brexiteers and the neo-Brexiteers in the cabinet Pizza Club, backed up by a letter signed by 170 MPs, stressed that they preferred no-deal to a long extension.

But MPs were alive to the possibility of an election – a course of action few could contemplate with alacrity after 2017. 'In those circumstances we would have to vote with Labour in a motion of no confidence to kick her out,' a leading Tory said. 'She can't be allowed near a general election.' Under the Fixed-term Parliaments Act, the rebels would have two weeks to install a leader who could win a confidence motion or see the Queen invite Jeremy Corbyn to form a government.

*   *   *

OUT OF THE QUESTION 523

On the evening of 31 March, a Sunday, May held a meeting in great secrecy at her constituency home in Sonning with Peter Kyle and Phil Wilson, the Labour MPs behind the amendment on a confirmatory referendum. They were accompanied by Tom Watson, Labour's deputy leader, to 'reassure the PM it was a serious proposition from our side'. In a 'long and detailed' conversation, May 'listened really intently' as Kyle told her a referendum was her only way out: 'Prime Minister, from where I sit, I cannot see you winning a third vote. I know you've been promised forty Labour votes who haven't turned up, but that isn't going to change. The pressure in our party is not coming from that direction, it's coming from the opposite direction. The numbers just are not there. And if you lose for a third time, there is nowhere else for you to go.'

May spoke of the threats of violence against MPs, particularly women, and expressed concern that another referendum would stir up further conflict. 'She was very open about her concern about the tone of politics and the simmering underbelly of threat,' Kyle said. 'She was worried about what that would mean if we were to go back and have another.' Kyle's response was simple: 'In my view, it's this or Boris Johnson in Number 10 by autumn. Then, we've opened the door to populism. The things you're worried about will be delivered writ large.'

Kyle recalled, 'Phil and I came out of the meeting full of respect for Theresa May; very understanding of the magnitude of decisions that she had to take, having the sense that she accepted the logic of the proposition.' Wilson despatched Kyle to 'go speak Tory' to the Conservatives while he worked on his own shadow whipping operation. There were numerous other dangerous liaisons. Kyle met 'four or five cabinet ministers' plus 'people very close to Theresa May, both within Number 10 and in her government'. On one occasion he was walking down a corridor 'and a hand came in from the side, and they'd just yank you into a room'. Another time, after a vote, he encountered 'a very senior government figure walking slowly past who just winked. I followed that figure down a corridor and into this empty office. We just sat for thirty minutes quickly just running through things.'

Kyle's description of a minister 'drawing a referendum ballot paper with different options on it' echoes conversations David Lidington had with Labour MPs. Lidington was privately interested in a two-stage referendum, which he assumed would be more palatable to Brexiteers, in which voters would have been asked first whether they wanted to leave the EU and second what sort of Brexit deal they wanted. 'That might work on a bit of paper in your office,' Kyle said. 'That's not going to fly in what could be deemed as a safe and fair election. The Electoral Commission isn't going to allow that. That's just weird. You can't have two propositions, where one of the propositions has two options.'

Cabinet lasted nearly eight hours on 2 April. 'The saddest moment' came first as Theresa May laid out why she needed to change the government's Brexit policy. 'I offered my resignation and still the deal didn't go through.' There was one attempt to cheer her up. When she referred to her offer to stand down, the energy minister Claire Perry yelled, 'Revoke it!' This sly play on the threat of Remainers overturning Brexit provoked widespread amusement. 'The whole room laughed but the PM was not laughing,' a cabinet source said.

Mick Davis and Brandon Lewis made a presentation based around the feasibility study drawn up by James Johnson. The pollster's numbers were not good. Labour was on course for a majority and was ahead of the Tories 'on all domestic issues', with the cost of living, the NHS and the environment topping voters' concerns. 'They basically said, "As things stand, based on the evidence, this is a terrible idea",' one of those in the room said. Davis concluded emphatically, 'I'm not in favour of this option – in fact I'm implacably opposed.'[1]

If there was an election, May would have to fight it on the basis that she was asking the public to support her deal and overrule Parliament. Johnson's polling analysis showed that having to ask for a second extension from the EU, violating the 29 March deadline, would undermine Conservative prospects. He predicted a great opening on the right where an insurgent force (inevitably led by Nigel Farage) would go on the attack because Britain had not yet left the EU. Lewis warned that Farage's soon-to-be-launched Brexit Party would do well in the European elections.

Ministers discussed how difficult it would be to write a manifesto which both Eurosceptics and Remainers could both sign up to. Philip Hammond couldn't risk a dig at the suicidal secrecy of 2017: 'We'd have to have a manifesto agreed in advance. We can't have it forced upon us without agreement again.' The prime minister 'rolled her eyes' at him. The chancellor also said of the public, 'They're not as resilient as they were in 1940 when they had to cope with doodlebugs', a remark greeted with similar weary bemusement by his colleagues.

There were other problems too. The Tory money men were reluctant to put their hands in their pockets for a prime minister who had thrown away a hard-won majority two years earlier. A cabinet minister said, 'It was an incredibly long cabinet. It began with us being told why we couldn't fight a general election as we would get absolutely marmalised. No donors, no money.' For once, every minister was united – there could not be an election.

Next up was Julian Smith, who made clear there was no way the deal would pass unless it was amended to attract more Labour votes. He calculated that of the 34 rebels (of whom 28 were ERG Spartans and six Bresisters), 26 were ultras who would never vote for the deal. Having tried and failed himself to get anywhere with Labour MPs, Smith was sceptical about the likely success of cross-party talks, but he also thought it was a logical next step. He told cabinet that unless they tried something they would face Parliament imposing a much softer Brexit or a referendum.

There was opposition, none more so than from Lewis, the party chairman. 'Brandon was concerned about how the party would feel,' a Number 10 official said. Andrea Leadsom and Gavin Williamson argued that talking to Labour would 'break the party'. The Leavers and neo-Leavers – Jeremy Hunt, Liz Truss, Penny Mordaunt and Sajid Javid – went into the meeting with the agreed line of, 'We need to threaten no-deal and get Labour MPs on side with that.'

What should an offer to Labour be? The two options were policy concessions or a referendum. David Lidington, David Gauke, Jeremy Wright, Karen Bradley and Caroline Nokes all suggested they give Labour a confirmatory vote. 'There were seven or eight Remainers in cabinet who either actively were then saying, "Maybe the referendum is the answer here", or were saying, "I could live with it",' a senior Number 10 official recalled. Philip Hammond agreed the only way to get more votes was to agree a customs union or a referendum. He preferred a customs union. A third way, backed by Damian Hinds and Greg Clark, would have seen indicative votes with 'elimination ballots', so Parliament could select its preferred option to put up against May's deal in a final meaningful vote. JoJo Penn was also pushing this solution in Number 10. The chief whip was firmly against.

The meeting broke for lunch and then reconvened as an official cabinet meeting. May asked whether ministers supported no-deal or an extension. Only Truss and Williamson opposed an extension. The chief secretary argued, 'We are in analysis paralysis, let's have some more national self-confidence in terms of no-deal.' In his memoir Barwell noted, 'several other ministers said they only supported a short one'.[2] The fact is that there was a clear majority in the room for only pursuing a short extension (and, by implication, pursuing no-deal instead if that did not work). Andrea Leadsom made notes in the meeting. 'I've taken down the numbers,' she said. 'It's 14–10 for a short extension.' May baulked. She was not one for votes.

Then the prime minister asked ministers to choose between using an extension to introduce the withdrawal agreement bill (an idea promoted by Chris Grayling which was largely friendless), hold preferential votes, or talk to Labour. The decisive moment came with a dual, but uncoordinated intervention by Michael Gove and Geoffrey Cox, who both argued that the government had to try to do a deal with Corbyn. Both believed they were within touching distance of losing the entire Brexit project to Bresistance forces in Parliament. Unlike the ERG, which sought a perfect Brexit, they were determined to leave the EU on almost any reasonable terms. Gove spoke halfway through the marathon meeting. 'Facts don't care about feelings,' he said. 'We have all got to stop thinking about what we want and focus on what is achievable. I mean, I would like to be the next James Bond, but that isn't going to happen. You can say that you want lobster Thermidor but if the only things in the canteen are corned beef and cabbage you've got to make a decision.' If there was an extension, he said, it would be the EU, not the cabinet, who decided its length. 'Brexiteers have to take action that is uncomfortable, or we will cede it to people who don't want Brexit at all.'

Cox spoke towards the end and argued that May should put the Labour Party on the spot: ask them what they would agree to and then offer it to them so they would be forced to accept. 'Prime Minister, it pains me deeply to say this,' Cox said, 'but the most overriding of all priorities is that we should just leave. The only option, therefore, is to look across the House and see if there are people who sincerely want to do what they've told the country they want to do, which is leave the European Union. Logic dictates that we move our red lines and make a big and bold offer to Labour.' Cox had appropriated the language David Cameron used when wooing the Liberal Democrats in 2010. Gove intervened again to support him.

Gavin Williamson was incandescent, calling the plan 'ridiculous', his voice raised. 'You can't trust Corbyn.' A Number 10 official said, 'He was the angriest person in the room by a mile.'

With the numbers evenly split between cross-party talks and preferential votes, May said they would try to engage with the opposition first, since that would not mean handing control to Parliament. Ministers were offered wine and asked to remain in the Cabinet Room while May went into the street to announce what had been decided.

Just as she had been at Chequers in July 2018, Penny Mordaunt was seething at the idea that the cabinet should be held hostage without the right to communicate with the outside world while the prime minister announced her version of events to the country. Mordaunt had refused to hand in her mobile phone, keeping it in her handbag outside the room, where it was not a security threat. When she nipped to the toilet she saw a text message from Chris Heaton-Harris, the DExEU minister, which revealed that the cabinet had been shown the wrong papers from the Borders Delivery Group on the consequences of no-deal. The BDG had downgraded the risk, but the cabinet had seen old papers with a higher risk rating. It smacked of conspiracy rather than cock-up.

Mordaunt had arranged for a group of school children to come to Parliament. They were waiting for her at the Commons education centre. Journalists were being told the cabinet was all together drinking wine to celebrate their harmonious decision-making. Now began one of the most gloriously farcical episodes of the dying days of the May government as a member of her cabinet made a desperate break for freedom.

Mordaunt slipped out of the room, gathered her things and made her way to the pod airlock-style doors between 10 Downing Street and the Cabinet Office. She could not leave by the front entrance, where the press pack was gathered for May's statement, but she hoped to slip into the street through 70 Whitehall. Mordaunt pressed the button to speak to the security control room: 'Hi, it's the secretary of state, can I just pop through. I'm just heading out.'

A disembodied voice came through the intercom: 'We've been told not to let you out.'

Mordaunt said, 'Look, I've got a meeting to go to. I'm not going out the front, but I really want to go.'

'I'm sorry. We can't let you go.'

Cursing the lockdown, Mordaunt then saw someone approaching. She seized her chance. 'Could you help me? I don't have a pass to get out.' The unsuspecting official swiped their card and Mordaunt was through. She now headed down a corridor towards the exit, where more pod doors lay between her and freedom. At that point a security guard barred her way. He was polite but firm: 'I'm terribly sorry, ma'am, but we've been told not to let you out.'

Mordaunt responded in kind: 'I know. You're just doing your job. But let's be realistic; you're not going to physically stop me.' A pause. 'I mean, you can try.' Mordaunt was a statuesque presence. If the guard considered how to grapple with her without being disciplined for assaulting a cabinet minister, he did not do so for long.

Instead, he muttered, 'No, I've just been told to …'

'Rest assured, you've done your duty, but I am leaving this building.'

'Fair enough, ma'am,' the guard said, stepping aside.

At the final set of pods, Mordaunt deployed charm rather than bluster and was allowed through. She had already called her driver to get round to 70 Whitehall. Like the tunnellers of the Great Escape, she burst into the fresh air of freedom and was quickly on her way to Parliament.

Back in the Cabinet Room, Mordaunt's absence was causing concern. 'There were fears Penny would resign,' a cabinet colleague recalled. 'She had fled and we were all kettled as the prime minister made the statement.' The only sadness about this episode was that it happened on 2 April rather than a day earlier on April Fool's Day.

In her statement, around 6.30 p.m., May said, 'Today I am taking action to break the logjam. I am offering to sit down with the leader of the opposition and to try to agree a plan – that we both would stick to – to ensure that we leave the European Union and that we do so with a deal. Any plan would have to agree the current withdrawal agreement … The ideal outcome of this process would be to agree an approach on a future relationship … that both the leader of the opposition and I could put to the House for approval.' She then spelled out that, if there was no agreement, they could put different options to MPs and would agree to be bound by the outcome – all with a deadline of 22 May, so that the UK did not need to take part in European Parliament elections.

The decision was met with fury by Brexiteers. The ERG watched the speech in Committee Room 15 and there were audible gasps as May announced her plan. When Mark Francois later encountered Andrew Bowie, May's PPS, he 'marched past, a little round ball of red anger,' an MP witness recalled. 'Well you've bloody done it now,' Francois exclaimed. 'You've done a deal with a Marxist!' The MP said, 'It was said with such gusto and bubbly fury that I couldn't help but burst into laughter.'

The following day Nigel Adams and Chris Heaton-Harris both resigned. Quitting his post in DExEU, Heaton-Harris was angry that the preparations he had been making for no-deal would not now be used. In his resignation letter, he wrote, 'These preparations are well advanced … I do not believe the briefings you have received on these matters recently have reflected all they have achieved.' He added, 'Every time we seek an extension to this process, we diminish faith in our political system … I simply cannot support any further extension.'

Spluttering rage was widespread that week. Most Tory MPs regarded Corbyn as a serious threat to the economy and national security. A former cabinet minister said, 'Why would you invite someone into your house who wants to blow it up?' Another leading Tory said, 'She's the worst prime minister since Lord North', who lost the American colonies. 'The only difference is that Lord North gave away another country and she is giving away this one.'

The decision to talk to Labour triggered a revolt among the Tory grassroots which opened up a new front against May, one that would play a key role in forcing the prime minister from office. Party members began quitting in high numbers. On 23 February constituency association chairmen on the party's National Convention had met in Oxford and passed a motion demanding that the prime minister keep no-deal on the table, delay leaving no later than the European elections and rule out a referendum. Now they wrote to Brandon Lewis warning that failing to stick to May's public promises would 'betray the 2016 People's Vote and damage democracy and our party for a generation'. Branding Corbyn 'a Marxist who befriends terrorists', the association chairmen wrote, 'Having spent a considerable amount of capital telling the country that Mr Corbyn is not fit to govern, our Conservative prime minister has invited him into the heart of government and is taking instructions from the Labour Party.' This was 'the last straw' for many activists 'now voting with their feet'. They went on, 'We have therefore concluded, after a lot of heartache, that Mrs May needs to step aside as soon as possible, so that a Brexit-supporting prime minister can take up the reins.'

Despite failing to oust May the previous December, the ERG began demanding another vote of no confidence. Andrew Bridgen, who was to letters of no confidence what Imelda Marcos was to shoes, wrote this time: 'The prime minister is no longer fit to run this country. She must be stopped before she gives away our once-in-a-lifetime chance to unshackle ourselves from the chains of the European Union.' Others in the ERG threatened to down tools and stop voting for the government.

While Conservative Party rules stated that May could not be challenged for a year, MPs said Graham Brady, chairman of the 1922 Committee, would have to tell her to go if he received letters from more than half the parliamentary party. 'If she doesn't listen, we will have to change the party's rules,' one said. In Downing Street, Gavin Barwell thought his boss was safe. It was reported that, to change the twelve-month rule, the Conservative Party constitution had to be rewritten, a National Convention of grassroots Tories called and even that a petition of 10,000 members was required. This was nonsense. For weeks, the ERG leadership had been getting MPs on the executive of the 1922 Committee to ask Brady for a copy of the rules. He repeatedly refused. Unknown to Brady, Christopher Howarth, the ERG's chief research man (the R in the ERG), already had a copy – and he knew it was much easier to get rid of May.

The only two former chairmen of the 1922 still alive were Michael Spicer and Archie Hamilton, both now Tory peers. Spicer, who was terminally ill, was also the founder of the ERG and still attended some of their Wednesday meetings when his health permitted. Howarth, who lived and breathed a purist form of Euroscepticism that brooked no compromise and had advised Mark Francois when he was shadow Europe minister, spoke to Spicer, who told him he had given all his papers, including the only other copy of the 1922 Committee statutes to the Bodleian Library in Oxford. From there Howarth retrieved the rules.

The executive of the 1922 Committee was split over whether there should be another leadership contest but, with the exception of Brady, believed it was complicated. To dissuade them from acting, Downing Street threatened legal action if an effort was made to circumvent the twelve-month rule. Brady told colleagues he was taking legal advice. 'He was just stalling,' Howarth said. 'We had a copy of it. We knew what it said. The key thing is that the rules aren't really rules, they say that the '22 can just change the rules. You don't need a lawyer to read it.'

Howarth penned an article for the *Telegraph* and visited Spicer in the Cromwell Road hospital to get his approval to publish it in his and Hamilton's names. Spicer told his nurse Howarth was 'here to save the country'.[3] On 13 April, the article blew up the notion of an inviolable rule. 'The current rules are not designed to facilitate the toppling of a sitting prime minister, but nor are they designed to protect a prime minister in office from the party's elected representatives in the House of Commons,' the piece said. 'This rule has been interpreted as being immovable ... This is not the case.' They concluded, 'Conservative MPs are responsible for their party. If they wish to change these rules there is nothing standing in their way.'[4] From then on, the mood in the 1922 executive began to move against Brady and towards a rule change. 'They say it was that article that unlocked it all,' Howarth recalled. Spicer lived long enough to know that 'Brexit was going to happen in a reasonable way'.

The man most keenly awaiting a leadership election stepped up his planning. Boris Johnson condemned May's plan. 'It is very disappointing that the cabinet has decided to entrust the final handling of Brexit to Jeremy Corbyn and the Labour Party,' he tweeted. Johnson was watching May make her statement on television in his parliamentary office when Oliver Lewis arrived to see him. Lewis, head of research on Vote Leave, had been informally providing advice on the small print of the treaty and the Northern Ireland Protocol to Johnson for months. With May now making her final, forlorn, throw of the dice, Johnson was already thinking about what he might do if he succeeded her.

'I want you to come on board,' Johnson told him. Lewis had also had an approach from Dominic Raab, who had signed up Paul Stephenson, the communications director of Vote Leave. But Lewis thought a general election was a likely outcome of the Brexit impasse and, having seen how Johnson fought when his career was on the line in 2016, he believed Johnson was much more likely to win.

Lewis also suggested that Johnson would have to get Dominic Cummings on board. Unknown to most Tories, Johnson and his former special advisers David Frost and Lee Cain, plus Munira Mirza, Johnson's deputy mayor in London, had held meetings with Vote Leave's campaign director, both as foreign secretary and afterwards. These conversations, which took place on Sundays around once a month during 2018, were kept very tight. Cummings often met Johnson one-on-one at the kitchen table of Jake Berry and his wife Alice Robinson, Johnson's former PA. The couple had a flat near when Johnson was renting. Cummings told Vote Leave allies he used these sessions to 'try to programme Boris and get him pointing in the right direction'. One source in the loop recalled, 'He was meeting Dom on a reasonably regular basis. The gist of those conversations was, "How do we get rid of her? And what does it look like afterwards?"' Many of the MPs who Johnson would need to support him in a leadership bid hated Cummings, a feeling which was more than reciprocated. At this stage, however, Cummings had little intention of working with Johnson again. He told one associate in 2018, 'Boris won't take sensible advice about what to do, because he can't. He is what he is. He will never change. We can't risk everything against Corbyn on putting someone like that in Downing Street.' Nonetheless, just as he had mapped out a strategy for winning the 2016 referendum in 2014, Cummings knew what an election campaign should look like: 'Investment in the NHS, cutting immigration, cutting taxes; that's what the Tories have to do to win the next election. If they do that, they'll smash Corbyn into small pieces. Even with a beta leader, an alpha team could win quite easily.'

The roll call of days of high drama in the Commons became wearying during the Brexit process, but 3 April 2019 ranked with any of them for its nail-biting tension. The main event was the historic attempt by back-benchers to pass a bill of their own design, opposed by the government, for the first time in modern political history. The legislation in question was the Letwin-Grieve project, fronted by Yvette Cooper, the inelegantly titled European Union (Withdrawal) (No. 5) Bill, designed to force the prime minister to propose a motion to extend Article 50, preventing no-deal.

First, however, there was an effort to pass an amendment from Hilary Benn to grant parliamentary time for another round of indicative votes the following Monday, a plan dismissed by Tory Bob Seely as 'a Strictly Come Brexit dance off'. When the votes were counted at 5 p.m. the result was a tie 310–310. Speaker Bercow announced, 'In accordance with prec-edent, and on the principle that important decisions should not be taken except by a majority, I cast my vote with the Noes, so the Noes have it. By casting vote, it is 311 to 310. That is the proper way in which to proceed.' The last time a speaker had broken a tie was in 1993 when Betty Boothroyd did so over the Maastricht Treaty.

On a frenzied day, the Cooper bill then faced a crunch vote on whether it should be allowed to proceed. The Bresistance eked out a knife-edge victory, prevailing by one vote, 312–311. Cooper and Letwin then had just six hours to pass the bill's second reading, committee stage and third reading. It passed its second reading at 7 p.m. by a margin of five votes. It culminated in a febrile denouement at 11.09 p.m. with the vote on third reading. The Cooper bill became law by one vote, 313–312. John Bercow's January ruling that MPs could seize control of the Commons timetable had, for good or ill, paved the way for history to be made.

The bill was supported by fourteen Tories,[5] while another six abstained. Astonishingly, seventeen of the twenty rebels were former ministers, seven of whom had served in cabinet.

Paleosceptic Bill Cash made a point of order, attacking what he viewed as a 'reprehensible' constitutional precedent. The following day the roof of the Commons chamber began to leak. A fellow Spartan said, 'Bill thought it was because lightning literally struck the roof at the time of his point of order the night before. Parliament was being swept away in a biblical intervention.'

Mark Francois also summoned biblical fury, abandoning his usual Churchillian rhetoric to invoke Jesus Christ on the Bresisters: 'Forgive them, Father, for they know not what they do.'

What they had done was show, for the first time in living memory, that Parliament could dictate to a government with no majority.

Next it was the official opposition's turn.

MATING PORCUPINES

The Cross-Party Talks

3 April to 17 May 2019

Geoffrey Cox had suggested that Theresa May open talks with Labour with a 'big, bold offer'. Yet when the prime minister met Jeremy Corbyn on Wednesday 3 April, she offered the same enigmatic face to the leader of the opposition which had bemused MPs and ministers for three years. May's chief of staff Gavin Barwell and her deputy David Lidington used an intermediary to tell Labour that the prime minister would move towards their position on a customs union. 'The leader's office was told she would effectively offer Corbyn something like his own plan in exchange for support,' a member of Corbyn's team said. 'We expected them to do something big to build trust and then work on the little things, rather than the other way around.' Instead, the first session was very much, what Barwell was to describe as a 'capture exercise', where the Tory team just tried to get the Labour people talking.

Corbyn turned up with Keir Starmer, the shadow Brexit secretary, Rebecca Long-Bailey, the shadow business secretary, Labour's chief whip Nick Brown, plus Seumas Milne, his chief Svengali, and Andrew Fisher, his policy chief. Starmer was sceptical about how much the government had thought the exercise through. There had been no discreet outreach from David Lidington beforehand and he learned of the plan for talks only when May announced it. He received a message from Sabine Weyand in Brussels: 'Did you know about this, Keir?' It was clear the Commission had no idea either. 'It seemed a desperate last bid to buy a bit of road,' Starmer said.

Emily Thornberry, the shadow foreign secretary, emailed colleagues to demand that any deal agreed come with a referendum and that the shadow cabinet should vote on it. For this act of insubordination, LOTO banned her from attending the Nato summit later that year.

Lidington led for the Conservatives in the room, with Barwell doing most of the staff work behind the scenes. 'Gavin ran it,' an official said. 'It wasn't an Olly [Robbins] run exercise in the way that just about everything else had been.' Also on the team were Julian Smith, the chief whip; Steve Barclay, the Brexit secretary; and Greg Clark, the business secretary. Lidington politely asked a lot of questions, to try to properly understand Labour's position. 'You say this. What does that mean?' Away from the public point-scoring, the government needed to know where the opposition's red lines were really drawn. 'Is there actually anything in the withdrawal agreement you're unhappy with?'

The Labour side was quick to make clear that they were concerned about the lack of workers' rights in the backstop. Starmer also put customs, environmental protections and a referendum on the table. And if any deal was to survive, how could the Tories guarantee that anything May agreed would survive contact with a new prime minister, who would likely take a tougher line than her?

More than one participant looked around the room at the awkward gathering and pinched themselves. 'It was like meeting your partner's parents,' Starmer joked.[1] It was no less strange for the Tories to be in a room with implacable enemies. The first time Lidington met Starmer, on 13 February, the shadow Brexit secretary had turned up with Jon Trickett, a Corbynite frontbencher, and Milne. He told colleagues afterwards, 'It was reminiscent of when I used to have meetings with Russian or Chinese ambassadors and they had their minders from the embassy.' Lidington did have one jokey exchange with Milne, asking him whether in a revolution it would be 'me or Keir in front of the firing squad'. Milne replied deadpan, 'It is a matter of sequence, not principle.'

To many pro-dealers, People's Voters and revanchist Remainers, the cross-party talks were two years too late. May came to them not as a dominant prime minister seeking to drive consensus, but as a politician on life support, desperately seeking a life raft to cling to.

Corbyn was also seriously weakened from his heyday in the second half of 2017. The Labour leader, whose passions were socialist solidarity, Palestine and South America, was not interested in EU policy but risked becoming defined by it. His encounter with May was described by one participant as 'the most constipated meeting', with follow-up briefings in 'the most dreadful phone calls'. Corbyn was by now – as Pogrund and Maguire have chronicled – 'psychologically incapable of leading',[2] in the grip of something resembling a breakdown, with growing rumours about his physical health, which led his diary secretary to hand him a pillow and duvet for afternoon 'nap time'.[3]

When May's deal was published in November 2018, Starmer read it in his loft that evening and briefed the shadow cabinet the next day. They could scarcely believe it when Corbyn interrupted and asked, 'What's this backstop?'[4] In Brexit meetings, Corbyn typically spoke and then sat mute as Milne, Fisher and Murphy attempted to clarify what he meant, in front of him, while the leader contemplated his phone. A political aide said, 'He would read something out at the start of a meeting, but Jeremy wouldn't engage in the debate. He wouldn't wrap up at the end. You often left none the wiser about what had been agreed.' In another meeting, Corbyn ignored the Brexit discussion and was overheard asking Thornberry about an international court ruling on the Chagos Islanders, another of his anti-colonial enthusiasms. 'He had a five-minute conversation with her about how to respond, while there was a discussion unfolding about Brexit,' a source recounted. 'He wanted to focus on his little passions.'

The story also circulated that when Corbyn met António Costa, the Portuguese prime minister, at a meeting of European socialists in Madrid, the Labour leader mistakenly praised him for authoring a Commons motion on EU citizens' rights, which had actually been tabled by the Conservative MP Alberto Costa.[5] The Commission had no more faith in Corbyn's grasp of the issues. When he visited Brussels in February 2018, he seemed out of his depth. Martin Selmayr was staggered to discover that Corbyn did not even have the prime minister's mobile number. 'Mr Corbyn looked at Martin like he came from another planet,' said an EU official who sat in the meetings. 'Keir Starmer knew a lot, but Jeremy Corbyn didn't sound like he really knew what the withdrawal agreement and the political declaration were.'

This was disputed by LOTO. 'I remember being on the train with him down to Plymouth and he read the entire deal and the political declaration from cover to cover on a Saturday morning,' one close aide recalled. 'He thought it was a big sellout that could lead to a race to the bottom –

and that our negotiating team had the wool pulled over their eyes.' The same aide did acknowledge, though, that Corbyn's abilities were in decline: 'He got worn down over time and lost his mojo.'

The cross-party talks continued the following day, Thursday 4 April, in the Cabinet Office, but without the leaders present. The negotiations were established as a formal government committee to consult with the opposition. The civil service treated it the same way as they had the Lib-Lab pact in the 1970s and the coalition talks in 2010. Officials were so excited they ordered luxury sandwiches from a catering range ministers had never seen before. Keir Starmer recalled, 'The first time I went, they had these really fantastic sandwiches. The next time, they're lesser grade sandwiches. Eventually the sandwiches were removed. By the time we got to the last meeting, it was water and a digestive biscuit.'[6]

David Lidington led for the government, suggesting they tackle each of Labour's asks. 'There was goods regulation, customs, services regulation, security, agencies, workers' rights, environmental protection and a second referendum,' a senior government official recalled. 'Those are the eight things we talked about.'

They began with customs. Starmer explained that Labour wanted a comprehensive customs union and stated that the words 'permanent customs union' needed to be included in any cross-party deal. This was where Team May's mask slipped. Lidington and Barwell argued that the backstop amounted to a customs union in all but name. Indeed, as Barwell admitted later, 'The political declaration effectively committed the government to what the World Trade Organisation would term a customs union, but a novel one that allowed for an independent trade policy.'[7] The point was reinforced by Oliver Robbins, who was on hand to provide advice. This was emphatically not what cabinet ministers were told, either at Chequers the previous July, or in November when they were asked to endorse the deal. A cabinet minister said, 'In the Labour talks, Olly was saying, "Legally, under GATT [the General Agreement on Tariffs and Trade], this is a customs union. We've just called it a customs arrangement." That isn't what they were saying at Chequers.' Barclay, the sole Brexiteer on the government team, felt Robbins had misled ministers. Barwell conceded in his memoir that the words 'customs union' were not deployed to describe May's deal 'because the phrase had become toxic for many Conservative MPs'.[8]

To some in Labour, Starmer's insistence on the wording was superfluous; what mattered was the substance. One member of LOTO said, 'They can call it "Alan" if they want to, but it needs to have a common external tariff and comply with the WTO definition of a customs union.' However, there was suspicion that the Number 10 negotiators were trying to keep May's moribund deal alive. 'The first few meetings were spent with them trying to sell us the deal,' a Labour source said. 'Saying, "If you look hard enough, it's much better than you think".'

Topic two was alignment with the single market. Rebecca Long-Bailey pressed for improvements to workers' rights and environmental standards and a guarantee that these would be no lower in the UK than the EU. The negotiations focused, in part, on how to give domestic legal force to any deal. Starmer questioned how they could be embedded. 'Let's be honest – Boris Johnson has said that we should junk half of this stuff,' he complained.[9] Labour wanted separate legislation on workers' rights with the political declaration written into the government's withdrawal bill. Some called it the 'Boris lock'. Labour called it 'sustainability'.

Starmer also pushed for full alignment with EU rules. It was down to Robbins and his officials to point out that there were negotiating risks in committing to alignment without also securing additional market access, something Brussels was not going to concede.[10] It was the first example of what Tory ministers saw as an 'education process' for the Labour team in the realities of what had really been going on for the last two years. A Number 10 adviser recalled, 'Labour had no fucking clue what they were talking about.' A cabinet minister agreed: 'I had forgotten what it was like. Even the best opposition spokesman is bound to know less than the minister because you are not living it every day.'

On security cooperation and British membership of European agencies, Barwell said, 'We quickly convinced them that we agreed with them. The problem was with the European Union, not us, once we'd explained the detail of what we'd tried, and why certain things hadn't been achievable. Olly was very good at that. On workers' rights, basically, we were prepared to concede what they were asking for.'

Starmer's biggest demand was for a referendum. In the very first meeting, he told the prime minister, 'If you want a stable majority that is going to get the deal over the line, and then get all of the implementation done, it will need to hold for many votes. If you want a stable majority, you're going to have to embrace it because you're not getting a majority of Labour MPs on board if you don't have an ability to go back to the public on this.' Starmer knew May's views but tried to pre-empt them: 'I completely appreciate that in principle we are in a different place, but we've got to be honest about where the numbers are.'

'Let's concentrate on substance first,' May replied. Starmer, who had dealt with her when she was home secretary, told aides it was 'Classic Theresa May'. He had more respect for her than many in her own party, but her 'let's not get into that' response felt inauspicious to the shadow Brexit secretary.

It was Barclay who pointed out that the purpose of the negotiations was to find a compromise which could win a Commons majority without a confirmatory vote. 'If we were prepared to concede a second referendum, we wouldn't have to talk to you,' the Brexit secretary said. 'We'd have just got our deal through. Your MPs are queuing up to tell us they'll vote for our deal with a second referendum.'

After the meeting, the Tories tried to write up what they thought they had learned of Labour's wish list to find a mutually acceptable landing zone. On several subjects, it was still not clear. Before the talks Milne, who was a full-blown Lexiteer, had briefed the media that it was Labour policy to end free movement. In the room, Starmer suggested he wanted to reopen the issue. The shadow Brexit secretary was clearly fixated on a referendum, an idea which seemed to leave Milne cold. 'I did not see them have cross words in the room,' a cabinet minister said. The looks were enough. 'There were a number of occasions where I would catch Seumas Milne's eye and I would think: *I don't think he's on the same page as Keir*,' another cabinet minister said. 'In the same way as in the Red Army you always had a political commissar next to the officer to make sure that the officer doesn't tell the troops to retreat, he was there. It wasn't the case that he would put a bullet in the back of Keir's head if he didn't obey orders, but you did sometimes get that impression.' A Downing Street official said, 'Seumas Milne told one of our political people there that he had voted for Brexit.'

From Starmer's viewpoint, the Tories were also divided. Lidington and Hammond seemed driven by fear that May would fall and be replaced by something worse. Lidington appeared optimistic, Hammond hopeful but not optimistic. Barclay, Starmer thought, just wanted to get Labour to back the existing deal. Both Downing Street and Labour wanted to 'Boris proof' any agreement to ensure a Johnson government could not unpick it.

Starmer also unearthed Tory tensions when he quizzed them about their priorities. The Conservatives wanted the benefits of a customs union but also an independent trade policy. 'Assuming the EU won't agree to that, what's your default?' he asked. 'Which is your priority?' It seemed to him that Lidington would opt for a customs union, Barclay for an independent trade policy. 'David Lidington would say something, and then Julian Smith the chief whip would pull a face,' he recalled.[11] Andrew Fisher said, 'You'd love to play poker with some of these people. Some of them almost had their head in their hands when things were being said. Julian Smith, every time somebody said, "Oh, well that won't get through Parliament", or, "We think we could get that through Parliament", he was going, "Oh, God" … as if to say, "You haven't got a clue."'[12]

On Friday 5 April, Barwell took the same route as Penny Mordaunt earlier that week and snuck through the link door from Number 10 to the Cabinet Office and out into the street via 70 Whitehall. A broadcast correspondent thrust a microphone into his face and asked how the talks were going. He bluffed: 'I'm a civil servant. I can't comment.' The reporter did not notice the unmarked brown envelope he was carrying. It contained a letter outlining the government's initial offer to Labour, which he was taking over the road to LOTO. 'I was laughing to myself as I walked off down the street,' he recalled.

Starmer and Long-Bailey responded coldly, but the following day they set out specific concerns that the government should enshrine workers' rights in domestic law, change the political declaration and complained the Tories had simply restated their position on customs. Barwell could see they had a point; the Tory wording had been deliberately ambiguous given the sensitivities on their own side. The Conservatives also enjoyed a masterpiece of obfuscatory drafting in Labour's response on a referendum: 'There is growing support in Parliament – especially in opposition parties – that any deal should be put to a confirmatory vote. Labour has made clear that we would back a public vote for any deal we did not believe protected UK living standards and industry.'[13] The first sentence was a nod to Starmer's demands, the second suggested it might not be necessary.

The government sent a short note back, clarifying that they were prepared to 'seek changes to the political declaration', and to see agreements 'entrenched in UK law'. The key line was the clarification that the government was offering 'the benefits of a customs union in all scenarios' and 'to enshrine this commitment in domestic legislation'.[14] Had it leaked, the reaction of the ERG and others might have been enough to end May's premiership there and then.

After the first session, there was a change in personnel on both sides which injected new energy. John McDonnell and Philip Hammond were added to discuss financial issues, along with Michael Gove and Sue Hayman, his shadow on the environment. The idea came from Lucy Powell and Nick Boles, who believed the work they had done on Common Market 2.0, which Labour had ended up voting for, would be the natural basis of any cross-party deal. Oliver Letwin introduced Gove to Powell and, three days after he left the party, Boles set up a WhatsApp group, called 'Mating Porcupines' to describe the spiky and awkward couplings under way in the Cabinet Office. Powell gave Gove McDonnell's mobile number and the environment secretary texted the shadow chancellor suggesting that the two sides add their Treasury and environment spokesmen. 'The purpose was not so much to get Philip in but to get McDonnell in, not so much to get Sue in as to get Gove in,' a source said. 'Lucy thought that McDonnell in would help deliver the Labour Party, Michael in would [also] help.'

Throughout the talks the members of Mating Porcupines operated a back channel, secret until now, which linked Powell, Letwin and Boles with Gove, David Lidington and Julian Smith. This group was also in touch with James McBride, a former Labour staffer who had worked on the Norway option for Hanbury Strategy, a public affairs company hired by Boles. McBride was crucial since he was close to Andrew Fisher, Corbyn's head of policy and a member of the negotiating team. It was Fisher who suggested to Gavin Barwell, on 8 April, that McDonnell, Hayman, Hammond and Gove be added to the cast list.

The Mating Porcupines group was the source of advice to negotiators on both sides, able to cut through some of the performative drama and allow discussions to take place about the talks without Starmer present. 'There were nightly calls with Lidington, Michael and with Julian and then to Lucy and then to McBride,' a source said. 'It was quite an intensive process.' Fisher, via McBride, was 'able to say, for instance, when the Tories came out with something completely useless', a source said. The message would then go to Gove and Lidington. In his role as matchmaker, Boles felt he had more influence now he had quit the Tories than he ever had inside the party. Letwin recalled, 'We tried to make sure that each party to those negotiations knew what were really the bottom lines of the other side, in an effort for them to be able to consummate some deal that didn't cross the red lines of either side. There were moments when I became very optimistic that was exactly going to happen.'[15]

Tutored by Powell, Gove made a simple argument with force when the talks resumed on 9 April: 'There is a sufficient amount that both sides can agree on to get the withdrawal agreement bill through and then a future Labour prime minister can always, if he wants to, go for a full-fat customs union. And a future Tory prime minister if they want to can always go for Canada plus.'

Gove sought to impress the Labour contingent with his knowledge of their party, holding a Socratic dialogue with himself as he mapped out how the different factions might respond. He had been a Labour Party member during the 1983 election, but this performance was greeted with a mixture of amusement and irritation by Starmer and his colleagues. 'He had a profound misunderstanding of Labour politics,' a Labour source said. 'What he thought we could say to our members and to the PLP to get everything over the line, particularly on things like customs, was well wide of the mark.'

Yet from the start Gove seemed to develop a curious bromance with McDonnell. In one monologue, designed to dissuade Labour demands for alignment with single market rules, Gove said, 'I can't see why you would want to have single market alignment on financial services. Surely the whole point of electing a Labour government is to have democratic control over international capital and the last thing anyone in the movement would want is to have the neo-liberal rules of Brussels imposed on a democratic socialist government.' McDonnell replied, 'Thank you, comrade.'

On another occasion, McDonnell said he had to leave. 'I've got a hospital appointment at four o'clock,' the shadow chancellor explained. 'It's a matter of life and death.' There was a momentary pause before McDonnell delivered the punchline: 'If I don't make it, my wife will kill me.' Despite his jokes, McDonnell seemed, to the Tories, to be serious about exploring a deal. 'McDonnell was acting as the convenor and compromiser on the Labour side,' a cabinet minister said. 'He was trying to bring together different positions.' Barwell was 'very impressed with him'.[16] Privately, McDonnell was less optimistic, complaining as he headed to one session that talking to the Tories was 'like negotiating with a company going into administration'.[17]

Starmer's stance was that Labour would need a confirmatory public vote on no-deal or any deal that was 'bad for the economy'. This was a sufficiently nebulous construction that Barwell asked, 'Does that mean that if we had a deal that you judge was good for the economy, it would not need a second referendum?'

Starmer said, 'We'd have to consult that party.'

Milne agreed with Barwell's proposition: 'That is the logic of what's in the letter we've written to you.'

The one sour note of the second round of talks came at the end when Julian Smith tried to get the Labour team to agree a timetable for the withdrawal agreement bill and was rebuffed. Starmer and McDonnell both wanted to see draft legislation and changes to the political declaration first. Barwell realised there was very little hope that May could secure Brexit by 22 May, after which the UK would have to take part in European elections. They were an existential threat to a Conservative Party which had spent three years failing to leave the EU.

While the talks continued with minimal leaking, the pressure built on May in both Brussels and Westminster. On 5 April, the prime minister wrote to Donald Tusk asking for a new extension until 30 June. The following day Tony Blair contacted Barwell to warn that EU leaders wanted a longer extension. As soon as the prime minister arrived in Brussels on the 10th, Tusk confirmed her worst fears and warned that Emmanuel Macron had gone AWOL, resisting attempts by the Council president to contact him.

May sat, once more, in Tim Barrow's residence as the other leaders on the European Council decided Britain's fate without her. This was, if anything, a more unpleasant experience for Barwell than the first extension, not least because MPs wrongly assumed the Europeans would oblige with alacrity. 'On the second occasion, it was not a done deal that was going to happen,' Barwell recalled. 'There were people in the room who were trying to stop it happening.'

Top of the list, of course, was Macron, playing his signature role as the Gallic stage villain. The French president stepped in when António Costa, the Portuguese premier, advocated an extension for 'as long as possible'. Macron said, 'This is absolutely ludicrous!' He pushed for a short extension in the hope that would force the deal through. May's team feared, instead, that it would encourage the hardliners to believe no-deal was within their grasp. The two officials in the room, Jeppe Tranholm-Mikkelsen for the Council and Martin Selmayr for the Commission, were in despair. It was Angela Merkel who finally intervened to force a resolution. The Council agreed an extension to 31 October, much longer than May had wanted. By moving the deadline back another six months, any hope she had of persuading MPs to back her plan to avoid no-deal was gone. Patience with May was wearing very thin in Brussels.

Her bigger problem, James Johnson's polling soon revealed, was that this extension, which killed the revised Brexit date of 12 April, marked the final breach between May and the electorate. Tory support and May's personal approval rating dropped off a cliff. 'The key moment for the polling decline is actually 12 April, not 29 March, when we went past the second extension,' he said. 'Before that, people were willing to say, "Give her a chance." But that was when the polls changed and opinion shifted.' The shift coincided with the formal launch of the Brexit Party, which went from a start-up to a political powerhouse in just three weeks.

Back in London, Barwell met Andrew Fisher on 11 April. The two chief sherpas knew each other already since Fisher had been an activist in Barwell's old seat of Croydon Central, attending his public meetings to make the case for the hard left. Fisher was always polite and Barwell had a high opinion of him. 'He's across the detail,' the chief of staff told colleagues. During seven weeks of talks, they met in May's and Corbyn's Commons offices. 'Insofar as progress is made, the progress is really made between Barwell and Andrew Fisher,' a cabinet minister said.

Working groups had also been set up on the environment, the economy and financial services. Relations were cordial in the environment group, where Gove used Labour's Sue Hayman to help him win ongoing Whitehall battles with Philip Hammond. Hayman raised a series of issues of concern to green pressure groups and NGOs. 'The irony is most, though not all, of the things that she wanted were things Michael was going to do anyway, or things he had been trying to persuade Phil we should do,' a Tory source said. When Hayman had finished speaking, Hammond handed Gove a note. It said, 'Michael, how much did you pay her?'

Gove was also able to persuade the Labour team to drop their demand for Britain to copy all EU environmental rules. 'On environmental protections, Michael did quite a skilful job,' a Number 10 official said. 'They were initially asking for dynamic alignment, and he found a few good examples of things where they wouldn't want to follow EU rules. He managed to get them off dynamic alignment.'

Starmer was absent for the third round of talks on 12 April, leaving McDonnell to lead for Labour. Barwell recalled, 'The addition of John made a massive difference.' The shadow chancellor was perceptive, comparing the Tories' use of 'constructive ambiguity' in their language on customs, to a 'composite Labour conference motion'.[18] He also teased Starmer behind his back, revealing, 'At every meeting we're obliged to raise the issue of a confirmatory vote.'[19]

They made good progress on workers' rights, the government agreeing to put a statutory duty on ministers to enhance protections through the joint committee which would govern UK–EU relations after Brexit (an alternative to reopening the withdrawal agreement). This was the nearest Labour was going to get to a 'Boris lock'. 'What you could not do is make something proof against a general election result that gives a government a majority and a mandate,' a cabinet minister explained. 'But what we did offer were a number of legislative changes that would have ensured that it would become a legal duty to pursue certain objectives following the political declaration.' More immediately, the government also agreed to draw up a separate bespoke bill to enhance workers' rights.

However, when, three days later, Downing Street and Labour swapped their latest papers, it was clear that the government had still not given adequate reassurances on customs. May held a conference call with ministers on 17 April, where they agreed to plough on, 'but only for lack of a better option,' Barwell recalled.

In the Labour team WhatsApp group, there was little enthusiasm for intensive talks. 'I'm due to go on holiday!' Hayman complained when the prospect of talks over the Easter recess were proposed. 'Our team ... ALL OF THEM ... need a break,' Corbyn insisted.[20]

That evening Andrew Fisher raced home to watch Tottenham Hotspur's Champions League quarter-final with Manchester City in his local pub. As half-time approached, City were already 3–2 up, but Spurs were winning the tie on away goals.[21] Then Oliver Letwin phoned him. 'It was the most surreal conversation I've ever had,' he recalled. 'Have you got a minute to chat?' Letwin asked. 'Yes, I've got fifteen,' said Fisher as the whistle went for the interval. 'We had this conversation and he's telling me, "Theresa May is doing this and, actually, if you offer this—"' The chief porcupine was still trying to get the two sides to mate. 'Oliver Letwin, I think, genuinely did want a compromise,' Fisher said. But, 'he had no control over the Conservative Party' and 'he was very isolated'.[22]

On 23 April, ministers met in person. Williamson, Liz Truss, Chris Grayling and Penny Mordaunt called for the withdrawal agreement bill to be introduced, to dare Labour to vote it down. Julian Smith and Andrea Leadsom suggested a package of measures also be announced based on what had been agreed with Labour, plus proposals designed to appeal to the DUP and something more on alternative arrangements for Tory backbenchers.[23]

In the fourth round of talks, that day, Smith suggested they introduce an amended bill, but let MPs decide on the two most controversial issues – customs and a referendum, on the basis that it was 'better for things to be done to us than for us to do them'. The chief whip thought Parliament would back Labour on membership of a customs union but back the Tories in ruling out a referendum. 'John McDonnell seemed interested,' Barwell noted.[24]

Further ministerial calls followed on 26 April and 28 April, May wondering whether it was time to bring the talks to a close. In the end they agreed that Lidington would send another proposal to Labour outlining the specific changes they were proposing to the political declaration, the new clauses for the withdrawal agreement bill and draft clauses for the workers' rights bill.

This was the basis of discussions in the fifth negotiating session later on the 28th. Starmer seemed to be playing for time, saying Labour could not back a bill until a new deal had been agreed with Brussels. Milne, by contrast, wanted only 'proof of movement'. He felt there were PR advantages to negotiating at the heart of Whitehall on equal terms with the prime minister's team. To the irritation of McDonnell and Starmer, Milne delighted in using the front door to 70 Whitehall, performatively wading through the press scrum, while the shadow chancellor slipped out of the back unobserved. 'He thought it would make Jeremy look like a prime minister in waiting,' said a colleague. 'I wonder if he thought it was the only chance he would ever get to swan around like Billy Big Bollocks.'

As far as the Tories (and some on his own side) were concerned, Keir Starmer was the problem. From the very first meeting, the shadow Brexit secretary seemed to have one goal only, to get a referendum or to scupper the talks. Starmer raised the prospect of a referendum in every single meeting. 'You can read our politics; there is a section of our party that is committed to a referendum,' he explained.

Gove hit back, 'It's also the case that there is a section of the party, the respect the result group, that do want a deal and therefore it must be a judgement for you about where to draw these lines.'

Nonetheless, when Barwell and Fisher met on 1 May, to start work on a 'What We've Agreed' document, it was possible to imagine Labour not whipping against the withdrawal legislation. If this was the high point of the talks, the politics outside the negotiating room were now careening away from Theresa May.

On 1 May, the prime minister was in Northern Ireland attending the funeral of Lyra McKee, a journalist gunned down by a Real IRA sniper, reinforcing her views about the spiralling security concerns in the province. At home, she lost another cabinet minister over concerns about security. Steven Swinford, the deputy political editor of the *Telegraph*, revealed that the National Security Council had decided to hand Huawei, the Chinese telecoms giant, the green light to build part of Britain's 5G mobile phone network, despite security concerns. The story caused uproar since the proceedings of the NSC were supposed to be more tightly controlled than the perennially leaky cabinet.

Gavin Williamson, the defence secretary, was already a marked man. In June 2018, he and his special adviser, Rob Golledge, had been blamed for a *Mail on Sunday* story recounting a conversation Williamson had with senior officers, in which he boasted that he would bring down the PM if she did not give him £20 billion for the armed forces. 'I made her, and I can break her,' he said.

Without consulting May, Gavin Barwell and Mark Sedwill, the cabinet secretary who doubled as national security adviser, announced a leak inquiry, bouncing the PM into approving it retrospectively. For once it was a serious probe, precisely because Barwell wanted Williamson out. The security services discovered that Swinford had called half a dozen cabinet ministers. Of those calls, Williamson's was the first and the longest. A senior civil servant said, 'There was an eleven-minute conversation between Steve Swinford and Gavin Williamson in the only time window when the leak could have happened.'

Summoned to see May in her Commons office, Williamson arrived to find the prime minister seated at the vast table alongside Dominic Fortescue, the head of the government security group, who had conducted the leak inquiry, having been despatched to locate and interrogate Williamson. The defence secretary sat down opposite. To make it look like he was not the only cabinet minister facing a serious grilling, Helen MacNamara went to interview the very innocent Greg Clark. Poring over his extraordinarily dull WhatsApps, MacNamara found herself thinking: *Please tell me you have another phone.*

The meeting was staged to ensure that Williamson had none of his special advisers present. Downing Street expected fireworks. Peter Hill, May's PPS, was so frightened of Williamson's temper, that he refused to sit in the meeting. The defence secretary immediately protested his innocence: 'It wasn't me!'

May calmly reeled off the evidence and said, 'Gavin, it's particularly upsetting that you have done this, given how we've worked together. It's clear to me that you have breached national security, you cannot serve in the cabinet, you're going to have to resign.'

Williamson played for time: 'Can I have some time to think about it?'

May, matter-of-factly, delivered the bullet. Looking at her watch, she said, 'It's being announced in five minutes. You'll be staying here until then.' She always planned to sack him on the spot and ensure Williamson would not have time to spin his dismissal before it was announced. He could not believe the woman he had helped install, someone he believed he could push around, had him in checkmate. 'She was pleasingly ruthless,' a witness said. 'He went absolutely bananas.'

Realising the game was up, Williamson got to his feet and leaned across the table and pointed his finger in May's face. He said coldly, 'You're going to regret this. I'm going to end you.'

May kept her composure. 'Thank you, Gavin,' she said. 'You'll be staying in here.'

Williamson always maintained his innocence, insisting Swinford already had the story when he rang and that most of their conversation concerned the upcoming local elections. Senior sources say the original tip-off came from one of the defence secretary's special advisers. But Williamson's assertion that he did not even have Swinford's number in his mobile phone raised suspicions that he protested too much. Swinford was a prolific story-getter and Williamson a prolific briefer. His colleagues had little sympathy for Williamson, who had helped remove Michael Fallon to get the job in the first place.

May was refusing to bring down the curtain on her premiership. On 2 May, the electorate began to do it for her. The local elections were a massacre for the Conservatives. Party strategists predicted the loss of 800 to 1,000 councillors. In the end they haemorrhaged 1,330, losing control of 44 councils at the same time.

It might have been worse: the Brexit Party was not contesting these seats and the Tory national vote share was the same as that of Labour, 28 per cent. Corbyn's party also lost six councils and 84 councillors, a sign that the electorate was punishing both main parties for the paralysis in Parliament. 'I think it only really sank in for Labour with the May local elections and then European elections that they too own the pain of delivering this,' a senior Number 10 political aide recalled. 'I think they thought they could just sit back and the Tories would suffer. They were losing seats in heartland areas and Brexity areas and you could see that was a surprise to them.'

Amid the Tory gloom, there were signs that the electoral map had been redrawn by Brexit. The Conservatives actually gained seats in pro-Leave areas of North-East Derbyshire; they topped the poll in Stoke-on-Trent and even took control of Walsall council. Nonetheless, Brexiteers nervously looked at the big winners, the pro-Remain Liberal Democrats, who gained 10 councils and 744 councillors (and the Greens, who picked up 198 seats), and saw a new threat to Brexit.

In an ERG meeting that week, Owen Paterson said, 'We are in a jumbo jet heading straight for the ground and we need to wrest control of the aircraft ASAP.' The local election results prompted Iain Duncan Smith to finally go public with a demand that May resign.

*   *   *

Before the sixth meeting on 6 May, the Tories circulated the 'What We've Agreed' document. Leaks suggested the two sides were close to agreement. In reality, there were still fundamental differences on customs and a referendum. To put Starmer on the spot, the Conservatives asked him to name Labour's price for a deal. 'We essentially said, "Tell us what you really, really want and then we will tell you whether or not it is do-able",' a minister recalled.

This produced a moment recounted with glee by everyone who saw it. Starmer said, 'We are still unhappy with the language in the document you've set out on customs.'

Barwell, very politely, replied, 'Just so you're aware, I just cut and pasted it from Jeremy Corbyn's letter of 22 April.' Starmer had been caught out theatrically objecting to his own demands. He sat 'po-faced' as 'everyone burst out laughing'. A witness said, 'Keir was busted. There was basically nothing we could have said, including cutting and pasting what they said, that would have got Keir Starmer [on board], whose prime motive was to crash the talks, because he didn't want to deliver Brexit.' Starmer's team briefed the media that what was on offer was 'politically and legally worthless'.[25]

A cabinet minister in the talks said, 'The two issues where we couldn't bridge the gap were customs and the referendum.' A Downing Street sage observed, 'Chequers was ultimately a customs union, but we couldn't call it that. And Labour kept calling for a customs union, but what they were asking for wasn't one.'

In round seven of the talks, on 7 May, Steve Barclay questioned whether there was any point continuing. The Brexit secretary was 'very sceptical', telling colleagues, 'There's no good them helping us get the meaningful vote won and then killing us down the road.' If a deal was done, it would have to hold together through every stage of a parliamentary bill. 'I think Steve had a deep mistrust of the Labour Party's motives,' a cabinet colleague said.

But when he voiced this in the negotiations, McDonnell gave a powerful response: 'We are not taking all the political pain of doing a deal with Tories for that deal then to collapse. If we say to you, "We're in", we're in to the end to get the thing over the line.' For that reason, however, McDonnell added, 'We are not going to therefore take the decision to say, "We're in" lightly. It's going to take quite a lot.' Another cabinet minister said, 'I think they did want to make this work. We did. It was not a pretend exercise.'

Starmer, in turn, had grave doubts about the lengths the government was prepared to go to. He had warned Lidington, 'If your intention is to present the same two documents to Parliament and get a majority, it isn't going to work. You're going to have to change at least the political declaration.' By the time of the second meeting, the Tories were only promising to use their 'best endeavours' to get changes. Fearful of a Brexiteer successor to May, this was not enough for Starmer. 'The first part of any lock against an incoming prime minister has to be, at the very least, that changes have been secured which the EU27 have agreed.' He wrote to Lidington, seeking to gauge how serious he was. Lidington called him and said, 'Yes, we are serious about this.'

Starmer kept pressing. 'How long is it going to take for these changes to be negotiated with the EU?' he asked. Robbins questioned his Brussels counterparts and was told 'four to six weeks' for simple changes. Starmer said later, 'I didn't see how we could sign up to anything that didn't have a different agreement we were voting on. Everyone goes on about the referendum and me being difficult. But that was actually what we were talking about most of the time. I couldn't see the Labour Party signing off on promises by the government to see if they could get changes and in the meantime vote through the deal. I was worried that they hadn't done the groundwork with the EU.'

Some officials in the talks regarded Starmer's position as disingenuous. 'Keir was quite enjoying playing with the Tories,' one said. 'He knew they needed him – and I suspect had no intention of doing any deal at any point.'

But the government never put Starmer on the back foot. As the negotiations descended into the weeds, Geoffrey Cox's original strategy for the talks had been lost. 'His take was that we should offer Labour everything,' said a civil servant in the talks. 'Ask what they want, give it to them and they can't refuse to vote for it. But, over time, we got into these talks, with the government trying to give away as little as possible. Had the government gone in and said to Keir, you can have whatever you want, would they have gone for it?' The conclusion must be that a demand for a second referendum, Starmer's bottom line, would have scuppered the negotiations, but moving swiftly to give Labour what they wanted in other areas would have piled political pressure on them to let the Commons decide on a referendum.

Some of May's aides and several cabinet ministers feared Labour were milking the talks, stringing the Number 10 team along. Raoul Ruparel always thought the efforts were doomed. He expressed concern to colleagues that Barwell and Lidington were 'putting too much skin in the game'. He argued that the more concessions they gave Labour, the more they could use against Number 10. He was not alone. A Downing Street aide said, 'We gave them workers' rights, we set out our position on a potential compromise. They just sucked stuff out of us and they got us to a position where they could drag us far enough away [from Tory MPs] that it killed us.' Those in the talks shared some of these frustrations. 'What concerned me is that they were much less willing to volunteer specific counter proposals,' a cabinet minister said. 'They wanted us to make the running the whole time.' Cabinet colleagues defend Lidington against the charge of naivety. 'I think he felt he had an obligation to try, try and try again,' one said. Barwell, a colleague recalled, 'always held out more hope that it would work than most'.

Julian Smith warned the Labour contingent that they faced 'electoral disaster' as well as the Conservatives if they failed to get Brexit through. 'It's in your interests to resolve this.' He had a 'fairly big bust-up' with Starmer in the lower committee corridor over the shadow Brexit secretary's tendency to argue like 'an exceptionally good barrister' over the detail, while missing the bigger picture. 'Where do you think this is going to end?' Smith shouted. Later, he concluded he had underestimated Starmer's ambition. To become Labour leader, Starmer had to champion a referendum and oppose a deal with the Tories. That was Starmer's assessment of *his* interests, that was where *he* thought it would end.

Despite the clashes, when Starmer's father fell ill and died during the talks, both Smith and Steve Barclay wrote him 'very personal letters'. Starmer recalled, 'Not just condolences, but about what happened when their father had died. That was a real moment. That really matters.'[26]

With the politicians unable to find a way through, their most senior aides began a series of secret meetings to try to do their own deal. On 9 May, Barwell, Gibb and Robbins met up with Milne and Fisher in Corbyn's office. The Downing Street delegation slipped into Norman Shaw North through the Derby Gate entrance next to the Red Lion pub. This was prudent but was a remarkable gesture on the part of May's aides. Jonno Evans, who had replaced Catherine Page as May's principal private secretary for Europe, also joined some of the sessions, along with James Wild, an adviser to Lidington. 'They were much more productive,' one of the participants said.

Milne described a referendum as 'a totem' in the party but when Gibb pressed him on what he thought about the idea, Milne replied, 'Opinions differ.'[27] With Starmer not present, Milne was 'more explicit that he was trying to find a way that doesn't involve a referendum', a senior Tory said. Fisher thought one might be needed to keep the Labour Party intact.

The following day Karie Murphy turned up, her mood as inflamed as her hair. Corbyn's gatekeeper played up her working-class credentials and said, 'I'm going to call through all the shit and just tell you, I'm a trade union negotiator.' She then relayed details of conversations on her weekly train from London to Glasgow to care for her sick mother. Her fellow passengers were sick of hearing about Brexit. 'Forget the technicalities,' she said, 'they only want it over and fucking done with.'[28] Murphy criticised the constant 'hokey cokey' of documents flying backwards and forwards and demanded a decision be made. Barwell hit back, wanting to know what it would actually take to get Labour over the line.

Despite Murphy's bluntness, these talks were good-natured. As ex-journalists of a similar vintage, Gibb and Milne had known each other for years and trust had developed between Barwell and Fisher. Fisher sat, laptop open, asking technical questions, 'the body language of someone that was investing a lot of time, someone who is serious'. The two sides got as far as discussing how they would jointly handle the communications of announcing that they had a deal. 'Nothing leaked out of those meetings,' a source said. The secrecy unnerved Julian Smith, who warned Barwell it was 'toxic' to bypass the cabinet.

Milne's view was that they needed to demonstrate progress, but he wasn't sure Labour could yet announce that they would vote for the bill. Barwell wrote a memo to May and Smith outlining the options:

1) A deal with Labour and a second reading of the bill on 22 May
2) With Labour's consent, announce the date of the second reading after the recess and table a programme motion to show that the legislation could be passed by the summer

3) 'Preferential votes'

4) Proceed with the bill on 22 May without a deal

When he discussed the options with Andrew Fisher on 13 May, Barwell added a fifth: breaking the withdrawal agreement into several smaller bills. Fisher was clear that Labour's preference was for indicative votes. That afternoon, in the eighth round of talks, the small group heard the same view from Milne. One of the Tories present said, 'He was making it clear that some kind of indicative vote process which could take responsibility for the decisions away from the leadership and put it in the hands of Parliament was the preferred route.' There was one problem: indicative votes would require the cooperation of the Labour whips' office. 'All nine of them were second referendum diehards.'

A government figure in the talks said, 'It felt like the Seumas-Andrew Fisher-world were engaging seriously but truthfully didn't understand the issues well enough to know whether they were getting screwed.' A civil servant who witnessed the interactions said, 'The Milne Labour crowd and the Barwell Tories could have done a deal, did want to do the deal, but they didn't feel they were able to.' There was never a likelihood of a 'Rose Garden moment' with May and Corbyn announcing agreement like Cameron and Clegg in 2010. But an ally of Milne said, 'What could have been possible was if the agreements reached between negotiating teams were handed to backbenchers on either side, who put them forward as amendments, then we both whip in a soft way in the hope that it gets through.' Barwell observed, 'Their negotiating team contained people who you felt, privately, wanted Brexit to go ahead but without Labour's fingerprints being on it.'[29]

However, it was also becoming clear that, even during the time of the talks, the sands were shifting on the Labour benches. A cabinet minister said, 'McDonnell, particularly, came to recognise that it was impossible to put a deal together that would satisfy the Labour Party without doing more on the second referendum than we were prepared to offer.'

More fundamentally, six weeks into historic talks between the government and the official opposition, neither group of politicians and officials was able to carry their MPs with them. 'They couldn't deliver their votes and we couldn't deliver our votes,' Robbie Gibb said. Starmer was quick to seize on the parliamentary arithmetic. 'If there's no second referendum, there is a group of Labour MPs – and in my opinion it's over 100, it may be as high as 150 – who will not vote for your deal,' he said. 'I'm assuming that the compromises you're going to make on customs will reduce the number of Tories who will vote for this. You begin to run into a danger that there aren't enough combined Conservative and Labour MPs to get through whatever our compromise is.' Barwell recalled, 'That is what ultimately killed the talks.'

On the morning of 14 May, the group of nine cabinet ministers who May had chosen to consult about the negotiations held fractious discussions. Michael Gove argued that they should fight for compromise, since leaving the EU would scupper the rise of the Brexit Party of Nigel Farage, who he branded 'a charlatan'. He added, 'Keir Starmer is harder to please than anyone I've ever met.' Liz Truss bluntly warned that the decision approaching was one of binary extremes: no-deal or revoke.[30]

That afternoon, May met Corbyn to tell him the government would hold a second reading of the bill in the week beginning 4 June, just after the Whitsun recess, but would switch to indicative votes if that was what Labour preferred. Nick Brown, the Labour chief whip, told her she could pass the bill if she also offered a referendum. 'If I was prepared to support a referendum I would have done it weeks ago and saved myself a lot of pain,' she replied.[31]

On the 15th, Barwell, Gibb and Robbins met Milne and Fisher to work out which issues should be settled by indicative votes and which could be addressed in the bill, but by now the process was breaking down. Nick Brown told Julian Smith he would not support any indicative votes.

Opposition to continuing had been growing in Labour ranks for weeks. By the time they entered the third week of seven, Corbyn was asking how Labour might escape the talks. Like the EU, the Labour Party did not trust May to deliver on her promises and worried what Boris Johnson would do next. Fisher explained, 'Even if they'd offered everything we wanted, there was just no guarantee it would happen. Why would we risk a huge backlash from the PLP, our own support base within the party, and our own voter coalition, for signing up to something with Theresa May, that is then going to fall apart the next week?'[32]

While the Tories thought they were getting somewhere, in reality Labour high command took the decision to pull out of the talks as early as 8 May, even before the small group meetings of aides had begun. On that day, Corbyn's operations manager Janet Chapman circulated a note summing up the conclusions of the meeting. The departure would be 'choreographed ... due to disarray of government'.[33]

Through their secret back channel, Boles, Letwin and Powell lobbied hard that the only viable solution was Common Market 2.0, something which Labour had already endorsed but which the government did not offer Corbyn in full. 'We were smashing our heads against the wall because it was so obvious that the only place they could land was roughly where Common Market 2.0 was, particularly on customs,' said one of those involved. Crucially, this did not require Number 10 to explicitly endorse a customs union, since the proposal (which Labour had previously supported) talked about a customs arrangement with a common external tariff and the union customs code. Barwell could have made Labour's life more awkward by adopting exactly the same language as Common Market 2.0. 'Labour signed up to it once, and they did say, "Yes, we will sign up to it in a cross-party deal",' one of the Mating Porcupines group said. 'The problem was getting the May government to adopt those words. They kept saying different words such as "which achieves the same outcome" or "which is like ..." But those weren't the words Labour signed off on.'

The final straw came on 16 May, when Barwell sent Fisher the proposed text of the government's legislation on customs. It was nowhere near what Labour needed. 'Seumas and Andrew would come back from meetings and we'd go through their notes,' a colleague said. 'Then we'd get a piece of paper that then didn't have [what was agreed]. May had obviously said No.' Corbyn ordered his team, 'Shut this down, this is nonsense, this is mad.'[34]

One of the most unusual exercises in cross-party cooperation in recent British history came to an end on 17 May. A senior official in Number 10 recalled, 'I remember the morning meeting. The discussion was, if we offer Labour a customs union will that be enough to get them over the line? To which the answer was no. If we were to offer them a second referendum, would that get them over the line? To which the answer was no. That might have been enough for Starmer but Corbyn wouldn't have wanted it. At that point, it was basically checkmate. There is no way you can move. My view was anything that will get Labour over the line will destroy the government or render it irrelevant. I just think the whole exercise was pointless.'

If it ended with frustration in Number 10, it did so, on Labour's side, in a cascade of farce. Corbyn and his aides were due to meet at 8.30 a.m. at the Labour leader's favourite neighbourhood café, before a short journey to record a speech at 9.30 a.m., which would be dropped unannounced on social media, kicking the stool away from May. The plan was upended by incompetence. As Jack Bond, Labour's social media man, and Jack McKenna, his spin doctor, waited in the café, they were informed that no one had booked Corbyn a car. Bond sent his father, a taxi driver, to the rescue. However, the leader did not appear until 9.20 a.m., fifty minutes late, Milne at 9.55 a.m., long after the clip was supposed to have been filmed. While they waited, Corbyn 'munched peaceably' on a quiche. His briefing only finished at 10.10 a.m. and the recorded message was cancelled. The press, who had been told to assemble for an announcement, were kept waiting for more than an hour and gave Corbyn a rough ride. 'That was terrible,' he complained afterwards.[35] It was also par for the course.

Corbyn had written to May declaring that 'the talks between us have gone as far as they can'. He blamed the failure to 'bridge important gaps' on customs and a referendum, as well as 'the increasing weakness and instability of your government', which had undermined Labour's trust that anything 'agreed between us' would be durable. Starmer said, 'They failed, mainly because we took the view the government couldn't deliver on it and, frankly, because you could never lock it against someone like Boris Johnson coming in.'[36]

However, the sub-*Thick of It* shenanigans in north London meant Downing Street had time to frame events their own way, issuing a statement blaming the collapse of talks on the lack of a 'common position in Labour about whether they want to deliver Brexit or hold a second referendum which could reverse it'.

Oliver Letwin blamed the failure of the talks on the total absence of mutual understanding or sympathy between May and Corbyn: 'If it had been David Cameron and Ed Miliband or John Major and Tony Blair … you can think of all sorts of pairings where probably that would have led … to a cross-party consensus, which probably then would have become the solution. But it wasn't to be.'[37] Some cabinet ministers wondered why May had not taken charge of the negotiations on which her future hung. 'I think that was a major fail by the prime minister,' one said. 'There was a consistent lack of personal engagement.' Her successor would demonstrate the benefits of direct contact and personal chemistry with other leaders.

In truth, the largest unbridgeable gaps were between both leaderships and their parties. A senior Number 10 official said, 'The [Labour] leader's office did not have the political room to do what they wanted to do, which was to get this done.'

Yet there were other ways to approach the talks. May never made Labour the big, bold public offer which Geoffrey Cox had recommended, a move that might have put pressure on Corbyn to account for his own choices. The government failed to follow the advice of the Mating Porcupines group, offering a deal which Labour had already voted for. 'Originally when we went into the cross-party talks it was a cold, hard policy to dip their hands in the blood too,' a Number 10 aide complained. 'Somehow it transmogrified into trying to find a genuine compromise. It seemed to me, even at the time, that there was nothing in it for Labour but to watch the tensions of it tear the Conservative Party apart.'

The Tories also failed to pin Labour down on a referendum – the choices on the ballot paper, the questions that would be asked. A Number 10 aide said, 'On the referendum, I have always thought that we should have forced them to choose. The whole point was that it was their weak spot and we should have just said to them, "What do you want to put in a referendum? Tell us what the question is going to be." Then we would have applied pressure on them and then try and get some of the Leave Labour MPs to come over to us and support an eventual deal.'

Like Robbins' negotiations with the EU, the cross-party talks and the document they generated was a technical compromise which represented a subtle triumph of the negotiator's art. 'There was a landing zone,' Barwell said. The agreement saw a deal on workers' rights and environmental protections. It would have led to Britain aligning with the EU on goods regulation (as Chequers envisaged), creating the benefits of a customs union without technical membership of it, but no alignment on services. It then left each side with a plan for the future the other regarded as a unicorn. The Tories could enter a general election promising to negotiate a free trade deal on services, something Labour regarded as impossible. Labour's manifesto would have promised membership of a customs union with a say on trade deals, something the Tories were confident the EU would not grant. But this deal was, by the spring of 2019, politically unpalatable for either main party. 'The final version of that document was something that most of the front benches of both parties could've lived with,' Barwell said. 'The problem with it was it probably wouldn't have commanded a majority in the House.'

Looking back, the failure of the talks killed the last chance of a soft Brexit. At that point, in mid-May, however, Labour felt it could block no-deal and win an election; Remainers felt they could get a referendum and overturn the 2016 result; and the ERG believed they could get a new leader who would secure no-deal.

The only certainty was that May had failed in the central mission she set herself. All that remained was the *coup de grâce*.

KNIVES OUT

The End of May

21 April to 24 May 2019

Labour stopped May's Brexit deal in its tracks, but it would be the Conservative Party who would finally force her from office. The prime minister's support, among the public and her MPs, had been in freefall since mid-April, when a poll suggested the Brexit Party, whose emergence was a direct response to May's failure to deliver on the referendum result, was on course to top the ballot in the upcoming European elections.

On 21 April, it was announced that the most senior grassroots activists would debate a motion of no confidence in May. Two days later, Graham Brady told the prime minister that moves were afoot on the 1922 executive to change the rules so that she could be challenged again – the result of Christopher Howarth's mission to filch the rulebook from the Bodleian. Brady suggested she name the date when she would stand down or engineer a no-confidence vote herself, as John Major had in 1995. This suggestion was greeted with 'a pretty punchy response,' Barwell recalled.[1] May made clear she had promised to go in exchange for votes which never materialised. 'I understand, Prime Minister,' Brady said. 'But the situation is ugly and my fear is that it is going to get worse.'

On 30 April, Brady returned to Downing Street. 'The party is angry, Prime Minister,' he warned. 'Colleagues' (the 1922 chairman's preferred description of MPs when at their least collegiate) were concerned that May would try to hang on to power if she did not get her deal through. At this, the prime minister snapped: 'If anyone thinks I'm sitting here trying to avoid getting Brexit done in order to cling on as long as possible, they really don't understand me!'[2] Her aides were sick of Brady's interventions. A political adviser said, 'You can't run a government with a weekly emissary from the executive of the '22.'

Two weeks later, Brady had had enough. On Saturday 11 May, he publicly called for May to set a date for her resignation. That same week, even the loyalists were heading for the lifeboats. Chris Grayling, who had served in Tory ranks alongside May since they were both councillors together twenty years earlier, privately told friends that she was finished.

On the 16th, the day before Corbyn pulled the plug on the cross-party talks, May met the executive of the 1922 Committee in Downing Street. Afterwards, Brady issued a statement announcing that, after the second reading of the bill, he and May would meet 'to agree a timetable for the election of a new leader of the Conservative Party'.

There was one last attempt to do a Brexit deal. May would put forward the withdrawal agreement bill, hung with the baubles her government had conceded to Labour. Letwin, Boles and the other Mating Porcupines were 'strongly encouraged' by May's team to try to build a coalition of support behind the plan in the cabinet. They immediately ran into problems. Key figures like Jeremy Hunt and Sajid Javid were no longer prepared to back the prime minister. 'It was nixed by the people running for leader,' said one.

The Downing Street team had only one card left. They could not offer a second referendum but Barwell, Lidington and Julian Smith were now of the view that giving Parliament a vote on a referendum, in exchange for backing May's deal, was the only way left of passing it. A fellow cabinet minister said, 'Julian thought a concessional referendum is what was required in order to win the vote.' Phillip Lee, an old friend, said Smith, a devout Remainer, 'struggled' with Brexit. 'Which is actually why, at the very end of the May administration, he tried to bump the Cabinet into supporting a second referendum … It was him.'[3]

The idea did make some progress with the Tory Bresisters who had held out against May in the three meaningful votes. In small groups, the rebels were worked on by the chief whip. In one of these meetings, Dominic Grieve, her most implacable opponent from the left of the party, agreed finally that he would support her. 'Yes, this will do,' he said, an intervention which took others with him. Most of the holdouts were persuaded. 'In the last seventy-two hours of Theresa's leadership, before she agreed to go, there was a real final attempt to do a deal,' a former minister said. 'It was Julian and Barwell trying to save the day. But she had the rug pulled from under her by the '22.'

As Starmer and others had calculated, a plan liable to win over the Tory Remainer rebels was likely to cost May more support at the other end from the Brexiteers. Labour MP Stephen Doughty, the Bresistance whip, had back channel talks with Smith and several cabinet ministers. He believed he could deliver 180 Labour votes for a referendum, enough to compensate for the 100 Tories likely to oppose it, but May's reluctance caused things to stall. 'The problem was Theresa May,' a Bresister said. 'We went through the maths with them multiple times, down to the level of individual names, but she wouldn't do it.'

These moves were the dying twitches of a government which was now a victim rather than the master of events. 'It became like a fish trying to get off a hook,' said one Number 10 official, loyal to the end. 'You just thrash around in different directions that are contradictory because all you want to do is get off the hook. The last few months were pretty pitiless and punishing. Nobody felt that more keenly than her. Everybody was exhausted.' The same was true for those who had tried to thwart her. A leading Bresister said, 'Every day there was strain and stress, let alone if you were getting threats or abuse. People were on the phone from seven o'clock in the morning till one o'clock at night, day after day and every holiday. Every single thing you're doing has some huge complication, people are trying to get one over on one another.'

May's authority was now under open assault from both wings of the party. Michael Heseltine wrote in the *Sunday Times* that he would 'lend' his vote to the Liberal Democrats in the upcoming European elections, saying he was 'not prepared to indulge in this act of national sacrifice by voting for Brexit'. The former leadership contender, now eighty-six, was summoned from the Chelsea Flower Show to see the Lords' chief whip and told he would have the whip suspended. One Downing Street source claimed the veteran peer shed a tear when he was informed. Another recalled, 'He went straight from there to a gathering of the surviving members of Mrs Thatcher's first government to celebrate the fortieth anniversary. He walked in and Norman Tebbit looked up and said, "This is only for Conservatives, you know." I gather they took two photos, one with him, one without him.' Brexit was often blamed for every battle in the Conservative civil war; this was a reminder that hatreds ran deep, none deeper than Thatcher's defenestration twenty-nine years earlier.

Cabinet the following day, Tuesday 21 May, was the prime minister's final, desperate, play. The government was to publish an amended withdrawal agreement bill two days later and ministers had to decide what would be in it. They were split down the middle, clear on what they did not want, vague on what they did. There was agreement to add what had been agreed with Labour and the DUP, plus a clause on alternative arrangements, with a vote to determine the government's position on a customs union. Most toxic, was the suggestion that the government might have to find time for a debate or even a vote on a second referendum.

The atmosphere was sulphurous, with ministers either enraged at what was proposed or cantankerous that the course of action they had previously advocated had led to this point. Liam Fox was 'vociferous' in his objections, Andrea Leadsom, who would have to present the bill, similarly pained. Liz Truss, ever more assertive in her role as the zealous convert, pressed for no-deal to become government policy. David Mundell, the Scottish secretary, objected to another referendum because it would set a precedent the nationalists north of the border could exploit. Geoffrey Cox launched into what one witness called his 'up with this, I will not put act' a few short weeks after loudly proposing a big bold offer to Labour. 'There was much eye rolling around the table,' one of those present said. 'This was what he was championing six weeks earlier.' Julian Smith did more than roll his eyes, 'barracking' Cox for 'trying to deny' his parentage of the mess. Most notably, Brandon Lewis, usually a byword for loyal pragmatism, warned May she was sailing too close to the wind. 'We have got to be clear that this is about facilitating their vote, not supporting it in any shape or form,' the chairman said. 'If you [look like you're backing a referendum], then we will have an absolute raft of no-confidence votes. The party will go apoplectic and rightly so.'

The results of the meeting were contested. As far as May's team were concerned, she had won the right to offer a vote in the Commons on whether to attach a referendum to her deal. Yet there was ambiguity about whether the government should feel bound by the results of a vote, something May did not address in her final comments. 'The second referendum thing and what we said about adhering to it or not, she did not have it in her summing up,' a Europe adviser admitted.

Barwell recalled, 'The prime minister said that cabinet had agreed we should offer a vote between two customs options and Parliamentary time for a decision on a confirmatory vote, with neither put on the face of the bill.'[4] Yet when May set out her case in a speech at the offices of PwC, offering MPs 'one last chance', she went further: 'The government will … include in the withdrawal agreement bill … a requirement to vote on whether to hold a second referendum.' The impression left was of a government advocating a vote, rather than merely facilitating one.

As Brexit secretary, Steve Barclay was the first minister to see the text of the proposed withdrawal bill at 9 a.m. the next day. If MPs voted for a second referendum, the government 'will make arrangements for a referendum,' it read. 'This is absolutely nuts,' he pronounced. He and his special adviser, Stephanie Lis, read it eight times then got an official, Jo Key, to check that they were right that it violated what had been pledged in cabinet. When they protested to Number 10, Ed de Minckwitz enraged Lis by suggesting neither she nor her minister understood what they were talking about.

Following demands by Leadsom, cabinet ministers were permitted to read the bill in a sealed room without their mobile phones. She recalled reading the offending passage: 'This was a real shock, and totally unacceptable. That could mean the end of Brexit, and certainly the end of public faith in the political process.' Assuming it must be a 'drafting error', Leadsom phoned Barclay, who confirmed that was now the position. She messaged the Pizza Club and they convened in her office.[5]

The scale of May's plight only became clear to outsiders at PMQs the following day. As the prime minister stood at the despatch box, the front bench to her left was almost deserted. Behind her, one after another, hardline Brexiteers (Ranil Jayawardena, Iain Duncan Smith, Owen Paterson and Mark Francois) got to their feet to condemn May's handling of criminal inquiries into soldiers who had fought in Northern Ireland – a convenient proxy for their fury at her handling of Brexit. The contributions were contemptuous (Francois accused her of 'pandering to the IRA') and coordinated. May was tethered prey. Julian Smith smelled a Gavin Williamson operation, telling colleagues it was 'Gavin's revenge' for his sacking as defence secretary.

Sitting in the press seats above, lobby journalists made a mental note of the absentees. It was quickly clear that the Pizza Club ministers had withdrawn their support. A watching backbench Brexiteer said,

'Everyone knew it was over. Graham Brady said he would be seeing the 1922 executive that day and May on Friday. He recommended that people write to him to issue additional letters expressing a lack of confidence, because if you had over 50 per cent of the party doing so it would strengthen his hand in that meeting.'

When the '22 executive met that evening, they held a second vote on whether to change the leadership rules so that May could be removed before the usual twelve-month time limit was exhausted. They did so in secret. Each MP wrote 'Yes' or 'No' on a piece of paper and folded it. The votes were collected and sealed in an envelope. 'Brady would threaten to open the envelope in his Friday meeting with May if she did not agree with a departure date,' an MP said. Christopher Howarth's sleuthing had delivered the rebels a stealth weapon. The result remains unknown and the envelope was deposited in the Bodleian Library. By then it was all but over anyway.

At around 2.30 p.m., after May's statement to the Commons, which followed PMQs that Wednesday, Barwell, JoJo Penn and Stephen Parkinson spoke and agreed that May had 'run out of road'. The chief of staff had a painful conversation with the prime minister, telling her, 'I don't have any other tricks up my sleeve. I don't know what else we can try now. Probably, we need to let someone else have a go and see if they can do it.'[6] He recalled, 'I think she knew it was time to stand down – she didn't need too much persuading.'[7] May had already discussed the issue with her husband, Philip. Barwell let a handful of aides into the secret, including Robbie Gibb, James Slack, Paul Harrison and James Marshall. Gibb pushed for a quick announcement, but with the following day, Thursday 23rd, being polling day for the European elections, the inner circle decided to delay the announcement until the Friday.

Throughout Wednesday, Leadsom had sent repeated text messages to Barwell, Smith and even to May, urging them to ditch the bill. She got no replies. Liam Fox also texted Barwell complaining that the draft bill 'is not what we agreed in cabinet' and 'I cannot agree to it being published'. For Fox it was a 'heart-tugging moment'. He was 'withdrawing support', leaving May with no significant Brexiteer allies, a move he knew would 'perhaps even bring her down'.[8]

At 5.30 p.m. Leadsom was due to see the Queen, in her capacity as lord president of the Privy Council. She told her team that if she had not got a reply by the time she got back, she would resign. Leadsom was to provide the bookends to May's time in office. Her decision to stand down in 2016 had gifted the premiership to her rival. May had pledged in their conversation then to deliver Brexit. She had manifestly failed. Leadsom, despite her reservations, had remained loyal. There was symbolism in her decision to pull the plug. She rang May and said, 'This is the call I never wanted to make. I always wanted to support you to get Brexit done, but I'm afraid the second referendum clause in the withdrawal bill is something I cannot support and therefore I'm so sorry but I'm phoning to offer you my resignation.' After an uncomfortable pause May, gauche to the last, asked what part of the bill she was concerned about and even suggested they talk about it. Leadsom, sensing a play for time, knowing she had 'lost confidence' in May, insisted she had to go.

As a leading Tory Remainer observed, 'They tried to bump the cabinet and that's when it all went pop.' In the aftermath, May considered bringing back her friend Damian Green as Leadsom's replacement. The PM consulted David Lidington, who thought it difficult. The job went to Mel Stride, a close ally of Michael Gove. His sixty-three days in post was one of the shortest cabinet tenures ever, until the events of autumn 2022 tore up all those records.

Leadsom was a proud woman, who saw herself as someone who had taken a stand on principle. To some fellow Brexiteers it was a little late to expect plaudits. At a summer party organised by Nigel Adams and Chris Heaton-Harris that evening, Leadsom arrived but stood apart, with no one really talking to her. When Stewart Jackson, who had previously criticised her for not resigning from the cabinet, approached, she was indignant: 'It was me that pushed her over the edge. She wouldn't have gone without me.'

Unaware of May's decision to resign, Jeremy Hunt joined Javid in requesting an audience with her. Barwell delayed Javid's until the morning. Graham Brady let it be known that he wanted to see May on Friday morning to tell her to quit. The prime minister's audience with Hunt that Thursday afternoon was evidence of her determination to put one over on the men who had spent three years telling her what to do, or supreme confirmation that she was a detached oddity. She had told Lidington, Smith and Brandon Lewis of her intention to resign several hours earlier. A female Brexiteer said, 'I sided with May. Why should she give them the dignity of a showboating showdown from cabinet ministers who have

hitherto been too pathetic to challenge her, but now wanted to grand-
stand to shore up their position for a leadership contest?'

That evening Raoul Ruparel called Julian Smith and said, 'It is over.'
In the corridor outside the Strangers' Bar in the Commons, Lis and a
group of special advisers, including Olivia Robey and Liam Booth-Smith,
ran into de Minckwitz. 'Time's up,' he admitted. 'We know.'

May and Philip went back to her constituency home in Sonning to
look at the draft resignation speech written for her by Keelan Carr. May
asked for the words 'I am the second female prime minister but I won't
be the last' to be inserted.

At 9 a.m. on Friday, Brady came to Number 10. Before the chairman
of the '22 could deliver his message, May told him she was quitting.
Watched by Barwell, Smith and Lewis, she then said, 'Before you leave
the building, I want you to tell me whether you're going to be a candidate.'

Brady was supposed to be the returning officer for the leadership election, a role he could hardly perform if he was going to run. The 1922
chairman had never served in the cabinet, but he had resigned from
David Cameron's team over grammar schools, a matter of principle that
endeared him to the right. Having put his name to the Brady amendment, which had briefly brought Tory MPs together, some sought to
persuade him that only he could unite the party. He went to a side room.
Brady told Seldon he 'decided there and then' he would recuse himself.[9]
That is not how May's team remember it. They say he spent some time
agonising. He need not have recused himself. 'The idea had dawned on
him that he might be leader,' a Downing Street adviser remarked, acidly.
'But it didn't seem to dawn on anyone else.'

May walked alone to the lectern in the street, the second prime minister
in three years to undergo ritual public resignation (there would soon be
two more), the famous black door looming behind like a forbidding
warning from Dante ('abandon hope, all ye who enter here') or Enoch
Powell ('all political careers end in failure') about the weight of the office.

May spoke of how she had 'striven' to 'honour the result of the EU
referendum' but admitted she had failed. 'It is in the best interests of the
country for a new prime minister to lead that effort ... It is, and will
always remain, a matter of deep regret to me that I have not been able to
deliver Brexit.' She dwelt a little on domestic policy, an agenda derailed,

in part, by Brexit and her quest to tackle the 'burning injustices' of society, incinerated in the electoral inferno of 2017. She concluded, 'I will shortly leave the job that it has been the honour of my life to hold – the second female prime minister but certainly not the last. I do so with no ill will, but with enormous and enduring gratitude to have had the opportunity to serve the country I love.' As she reached the last few words, the least publicly emotional prime minister for decades was overcome, her final utterances a strangulated blub, fighting tears and losing as she retreated through the door. Watching in the street, her husband Philip grimaced. He turned to Barwell and mouthed, 'Oh, crikey.'

Keelan Carr, who helped May write her valedictory, watched on the television in his office, a room that had once been occupied by Margaret Thatcher's spin doctor Bernard Ingham. When May came back into the foyer there was applause from civil servants and spads.

In the haven of Number 10, that gilded cage, May said to Barwell, 'I'm sorry I cried.' He replied, 'Please don't apologise. You have absolutely nothing to apologise for.'[10] The chief of staff had wanted his boss to show more emotion for months, but now that she had May felt it had undermined her. 'You wait and see. The papers will use those pictures differently because I'm a woman.'[11] She said ruefully later, 'If a male prime minister's voice had broken up, it would have been said "what great patriotism, they really love their country". But if a female prime minister does it, it is "why is she crying?".'[12] It was a sad epitaph for a career limited by her posture of enigmatic defensiveness that May concluded at its end that she had shown weakness by seeming human. 'The thing that struck me about the speech is that she basically left the hardest line to say to last,' a member of the comms team said. 'All the time you're out there you know you've still got it to come.'

Upstairs, in the pillared room, May paid tribute to her chief of staff and her husband, who had been with her all the way on her journey from councillor to prime minister. 'There was a lot of emotion in the room,' a spad recalled. 'It wasn't weeping and it wasn't sobbing. Everyone was laughing with tears in their eyes. Everyone was happy to think about the experience they'd had together. There was a sense of quiet pride in her and what had been achieved even though it hadn't been successful.'

* * *

May resigned as leader of the Conservative Party but would remain prime minister while her successor was elected. As she walked back into Number 10, Barwell convened a meeting of key aides. 'Right, we've got seven weeks and five days. What can we do? It can't be anything requiring primary legislation because we haven't got time to pass it.'[13]

May's quest for a political legacy beyond Brexit put her on a collision course with Philip Hammond, the chancellor, who was even more reluctant than usual to open the public purse. Robbie Gibb had booked Brandon Lewis onto *The Andrew Marr Show*, to explain the European election results and give May a send-off. Hammond's office called the producers directly behind his back and he appeared instead. Gibb was apoplectic, seeing this as the action of a minister who was not a team player. There was 'a huge row' and Gibb did not speak to Hammond for the rest of their time in government.

In this period May represented Britain at the D-Day commemorations, and announced that the UK would legislate to achieve net zero for carbon emissions by 2050, the first major economy to do so. At every turn, Hammond dug in. She wanted investment in mental health, parental leave and a school funding plan. Hammond said, 'Once a prime minister has announced that they are retiring on a certain date, they can't then say, "I think I'll just launch a five-year multi-billion-pound policy agenda." That would have been completely wrong. She was very nonplussed by my lack of cooperation, but I'm afraid this was an issue that I just felt was a straightforward right-and-wrong thing.'[14] But that was not the full story. A 'nakedly transactional'[15] chancellor agreed to hand over the cash for schools if May legislated to ensure MPs had a veto over no-deal which would give him a free vote. It was not granted and Hammond agreed just one year of extra spending. 'Quite a chunk of her domestic achievements were in those last eight weeks,' Barwell said. 'The net zero announcement is probably the biggest single long-term thing she did ... She looks back on that period with a certain degree of wistfulness, as: "What would my time of Prime Minister have been like if I didn't have Brexit?"'[16]

From Hammond's point of view he, unlike many others, had achieved what he wanted on Brexit. 'I will go to my grave convinced that what I did between October 2016 and early 2019 was a significant factor in stopping us going for a hard Brexit,' he said. 'Moving her away from her initial instinct to do a very hard Brexit and helping her to see how damaging that would be. Although it was massively painful at times, because it was like wading through treacle, that it was worth doing. In early 2017, she was absolutely up for no-deal. By the end, she was one of the hardest-line people that no-deal was simply not acceptable. She never said that in public but in private that is where she was: "We cannot have no deal. It would be a catastrophe for the country." I am claiming some share of the credit for that. That's why I stayed in and did what I had to do.'

In mid-July, May had a rapprochement with Fiona Hill, who attended a dinner in Number 10 on modern slavery, an issue close to both of their hearts. When May's resignation honours list was announced on 10 September, Hill and Nick Timothy were both given CBEs for helping her to power. Barwell, JoJo Penn and Stephen Parkinson all went to the Lords but several in the building felt that gongs for Hill and Timothy were a ploy by Gibb to distract the media from his own knighthood, a questionable reward for spin doctors which began with Craig Oliver, whose 'K' May had publicly condemned less than a year earlier.

She remained haunted by what might have been at MV3. Midway through the leadership election, she invited Phillip Lee for gin and tonic in the Downing Street flat. 'They told me if I named the date, they'd give me their support,' she said.

Lee, who thought the ERG were liars, looked at her and said, as gently as he could, 'That was never going to happen.' May looked at the floor.[17]

On 30 June, the lame duck prime minister attended her final European Council meeting. Her fellow leaders mouthed supportive bromides but, in truth, they were not sorry to see the back of her and the paralysis she had brought to European affairs. The only people allowed to sit around the Council table were heads of government and heads of state. May was tired, having just returned from Japan. The prospect of another interminable dinner palled. Paul Harrison offered a mischievous suggestion: 'There is one other person who can sit in that chair. The Queen. Why don't you just say "Your Majesty, do you fancy it?"' There was laughter from aides.

May silently raised an eyebrow – a woman similar to her monarch in her devotion to duty, but whose inability to connect with the public, as Elizabeth II did, fatally eroded her ability to do her job effectively.

Her political collapse had left the way clear for two new political parties, both driven by Brexit, to try to fill the vacuum. One failed utterly, the other learned the lessons she ignored and would shape the future of the Conservative Party and of Brexit. In so doing it inflicted on May the most humiliating election result in her beloved party's history.

OUTSIDERS

The Rise of the Brexit Party and the Fall of the Tiggers

26 May 2019

The transformation of the Independent Group into Change UK, the party which fought the European elections, was an object lesson in how not to do politics. The Tiggers had not long split from the Labour Party when they began to split in two themselves. Divisions opened between those who wanted to champion a new politics driven by a grassroots movement and those who believed they would only have influence if they quickly sought election. 'We allowed far too much focus on the day of departure and not enough focus on what was going to happen afterwards,' Angela Smith recalled. 'That was where we went wrong.'

To Gavin Shuker, polling showed that the biggest driver of support to the new project was the tone that they adopted. This view was shared by Luciana Berger, who had not left one toxic culture only to create a new one. Smith was firmly with them. To Chris Leslie, the point of the enterprise was to build something that could get him and others elected. 'If we wanted to do more than simply signal our virtue and feel comfortable as individuals, we would eventually have to develop into a political party,' he said. 'It's all very well talking about broken politics and the need to change it, but you have to offer the public a vehicle that they could potentially come behind and support.' Anna Soubry was Leslie's biggest cheerleader. As a barrister and former television presenter, Soubry was a strong media performer, but she surprised her fellow MPs early on when she turned to Leslie and said, 'I rely on this man for political analysis. I trust his analysis on everything.'

To the 'new politics' crowd, Leslie's objection to the aggressive machinist culture of the Labour Party was merely that it was the hard left who were running it. Two weeks after the breakaway, Leslie turned to a fellow MP and said, 'I'm not really bothered about this realignment thing. I just want to make sure that Jeremy Corbyn never becomes prime minister.' It felt like a 'smack in the mouth', a 'betrayal' to those who had shared months of planning for the new venture.

In truth, they were already too late. When enquiries were made with the Electoral Commission, the watchdog in charge of registering political parties and their donations, they were informed that the process took three months. 'When we left in February, by that time it was too late, by about two or three weeks, to register as a party for the May local elections,' one said. 'We would had to have jumped in the January.' The first time the public could go to the polls to support them, the Tiggers would not be on the ballot paper.

They were in time to fight European elections at the end of May but had to make a snap decision about whether to stand. Shuker, Berger and Smith had doubts. Leslie, Joan Ryan and Soubry thought it would be ridiculous not to. Umunna started on the fence, but Leslie won him over. In the end, there was unanimous agreement. 'We thought the risks were much bigger to not fight it,' Ryan recalled. To Heidi Allen, the Tiggers' strong showing in the polls meant there was a 'feelgood factor' which they had to exploit. She felt 'obliged', she told colleagues, admitting privately later, 'It became a bit too addictive not to do it.'

The next decision was whether to stand candidates everywhere. Sarah Wollaston suggested that they focus on one region and 'do a small number well' rather than spreading resources too thinly. 'We're trying to run before we can walk,' she warned. Berger argued it would be 'absolutely ridiculous' to try to find and vet enough candidates in time. Leslie, Umunna and Soubry wanted to go big and their determination carried the day. 'You have to take risks in politics,' Leslie argued.

Leslie understood how power was obtained and exercised in a political party. When discussions turned to forming one, he turned up with a draft constitution he had written. 'I think his view was "We'll let Chuka be the leader, I'll really hold the power and my wife will run the organisation",' a colleague said. Leslie's wife, Nicola Murphy, became the statutory 'nominating office' demanded by the Electoral Commission. The watchdog also required a party to have a treasurer. Soubry brought in her partner, Neil Davidson, to do the job. To Shuker, this was exactly the kind of 'stitch-up' he had left Labour to avoid. 'Chris and Anna basically instigated a power grab,' one MP said. Leslie became the election coordinator, taking control of candidate selection with the help of Soubry and Mike Gapes. 'Effectively he was running the party,' another MP said.

The Electoral Commission also required a political party to have a leader. Most assumed it would be Umunna. 'When the three Conservatives joined, in their minds they were joining Chuka's new party,' said one of the former Labour MPs. Joan Ryan and Ann Coffey thought him the 'obvious' choice. Shuker, Smith and Berger were concerned Umunna's elevation would deter other Labour MPs from joining them. Shuker showed Umunna a list of twenty MPs who had expressed concerns to him about it being 'the Chris and Chuka show'.

The decisive voice was Berger's. Having had her second baby, she was absent but, via Shuker, she signalled that if Umunna was put in charge she might leave. 'We all were up for Chuka,' another MP said. 'But Luciana decided to veto it.' Berger wanted a permanent leader elected at a special conference later in the year. Some thought she wanted to delay until she could run herself, though Berger said she had no interest in the leadership. Some believed Shuker wanted Berger to lead. Others reflected that she and Umunna had briefly been in a relationship after they entered Parliament and wondered if ancient history was getting in the way.

There was a 'heated' meeting in which a majority of the MPs backed Umunna. The following day, at a second gathering in Wollaston's office. Umunna announced, 'I'm not prepared to push this, I will stand aside.' He was seen by some MPs jealous of his prominence and looks as a narcissist, but here he made a selfless decision. 'Chuka agreed not to be leader,' a colleague said. 'Personally, I think that was a big mistake. He understood that if Luciana was threatening to walk that would be pretty catastrophic.' Another member of the group saw a man who was not nearly as ruthless as he was depicted. 'Chuka is a lovely gentle man,' said one of the female MPs. 'He's very, very bright. I think he's probably been told all the time that he should be leader but he's not a leader.'

With the frontrunner disqualifying himself, a replacement was needed. Soubry was vocal in her support for Leslie, but he was not interested. Nor would she do it herself. Leslie whispered in Heidi Allen's ear, 'Well, it needs to be you.' Allen was shocked. She had never thought of herself as a leader 'in a month of Sundays'. She was the least experienced MP of the eleven and a loose cannon with the media, openly admitting the concept of party loyalty 'is lost on me'. But the group saw benefits in presenting a fresh face. With Umunna still chief spokesman, there was logic too in having a man and a woman, an ex-Tory and an ex-Labour MP as the public face of the Tiggers. It was 29 March, the day of the third meaningful vote, and into the maelstrom of their first election the newest kids on the block thrust someone Allen's colleagues privately regarded as 'obviously very untested' and 'not qualified to be leader'.

Allen inherited a party in which small divisions were becoming deep fissures. 'The problem with only having eleven of you meant that everybody took part in every decision,' one Tigger recalled. 'People started being able to veto things. It was really quite painful.' To speed things up, Leslie set up a management committee, chaired by Umunna, which included only eight of the eleven MPs, angering the other three. Soubry, one of the biggest personalities in Parliament, was viewed by Shuker and Smith as bombastic and domineering.

When the call went out for people to stand as candidates in mid-April, they were inundated with 3,700 applicants. After an initial sift, to reduce the number to 120, Leslie, Soubry and Gapes spent the whole of Easter weekend interviewing potential candidates. They did well at weeding out problematic people, but inevitably a couple slipped through the net, including one who had said something rude about Romanians and another who had sent misogynistic tweets as a student. Both were kicked out.

There was still no agreement about policy. Umunna suggested they secure a debate on proportional representation, natural terrain for a wannabe third party seeking a realignment of politics. Angela Smith, who was a convert to the PR cause, secured a Westminster Hall debate and asked the others to turn up and support her. Leslie, who had missed the original discussion, erupted: 'No, no, no, we're not having that. We're not supporting PR.' Smith was furious.

They still didn't have a logo or a name. Umunna got a branding agency he knew to draw up some designs, which were shared during a conference call on the Signal app. One had vertical stripes, others had horizontal stripes and a third a rainbow of colours, but that looked too like a gay pride logo. They picked an image with horizontal black and white lines. 'They thought it looked like a tiger, for the Tiggers,' said one despairing MP. The monochrome was more zebra than tiger. When it was unveiled, most people thought first of a supermarket bar code.

'The Electoral Commission rejected our first name,' Gapes said. 'We had to find another name with about two days' notice. We originally wanted the Independent Group for Change and they wouldn't allow it. We finally said we'll call ourselves Change UK.' Even that became a problem when the campaign website change.org threatened to sue. To prevent legal action an absurd agreement was drawn up that the Tiggers would keep the name but refrain from mentioning it during the election campaign. Each MP was asked to sign an undertaking. Wollaston thought this nonsense and refused to do so. Change.org was informed that they would be responsible for the party not being able to stand candidates and they backed off.

Brexit had been the strongest thing holding them together, but it was also what drove them apart. The Tiggers' failure to stand in the local elections ceded the playing field to the Lib Dems and the Greens, both of whom performed well. Vince Cable led the Lib Dems to gains of 704 council seats and a national equivalent vote share of 19 per cent, just nine points behind both the Tories and Labour. Independents got more than 11 per cent of the vote, so the potential was there for a group like Change UK. But as Joan Ryan recalled, 'The Lib Dems became identified once again as the party of the protest vote. They became the repository of the Remain vote.' Leslie admitted, 'With hindsight if we had jumped a few weeks earlier history might have been slightly different because we were actually riding quite high in that period in February and March.'

YouGov's first poll after the February breakaway put the Tiggers on 14 per cent, double the Lib Dems on 7 per cent. A week later, TIG got its best ever poll showing in another YouGov survey with 18 per cent, while the Lib Dems languished on just 6 per cent. However, the last time the Tiggers led the Lib Dems was in a ComRes poll published on 16 April. YouGov's last survey before the local elections had the Lib Dems on 13 per cent, ten points clear of the Tiggers.[1]

From the beginning, Shuker was conscious that for any breakaway to be a long-term success, it would need to attract Lib Dem defectors, absorb or merge with the third party or come to an accommodation with it. He envisaged a political force polling over 20 per cent nationally with at least thirty-five MPs, enough to ensure that the broadcasting watchdog Ofcom designated them as a major party, which guaranteed airtime. His view was that the way to prosper was to grow the Independent Group until it was a force to be reckoned with. It would also be far easier to persuade Labour and Tory MPs to join something new than jump straight to the Lib Dems.

However, as the Lib Dems began to prosper again, those who were disgruntled that Change UK seemed destined for failure began to reconsider. Shuker, Smith, Berger, Wollaston and Allen were all unhappy with the direction forged by Leslie and Soubry and began to talk to discuss their concerns over the culture of the party. They then looped in Umunna.

Mike Gapes could see that Umunna was losing heart. On the train back from a rally in Manchester, Umunna said, 'I don't think it's going to work.' Gapes, who believed they had to fight on, said, 'We've only just started.'

Gapes, Leslie, Soubry, Ryan and Coffey had little time for the Lib Dems, who they accused of 'dirty tricks'. One MP in this faction said, 'They were claiming that some of our candidates had gone over to them. They were even registering websites in our name under their ownership.' These were classic black arts techniques. Another Lib Dem gambit exploited a general misunderstanding about the rules of European elections. Vince Cable, the Lib Dem leader, offered a 'remain alliance' to the Greens and Change UK. It was a publicity stunt because electoral law made it illegal. Under the D'Hondt list system, used to determine how many MEPs each party received, a joint list of different parties was impossible. An MP explained, 'You have to register a separate party with the Electoral Commission which would have its own list and logo. But the Liberal Democrats succeeded in spinning this lie.'

The D'Hondt system was also responsible for the final collapse. Heidi Allen was sent statistical analysis showing that even a relatively poor showing by Change UK would split the Remain vote and let in more Brexiteers. Allen was leaned on by Lib Dem high command and became uncomfortable, Wollaston too. On one conference call, Allen said, 'We need to think carefully about pulling back and doing a deal and working collaboratively.' This prompted an expletive-laden reply from Soubry.

At the same time, suspicions were growing that the six who had started caucusing separately were already in talks to join the Lib Dems. 'The Lib Dems circled Heidi,' another MP said. 'She got seduced by this idea that we should somehow stand down.'

Everything came to a head on Monday 20 May, three days before polling day, when the MPs gathered in a meeting room on the upper committee corridor in the Commons. Allen made the case that Change UK should recommend tactical voting, publicly urging their supporters to back the Lib Dems or the Greens where Change UK had little chance of getting seats – everywhere outside London and the South-East. She was backed by Wollaston, who thought Change UK candidates in the South-West should be allowed to publicly endorse the Lib Dems. Umunna did not speak out, Berger was 'silent', Shuker increasingly withdrawn. The other five MPs were aghast and pointed out that compliance with electoral law made explicit statements backing other parties difficult. It was too late to stand down candidates or change leaflets. More importantly, Leslie and his allies argued, it was morally wrong to pull the plug on candidates who had gone out on a limb to join the new party. 'Think how they'll feel,' Leslie said. 'We've made this decision, we're committed to it.'

Allen felt so strongly about Brexit that she threatened to resign. She said, 'If nobody agrees with me and I'm completely out on a limb, then maybe it's best that I stand down and you can all get on with it, I don't want to be a thorn in the side.' The others sought to convince her that this would be the ultimate act of self-sabotage. 'Imagine the leader doing that to a party in the last few days of a campaign,' one MP said. 'It was absolutely mortifying. It would have been a selfish, self-indulgent thing.'

Privately, Allen's faction had already decided Change UK had no future. 'Half of us knew that we would walk away afterwards,' one of these MPs admitted. 'That half of us still felt very strongly that politics needed to change, needed to be not party first if we were going to do things differently.'

In return for Allen not going public with her thoughts and not walking out, she pressed for Leslie to turn off Change UK's social media messaging for the rest of the campaign. Rather than stand down, the new party would stop urging the public to vote for it outside London. 'Chris was utterly distressed,' a colleague said.

Neither side kept to the deal. Leslie switched off the social media, then switched it back on again for the final two days. His view, shared by the more seasoned MPs – Gapes, Soubry, Ryan and Coffey – was that a life in Parliament meant taking the rough with the smooth. You couldn't just run away at the first setback.

On 22 May, the day before voters went to the polls, Allen gave an interview to *Channel 4 News*. Asked by presenter Cathy Newman whether there should be tactical voting, her response was astonishingly unguarded: 'I guess it depends whether you are asking me as the Change leader or me as Heidi. As Heidi, yes, I do have huge sympathy and I understand why people would do that. At the end of the day, all I want is one more vote than Nigel Farage … Frankly, if that means you have to vote differently in some parts of the country to others to ensure that, then I have no issue with people doing that at all.' The idea that a party leader could offer their views in a personal capacity was naive in the extreme.

To the Leslie faction, Allen had just blown up Change UK's campaign because of Brexit's 'higher calling'. She then proceeded to wash the party's dirty linen in public. Newman had been tipped off about the row two days earlier. 'There was a significant difference in opinion,' Allen conceded. 'A good chunk of us in the group did want to recommend tactical voting across the UK.' Asked if she threatened to resign, she said, 'Yes, yes, I did … Had it been left to me, I would absolutely have advised tactical voting.' Now, in effect, she had.

Allen's allies believed she was briefed against and ambushed. 'She was on the receiving end of a drive-by shooting,' a close ally said. In the other camp, an MP said, 'She admitted she had no leadership qualifications and she was absolutely right on that one.'

Over the next three days, as the votes were counted, the space they had opened up for a new party was closed down. The Lib Dems won 19.6 per cent of the vote, not far short of Labour and the Tories combined and went home with 16 MEPS, a gain of fifteen. Change UK got 3.3 per cent and won nothing. The machinists thought the idealists had cost them a chance of securing 7 or 8 per cent, enough to win an MEP in London and another in the South-East, a meaningful platform to build from. The new politics brigade blamed the haste of the new party faction for the disaster. 'It was a massive mistake,' Angela Smith said later. 'The decision to stand and register I think destroyed our credibility. We tried to run before we could walk. It was an embarrassment, frankly.'

The Lib Dems attracted votes from Remain supporters disgruntled with Labour, who ended up with just 13.7 per cent of the vote and saw its contingent of MEPs halved to ten. In Scotland, Labour slipped to fifth place, prompting the Corbynite leader of Scottish Labour, Richard Leonard, to demand that Labour become a 'Remain party'.

The defectors included Alastair Campbell, who revealed he had voted Lib Dem for the first time in his life over Brexit. Five days later his party

membership was terminated. Campbell was bang to rights according to
the Labour rulebook, but drily noted that summary justice was quicker
for him than Corbynites accused of antisemitism. A round of 'I'm
Spartacus' tributes from ageing Blairites followed. Charles Clarke and
Cherie Blair both said they too had voted Lib Dem, while Bob Ainsworth
voted Green.

The following week, 4 June, the MPs of Change UK gathered for a
'horrible meeting' in Sarah Wollaston's office. There was no shouting or
nastiness, just a 'sad and quiet' realisation that the experiment was over.
One said, 'It was like a couple that knows they are going to get divorced,
sitting down talking about who's going to get the chairs and who's going
to get the dining table', or in this case clearing up the financial and
compliance returns to the Electoral Commission. Berger turned up with
her baby in a buggy and changed a dirty nappy, a metaphor for the
mood.

Allen, Wollaston, Smith, Berger and Shuker all said they would return
to being independents. Umunna decided to join them. Leslie, Gapes,
Soubry, Ryan and Coffey agreed to remain together. Leslie still saw the
possibility of a wider realignment involving One Nation Tories and
figures alienated from their party by Brexit like Nick Boles and Dominic
Grieve.

The following day there was another meeting to go over further details
of the separation. Joan Ryan confronted the six splitters. 'Are you going
to the Lib Dems?' she asked. They all denied it. 'You are. When are you
joining the Lib Dems? I know you are.' Some of them could not look her
in the eye. Eight days later, on 13 June, Umunna joined the Lib Dems. By
October, Wollaston, Berger, Smith and Allen had done so as well.

Perhaps there was a parallel universe in which it might have worked. One
where Tom Watson did not stop more Labour MPs following the original seven out of the door. One where the People's Vote campaign had not
already become a lifeboat for those disillusioned with the leadership of
Corbyn and May. One where their greatest asset, Luciana Berger, was not
absent after the launch. One where Berger did not block Chuka Umunna,
the most high-profile figure, from taking on the leadership. They failed
too because others lacked their political courage. Berger said she 'had
time for every single one' of her fellow Tiggers, 'because they had the
courage and the balls to at least try and change things'. She saw those

who sat on their hands during the Brexit wars as 'bystanders', adding, 'I think so many people on both sides shirked that responsibility.'

The paradox of the Tiggers was that half of them understood that voters were crying out for a party that did things differently, who felt disenfranchised by a broken political system. Yet what Chris Leslie and his allies understood was that politics is ultimately about power and power in Britain comes from elections, from serving in the legislature. Without power, idealism has no practical means of implementing itself.

Heidi Allen concluded they moved too soon to become a party. 'We should have stayed as we were, as Switzerland in the centre of the House of Commons, a neutral safe space that other MPs might have been brave enough to jump to, where something new could grow.'

The bigger mistake, in retrospect, was not to become a party earlier. The most likely scenario for success was one where they stood in the local elections, when they were outpolling the Lib Dems by a factor of two or three. Perhaps then, it might have been Change UK picking up 700 council seats in early May and 19 MEPs a few weeks later. From that platform they could have eclipsed the Lib Dems as the main Remain party. Ann Coffey said later, 'We failed to understand – and really we should have understood six months before – that the Lib Dems were going to do well at the local elections.'

The Tiggers were not irrelevant; they did redirect the currents of Brexit. Angela Smith saw two legacies: 'Corbyn couldn't become caretaker PM because of the people who left. It could also be argued that we created a space for the Lib Dems as well, to reassert the importance of a credible centre ground alternative.' Heidi Allen offered this: 'When we jumped, we did nudge Labour to move closer to Remain, we did nudge some of the Tories across the line. So we played a part.'

A group which had formed, in large part, because of disgust at the main parties' handling of Brexit was eventually torn apart because half of its adherents put their allegiance to Remain above the interests of their new party. The episode highlighted too how even a group of highly experienced political operators could fail if they were only able to decide what they were against, rather than what they were for, lacked clear and able leadership and had not staked out in advance where they wanted to go.

The party which won the European elections was the mirror image of Change UK. The Brexit Party was formed even later and harboured some of the most eccentric operators in British politics. But it had one clear objective – to pile pressure on the government to deliver Brexit – and had at its helm a decisive and charismatic leader who had a case to be the most influential British politician of the decade either side of Brexit.

'You guys are going to be very happy,' the voice said. 'You're way ahead in the polls.' It was Saturday evening, 20 April, eight days after the Brexit Party had launched its European election campaign and the message reached Richard Tice that one of the *Mail on Sunday* political team had been in touch. A poll in the week had put them on 27 per cent, with Labour on 22 per cent, the Tories having slumped to 15 per cent. Tory voters were defecting to Nigel Farage's new electoral vehicle. What the new Survation survey showed, however, was that this was not confined to voters, but also Conservative members and even the party's elected representatives. Four out of ten Tory councillors were planning to vote for the Brexit Party and three quarters wanted Theresa May to resign.[2] 'The prime minister has destroyed the Conservative Party,' one of the eight hundred councillors contacted by the pollster declared.[3] 'Basically, the die was then cast,' Tice recalled. 'We knew from that moment that basically we would win. It was just a question of how big could we make it and, therefore, how big an impact that would have.'[4]

Tice, a city smoothie with well-cut hair and suits, earned his money from property investment and his Euroscepticism from the campaign against the euro, when he was a director of Business for Sterling. In 2012 he met Nigel Farage and tore up his Conservative Party membership card. He gave Ukip £20,000 for the 2014 European elections, which Farage's party won. In early 2015, before the general election, he met Matthew Elliott from Business for Britain, who would go on to set up Vote Leave, to ask what the plan was for the referendum which David Cameron had promised. When Elliott said they would wait for the prime minister to complete his renegotiation with Brussels before running a short Leave referendum campaign, Tice was horrified. 'That is ridiculous,' he said. 'That is way too late, you will have missed the boat and you will lose.'[5] Within a week he had been introduced to Arron Banks and Andy Wigmore. They joined forces to found Leave.EU, backed by £50,000 of Tice's money – the so-called 'Bad Boys of Brexit' who fought Vote Leave for the designation of official campaign.

After the referendum, in July 2016, Vote Leave had to disband by law. Seeing the 'hysterical response of Remainer MPs' to the Leave vote, Tice decided Brexiteers needed a new organisation so that journalists had somewhere to get a balancing opinion. He approached John Longworth, who had resigned as director general of the British Chambers of Commerce in 2016 and become chairman of the Vote Leave business council, to see if he wanted to help. Longworth believed EU membership had 'infantilised' Britain, reducing the Mother of Parliaments to a version of a county council. 'I was convinced that we hadn't won, we'd just temporarily planted our flag at the top of the hill,' he said. When Elliott, to whom he had also been talking, said it would be a mistake to start something new, that they would look like 'the Japanese soldier still fighting in the jungle in the 1960s', Longworth contacted Tice and they became co-chairmen of Leave Means Leave.

Tice's old comrade in arms, Arron Banks, had a different idea to keep the Tories honest and save Brexit. In early 2018, Banks used his mailing list to encourage supporters of Leave.EU to join the Conservative Party so that they could vote for a Brexiteer in the next leadership contest. Banks pointed out that with Tory membership at an all-time low at around 70,000, 'the arrival of 20,000 Ukip members could make a real impact'. Remainers like Dr Phillip Lee cried foul about this 'entryism', warning, 'I don't want our Party to be hijacked by people on the extreme as Labour has been.'[6]

The Chequers deal in July 2018 energised Eurosceptics. By August, Tice had got Farage to join Leave Means Leave as vice chairman. They raised £1 million that month and in September began a series of rallies, starting with one in Bolton attended by 1,600 people. 'It was basically a vehicle for Nigel and Brexiteer MPs to get their views out in the press,' a party official said. It was also a response to the 'wall to wall' coverage the BBC was giving to the People's Vote campaign. Leave Means Leave was determined to be the official Leave campaign if it came to another vote.

After May's November deal (described by Farage as 'probably the worst deal in history'), they began to ramp up their activities, lobbying MPs to reject May's plan in the three meaningful votes and arming Brexiteers with facts and figures for broadcast appearances. It was clear that a new party might be needed, but the time was not yet right. 'Our polling showed us that it wasn't yet bad enough,' Tice said. 'People didn't realise how badly it was going.'[7]

* * *

There was also a rival outfit, run by businessman Jeremy Hosking. On 11 October 2018, one of Hosking's sidekicks met Steve Baker for lunch in Parliament to explore the chances of ERG MPs leaving the Tory party and setting up a breakaway of their own. Hosking was devising a campaign called 'Brexit Express', which would see campaigners tour the country by train. Baker advised against efforts to start a new party. 'It's not a good idea,' he said. 'If we get into that territory, we're likely to just split the centre-right vote. The money would be better spent helping the Conservative Party do the right thing.'

That autumn, Hosking registered Brexit Express with the Electoral Commission. He continued wooing Baker. They met in person, with others, on 28 February 2019. Their hope was that Baker would lead fifty ERG Conservatives out of the party. Baker felt he had to explain the political facts of life. 'We will end up fishing in the same pool, splitting the vote and letting our opponents win. Look, I'm not going to do it, nor are the fifty others.' On 18 April that year, Baker gave the same message to Tice and Lucy Harris, one of the Brexit Party's MEP candidates.

While Hosking's project came to nothing, he became one of the Brexit Party's early donors. The biggest was a tech and cryptocurrency millionaire, Christopher Harborne, who was to twice give the Brexit Party £3 million. Educated at Westminster, Cambridge University and INSEAD, the European business school, Harborne was a twenty-four-carat member of the establishment, but his business interests made him a disruptor. He also held Thai citizenship under the name Chakrit Sakunkrit. 'He's a very humble man, he wears M&S suits and eats meal deals,' a party source said. The issue was that Harborne was non-domiciled for tax purposes and could only spend ninety days a year in the UK. Party officials feared the media attention would drive him away. Hosking stepped in and gave £200,000, telling the press he was the main donor to distract attention.

Harborne's money was tapped by Chris Bruni-Lowe, Farage's long-standing collaborator on polling and messaging, who played a key role in Ukip's activities during the referendum campaign in 2016. Their goal was to get rid of May and persuade the public that a no-deal Brexit would not be the disaster that many feared. Bruni-Lowe tested endlessly, asking the same questions in different ways, making minor changes to messages to see which forms of words polled best.

Two arguments had traction. 'People on both Leave and Remain felt Britain had been humiliated,' a party official recalled. 'The best way to get people to think that no-deal was good was to talk about the money.' The polling showed that voters deeply resented May's divorce settlement with the EU. 'People thought, "Why are we giving £39 billion to the EU for nothing in return",' the source said. Bruni-Lowe was assisted by the new head of digital, Steven Edginton. He pumped out videos and other social media content arguing that May had humiliated Britain, lines like 'no deal, no problem' and calls to repatriate the cash. 'The £39 billion was the new £350 million – trying to get that into voters' minds,' a party source said.

The final killer argument played neatly into Farage's outsider status. 'Voters were fucked off with politicians, they hated all politicians,' the official said. 'Theresa May had completely destroyed public trust in politics.' Like the Tiggers, the Brexit Party would seize on the 'time for a change' argument.

The plan was to wait until May had failed to deliver Brexit on 29 March, a moment Leave Means Leave content labelled 'the betrayal', and then launch the new party. The big idea to generate drama around the 29th was Richard Tice's. There would be a nationwide 'March to Leave', starting in Sunderland – where the Brexit vote in 2016 had signalled the beginning of the Leave earthquake – culminating in a rally in Parliament Square on what was supposed to be Brexit day. 'Theresa May was our best ally in this,' a Brexit Party official said. 'She had built up 29 March as this huge day in voters' minds, they thought this was the day we're going to leave. So when we didn't, the Tories nosedived in the opinion polls. Leave Means Leave helped get that in the public consciousness.'

The march was a peculiarly British affair, attracting eccentrics and Brexiteers who marched part of the route with around one hundred diehards. To those who got misty-eyed at the reclamation of sovereignty, it was a pilgrimage for democracy to the centre of resurgent Remainer opinion. To others it was a bit of a circus. It might have been literally so if Tice had had his way. 'Richard wanted people on stilts, he wanted jugglers and he wanted camels,' a bemused colleague recalled. 'He wanted a whole circus because he thought this would be a fantastic way to get the media drawn in. He came up with a load of ideas which got shot down pretty quickly. He wants to be Boris, and he sees Boris with the two flags and zipwire, Richard thinks let's do ridiculous things and get more coverage.' When Tice had been the third wheel in Leave.EU alongside Banks and Wigmore, he had been seen as the strait-laced one of the operation. No more. 'Richard was a buccaneer,' a close ally said.

Even without the camels, the march itself was a headache for the organisers. The core group of walkers were devout believers, in all their technicolour glory. 'People were quitting their jobs, flying in from all over the world to go on this march,' a party official said. 'They were shagging each other, they were bitching about each other and the Leave Means Leave staff who had to go on the march with them were driven mental because they were in this environment like a reality TV show, where they had to look after these old nutters.' The marchers were given a free dinner every evening at a Wetherspoons pub, owned by Brexiteer Tim Martin. The quality of the cuisine led to a mutiny among the marchers.

Some got trench foot from all the marching and had to drop out, but in towns like Doncaster, where the marchers arrived at 4 p.m. one day, they were greeted with cheering and people hooting their car horns. 'The idea that the red wall doesn't get this or isn't interested or doesn't want this is complete rubbish,' said one marcher, 'because these constituencies in the North, Doncaster, were absolutely passionate about Brexit.'

Leave Means Leave had also hired a firm which usually made music videos for rap artists to make a mini film for each day of the march. 'One day, they sent us a video that was just about a toilet, promoting this guy called "Mr Loo", a portaloo guy, who had joined them on the march,' a staffer recalled. 'It was a two-minute video with everyone saying his toilet was fantastic.' Back in London, officials asked each other, 'What the fuck is this?' Sadly, Mr Loo's advert was never released.

On one of the legs, Farage took John Longworth aside and asked whether he would be interested in becoming an MEP if he set up a new party to run in the European elections. Longworth agreed and became the lead candidate for Yorkshire. 'I'd come to the conclusion by that point that the only thing that works with parliamentarians is to frighten them, make them think they're going to lose,' he said. 'We needed to frighten the Tories.'

The march, despite its eccentricities, was a success. It arrived in London on a glorious sunny day and several thousand people gathered in Parliament Square to hear from Tice, Longworth, broadcaster Julia

Hartley-Brewer, *Spiked* editor Brendan O'Neill, Labour MP Kate Hoey, the DUP's Ian Paisley Jr and Wetherspoons man Martin. Tice thanked gel trainers and 'two-skin socks' for saving his feet from evisceration as he arrived in the company of a group of protesters singing 'Bye bye, EU, bye bye, EU' to the tune of 'Auld Lang Syne'.[8] Mark Francois and Peter Bone came over from the Commons to address the rally.

Tommy Robinson, Ukip's Gerard Batten and a gang of far-right activists set up a rival Make Brexit Happen sound stage, which marred proceedings, but by then Farage had inoculated himself from such associations by ensuring his new project looked very different from Ukip.

The Brexit Party suffered its own birth pangs. It was established not as a party but as a company – 'The Brexit Party Limited' – incorporated with Companies House on 23 November 2018. 'We came to the conclusion long before Christmas that we were not leaving on 29 March, so we had to be getting ourselves ready,' said Gawain Towler, who would be the party's spokesman. A formal announcement was made on 20 January 2019 by Catherine Blaiklock, a former Ukip economics spokesman who was the Brexit Party's administrator and founding leader. By the start of February, they had raised £1 million and more than two hundred people had offered to stand as candidates. On 5 February, thirteen days before the Tiggers left Labour, the Brexit Party was registered with the Electoral Commission in time to run candidates in both the local and European elections. Farage, who had formally left Ukip in December and was now an independent MEP, said on 8 February that he would stand for the Brexit Party if there were European elections.

Blaiklock was not popular with the Leave Means Leave people with whom she was sharing an office. She was also a liability. Blaiklock resigned on 20 March over Islamophobic messages on Twitter, including re-tweets of messages by Tommy Robinson, leader of the English Defence League, and Mark Collett, an ex-BNP activist who was the subject of the 2002 documentary *Young, Nazi and Proud*. 'Nigel kept everything at an arm's length until the Brexit Party was created,' said Towler. 'He gave Catherine Blaiklock the nod, unaware that she was a raging loon.'[9]

Two weeks later, the party treasurer Mick McGough, also a long-standing UKipper, also stood down after a *Guardian* investigation uncovered antisemitic and homophobic social media comments he had posted in

2017.[10] Towler recalled, 'I was sitting in this tiny little office in a shared space in Victoria Street. I was the only person left. Nigel was going to take over but … he had to step up two weeks earlier than the plan, which was in some ways good because it gave us a bit more time to find the 86 candidates for the European elections that we needed.'[11]

When Farage took over as leader, he dismissed the departures as 'teething problems'. Behind the scenes, however, neither had completely left. 'Mick McGough controlled the bank account for the Brexit Party,' a source revealed. 'We had a ridiculous battle for months on end, where every single bit of expenditure had to go through Mick McGough.' Andrew Reid, who worked with Farage in his UKIP days and was the closest thing the party had to a chief operating officer, recalled, 'There was £200,000 of supporters' donations in a PayPal account which we couldn't get to.' Since the party was established as a company, Blaiklock was the sole owner and sole shareholder and controlled the PayPal account. 'She gave Mick the login details and he penetrated the account far enough to change the password. But then it rejected his ID details and refused to let him do anything else,' Reid wrote in his account of the formative chaos.[12]

Those on the payroll included Farage's sidekick 'Posh George' Cottrell and his spin doctor Dan Jukes, but the goal was to get a broader selection of candidates than Ukip – and to ensure they were not closet racists and conspiracy theorists. Immigration would barely be mentioned in the campaign. A remarkable number of staff were ex-communists. Lesley Katon, a filmmaker who had been a producer on *The Weakest Link*, came from city consultancy Pagefield to be head of candidates. In the early 1980s Katon had been one of the women protesting at Greenham Common against US cruise missiles. On the other side of the fence then was army officer Toby Vintcent, now the Brexit Party's promoter. Mick Hume, a self-styled 'libertarian Marxist' who had launched both *Living Marxism* and *Spiked*, became director of communications.

Towler said, 'The only thing that united everybody in the party was a belief in democracy and the belief that the referendum should be respected. Period. That was it.'[13] They received more than a thousand applications and selected candidates who were notably ethnically diverse. 'We wanted high-profile people from a cross-party or no-party basis who would get people thinking,' Tice explained. 'They all paid £100, so that was quite a useful fundraiser. Hundreds of people got interviewed.'[14]

There were also prominent Conservative defectors. Annunziata Rees-Mogg, sister of Jacob, offered to stand, as did the former shadow home secretary Ann Widdecombe. When Widdecombe was selected as the lead candidate for the South-West, she received an email from CCHQ telling her she could not remain in the Conservative Party. To their surprise, she replied with a 'charming' note saying, 'I thought that would be the case' and wishing everyone well in her old party.

The most surprising attendee at the Parliament Square rally and the least likely MEP candidate was Claire Fox, the director of the Institute of Ideas think tank, a former member of the Revolutionary Communist Party, which defended the IRA bombing of Warrington. A regular on *The Moral Maze* and *Question Time*, she had attracted controversy after standing up for Gary Glitter's right to download child porn. But as a left-wing Brexiteer, she shared the view of Tony Benn and Peter Shore that the EU was an unelected and unaccountable body that was 'a threat to popular sovereignty'. The EU, she believed, had imposed its vision without ever creating the 'demos' of public support to justify it.

Fox's story and her role in the Brexit Party is one of the most fascinating footnotes to the period since, as a deep thinker, she was able to explain important characteristics of Leave voters, which many in the Remain universe (including most of Fox's left-wing friends) failed to grasp. She concluded during the referendum campaign that it was not Nigel Farage and Boris Johnson who had radicalised Leavers but the Remainers themselves. Fox saw how the pledge that their vote would count for something 'captured the imagination' of working-class voters. She then saw how Remainers 'started to attack those people who were considering leaving'. She recalled, 'There was a group of pretty establishment figures saying, "We don't trust you, because you're all racist", or, "You don't understand it", or, "You're xenophobic, and you're all Little Englanders". That galvanised a popular reaction … Ordinary voters – millions and millions of them – realised that something was at stake, and they took it seriously.'[15]

Fox felt the same process of radicalisation happening to her. At a literary event the chair told the audience, 'It's good to be amongst friends. Does anyone here know anyone who's going to vote Leave?' Everybody laughed. They laughed again when Fox said, 'Me!' They thought she was joking. 'It was: you can't be at a literary event in Waterstones and be a Leaver,' she recalled. Afterwards three or four people sidled up to her and said, 'I'm voting Leave, too, but don't tell anyone.'[16]

On referendum night, in the green room of a television studio, Fox had friends 'screaming in my face' in outrage at the result. After the referendum, the attitude of Remainers further radicalised the Leavers. 'The speed with which they started to demonise Leave voters became the preoccupation of Leave voters,' she said.[17] By the start of 2019, she was worried, 'because people were getting very angry and disillusioned with the democratic process, and felt totally betrayed ... I'd got to the point where I just didn't believe we were ever going to leave.'

The week before the 29 March rally, Fox attended a left-Leave meeting and spoke from the floor. In the pub afterwards she was approached by a tall man in the clothes of a country squire. 'Would you be interested in speaking at the rally?' he asked. Fox did not yet know Gawain Towler. 'I'm not speaking at a rally with Farage,' she said. The presence of Kate Hoey, the Labour MP, and Paul Embery, a Fire Brigades Union official, prompted a change of mind. 'I loved that day,' she recalled. 'It was joyous, and it was democratic, and it was authentic.'[18]

Soon afterwards she was asked to meet Farage and Tice who urged her to stand. She refused, telling Farage, 'You're associated with racism far too much for me.' An Asian friend who had voted Remain talked her round. 'Nigel Farage is not a racist,' the friend said. 'But whereas I can smell a racist at ten paces, Nigel Farage can't.' Fox thought this persuasive. 'We have betrayed a democratic vote,' the friend said. 'If you can stand and not leave it up to Farage and his mates, but show that there are other people, then you should do it.' Fox told Farage she would back him but not stand. A week later, after Labour's David Lammy compared the ERG to the Nazis, she phoned Farage and said, 'I'm going to do it.' She remembered, 'My family and friends were pretty outraged.'[19]

The formal launch came on 12 April. In the run-up, Chris Bruni-Lowe and Steven Edginton had daily meetings about the messaging, another area where the Brexit Party did not conform to type. The original slogan was going to be 'Fighting back' or 'Teach them a lesson' but these were only popular with 30 per cent of voters, the hardcore. Bruni-Lowe's research from Leave Means Leave showed that there was a better message: 'Change Politics for Good'. A party official recalled, 'They painted buses with "Fighting back" on and then had to repaint them with this new slogan because it bombed.' Tice said, 'People, even when they are frustrated and angry, want an uplifting, positive message. They don't want a message of war.'[20] The Brexit Party 'stole' the wording of tweets by

Change UK about defending democracy and the change narrative to press their case.

It may be the supreme irony that the party set up to change politics was beaten hollow by the party which represented the people who thought they had already done so – with their vote to Leave. During the European election campaign, Fox found Brexit Party voters 'highly politicised' with 'well-informed opinions'. She said, 'Brexit had come to represent more than Brexit. People were saying, "We need to change politics for good. We need to change everything. We are fed up with being done to and treated like dirt, treated with contempt. We now want a say in British politics. We've got our voice back."'[21] To these voters, Brexit was not the goal, it was the start of a revolt by people who had felt excluded for decades, people who had seen the mechanisms through which they had previously asserted their views, like the trade unions, lose influence. Tice agreed: 'The truth is that many people who voted Brexit from the regions felt left behind, felt ignored, their areas had underinvestment. People just felt that the political system wasn't working in any way, so there was an appetite for change, an appetite for something different.'[22]

This sentiment combined with 'fear that a Remain alliance was trying to scupper the votes of ordinary people' and fury at MPs for enabling it. 'The hatred for what was happening in Parliament was palpable,' Fox said. 'People were furious. Leavers needed a psychological win.' They wanted, she concluded, 'proof that our vote in 2016 counted'.[23]

The desire to do anything to win explains the Brexit Party's success in the European elections, the way Boris Johnson behaved soon afterwards and his victory in the subsequent general election. It also led to a profound indifference to how Brexit was achieved and a belief that no-deal was far preferable to no Brexit. 'People do not think that you need a deal, because the deal was never what it was about,' Fox recalled. 'They prefer to have no-deal than something which could be seen to give the EU jurisdiction over UK sovereignty, in any way.'[24]

Such a stance was incomprehensible to Remainers and pro-dealers, let alone the European Commission. The biggest discord over Brexit was between those whose concern was the nature of the trading relationship and those who simply wanted the UK to make its own decisions, who put a limitless value on sovereignty. 'It's absolutely nothing to do with concrete benefits, it never was,' Fox said. 'It never, ever, ever, ever, ever was. That's why all those people who were told they would lose their jobs if they voted to leave voted to leave regardless.'[25] The same applied to opposition to the European Court of Justice, an institution largely invisible to them. 'They understood what the ECJ meant, which is a court that's got nothing to do with the UK,' Fox said. 'They have to take the diktats of that court. That's what people don't like. That's what they fought against.'[26]

Tapping into these strong currents of opinion, the Brexit Party targeted, almost exclusively, Labour working-class voters. Edginton crafted videos of arch Remainer Lord Adonis telling Brexiteers not to vote Labour and they made films showing that Labour was on the side of the working class under Eurosceptic Tony Benn in the 1970s and that changed when pro-EU Tony Blair won in 1997. The Brexit Party racked up 250 million online impressions in six weeks, more than any other party. Even the *Guardian* proclaimed it a great digital campaign, praise which unnerved Farage, who was more used to media brickbats. 'Nigel was so used to being battered by the press, he was pissed off and angry that there was so much positive coverage,' a colleague said. 'He would come in fuming and bewildered that this was happening.'

Despite the public success, those who worked on the campaign say it was a 'complete clusterfuck' behind the scenes. 'People were running around like headless chickens,' a staffer recalled. Personalities clashed. 'Richard Tice made a huge list of enemies,' a party source said. 'We had an IT contractor who would charge double for any job involving Richard, which he called the "Tice Tax".' Tice may have been out of sorts since he was having a difficult time, personally: 'My mother died in the middle of the [campaign], so I had to bury her in the middle of the election.'[27]

Two days before the election, the Electoral Commission raided the Brexit Party's offices, following a speech by Gordon Brown in which he claimed irregularities with their fundraising. The former prime minister said democracy would be damaged if the Brexit Party was allowed to accept foreign and untraceable donations via PayPal – a curious target since it was used by millions of people to make online purchases. Political gifts of under £500 did not have to be declared.

The probe came as a surprise to Farage, who claimed Brexit Party officials had visited the Electoral Commission the week before. 'They said they were perfectly happy with our procedures and gave us a clean bill of health. We asked them to put that in writing, they didn't do so. We then said, "Why don't you come into our offices and see our systems." "Oh no," they said, "we are too busy before the election to do that."' Farage pointed out, accurately, that the board of the commission were all Remain supporters and accused them of 'an outrageous act of political interference'. It was left to Tice to deny the specific allegation. 'The Brexit Party only receives money in sterling,' he said, offering the BBC the chance to send someone to 'look at our PayPal account'.

None of it mattered. When the results were counted, the Brexit Party romped to victory. Farage secured 5.2 million votes, 30.4 per cent of the total and won 29 seats in the European Parliament. The Lib Dems, flying the flag for Remain, took 16 and Labour just 10. A Brexit Party official tweeted out after the result, 'It took the Labour Party forty-five years to win the popular vote, the Brexit Party did it within forty-five days.'

Labour was hamstrung by LOTO's fudged position on a referendum. Keir Starmer and Tom Watson had wanted to offer a referendum on any deal. Richard Corbett, the leader of Labour's MEPs, and Emily Thornberry also thrashed out 'referendum and remain' language for the manifesto. Instead, the party went into the campaign promising only to hold a referendum if it was a deal which did not meet their demands. 'It was massively complicated,' a shadow minister recalled.

Labour finished fifth in Scotland and third in Wales, their worst performances ever. Richard Leonard, the leader of the Scottish Labour Party, and Mark Drakeford, the first minister in Wales, both came out straight after the result to back a People's Vote in all circumstances. Starmer said, 'In those EU elections, lots of Labour voters deserted us for the other parties. Most of the analysis shows that for every one voter we lost to the Brexit Party, we lost three to Remain parties.'[28]

Even Brexit Party officials were surprised by the meltdown in the Conservative vote. Theresa May's final act as prime minister was to slump to fifth place with just 8.8 per cent, the worst result for the Tories in any national election in more than a century. They won just four seats. 'We had people from CCHQ voting for the Brexit Party,' a source said. 'Tory MPs voting Brexit Party, Tory cabinet ministers voting Brexit Party.'

The European elections of 2019 were a watershed moment. Two new parties had tried to represent the twin poles of the Brexit divide. Change UK was late to the party, unclear in its aims, weak in its leadership and internally divided. The Brexit Party was the most successful electoral vehicle since Vote Leave. It had prepared in advance, researched the arguments which worked, launched at the right time, had a clear and limited goal on which each of its candidates agreed, plus strong leadership. It was proof that coherent political strategy can trump professionalism.

Claire Fox said, 'If there hadn't been this assault on the electorate after the referendum result, which then consolidated Leavers as Leavers, with Remainers also emerging as an identity rather than just a vote in a referendum, then I think that populist revolt around Brexit would have been a moment that would not have lasted. After four years of feeling under assault, it became a politicised movement.'[29]

May resigned on 24 May, the day after the European elections. The results came two days later, a posthumous political humiliation. Having suffered the worst ever parliamentary defeat four months earlier, the prime minister now led her party, one of the greatest election-winning forces in the Western world, into its most abject defeat in history. If they were to survive, the Conservatives had to abandon May's attempts to please everyone. The only way they could defeat the Brexit Party was to become a more successful version of it. That is what all of May's would-be successors set out to achieve.

PART FIVE

TIME OUT

COMETH THE HOUR ...

June to July 2019

DÉJÀ BLUE

The Leadership Election

July 2019

The Conservative Party leadership contest of 2019 was the political equivalent of the Grand National: a crowded field with few thoroughbreds which was more a test of endurance than class. Under Tory rules, MPs would whittle down the field to two candidates, who would then fight it out for the votes of the grassroots membership. The assumption of MPs and media was that the run-off would be between an establishment big beast or Remainer and the flag-carrier for the Brexiteers.

When it began, Boris Johnson might have been the logical choice for many outside Westminster to solve the Brexit conundrum that he, more than anyone else, had created. But within SW1 there was a perception that MPs – many of whom regarded him as self-serving, disorganised and unreliable – might not rally to his cause in sufficient numbers.

The first two candidates out of the blocks were Jeremy Hunt and Dominic Raab, with Sajid Javid positioning himself as heir presumptive in cabinet meetings. Hunt, the foreign secretary, had quietly wooed MPs funnelled to him by his 'whips', Philip Dunne and Robert Goodwill. 'Jeremy was clearly way more advanced than anybody else at that point,' a special adviser recalled. Rival camps claimed he already had 75 backers. This was nonsense designed to damage him when the voting started.

Hunt's main rival on the establishment 'track' was Javid. The home secretary made sure everyone knew he was the son of a bus driver, but MPs struggled to recall anything memorable he had done in four cabinet posts. Even his critics expected Javid to be organised. In the event, while other candidates began to unveil supporters and put out launch videos, Javid was left standing. Spending two hours a day signing warrants was not a great platform from which to campaign for the leadership. Javid had little Commons organisation and rival camps watched bemused as he stalked big-name cabinet endorsements while Hunt, realising that every Tory MP's vote was worth the same, racked up the numbers on the backbenches. 'He didn't have anything resembling a proper operation when it mattered,' a rival adviser said. After viewing Javid's soporific launch video, a senior minister remarked, 'I expect a speak-your-weight machine would be a better communicator than Theresa, but people looked at Saj and thought he was not ready.'

Aware he was in trouble, Javid hired Matthew Elliott, the chief executive of Vote Leave, to run the campaign. Elliott brought in journalist Andy Silvester to run the comms. He quickly set up a WhatsApp group to communicate with lobby journalists (an innovation which was copied by every other campaign and special adviser thereafter).

Javid's weakness encouraged others to try their hand. Some of them – including James Cleverly, Sam Gyimah and Kit Malthouse – quickly discovered that their high hopes exceeded other people's low expectations. Johnny Mercer paid for 'strategic counsel' from former Cameron spin doctor Andy Coulson on how to navigate his path to power, but failed to locate it. Matt Hancock and Rory Stewart hoped to fight Hunt for the One Nation wing of the party and catch lightning in a bottle.

The most intriguing, though, was Michael Gove. News that Sunday that the environment secretary would run electrified the race, setting up a repeat of the 2016 Johnson-Gove psychodrama. Gove was despised by hardline Brexiteers for his fears of no-deal and his willingness to support May's compromises. But he could still attract serious Remainers and Brexit pragmatists. His support grew after his barnstorming speech in the January no-confidence debate. John Hayes introduced him to Mel Stride, one of the best-connected MPs, who ran a dining club called Deep Blue at his Chelsea home. Stride and his friend Guy Opperman became effective whips for Gove. The inaugural team dinner included Hayes, Liz Truss, Nicky Morgan, George Eustice, Tom Tugendhat and Kemi Badenoch. There might have been more if Gove had committed earlier to running. Potential supporters like Greg Hands and Shailesh Vara went elsewhere. Others, such as Nadhim Zahawi, were flaky. 'He offered to run Michael's campaign,' a Gove ally said. 'Within ten days, he was Raab's chief executive. Then he was on Jeremy Hunt's team for a week – and he ended up with Boris.' However when, in early May, the Goveites staged a rally in a pub called the Surprise, he could count on at least 25 votes, a respectable base from which to build.

In early 2019, the perceived frontrunner on the Brexiteer 'track' was Raab, the former Brexit secretary. He built a good operation, which included Paul Stephenson, the communications chief of Vote Leave, widely seen as the best Tory spin doctor of his generation. But Raab was a flawed candidate; as Brexit secretary he lost private office staff as others misplaced spectacles. Civil servants regarded him as a martinet with 'a woman problem'. This he tried to neutralise with a biographical *Sunday Times Magazine* interview in early May, pictured with his wife Erica. But when Andrew Marr quizzed him about a comment, made in 2011, that feminists were 'obnoxious bigots', Raab doubled down, telling the *Spectator* he was not a 'feminist', a boast which soon backfired.

Raab's stumbles encouraged other Brexiteers to challenge Johnson. These included Esther McVey, Andrea Leadsom and even Steve Baker. On 10 January, Baker discussed the leadership with his sounding board Christopher Montgomery. Baker's diary was peppered with references to people encouraging him to run throughout April and May 2019. On 29 May, he was fourth in the ConservativeHome list of the most popular senior Tories with the grassroots, but ruled himself out on 1 June after just two MPs pressed 'enthusiastically' to sign his nomination papers.

Boris Johnson might have looked like a cart horse (or as *Guardian* columnist Marina Hyde put it, 'an Oxfam donation bag torn open by a fox'),[1] but as an election winner he was the one proven thoroughbred in the field. Yet for six months, he had presided over exactly what sceptical MPs most feared – a disorganised mess. Since his resignation from the cabinet the previous July, Johnson had been exiled to a poky and decaying office in 1 Parliament Street. There, a proto-campaign team took shape: Lee Cain, Oliver Lewis, Conor Burns, Jacob Rees-Mogg, Anne-Marie Trevelyan, Nadine Dorries, Charlie Elphicke and Ranil Jayawardena. On 19 December, Steve Baker recorded in his diary that he was asked to run the national campaign for Johnson, after the MPs had voted. One of Johnson's advisers recalled, 'He started promising various different things to lots of people.' Jayawardena and Lewis were both told to take charge of policy. Even Johnson's announcement that he would run was unplanned. On 16 May, more than a week before May resigned, he said publicly 'Of course I'm going to go for it.' Typically, he just spoke his mind. 'We had no idea he was going to do that,' an aide revealed. Surveying the chaos, Dominic Cummings texted Lewis, 'I want nothing to do with this. It's not going to work.'

Three things made Johnson the favourite. The first was the failure of MV3 on 29 March, the original Brexit day. The second was his decision to recruit James Wharton, who had lost his Stockton South seat in the 2017 election, as campaign manager, and Gavin Williamson as chief whip. (A cabinet minister joked, 'You've got to have Gavin on side otherwise he'll launch a military coup against you.') They formed a triumvirate with Grant Shapps, who had been compiling a spreadsheet on the views of MPs since his attempted coup against Theresa May in the autumn of 2017.[2] Twenty months earlier, Williamson had denounced Shapps publicly. Now he joked, 'You turned out to be right after all!'

Shapps spent his time on the backbenches reading Robert Caro's four-volume biography of Lyndon Johnson, absorbing LBJ's lessons on 'how to count'. As a centrist Remainer with a business background, Shapps first assumed he would support Hunt, but then concluded a Brexiteer was needed. Recalling the final scene of *Darkest Hour* where it is said of Churchill that he 'mobilised the English language and sent it into battle', he concluded Johnson was the party's best hope. Johnson loyalists detected opportunism. An MP said, 'Grant came along when his spreadsheet showed Boris at fifty per cent plus one, because he knew Boris was going to win.' Johnson knew he needed a professional organisation if he was to broaden his appeal beyond the Brexiteer right. In a grim assessment of his core support, he remarked, 'We've cornered the market in sex pests', a comment that would come back to bite him. When he saw Shapps, he solemnly declared, 'You will run the data and I will do what you say.'

Shapps's first law of the spreadsheet was 'everybody is against you until proven otherwise'. This forced Back Boris to be relentless and thorough in their contacts with MPs. His second rule was 'own the data', countering a mistake Johnson had made in 2016 when Gove's advisers controlled his supporter list. Shapps also stole from a book called *Principles* by Ray Dalio, a hedge fund billionaire, who assigned a 'believability weight' to everything he heard. Shapps used algorithms to weigh each 'data point' gathered from MPs. He then assigned a supportiveness percentage to each MP. By assigning fractional probabilities, the system compensated for the lies and self-deception which hamper 'counting'. Shapps explained to a friend, 'We never thought we were getting everyone right, we just thought that on average we were getting people right.' He was careful only to move people slowly towards 100 per cent as more evidence was accrued. Even when MPs reached 100 per cent, Shapps only trusted the number if they went 'extra-curricular' – making a speech, tweeting their support, telling their local paper, or becoming a 'handler'. 'We don't go out and spin numbers,' he told colleagues. 'I don't care if we're behind in declarations with two weeks to go. What I care about is we genuinely have people on side.'

To minimise leaks, Shapps refused to let the garrulous Johnson see the raw data. Instead, he supplied a colour-coded chart, which marked MPs with a deeper blue, the more committed they were, so the candidate had a visual impression of progress without blurting out the numbers to MPs and media friends.

Even before the leadership contest, Shapps had used his methodology to more accurately calculate the number of Tory rebels at MV3 than Julian Smith, winning a meal at Nando's off the chief whip. During the campaign, a small group met at 9.30 a.m. in Shapps's office, which included Williamson, Wharton if he was free, key lieutenants Nigel Adams, Simon Clarke, Anne-Marie Trevelyan, Graham Stuart, Charlie Elphicke and Ellie Lyons. They would decide who to target that day based on Shapps's data – sometimes supporters of a candidate about to drop out; on one occasion a push to turn 50 per cent MPs into 75 per centers. A second meeting followed at 10 a.m. in Williamson's office, where the battalion of 'handlers', the campaign foot soldiers, were given their marching orders.

Shapps also enlisted the help of Carrie Symonds. Johnson's instinct was to phone random MPs on a hunch. Wharton and Shapps asked Symonds to ensure that he only called those who the spreadsheet had identified. 'Carrie was really helpful. They made her the taskmaster,' an MP said. Williamson's team gathered evidence that Chloe Smith, who they never suspected would back Johnson, was in play. Symonds told him to make the call. Twenty minutes later she messaged Shapps to say, 'Boris would never have called her in a million years had it not been put on the list and said it was worth a go. He's very pleased.'

Not all these conversations were easy. In private, MPs exploited Johnson's desire for their votes to tell him what they thought of him.

'People said the most outrageously blunt things: "My concern about you, Boris, is with your philandering",' an ally reflected. 'There's something about Boris that gives the public and his colleagues permission to be ultra direct with him and not feel embarrassed. It is both his greatest strength and the source of his greatest weakness. He's sensitive, and that upsets him, and people think it doesn't.' Conor Burns, Johnson's parliamentary private secretary, sat in on most of these meetings and came to his aid when one truculent female MP marched into his office and complained, 'This is like going to the doctor. Your staff are rude and you kept me waiting. Why should I vote for you? You don't even come into the chamber to listen to my speeches.'

The MP was not a renowned orator but Johnson, busking it, declared, 'That's unfair. I recall a very fine speech that you made two months ago, on the withdrawal agreement.'

'I've never spoken on the withdrawal agreement,' she snapped.

Burns texted Johnson's PA in the outer office who quickly searched the parliamentary database and discovered just such a speech. Burns interjected to inform the MP. 'You see,' Johnson declared, 'I paid more attention to your speeches in the chamber than you do yourself.' The MP did not, in the end, vote for him.

The common refrain of many MPs was, 'Boris, I get that you can campaign, but you're not capable of doing the job.' Johnson's response was not to compare himself to Churchill but to another charismatic campaigner whose governing skills were always doubted: 'My political inspiration is Ronald Reagan. I want to be out there sowing optimism and selling the mission. I'm not afraid to have big personalities around me, unlike Mrs May, who's like one of those giant Yucca trees in the Brazilian rainforest under whose shade everything dies. I'm going to be the chairman of the board and I am going to have a Number 10 that empowers big figures who are going to be the delivery figures in the key departments.' This was a model which might have worked, but it was not to be the one Johnson eventually adopted.

Nonetheless, as the votes came his way, Johnson, like Reagan, was a happy warrior. 'Boris wanted to show Carrie,' another Tory observed. 'He blew up his life, only winning would be worth it.'

Shapps knew he had better intelligence than the other campaigns, not least because he received a text from Rory Stewart and phone calls from Esther McVey and Sam Gyimah asking him to help them, unaware he was working for Johnson. Shapps explained he could not help but suggested several MPs Gyimah might call. 'Are they backing me?' Gyimah asked, oblivious of his own base. When a Gove supporter approached Shapps, he explained he was 'with Boris'. The MP admitted he had also been to see Johnson. 'I know,' said Shapps. 'You saw him at two o'clock and your main issues are this, this and this, you are now considering this and your constituency chairman thinks this.' The MP was floored.

The third and final game changer for Johnson was the European election result. Staring at a national vote share of 9.1 per cent, MPs turned to the candidate they knew was flawed but who was a proven vote winner. 'Before that, we were doing well,' said a member of Raab's team. 'After that, Boris was ahead and pulling away.'

Johnson's growing confidence and his determination to leave the EU come what may on 31 October torpedoed the possibility of a pact with Amber Rudd to unite right and left of the party, a Frankenstein creation dubbed 'BAmber' by its advocates. For two years Johnson had been telling Rudd, 'Let's do this together', hinting she might be his chancellor. She went for dinner with the couple at Carrie Symonds' flat in Kennington before Christmas 2018 and asked how Johnson would persuade the ERG to vote for a Brexit deal to avoid no-deal. Unsatisfied, she concluded, 'I don't see how you're going to protect the economy.' In late May 2019, Johnson went for drinks at Rudd's house to ask her to 'be part of' his team, floating the idea of Rudd as 'my Prescott'. Her team promoted the idea of 'BAmber' to gauge reaction among her allies. 'She got quite a lot of backlash from her Remainer friends,' an ally said. 'People like Ruth Davidson, John Major and Michael Heseltine. That put her off.' The relief among the Brexiteers of Team Boris was palpable.

On 18 March, Rudd and Nicky Morgan established the One Nation caucus, to ensure their faction would have a say in the outcome of the leadership election. 'It was deliberately set up as a counterweight to the ERG,' Rudd said. It became the key constituency for the candidates on the establishment side of the draw. Rudd told Hancock, the health secretary, that she hoped he would run, but did not explicitly promise to back him. Gove had also approached Hancock after a dinner in January 2019 to say, 'Matt, one day you could be the prime minister.' It was a conclusion Hancock had already come to. On hearing later that Hancock was running, Gove – who would have preferred a free run at his supporters – said, 'Every corporal has a field marshal's baton in his backpack.' Hancock, believing he had Rudd's support, began the campaign hoping to be the freshest face, a position from which William Hague in 1997, Iain Duncan Smith in 2001 and Liam Fox in 2005 had all prospered. Yet he was quickly eclipsed by Rory Stewart, the international development secretary.

Stewart began a walking tour around Britain, releasing eccentric videos of his interactions with the public on social media. The first was shot in Kew Gardens on a tripod-mounted iPhone, but Stewart stuck his hand out towards the lens as if filming a selfie, the first case of a politician faking a video to make it look more amateurish. The following day he admitted once smoking opium in Iran. Soon strangeness was his leitmotif. He described himself in one interview as 'the Trumpian anti-Trump'.

Stewart's core team was his wife, Shoshana, who ran their Kabul-based charity, Turquoise Mountain, plus a raft of former May staffers: pollster James Johnson, strategist Chris Wilkins, spinner Lizzie Loudon (and Ramsay Jones, a former Scotland Office spad, who stepped in when Loudon went on maternity leave). Attempts to hold formal meetings were doomed. 'I soon learnt with Rory you don't do that,' one aide said. 'He sets the strategy and you've got to be with him. You had to run to keep up, literally.' After years of miserable calculation with a prime minister who did not seem to know her own mind, the Mayites found Stewart's instinctual campaign liberating. 'If you put a piece of paper with some lines in front of Theresa she might rearrange the paragraph order,' one said. 'If you put that in front of Rory, he wouldn't even look at it because he's got his own ideas.'

On Brexit, however, his big idea was May's. Stewart said he would seek to get more MPs behind her deal, refusing to rule out a permanent customs union. Phillip Lee and Guto Bebb tried, in vain, to persuade him to back a second referendum instead. 'What is the point of having a pitch for a soft Brexit outcome?' Lee asked. 'You're going to lose.' Stewart was unpersuaded.

On 4 June, the One Nation group hosted the first formal hustings, which were dominated by Brexit. The running had been made by Johnson on 24 May, just a few hours after May resigned. At a conference in the Swiss town of Interlaken, he declared, 'We will leave the EU on 31 October, deal or no-deal.' It was what Brexiteers had wanted to hear for two years. At the hustings, Johnson got loud support – and the front pages of the newspapers – by warning that the Tories faced 'potential extinction' if they failed to leave the EU by the end of October.

The most important meeting of the day for Johnson had taken place earlier, when the ERG met to decide who to support. The hard Brexiteers wanted just one candidate, to avoid splitting their vote and allowing a Remainer to emerge victorious as May had in 2016. It was a straight fight between Johnson and Raab. Those sitting in judgement were the Paleosceptic grandees and Spartans: Iain Duncan Smith, Bill Cash, Owen Paterson, John Redwood, Bernard Jenkin, Priti Patel, Mark Francois and Steve Baker. Jacob Rees-Mogg recused himself as a committed Johnson supporter. Raab told the ERG he would adopt the Malthouse Compromise as government policy. Johnson told the group what they wanted to hear: 'The withdrawal agreement is dead.' At Christopher Montgomery's suggestion, Steve Baker asked, 'Will you employ Dominic Cummings?' and Johnson was clear: 'No chance!' Baker recorded in his diary 'Back Boris! (Not Dom)'. Not trusting Johnson, a smaller group of ERG grandees called him back the following day. 'He gave exactly the answer they wanted to hear to all the questions,' a source said.

Johnson also paid lip service to the idea, advocated since the spring by Rees-Mogg and Duncan Smith, that the UK could use Article XXIV of the General Agreement on Tariffs and Trade (GATT) – the World Trade Organisation's rulebook on trade in goods – to secure a zero tariff, zero quota agreement with the EU in the event of no-deal. Rees-Mogg claimed WTO rules would allow the UK a ten-year grace period to negotiate a free trade agreement. In effect, Brexiteers citing 'GATT XXIV' believed there was no risk at all from no-deal. But, as Vote Leave's Oliver Lewis explained, a grace period could only be achieved if both sides agreed they were working towards a deal, and if they were prepared to file the details of the proposed treaty. In other words, there would still have to be some sort of agreement with the EU. Duncan Smith advocated a 'standstill' deal allowed under GATT XXIV, but Britain already had a deal where rules wouldn't change; that's what the transition period was. Lewis implored Johnson not to give credence to the idea, but his approach was to say what was needed to achieve his immediate goal and deal with the consequences later. Both Lewis and Geoffrey Cox were asked to devise a

Brexit plan. Cox told Johnson he should 'take Theresa May's deal and switch off the backstop bit by bit' – precisely what Cox had tried and failed to negotiate in February and March. To make matters worse, Duncan Smith thought he was the senior adviser and Baker believed he was going to be made Brexit secretary. 'It was basically just chaos at this stage,' one adviser said.

Raab created waves at the One Nation hustings by saying he was prepared to prorogue Parliament to sideline MPs and secure Brexit on 31 October. 'We risk Parliament blocking no-deal and the EU blocking a better deal, so we need a new approach,' he said. This was the first public mention of prorogation, constitutional arcana on which every commentator soon feigned expertise. The idea met with revulsion from Amber Rudd, who said, 'It's outrageous. We are not Stuart kings.' Johnson's team were irritated with Raab for publicising the issue. 'If you announce in advance, it defeats the purpose,' one said. Johnson told the hustings he was not interested in 'archaic' mechanisms, not ruling it out, but not setting hares running either. The episode made him seem less extreme than Raab.

The centrist candidates found themselves struggling for definition. Javid said he would not take no-deal off the table but added, 'We will not beat the Brexit Party by becoming the Brexit Party.' Hancock was the first to rule out no-deal, a position matched by Hunt, who ditched his cabinet positioning under May and branded it 'political suicide'.

Johnson became the vanishingly short-priced favourite on 5 June, when he received the endorsement of three of the brightest young MPs: Rishi Sunak, Oliver Dowden and Robert Jenrick. In a joint article for *The Times* headlined 'The Tories are in deep peril. Only Boris Johnson can save us', they argued that Johnson alone could defeat the 'twin threats' of Nigel Farage and Jeremy Corbyn. They hailed his 'instant credibility' on Brexit and his 'sense of excitement and hope' about the future.

The endorsement had been initiated by Carrie Symonds, who was keen for Johnson to get prominent support beyond the fossilised Tory right. She approached Sunak, who got the other two on board. Sunak had shocked David Cameron and George Osborne by backing Brexit,[3] a decision which prompted Osborne to declare, 'We're fucked.' The sentiment was one now shared by Gove, who had been backed by both Sunak and Jenrick in 2016. Dowden, who backed May three years earlier, told friends, 'These are populist times and we need a populist prime minister.'

In her office in Downing Street, Theresa May saw the article and turned to her aides. 'Oh my God,' she said. 'This means Boris has won.'

Gove soon had more to worry about than endorsements. Around noon on Friday 7 June, he was contacted by Simon Walters, the veteran mischief-maker at the *Daily Mail* to be told that the paper was planning to serialise a biography of the environment secretary, by the journalist Owen Bennett, which revealed that Gove had once taken cocaine. Bennett had got in touch three weeks earlier, as he was finalising his manuscript, to reveal details of Gove's birth, adoption and mother which he had never known. 'Michael was quite shaken by that,' a friend revealed. 'That was the first time we realised Owen hadn't told us everything that was in the book.' The first they knew about the cocaine was when Walters called.

The environment secretary gathered his team – Henry Cook, Henry Newman, Josh Grimstone and Declan Lyons. It was not until 4 p.m. that they saw the extract and knew what they were dealing with. It revealed that on the evening in July 2016 when he withdrew support from Boris Johnson and decided to run himself, his spads had asked Gove if there were any skeletons in his closet. Gove admitted that he had used cocaine.

Team Gove mulled the option of him giving 'the Cameron answer' – that he had not done drugs since going into politics. But they concluded it would only fuel the story. 'Owen's account of 2016 says we advised him to use the Cameron line, so to use it now would be doubly evasive,' an aide said. It was Gove's campaign launch the following Monday. 'It will dominate everything,' he said. 'I'm not going to lie about it.'

Saturday evening brought more peril. The *Mail on Sunday* splashed on claims that Gove snorted coke at a party just hours after writing a column for *The Times* condemning middle-class drug use. His future in the contest hung in the balance. Before 'coke-gate', Gove was 'neck and neck' with Hunt for the right to take on Johnson. The *Telegraph*, for which Johnson wrote a column, declared Gove's campaign 'dead'. In fact, his supporters were not deserting but 'people were more reluctant to come out publicly,' an ally said. On Sunday morning, he endured a torrid time with Andrew Marr, admitting 'drugs wreck lives' and that his cocaine use was a 'mistake which I profoundly regret'.

At 5 p.m. that day, he was reading out his launch speech to Cook, Newman and Grimstone. 'It was all a bit pedestrian,' one recalled. They suggested he put the text aside. Gove spoke off the cuff. 'It was so much more powerful,' an aide said. 'That's the point we thought, "We can punch through this and smash it tomorrow."' They messaged the campaign WhatsApp group, 'Let Gove be Gove.' A cabinet minister wooed by Gove said he defined himself as 'the capable side of Brexit' in contrast to Johnson. Asked why he had turned on Johnson in 2016, Gove replied, 'It was his appetite for risk – not just in his private life, but risk in everything he does.'

That weekend, Javid got the backing of three Home Office ministers – Caroline Nokes, Victoria Atkins and Baroness Williams – and Ruth Davidson, who had been a friend since he beat her to the Bromsgrove selection in 2010. The leader of the Scottish Tories had planned to attack Johnson, who she despised, but she was talked out of it, in part by Amber Rudd. A Tory political adviser also revealed, 'Carrie told me over lunch that Boris spoke to [Ruth], Boris calmed her down.'

Rudd, having flirted with Johnson and then told Gove she would back Hancock, before switching to him in the later rounds, now decided to back Hunt because he was 'the most anti-no-deal'. Hancock was furious and his supporters phoned MPs to complain about her behaviour. A Rudd ally explained, 'She really didn't like the campaign Hancock was running. She thought the guy had absolutely no fucking chance.'

On the evening of Saturday 8 June, both Steve Baker and Priti Patel joined Back Boris. The following day it was Alun Cairns, the Welsh secretary, and Chris Grayling. Prepping for his first campaign interview, with the *Sunday Times*, Johnson told aides, 'We probably are going to have to go for no-deal, aren't we?'

Hunt had other plans. He revealed on 9 June that he had spoken to Angela Merkel and was confident she would negotiate over the backstop. When they met at D-Day commemorations a few days earlier, the German chancellor had referred to it as a 'British Isles problem' requiring a solution agreed by Ireland and the UK. 'Of course we can find a deal,' she said. Hunt told aides, 'She even hinted that she wouldn't accept a deal that trapped Germany in the customs union if Germany was leaving.'

On the morning of Monday 10 June, Johnson was in the *Telegraph* pledging to raise the threshold at which people started paying the 40p rate of income tax from £50,000 to £80,000, an £8.9 billion tax cut benefiting three million families, but a curious choice when Johnson was wooing the party left. When the article dropped, Gavin Williamson 'bollocked' Oliver Lewis. 'There was a lot of effing and blinding,' a source said. 'Gavin did a lot of shouting.' In actual fact the blame lay with Liz Truss.

That same day five candidates staged campaign launches: Hancock, Raab, Esther McVey, Hunt and finally Gove. Hancock had hoped his speech would be memorable because he made it with no notes. Unfortunately, the decision to position himself in front of a wall of glass as the rain thundered down outside meant he could hardly be seen or heard. 'He looked like an IRA mole being interviewed in silhouette,' Michael Deacon, the *Telegraph*'s sketchwriter, noted. Of the main contenders, Hunt made news by unveiling Penny Mordaunt as a supporter, alongside Rudd, whose face was 'like thunder' as Mordaunt was hailed as the bigger coup.

Gove's priority was to show MPs that he still had his mojo. His extempore speech went well but he was pressed on his drug use and his relationship with Johnson. Irritated by briefings from Back Boris that he might withdraw, he noted that in 2016 it had been Boris who had pulled stumps. 'If I get through to the final two against Mr Johnson, this is what I will say to him: "Mr Johnson, whatever you do, don't pull out, I know you have before".' Gove pleaded ignorance when the comment was interpreted as a sexual slur about Johnson's priapic past. But his team knew the best way to avoid another day of cocaine headlines was to give the media a story about the Johnson-Gove psychodrama. 'We did want to show that Michael was the one to take on Boris,' an aide said. 'We did decide to go strong on Boris, definitely.'

Johnson's launch was not until Wednesday morning, 12 June. The sense of it being the main event after the trailers was hard to shake. When Johnson sought the backing of Johnny Mercer, the former soldier proclaimed, 'We're going to do this together, my friend. I'll introduce you when you come to Plymouth and then everywhere else. It's you and me.' Johnson's allies were somewhat disturbed when Mercer emerged clutching the wrong end of the stick. 'He told everyone he and Boris were on a "joint ticket",' one said. 'We had to unfold that.' When the press assembled for the launch on Carlton House Terrace, it was Geoffrey Cox, instead, who took to the podium to introduce him. The attorney general barely knew Johnson, but had concluded he was 'the man for the time'. Over breakfast at the Corinthia Hotel, Johnson asked Cox, 'What do you want?' He primly replied, 'We shouldn't be talking about things like that.' The one request he made was that he be 'central to Brexit policy'.

Also present at the launch, to the consternation of Johnson's team who had no idea she was due to attend, was Carrie Symonds, who at that point had never been seen in public as his paramour. Shortly before the event began, Alice Robinson, Johnson's parliamentary office manager, warned Conor Burns, 'We've got a problem. Carrie is five minutes away with Nimco Ali.'

Burns found Johnson preparing for his speech. 'Carrie's coming?'

'I'm so sorry,' Johnson blustered. 'I completely forgot ...'

'Fuck off, you did,' Burns exclaimed. 'Who is handling the arrival?' They had no security or police protection to help clear a path through the phalanx of photographers outside.

'I suppose you are,' said Johnson, enjoying Burns' discomfort.

Burns greeted the car and was clobbered by a cameraman. Symonds was smuggled into the event by a rear door while Burns tried to secure a seat for her at the front, where two rows had been reserved for MPs and ministers. Ranil Jayawardena refused to move, declaring grandly, 'I'm an MP.' Eventually John Whittingdale, her old boss, came to Burns' rescue and secured Symonds a seat.

In the first ballot, the following day, 13 June, Johnson's position as front-runner was confirmed. He got 114 votes, more than a third of the parliamentary party, enough to guarantee a place in the final run-off. It had always seemed like a battle for second place. Now it was. Gove was third with 37 votes but had done better than he feared. 'We worried that one or two people were going to flake off,' a friend said. Hunt was just six votes ahead of him, rather than the 10 to 15 Gove had expected. Raab, fourth on 27, and Javid behind him on 23, failed to live up to their high expectations at the turn of the year. Javid's spokesman, Andy Silvester, grimly spun former journalistic colleagues that the home secretary had secured 'a strong fifth' place. Hancock, on 20, got one more vote than Rory Stewart, but Stewart's emergence killed his chances. The 1922 Committee, fearing an endless contest, had imposed thresholds to ensure only viable contenders continued. Andrea Leadsom (11), Mark Harper (10) and Esther McVey (9) all failed to reach the target of 17.

That night Hancock suggested to Gove that they meet and invite Stewart. When he had first decided to run, Hancock had told Gove he would back him if he dropped out of the contest. The following morning, Gove and Stewart had breakfast at Mel Stride's house to try and come to a deal. Hancock did not turn up and announced he was pulling out. Gove wanted Stewart to back him, but Stewart refused: 'Michael, you should back me. Even though you've got the numbers, I've got the momentum.'

Later, Gove went to see Hancock. He said, 'The two of us together could win this and even if we don't, we will run Boris so close it will be impossible for him to ignore the arguments we've made.' He offered Hancock any job he wanted. Hancock said he needed to think about it. Over the weekend, Gove recruited intermediaries to lean on the health secretary, among them Ruth Davidson, Cameron staffers Ameet Gill and Daniel Korski plus Alex Chalk. They argued it would be 'choppy' if he backed Johnson, following his opposition to no-deal. David Cameron phoned Hancock and told him not to back Johnson but said he did not need to commit to anyone to have a bright future. However, George Osborne, Jamie Njoku-Goodwin, his special adviser, and Adam Atashzai, another ex-Cameron aide, all concluded that Johnson was going to win and urged Hancock to get on board and seek a promotion. Fifteen minutes after the first debate, on the Sunday evening, a sheepish Hancock called Gove to say he was backing Johnson. His op-ed endorsement dropped minutes later, good publicity for the frontrunner, who had taken a pounding in the media for refusing to turn up to the debate.

The ninety-minute broadcast was Rory Stewart's coming out party and cemented his status as the most popular Conservative with non-Tories – a role with limitations in a contest decided by party members. Stewart essayed a puny-framed but big-brained vibe to attack the 'machismo' of the other four candidates over their Brexit pledges. 'Everyone is saying "I'm tougher",' he complained. 'Everyone is like, "trust me, I'm the guy, I can defeat the impossible odds". And I'm accused of being a defeatist by trying to be realistic. It reminds me of trying to cram a whole series of rubbish bags into the rubbish bin ... I was tempted to say, "believe in the bin, believe in Britain". It's nonsense.' The Twitterati seized on this mockery of the Brexiteers and #believeinthebin began to trend online.

Stewart, Hunt, Gove and Javid condemned Raab's refusal to rule out prorogation. Javid called it the action of 'a dictator ... You don't deliver

on democracy by trashing democracy.' It was left to Hunt to challenge
Banquo's ghost at the empty podium: 'Where is Boris? If his team won't
let him out to debate with five pretty friendly colleagues, how is he going
to get on with twenty-seven European colleagues?' The Back Boris team
saw little to gain and everything to lose by turning up. Johnson was again
the lone absentee at a hustings arranged by the parliamentary lobby on
the 17th, which Gove compared to 'Hamlet without the prince'.

These absences did nothing to dent Johnson's momentum. In the
second ballot, on 18 June, he surged further ahead, securing 126 votes.
Gove (41) closed the gap a little to Hunt (46), but Raab (30) was eliminated. While Javid jumped 10 votes to 33, the big story was that they were
both overtaken by Rory Stewart, who nearly doubled his share from 19 to
37. Some of Stewart's extra supporters came from the pool of Hancock's
20 backers but he had also succeeded in capturing a moment. One MP
told a member of Gove's campaign team, 'I declared for someone else,
but I voted for Rory because I thought it was fun.'

There were accusations of chicanery by Williamson, artificially lifting
Stewart – who Johnson was confident of obliterating with a Eurosceptic
membership – as a rival to Gove and Hunt. Williamson personally
controlled a staggering 90 votes from MPs who had passed him their
proxy. The Stewart camp said they could positively account for 36 of the
37. The other vote was believed to be Theresa May, but she was not
saying. Paul Harrison, her press secretary, asked the PM, 'Have you even
told Philip, your husband?' and recalled, 'She looked absolutely aghast.'
May replied indignantly, 'No, absolutely not!'[4]

It briefly seemed possible that Stewart could catch fire and become
Johnson's opponent in the run-off. 'If we get through, it is going to be
ugly,' Stewart told his team. 'It is going to be horrible. It will be Cicero,
saving the Republic from a monster.'

In the third debate on the BBC, on the evening of the 18th, an irritated
Gove roughed up Stewart over his Brexit policy. No longer a novelty
outsider, the MP for Penrith and The Border seemed unprepared for the
spotlight and becoming the focus of attacks. The cameras caught him
looking bored while the others spoke. At one point his body sagged like
a mime artist acting out a sigh as the five contenders perched on bar
stools like an ageing boy band on their third farewell tour. Stewart even
suggested there should not be tax cuts for fifteen years. His plan in debate
prep had been to take on Johnson directly, as he had confronted Raab in

the first debate. But they were positioned on opposite sides of the stage. 'There was no room for conversation,' an aide complained. 'It was a set of mini speeches.' This suited Johnson. The frontrunner was hardly at his best, but he fended off questions about his past comments about Muslims and offered only vague explanations about what a Brexit deal would look like, referring to GATT XXIV as 'Article 24 or whatever it is ...'

The Stewart surge came to a crashing halt in the third ballot the following day, 19 June. His eccentric behaviour in the debate led MPs to conclude that he wasn't ready. Stewart lost ten votes, dropping to 27. Finishing below Javid (38) again, he was eliminated. Hunt and Gove had successfully put the frighteners on supporters who flirted with Stewart in round two. The battle for second place tightened. Gove advanced to 51, just three behind Hunt. Johnson was miles clear on 143. Shapps had sealed his prediction in an envelope. Conor Burns took a picture as Johnson opened it and saw: 143. 'Ridiculous!' he exclaimed. 'He was pretty blown away,' a witness said. 'He thought it was black magic.'

The primary goal of the Johnson camp was to avoid a run-off with Gove, the only candidate who Johnson believed might rough him up in a run-off. They played hardball. 'Our MPs were told, directly in some cases, that if you go for Michael, you will never have another job,' one of Gove's allies said. They also warned that putting Gove into the final two would fuel the psychodrama: 'He's spent the whole campaign attacking Boris, that's not good for party unity.' It was a line Hunt's team was also happy to peddle.

There were also claims of dirty tricks by the Johnson camp. At least one MP supporting another candidate was threatened with the exposure of sexual secrets. 'He was left broken,' a friend said. 'It was really quite horrible.' The MP in question did not change their vote but refused to do or say anything publicly to support his preferred candidate. Williamson, of course, denied that he had anything to do with such activities.

The final two rounds of MPs voting were held on the same day, 20 June. In the morning, Johnson advanced to 157, a milestone since it was more than half of the parliamentary party, while Javid went backwards and was eliminated with 34 votes. The big news was that Gove had overtaken Hunt and was now second on 61, two ahead of the foreign secretary.

Half an hour before the final result was declared, Gove received a call from one of Javid's people suggesting that more than enough of his supporters would break for Gove. 'You're in the final round,' the source said. The environment secretary was in his campaign headquarters, a supporter's flat on Victoria Street, when Graham Brady read out the result. Alphabetically, Gove was first. He had 75 votes. His team felt 80 votes would be safe; this was no man's land. In Hunt's headquarters, the foreign secretary turned to his team and said, 'Oh, Michael's got it.' Then the axe fell. Brady announced that Hunt had 77. He had leaped back into second place. By the end of the contest, Johnson had seventy-seven 'handlers' gathering information from fellow MPs; his core team was as big as Hunt's entire voter base.

A whip said, 'Boris's team did not want MG in that final. A number of proxies went to Jeremy Hunt to ensure that it was him in the final.' Johnson and Williamson denied sanctioning such an operation but chicanery was not difficult to deduce since Johnson's total only went up by three when at least four of Javid's backers had publicly declared for him between the final two ballots. 'A dozen or more votes were lent to Hunt in the final round,' a Gove ally claimed later. 'We knew we were getting 14 or 15. We had Jeremy picking up three or four, and he got 18 extra votes.' Even Shapps told friends after the event that his spreadsheet showed some of Johnson's votes had gone walkabout. The final number of people listed on the spreadsheet as 'extra-curricular' for Johnson, having made a public declaration of support, was 168. Yet he only got 160 votes. Shapps thought some MPs took it upon themselves to vote for Hunt to keep Gove out, enough to make the difference. Another MP in Johnson's team claimed however, 'It was done with the proxies.'

Despite Johnson's emphatic win, one senior supporter looked at the figure of 160 and smelled trouble ahead. 'It was guaranteed that he was going to the final two, he was nailed on to win and he could still only command just about half of the parliamentary party. That should have given them sleepless nights in Downing Street.' Gove was '90 per cent disappointed, 10 per cent relieved', but also sanguine. 'Them's the rules,' he told his team. He was irritated but also perversely flattered. Had he got through, he would have challenged Johnson's claim that he could scrap the entire Northern Ireland Protocol and strike a deal based on GATT XXIV. While Johnson would probably have won, he would have been on edge and more likely to make errors.

As the run-off began, Tory MPs, the grassroots membership and the country at large expected Johnson to win. Some did so with hope, others with the feeling that Brexit was a mess of his creation and it was right that he deal with it. Raoul Ruparel put it best, telling friends that Johnson's arrival in Number 10 would be like José Mourinho returning to Chelsea, six years after his first spell in charge. 'With every manager until then, people said, "Why is it not Mourinho?" They were never going to succeed with his ghost looming over them. Until Boris has a shot, and succeeds or fails, they are not going to face up to what other choices they have.'

The race was Johnson's to lose. 'The only person who can defeat Boris now,' Lee Cain remarked, 'is Boris himself.' Characteristically, he came close to doing just that.

ROUT

Boris v Hunt

July 2019

Lee Cain rang Boris Johnson. It was one of those calls that you only made when you worked for him. People called his personal life chaotic, they called it colourful, but there was one thing you learned fast when you worked for him: it was none of your business. It was a lesson Guto Harri and Will Walden, his spin doctors at City Hall, had learned years ago. Cain had just come off the phone from Jim Waterson, the media editor of the *Guardian*, who had received a 'ring-in' from a neighbour of Carrie Symonds, who lived in an elegant first-floor flat in a Victorian mansion block overlooking a square in Kennington, south London. The paper was about to run a story saying the police had been called to an altercation between the couple the night before. Heated exchanges between Johnson and Symonds had been recorded by the couple next door. Johnson answered. 'It's not true, is it?' Cain asked.

There was a pause. 'Nope, no, no, not true. Just say it's not true.'

Cain waited a moment. The pause was like a poker tell. 'Of course, if the police were called, there would be a record of that,' he said, 'so it shouldn't be too hard for anyone to stand up. If it's not true, I'll just knock it down.'

Another long silence, then Johnson's voice: 'I'll call you back.' When he did so the instructions were from the age-old Boris playbook: 'Go doggo.' Say nothing, hope it goes away. Not for the first or last time, Johnson showed that his first instinct, with his back to the wall, was to lie.

The tape was lurid. The neighbour said they heard a woman screaming followed by 'slamming and banging'. The report continued, 'At one point Symonds could be heard telling Johnson to "get off me" and "get out of my flat" … Johnson can be heard refusing to leave the flat and telling Symonds to "get off my fucking laptop" before there is a loud crashing noise. Symonds is heard saying Johnson had ruined a sofa with red wine: "You just don't care for anything because you're spoilt. You have no care for money or anything."' The neighbour told the paper, 'There was a smashing sound of what sounded like plates. There was a couple of very loud screams that I'm certain were Carrie and she was shouting to "get out" a lot.'[1] The neighbour said they tried knocking on the door but got no reply, so they dialled 999. Within minutes two police cars and a van turned up. After initially denying that they had any record of a domestic incident, when Waterson provided the case number, a Met spokesman issued a statement: 'At 00:24 hrs on Friday, 21 June, police responded to a call from a local resident. The caller was concerned for the welfare of a female neighbour. Police attended and spoke to all occupants of the address, who were all safe and well. There were no offences or concerns apparent to the officers and there was no cause for police action.'

Here was everything some had feared about Johnson: his chaotic existence, his turbulent private life. Speculation was rife about what Symonds had found on his laptop. Those who had known and disliked his narcissism for years saw truth in her complaint that he was 'spoilt' and had 'no care' for the property or feelings of others.

The *Guardian* put the story online at 7.12 p.m. and Waterson, now abroad, basked in the glory of a stone-cold scoop. Yet the paper had published in time for their rivals to pick up the story. Every national newspaper splashed the story with the exception of the *Guardian*, which was forced to 'reverse ferret' in the second edition.

Throughout Friday evening, Johnson's team had no idea exactly what had happened, or whether the tape was about to be released, which could have sunk his hopes of the premiership. On Saturday, however, Symonds and her allies went to war on Johnson's behalf, Carrie briefing some journalists directly. Details of the neighbours, Tom Penn and Eve Leigh, emerged, left-wing activists who had shouted abuse at Johnson in the past. 'Just gave Boris Johnson the finger,' Leigh boasted online a week earlier. Yet, as reporters swarmed to the scene, they found Johnson's car, full of rubbish, with a confetti of parking tickets shoved under the wiper blades – more evidence of a man who did not think the normal rules applied to him.

The 'spat in the flat' led to an orgy of character studies of Johnson by long-time critics, none more so than Max Hastings, the former *Telegraph* editor who sent Johnson to Brussels, where he created the 'bendy banana' genre of EU reporting, ground zero on the road to Brexit. Hastings had seemed for years to be seeking redemption from polite society for this appointment. His piece for the *Guardian* the following Monday noted, 'There is room for debate about whether he is a scoundrel or mere rogue, but not much about his moral bankruptcy, rooted in a contempt for truth … He is unfit for national office, because it seems he cares for no interest save his own fame and gratification … His premiership will almost certainly reveal a contempt for rules, precedent, order and stability.' He predicted Johnson could survive as prime minister 'for three or four years, shambling from one embarrassment and debacle to another, of which Brexit may prove the least … The experience of the premiership will lay bare his absolute unfitness for it.'[2]

There was much here that would prove to be prescient, but little attempt to understand Johnson's appeal to those who did not share Hastings' world view, or to admit that his appeal lay precisely in the fact that Johnson was a demi-rogue living a chaotic existence with which many voters could identify. In May 2021 Janice Turner, a left-of-centre *Times* columnist, who readily admitted her friends were 'Boris-haters', observed, 'The truth is Johnson's supporters haven't just "priced in" his manifest character flaws, they actually find them reassuring. With his six (or so) children, two divorces, a late-life toddler, demanding new girl-friend, weight problem and propensity for gaffes, his life is a blur of chaos and drama. In popular parlance he is a "messy bitch" but so are many of us.'[3] She quoted an observation about the appeal of Donald Trump: 'The white working class resents professionals but admires the rich.' Turner added, 'To them, lawyers and teachers are chiding do-gooders, telling them how to live, judging their flaky parenting or flashy homes – whereas the rich don't pretend to be paragons. Trump, with his model wife, hamburger habit and fake tan, was just a trucker after a lottery win. Boris undercuts his elite education and privilege with a dissolute lifestyle which is both genuine and contrived.' If anything better has been written about Johnson's appeal, I am yet to read it.

The spat in the flat might have enhanced Johnson's appeal with the country's messy bitches but it caused debilitating chaos in Johnsonworld. Both Lynton Crosby and Will Walden, his two most enduring advisers, believed the presence of Carrie Symonds was a distraction and potentially a disaster. 'Lynton and Will were livid,' a colleague recalled. 'They sat him down that weekend and told him, "If you're going to get rid of her, now's the time to get rid of her. You've had your fun, wave goodbye."' Crosby was blunt. 'When your dick gets hard, your mind goes soft,' the Australian said. He told Johnson the premiership was in his grasp, but he saw a man unprepared to make the sacrifices needed to win power: 'You have to pay a price.' Crosby was fond of recalling the former Australian prime minister Bob Hawke, a notorious drinker and philanderer, who won the 1983 general election and immediately gave up alcohol and womanising until he was out of power – when he promptly left his wife for his biographer. 'Lynton made his position very, very clear,' a colleague said. 'It was pretty brutal, but Boris wasn't going to choose that path.'

Walden suggested Symonds 'take a step back' for a few weeks while he secured the keys to Number 10. Neither Crosby, Walden nor Mark Fullbrook, Crosby's business partner, had learned of the spat in the flat until Friday evening, just before the story broke. 'The fightback could have been handled much better if he'd bothered to tell the truth on the Friday morning,' a campaign source said. 'We lost sixteen hours which sent everyone into a tailspin.' There was talk of making Johnson do a press conference to explain himself, which Cain advised against.

Symonds' critics saw a young woman devoted to the dramas of Westminster, unlike Johnson's estranged wife Marina Wheeler, who had been a stabilising presence. 'I never recall a situation where Marina was screaming in his ear about something,' one ally remarked. They assumed, wrongly, that Symonds was a passing fancy, just the paramour present when the leadership music stopped.

Long before the spat in the flat, Symonds' influence over the campaign irked those trying to keep the show on the road. Cain, while keen to avoid her ire, was unsighted by her shadow briefing operation, including the release, that weekend, of a reconciliation picture of the couple, which had actually been taken weeks before. Wharton and Williamson became annoyed with her demands to attend events. 'They'd deliberately send her off places just to keep her out the way,' a campaign aide said. 'They'd put Carrie in cars and tell the driver to go the long way, get lost so she would be late for events or miss them so they just wouldn't have to deal with her.' Another Johnson ally said, 'The issue was the distraction that all of it caused him. Boris mistook opposition to Carrie as being personal as opposed to professional. We needed to get on and do a job. He was constantly being distracted during preparation for debates and TV appearances. There were paparazzi at the door, and her complaining and needing him back frustrated a lot of people.' After a debate in Manchester, Johnson was supposed to spend the night there so he could get a proper rest. Instead, he forced his protection officers to race through the night to drive him home to Symonds. One disgruntled aide asked Johnson, 'How are you going to negotiate your way around the EU if you can't negotiate with your girlfriend?'

Nothing caused more awkwardness than Symonds' attempt to get a campaign job for her friend Ben Mallet, a twenty-something political operator who had worked on London mayoral campaigns. When Mallet arrived at campaign headquarters, purposefully clutching a briefcase, it became clear that Symonds had told him he could be chief of staff. The others were having none of this. Symonds kept up a campaign, badgering Johnson, who repeatedly called aides to ask, 'Can't you just *call* him chief of staff?' In the end Wharton took Mallet aside and said, 'You seem a nice kid, but let's be clear what's happening here: this campaign is run by me, Gavin and Lee. You can be part of the team. It will be interesting. But if you go against us, you're fucked.'

That did not stop Symonds, who was trying to persuade Cummings to get properly involved, taking Mallet along when she and Johnson met the Vote Leave supremo for dinner. Cain and Wharton were both excluded. 'Why isn't Lee here?' Cummings snapped. 'This is fucking preposterous.' There was one advantage to Cain's exclusion. When Harry Cole was tipped off that he and Johnson had met Cummings to discuss the leadership, the spin doctor was able to kill the story by saying, truthfully, 'It's not true. I haven't had dinner with Boris and Dom.' Privately, he urged Cummings not to get involved – yet. 'It's carnage and he's a shambles,' Cain said. 'If you come in, you'll just be part of the shambles. We're going to win anyway. At the end of it, he's going to look around and his rat brain is going to decide he needs someone to grip Number 10.' This proved to be shrewd.

Symonds tried to block other appointments, among them Richard Holden, a former Tory press officer and special adviser at the MoD. He had fought and won a court case to clear his name after accusations of sexual assault at a party. At Symonds' urging, her old boss Sajid Javid had given evidence about what one of Holden's accusers had told him. Legally and morally, Holden was exonerated, but Symonds didn't want him near the campaign. She also pressured Johnson to get rid of Williamson's special adviser Ellie Lyons. Cain and Wharton told Johnson he would have to conduct the sackings himself and then briefed Politico's Playbook email that both were on the team.

On the evening of Sunday 24th, two days after the spat in the flat story broke, there was a lengthy crisis meeting between Johnson, his campaign managers and Mark Fullbrook of CTF, at which it was agreed that Fullbrook – who had previously run Zac Goldsmith's unsuccessful 2016 London mayoral campaign – would take day-to-day control of the ground war to win over the membership. At 4 p.m. on Monday 25th, Fullbrook gave a presentation in the Thatcher Room in Portcullis House to MPs backing Johnson. He told them a centralised media strategy had been imposed, with MPs told to refer all national media bids back to campaign HQ. Fullbrook unveiled a new mission statement for the campaign, outlining the argument they needed to make on Johnson's behalf. One MP said, 'There are three messages: "Boris will deliver Brexit on 31 October; Boris will reunite the party and the country; and Boris will beat Jeremy Corbyn." That's all we are allowed to say.' These messages had been a feature of the campaign for weeks, but Fullbrook made clear that they would now be rigidly enforced. He did so, though, in a manner MPs found high-handed.

The other appointment that week was of Iain Duncan Smith, the Paleosceptic grandee, as chairman of the campaign. 'The first we knew of it was when IDS walked in and told everyone he was in charge,' said one campaign staffer. 'We'd have to have these meetings where we'd all nod along to our dear leader Iain and then, as soon as he left, we'd re-do the whole thing and carry on with whatever we were doing anyway.' Aides claim Duncan Smith was so unfamiliar with the rest of the team that, on one occasion, he walked into campaign headquarters in Lord North Street, saw someone he didn't recognise and turned tail. 'That was my favourite moment,' one said. 'He goes, "Wrong building", and turns around and walks out.' As one MP put it, 'IDS has been made fat control-ler but he hasn't been given any trains to play with.' As an ERG-reassurance exercise the appointment made some sense, but no one seems to have told Duncan Smith he was window dressing. On another occasion, not long before Johnson became prime minister, Duncan

Smith repeatedly phoned the candidate to try to convene a strategy discussion. Johnson dodged the calls. IDS announced he was coming to HQ. Johnson ordered his entire team upstairs to hide, where they stayed, sniggering, while Duncan Smith hammered futilely on the door, ringing the bell. There may not be a more ridiculous episode in the entire Brexit period.

While the new generals displayed their epaulettes, it was left to the NCOs to keep the show on the road: Lee Cain, Oliver Lewis, the head of operations Shelley Williams-Walker. New recruits: Damon Poole, another Vote Leave alumnus, Rosie Bate-Williams and Ed Oldfield, an affable youngster whose father was a prominent donor, bolstered the team. All around them ambitious MPs like Sunak and Hancock manoeuvring for position, the ERG trying to seize control of Brexit policy, bits of CTF making announcements and Duncan Smith throwing his weight around. All this while campaign staff perched on 'little tiny chairs that gave you back pain'. One said, 'There was literally piss on the carpet, the wifi didn't work. I'd perch on a sofa trying to buy BT Openreach when it went down.'

CTF personnel were supposed to be running the membership phase of the operation. But when Cain asked for their plan and the media announcements he would need to make, there was silence. 'It was a six-bomb shitshow after Fullbrook came in,' a colleague recalled. 'The grid was all over the shop. There was no plan and no coordination. What I always remember is Fullbrook pushing for us to announce that we'd support a royal yacht,' another aide said – a campaign run by the *Telegraph*'s professional nostalgic Chris Hope.

This characterisation of CTF's role was regarded as unfair by other campaign officials. 'I thought [David] Canzini and Fullbrook did a pretty decent job with the grassroots campaign,' one said. 'The Vote Leavers weren't really involved in that side of things.' Nonetheless even a friendly cabinet minister admitted, 'It is true that there was a lack of coordination between phase one and phase two. It was knocked sideways by the Carrie row, but everyone thought that someone else was handling the transition.'

The NCOs escaped to plot in a bedroom upstairs. It was evident to Cain and Lewis that Johnson could not run a government in the same manner as the campaign. 'Unless we have someone really tough to grapple with the machine, we're going to get screwed,' Lewis observed. Cain agreed, 'If we go in and Sedwill pulls Boris aside and tells him, "You can't do no-deal", it will be all over before it's started.' Over dinner, Lewis told Cummings, 'You've got to come on board.' Cummings was unmoved, recalling Cain's advice to stay out. During a bedroom summit on 25 June, Cain and Lewis concluded: 'We've got to take control of this.' They went downstairs to the whiteboard, on which Fullbrook had scrawled the beginnings of a grid, and wiped it clean. In its place they wrote Vote Leave pledges, an echo of the alternative government which Johnson and Gove had proposed in the referendum campaign.[4] An Australian-style points-based system. Tighter immigration controls. 'Boom, boom, boom.' Fullbrook walked in, paused, then took out his phone and took a picture of the whiteboard. 'For the scrapbook,' he said, then left.

Lewis tried to persuade Johnson to make the immigration pledges: 'You have got to commit to this as an example of what you voted for when you voted for Brexit and what you're going to deliver.' The candidate was suspicious. 'Is this really a winning idea or is this a Dom thing?' he asked. Lewis won the argument and Johnson went public with the plan the following day. Sam Coates, one of the bigger cynics and better journalists, observed, 'This is an announcement designed to do absolutely nothing except get the words "Boris Johnson" and an "Australian-style points system" into the same headline.' However cynical, it worked. The spat in the flat was no longer top of the news. 'The game is back on,' Lewis said.

Not all policy was in the hands of the NCOs, though. The first cabinet minister to endorse Johnson was Liz Truss, the chief secretary to the Treasury. Having got in early, she had been made head of policy, to the consternation and irritation of Johnson's backroom staff. If the plan was to keep her out of the public eye, it swiftly backfired. The £80,000 income tax threshold policy reflected Truss's near-religious zeal for tax cutting. She began briefing the media about the radical plans she was considering: a 'no-deal budget' packed with tax cuts and a bonfire of regulation. Scrapping half a dozen major Whitehall departments. It was unfair to blame Truss for every policy leak. She was only responsible, according to one estimate, for 'about 90 per cent' of the stories.

In the midst of this chaos, on 25 June, Johnson did an interview with talkRADIO, whose political correspondent Ross Kempsell knew both Johnson and Symonds. In it Johnson made the eccentric admission that he liked to relax by painting old fruit boxes so they resembled red London buses. To distract attention from the spat in the flat, he hardened his line on Brexit. He first claimed Theresa May had never 'really wanted to come out' of the EU and condemned the 'morosity and gloom' of her government. Then he added, 'We are getting ready to come out on 31 October, come what may,' he said.

'Do or die?' Kempsell asked.

Johnson repeated the line: 'Do or die, come what may.' It was the key quote of the campaign. None was more relieved than Kempsell, who had failed to get Johnson to give him a quote on sport to please his employers.

Jeremy Hunt's team met in the Conrad Hotel next to St James's Park tube on the Friday morning after the result was in. Christina Robinson, his long-time spin doctor, and Tim Smith, the foreign secretary's media spad, both messaged Jason Stein, former adviser to Amber Rudd, asking him to join the team. Ben Mascall, a former comms adviser to David Cameron and the Remain campaign, was there. With Sue Beebe and Ed Jones vying to be chief of staff and Adam Smith doing policy, there was the nucleus of a good operation. Phil Collins, a former speechwriter to Tony Blair, who had lost his column at *The Times*, helped craft Hunt's speeches. However, it was quickly clear the operation was not ready for a six-week campaign. 'We were so focused on getting to the final two, rightly,' a campaign aide said. 'We then had no plan for the campaign. We literally had no grid. We didn't have enough people. We were a complete insurgency.'

At the end of that first meeting, Robinson called Hunt on speaker-phone and explained that the team's view was that he should go on the attack against Johnson for dodging scrutiny. After a short debate, Robinson said, 'Everyone shut up and come up with some zingers.' One of those present said, 'It was Sue and Christina who got him being more aggressive.' Hunt had already concluded that to avoid the role of 'the party's useful idiot', forced to tour the hustings in a vain attempt to prevent a foregone conclusion, he would not be a supine opponent. Robinson wanted 'doers not thinkers', one reason why the hyper-aggressive Stein got the call. 'We got pretty sick of Tory illuminati joining conference calls to offer us strategic advice,' a colleague said. Stein ended up running the campaign's weekend media operation, doing so with tactical acumen and uncompromising zeal. 'We are at war,' he told friends.

Hunt decreed that there would be no mention of the spat in the flat. 'We're arguing about the future of the country, not the arguments people have whilst being spied on in the privacy of their own home.' But on 24 June, the Monday after Johnson's Kennington altercation, Hunt laid into him for failing to agree to a *Sky News* televised debate. 'He is being a coward,' the foreign secretary said. 'It is cowardice not to appear in head-to-head debates.' His team had polled the issue and party members agreed it was 'disrespectful' for Johnson to duck debates, so Hunt deployed that line too. He concluded, 'I promise Boris Johnson the fight of his life.'

The following day, Johnson wrote to Hunt demanding to know if he would commit to leave the EU on 31 October 'no matter what'. The newly feisty Hunt tweeted back, 'Hi Boris, it's good to talk. But no need for snail-mail, why not turn up to Sky tonight and I'll give you full and frank answers?' He ended with the hashtag '#BoJoNoShow'. This was not what Johnson was expecting. Hunt was fifty-two and in fifteen years of front-line politics he had never felt so free to say what he thought. He knew it was high risk, but he had little to lose. 'If I go to the backbenches, I go to the backbenches,' he said. A Hunt adviser recalled, 'We were given an enormous boost by the Carrie/Boris stuff on the Friday. We then came up with "coward", which worked for us for three or four days while we worked out what the fuck our policies were.'

Hunt picked a handful of themes: his experience as an entrepreneur, a plan to raise defence spending to 3 per cent of GDP, to cut corporation tax and his vision of a new Silicon Valley tech hub in the UK. 'The grand strategy was: be the person best qualified to do the job and also show new sides of yourself,' a senior Hunt adviser said.

On 1 July, Hunt made a keynote speech on Brexit. He thought Johnson's 'do or die' approach to the 31 October deadline unrealistic and was brave enough to say so. Later, Hunt felt as if he had played into Johnson's hands, telling friends, 'I wasn't smart enough to realise that what he was trying to do was create some immediate Brexit blue water between him and me, and that he needed me to go against it.' To balance his reluctance to commit to the Halloween deadline or to countenance prorogation, Hunt announced that he regarded no-deal as the default outcome of discussions with the EU: 'From the start of my premiership, I will work on the basis we are leaving on 31st October without a deal unless the commission changes its position.' He also revealed that Stephen Harper, the former Canadian prime minister, had agreed to be his lead negotiator for a Canada-style trade deal. In one regard, Hunt went further than Johnson: 'As prime minister I will make a judgment on 30th September as to whether there is a realistic chance of a new deal being agreed that can pass the House of Commons.' If that wasn't the case, 'I will immediately cease all discussions with the European Union and focus the whole country's attention on no-deal preparations.'

The speech hit its mark. Ed Jones had a good relationship with YouGov and got early intelligence on their polling. Their first major survey of the campaign, on 24 June, with fieldwork conducted before the spat in the flat, had put Johnson on 74 per cent, with the foreign secretary trailing badly on 26 per cent. Now YouGov's returns showed that a high proportion of undecided voters were breaking for Hunt and that he was gaining with women too. Anecdotally, those running the hustings, including broadcaster Iain Dale, told Team Hunt they detected no switching to Johnson but some to Hunt. 'The no-deal speech landed well,' a campaign aide recalled. 'At that point we were unquestionably having a better campaign. That was the first time we genuinely thought that we had a chance. What killed us was fox hunting.'

The following morning, on a conference call, Jason Stein pressed for Hunt to do an article with the *Telegraph* for 4 July, both American Independence Day and the day the leadership ballots went out to members. The idea was to play up Britain's close links with the US, attacking Corbyn as a menace to the Western alliance and argue that Hunt was best placed to defeat him. Stein worked up the article and sold it hard to Gordon Rayner, the paper's political editor. Hunt followed up with the editor, Chris Evans. When the front page dropped on Wednesday evening, Stein was praised as a 'magician'. On one of the most important days of the campaign, Boris Johnson's own paper, the voice of the Tory grassroots, had the splash headline, 'Hunt: I'm the man to beat Corbyn'.

Within minutes triumph turned to disaster. Buried in the story were comments Hunt had made about fox hunting, in a separate podcast interview with the *Telegraph*'s Chris Hope. The wily veteran asked whether he would support a free vote on overturning the ban on fox hunting and Hunt walked into the trap. Tory MP WhatsApp groups went into meltdown and every other paper picked up on fox hunting, ignoring the carefully planned story the campaign wanted. It was an unforced error, and one which derailed Hunt's big interview on the *Today* programme the next morning, where he had to spend valuable time dealing with hunting. 'That was a genuine momentum killer,' an aide recalled. 'It deflated everyone. We never really recovered, honestly.'

The first debate was on the Tuesday evening, 9 July. Hunt prepared with sessions on Sunday and Monday, Greg Hands playing Johnson, aptly since his impersonation consisted of 'a lot of hands' waving. Even his own side admitted Hunt 'did not land any zingers' but his main goal was to implant his Brexit policy in the public consciousness. 'The main thing we wanted to get out of that debate was the idea that he was serious about no-deal,' a Hunt campaign source said. 'We've prepared for no-deal and he hasn't.' Johnson counterattacked, focusing on Hunt's refusal to commit to the 31 October deadline.

Johnson's worst moment was only tangentially connected with Brexit. On the evening of 7 July, the *Mail on Sunday* had splashed on a leak of government diplomatic telegrams ('diptels' in Whitehall jargon) written by Sir Kim Darroch, the British ambassador in Washington, which described Donald Trump as 'radiating insecurity' and called his early administration 'inept', 'incompetent' and 'uniquely dysfunctional'. They provoked a full-blown diplomatic incident. Trump denounced Darroch on Twitter as 'wacky', 'a very stupid guy', a 'pompous fool' and 'not well liked within the US', before declaring, 'We will no longer deal with him.' For good measure, he also called May's handling of Brexit a 'disaster'. 'I told her how it should be done, but she decided to go another way,' he wrote.

The diptels had been leaked to Steven Edginton, a budding journalist working on the Brexit Party's digital operations. He gave the story to Isabel Oakeshott, a Fleet Street veteran who was in a relationship with Richard Tice, the chairman of the Brexit Party. Darroch believed the leaks were a coordinated effort to have him removed and replaced by Brexit Party leader Nigel Farage, a close ally of Trump. In Washington, the president called John Bolton, his national security adviser, at 7 a.m. and said, 'Get him out of here.' Bolton phoned Mark Sedwill with the news: 'This isn't going to end well, you've got to pull him out.' Sedwill pushed back saying an ambassador could not simply be 'run out of town'.[5] Downing Street issued a statement giving 'full support' to

Darroch. But in the debate Johnson, who was foreign secretary when some of the cables were written, repeatedly refused to say if he would keep Darroch as ambassador (perhaps concerned about upsetting Trump, whose support he would need to secure a trade deal with the US). Alan Duncan, his old colleague at the Foreign Office, accused Johnson of throwing Darroch 'under a bus'.

Darroch resigned the following day. Johnson, frantic that he would be blamed, phoned to say how sorry he was that Darroch was going. Nervously, he expressed hope it was nothing to do with him. Darroch replied that Johnson's comments were 'not helpful'. Trump's demand that he be fired was a breach of protocol and Johnson probably correctly judged the ambassador's position to be untenable. Nonetheless, it would have been better for Johnson to say it was for Britain to appoint its representatives rather than adopt the supine stance he did.

Three days later, Johnson suffered another dicey television encounter, this time with Andrew Neil, who focused mercilessly on his advocacy of GATT XXIV. Johnson said it would be 'attractive' to have a tariff-free 'standstill … until such time as we do a free trade deal'. Dripping with hubris, he even berated the interviewer: 'Andrew, get the detail right. It's Article XXIV, paragraph 5B.' Neil delivered the *coup de grâce*: 'How would you handle paragraph 5C?' A flustered Johnson waved a hand and said, 'I would confide entirely in paragraph 5B.' The same question followed, then the same answer. Neil tried again, 'Do you know what's in paragraph 5C?' Knowing the game was up, Johnson replied, 'No.' Neil explained, '5C says you don't just need the EU's approval, you need to agree with the EU the shape of a future trade agreement and a timetable.' Johnson drew two conclusions, the first immediately evident as mentions of GATT XXIV disappeared from his public comments. The second was that he would not subject himself to a grilling from Neil again with the premiership on the line.

The GATT XXIV farce had occurred because Johnson let Oliver Lewis, David Frost, Geoffrey Cox, Iain Duncan Smith and Steve Baker all think they were formulating his Brexit policy. Lewis, Frost and Cox all thought GATT XXIV 'headbanging nonsense' and 'the land of the cuckoo'. But as one of them put it, 'There are some people who make up their minds by methodical and careful study of a problem and there are other people who make up their minds by deliberately allowing conflicting clans to fight it out in front of them. That's Boris's way.'

Lewis told Johnson he had to convince the EU that he was serious about no-deal: 'You've got to go hardcore with them.' Cox urged him to pursue a three-pronged strategy. 'As soon as you get in, you're going to have to see if you can get a deal,' he said. 'But you should also prepare flat out for an election. That's where this is going.' He said Johnson would have to justify an election too: 'The obvious narrative is that you've got a dysfunctional Parliament, blocking the democratic desire and will of the British people. You have to show that at every cost.' The third prong, he argued, as a strategy for both getting a deal and winning an election, was to prepare 'outright for no-deal'. He recommended a cabinet committee solely to prepare for no-deal, chaired by Michael Gove, as well as a strategy committee of senior ministers, chaired by Johnson.

Johnson accepted much of Cox's analysis but ignored his view that there could be a tweak to the backstop. In the final head-to-head debate on 15 July, hosted by the *Sun* and talkRADIO, Johnson said, 'No to time limits or unilateral escape hatches, or elaborate devices, codicils that you could apply to the backstop. It has been devised by this country as an instrument of our own incarceration within the customs union and single market.' Hunt agreed: 'The backstop as it is, is dead. I don't think tweaking it with a time limit will do the trick. We have got to find a new way.' Amber Rudd watched in despair, telling friends both candidates were playing a game of 'my Brexit is harder than yours'.

Beyond a hard line on the protocol and the 31 October deadline, other key Brexit issues remained unresolved by Johnson during the campaign. Indeed, it was not clear he understood them all. After an aide used a whiteboard to outline a timeline for the Brexit battle ahead, Johnson replied, 'That's really interesting. Explain to me again, why can't we just join the EEA.' The aide was flabbergasted.

MPs would have had grounds for further consternation if they knew who else Johnson was consulting about Brexit. At this stage, he wanted Dominic Cummings' ideas, rather than him on the team. 'We obviously knew that having Dom anywhere near the campaign was incredibly toxic so kept him very quiet,' a colleague said. Since Vote Leave had ridden roughshod over the views of the Paleosceptics, most ERG leaders detested Cummings, seeing him as an arriviste. As Christopher Montgomery said at the time, 'I could go to a meeting of ERG MPs and say we're going to join a federal European republic, or Dominic Cummings is going to be running the country, and a majority of them would say we're going to take the federal European republic. The ultimate poison pill for Boris would be any association with Cummings.' Conor Burns was in the car with Johnson in mid-June when he took a call from Symonds to talk about her attempts to get Cummings permanently on the team. When he hung up, Johnson said, 'You can't tell anyone.' Burns replied, 'I won't, but I hope you know what you're doing.'

Cox's idea that Gove should take charge of no-deal preparations was sensible, but it could not happen until the psychodrama which had gripped the Tory party for three years was resolved. Boris Johnson and David Cameron had a private rapprochement. The London *Evening Standard*, edited by George Osborne, endorsed Johnson for the leadership, saying he was 'the candidate who might just get Britain feeling good about itself again'. But neither Cameron nor Johnson was reconciled with Gove, who had betrayed first one and then the other in 2016. Friends of Gove saw a double standard – the two old Etonians reviving a friendly rivalry while the orphan kid from Aberdeen was held to a different standard.

The thaw began after Gove's speech in the no-confidence debate in January 2019. Cameron texted him to say 'well done'. A while later Gove suggested a drink. 'Why not?' said Cameron, but they waited until after the leadership election. Cameron recommended 5 Hertford Street. The owner, Robin Birley, had a private sitting room upstairs where they could meet in private. Gove arrived early for the dinner on 1 July. But when he confided his purpose to the doorman, a staff member announced loudly, 'Mr Gove is seeing David Cameron.' When Cameron arrived, the room had not been cleared, so at least five Tory donors and thirty others saw him order a whisky and soda and Gove a glass of white wine.[6]

Cameron wanted to clear the air before his criticisms of Gove's behaviour in 2016 were published in his memoir. He spent the first five minutes getting things off his chest. He was candid but, Gove thought, generous. Things were more complicated, in his view, yet there was no point contesting what Cameron said. 'That's completely fair,' he said. 'I completely understand.' There followed a forty-minute chat about the Conservative Party, life, the universe and everything. The two men had not spoken at all since Cameron left Number 10.

Two weeks later, on 16 July, Gove made a speech praising Johnson and pitching for a job in his cabinet. It came about after Gove requested a meeting. They talked for forty minutes in Johnson's office, room 471 in Portcullis House. Gove's betrayal in 2016 still stung. Johnson told aides, 'He's never really apologised.' If he was to give Gove a cabinet job, he needed to know he would not be betrayed again. He also needed reassurance that Gove was prepared to risk no-deal. 'Michael, you bailed on me last time,' Johnson said. 'You stuck in May's cabinet even though you know the withdrawal agreement and Chequers is a bit of a stinker. My worry is that you will go soft and bail again. Part of the strategy is to say to Europe, "Unless we get what we want, it's no-deal."'

Gove, in response, was frank and emollient. 'I do have worries about no-deal, but you will win and you will have a mandate. I have said throughout that no-deal is better than no Brexit. Whether or not you put me in your government, I won't be causing trouble, I will be supporting you in getting it done.' He then summoned the spirit of Vote Leave: 'We started this; we have got to finish it.'

They had a second conversation, by phone, the following Sunday. Gove concluded that Johnson was searching for a public olive branch, something to convince sceptics in his own team that inviting him into government would not mean putting a psychopath in the driving seat. In his speech, in Kew, Gove said both Johnson and Hunt would be 'great prime ministers – we can trust them both to do the right thing on every critical issue'. He added, 'I won't say who I'm going to vote for. It will be the love that dare not speak its name', but asked about his previous claim that Johnson was unfit to be prime minister, he said that was 'based on events at that time'. He concluded, 'Whoever is the prime minister, if they wanted me to serve in their government, I would be happy to do so. If they wanted to send me to the backbenches I would completely understand.'

The other big beast to seek terms with Johnson was Amber Rudd. Most of his team did not want him to give her a job. Her aides told her she had a choice to make. On 6 July, Jason Stein emailed Eleanor Shawcross concerned that Rudd would 'effectively resign her seat in the cabinet out of pride'. If she was not prepared, in extremis, to accept no-deal, 'then she is gone'. Stein saw that a Johnson government would essentially have the same headline policy as May's: securing a deal while preparing for no-deal – though this time they would mean it. 'No different to the government she currently serves. My view is always: stay to shape things.' He proposed a 'pivot' which would unfold via a grid of media interviews.

Together Shawcross and Stein took Rudd through her options. 'Do you accept Theresa May's deal is dead?' Rudd did. 'Do you accept that if the EU don't give us anything, it is a general election or no-deal?' Rudd agreed. Finally, which was worse? A Labour government under Jeremy Corbyn or no-deal? As a former home secretary, she feared Corbyn would make Britain 'face East not West'. She could not imagine him going to the offices of MI5 and MI6. Rudd consulted David Lidington, David Gauke and Greg Clark, none of whom wished to serve a Johnson government set on no-deal. However, Clark told her, 'Having you there arguing that no-deal is going to be destructive is going to be important.' Rudd wanted the EU to compromise, but if they did so, she thought the ERG had to compromise too and Johnson should be prepared to face them down. But she also knew that if she was demanding flexibility of others, she had to show flexibility herself. Rudd also wanted to be in cabinet. 'She's not in politics to cut ribbons, she's in it to make decisions and be in the thick of it,' a close ally said. 'She knew she had to compromise.'

What her aides called the AEP – 'Amber's elegant pivot' – unfolded through a piece for the *Times*'s Red Box blog, a *Good Morning Britain* interview and then with LBC, where the story finally took off when Ross Kempsell, tipped off by Stein, tweeted the significance of her comments.

An irate Philip Hammond texted Rudd to complain. She, in turn, was irritated with the chancellor, telling friends, 'Hammond's like a retreating army, blowing stuff up as he goes, I don't want to be caught in his crossfire.' Rudd was also self-critical. Her allies had tried a third meaningful vote, they had tried indicative votes, they had tried talks with Labour – all had failed. 'There's a point at which you have to ask yourself, am I right?' Hammond was not alone in being appalled. A former minister said, 'The problem with Amber is that she has got a soft spot for Boris, like many women do. He has an ability to be the vulnerable guy – and then suddenly, too late they are pregnant.' Rudd's pivot was eventually regretted by both her and Johnson.

Not everyone who bargained with Johnson was successful. Shailesh Vara, who had never risen above number two in the Northern Ireland Office, demanded membership of the Privy Council and told the presumptive prime minister he would only accept one of five cabinet jobs: trade, justice, culture, international development or Northern Ireland. 'Don't call me if it's a minister of state role,' he said. When Vara left, Johnson turned to an ally and said, 'Put it this way, I don't think his phone is going to be ringing.' It did not.

Johnson received both Claire Perry and Rory Stewart on the same day, Perry in the morning and Stewart in the afternoon. Stewart told Johnson's team he wanted Eddie Lister present as well as Burns: 'I want multiple witnesses.' Stewart showed little intention of voting for Johnson and bemoaned the 'terrible mistake' the party was about to make by electing him. To the consternation of Johnson's seconds, Stewart then summoned the chutzpah that perhaps only Old Etonians can muster at such moments, and suggested Johnson make him chairman of the COP26 climate summit, which Britain was to host the following year. Eyes rolled that one of Johnson's bitterest critics was still prepared to trade his vote. But it was not to be. Johnson replied, 'Rory. I'm sorry, my friend. I sold that particular elephant this morning to Claire.'

There were, by now, scarcely any doubts that he would win. Asked by a friend if anything could stop Boris, his brother Jo replied, 'I suppose if he had killed someone.' Then he paused and added, 'I mean if someone found out that he had killed someone.'

While Johnson, Gove and Cameron buried the hatchet, senior Labour figures continued to insert it in each other's backs. The divisions concerned both Brexit and the continuing antisemitism crisis gripping the party. First, two of Jeremy Corbyn's closest allies – shadow chancellor John McDonnell and Diane Abbott, the shadow home secretary – called on him to fire his most senior aides Seumas Milne and Karie Murphy and back a referendum. With a Labour conference in September expected to vote for a referendum, a source said, 'Diane and John's view is that we should do it now so we aren't forced into it.' In a meeting on 27 June, Abbott told Corbyn his leadership would be damaged, perhaps mortally, unless he changed Labour's Brexit policy. At the *Spectator*'s summer party, Abbott approached journalists to say, 'The Scottish Labour Party has moved to referendum and remain. The Welsh party has moved to referendum and remain. The only reason the English party hasn't moved is Karie and Seumas.' She added, 'They are keeping him captive.'

This came as eight former Labour Party staffers – including Iain McNicol, the former general secretary and Sam Matthews, the former head of investigations – broke gagging orders to speak to the BBC's

Panorama programme, broadcast on 10 July, about the way Corbyn's team handled claims of antisemitism. The whistleblowers said the party's system for dealing with complaints was bedevilled by delays, inaction and interference from the leader's office. It tainted Corbyn further as a credible leader.

Philip Hammond finally broke cover to join the Bresistance on 18 July, just five days before Theresa May left Downing Street. At the start of the leadership contest he told Johnson he was considering backing him, believing that he was a 'bloody good sales person' and he 'might be able to persuade the hardliners to accept some hard truths'. When Johnson talked about leaving on 31 October 'do or die', he assumed it was classic Johnson bluster. But when they met it was clear this was not for show. Hammond said later, 'Very uncharacteristically for Boris he said exactly the same in private meetings in that period as he was saying in public, which Boris has never done. Actually, Boris has never said exactly the same in any two meetings.' Johnson tried to buy him off with a peerage and an international role. Hammond took this to be an invitation to go away and keep quiet and declined the offer.

Instead, fearing 'catastrophe', he joined the rebels during the vote on an amendment to the Northern Ireland (Executive Formation) Bill – tabled by Labour's Hilary Benn and Tory Alistair Burt – seeking to prevent a future government from proroguing Parliament to ensure a no-deal Brexit. John Bercow accepted the amendment, even though a similar effort by Dominic Grieve a week earlier had been rejected by deputy speaker Eleanor Laing, who ruled it was beyond the scope of the bill. It passed by 315 votes to 274, a majority of 41, a big win for the rebels. Since Hunt had ruled out proroguing, it was targeted at Johnson. Margot James, a culture minister, resigned to back the amendment and Keith Simpson voted against the government for the first time in his twenty-two years as an MP. Hammond, Gauke, Clark and Rory Stewart all broke a three-line whip to abstain. Colin Johnson, a Back Boris supporter, wrote in a Tory WhatsApp group, 'They should all be fired. This is a team game.'

Rudd was privately withering about Hammond's late conversion to rebellion, telling an ally, 'Now Philip has decided he has not got a future, he has got his mojo.' To Dominic Grieve, 'Philip was finally liberated'. Grieve had got the ball rolling nine days earlier with an amendment, passed by just one vote, requiring a minister to report to the Commons every two weeks until December on the progress of talks on restoring the Northern Ireland assembly. This was a procedural device to ensure that Parliament could not be mothballed as 31 October approached. The Lords then strengthened it further, so the fortnightly reports would have to be debated within five calendar days, ensuring the Commons had to sit. The Benn-Burt amendment then stipulated that if Parliament was prorogued it would have to sit on the day demanded and for the following five weekdays. Before Johnson even had a grip on the reins of power, his opponents were preparing to prise his fingers loose.

On 21 July, Hammond announced that he was planning to resign from the cabinet even before Theresa May's final day. He told Andrew Marr, 'I'm not going to be sacked because I'm going to resign before we get to that point, assuming that Boris Johnson becomes the next prime minister.' The same day it emerged that Margot James and six other Tories were in talks with the Lib Dems. David Gauke also confirmed he would quit. Three weeks earlier, the justice secretary had survived a vote of no confidence held by his constituency party in South West Hertfordshire. Johnson called to congratulate him and express pleasure that he had survived. Nonetheless, what pro-dealers saw as a theological witch hunt was taking its toll. The first to resign was Alan Duncan, who went on Monday 22 July, issuing a swipe at Johnson over his handling of the Nazanin Zaghari-Ratcliffe case.

The Lib Dem attempt to woo rebel Tories intensified when Jo Swinson was elected Lib Dem leader on 22 July, beating rival Ed Davey with 63 per cent of the vote. In her acceptance speech, she said, 'My message to MPs in other parties who share our values is this: if you believe our country deserves better, that we can stop Brexit, that we can stop Johnson, Farage and Corbyn, then work with us, join us. My door is always open.' Tom Watson sent a congratulatory tweet, adding, 'I hope we can work together to stop a disastrous no-deal Brexit.'

The other person moving on was Oliver Robbins. Even Hunt had indicated that he wanted fresh blood in the negotiating team and Robbins was a hate figure to many Johnsonites. It was a low moment for Robbins, who did not want the job in the first place but had devoted three years of his life to it. Like May, he told friends he regarded it as his 'duty' to 'see it through'. One of Robbins' close colleagues had missed his best friend's memorial service because he was in Brussels. Another's mother-in-law had died while they were on the Eurostar. 'But we fucking well kept going,' a senior negotiator recalled. Politics is a hard business for officials as well as those at the mercy of the electorate. After twenty-three years in Whitehall, he would sit tight, await a new master and tell them the truth as he saw it. But he admitted to a friend he was 'not the neutral figure I wish I was'.

Robbins was present and praised by Theresa May at her final cabinet as prime minister on the morning of Wednesday 23 July. She told ministers they should be 'proud' of what they had done. She spoke of the Union and public service, the two creeds which had defined her time in Downing Street. An enigma even to her closest aides, she became tearful as she drew down the curtain on a premiership which had promised much and delivered little. May began to leave and the ministers started banging the table and then stood and clapped. Then David Lidington said, 'This is one occasion, Prime Minister, where I can't allow you to have the last word.' A cabinet minister said, 'He offered a very generous tribute.' Michael Gove crept out to retrieve the presents the cabinet had bought her – a handbag from Liberty and a necklace from Lalique. Gove's whip-round had raised £1,500. There was money left over because the man who sold the necklace was a fan of May's and gave a discount – a poignant reminder that the respect in which she was held was not matched by her political ability.

In Downing Street, after May's final PMQs, the mood was light. 'People were coming in to hand over their resignations,' an aide recalled. 'As I left, Karen Bradley walked in and gave her a big hug.' Lidington did not resign but told the prime minister he was leaving the government with her. Then it was Hammond's turn. Gauke and Rory Stewart followed suit.

Two hours before the leadership result was announced, Anne Milton resigned, citing 'grave concerns' about no-deal. A colleague had once said to her, 'If you're going to resign, make sure somebody notices.' Milton had raised four children not to tell lies. Johnson, she told one colleague, Danny Kruger, 'falls short of a standard of behaviour that I would expect of my children'. Kruger defended Johnson: 'You know what Boris is like …' Milton responded, 'That is an absolutely outrageous thing to say. Do you think that anybody is excused poor behaviour because they're that sort of person?' Taken aback, Kruger blurted, 'I'm jolly glad you're not my mother.' Milton had the last word: 'If I was your mother, you would know how to behave.' Kruger's mother was the television chef Prue Leith, judge of *The Great British Bake Off*. History does not record if Kruger retreated from this confrontation with a soggy bottom.

May's Downing Street advisers left at ten to three, ten minutes before their replacements were let into the building, a quietly surreal as well as a peaceful handover of power. 'It's quite weird,' one said. 'You walk out and there are two civil servants waiting. One says, "Give me your pass", and hands over a piece of paper containing security information. One says, "Give me your phone." And that was literally it. Then you walk out the front door and it's like those films where characters just walk off into the crowd into the middle distance. No one knows who you are. It's a really strange feeling.' They all went to the Young Vic and got drunk.

Twenty minutes before noon, Johnson and Hunt were taken into a side room at the QEII Centre across the square from Parliament and told the result. Johnson had won with 66 per cent of the vote. Hunt's 34 per cent was 10 points higher than the first YouGov poll had suggested. He had done better than David Davis against David Cameron in 2005.

In the quiet before the public was informed, Hunt seized his chance to talk to Johnson alone. He offered to help unite the party and become a senior lieutenant. 'I would love to be your foreign secretary,' he said. 'I'd like to be for you what Simon Milton was to you for mayor. I'll do a terrific job for you.' This was not music to Johnson's ears. He and his team had concluded that they were going to be in a dogfight with Brussels and Parliament and needed a cabinet of loyalists. 'I think we've got to have change in all those top jobs,' he said, effectively demoting Hunt. He also wanted a Brexiteer as foreign secretary. There had been media rumours that Hunt would be offered defence. Ed Jones had got drunk with a couple of Johnson's team the week before and left with the impression that their idea of unity was for his boss to 'suck it up'. Hunt said, 'Look, I wouldn't do defence. If that's all you want me to do, then let me know today and I'll say I'm stepping down and it won't complicate your reshuffle.'

(If the positions were reversed, Hunt would have made Johnson his deputy prime minister with joint responsibility for delivering Brexit. 'It was going to be a very generous offer,' an ally said.)

At noon they filed into the main auditorium and the result was announced by Brandon Lewis, the party chairman. Johnson gave an eccentrically frivolous acceptance speech. 'There will be people here who will wonder quite what they have done,' he acknowledged. They were certainly doing so when Johnson noted that his campaign mantra – deliver (Brexit), unite (the country) and defeat (Jeremy Corbyn) – 'spells DUD, but they forgot the final E my friends, E for energise. I say to all the doubters: Dude, we are going to energise the country.'

Johnson returned to Parliament to begin crafting his cabinet. Hunt had heard nothing since their conversation in the QEII. Ministers who were to be sacked were summoned. They included James Brokenshire, who had backed Johnson, and Penny Mordaunt, who, pointedly, had not. One after another they took to Twitter to announce their departures. 'David Mundell was shocked,' a Johnson adviser said. 'Penny was really, really upset and angry. She just couldn't quite believe it. Brokenshire was surprised. Karen Bradley was quite phlegmatic.' Having been fired, the Northern Ireland secretary said to herself as she left the prime minister's office, 'Oh well.'

At 5.45 p.m., Hunt was summoned. Johnson offered him defence. It made the decision easy. 'I'm not going to take Penny's job,' Hunt said. 'She's been a real superstar and a good defence secretary.' Hunt, with May, was the only cabinet minister left who had served since 2010. He could not have people saying that Mordaunt backed him and then he took her job. Johnson and the chief whip, Mark Spencer, tried to persuade him to change his mind. A suggestion was made that Hunt might return to the Foreign Office once Brexit was done. Spencer was a hefty figure dubbed 'big farmer' by Johnson for his agricultural background, but when Hunt was unpersuaded, the chief whip became 'very emotional'. A witness said, 'Spencer was welling up. I think Mark found it all quite hard.'

When Julian Smith ceased to be chief whip, he went to the Clarence pub and got drunk. His wife had taken him to McDonald's to sober up when he was called back to Number 10 to be made Northern Ireland secretary. 'I've been to the pub,' he admitted. Johnson was understanding. Next he saw Helen MacNamara for his compliance and ethics clearance. She took one look at him and said, 'We'd better do this tomorrow.'

The following day, the one he had waited for since he was a small boy dreaming of becoming World King, Johnson made a late change to the speech he planned to give to the nation in Downing Street just before he left for the palace occupied by a real queen. The Number 10 man in charge of the podium showed the printed version to Will Walden, who had helped craft it that morning with Johnson, David Frost, Alex Crowley and Munira Mirza. Checking it against the final copy in his WhatsApp, he exclaimed: 'It's the wrong fucking speech.'

'How much is missing?'

'One paragraph,' said Walden, 'but it's a key paragraph.'

The admin staff went into meltdown. The new prime minister's car was already on its way back down the Mall. The speech was reprinted. Walden checked it. The podium man walked out of the black door and swapped the folders. Thirty seconds later, Johnson's car pulled up.

The speech was an awkward amalgam of Johnsonisms (hailing England, Scotland, Wales and Northern Ireland as 'the awesome foursome') and Harry Truman ('never mind the backstop – the buck stops here'). He paid tribute to the 'fortitude and patience' of May, words reminiscent of the school report for a hard-working pupil who failed the exam because they read the question wrong. Rounding on those who believed that 'in this home of democracy we are incapable of honouring a basic democratic mandate', he declared, 'Those critics are wrong. The doubters, the doomsters, the gloomsters – they are going to get it wrong again. The people who bet against Britain are going to lose their shirts.' Johnson vowed to leave the EU on 31 October 'no ifs or buts', and do 'a better deal that will maximise the opportunities of Brexit'.

It would not be as simple as that, of course. The EU's red lines were unaltered, the parliamentary arithmetic the same, the opponents of Brexit, if anything, emboldened by May's failure. Reflecting on the task facing Johnson, a former minister said, 'He has got no choice but to be a great prime minister.' Another was pithier: 'He thinks he's Winston Churchill. He'd fucking better be!'

One cabinet minister who resigned was angry rather than sad at the changing of the guard: 'It's a coup. Vote Leave has seized power.' When he spoke, the minister did not know how accurate he was, since the full extent of the takeover would only become clear the following day.

When Boris Johnson walked through the famous black door for the first time as prime minister, he allowed himself the briefest glimpse to the left. There in the shadows stood the other man who had done most to bring about Brexit: Dominic Cummings. The black door closed behind them. Brexit was their project. Theresa May nearly broke it. Now they owned it.

Conclusion

THERESA MAY: A STUDY IN FAILURE

In her own terms, Theresa May failed as prime minister. Her stated political goal, held with near-missionary zeal, was to deliver on the EU referendum result and to tackle the 'burning injustices' which drove large numbers of Leave voters to back Brexit in the first place. In the end, her slowness to understand Brexit and her inability to either deliver it or handle the consequences, swamped any prospect of dealing with some of the causes of it.

Her allies saw a serious, methodical, honest, evidence-based and fanatically hard-working leader who faced an all-but-impossible task. They saw someone who tried to do the right thing for her country, but who failed because those who supported Brexit refused to vote for a Brexit deal and those Remainers who said they would honour the 2016 result were similarly disingenuous.

Her critics saw a politician of limited personality, flair or vision with a near-pathological distaste for the modern media (who nevertheless continued to cheerlead for her government and deal), who was slow to identify a political destination or a means of getting there, and whose mulish stubbornness meant she clung too long to solutions which were no longer viable in Westminster, Brussels or both. To these people, May was a politician whose views remained frustratingly opaque to nearly everyone she spoke to outside her inner circle and who seemed unable to galvanise the large number of MPs and voters who for most of 2017 and 2018 would have been happy to be led to a destination which might have commanded a majority in the Commons. Nor did she persuade EU leaders that she had a vision of future relations which was viable, or the ability to win parliamentary approval for the deals they did strike. May found herself locked in a vicious circle in which her failure to deliver in Brussels undermined her at home, while Parliament's growing militancy limited her freedom of manoeuvre in the negotiations. In the end, the European Commission – and even more, the European Council and the member states they represented – were reluctant to grant further concessions because they did not think her temperamentally or numerically capable of securing a majority in Parliament.

One of her most loyal Downing Street aides said, 'Having known two prime ministers well, the job of prime minister is an impossible one. No prime minister has the full skill set. She had some virtues in abundance: courage, determination, a sense of duty, a sincerity, an intelligence that allows her to understand the policy issues. Without those, she couldn't have got nearly as far as she did. However, she also lacked some other things that might have been useful. But had she been a different person, she wouldn't have had the virtues that allowed her to get as far as she did.' However, even loyalists could see that something was missing. Robbie Gibb, her director of communications, told a friend that he knew every cabinet minister better than the prime minister. Another aide said, 'Her qualities are more obvious in private than they are in public and her weaknesses are more obvious in public than they are in private. She's incredibly shy.'

There can be no disagreement about the daunting scale of May's task. Tackling Brexit was arguably the most difficult domestic policy issue to resolve in a century. Only the Great Depression, the economic crash and industrial strife of the mid-1970s and the Covid-19 pandemic stand comparison as full spectrum economic and social crises engulfing every branch of government. Brexit was a constitutional, economic, diplomatic, bureaucratic and technical challenge. It would have taxed even the most able political leader. As Ivan Rogers, her first ambassador to the EU, observed:

Brexit is a revolution; it's the biggest regime change in British governance for at least fifty years but probably longer. It involves everybody, and then suddenly a whole load of people, who've never thought seriously about any of these questions before, are confronted with massive radical institutional changes, which involve changing the construction of our own state to resume control over things that we hadn't fully thought about for forty-five or fifty years. And you're having to run the most complex negotiation in history where, let's face it, you're the junior partner and the other side can beat you up quite badly, and has more of the levers, at the same time as re-engineering your state. And they know your negotiating positions on most of the key stuff, because, oddly enough, they have been representing the UK in multiple big negotiations … The other side is clever, astute, knowledgeable and it knows all your positions. And, at the same time, you are having to demonstrate to a bunch of revolutionaries, who think that you're basically all paid-up Remoaners who are just completely bought in to the existing system, that your heart is in it. So it's a massive set of problems, hugely corrosive.[1]

It may seem a fatuous point, but Brexit was something British politicians and the Whitehall machine had not done before. There was no collective memory of how to go about it as there is with most set-piece political moments, from announcing a budget to launching military action. 'It's the first time we had done Brexit,' a Number 10 aide said. 'You live your life forwards, but you analyse it backwards. Brexit was a huge challenge for the government to take on – one that it hadn't prepared itself for and there wasn't a textbook for. If we did it again, we might do things in a different way.'

In some ways May was an appropriate leader for the times. She really was a dedicated public servant who believed in service. She did work hard and voters ought to want politicians who are serious, hard-working and dedicated. The word aide after aide used when discussing her was 'resilience', which she had in abundance. 'I remember Amber Rudd during the three weeks of sustained media fire over Windrush,' a Number 10 aide said. 'God love Amber, she looked like she'd been run over by a herd of elephants by the end of it. The PM gets that before breakfast.' Another compared May to the words of 'Deep Throat', the secret source in *All the President's Men*, about G. Gordon Liddy, the orchestrator of the Watergate burglary. Liddy could hold his hand in an open flame until his flesh seared. 'What's the trick?' someone asked. Liddy replied, 'The trick is not minding.'

Theresa May did mind the setbacks and humiliations – accounts of her distress and tears at moments of lost hope attest to that. But even in private she was restrained. 'I've seen her put her head on the desk in exasperation and throw her hands up,' a member of her private office said. 'She once called something "fucking ridiculous" and then immediately said, "Excuse me, excuse me."' May absorbed the political torture to which she was subjected. As early as October 2018, when she still had nine months of relentless misery ahead of her, one of May's cabinet colleagues remarked, 'Any man would have resigned by now.'

But she was resilient to a fault. May was so determined to show that a woman was tougher than the dilettante men who packed her cabinet that she seldom showed her feelings or, more importantly, changed her plans when the irresistible force of her will collided head on with the various immovable objects in Parliament. For May, political resilience was not plotting a new route, it was trying the same one again and again.

It is fair to ask how much anyone can be expected to transcend their character and personality flaws. To say she should have been a better communicator and more collaborative with her cabinet is both self-evident and pointless, since she was not. Had she had those attributes she would not have been Theresa May. But it is also fair to judge whether she understood her limitations, sought to work on her deficiencies or to appoint aides who could help compensate for them. For someone who had wanted to be prime minister since at least the age of eighteen, it is reasonable to ask why she had not worked to improve her presentation. The truth is that she thought issues of style were vacuous next to the substance of policy. That would be a flawed judgement in normal times; as the first prime minister after Brexit, it was a catastrophic one for both her and the country she loved. Presentation was not an optional extra, the very definition of leadership is to persuade, otherwise no one – voters, ministers or MPs – will follow where you want to go. Theresa May's disdain for whistling left her as a Pied Piper with no pursuers.

It went beyond presentation, as well. Throughout the Brexit years, the British government was held hostage by the personalities of the five prime ministers who did the job – the structures, organisation, goals and impulses shaped by successively: a blasé public schoolboy, an indecisive introvert, a self-centred extrovert, an untrammelled ideologue, and the school swot with little feel for politics.

May believed, like Gordon Brown (and later Rishi Sunak), that by staring at a problem for long enough she could come up with the perfect solution – and shared the Brownite belief that having stared so much, the contrary views of others must be wrong. Like Brown, she underestimated the step up from being a heavyweight cabinet minister with close command of a brief to the top job of prime minister, where moving at pace and with vision is a basic requirement. A fellow female cabinet minister said, 'May, in the nicest sense, is made worse by being a female politician, because we don't like to make decisions unless we're at least 90 per cent certain of our facts, while the average male politician will do it on 10 per cent, and wing it.' May did not trust her own instincts. The novelist Robert Harris, who understood Homo Politico (ancient, modern, real and fictional), identified a 'lack of largeness of character that is necessary if you are going to get to the very top'. He said, 'If you put in a novel a prime minister that doesn't like speaking in public, that can't take a decision, that's incredibly shy, you would say there's no way someone like that would even want to be prime minister, let alone get the job.'

Many of May's allies quietly accept her presentational limitations, but her record on substance was nearly as questionable as it was on style. May had none of the blunt political brutality which made Brown and his sidekick Ed Balls such effective operators when he was chancellor. Unlike Brown, when crisis presented itself at her door, she shrank where Brown (and his chancellor Alistair Darling) rose to the occasion during the global financial crisis, grasping the government and much of the international community by the scruff of the neck with a clear vision of what needed to be done and deploying a bulldozer spirit in pursuit of that goal. Only when it came to Syria and Salisbury, where May had muscle memory of security issues from her Home Office days, was she assured and impressive.

May almost never stepped back, as the Brexiteers begged her to do, to think about her strategic approach to the negotiations – whether to make leverage of no-deal preparations, whether to turn the table over and make the talks a performance. She took two years to decide what the deal should look like and seemingly no time over how she should persuade others to join her at that destination. She was reactive not proactive, the victim of events, rather than their master.

It was not May's fault that, when she became leader, she lacked a full awareness of what Brexit would entail and an understanding of the interplay between the opportunities and constraints of the single market, the customs union, immigration and supply chains. The same was true of most of her cabinet and a disturbing number of Whitehall officials, who all embarked on a journey of revelation in the second half of 2016.

She was not helped by the truncation of the leadership election, when Andrea Leadsom withdrew and handed her the premiership without a fight. Barwell speculated: 'If Andrea had carried on and [May] adopted a "Brexit means Brexit but we also have to remember the Union, we've got to get some solution that works on all fronts" [position], versus Andrea taking a more absolutist position, and she'd won a convincing majority ... then I think she'd have been in a stronger position ... She hadn't won the argument for that policy with the mass membership.'[2]

It was May's fault that, lacking any experience of the Treasury or any real feel for economics, she appointed Sedwill, a securocrat with no Treasury background either, to replace Heywood as cabinet secretary. Neither prevented an ill-thought-out machinery of government reorganisation which most came to believe was, at best, pointless and, at worst, counterproductive. DExEU's role could have been performed by the Cabinet Office and May didn't seem to realise that creating the Department for International Trade itself sent a message that she was leaving the customs union.

Among the original sins of the May government was the decision to appoint Oliver Robbins as both the permanent secretary of DExEU and the prime minister's personal sherpa. Gavin Barwell reflected, 'I think with Olly – and I take some responsibility for this – we never really got it right in terms of his relationship with the DExEU Secretary, as well as the prime minister. He always saw himself as the prime minister's Sherpa. I have quite a bit of sympathy with DD [David Davis], who found it very frustrating.'[3]

Robbins had his faults, but the worst of them, his secrecy and disregard for some ministers, were colossally exacerbated by May's own personality, which was, if anything, more closed and less trusting of elected politicians than Robbins'. It was May, of course, perhaps recognising a kindred spirit, who appointed Robbins and empowered him far beyond any of her cabinet. The evidence suggests he was prepared to deliver Brexit and was determined to find a solution to the challenge set for him. But, like most civil servants, he regarded it as his duty to identify problems and work for solutions, rather than to challenge the fundamental premise of his instructions. This led the negotiation into the weeds of tactical solutions within tramlines set primarily in Brussels.

It was not May's fault that, when she got the job, she did not know where she wanted to take post-Brexit Britain. Only some lifelong Brexiteers had a firm view of that (a vision of absolutist sovereignty which brooked little compromise with the realities of an interconnected world). And the statements of some Brexiteers during the campaign, Nigel Farage included, who happily said they would stay in the single market, was either evidence of ignorance or deception.

Yet May showed no inclination to consult (or make complicit) the Brexiteer big beasts. She made great play of appointing David Davis, Boris Johnson and Liam Fox to her cabinet in 2016 and then proceeded to neuter them. Davis was supplanted by Robbins, Johnson was consciously excluded from decisions on Brexit and Fox's department was effectively neutered once May decided on customs union membership by any other name. 'She'd appointed these guys in order to appease the party and say, "I've put Brexiteers in charge of DIT, Foreign Office and DExEU",' Ivan Rogers said. 'But she obviously made utterly clear very early on to Jeremy and to Olly that, "I don't want any of these people in the room when I actually decide what I want to do."'

May might have done better to give the Brexiteers their head in Brexit policymaking and if, as her loyalists would argue, the impossibilities and inconsistencies of their positions were exposed, they would have had full ownership of the compromises and imperfections of the outcome – that or they might have made more progress than her with the EU. It is also the case that if these four men had declared a deal of May's to be Brexit, the bulk of the public and a preponderance of Leave voters would have accepted it as such.

Instead, she made it easy for Davis and Johnson to retreat to a position of purity where the ERG ensured a sizeable chunk of future leadership votes would reside, rather than force them to confront Bismarck's quest for 'the next best'. None of the four, after all, were Maastricht-era rebels with an absolutist position. Johnson, in those days, was a highly critical supporter of EU membership and Davis had been a government whip on the Maastricht legislation.

Michael Gove, arguably the most talented of the four as a departmental minister, was excluded altogether from May's first cabinet and then, when the 2017 election forced a rethink, he was never trusted or consulted even when he had demonstrated his more nuanced views of no-deal than Johnson, Davis or Dominic Raab.

With the cabinet Leavers sidelined, May allowed herself to be seduced by the inflexible certainties of Nick Timothy and the ERG into mapping out a vision which boxed her in to a position that was perilous to hold before the 2017 election and arguably would be inevitably overrun after it. May's secrecy and Timothy's certainty combined at the party conference in 2016 to draw red lines which reduced her room for manoeuvre. 'She then spent practically the following eighteen months either side of the election, up until Chequers, trying inch by inch to undo some of the worst consequences of having impaled herself on the ridiculous hooks of that conference speech,' Rogers observed. 'But every inch she moved of course just cost her more with the party. They always had to blame the courtiers, primarily Olly, for the errors, and not the queen herself.'

It was also May's fault that she took so long to crystallise her thoughts, to force her ministers to join her in deciding or then to confront the contradictions of their positions.

While some members of the cabinet think Robbins had an agenda and pushed May in the direction always desired by the Treasury and the civil service, towards geosynchronous orbit with the EU, Rogers thought the problem was actually that Robbins' initial ignorance of EU affairs meant it took him too long to see a viable landing zone for a deal. 'The key EU players think the tragedy of Olly is that he worked out where he might have to get, too late,' Rogers said. 'By the time he had got there, he'd become public enemy number one within the Tory party.'

Because May could not make her mind up, Robbins frequently worked with the Commission team in almost a collective endeavour to devise a solution to satisfy May, rather than making firm demands from a position of strength. A senior member of Robbins' negotiating team recalled, 'I think the biggest single lesson was that it was never a political process in Parliament or with the Europeans. It was a technocratic process. This is why I think it needed a Brexiteer prime minister. The person who decides it, has to believe it. She believed it was her duty to do it, but she never believed it was the right idea. It meant there wasn't a Brexit blueprint that the machine could follow. The bureaucracy did what it always does, which is to fill the space with a bunch of process. It was a technocratic success, but it was a political failure.' One of the rare Brexiteers who worked in May's Number 10 said, 'I think she fell into the Cameron trap of negotiating on the basis of what they [the EU] would accept.'

David Davis said, 'In any negotiation, you have got to maintain a certain level of confidence. And one of the reasons we didn't do as well as we should have done, is we weren't confident enough. Not too glib, not too confident, but not confident enough.'[4] He, like his successor, Dominic Raab, thought the way May sidelined elected ministers was constitutionally questionable.

One of May's Europe advisers was also disturbed by the prime minister's lack of interest in negotiating tactics. 'I have deep respect and admiration for her, but the strangest thing I found was her singular lack of curiosity,' the aide said. 'The weirdest thing for a politician is that she didn't seem particularly interested in the politics. Working for David Cameron, the view was: politics is a game and you need to win at it. And the way you win at it is by working out what your opponents are doing.'

The one tactic on which she and Davis agreed – seeking to divide and rule – between the member state power brokers did not work. 'They nearly always thought they could unpick the solidarity of the twenty-seven, and they proved wrong over and over again,' said Rogers.[5] Stefaan De Rynck, of the Commission, reflected, 'My personal view would be that the UK underestimated what Brexit means, in terms of influence over the other EU countries. Sometimes you got the impression that the UK thought it was still part of the EU's game against the Commission, which is sometimes what members of the Council do in the classic EU decision-making process. The Commission proposes something, and members of the Council get together to shift it, to change it, to kill part of it, or to add stuff. The UK was trying to build some kind of alliance to sway that EU machine in its favour, which was a total underestimation of the serious implications of Brexit, in terms of putting yourself outside of EU power and EU influence.'[6]

The lack of thought about negotiating strategy led directly to the two foundational errors in early 2017 – triggering Article 50 with no clue what Brexit to pursue and accepting the sequencing plans which elevated the Northern Irish border into the critical focus of the entire exit negotiation. Yes, it would have been politically difficult to delay triggering Article 50, but May seems not even to have seriously contemplated doing so, despite the benefits being obvious to such opposites on Brexit as Ivan Rogers and Dominic Cummings. A DExEU political adviser said, 'Tracing back to the original sin in the process is quite a difficult thing to do. But doing that without a very clear sense of what she wanted was a total abdication of responsibility and was a big mistake.'

A senior British diplomat with extensive experience of Brussels explained how May might have done things differently:

> They did everything in the wrong order. You go away for six months and get the civil service to work out all the implications of no-deal Brexit. How do you do it with minimal damage, and what are the consequences? How do you disentangle a thousand different bits of interaction between the UK and the EU? You develop a package on all that. You start then talking informally to the EU and say 'We're going to leave. We're not going to pay any bills because we don't really need to. We've got it all worked out how we'd leave, and we've got all our lorry parks sorted out in Kent, but if you'd like to talk, we're ready to talk about the future trade deal. Whether we pay anything will be dependent on what kind of future trade deal you want with us.' Then you're in a good position; you've got some leverage. Meanwhile, you need to have a much better idea of what the opinion is among MPs. You don't just lob some package at Parliament and say, 'What do you think?' You work out where parliamentary opinion is. Maybe you publish a white paper, maybe you go public and say 'These are the options' and then you start negotiating for the option that you think will command parliamentary support. That's when you put the Article 50 letter in.

The most obvious omission in May's negotiating arsenal was her failure either to neutralise the domestic risks of no-deal or to weaponise the threat of it during the negotiations. Having raised the possibility of no-deal in January 2017, when she proclaimed at Lancaster House that it was better than a bad deal, the government did almost nothing to mean-ingfully prepare for it until the spring of 2018, and nothing publicly until that summer. Only in December, with a little over three months to go before the putative date of Brexit, did no-deal prep become a top priority of government. There was a respectable argument that Britain would have done better in the negotiations if the EU had regarded it as more plausible that the UK could walk away (a counterfactual that was to be tested in the second half of 2019), but also that preparing for no-deal was actually the best way to avoid it. In either scenario, the responsible course of action was to prepare as fully as possible. Having raised the salience of the issue, this was not done until it was much too late.

Arguably the greatest disaster, since it ought to have been a red line on which Britain fought hard, was sequencing. For a process-driven prime minister, it is remarkable that she did not understand how damaging it would be to agree to the EU's structure for the talks immediately after the general election. Gavin Barwell, who arrived in Number 10 only after the point was conceded, said, 'It may well have been impossible to avoid it, but it was a major factor in what followed. Sequencing was the genesis of the backstop, which is ultimately what stopped the deal getting through Parliament.'[7] Whatever appetite there had been for Davis's 'fight of the summer' was washed away by the shattered morale and instability unleashed by the 2017 election debacle.

Sequencing not only elevated Northern Ireland to centre stage, it also relegated talk about the future relationship to the wings. With that went the ability for May to say to the Brexiteers, 'You may not like the withdrawal agreement, but you can shape the final trade deal.' Putting the future up in lights might have allowed May to keep Davis and Johnson on board. Barwell added, 'It would have been much easier to handle politically, if we were talking about all those things together.'[8] Another political aide recalled, 'One of the more productive strategies would have been to have the mother of all rows about what sort of trade deal we should have.'

The same passive approach was taken to the Joint Report, the creation of the backstop and the failure even to try to write a British legal text. 'If we put our own text out there, might that have helped?' Barwell mused. 'I suppose it's a valid argument to say, "Given they did it, shouldn't you have responded or beaten them to it?" I suppose.'[9]

The Joint Report flowed from the decisions taken by a weakened May in the aftermath of the general election setback. 'Some of the language changed pre- and post-election,' a senior aide said. '"No return to the borders of the past" in Northern Ireland became "no border". Keeping trade "as frictionless as possible" became "frictionless trade". They were symbols of the move towards a softer Brexit.' A member of Vote Leave, watching the whole thing unfold with horror, said, 'May signed up to a bunch of axioms that were a catastrophe when pulled together. One was there must be no change whatsoever to North/South trade. The second was the EU's external customs frontier must be protected and the third was there must be no substantial change to EU law because Brexit was a UK decision. Put all those things together, it was a disaster. You could take any two of those and you could've done a deal. All three together made them the unholy trinity. One that Vote Leave would have rejected was the idea that the EU did not have to make any changes to its legal order.' In Northern Ireland, they would have argued, as they did later, 'We've all got to prioritise peace and kids not getting killed over anything else. But that's not what they did in the May government's wisdom.'

This is where the EU has questions to answer as well. Barnier, Juncker and Tusk deserve plaudits for the way they kept the twenty-seven member states on the same page, something which was far from a given when the process started. The document outlining how the talks would proceed, written by Tusk's aides Jeppe Tranholm-Mikkelsen and Piotr Serafin, showed they had prepared in a way that the British state had not.

In piling blame upon Theresa May's miscalculations, it is only fair to say that the EU and the Irish were not blameless either on the issue of Northern Ireland, where legalistic literalism triumphed over the long-standing history of political fungibility in the province. Brussels was prepared to tolerate zero risk of single market contamination, when a more can-do approach on technology, which acknowledged the unique circumstances of the North-South border, would have borne fruit. By 2022 the real-time monitoring of goods movements (alternative arrangements by another name) was a reality and there is reason to think it could have been accomplished more quickly with a little more political will.

Brexit Britain should not have expected favours from a club it was leaving, but the EU's approach rendered its claims to be a guardian of the peace process rather hollow. JoJo Penn, May's deputy chief of staff, admitted, 'Something that we did find hard throughout was a bit of a sense that Northern Ireland/Ireland was a unique situation because of the Good Friday Agreement, so it needed a unique or different approach. Whereas ... for the EU side ... the integrity of the single market and the single market's border, was the overriding concern when it came to resolving the issue in Northern Ireland.'[10]

The Irish, too, during the period of *No Way Out*, chose to play hard-ball, particularly in the run-up to the Joint Report, when the Varadkar government took advantage of May's domestic situation. 'The Irish took a hard line,' a Number 10 Europe adviser said. 'We were far too often far too optimistic about what was required. The desire to give some future certainty to the economy was very high in our minds, so we were very keen to have an agreement that there should be a transition/implementation period. The EU knew that, and they exploited that hard.' A second EU adviser said, 'The Irish were very concerned about North-South but showed no concern about East-West borders.' Only in the summer of 2019 did Leo Varadkar concede privately to May that his rigid insistence on sequencing might have been a mistake.

Had Britain managed to get discussion of the political agreement alongside the withdrawal agreement, Northern Ireland might have been the key which unlocked the whole deal, rather than the problem which derailed it. 'If you listen to Bertie Ahern, or any sensible elder statesman from Ireland, their view was pretty close to the British view,' said one of May's senior aides. 'As soon as you get an agreement that technology can work between Northern Ireland and the Republic of Ireland, there's no way the Dutch ports wouldn't say, "You've got all this technology for Northern Ireland, we want the same deal." If you got Northern Ireland right at the beginning that could potentially have worked for the UK–EU border as well.'

In the autumn of 2018, Juncker and Selmayr, in particular, realised that the EU might have been too successful. They had not just boxed the prime minister in, they had almost asphyxiated their main interlocutor. It was the Commission – rather than the Council or the member states – which was the driving force of compromise, an inversion of the popular media depiction of Juncker as a truculent drunken federalist and Selmayr as the 'monster' of Brussels. However, none of this might have been necessary if the EU had thought a little more about the strategic relationship it wanted with the UK over the decades to come, rather than leave London to take the lead.

May was right that Britain's historic ties to the EU made it logical and essential to secure a bespoke deal. She was right that simply sitting on one of Michel Barnier's steps was neither desirable nor politically tenable at home. But she was also too stubborn to realise that playing Barnier's game a little, presenting British decisions in EU language, offering some sort of 'concept' of the future relationship, as craved by everyone from Selmayr to Guy Verhofstadt, would have helped her achieve what she wanted. The one time an idea of an association agreement was proposed, it was rejected for no discernible good reason.

The deal had many moving parts but in essence the game was simple. 'They'd like to be able to impose on us their regulation without giving us access to their market, and we'd like access to their market without any of their regulations,' a senior cabinet minister said. 'Somewhere in the middle there's got to be a landing ground.'

So what did Theresa May actually believe about Brexit? Another senior cabinet minister said early in the iterative process, 'I think the only two things she certainly believes are that we have to deliver on the referendum result and we have to end freedom of movement. Those are the only real red lines.' On control of the border, May was by far the most hardline in her government. Most Brexiteers wanted control and a system which did not discriminate in favour of EU nationals over other countries with which Britain had strong links, rather than a drastic reduction in immigration. May, correctly, felt many Leave voters wanted the numbers to come down as well. 'She looks at all the public schoolboys and she thinks that they don't really understand ordinary people,' the cabinet minister said, 'And there's the Berkshire vicarage element where she believes that people don't have jobs because they have been taken by immigrants.' Philip Hammond disagreed vociferously with May on immigration but agreed it was her initial priority: 'She will have seen this through the prism of immigration and security. For her, the economy would have been very much a secondary thing. She didn't really have a deep interest in how the economy worked.'[11]

This opening position was then modified in two important ways. First, Hammond and Greg Clark, the business secretary, convinced the prime minister, by the autumn of 2017, that she needed to achieve as near-frictionless trade as possible or established supply chains would collapse.

The fourth, final and, in the end, most significant element for Theresa May was when she grasped the potential dangers of a hard Brexit to the Union. Philip Rycroft, who was Robbins' deputy at DExEU and then his successor as permanent secretary, said, 'It took the prime minister a long time – post-Lancaster House, when she'd sprayed all the red lines all over the place – to work out just how fundamental this was for the Union.'[12] This was an issue that gradually came to the fore during 2018 and was, following her visit to Belfast in early 2019, May's overarching motivation. A senior cabinet minister said, 'Her view on no-deal economics was that it would be bad and damaging but could, over time, be weathered. However if you started to see the break-up of the UK, that is irreversible.' Kirsty Buchanan, her deputy press secretary, concluded 'Theresa May gave up her premiership for' that judgement.

Yet May never made a speech to the country, or ever sat down with her cabinet, clearly explaining her beliefs and the hierarchy of her concerns. Instead, she allowed a free for all in her cabinet, with ministers pressing very different priorities, until the final moments of the second Chequers summit in July 2018. By then, her cabinet was so used to having carte blanche that being asked to fall into line was a resigning matter.

May was a believer in cabinet government and her top team included a greater cross-section of Tory talent than the three governments which followed hers – but it fundamentally did not work. It took from July 2016 until February 2018 before the prime minister even attempted to achieve a collective view about what to ask for, and until July 2018 when it was finally decided. A very senior civil servant said, 'She was trying to do something which doesn't work in our country. You cannot have a cabinet that disagrees with itself about something so profound. Nothing works. Cabinet government allows you to thrash things out. Life is complicated. There are at least two views on everything. You can either save the environment or you can build a road. Cabinet lets us work out what to do.' But, on Brexit, a good-mannered disagreement became impossible, so existential did the issues feel to Brexiteers and Bresisters. 'Toxicity set in,' the mandarin said. 'They didn't trust each other. It was deeply, deeply emotional on both sides.'

The determination to win the internal battle and be seen to do so, coupled with mutual suspicion and distrust, led to leaking from cabinet on a scale probably never seen before. This in turn created a vicious circle where the battles in the room were fought out, often just minutes later, with selective briefing of journalists only too happy to share the latest rows on Twitter. Julian Smith, the chief whip, said, 'At the time where our prime minister needed to be able to have conversations with all of her cabinet ministers and be sure that those would not enter the public domain, she had a situation where that was very difficult.' Another cabinet minister found himself in a small meeting in the Thatcher study in February 2019: 'She got seven or eight senior ministers together. For me, it was exactly what government should be – a proper political decision, where people weren't being sycophantic and a range of views. And then something from that leaked and I just thought, for fuck's sake.'

Many ministers would argue that the prime minister's refusal to reveal her true intentions led people to fight their battles in public. 'You sit there and you tell her what you think and it's never clear whether she has registered what you are saying or not,' a senior minister complained. Another cabinet minister said, 'We have to say things in cabinet so that everybody else can witness what we've said, and it'll be written down in the minutes and then there is some record that we've said it to her. Because if you say it in a private meeting, it has no impact. Whereas with David Cameron, you'd just walk into his office and say, "I'm not going to say this in cabinet, because I don't want to embarrass you, but this is what I really think and this is what you should do." He'd say, "Thank you very much", and agree with you or not.'

There was a huge opportunity cost to May's indecision, caution and her obsessive need to plod through an iterative process rather than to work out where things were heading and take a risk to get ahead of events. The first was credibility. One of Jeremy Hunt's aides in the Foreign Office remarked, 'Jeremy's view, going round the world, was that it was not the fact we were leaving the EU that was damaging our reputation. It was the fact that we were fannying about so much.'

The more important issue was that May's unwillingness to drive events meant that her positioning became, in large part, a reaction to the initiatives of others. Other MPs did not sit idle, they caucused and organised and, in the process, became more militant, on both sides of the Brexit divide. Political prizes which might have been obtainable in the spring of 2018 were, by the autumn, impossible dreams. Hard Brexit in 2016 was leaving the single market and customs union and by the spring of 2019 it meant leaving on WTO terms with no-deal.

One of the shrewdest members of May's inner circle said, 'We have to accept responsibility. When we set off, there was a group of people on the Remain side who accepted the referendum but were fighting to keep us in the single market and customs union. Another group on the other side, who had spent their entire lives wanting to be out of the EU, were prepared to leave with a deal and were prepared to pay the £39 billion and were prepared to have an implementation period. Somehow these two groups got so pushed apart that some lost all interest in having a deal and the other group wanted a referendum to remain. We were still walking down the middle of the road waiting to get hammered by a bus coming in any direction.' The source added, 'One of the mistakes we made is that we zig-zagged from one group to another. As we came across a horror show amendment from the Remain side, we pivoted in one direction to try and win a vote by three. As the trouble came from the other side, we pivoted back towards a much harder position on Brexit to avoid it. Every time we won those votes by three or four, we lost trust. It was the zig-zags that really cost us.' The sense that their party was leaving them, not the other way around, was to be a common theme on both sides of the Brexit divide. It was May's tragedy that both Brexiteers and Remainers concluded at key moments that the prime minister had sided with the other group.

It was understandable that she began her premiership seeking to find a solution which could command a Commons majority solely from Conservative (and DUP) votes, but it was her mistake that, when that became unrealistic, she was too rigid in her tribal loyalties to entertain the idea of a broader cross-party solution. The presence of the equally inflexible (and to many Tory MPs) politically reprehensible Jeremy Corbyn at the other despatch box made her task more complicated.

The various Bresistance groups showed that cross-party working was not impossible, though they also demonstrated how difficult it was to forge consensus, but there were moments in 2016, 2017 and the spring of 2018 where it is perfectly possible to envisage one of the softer Brexit outcomes securing a majority in the House. Phillip Lee recalled, 'The only chance for a soft Brexit was at the point when there were 80 Labour MPs who were prepared to walk through the lobbies with the government to support a customs union or Norway. It was rejected by the government.'[13] Nicky Morgan agreed: 'In 2016, I think she could have got away with Norway.' A leading Labour member of the Bresistance added, 'I always thought that after she got in, she was going to form some cross-party negotiating commission, lock in Corbyn and Keir and come up with soft Brexit. Everybody would have to vote for it, even if there were some ultras at both ends. It would have swung through with 450 votes.'

An attempt at outreach – either in 2016, after the general election in 2017 or as she leached Conservative support in 2018 – would have been in keeping with the side of May's character that believed in doing the right thing for the country. It would have been wholly out of character for a leader who was a tribal Conservative. 'After the election, literally no one was making that argument, because it would've been fatal to try,' a Downing Street aide argued. 'The only means of proceeding was to try and keep as many people together in a big enough group for as long as you possibly could. The PM is conservative. She is a partisan politician.' A minister agreed: 'To Theresa, the Conservative Party is everything. She feels very strongly that it is only through the Conservative Party that good government can be delivered.' To dyed-in-the-wool Tories this was admirable and correct. To the vast majority of others, it was a conclusion that the Brexit years rendered absurd.

The fact that the public voted to Leave and the overwhelming majority of MPs voted to Remain was often highlighted as the systemic source of May's problems. Jeremy Hunt, her foreign secretary, identified a more subtle source of discord, telling aides, 'The problem is that she has selected a form of Brexit which is supported by Brexit voters but not by Brexit MPs.'

Instead of openly seeking a majority for the close economic Brexit May had concluded she needed, between March and July 2018, the prime minister performed a semi-private pivot which she failed to explain to moderate MPs who might have backed her and which left some Brexiteers convinced she had engaged in a grand deception. Others saw confusion rather than conspiracy. A senior Brexiteer, who served in later cabinets, said, 'I think most of the time people thought she was useless rather than devious. She didn't, off her own bat, have a clear or strong view on the European issue. Rather than being a devious Remainer who wanted to get us as closely tied into the EU as possible, it looked as if it was a bit of uselessness combined with fear. She was absolutely terrified of the consequences of Brexit and didn't believe that there was any positive from it. That made her decision-making fundamentally flawed as a prime minister in charge of Brexit.'

May morphed from indecisive to immovable. Having latched on to the Heath Robinson hybrid customs plan (with its many acronyms), she clung, almost alone, to a solution that was theoretically brilliant but practically and politically absurd, despite being repeatedly told by her Brexit secretary and (admittedly less emphatically) by her chief negotiator that it would not fly. 'It was such a clever scheme that nobody thought it could work in practice, including many British officials,' said Charles Grant of the Centre for European Reform.[14] Having watched Davis and Johnson resign over Chequers, she saw no reason to move, even when

Brussels told her (admittedly rudely and ineptly) it was a non-starter at Salzburg. A special adviser in another department said, 'She had very clear tramlines for her views and once she'd settled on them, you could never shift her, even when the facts changed.' A Downing Street Europe adviser concluded, 'One of the things that killed her was that she expended all her political capital on Chequers, which was never going to work.'

Philip Rycroft said, 'I think it was a brave attempt to reconcile the irreconcilable, but I think all of us who are a lot wiser after the event can probably say, "It was never going to fly."'[15] Justine Greening criticised May's failure to signpost her intentions: 'If you are going down a strategic route of hard Brexit, which is what she had articulated, then what you can't do is, 75 per cent of the way down there, suddenly get to Chequers and then tell everybody, the cabinet and the public, that suddenly it's a compromise, and we're doing soft Brexit now.'[16]

The withdrawal agreement May signed in November 2018 was hard won but truly satisfied no one. 'I think, technically, as a piece of negotiation and as a piece of drafting, the withdrawal agreement does the job that we were asked to do,' one of those who helped write the text argued. 'We also got a rather good deal on money, which was the thing that people thought might be a great sticking point.'

Politically, however, May did not tell Robbins to fight harder on the backstop, despite the clear signals that it would be a deal breaker for her party. Those MPs who say Robbins never asked for a time limit or exit clause were wrong. But the demand was not formalised or made a red line drawn in blood. May's aides give the impression they were happy for Dominic Raab to press the case, not so he could get anywhere but so he could be exposed to the impossibility of doing so. Elevating the importance of such a demand and then facing rejection would have been devastating for May, unless she was prepared to use such a setback to justify a pivot to a looser trade arrangement than Chequers. History suggests she was not willing to do that. However, it would have been wise, politically and optically, to be seen to try harder to get something which was now of elemental importance to her Brexit secretary and her backbenchers.

This was the moment when May should perhaps have considered another demonstrative row, turning over the table as she did after Salzburg. The prime minister's view and that of many of her aides was that this would have been pointless. 'She has said this to me in these terms, "If at any point it had been worth my while turning the table over I would have happily done it. But, the EU were watching everything that our Parliament was doing",' said one. 'They knew, no matter what she said in the room, she didn't have the authority to take us out without a deal. So it would not have made any difference. It may have cheered people up for twenty-four hours.' Yet there is an argument that this is precisely the kind of demonstration of determination which May needed at this and later points.

More importantly, there does not appear to have been any meaningful effort to seek a democratic lock on the backstop, giving the people of Northern Ireland a say over its imposition or its continued operation after a fixed period of time. When the Johnson government pushed for this a year later, both the Commission and the member states recognised the moral and political force of their argument. Had May got that in 2018, she might well have kept the DUP on board and with them a sizeable chunk of the ERG. Perhaps it needed another eight months of deadlock and misery before Brussels and Dublin were prepared to move, but neither May nor Robbins seems to have appreciated the potential for a Stormont lock.

May presented her November 2018 deal as the best of both worlds, as the only way of reconciling the conceptual freedoms of Brexit with the practical necessities of continuing economic prosperity and the political coherence of the Union. But even since Chequers she had not successfully rolled the pitch. 'She thinks this is a good deal,' one political aide said. 'She thought it through, analysed it. Maybe you could say she could have done more to ventilate these issues during the process and take people on the journey. When you got to the destination it made perfect sense to her, it made perfect sense to those who had worked on it. Perhaps for other people, it didn't make sense to them.'

There were alternatives. On the Brexiteer side, the desire was for a cleaner break from EU sovereignty, regardless of the practical economic difficulties. But there was also an alternative deal at the softer end which might have secured a Commons majority. Gavin Barwell said later, 'The best deal we could have got would have been alignment with the rules on goods so that you avoided the regulatory checks at the border. Not just NI to Ireland but UK to EU, and some kind of novel customs arrangement that avoided customs checks at the UK–EU border but, over time, would have given us some flexibility to vary our tariffs for third country trade deals.' As he acknowledged, 'The crux of this issue has always been that the Brexiteers are right to say the ability to do our own trade deals with other countries is an important part of what Brexit is all about.'[17] Reflecting after his departure from government, Philip Hammond said, 'I think a more realistic solution was a customs union between the UK and the European Union which would have allowed the relationship to be governed by treaty, with the courts of each entity interpreting, and then some kind of international body to deal with conflict-of-laws type issues. But this was never what the hardliners wanted, of course.'[18]

Throughout the period from November 2018 to the end of March 2019, the only way May could win a meaningful vote was to convince Remainers there was a danger of no-deal and Brexiteers there was a danger of no Brexit to get them to embrace her deal as the lesser evil. 'The thing that we were never been able to do is close things down to a binary choice so that we could get a majority for one option,' Gavin Barwell reflected. 'Brexit is a maze. And the rules of the maze are there are three doors out marked: deal, no-deal, revoke. And you can only leave the maze if you can get half of the participants to go through the same door at the same time. We were never able to do that, because we were never able to wedge shut one of the doors.'

The battles in Parliament came at a time when May's dawdling had left time and space for MPs to harden their views. If there had been a moment when MPs did not insist on their perfect solution to the detriment of good alternatives, that time had passed. Even Bismarck, the man of blood and iron, lived by the maxim that 'politics is the art of the possible, the attainable – the art of the next best'. But by 2019, those backing the People's Vote, Common Market 2.0 or membership of a customs union were not interested in 'the next best', when they might easily have cooperated to force the government down one of these paths.

At precisely the moment parliamentarians became an irresistible force, Theresa May made herself into an immovable object. Having concluded what was best at Chequers and in the deal, she then brooked no talk of a different approach. Yet this stubborn refusal to bend came from a position of terrible political vulnerability. As the commentator Steve Richards observed, 'May misread the political rhythms. She chose to act weakly when she was politically strong and then had no choice but to be assertively strong when she was pathetically weak. Before the [2017] election, when she was walking on water, she meekly told her party what it wanted to hear; that they could have their cake and eat it ... Then [in the spring of 2019] she reached out to a Labour leadership desperate to move on from Brexit and made the case for compromise. She did so when her internal opponents were ready to remove her.'[19]

The Spartans concluded once May had been removed and Johnson installed that their strategic truculence was triumphant. By standing firm in the face of all compromise they had blocked a soft Brexit and secured a Brexiteer prime minister willing, ostensibly, to do their bidding. But this was only ever a marginal victory. Around 95 per cent of the withdrawal agreement Johnson finally signed was negotiated by Oliver Robbins, not his point man David Frost. The negotiations in 2018 and early 2019 irrevocably shaped the debates which followed and bound both Johnson and Frost's hands. The Spartans were still complaining about the 2019 withdrawal agreement and the 2020 trade deal in 2024.

They would have been better to oust May in July 2018, rather than wait a year. Instead, the hardliners maintained their polite loyalty to the prime minister until, from their point of view, it was far too late. Had Davis, Johnson and Gove moved against her in December 2017 or earlier in May or June 2018 when it was beginning to become clear that May was on a very different page to them, things might have turned out differently. Even when Davis and Johnson did resign in July 2018, neither made any concerted effort to remove the prime minister. Both could have done so, with Philip Hammond's assistance, after the general election.

The case of Davis is both the most peculiar and the most understandable. The Brexit secretary, as his letters to May show, had far more idea than Johnson or Gove what was really going on – and he predicted pretty much every misfortune which would befall May if she continued on the path she had chosen. But Davis was also the most loyal, grateful for her patronage and unwilling to betray her. 'He was right on sequencing, he was right about the Northern Ireland Protocol,' a close ally said. 'He was right about alignment and Chequers I, he was right that soft Brexit wasn't going to fly. He was right that Chequers II would bomb. If we knew then what we know now, he should have gone and he should have said, "I've got a public duty to say you've failed. You blew it, you've put Brexit in jeopardy. We need someone else at the helm."'

From that point forward, the Brexiteers resolved to oppose May's approach but, rather than remove her, they left the prime minister in a state of miserable suspended animation as ardent Brexiteers found reasons not to vote for Brexit. 'You felt there were some people who would literally do anything for Brexit other than vote for it,' Barwell observed. Julian Smith rightly noted that the longer it went on, the more militant the Eurosceptics became: 'There was definitely a shift from some Brexiteers. If you'd asked them three years ago, "Would you be happy with the prime minister's deal?" they'd have bitten your arm off ... There was a purification process.' Had May and Smith been more clear-eyed, they might reasonably have concluded that the Tory right was never satisfied and spent the time in which they tacked away from the ERG by stealth rolling the pitch for compromise, rather than denying that this was her new path. The problem for May was that the same purification process and hardening of views was also the case with the anti-Brexit MPs.

May clung to the notion that her MPs would ultimately fold. She herself cared much more about her party than about the EU, but she seems not to have noticed that others, on both flanks of her party, felt differently. A civil servant in the government legal department said, 'I found the wilful blindness both from her and from Julian Smith about their ability to get Parliament to agree it, pretty astonishing. They lost vote after vote, and yet somehow thought they could bludgeon Parliament into agreeing. Politically, she was in cloud cuckoo land.' JoJo Penn admitted afterwards, 'I think there was probably a point at which, after the opposition to Chequers had grown within our own backbenches, that we should have reassessed how possible it was to get a deal through based on that model.'[20] Phillip Lee said, 'Theresa May had a narrow window to reset her strategy, in early January 2019. She had a further opportunity in April when the indicative votes process showed that the option with the most support was a second referendum. There was never the parliamentary majority needed to get a soft Brexit through without the second referendum as well.' In the first half of 2018, that was not true, but it was demonstrably so by the time Robbins returned from Brussels with the deal.

Perhaps May's only chance of winning the meaningful vote was right at the beginning, if she had called it for the day after the deal was signed in November 2018 – but that would have necessitated some pitch rolling and bringing the communications team into the picture earlier, so they could launch a twenty-four-hour propaganda blitz to persuade MPs of its virtues.

Others make a case that May would also have been better off taking her first big loss in MV1 before Christmas, rather than waiting until mid-January, not least because the whips failed to move the numbers at all in the intervening month. That would have bought more time to convert people before the crucial 29 March deadline. These suggestions, however, are probably sticking plasters on a gunshot wound.

The Bresisters miscalculated as well, of course. The pro-dealers, whose only common interest was in preventing no-deal, saw that as an end in itself. But to Downing Street officials it was simply delaying the day when they would have to endorse a deal or a referendum. JoJo Penn called 'no to no-deal' a 'false option'. She said, 'Having triggered Article 50 the options are: do a deal, leave with no-deal, maybe have an extension and have a second referendum, or revoke the whole process. "No to no deal" without a deal that you're in favour of … created a dynamic that was not conducive to finding a way forwards and I think upset the balance.'[21]

To those who were fighting for a referendum, the pro-dealers in the cabinet – Hammond, Rudd, Gauke and Clark – morphed too late from the Croissant Club talking shop into the Rebel Alliance, the chancellor even later than the others. May neither listened to them nor stripped them of the whip during the abstention rebellion in March 2019, an action which simultaneously drew attention to her lack of authority and exacerbated it. Phillip Lee recalled, 'The moment was Christmas 2018. If a cabinet minister had gone in that period immediately after the confidence vote then I think we would have won, but we couldn't get them to do it.'[22] Lee also accused May and Norway advocates like Nick Boles and Oliver Letwin of misjudgement: 'They got it wrong. It was never going to happen. The only options were a hard Brexit, which is effectively where we've ended up, or a second referendum.'[23]

The Rebel Alliance, in turn, looked askance at those who refused to back a soft Brexit because they wanted a referendum instead. Greg Clark said, 'It is ironic that the people who defeated it were the people who wanted to have a close relationship with the European Union, but were sufficiently purist that they wanted to run a second referendum or remain and weren't prepared to support what I thought was a fair response to the verdict of the referendum.'

Despite all this, Theresa May actually got quite close to passing her deal. Without John Bercow's support for Grieve and Letwin's challenge to the parliamentary conventions, she might well have done so. By allow-ing MPs to take control of the Commons timetable, to pass legislation opposing no-deal, for the first time in history, the speaker (justified or not) changed the rules of the game and consequently its outcome.

That was one constitutional impediment to the government's success, the other was the existence of the Fixed-term Parliaments Act, which made it impossible for Downing Street to drum up votes on its own side by threatening a general election to force MPs into line. This held the government in a state of paralysis, neither able to move forward nor to give the public a chance to overrule Parliament. 'MPs, at some point, have to decide whether they have confidence in the government or not,' JoJo Penn said later. 'You can't have an option of rejecting the govern-ment, the government having no majority on something that they could say is a confidence issue, but we're not going to … change it.' This, she said, 'created false options which didn't help the process for coming to a conclusion or a decision'.[24]

Kirsty Buchanan said, 'It was one of those achingly close things but there was always a piece of the jigsaw that needed to slot into place and it just never quite landed at the right time. But for Bercow, but for Geoffrey Cox's advice we might have carried the DUP.'

Some decisions, which seemed necessary at the time, looked in retro-spect like horrific own goals, including allowing the attorney general's legal advice to assume totemic significance. To some degree the govern-ment's hand was forced by both the Bresistance and the Spartans, but the superannuated drama of Geoffrey Cox's verdict on 29 March cost May dearly. No other single moment in the Brexit years would so clearly have put history on a different path. 'Imagine if the government worked like this all the time,' said a member of the negotiating team, whose work in the weeds of the backstop was torpedoed by Cox's verdict. 'For every policy, or thing you did, you publish legal advice on what was shit about it. It was such a weird thing to happen.' It was also the pivot on which May's premiership turned. From then on she was impaled.

By the end, a good number of May's aides concluded that, since she had failed to deliver Brexit, no one else could have done so either. 'It might just be an impossible ask because of the maths of it,' a special adviser in Number 10 said in those final weeks. 'Ultimately, everything is about the numbers and if the numbers don't work, no amount of wishing it is going to change the simple mathematical reality.'

The parliamentary arithmetic, of course, was a catastrophe of May's own creation. Her desperate performance in the 2017 election was the direct cause of her problems on Brexit. 'She created that Parliament,' a less forgiving Number 10 adviser said. 'It was the election that produced it. There's no point having a go at Parliament for not doing its job – you produced this situation.'

Stepping back, May was diligent in exploring all the implications of Brexit, but in adopting a defensive crouch, she also ensured there was little effort made to calculate the potential opportunities presented by leaving EU rules behind, still less exploit them. And her posture encouraged the EU to dictate terms, in both the structure and substance of the negotiations.

The Brexiteers were many things – fanatical, casual about the facts, often deluded about reality, disloyal – but they understood far better than May what strategy the moment required. Some of them naively believed that people they had spent three decades maligning for pursuing a crazed political project would put aside their hard-won unity to seek a deal of mutual economic benefit. They wished away every warning about the potential downsides. On nearly every detailed issue they seemed delusionally optimistic. But on strategy they understood the game better than May. It is hard not to conclude that a Brexiteer prime minister with a buccaneering strategy – reined in by a civil service punctilious about the details – would have served Britain better than a cautious Remainer who became a captive of a process drawn up by her opponents and the judgements of a communautaire chief negotiator about what was negotiable, who refused ever to kick over the table and change the dynamic of a losing game. In their memoirs of the negotiations Michel Barnier and Stefaan De Rynck are adamant that they were never impressed by Boris Johnson's tougher approach, that Britain was really only ever going to get what it was given. But the events of late 2019 and 2020 do not support this conclusion. There were people in Brussels and, more significantly, in Dublin, who thought no-deal was possible and gave more ground as a consequence. It is a simple fact that Johnson was offered things which May was not.

This foray into counterfactual speculation does not mean, though, that May talking tough would have got the job done. First, it was not her style. Asking May to come out fighting would have been the equivalent of sending her idol Geoffrey Boycott out to bat in a T20 game and expect him to reverse scoop a full-length ball over the keeper for six. Part of the way you make a hardball strategy work is to make the other side believe you are capable of swinging the bat and walking away, risking mutual harm. Barnier, Selmayr and others in the EU apparatus are clear that they never believed May would make no-deal her policy. After the general election setback, May arguably did not have the numbers in Parliament to take on a high-risk strategy, even if she had been so inclined. That, in turn, meant the Commission had serious doubts that the concessions they granted could be delivered. Chris Grayling, perhaps the most loyal Mayite among the cabinet Brexiteers, said, 'The consequence of that election was she had no majority, there was a Remain majority in the House of Commons, and she was simply not in a position to emphatically say, "Right, we are going to play hardball", because behind her there were a lot of people with sharp knives.'[25]

The suspicion remains that May would have been better emphatically embracing either a hard or soft Brexit before the end of 2017. By the spring of 2019, her options had narrowed so the only hard option was no-deal and the only soft option meant backing a referendum, which would have meant splitting her party down the middle. 'The PM was always very, very clear that she was not prepared to sanction a second referendum,' Barwell recalled. 'She felt that was saying to voters, "You told us what you wanted, and we're now going back and saying to you, 'Are you sure?'" Other countries have these second referendums when the government gets given an answer it doesn't like. We shouldn't be like that. We have to honour the result. It was always clear she wasn't going to countenance that.'[26]

Given her opposition to a referendum, it is odd the government did not try a third but binding round of indicative votes with transferable voting in an attempt to find common ground across the chamber. Penn was among the Number 10 aides who were pushing that idea.

Instead, May tried to find a deal with the Labour front bench which, by then, had itself become fatally detached from its backbench and grassroots opinion. It is fatuous to blame the opposition for a government's failure but Jeremy Corbyn and his closest aides might have benefited if they had been cuter in their approach to the Commons votes, given that the Labour leader did not really want to commit himself one way or the other. 'I think the way that Labour could've enabled Brexit to happen would've been to whip less strongly those backbench MPs who may have been prepared to vote for a deal,' JoJo Penn observed.[27] Instead, by the time the two teams sat down together in April 2019, Corbyn and Seumas Milne were no more capable of taking their party with them than was May. By then Keir Starmer was positioning himself for a future leadership contest with just as much dedication as Boris Johnson.

May's final roll of the dice – the offer of a Commons vote on a referendum – was ambiguous. The conventional wisdom was that, by this point, the Commons would have backed a confirmatory vote if it had come to a vote. Both Barwell and Leadsom, in their memoirs, saw it as inevitable that the advocates of a second referendum would have won. But even Dominic Grieve was not sure. He told a friend afterwards, 'I think the irony is she probably would have defeated a second referendum.' In that scenario, even if passing the deal would not have been enough to save her premiership (and things had probably gone too far for that), May's political legacy might have looked very different.

How will history judge Theresa May? One of her political aides rightly observed that the memories of contemporaries who found her company agonising would fade and future historians might see her differently. 'With prime ministers, because we are so overexposed to them, you only feel the shoe where it pinches, you only feel the bits of her premiership where it's annoying,' the adviser said. 'This is why some premiers who are a bit underrated in their time have their reputations revised up. At the time, you only notice the things that annoy you about them, but in hindsight the other qualities come through. I think she has a lot of very fine qualities you want in a prime minister. History will judge her more kindly.'

The outlines of what may become the revisionist view of her political achievements are dimly visible. Some will argue that her quiet marshalling of the Brexit settlement away from no-deal prevented worse turmoil. Others, that by never quite committing to one interpretation of Brexit throughout 2017 and much of 2018, May kept her party together for far longer than a more ideological figure would have.

Historians of all generations will conclude that the nation had much to thank Theresa May, the woman, for: her dedication, her service, her resilience, her effort. Given different circumstances, she might have been a good prime minister. The response to the chemical weapons attacks in Salisbury and Syria, and the final month of domestic activism, gave hints of what might have been.

Nor should we forget the human inside the politician. 'One of the areas she is entitled to feel sad about,' a Downing Street aide said, 'is she was told at quite a lot of points that if she just did this, "We will get it over the line". And every time she did it at great political cost, it failed.' Another Number 10 adviser said, 'Again and again, in order to do her best by what her party and her colleagues wanted, she batted strongly for stuff she thought she was highly unlikely to get. She did it anyway. They never gave her the credit she deserved for that.' In her final newspaper interview as prime minister, May revealed a little of the frustration: 'I did everything I could to get it over the line! I was willing to sit down with Jeremy Corbyn, willing to sacrifice my premiership – give up my job!'[28]

But it is also hard not to conclude that Brexit required a highly skilled political operator and May's virtues were profoundly ill-suited to the fast-moving media and ideological environment of the 2010s. Dealt a bad hand, she proceeded to give away the few aces she had, showed repeatedly she did not really understand the rules of the game and sent Oliver Robbins to ask her opponents how she ought to play her cards. Most importantly, perhaps, she never showed any willingness to turn over the table and bring the game to a crashing halt, or even credibly threaten to do so. Brexit was a task crying out for decisive leadership, for a politician who knew where they wanted to go, armed with the powers of persuasion to take a country with her. When she set off, May did not know where she was going or understand the need for speed. When she worked out where she was headed, she concealed it from both factions of Tory MPs, only to discover that neither side liked her chosen destination very much.

One of the key questions is whether the agony of the nineteen months between the Joint Report and May's defenestration, covered in *No Way Out*, was necessary, for her or for the country. In a perverse way, May's premiership, in trying many options – hard Brexit, soft Brexit, cross-party working and even, in the end, flirting with another referendum – left each tributary dry. What remained untried, in the manner of Sherlock Holmes's dictum ('Once you eliminate the impossible, whatever remains, no matter how improbable, must be the truth'), was the only course of action left. One of the younger Spartans said, 'We had a terrible leader, an impossible task, a hung Parliament. But I've asked myself, philosophically, did the last few years need to happen? I think the country needed it proven that there was no middle way.' Theresa May never fully accepted that the real choice was a hard Brexit or referendum and revoke but by her actions, she left that as the binary choice facing the nation. As in nature, so too in politics every action has an equal and opposite reaction. Having tried yin ('retractive, passive and receptive'), the Tory party would now opt for yang ('active, repelling and expansive').

May would hate this valediction, but in the final analysis her premiership so exhausted the possibilities of Remain pessimism, of cautious, details-oriented technocratic grinding, of stilted, charisma-free communication, that she not only made possible the premiership of Boris Johnson – a Brexiteer optimist and gambler, a big-picture improviser and an arresting speaker – she made it inevitable. More than that, for the overwhelming majority of her own party, she made Johnson *necessary* if the referendum result was to be respected. In so doing the advocate of caution and duty bequeathed the country a successor prepared to risk chaos to get what he wanted.

THE MEANINGFUL VOTES AND INDICATIVE VOTES

The First Meaningful Vote (MV1), 15 January 2019

	AYES	*NOES*	*MAJORITY*
TOTAL	**202**	**432**	**-230**
Con	196	118	
Lab	3	248	
SNP	–	35	
LD	–	11	
DUP	–	10	
PC	–	4	
Green	–	1	
Ind	3	5	

The majority of 230 against the government was the largest in parliamentary history

The Second Meaningful Vote (MV2), 12 March 2019

	AYES	NOES	MAJORITY
TOTAL	**242**	**391**	**-149**
Con	235	75	
Lab	3	238	
SNP	–	35	
LD	–	11	
DUP	–	10	
PC	–	4	
Green	–	1	
Ind	4	17	

The majority of 149 against the government was the fourth largest in parliamentary history

First Round of Indicative Votes, 27 March 2019

Motion	Proposer	AYES	NOES	ABS	MAJ
No-deal	John Baron	160	400	74	-240
Common Mkt 2.0	Nick Boles	189	283	162	-94
EFTA	George Eustice	64	377	193	-313
Customs union	Ken Clarke	265	271	98	-6
Labour's plan	Jeremy Corbyn	237	307	90	-70
Revoke A50 to avoid no-deal	Joanna Cherry	184	293	157	-109
Referendum	Margaret Beckett	268	295	71	-27
Managed no-deal	Marcus Fysh	139	422	73	-283

The Third Meaningful Vote (MV3), 29 March 2019

	AYES	*NOES*	*MAJORITY*
TOTAL	**286**	**344**	**-58**
Con	277	34	
Lab	5	234	
SNP	–	34	
LD	–	11	
DUP	–	10	
PC	–	4	
Green	–	1	
Ind	4	16	

Tory rebels at MV3

28 'Spartans': Adam Afriyie, Steve Baker, John Baron, Peter Bone, Suella Braverman, Andrew Bridgen, Bill Cash, Christopher Chope, James Duddridge, Mark Francois, Marcus Fysh, Philip Hollobone, Adam Holloway, Ranil Jayawardena, Bernard Jenkin, Andrea Jenkyns, David Jones, Julian Lewis, Julia Lopez, Craig Mackinlay, Anne Marie Morris, Priti Patel, Owen Paterson, John Redwood, Laurence Robertson, Andrew Rosindell, Lee Rowley and Theresa Villiers

6 'Bresisters': Guto Bebb, Justine Greening, Dominic Grieve, Sam Gyimah, Jo Johnson and Phillip Lee

Second Round of Indicative Votes, 1 April 2019

Motion	*Proposer*	*AYES*	*NOES*	*ABS*	*MAJ*
Customs union	Ken Clarke	273	276	85	-3
Common Mkt 2.0	Nick Boles	261	282	91	-21
Confirmatory public vote	Peter Kyle & Phil Wilson	280	292	62	-12
Revoke A50 to avoid no-deal	Joanna Cherry	191	292	151	-101

Appendix II

THE 2019 LOCAL AND EUROPEAN ELECTIONS

Local Council elections, 2 May 2019

	Pop. Vote	Councils	Councillors
Conservatives	28%	93 (-44)	3,564 (-1,330)
Labour	28%	84 (-6)	2,021 (-84)
Lib Dems	19%	18 (+10)	1,351 (+704)
Green	9.2%	273 (+198)	
Ukip	4.5%	31 (-145)	
Others	11.4%	2 (+2)	1,179 (+662)
DUP			122 (-8)
Sinn Féin			105 (nc)

European elections, 23 May 2019

	Pop. Vote	MEPs
Brexit Party	30.5%	29 (+29)
Lib Dems	19.6%	16 (+15)
Labour	13.6%	10 (-10)
Green	11.8%	7 (+4)
Conservatives	8.8%	4 (-15)
SNP	3.6%	3 (+1)
Change UK	3.3%	0
Ukip	3.2%	0 (-24)
Plaid Cymru	1.0%	1 (nc)
Sinn Féin	0.7%	1 (nc)
DUP	0.7%	1 (nc)
Alliance	0.6%	1 (+1)

The Conservative share of the popular vote was their lowest ever in a national election

THE 2019 CONSERVATIVE PARTY LEADERSHIP ELECTION

1st MPs' Ballot – 13 June 2019

1	Boris Johnson	114	
2	Jeremy Hunt	43	
3	Michael Gove	37	
4	Dominic Raab	27	
5	Sajid Javid	23	
6	Matt Hancock	20	(withdrawn)
7	Rory Stewart	19	
8	Andrea Leadsom	11	(eliminated)
9	Mark Harper	10	(e)
10	Esther McVey	9	(e)
	James Cleverly		(wd)
	Sam Gyimah		(wd)
	Kit Malthouse		(wd)

2nd MPs' Ballot – 18 June 2019

1	Boris Johnson	126	
2	Jeremy Hunt	46	
3	Michael Gove	41	
4	Rory Stewart	37	
5	Sajid Javid	33	
6	Dominic Raab	30	(e)

3rd MPs' Ballot – 19 June 2019

1	Boris Johnson	143	
2	Jeremy Hunt	54	
3	Michael Gove	51	
4	Sajid Javid	38	
5	Rory Stewart	27	(e)

4th MPs' Ballot – 20 June 2019

1	Boris Johnson	157	
2	Michael Gove	61	
3	Jeremy Hunt	59	
4	Sajid Javid	34	(e)

5th MPs' Ballot – 20 June 2019

1	Boris Johnson	160	
2	Jeremy Hunt	77	
3	Michael Gove	75	(e)

Final Ballot – 23 July 2019

1	Boris Johnson	92,153 (66.4%)
2	Jeremy Hunt	46,656 (33.6%)

ILLUSTRATIONS

Theresa May boards an early morning flight (Number 10/Crown copyright)
May with Jean-Claude Juncker (Associated Press/Alamy Stock Photo)
The crunch lunch (Eric Vidal/Reuters)
Barnier's notorious 'staircase' graphic (© European Union, 2023)
The first Chequers meeting (Number 10/Crown copyright)
The second Chequers meeting (Number 10/Crown copyright)
Martin Selmayr (FREDERICK FLORIN/Getty Images)
Attorney general Geoffrey Cox (Xinhua/Alamy Stock Photo)
John Bercow (PA Images/Alamy Stock Photo)
The Task Force 50 negotiating team (Thierry Monasse/Getty Images)
May confronts Juncker (© European Union, 2023)
Gavin Barwell (Bloomberg/Getty Images)
Oliver Letwin (Leon Neal/Getty Images)
Dominic Grieve (Vickie Flores/Getty Images)
Jacob Rees-Mogg and Steve Baker (Peter Nicholls/Reuters)
'Dancing Queen' (PA Images/Alamy Stock Photo)
Boris Johnson (Jeff J Mitchell/Getty Images)
Theresa May resigns in tears (Leon Neal/Getty Images)

BIBLIOGRAPHY

Baldwin, Tom, *Keir Starmer: The Biography*, William Collins, 2024
Barnier, Michel, *My Secret Brexit Diary*, Polity Press, 2021
Barwell, Gavin, *Chief of Staff: Notes from Downing Street*, Atlantic Books, 2021
Bercow, John, *Unspeakable: The Autobiography*, Weidenfeld & Nicolson, 2020
Bower, Tom, *Boris Johnson: The Gambler*, WH Allen, 2020
Connelly, Tony, *Brexit and Ireland: The Dangers, the Opportunities, and the Inside Story of the Irish Response*, Penguin Books, 2017, 2018
Cook, Chris, *Defeated By Brexit*, Tortoise Media, 2019
De Rynck, Stefaan, *Inside the Deal: How the EU Got Brexit Done*, Agenda, 2023
Desmet, Lode and Stourton, Edward, *Blind Man's Brexit: How the EU Took Control of Brexit*, Simon & Schuster, 2019
Foster, Peter, *What Went Wrong With Brexit and What We Can Do About It*, Canongate, 2023
Francois, Mark, *Spartan Victory: The Inside Story of the Battle for Brexit*, Kindle Direct Publishing, 2021
Grey, Chris, *Brexit Unfolded: How No One Got What They Wanted (and Why They Were Never Going To)*, Biteback, 2021, 2023
Heywood, Suzanne, *What Does Jeremy Think?*, William Collins, 2021
Leadsom, Andrea, *Snakes and Ladders: Navigating the Ups and Downs of Politics*, Biteback, 2022
May, Theresa, *The Abuse of Power: Confronting Injustice in Public Life*, Headline, 2023

Pogrund, Gabriel and Maguire, Patrick, *Left Out: The Inside Story of Labour Under Corbyn*, Bodley Head, 2020

Reid, Andrew with Carr, Simon, *The Art of the Impossible: The Inside Story of the Brexit Party*, Biteback, 2023

Riley-Smith, Ben, *The Right to Rule: 13 Years, Five Prime Ministers and the Implosion of the Tories*, Hachette, 2023

Russell, Meg and James, Lisa, *The Parliamentary Battle Over Brexit.* OUP, 2023

Seldon, Anthony with Newell, Raymond, *May at 10*, Biteback, 2019

Whiteley; Clarke; Goodwin and Stewart, *Brexit Britain: The Consequences of the Vote to Leave the European Union*, CUP, 2023

NOTES

A full index of Brexit Witness Archive interviews, by UK in a Changing Europe, can be found online at: https://ukandeu.ac.uk/the-brexit-witness-archive/

Each transcript is available at: https://ukandeu.ac.uk/the-brexit-witness-archive/firstname-surname/

Chapter 1: Original Sin

1. *Britain's Brexit Crisis*, BBC1, 18 Jul 2019
2. David Davis, 8 Jul 2021, Brexit Witness Archive, UKICE, p.39
3. Boris Johnson thinks he's in control, *The Atlantic*, 31 Oct 2019
4. Gavin Barwell, 1 & 25 Sep 2020, Brexit Witness Archive, UKICE, p.17
5. Ibid., p.16
6. Denzil Davidson, 14 Sep 2020, Brexit Witness Archive, UKICE, p.20
7. David Davis, 8 Jul 2021, Brexit Witness Archive, UKICE, p.27
8. Boris Johnson: Theresa May misled me over Brexit, and mustn't copy Jeremy Corbyn, *Sunday Times*, 30 Sep 2018
9. 10 things that stopped Brexit happening, BBC website, 18 Jul 2019
10. Denzil Davidson, 14 Sep 2020, Brexit Witness Archive, UKICE, p.11
11. Ibid., p.21

Chapter 2: The Monogrammed Mutineer

1. The fifteen 'mutineers' were Grieve, Heidi Allen, Ken Clarke, Vicky Ford, Stephen Hammond, Oliver Heald, Jeremy Lefroy, Paul Masterson, Nicky Morgan, Jonathan Djanogly, Bob Neill, Antoinette Sandbach, Anna Soubry, Tom Tugendhat and Sarah Wollaston
2. Tory Brexit rebels inflict major defeat on Theresa May, *Guardian*, 14 Dec 2017

Chapter 3: Out Manoeuvred

1. Denzil Davidson, 14 Sep 2020, Brexit Witness Archive, UKICE, p.9
2. Ivan Rogers, 27 Nov 2020, Brexit Witness Archive, UKICE, pp.46–7
3. Prior to the 2015 general election, Cameron had not even expected to hold the referendum. In 2019, Oliver Letwin confirmed what had long been suspected, that Cameron was ready to drop his pledge to sign a new coalition

deal with the Liberal Democrats. 'I had prepared documents ready to sign on that basis,' Letwin said. (Oliver Letwin, 11 Dec 2020, Brexit Witness Archive, UKICE, p.4)

4. Defeated by Brexit, Part I: Forgetting our history, Tortoise, 18 May 2019
5. *The Brexit Prime Minister*, Radio 4, Episode 1, 11 Mar 2019
6. *Britain's Brexit Crisis*, BBC1, 18 Jul 2019
7. 10 things that stopped Brexit happening, BBC website, 18 Jul 2019
8. Ibid.
9. *Britain's Brexit Crisis*, BBC1, 18 Jul 2019
10. *The Brexit Prime Minister*, Radio 4, Episode 1, 11 Mar 2019
11. Ibid.
12. Ibid., Episode 2, 18 Mar 2019
13. Gavin Barwell, 1 & 25 Sep 2020, Brexit Witness Archive, UKICE, p.24
14. Ivan Rogers, 27 Nov 2020, Brexit Witness Archive, UKICE, p.45
15. Oliver Letwin, 11 Dec 2020, Brexit Witness Archive, UKICE, pp.11–12
16. *The Brexit Prime Minister*, Radio 4, Episode 1, 11 Mar 2019
17. Gavin Barwell, 1 & 25 Sep 2020, Brexit Witness Archive, UKICE, p.4
18. Denzil Davidson, 14 Sep 2020, Brexit Witness Archive, UKICE, p.16
19. David Davis, 8 Jul 2021, Brexit Witness Archive, UKICE, p.11
20. Philip Hammond, 13 & 20 Nov 2020, Brexit Witness Archive, UKICE, p.13
21. *The Brexit Prime Minister*, Radio 4, Episode 1, 11 Mar 2019
22. Joanna Penn, 16 Oct & 17 Nov 2020, Brexit Witness Archive, UKICE, p.8
23. Heywood, Suzanne, *What Does Jeremy Think?: Jeremy Heywood and the Making of Modern Britain*, William Collins, 2021, p.455
24. Seldon, Anthony and Newell, Raymond, *May at 10*, Biteback, 2019, p.106
25. The other irony, recalled by Oliver Letwin, who was briefly in charge of

Brexit policy between referendum day and May's arrival in Downing Street, was that May was 'pretty resistant' to Robbins taking the job. 'She did give way, not altogether willingly,' Letwin said. 'She became an enthusiast for the proposition only once it became clear that she was likely to become the next prime minister.' (Oliver Letwin, 11 Dec 2020, Brexit Witness Archive, UKICE, p.10)

26. David Davis, 8 Jul 2021, Brexit Witness Archive, UKICE, p.16
27. Ibid., p.24
28. *The Brexit Prime Minister*, Radio 4, Episode 1, 11 Mar 2019
29. David Davis, 8 Jul 2021, Brexit Witness Archive, UKICE, p.43
30. Ivan Rogers, 27 Nov 2020, Brexit Witness Archive, UKICE, p.55
31. 10 things that stopped Brexit happening, BBC website, 18 Jul 2019
32. *Britain's Brexit Crisis*, BBC1, 18 Jul 2019
33. Philip Hammond, 13 & 20 Nov 2020, Brexit Witness Archive, UKICE, p.14
34. *The Brexit Prime Minister*, Radio 4, Episode 1, 11 Mar 2019
35. Ibid.
36. Ibid., Episode 3, 25 Mar 2019
37. *Britain's Brexit Crisis*, BBC1, 18 Jul 2019
38. 10 things that stopped Brexit happening, BBC website, 18 Jul 2019
39. Denzil Davidson, 14 Sep 2020, Brexit Witness Archive, UKICE, p.10
40. Seldon and Newell, *May at 10*, p.130
41. Philip Hammond, 13 & 20 Nov 2020, Brexit Witness Archive, UKICE, p.14
42. Ibid., pp.14–15
43. David Davis, 8 Jul 2021, Brexit Witness Archive, UKICE, p.15
44. Defeated by Brexit, Part IV: May's indecision, Tortoise, 19 May 2019
45. Keir Starmer, interview with Matt Forde, *The Political Party* podcast, Ep. 103, 3 Jul 2019
46. *The Brexit Prime Minister*, Radio 4, Episode 1, 11 Mar 2019

47. Ibid.
48. Seldon and Newell, *May at 10*, p.140
49. *Britain's Brexit Crisis*, BBC1, 18 Jul 2019
50. Ibid.
51. On the referendum #25: a letter to Tory MPs & donors on the Brexit shambles, Dominic Cummings's blog, 23 May 2018
52. Joanna Penn, 16 Oct & 17 Nov 2020, Brexit Witness Archive, UKICE, p.4
53. Chris Grayling, 21 Oct 2020, Brexit Witness Archive, UKICE, p.9
54. Seldon and Newell, *May at 10*, pp.145–6
55. Gavin Barwell, 1 & 25 Sep 2020, Brexit Witness Archive, UKICE, p.2
56. Joanna Penn, 16 Oct & 17 Nov 2020, Brexit Witness Archive, UKICE, p.9
57. Gavin Barwell, 1 & 25 Sep 2020, Brexit Witness Archive, UKICE, pp.47–8
58. Keir Starmer, *The Political Party* podcast, Ep. 103, 3 Jul 2019
59. Oliver Letwin, 11 Dec 2020, Brexit Witness Archive, UKICE, p.15
60. David Davis, 8 Jul 2021, Brexit Witness Archive, UKICE, p.19
61. *Britain's Brexit Crisis*, BBC1, 18 Jul 2019
62. Stefaan De Rynck, 1 & 15 Mar 2021, Brexit Witness Archive, UKICE, p.13
63. David Davis, 8 Jul 2021, Brexit Witness Archive, UKICE, p.20
64. *Britain's Brexit Crisis*, BBC1, 18 Jul 2019
65. Ibid.
66. Ibid.
67. Ibid.
68. Philip Rycroft, 26 Jun 2020, Brexit Witness Archive, UKICE, p.15
69. The long and winding road to Brexit, *The Times*, 25 Mar 2019
70. Philip Hammond, 13 & 20 Nov 2020, Brexit Witness Archive, UKICE, pp.22–3
71. Defeated by Brexit, Part V: Held at the border, Tortoise, 25 May 2019

Chapter 4: Clear Out
1. I won't keep my silence: Michael Fallon lunged at me after our lunch, *Observer*, 5 Nov 2017
2. Leadsom, Andrea, *Snakes and Ladders: Navigating the Ups and Downs of Politics*, Biteback, 2022, pp.204–6
3. Kate Maltby: Damian Green probably has no idea how awkward I felt, *The Times*, 1 Nov 2017
4. Suella Fernandes, as she then was, married Rael Braverman in March 2018. For simplicity's sake, I have used Braverman, the name she was known by for the vast bulk of this book, throughout.

Chapter 5: Cop Out
1. Steve Baker, House of Commons Hansard, 18 Jul 2018, Col. 487
2. Defeated by Brexit, Part VI: Things fall apart, Tortoise, 25 May 2019
3. Seldon and Newell, *May at 10*, p.110
4. *The Brexit Prime Minister*, Radio 4, Episode 1, 11 Mar 2019
5. Ibid., Ep. 2, 18 Mar 2019
6. This leaked government Brexit analysis says the UK will be worse off in every scenario, BuzzFeed, 29 Jan 2018
7. Baker also spread allegations that a German government official had been appointed to run 'black ops' against Britain. 'That bloke was in fact quite a good contact for the British embassy in Berlin, who subsequently was less interested in talking to them,' a frustrated official complained.
8. Heywood, *What Does Jeremy Think?*, p.496
9. Steve Baker interview, *Political Thinking with Nick Robinson* podcast, 22 Jan 2022
10. *Britain's Brexit Crisis*, BBC1, 18 Jul 2019
11. Gavin Barwell, House of Lords Hansard, 13 Jan 2020, Col. 466
12. *Britain's Brexit Crisis*, BBC1, 18 Jul 2019

13. Ibid.
14. Gavin Barwell, 1 & 25 Sep 2020, Brexit Witness Archive, UKICE, p.26
15. Raoul Ruparel, 11 Aug 2020, Brexit Witness Archive, UKICE, p.18
16. Ibid.
17. Desmet, Lode and Stourton, Edward, *Blind Man's Brexit: How the EU Took Control of Brexit*, Simon & Schuster, 2019, p.184
18. Ibid., p.198
19. Stefaan De Rynck, 1 & 15 Mar 2021, Brexit Witness Archive, UKICE, pp.15–16
20. Ibid., pp.11–12
21. Desmet and Stourton, *Blind Man's Brexit*, p.199
22. Seldon and Newell, *May at 10*, p.415
23. 10 things that stopped Brexit happening, BBC website, 18 Jul 2019
24. Denzil Davidson, 14 Sep 2020, Brexit Witness Archive, UKICE, pp.20–21
25. EU stands firm over Northern Ireland border, *Financial Times*, 25 Feb 2018
26. Desmet and Stourton, *Blind Man's Brexit*, p.211
27. Ibid., p.208
28. Defeated by Brexit, Part VI: Things fall apart, Tortoise, 25 May 2019

Chapter 6: Poison
1. Pogrund, Gabriel and Maguire, Patrick, *Left Out: The Inside Story of Labour Under Corbyn*, Bodley Head, 2020, p.80
2. *Corbynism: The Post-Mortem*, hosted by Oz Katerji, Ep. 1, Labour's Institutional Antisemitism Crisis, 17 Jan 2020
3. Jeremy Corbyn told by veteran Jewish MP 'You're a f***ing anti-semite and a racist', HuffPost, 17 Jul 2018
4. The *Jewish Chronicle*, *Jewish News* and the *Jewish Telegraph*

Chapter 7: Revealed Preferences
1. Philip Hammond, 13 & 20 Nov 2020, Brexit Witness Archive, UKICE, p.23

2. *The Brexit Prime Minister*, Radio 4, Episode 2, 18 Mar 2019
3. Ibid.
4. Philip Hammond, 13 & 20 Nov 2020, Brexit Witness Archive, UKICE, p.21
5. Heywood, *What Does Jeremy Think?*, p.466
6. Ibid., p.484
7. Defeated by Brexit, Part VI: Things fall apart, Tortoise, 25 May 2019
8. David Davis letter to Theresa May, Our future relationship on customs, 24 Apr 2018
9. Gavin Barwell, 1 & 25 Sep 2020, Brexit Witness Archive, UKICE, p.21
10. David Davis, 8 Jul 2021, Brexit Witness Archive, UKICE, p.25
11. EU rejects Theresa May's Brexit Irish border solution as doubts grow over whether UK can leave customs union, *Daily Telegraph*, 20 Apr 2018
12. Denzil Davidson, 14 Sep 2020, Brexit Witness Archive, UKICE, p.17
13. Defeated by Brexit, Part VI: Things fall apart, Tortoise, 25 May 2019
14. Desmet and Stourton, *Blind Man's Brexit*, p.211
15. Ibid., pp.231–2
16. Defeated by Brexit, Part VI: Things fall apart, Tortoise, 25 May 2019
17. Bang goes Brexit if we fall for this customs con trick, *Mail on Sunday*, 21 Apr 2018
18. Desmet and Stourton, *Blind Man's Brexit*, p.231
19. David Davis, 8 Jul 2021, Brexit Witness Archive, UKICE, p.30

Chapter 8: Ruled Out
1. *Britain's Brexit Crisis*, BBC1, 18 Jul 2019
2. Ibid.
3. Remainer MPs bring 'ideas and solutions' to meeting with Barnier, *Guardian*, 15 Jan 2018
4. Desmet and Stourton, *Blind Man's Brexit*, p.194
5. Stefaan De Rynck, 1 & 15 Mar 2021, Brexit Witness Archive, UKICE, p.24

6. Henry Zeffman, Twitter, 18 Apr 2018
7. Phillip Lee, 9 Apr 2021, Brexit Witness Archive, UKICE, p.9
8. Ibid., p.11
9. May escapes Brexit bill defeat as Tory rebels accept concessions, *Guardian*, 12 Jun 2018
10. If no-deal seemed likely, da Costa's blueprint said the government would have to put a motion before Parliament which MPs could approve, reject or amend. If no-deal was rejected the government would have twenty-eight days to come up with another plan or there would be an election.
11. Abraham Lincoln's reply, First Debate with Stephen A. Douglas, 21 Aug 1858, quoted in *Team of Rivals: The Political Genius of Abraham Lincoln*, by Doris Kearns Goodwin, Simon & Schuster, 2005, p.206

Chapter 9: Chequers Mate
1. Gove shows uncustomary anger, *Sun*, 29 Jun 2018
2. Gavin Barwell, 1 & 25 Sep 2020, Brexit Witness Archive, UKICE, p.28
3. David Davis, 8 Jul 2021, Brexit Witness Archive, UKICE, p.32
4. *The Brexit Prime Minister*, Radio 4, Episode 2, 18 Mar 2019
5. *Britain's Brexit Crisis*, BBC1, 18 Jul 2019
6. *The Brexit Prime Minister*, Radio 4, Episode 2, 18 Mar 2019
7. Ed de Minckwitz had been charged with devising a new acronym to distinguish the new plan from the New Customs Partnership (NCP)
8. David Davis, 8 Jul 2021, Brexit Witness Archive, UKICE, p.32
9. Gramsci stole the formulation from the French Nobel laureate Romain Rolland
10. *The Brexit Prime Minister*, Radio 4, Episode 2, 18 Mar 2019
11. *Britain's Brexit Crisis*, BBC1, 18 Jul 2019
12. One other source recalled Johnson describing the plan as 'fucking bullshit'
13. David Davis, 8 Jul 2021, Brexit Witness Archive, UKICE, p.32
14. *The Brexit Prime Minister*, Radio 4, Episode 2, 18 Mar 2019
15. *Britain's Brexit Crisis*, BBC1, 18 Jul 2019
16. Seldon and Newell, *May at 10*, p.434
17. Ibid., p.436
18. David Davis, 8 Jul 2021, Brexit Witness Archive, UKICE, p.33
19. Gavin Barwell, 1 & 25 Sep 2020, Brexit Witness Archive, UKICE, p.27

Chapter 10: Brexodus
1. Heywood, *What Does Jeremy Think?*, p.505
2. David Davis, 8 Jul 2021, Brexit Witness Archive, UKICE, p.36
3. Ibid., p.34
4. Ibid., p.37
5. Seldon and Newell, *May at 10*, p.443
6. David Davis, 8 Jul 2021, Brexit Witness Archive, UKICE, p.34
7. Leadsom, *Snakes and Ladders*, p.212
8. Ibid., p.211
9. May has wrecked Brexit … US deal is off, *Sun*, 13 Jul 2018
10. Ibid.
11. Inside the bunker as Brexit was betrayed, *Daily Mail*, 27 Jul 2019

Chapter 11: 'Chuck Chequers!'
1. Dominic Cummings interview with Steve Hsu, *Manifold* podcast, Ep. 28, 19 Jan 2023
2. Theresa May's election boss Lynton Crosby tries to scupper her Brexit deal, *Sunday Times*, 2 Sep 2018
3. Facebook ads by Lynton Crosby's firm 'part of push for hard Brexit', *Guardian*, 22 Apr 2019
4. Barker played on George Michael's Symphonica tour and did the saxophone solo on 'Cowboys and Angels'

Chapter 12: Chequers Goes Pop!

1. Transcript of interview with Dominic Raab, an edited version of which appeared in the *Sunday Times*, 16 Nov 2018
2. Desmet and Stourton, *Blind Man's Brexit*, p.271
3. Gavin Barwell, 1 & 25 Sep 2020, Brexit Witness Archive, UKICE, p.3
4. *Britain's Brexit Crisis*, BBC1, 18 Jul 2019
5. Ibid.
6. Desmet and Stourton, *Blind Man's Brexit*, p.291
7. *Britain's Brexit Crisis*, BBC1, 18 Jul 2019
8. Ibid.
9. Desmet and Stourton, *Blind Man's Brexit*, pp.297–8
10. Stefaan De Rynck, 1 & 15 Mar 2021, Brexit Witness Archive, UKICE, pp.17–18
11. Gavin Barwell, 1 & 25 Sep 2020, Brexit Witness Archive, UKICE, p.29

Chapter 13: Out of Sight

1. The good, the spad and the ugly, *Times Red Box* podcast, 20 Jul 2019
2. How Merkel and Macron spent more time in the pub than listening to May's Brexit overtures, *Daily Telegraph*, 18 Oct 2018
3. Theresa May faces 'show trial' by Tory MPs, *Mail on Sunday*, 21 Oct 2018
4. Oliver Robbins memo to Theresa May, 2 Nov 2018
5. Ibid.
6. Email, Dominic Raab to Gavin Barwell, 8 Oct 2018, 10.35
7. Email, Gavin Barwell to Dominic Raab, 8 Oct 2018, 15.43
8. Dominic Raab memo to Oliver Robbins, attached to email, Matt Baugh to Catherine Page and others, 21 Oct 2018, 12.53
9. Email, Catherine Page to various, 21 Oct 2018, 13.39

10. Email, Matt Baugh to Catherine Page, Kay Withers and others, 21 Oct 2018, 17.58
11. Barnier, Michel, *My Secret Brexit Diary*, Polity, 2021, p.193
12. Letter, Dominic Raab to Theresa May, re dinner with Simon Coveney, 31 Oct 2018
13. Ibid.
14. Dominic Raab demands right to pull Britain out of EU backstop after three months, *Daily Telegraph*, 5 Nov 2018
15. Transcript of interview with Dominic Raab, an edited version of which appeared in the *Sunday Times*, 16 Nov 2018
16. Letter, Oliver Robbins to Theresa May, 2 Nov 2018
17. Ibid.
18. Heywood, *What Does Jeremy Think?*, p.508
19. Ibid., p.515
20. Selmayr's reputation as a schemer was cemented in February 2018 when he was promoted from head of Juncker's private office to become deputy secretary-general of the Commission. Literally minutes later, Juncker informed the Commissioners that the then secretary-general, Alexander Italianer, intended to retire, clearing the way for Selmayr to become the EU's top civil servant.
21. Barnier, *My Secret Brexit Diary*, p.193
22. *Britain's Brexit Crisis*, BBC1, 18 Jul 2019
23. Dominic Raab comments in: Email, Matt Baugh to Catherine Page and others, 28 Oct 2018, 14.23
24. Email, Raoul Ruparel to Gavin Barwell, 13 Nov 2018, 00.39; copied to others at 10.51
25. Seldon and Newell, *May at 10*, p.489
26. 'If a male PM weeps he's a patriot. If a woman does, they ask why': Brexit regrets, digs at Boris, and yes, mistakes. Theresa May's last No 10 interview reveals a leader whose

decency was never in doubt, *Daily Mail*, 11 Jul 2019

Chapter 14: Sellout?
1. Jacob Rees-Mogg rallies rebels with a bit of a coup at Westminster, *The Times*, 14 Nov 2018
2. Transcript of interview with Dominic Raab, an edited version of which appeared in the *Sunday Times*, 16 Nov 2018
3. Seldon and Newell, *May at 10*, p.490
4. Theresa May accused of betrayal as she unveils Brexit deal, *The Times*, 14 Nov 2018
5. Minister in 'meltdown' at end of five-hour cabinet marathon, *The Times*, 15 Nov 2018
6. *Britain's Brexit Crisis*, BBC1, 18 Jul 2019
7. Brexiteers sharpening their pens for letters of no confidence in May, *The Times*, 15 Nov 2018
8. *Britain's Brexit Crisis*, BBC1, 18 Jul 2019
9. Bercow, John, *Unspeakable: The Autobiography*, Weidenfeld & Nicolson, 2020, pp.369–70
10. Ashcroft, Michael, *Jacob's Ladder*, Biteback, 2019, p.274
11. Brexit: 'Stand up to Brussels bullies', Dominic Raab tells Theresa May, *Sunday Times*, 18 Nov 2018
12. The inside story of the no confidence vote, *House Magazine*, 17 Dec 2018

Chapter 15: *Zugzwang*
1. Hammond himself was arguing that Britain should not take a 'dogmatic' position on freedom of movement and that, since the economy would still require EU migrants, Britain might as well use that as a bargaining chip for greater market access
2. This was the same device that had been used to force David Davis to release the government's Brexit contingency plans in the spring
3. Bercow, *Unspeakable*, p.370

Chapter 16: No Confidence
1. *The Brexit Prime Minister*, Radio 4, Episode 3, 25 Mar 2019
2. Ibid.
3. Bercow, *Unspeakable*, p.372
4. The inside story of the no confidence vote, *House Magazine*, 17 Dec 2018
5. Ibid.
6. Ibid.
7. *The Brexit Prime Minister*, Radio 4, Episode 3, 25 Mar 2019
8. Gavin Barwell, 1 & 25 Sep 2020, Brexit Witness Archive, UKICE, p.32
9. *The Brexit Prime Minister*, Radio 4, Episode 3, 25 Mar 2019
10. *Guardian* live blog, 12 Dec 2018
11. Gibb told this story at his leaving do the following year

Chapter 17: 'Nebulous' Negotiations
1. *Britain's Brexit Crisis*, BBC1, 18 Jul 2019
2. Ibid.
3. Brexit: Theresa May invites Rees-Mogg to talks on healing rift, *The Times*, 21 Dec 2018

Chapter 18: Yellowhammered
1. Philip Rycroft, 26 Jun 2020, Brexit Witness Archive, UKICE, p.19
2. Hancock was also the indirect inspiration for Robert Harris's novel *The Second Sleep*, set hundreds of years after the collapse of Western civilisation. 'I was at a dinner and Matt Hancock was there and he said, "The average home used to have eight days' supply of food in it and now it is only two",' Harris recalled. 'That stuck in my mind. The idea of "six meals from barbarism" is one that my grandmother introduced me to years ago.'
3. Michael Gove 'decided to back May's Brexit after hearing how UK would run out of clean drinking water within DAYS of No Deal', *Mail on Sunday*, 24 Nov 2018
4. *Britain's Brexit Crisis*, BBC1, 18 Jul 2019

5. David Davis, 8 Jul 2021, Brexit Witness Archive, UKICE, p.42
6. *Britain's Brexit Crisis*, BBC1, 18 Jul 2019
7. Ibid.
8. Ibid.
9. Letter, Dominic Raab to Theresa May, 7 Sep 2018
10. To frighten the EU into believing we are serious about no-deal Brexit, the country has staged a fake traffic jam all the way to Dover, *Independent*, 7 Jan 2019
11. Chris Grayling, 21 Oct 2020, Brexit Witness Archive, UKICE, p.18
12. Ibid., pp.10–11, 15–16
13. Ibid., p.17
14. Philip Hammond, 13 & 20 Nov 2020, Brexit Witness Archive, UKICE, p.32

Chapter 19: Erskine Mayhem

1. Phillip Lee, 9 Apr 2021, Brexit Witness Archive, UKICE, pp.14–15
2. While MPs like Letwin and Grieve were experienced at writing amendments, the saying went that only Rees-Mogg and Chris Bryant, author of a two-volume history of Parliament, truly understood the arcana of procedure
3. John Bercow, 21 Jul 2020, Brexit Witness Archive, UKICE, p.19
4. Oliver Letwin, 11 Dec 2020, Brexit Witness Archive, UKICE, pp.17–18
5. Ken Clarke: Lunch with the FT, *Financial Times*, 10 Jan 2020
6. Tom Newton-Dunn, Twitter, 8 Jan 2019
7. Sam Coates, Twitter, 8 Jan 2019
8. John Bercow, 21 Jul 2020, Brexit Witness Archive, UKICE, p.21
9. Ibid., p.32
10. Ibid., p.7
11. Ibid., p.8
12. Ibid., pp.9–10
13. Ibid., p.17
14. This one quote came from Sebastian Whale's biography of the speaker, the rest I had already obtained from my own sources prior to the publication of his book. Whale, Sebastian, *John Bercow: Call to Order*, Biteback, 2020; extracted in *Mail on Sunday*, 21 Mar 2020
15. Bercow, *Unspeakable*, p.373
16. John Bercow, 21 Jul 2020, Brexit Witness Archive, UKICE, p.22
17. Ibid., p.23
18. Bercow, *Unspeakable*, p.373
19. John Bercow, 21 Jul 2020, Brexit Witness Archive, UKICE, p.23
20. Gavin Barwell, 1 & 25 Sep 2020, Brexit Witness Archive, UKICE, p.34
21. The seventeen Conservatives who backed the Grieve amendment were: Heidi Allen, Nick Boles, Ken Clarke, Jonathan Djanogly, Justine Greening, Dominic Grieve, Sam Gyimah, Jo Johnson, Phillip Lee, Oliver Letwin, Andrew Mitchell, Nicky Morgan, Bob Neill, Antoinette Sandbach, Anna Soubry, Ed Vaizey and Sarah Wollaston
22. Inside the bunker as Brexit was betrayed, *Daily Mail*, 27 Jul 2019

Chapter 20: Wipeout

1. Seldon and Newell, *May at 10*, p.518
2. BREXPENSIVE MISTAKE! Brussels boasts to EU27 that Theresa May's Brexit deal will tie Britain to following EU's rules for years to come, *Sun*, 14 Jan 2019
3. Tom Newton-Dunn, Twitter, 15 Jan 2019
4. Steven Swinford, Twitter, 15 Jan 2019
5. Jim Pickard, Twitter, 15 Jan 2019
6. Gavin Barwell, speech to the Institute for Government, 13 Jan 2020
7. Debbie Abrahams, Twitter, 15 Jan 2019
8. *The Brexit Prime Minister*, Radio 4, Episode 3, 25 Mar 2019
9. Welcome to the Westminster apocalypse. Have you thought about theocracy instead?, *Guardian*, 16 Jan 2019
10. Bercow, *Unspeakable*, pp.375–6

11. *The Brexit Prime Minister*, Radio 4, Episode 2, 18 Mar 2019
12. Philip Hammond, 13 & 20 Nov 2020, Brexit Witness Archive, UKICE, p.33

Chapter 21: A Way Out?
1. *The Brexit Prime Minister*, Radio 4, Episode 3, 25 Mar 2019
2. Gavin Barwell, 1 & 25 Sep 2020, Brexit Witness Archive, UKICE, p.31
3. Joanna Penn, 16 Oct & 17 Nov 2020, Brexit Witness Archive, UKICE, p.18
4. Malthouse Proposal, memo by Raoul Ruparel to the prime minister, 13 Feb 2019

Chapter 22: Walk Out
1. See *All Out War*, chapter 27
2. Andrew Fisher, 15 Jun 2022, Brexit Witness Archive, UKICE, pp.1–2
3. The mutiny did not unduly concern LOTO. Andrew Fisher recalled, 'There was a fairly big rebellion, but when you've had 172 MPs say they have no confidence in you as leader, 50 feels like progress.' (Andrew Fisher, 15 Jun 2022, Brexit Witness Archive, UKICE, p.12)
4. See *Fall Out*, chapters 12 to 25
5. Andrew Fisher, 15 Jun 2022, Brexit Witness Archive, UKICE, pp.17–18
6. Pogrund and Maguire, *Left Out*, p.66
7. Ibid., p.167
8. Keir Starmer, *The Political Party* podcast, Ep. 103, 3 Jul 2019
9. See *Fall Out*, chapter 9
10. Andrew Fisher, 15 Jun 2022, Brexit Witness Archive, UKICE, p.11
11. Pogrund and Maguire, *Left Out*, p.70
12. Ibid., p.72
13. Ibid., p.75
14. Andrew Fisher, 15 Jun 2022, Brexit Witness Archive, UKICE, p.19
15. Hilary Benn, Brexit Witness Archive, UKICE, p.15
16. CORBYN'S CURTAIN CALL: Furious MPs vow to 'COLLAPSE' leadership at SECRET MEETINGS, *Daily Express*, 7 Aug 2018

17. Far right comes out for Jeremy Corbyn, *The Times*, 25 Aug 2018
18. Tony Blair, interview with Nick Robinson, *Political Thinking* podcast, 7 Sep 2018
19. Tom Baldwin, 5 Jul 2021, Brexit Witness Archive, UKICE, p.15
20. Andrew Fisher, 15 Jun 2022, Brexit Witness Archive, UKICE, pp.20–1
21. Pogrund and Maguire, *Left Out*, p.128
22. Andrew Fisher, 15 Jun 2022, Brexit Witness Archive, UKICE, pp.25–6
23. Ibid.
24. Why Labour's leader has to perform a Brexit balancing act, *Guardian*, 17 Apr 2019
25. Pogrund and Maguire, *Left Out*, p.179
26. Rebel Labour MPs set to quit party and form centre group, *Observer*, 3 Feb 2019
27. Phillip Lee, 9 Apr 2021, Brexit Witness Archive, UKICE, p.12
28. Why Labour's leader has to perform a Brexit balancing act, *Guardian*, 17 Apr 2019
29. Caroline Flint, 29 Jan 2021, Brexit Witness Archive, UKICE, p.21
30. Why Labour's leader has to perform a Brexit balancing act, *Guardian*, 17 Apr 2019

Chapter 23: The Gaukeward Squad
1. Philip Hammond, 13 & 20 Nov 2020, Brexit Witness Archive, UKICE, p.20
2. *Britain's Brexit Crisis*, BBC1, 18 Jul 2019
3. Gavin Barwell, 1 & 25 Sep 2020, Brexit Witness Archive, UKICE, p.26
4. The name emerged over dinner when Paul Goodman, the editor of ConservativeHome, asked Mark Francois about the pressure he was under. 'Sometimes it feels like the bloody Spartans guarding the pass at Themopylae,' he replied. Goodman said, 'I like that, I'll write that.'

5. Theresa May funks Brexit vote as cabinet splits, *Sunday Times*, 24 Feb 2019
6. Breaking point: can either Labour or the Tories survive Brexit?, *Spectator*, 2 Mar 2019

Chapter 24: Cox's Codpiece
1. 'Cox's codpiece' was popularised by Steve Baker, but the phrase was first used by Daniel Moylan in conversation with Kit Malthouse, who mentioned it to Baker, who promptly tweeted it and got the credit
2. The author
3. The symbolism was delicious but misleading. Cox was a collector of paintings. He had paid £4,000 for the portrait and he had had it cleaned. It was now worth £25,000
4. De Rynck, *Inside the Deal: How the EU Got Brexit Done*, Agenda, 2023, p.153
5 'Hand on heart, I'll find a way to beat the backstop', *Mail on Sunday*, 10 Mar 2019
6. Chris Grayling, 21 Oct 2020, Brexit Witness Archive, UKICE, p.20
7. Pogrund and Maguire, *Left Out*, p.201
8. 'Hand on heart, I'll find a way to beat the backstop', *Mail on Sunday*, 10 Mar 2019
9. Ibid.
10. Gavin Barwell, 1 & 25 Sep 2020, Brexit Witness Archive, UKICE, p.48
11. The full text of Cox's legal advice can be found at: https://assets.publishing. service.gov.uk/government/uploads/ system/uploads/attachment_data/ file/785188/190312_-_Legal_Opinion_ on_Joint_Instrument_and_ Unilateral_Declaration_co.._____2_.pdf
12. *Political Thinking with Nick Robinson* podcast, 15 Mar 2019
13. Gavin Barwell, 1 & 25 Sep 2020, Brexit Witness Archive, UKICE, pp.32–3

14. David Davis, 8 Jul 2021, Brexit Witness Archive, UKICE, pp.37–8
15. Heather Stewart, Twitter, 18.37, 12 Mar 2019
16. Hannah Bardell, Twitter, 19.08, 12 Mar 2019

Chapter 25: Abstention Rebellion
1. David Mundell, Twitter, 13 Mar 2019
2. Theresa May planned to defeat herself, then decided not to defeat herself by defeating herself, then lost. To herself, *Independent*, 13 Mar 2019
3. https://twitter.com/tombarton/ status/1106560180819496962

Chapter 26: The Queen Sacrifice
1. David Natzler, Evidence to Exiting the European Union select committee, 31 Oct 2018
2. May, Theresa, *The Abuse of Power*, Headline, 2023, p.47
3. *The Brexit Prime Minister*, Radio 4, Episode 3, 25 Mar 2019
4. See *Fall Out*, chapter 26
5. Brexit chaos: Cracks emerge as EU squabbles over 'inevitable' no-deal, *The Times*, 22 Mar 2019
6. Spooked EU leaders turn tables on May in night of political drama, *Financial Times*, 22 Mar 2019
7. Phillip Lee, 9 Apr 2021, Brexit Witness Archive, UKICE, p.21
8. Everything up to 'none of us wants' is my reporting. The rest of the conversation comes from: Phillip Lee, 9 Apr 2021, Brexit Witness Archive, UKICE, pp.17–18
9. Theresa May maintains carry-on-regardless Brexit strategy, *Guardian*, 25 Mar 2019
10. Feelings run high and low as May tells Tories: I'm through, *Guardian*, 27 Mar 2019
11. A packed room and MPs in tears: Behind the scenes at the 1922 meeting where Theresa May announced her resignation, *Daily Telegraph*, 27 Mar 2019

12. Ibid.
13. Feelings run high and low as May tells Tories: I'm through, *Guardian*, 27 Mar 2019
14. Ibid.
15. Michael Deacon, Twitter, 27 Mar 2019
16. Oliver Letwin, 11 Dec 2020, Brexit Witness Archive, UKICE, pp.19–20
17. Why Labour's leader has to perform a Brexit balancing act, *Guardian*, 17 Apr 2019
18. Pogrund and Maguire, *Left Out*, pp.204–5
19. 10 things that stopped Brexit happening, BBC website, 18 Jul 2019
20. Mark Francois, *Spartan Victory*, p.15
21. Ibid., pp.294–5
22. Ibid., p.296
23. Caroline Flint, 29 Jan 2021, Brexit Witness Archive, UKICE, p.17
24. Gavin Barwell, 1 & 25 Sep 2020, Brexit Witness Archive, UKICE, p.36
25. Andrew Fisher, 15 Jun 2022, Brexit Witness Archive, UKICE, p.27
26. *Britain's Brexit Crisis*, BBC1, 18 Jul 2019
27. 'If a male PM weeps he's a patriot. If a woman does, they ask why': Brexit regrets, digs at Boris, and yes, mistakes. Theresa May's last No 10 interview reveals a leader whose decency was never in doubt, *Daily Mail*, 11 Jul 2019
28. Inside the bunker as Brexit was betrayed, *Daily Mail*, 27 Jul 2019

Chapter 27: Out of the Question
1. Barwell, *Chief of Staff*, p.355
2. Ibid., p.357
3. Mrs May: My part in her downfall, *The Critic*, Jul 2021
4. If Tory MPs wish to change the 1922 committee no confidence vote rules there is nothing standing in their way, *Daily Telegraph*, 13 Apr 2019
5. The fourteen Conservative MPs who backed the Cooper bill were: Guto Bebb, Steve Brine, Alistair Burt, Ken Clarke, Jonathan Djanogly, Justine Greening, Dominic Grieve, Sam Gyimah, Richard Harrington, Phillip Lee, Oliver Letwin, Antoinette Sandbach, Caroline Spelman and Ed Vaizey

Chapter 28: Mating Porcupines
1. Keir Starmer, *The Political Party* podcast, Ep. 103, 3 Jul 2019
2. Pogrund and Maguire, *Left Out*, p.191
3. Ibid., p.206
4. Pogrund and Maguire, *Left Out*, p.190
5. Corbyn's spokesman James Schneider denied this story to Pogrund and Maguire, but they included it in *Left Out* (p.202) and sources in LOTO told the author at the time, and since, that the incident did happen
6. Keir Starmer, *The Political Party* podcast, Ep. 103, 3 Jul 2019
7. Barwell, *Chief of Staff*, p.360
8. Ibid.
9. Pogrund and Maguire, *Left Out*, p.211
10. Barwell, *Chief of Staff*, p.360
11. Keir Starmer, *The Political Party* podcast, Ep. 103, 3 Jul 2019
12. Andrew Fisher, 15 Jun 2022, Brexit Witness Archive, UKICE, p.30
13. Barwell, *Chief of Staff*, p.362
14. Ibid., pp.362–3
15. Oliver Letwin, 11 Dec 2020, Brexit Witness Archive, UKICE, p.21
16. Gavin Barwell, 1 & 25 Sep 2020, Brexit Witness Archive, UKICE, p.41
17. Andrew Fisher, 15 Jun 2022, Brexit Witness Archive, UKICE, p.30
18. Barwell, *Chief of Staff*, p.365
19. Ibid., p.366
20. Pogrund and Maguire, *Left Out*, p.213
21. The game finished 4–3 to City, but Spurs went through on away goals after a late City strike was ruled out by VAR
22. Andrew Fisher, 15 Jun 2022, Brexit Witness Archive, UKICE, pp.27–8
23. Barwell, *Chief of Staff*, p.367
24. Ibid., pp.367–8
25. Pogrund and Maguire, *Left Out*, p.215

26. Keir Starmer, *The Political Party* podcast, Ep. 103, 3 Jul 2019
27. Barwell, *Chief of Staff*, p.372
28. Pogrund and Maguire, *Left Out*, p.215
29. Gavin Barwell, 1 & 25 Sep 2020, Brexit Witness Archive, UKICE, p.43
30. Barwell, *Chief of Staff*, p.374
31. Ibid.
32. Andrew Fisher, 15 Jun 2022, Brexit Witness Archive, UKICE, p.30
33. Pogrund and Maguire, *Left Out*, p.216
34. Ibid.
35. Ibid., p.217
36. Keir Starmer, *The Political Party* podcast, Ep. 103, 3 Jul 2019
37. Oliver Letwin, 11 Dec 2020, Brexit Witness Archive, UKICE, p.21

Chapter 29: Knives Out

1. Barwell, *Chief of Staff*, p.367
2. Ibid., pp.370–71
3. Phillip Lee, 9 Apr 2021, Brexit Witness Archive, UKICE, pp.9–10
4. Barwell, *Chief of Staff*, p.379
5. Leadsom, *Snakes and Ladders*, p.218
6. Gavin Barwell, 1 & 25 Sep 2020, Brexit Witness Archive, UKICE, p.44
7. Barwell, *Chief of Staff*, p.381
8. Seldon and Newell, *May at 10*, p.621
9. Ibid., p.624
10. Ibid.
11. Barwell, *Chief of Staff*, p.384
12. 'If a male PM weeps he's a patriot. If a woman does, they ask why': Brexit regrets, digs at Boris, and yes, mistakes. Theresa May's last No 10 interview reveals a leader whose decency was never in doubt, *Daily Mail*, 11 Jul 2019
13. Gavin Barwell, 1 & 25 Sep 2020, Brexit Witness Archive, UKICE, p.51
14. Philip Hammond, 13 & 20 Nov 2020, Brexit Witness Archive, UKICE, p.35
15. Barwell, *Chief of Staff*, p.387
16. Gavin Barwell, 1 & 25 Sep 2020, Brexit Witness Archive, UKICE, p.51
17. Phillip Lee, 9 Apr 2021, Brexit Witness Archive, UKICE, p.18

Chapter 30: Outsiders

1. These figures are all taken from Mark Pack's immensely useful PollBase spreadsheet of historic polling data, which can be downloaded at www.markpack.org.uk/opinion-polls/
2. 40% of Tory councillors back Farage, *Mail on Sunday*, 21 Apr 2019
3. A howl of rage from the shires, *Mail on Sunday*, 21 Apr 2019
4. Richard Tice, 11 Sep 2020, Brexit Witness Archive, UKICE, p.14
5. Ibid., p.4
6. Phillip Lee, Twitter, 17 Feb 2018
7. Richard Tice, 11 Sep 2020, Brexit Witness Archive, UKICE, p.11
8. 'Fighting for freedom': Inside the leave protest on what would have been Brexit day, *Guardian*, 29 Mar 2019
9. Gawain Towler, 10 Aug 2020, Brexit Witness Archive, UKICE, p.19
10. McGough referred to prominent Jewish politicians as being 'devoid of UK roots', dismissed Peter Mandelson as 'an old queen' and said foreigners came from 'bingo bongo land'. See Brexit party official removed after antisemitic posts, *Guardian*, 3 Apr 2019
11. Gawain Towler, 10 Aug 2020, Brexit Witness Archive, UKICE, p.20
12. Reid, Andrew, and Carr, Simon, *The Art of the Impossible: The Inside Story of the Brexit Party*, Biteback, pp.68–70
13. Gawain Towler, 10 Aug 2020, Brexit Witness Archive, UKICE, p.20
14. Richard Tice, 11 Sep 2020, Brexit Witness Archive, UKICE, p.13
15. Claire Fox, 6 Nov 2020, Brexit Witness Archive, UKICE, pp.4–5
16. Ibid., p.6
17. Ibid., p.13
18. Ibid., p.17
19. Ibid., p.18
20. Richard Tice, 11 Sep 2020, Brexit Witness Archive, UKICE, p.14
21. Claire Fox, 6 Nov 2020, Brexit Witness Archive, UKICE, p.20

22. Richard Tice, 11 Sep 2020, Brexit Witness Archive, UKICE, p.15
23. Claire Fox, 6 Nov 2020, Brexit Witness Archive, UKICE, pp.22–3
24. Ibid., p.23
25. Ibid., p.24
26. Ibid., p.25
27. Richard Tice, 11 Sep 2020, Brexit Witness Archive, UKICE, p.14
28. Keir Starmer, *The Political Party* podcast, Ep. 103, 3 Jul 2019
29. Claire Fox, 6 Nov 2020, Brexit Witness Archive, UKICE, pp.19–20

Chapter 31: Déjà Blue
1. Welcome to the Westminster apocalypse. Have you thought about theocracy instead?, *Guardian*, 16 Jan 2019
2. See *Fall Out*, chapter 27
3. See *All Out War*, chapter 10
4. The good, the spad and the ugly, *Times Red Box* podcast, 20 Jul 2019

Chapter 32: Rout
1. Boris Johnson: Police called to loud altercation at potential PM's home, *Guardian*, 21 Jun 2019
2. I was Boris Johnson's boss: He is utterly unfit to be prime minister, *Guardian*, 24 Jun 2019
3. Why Johnson will always get away with it, *The Times*, 1 May 2021
4. See *All Out War*, chapter 16
5. Revealed: Donald Trump ordered dismissal of UK ambassador Kim Darroch after leaked cables, *Daily Telegraph*, 4 Sep 2020
6. REVEALED: Michael Gove and David Cameron end their three-year feud over whisky and wine at exclusive private members' club in Mayfair, *Mail on Sunday*, 7 Jul 2019

Conclusion: Theresa May
1. Ivan Rogers, 27 Nov 2020, Brexit Witness Archive, UKICE, pp.56–7

2. Gavin Barwell, 1 & 25 Sep 2020, Brexit Witness Archive, UKICE, p.4
3. Ibid., p.46
4. *Britain's Brexit Crisis*, BBC1, 18 Jul 2019
5. Ivan Rogers, 27 Nov 2020, Brexit Witness Archive, UKICE, p.52
6. Stefaan De Rynck, 1 & 15 Mar 2021, Brexit Witness Archive, UKICE, p.19
7. Gavin Barwell, 1 & 25 Sep 2020, Brexit Witness Archive, UKICE, p.7
8. Gavin Barwell, Institute for Government, 13 Jan 2020
9. Gavin Barwell, 1 & 25 Sep 2020, Brexit Witness Archive, UKICE, p.18
10. Joanna Penn, 16 Oct & 17 Nov 2020, Brexit Witness Archive, UKICE, p.12
11. Philip Hammond, 13 & 20 Nov 2020, Brexit Witness Archive, UKICE, pp.15–16
12. Philip Rycroft, 26 Jun 2020, Brexit Witness Archive, UKICE, pp.13–14
13. Phillip Lee, 9 Apr 2021, Brexit Witness Archive, UKICE, p.7
14. *The Brexit Prime Minister*, Radio 4, Episode 2, 18 Mar 2019
15. Philip Rycroft, 26 Jun 2020, Brexit Witness Archive, UKICE, p.21
16. *The Brexit Prime Minister*, Radio 4, Episode 2, 18 Mar 2019
17. Gavin Barwell, 1 & 25 Sep 2020, Brexit Witness Archive, UKICE, p.10
18. Philip Hammond, 13 & 20 Nov 2020, Brexit Witness Archive, UKICE, p.34
19. May's might have beens, *New Statesman*, 22–28 Nov 2019
20. Joanna Penn, 16 Oct & 17 Nov 2020, Brexit Witness Archive, UKICE, p.14
21. Ibid., p.22
22. Phillip Lee, 9 Apr 2021, Brexit Witness Archive, UKICE, p.19
23. Ibid., p.13
24. Joanna Penn, 16 Oct & 17 Nov 2020, Brexit Witness Archive, UKICE, p.22
25. Chris Grayling, 21 Oct 2020, Brexit Witness Archive, UKICE, p.5
26. Gavin Barwell, 1 & 25 Sep 2020, Brexit Witness Archive, UKICE, p.42

27. Joanna Penn, 16 Oct & 17 Nov 2020, Brexit Witness Archive, UKICE, p.25
28. 'If a male PM weeps he's a patriot. If a woman does, they ask why': Brexit regrets, digs at Boris, and yes, mistakes. Theresa May's last No 10 interview reveals a leader whose decency was never in doubt, *Daily Mail*, 11 Jul 2019